THE LIFE OF SAMUEL H. WALKER

Dedicated to coauthor Jim Worsham with regret.
You left this life too soon.

THE LIFE OF SAMUEL H. WALKER

DAVID M. SULLIVAN AND JAMES WORSHAM

CASEMATE
Pennsylvania & Yorkshire

Published in the United States of America and Great Britain in 2025 by
CASEMATE PUBLISHERS
1950 Lawrence Road, Havertown, PA 19083, USA
and
47 Church Street, Barnsley, S70 2AS, UK

Copyright © 2025 David Sullivan and Patricia Worsham

Hardcover Edition: ISBN 978-1-63624-538-6
Digital Edition: ISBN 978-1-63624-539-3

A CIP record for this book is available from the British Library

All rights reserved. No part of this book may be reproduced or transmitted in any form or by any means, electronic or mechanical including photocopying, recording or by any information storage and retrieval system, without permission from the publisher in writing.

Printed and bound in the United Kingdom by CPI Group (UK) Ltd, Croydon, CR0 4YY
Typeset in India by DiTech Publishing Services

For a complete list of Casemate titles, please contact:

CASEMATE PUBLISHERS (US)
Telephone (610) 853-9131
Fax (610) 853-9146
Email: casemate@casematepublishers.com
www.casematepublishers.com

CASEMATE PUBLISHERS (UK)
Telephone (0)1226 734350
Email: casemate@casemateuk.com
www.casemateuk.com

Back cover image: Courtesy of Erik Christianson, sculptor.
Front cover image: Courtesy of Richard Luce.

The Publisher's authorised representative in the EU for product safety is Authorised Rep Compliance Ltd., Ground Floor, 71 Lower Baggot Street, Dublin D02 P593, Ireland.
www.arccompliance.com

Contents

Foreword

During the early years of the Texas Rangers, two remarkable figures emerged who profoundly influenced the future of Texas and the American West: Samuel Hamilton Walker and John "Jack" Coffee Hays. Their strengths and experience complemented one another, and their close friendship, leadership abilities, and innovation contributed to the outcome of a war, and the destiny of Texas and the American West.

Hays and Walker fused centuries-old traditions of horseback reconnaissance, mobility, and unconventional warfare from Native American, Hispanic, and Anglo-European cultures into an operational strategy forever identified with the Texas Rangers. Their exploits and successes on the battlefields of the Mexican–American War made an indelible impression on commanders who would later serve on both sides during the Civil War such as Ulysses S. Grant, Robert E. Lee, James Longstreet, William Sherman, and Stonewall Jackson.

Until now, there has been no comprehensive biography of Samuel Hamilton Walker. His remarkable life and contributions have been limited to summary overviews and passing mentions, leaving a significant gap in our understanding and insight into his contributions to history.

After years of meticulous research, distinguished historians David M. Sullivan and James Worsham have reassembled the letters, reports, and source material that trace Samuel Walker's short but pivotal life—from his family roots in Maryland to his death at age 30 in Huamantla, Mexico.

Both Walker and Hays were born in 1817, and they were profoundly influenced by the conflicts and westward expansion of their era. In 1836, Jack Hays arrived in Texas, as a 19-year-old surveyor from Tennessee who had helped map the new state of Mississippi. He had come at the behest of his relative by marriage, U.S. President Andrew Jackson. Hays was urged to see his godfather, Sam Houston, then president of the newly independent Republic of Texas.

Texas was now a republic—a new nation—largely because of the effectiveness, mobility, and asymmetrical warfare of the Texas Rangers and the Texian[1] Army, and militias against Santa Anna and the Mexican Army. Houston sent Hays to join the Texas Rangers in San Antonio where he quickly matured, adapted to the frontier environment, and demonstrated exceptional skill and leadership that soon propelled him to the rank of captain of his own company.

Hays learned the importance of mobile horseback tactics developed in the 1700s by the Spanish presidial *compañías volantes* (flying companies). He also learned the survival skills and strategies of the Native Americans required to navigate and survive in the challenging terrain of the Southwest. They were refined by the Texas Rangers on the frontier and in the War of Independence.

As Jack Hays was arriving in Texas, Samuel Walker joined a militia company involved in the Seminole campaign. He remained in Florida after his discharge and established himself in the lumber business. Initially successful, he found himself out of work when the economy of Florida collapsed.

In 1842, Samuel Walker arrived in Galveston, Texas, amid considerable turmoil. Recruited for Captain Jesse Billingsley's militia company, likely due to his military experience, Walker was tasked with defending against repeated attempts by Mexico to reclaim Texas through raids and an expedition led by Mexican General Adrián Woll. This gave Walker experience in two Ranger-type militia companies: working with the military, and as a scout or spy (some early Ranger companies were also called "spy companies").

After successfully repelling the Woll invasion, Walker took part in the ill-fated and "allegedly" unauthorized Mier Expedition into northern Mexico. This punitive mission—launched by a faction of the Texas militia—severely underestimated the Mexican Army, which included seasoned veterans experienced at handling rebellions against Santa Anna, and Native American raids.

Walker and other members of the Mier Expedition were captured. During his captivity, Walker observed the Mexican Army's organization and leadership closely, gaining insights into their operations that would prove to be invaluable during the Mexican–American War. He survived the notorious "Black Bean" episode and endured two years of imprisonment before escaping back to Texas.

When Walker returned to Texas, in 1844—at the age of 27—he joined Jack Hays' Ranger company. His strong friendship with Hays proved invaluable as the Mexican–American War approached.

During the Seminole War, Walker had become familiar with Samuel Colt's groundbreaking five-shot Paterson revolving pistol. Although the army rejected the pistol after trials—it was fragile and complex to reload—some army officers bought them independently, impressed by their innovative design and combat advantages. The Paterson's ability to fire five shots without reloading marked a significant improvement over the single-shot military pistols of the era.

Shortly after joining up with Hays, "Captain Jack" had acquired an improved version of this pistol for his men, the legendary Colt No. 5 Texas Paterson. Tested in combat at the battle of Walker Creek, about 15 to 20 Texas Rangers used the

Colt with devastating effect against an estimated 70 to 80 Comanche warriors. It became iconic with the Texas Rangers and changed horseback warfare.

When the Mexican–American War broke out in 1846, Gen. Zachary Taylor—then 65 years old and leading an inexperienced army—sought the assistance of the Texas Rangers and volunteer frontiersmen familiar with the region. Not having faced an organized foreign army since the War of 1812, Taylor recognized the need for seasoned fighters. He turned to figures like Sam Walker and Jack Hays, who had demonstrated their skills in horseback tactics, scouting, and knowledge of the terrain with the Texas Rangers against the formidable Comanche.

Seconded from the State of Texas to the U.S. Army as volunteers, some regular U.S. Army officers and opposing Mexican commanders criticized the Texians for their lack of discipline, rough appearance, independence, and ruthless ferocity. They frequently challenged the rigid central control and antiquated Napoleonic tactics. Mexican officers reportedly referred to them as "*irregulares, muy irregulars*" (highly irregular irregulars) due to their unconventional methods. The Mexican populace called them *Los Diablos Tejanos* (the Texan Devils) in a brutal war.

However, their expertise demonstrated the advantages of being able to "ride like a Mexican, trail like a Native American, shoot like a Tennessean, and fight like a very devil." More than once Walker and Hays kept supply lines from the coastal ports open, without which the army would have ground to a halt or disaster would have ensued.

For the most part they eschewed elaborate uniforms for adaptable frontier dress, and elected their own officers—based on competence—who commonly wore no uniform or insignia of rank. Ironically, this might have contributed to Walker's early death.

Fame soon followed Walker and Hays. Offered a commission in Company C of the new Regiment of Mounted Rifles, Walker accepted the post, but only after he completed his service as a lieutenant colonel of Texas troops. The Mexican–American War is considered the first war where reporters were actively embedded with the military. Journalists were given unprecedented access to the front lines, and their reports from the battlefield were published in newspapers across the United States, as depicted in Richard Caton Woodville's 1848 painting *War News from Mexico*. Capt. Sam Walker of the U.S. Regiment of Mounted Riflemen and Col. Jack Hays of the 1st Regiment of Texas Mounted Rifle Volunteers were good copy and became household names.

In 1847, Capt. Samuel Walker's name was forever linked to military technology through his collaboration with inventor Samuel Colt. During a recruiting trip back east in 1846, Walker approached Colt to propose a redesign of his Paterson repeating pistol. The Paterson had been a breakthrough compared to single-shot pistols and rifles, but it was becoming woefully obsolete as military technology advanced.

The "Texas" Paterson No. 5 performed well at close ranges up to 75 yards. Its .36-caliber round ball proved deadly against Comanche adversaries using bows or single-shot trade muskets, which were effective up to a comparable 60 yards.

However, the Mexican Army posed a different challenge. Mexican infantrymen, dragoons, and lancers were among the best-trained and equipped soldiers of the era, armed with British "Brown Bess" muskets or Baker rifles. These firearms had an effective range of up to 200 yards and fired .75- and .625-caliber balls, giving them nearly three times the range and twice the stopping power of the Paterson.

A single hit from the Paterson often failed to disable a Mexican infantryman or horseman at a distance. Moreover, the Paterson was fragile, prone to misfires, and required disassembly into three pieces for reloading. Held together by a single shim, some even fell apart due to the vibrations of riding.

Colt listened to Walker's concerns, and they created the iconic Walker Colt revolver. This new revolver fired a .44-caliber round or conical bullet at rifle-like velocities up to 150 yards. Weighing 4.5 pounds, it was designed as a "horse pistol" for saddle carry and held six shots, an improvement over the Paterson's five. Unlike its predecessor, the Walker Colt did not require disassembly to reload, making it a game-changer in combat. Colt presented Walker with two of the 1,100 made shortly before his death, and both have survived in the hands of collectors.

Samuel Hamilton Walker played a pivotal role on the Texas frontier and in the Mexican–American War, advancing military tactics and technology. His friendship and association with Jack Hays led to a realization among future leaders of the importance and effectiveness of asymmetrical and unconventional warfare, influencing guerilla raids and covert operations during the Civil War. They are still studied at the Military Academy at West Point, and the mobility, marksmanship, and adaptability demonstrated by the Texans are core elements in modern Special Forces doctrine.

Byron A. Johnson, Director
Texas Ranger Hall of Fame and Museum
Official Historical Center of the Texas Rangers

Introduction

Texas Ranger Capt. Samuel Hamilton Walker is probably best known as the co-designer of the first six-shot Colt revolver. It was initially issued to American soldiers in 1847 and known to historians and collectors as the "Walker Colt." But Walker's service to the Rangers and later the U.S. Regiment of Mounted Riflemen is also truly extraordinary. And he did it all before he was killed in action when only 30 years old.

His friends and influence took him far beyond Texas. He made the acquaintance of President of the United States James K. Polk and became friends with inventor Samuel Colt, and an even closer comrade with Texas Ranger Commander Col. John Coffee Hays. Walker's experience earned him the rank of lieutenant colonel of the 1st Regiment, Texas Mounted Volunteers; second-in-command of this "Texas Ranger Regiment" that fought at the battle of Monterrey.

But he was not originally a Texan. Samuel Hamilton Walker was born near Greenbelt, Maryland, on February 24, 1817. He began his military experience while still a teenager when he served as an enlisted soldier during the Second Seminole War of 1836–37 in Alabama and Florida. In spite of many later myths of his heroic actions during this war, he did not see combat. What he did encounter had an impact on him for the rest of his life. He endured officers who were brutal, immoral, and unjust. Later, as an officer himself, he remembered those days and treated those under his command fairly, but demanded discipline of his men and of himself.

After Walker had served his enlistment in the Seminole War, he and his older brother Nathan settled in Florida and went into business together. After a little more than two years, Nathan died. It was just a matter of time before Sam moved to Texas.

It was a turbulent time in Texas when Walker arrived there. Operating as an independent republic, Texas had problems both internal and external. The leaders of the Mexican government felt Texas's independence was a fraud and occasionally ordered major harassing raids deep into Texas; on more than one occasion Mexican troops attacked San Antonio. As a new resident of the fledgling Republic of Texas, Walker's patriotic enthusiasm caught up with him. After another raid on San Antonio, September 11, 1842, he joined a volunteer company under Capt. Jesse Billingsley and participated in a retaliatory raid into Mexico. Procrastination and poor planning doomed the attack. Billingsley's company served only three weeks before being disbanded. A few weeks later, a punitive expedition was formed under the command of Alexander Somervell. It broke up when Somervell and others decided nothing would be accomplished by continuing its foray into Mexico and orders were given for a retreat back to Texas. Not all agreed. The dissenters, Walker among them, elected William S. Fisher and pushed on toward the Mexican town of Mier. The decision proved to be disastrous. Walker and 240 others would be captured by the Mexicans in the town of Mier on December 25, 1842. He would be a prisoner for eight months.

During this time, he endured the hardships and humiliation of captivity. But what was hardest for him to bear was the loss of 18 friends who were executed in reaction to a failed escape attempt. The men who were shot were selected by a lottery known to history as the "Black Bean episode," except for Walker's company commander Ewen Cameron who was murdered later. Walker, who later was often called "Unlucky Walker," lucked out by drawing a white bean.

Even as a prisoner, he kept his focus. When beaten by a guard, he "returned the compliment" with a shovel. Afterward he told an officer that if the guard attacked him again, he would kill him. Walker made his escape from Mexico City's Santiago Prison, and with two other escapees crossed Mexico to the Gulf and then returned to Texas.

Joining the Texas Rangers in 1844, he earned a reputation as a daring Native American fighter and in the process became a close friend of Texas Ranger Commander, Capt. John Coffee Hays. He was among the 16 Rangers who made history at the June 8, 1844, battle of Walker Creek. For the first time, mounted Texians used Colt's Paterson five-shot revolvers to defeat nearly 80 Comanche; the most feared Native American enemy on horseback in Texas. They were extremely deadly; Walker was nearly killed by a warrior's lance in that engagement but he recovered and continued to serve with the Rangers.

When the Rangers were disbanded to organize one battle-ready formation at the start of the Mexican–American War, Walker continued his Texian service, first as a private in Capt. (Robert) Addison Gillespie's company, Texas Mounted Rangers (six months), from September 28, 1845, to March 28, 1846, and then mustered into service with Colonel Hays's 1st Regiment of Texas Mounted Rifle Volunteers on April 16, 1846. However, at the request of Gen. Zachary Taylor, he was made captain of his own company of scouts on April 21, serving in that capacity until his resignation on June 30. He returned to Hays's regiment and where he had been elected lieutenant colonel and second-in-command on June 24, 1846.

The Texas Rangers were hardly a military-looking group. They clothed and equipped themselves according to individual taste. Even Captain Hays, their commander, was plainly dressed: a blue roundabout (waist-length jacket), a black leather cap, and black pants, and nothing about him to denote that he belonged to the army or held any military rank in it. Lieutenant Colonel Walker likely wore a frontiersman's buckskin jacket and leather trousers. Hays's Rangers at Puebla were described as follows:

> Their uniforms were an outlandish assortment of long-tailed blue coats and bobtailed black ones; slouched felt hats, dirty panamas, and black leather caps. Most of them wore long bushy beards. Their horses were all sizes and breeds, Texas ponies and American thoroughbreds, but they were without exception, tough, mettlesome, and quick. Each Ranger carried a rifle and four pistols ... two old style single-shooters and two brand new six-shooters which they had just received out of Vera Cruz [January 4, 1847]. They also carried a short knife, hempen ropes, rawhide reatas, or hair lariats. They carried anything else they chose to be tied to their saddles.

Walker served until he was mustered out on October 2, 1846, leaving Texas service to accept a commission as captain of Company C, 1st Regiment, U.S. Mounted Riflemen. He recruited his company in Washington City; his home state of Maryland; Cincinnati, Ohio; Newport, Kentucky; and New Orleans, plus other cities and towns his travels took him to while on his way to physically take command of Company C. Numerous newspaper articles about his earlier heroic actions had recruits flocking to join his company.

When Captain Walker came east to visit family in Washington City or to go to Philadelphia or New York, he was mobbed by admirers. Even a Broadway play was produced with Captain Walker of the Texas Rangers as the main character.

Early in his life, Walker admitted he was "naturally fond of military glory." He both enjoyed and exploited the recognition that his reputation brought him. However, Walker did not welcome the attention of the press when it was inaccurate or distorted. Some of his critics wrote that all the reports of what he did were exaggerated. Still others even wrote of events that never happened at all. Resistant to attacks on his reputation, Sam was very sensitive to anyone who attempted to dim the luster of his image. He sized one critic up, branding him a "malicious scribbler who has been perhaps educated at public expense" who has been laboring "to injure my reputation."

Walker applied his popularity and perseverance to politics, and acquired government funding for new revolvers for his men. Captain Walker of the Mounted Rifles wanted to arm his new company with Colt revolvers that had proven effective when he was with the Rangers. He went to Sam Colt and then directly to the president to get a federal contract for new revolvers. Successful in his discussion with the president, he worked with Colt to design these federally contracted pistols; the first six-shot Colt revolver. Colt, whose earlier attempts at making the Paterson revolvers had left him bankrupt, was very grateful to Walker who had given him the opportunity to become perhaps the most well-known of all early American revolver makers, and so named this revolver the Walker Colt. The Walker Colt revolver, as the first six-shot Colt revolver, is today an icon in American firearms history.

Ironically, Walker also had an impact on another firearms manufacturer—Smith and Wesson. Approaching Edwin Wesson to make rifles for his company, Walker was never able to get financial backing to pay for them. Unfortunately, Edwin Wesson had already purchased steel to make them. With this debt over his head, he and his brother Daniel were forced into a temporary partnership with a Thomas Smith (not Horace Smith of the Smith & Wesson partnership).

While Sam Walker stories became legendary during his lifetime, his image was permanently engraved in steel on each one of his namesake presentation Colt revolvers. Sam and other Rangers are depicted on horseback with pistols in hand fighting Comanche on the Walker Colt cylinder—Rangers in the battle of Walker Creek—an event that would forever change Texas history. From the eventful day of the battle forward, Walker's name would be linked to the Rangers.

Texas Ranger Captain William J. McDonald once said of the Rangers, "No man in the wrong can stand up against a fellow that's in the right and keeps on acomin'." This became the motto of the Rangers who became known for their fierce dedication to duty. To them, no adversary who had done wrong would escape their resolve to do right and serve justice. Texas Ranger Sam Walker certainly fit that description of focused determination—no matter the odds.

Unlike the rough-and-ready image many had at the time of the 19th-century Rangers as hard drinking men who rolled their own cigarettes, the future Texas Ranger Sam Walker was nothing of the sort. In fact, he was an outspoken advocate of abstinence from alcohol and tobacco. He was indeed a unique Texas Ranger. While he may have been a teetotaler, he was a teetotaling terror to those who faced him in battle.

Sam Walker served in Mexico on horseback, first with the Rangers and then with the Mounted Rifles. Ironically, without his determination, Walker's Company C of the Mounted Rifles would have served on foot. When almost all of the regiment's horses were lost at sea on the way to Mexico, Walker—who was delayed recruiting his company as well as getting his new revolver designed and funded—had time to do something about the missing mounts. He got permission and purchased horses for his company—horses that did make it safely to Mexico. Thanks to Walker, his company of Mounted Riflemen were mounted and eventually armed with the most advanced cavalry weapon produced by the army—the revolver that bore his name. The 30-year-old former Ranger died in battle on October 9, 1847, with one of his new Walker Colts in his hand.

A television series named *Walker Texas Ranger* associated many viewers with a fictional modern Ranger who was portrayed by the black belt karate expert Chuck

Norris. Yet there was a real Walker Texas Ranger and he was nationally famous during his lifetime.

The following account of Sam Walker's life is based primarily on his own words, numerous letters preserved by the family that are now in the Texas State Archives, the Connecticut State Library, and the National Archives. All known letters Walker wrote or received are reproduced, most in their entirety. Punctuation has been added for the benefit of the reader, but misspellings and grammatical failings remain as they were written. Contemporary newspaper accounts, rare photographs, as well as diaries and memoirs were consulted and included. The decades of research by the authors dispel the elevated myths and half-truths found in many previously published articles dealing with Sam Walker's brief time on this earth. The facts reflect a life that needs no embellishment.

Samuel Hamilton Walker *ca.* 1842. (James Worsham collection)

CHAPTER I

Deep American Roots

Col. Ninian Beall, commander, Maryland Rangers. (www.geni.com)

In 1696, two Maryland men—one old and one young—briefly walked a tract of land in this their first meeting.[1] Unknown to each other, they shared a special bond. One was a veteran frontier Maryland Ranger[2] and the other was the ancestor of a famous Texas Ranger yet to be born. The older man, Col. Ninian Beall (the spelling of the family surname varied from account to account; Beale/Beall)[3] was the commander of the Maryland Rangers—the first such Native American-fighting force in America.

The younger man was Charles Walker, Sr., the great-great-grandfather of a man who, 150 years later, would be known not only in Maryland but also all over the East Coast as Sam Walker, the famous "Texican Ranger."

While Texas Ranger Walker would be famous during his lifetime, at this meeting 33-year-old Charles Walker would stand in awe of the reputation of the much older Colonel Beall. This war-hardened veteran had been a soldier all of his life—first as a Scot fighting the English and later as an experienced soldier in America fighting the indigenous people.

By 1678, Beall held the rank of captain and was put in command of 30 men to be raised in case of trouble with the natives. Twenty of the men were to be distributed among the plantations for defense of the houses; the other 10 to be constantly ranging about the head of the river according to the discretion of Captain Beall.

Neither Beall nor his soldiers nor any inhabitants were to offer any violence to the natives unless the natives first made an assault upon them. Those people whose homes were being guarded were to take care of the crops of those pressed into service as Rangers. From then on, the name "Rangers" was given to the small forces raised from time to time to protect the frontiers from sneak attacks by the natives.

Samuel H. Walker, Texas Ranger. (James Worsham collection)

Evidently the Native American situation was very fluid. Native American trouble was first noted by the council and a force of Rangers (30 men) was ordered into service on August 9, 1678. On August 20, Captain Beall was ordered to keep ranging at the head of the Patuxent River. By August 29, the situation must have eased, as the number of Rangers was reduced to 15; however, the settlers were not to relax in their precautions. As the council saw the situation, Common Rangers now under pay in Charles, Calvert, Anne Arundel, and Baltimore Counties were sufficient to let the natives see that they were awake and watchful. Rangers were to tell the frontier inhabitants that if any natives appeared, they were to fire three guns. Every house was to answer the alarm by firing one gun; then all were to repair to the place from whence three guns were fired, to assist them if need be.

The Archives of Maryland contain frequent references to Native American troubles during ensuing years. On each occasion Ninian Beall was called upon to investigate, confer, or fight.[4]

A meeting of Walker's ancestor with the 71-year-old Beall could not help but command physical attention; he was six feet, seven inches tall and had an unusually heavy growth of long, fiery red hair.

Ironically, the red hair was a trait the old Ranger and the future Texas Ranger would also share. Like the flaming long hair, Ranger Beall's life's flame would also be long, lasting nearly a century. He died peacefully at home near Upper Marlboro, Maryland, at 92 years old, and had 12 children. Sam Walker's life flame would end in a burst of glory; killed in battle in Mexico when he was thirty and never married.

In another series of coincidences between the two men, even after their deaths, both Rangers would be disinterred. Beall's body was removed from his grave and his second grave site remains unknown. Sam was disinterred four times. But his final grave is well marked today.

The legacy that began with Charles Walker, Sr. (born 1663), would continue through his son Charles, Jr. (born 1698); then to his son Isaac (born 1721); his son Nathan (born 1756); and then to his son, Texas Ranger Samuel Hamilton Walker (born 1817).

The chance meeting of Walker's ancestor with the famous Maryland Ranger is but one example of how facts in this fascinating man's life are more interesting than some of the legend that surrounds his life.[5]

One strongly held family tradition is that Sam Walker's homestead near Greenbelt, Maryland, was named Toaping Castle[6] after the ancestral home in Scotland. However, some family researchers have pointed out that the original land patent for Isaac Walker was called Toping Castle, not Toaping Castle. The old homestead sat behind the current gravesites of Walker's family on top of a hill (elevation 250 feet). Hence the name on the original land patent—Toping Castle. No site of a Walker Toaping Castle has been located in Scotland.

The Scottish heritage is definitely in the Walker family but apparently not where the passed-down ancestral story indicates. The story often retold, and that is even on the historical marker near the site of Toaping Castle, is based on fact but also includes information that has been changed as it has been passed down through the years.

Sam's grandfather Isaac Walker did not fight in Scotland against the English king. However, his grandfather, Dunkin (Duncan) Ferguson did. Dunkin Ferguson, a laborer from Belwether, Perth County, Scotland, was among the Scottish rebels taken prisoner three days after the battle of Preston, November 12, 1715, during the second Jacobite uprising of 1715–16 led by The Old Pretender—James, the former Stuart king of England. After being held in prison for eight months, he and 54 other Scotsmen were sent aboard the ship *Good Speed.* The ship left England on July 14, 1716, and arrived in Annapolis, Maryland, on October 18, where all were subsequently sold into indenture for seven years. Ferguson and fellow transportee John Mackewan were purchased by Capt. John Fendall, (1672–1734), the son of Josias Fendall, fourth proprietary governor of Maryland. Captain Fendall was a planter, justice of the peace, and member of Maryland's Lower House.[7] (Interestingly, Maryland Ranger Col. Ninian Beall was also transported to America as a prisoner of war of the English in the 1650s.)

The tradition that Sam's Ferguson grandmother was a Stuart has no basis in fact. Dunkin Ferguson married Catherine Clark Cameron (*ca.* 1700–*ca.* 1779) and from that union came two sons, William and John, and one daughter, Elizabeth (1730–99). She married Isaac Walker. She was a commoner, not Lady Elizabeth Stuart, kin to the Stuart Dynasty of Scotland.[8]

Long-standing Family Tradition

One reason the cast-iron markers near the site of Sam's home misstate the facts of Walker's heritage is because of the booklet published by his nephew and namesake Samuel Hamilton Walker, II. According to this family history written in 1889—"The Walkers of Toaping Castle, Maryland"—the Walkers came from Scotland. This account says in the early 18th century they fought against the enthronement of King George I of Scotland and England who, although married into the Scottish Stuart lineage, was German and rumored not able or willing to speak a word of English. After this resistance was crushed, the rebellious Walkers were sought "both at home and the colonies, as rebels and felons, with large rewards offered for their heads." Family tradition erroneously states they came to America in 1746. Family history further and also erroneously states:

> Isaac Walker and his brothers Charles and Nathan were thus forced to flee, with five hundred pounds offered for their heads, The brothers constructed a large white oak log house at the head waters of Bear Garden Branch, in Prince George's County, (Maryland) about nine miles northeast of what was afterwards called Washington, D.C. … They named the place "Toaping Castle,"[9]

> after their stronghold in the old country; and after they thought it safe to acknowledge their identity, and danger was over.[10]

Thus were the bits and pieces passed down through the generations in the Walker family and finally given credibility by placing it in print. This was the story of the Walker heritage that was passed down to Sam Walker. That combined with the national political climate into which he was born, as well as growing up so near the nation's capital would have an impact on him.

The year Samuel Hamilton Walker was born, 1817, was a most interesting time in American history. The human and natural events set the stage for Walker's enthusiastic patriotism that seemed to be a motivating force for him all of his life.

During the War of 1812, a few years before Walker's birth, the British had done much damage to the American self-image. In 1814, militiamen rallied to resist the invaders outside Washington and were routed at the battle of Bladensburg, and the British advanced inland over 40 miles to burn the Capitol, the president's house, and all other public buildings except the combined Post Office and Patent Office, and the Marine Barracks.

The War of 1812 had been a series of lackluster efforts on the battlefield by the American Army that nearly always resulted in a British victory. But then events took a turn against the British. Even though the British had been devastatingly effective at Bladensburg, it was a different story at Baltimore in 1814. It was there that Francis Scott Key, an eyewitness to the American spectacular, stubborn, and successful defense at Fort McHenry, wrote the words to what would become the National Anthem, "The Star-Spangled Banner."

On January 8, 1815, Gen. Andrew Jackson decisively defeated a British Army of hardened Napoleonic War veterans at the battle of New Orleans; ironically two weeks after the war had been concluded by the Treaty of Ghent, December 24, 1814. This surprised the nation as well as the world. Jackson's victory inspired Americans to begin to look at themselves with more confidence and promise. More importantly, the rest of the world began to step back and reevaluate this new nation that had taken root in the vast wilderness of the New World.

Walker was born February 24, 1817, at a time when many Americans were starting to enjoy their new national self-image. The awakening young giant of a new nation was rebuilding the burnt Capitol. On an "elevated portico" in front of the Capitol building, James Monroe took the oath of office as president on March 4, 1817, just over a week after Walker's birth. Soon Monroe and his family were installed in the whitewashed-restored president's house—from that time on to be known as the White House. Walker was born near Washington City[11] where he and his family were caught up one way or the other in the great expectations of the new nation.

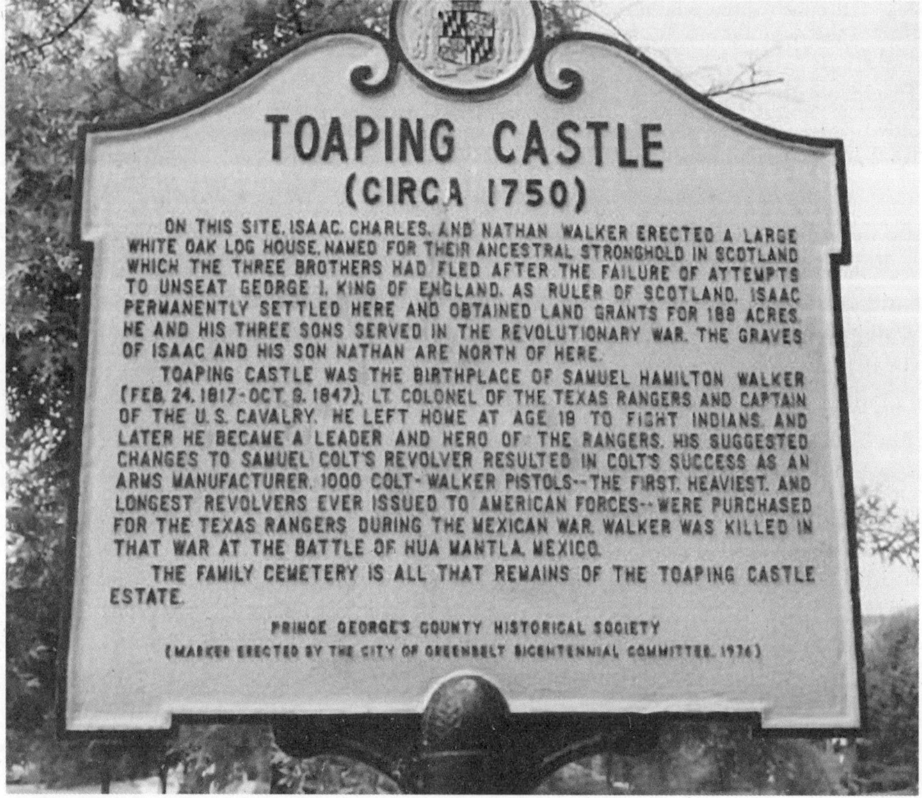

Prince George's County Historical Society marker noting the site of Toaping Castle, Samuel H. Walker's birthplace. (James Worsham collection)

The Prince George's County Historical Society marker erected by the City of Greenbelt Bicentennial Committee in 1976, is located near the family cemetery for the residence "Toaping Castle."

The marker, enshrining the partially fanciful Walker family tradition booklet states:

> On this site, Isaac, Charles, and Nathan Walker erected a large white oak log house, named for their ancestral stronghold in Scotland, which the three brothers had fled after the failure of attempts to unseat George I, King of England, as ruler of Scotland.

Isaac permanently settled here and obtained land grants for 188 acres. He and his three sons served in the Revolutionary War. The graves of Isaac and his son Nathan are north of here.

Toaping Castle was the birthplace of Samuel Hamilton Walker, U.S. soldier, Texas Ranger, Texas soldier, and captain of the U.S. Mounted Rifles. He left home at the age of 19 to fight the Seminoles and later became a leader and hero of the Rangers.

His suggested changes to Samuel Colt's revolver resulted in Colt's success as an arms manufacturer. One thousand Walker Colt pistols—the first six-shot, heaviest, and longest lengthwise revolvers ever issued to American forces—were purchased for the Texas Rangers and Mounted Riflemen during the Mexican–American War. Walker was killed in that war at the battle of Huamantla, Mexico.

CHAPTER 2

The Young Patriot and the Second Seminole War

Sam Walker was deeply patriotic. While his uncles Isaac, Samuel, and Charles were Revolutionary War veterans, his father Nathan—born in 1756 and the middle son—was needed at home to take charge of the farm and provide for the family. Nathan did not go to war until his older brothers Isaac, Samuel, and Charles returned from their service.[1] Eventually, Nathan served as a private in Capt. Thomas Beall's[2] Company of the Upper Battalion of Militia in Prince George's County, the same unit in which his brother Isaac was first lieutenant.[3]

Nathan married Nancy Baggerly (1775–1804) of Montgomery County in 1799 and to them were born three children, Henry (1798–1882), Nathan[4] (1802–1802) and Elizabeth Ann (1805–80). Nancy died six years later in 1805.[5]

Nathan married his second wife, Elizabeth Thomas (Sam's mother) of Charles County, Maryland, on October 4, 1810. Elizabeth was the widow of John Beck. Beck's nephew Rezin, would marry Nathan's daughter Elizabeth.[6]

Nathan and Elizabeth had Jonathan Thomas (1811–85), Nathan (1812–39), Catherine Beall (1814–1901), Jane Elizabeth Beall (1815–63), Samuel Hamilton (1817–47), Charles Edward (1818–1901), and Mary Thomas (1820–90). The patriarch of the family was a house carpenter by trade and a farmer by occupation. According to Walker "being of moderate circumstances, he gave us a common country education, and brought us up on hard work; having taught the eldest son the business of a house carpenter, he in turn taught the rest."[7] Walker would later use his carpentry skills in Florida to provide his livelihood, and his interest in detail carpentry construction led him to play an active part with Samuel Colt in designing the Walker Colt.

Walker no doubt grew up hearing the Revolutionary War stories of his father and uncles and, living so close to Washington City, it is not surprising he chose reading of America's patriotic past as a favorite pastime.

He recalled as a youth nothing so much interested him as to read of the "chivalry and noble deeds of our forefathers in the wars with Great Britain."[8] He certainly was aware of the effort of his countrymen to subdue and pacify the Native Americans of the Southeast, especially the Creeks in Alabama and the Seminoles in Florida.

Contemporary drawing of Fort Brooke, Florida, where Walker served in the Washington City Volunteers during the Second Seminole War in 1836. (Library of Congress photograph LC-DIG-pga-10851)

Following the defeat of the Creek Confederation by Gen. Andrew Jackson at the battle of Tohopeka, March 27, 1814, in the Creek War of 1813–14; a remnant of the Upper Creeks, known as the "Red Sticks," fled to Florida, then a Spanish possession. They were joined by other bands of the Creeks who were unwilling to live with their brothers who had sided with Jackson and relinquished title to two-thirds of their territory in the war-ending treaty that followed. They and their allies were known as Seminoles—"wild people" in the Muscogee language.[9]

A 19th-century sketch of Native Americans attacking Lt. Richard Scott's party. (Courtesy of the New York Public Library Digital Collection)

The First Seminole War, 1816–18, was a brutal affair that was marked by the November 30, 1817, Seminole ambush of 40 soldiers led by 1st Lt. Richard W. Scott, USA.[10] All but four were killed in what became known as the "Scott Massacre"; Lieutenant Scott being tortured by fire and burned at the stake.[11]

Led by Gen. Andrew Jackson, the scorched-earth retaliatory campaign that followed, drove the Seminoles out of western Spanish Florida and toward the central part of that territory.

After its acquisition from Spain by the United States in 1819–21, Florida became a magnet for white settlement. These settlers considered the Seminoles a hindrance to their agricultural endeavors and, more importantly, a threat to their very lives. They wanted the Seminoles out of Florida and their influential friends in Florida and Washington shared their sentiments. The Indian Removal Act of 1830; the Treaty of Payne's Landing, signed May 9, 1832, and ratified by the federal government in April 1834; and the Treaty of Fort Gibson, February 14, 1833, provided reservations for the Seminoles in the Arkansas territory. When the government demanded the natives begin immediate evacuation from Florida, the Seminoles—claiming their leaders who signed these treaties were coerced and believing they had many years before they had to leave—refused to move. Brig. Gen. Duncan L. Clinch[12] told the Seminoles if they refused to go peacefully, he would use force to compel them.

Tensions grew. Violence flared between whites and Seminoles; murders being committed by both. In August 1835, Pvt. Kinsley H. Dalton, 3d U.S. Artillery, was slain by Seminoles while delivering mail from Fort Brooke to Fort King. The attacks on white settlers caused Acting Governor G. R. Walker to mobilize five hundred militiamen. Col. John Warren, commanding a regiment of East Florida volunteers, was called out for active service by General Clinch. Ordered to scout for Seminoles, Warren detached his baggage train from his main force on December 18. It was attacked by Seminoles and captured. Six militiamen were killed and eight others wounded in a failed attempt to recapture it in what became known as the battle of Black Point.

On December 23, a detachment made up of soldiers from Company C, 2d U.S. Artillery, and Company B, 3d U.S. Artillery left Fort Brooke under the command of Maj. Francis L. Dade[13] to reinforce the undermanned Fort King. The Seminoles, well-prepared for this movement, ambushed the column on the 28th, killing all but three of the 108 officers and men. Of the three survivors; one was slain as he tried to escape, and another was so badly wounded that he died within days. Pvt. Ransome Clark was the only one left to tell the harrowing tale of the annihilation of Dade's column.

Col. Duncan Lamont Clinch. (Courtesy of Florida Memory)

On the 29th, General Clinch left Fort Drane with 250 Regulars and some 500 volunteers under Lt. Col. Alexander Fanning, Florida Militia,

The Dade Massacre by Ken Hughes. (Historical Association of Southern Florida, Inc.; Great American Color Co.; University of Miami Libraries)

intending to surprise the Seminoles in their camps some 35 miles away. On December 31, Clinch found the Withlacoochee River blocking his route to the Seminole camps. The natives established a defensive position on the opposite bank and fired on the soldiers who were attempting to cross the swollen river. Nevertheless, the Regulars, after some confusion, made their way across and formed ranks, all the while taking fire from the Seminoles. Three bayonet charges failed to dislodge the natives. Exhausted from their exertions, both sides gave up the fight. Clinch ordered his men back to Fort Drane. Four Regulars were killed and 52 were wounded.

When news of these military debacles reached Washington and spread throughout the United States, the national clamor for a military solution to the increasing violence was heard in Congress. The government, unable to satisfy the demand for additional Regulars in Florida, welcomed volunteers.[14] Sam Walker, eager to be among those who were called to avenge the deaths of Americans in Florida and inspired by American military heroes, was among the first to volunteer. Despite contemporary traditions that Walker had been conspicuous in combat during the Seminole War,[15] he did not have the glorious experience he anticipated. In fact, he details his less than fame-filled services in his 12-page *Brief observations on the conduct of the officers, and on the discipline of the army of the United States* (Appendix I) which he wrote and self-published four years later.

While Walker did not serve in combat during the Seminole War, it does not mean that he did not want to. To the contrary. In his own words, Sam admits to being "naturally fond of military glory" and becoming incensed upon reading local newspaper accounts of the "massacre of our citizens and soldiers in the Creek nation and in Florida." He wanted to fight, and enlisted for "purely patriotic motives" to "march to the rescue of his fellow-citizens,"[16] and "try his fortune on the field of battle on the first opportunity that presented itself." In May 1836, the 19-year-old Walker was enlisted by Captain of Light Infantry Benjamin Lloyd Beall,[17] and became a private in the Washington City Volunteers, 1st Regiment, 3d Brigade, District of Columbia Militia.

Benjamin Lloyd Beall. (Photograph in the public domain)

The officers and men of the Washington City Volunteers were mustered into federal service on June 1, 1836. Unfortunately, the very qualified Captain Beall, who had pledged to stay with his command, yielded to an offer of a captaincy in the 2d Regiment of Dragoons. 1st Lt. Edward B. Robinson,[18] next in command, was elected captain on June 13. Walker fairly commented that Robinson, formerly a soldier in the army, was a "tolerable expert in drilling." But Walker, who had his way with words, also described Robinson as "entirely destitute of moral principles and behavior."[19]

Robinson's amoral character would have a decided impact on Walker that would affect him for the rest of his life. Walker suffered at Robinson's hand, but he would also learn a most valuable lesson that served him well when he himself became an officer and had to lead men into harm's way—his concern for his men earned their loyalty and devotion, a characteristic that could hardly be said of many combat officers of the time.

On June 1, 1836, the Washington City Volunteers marched to Marine Barracks Washington (now almost entirely devoid of Marines, the bulk of them on their way to the scene of war under their commandant, Col. Archibald Henderson,[20]) where Walker and his comrades-in-arms were sworn into federal service. A few nights later, Robinson was accused of trying to "force the door of the quarters of where some of the absent soldiers' families were, but their calls of alarm forced him to jump the wall and escape." Although he was recognized, Robinson was able to find men to provide him with an alibi.[21]

That June, the Washington Volunteers took a steamboat to Charleston, South Carolina; marched to Augusta, Georgia; and finally arrived in Columbus, Georgia, in July. In August, it was in Tallassee, Alabama, where it was attached to Colonel Henderson's U.S. Marine Battalion.

While in the Creek nation of south Alabama, Walker—like many other soldiers—"got completely barefoot. And having moved to a new encampment where the earth was completely covered with briars." Because of the vulnerable condition of his bare feet, Orderly Sergeant George Cochran did not detail Walker to be among those to clear up the area. "I was sitting down writing on a drumhead," Walker recalled. Captain Robinson asked the sergeant why Private Walker was not working on clearing the area. The sergeant told him, and Robinson exploded. Walker said "he swore that I should go any how; he said he did not care a d—n if I was barefooted, and ordered me to go." Walker responded by saying he would go and added the captain may have reacted the way he did because he assumed Walker was writing a letter to his father seeking his own discharge. He assured Captain Robinson, according to Walker "in a very respectful manner," that he was not writing such a correspondence. Robinson then called for a guard and had Sam escorted to the guard tent charging him with "insolence and disobedience." He was then called before Col. Archibald Henderson.

Archibald Henderson, shown here at the time of the Second Seminole War as Colonel and Commandant, United States Marine Corps. (Portrait by Col. H. Avery Chenoweth, USMCR [Retired], National Museum of the Marine Corps)

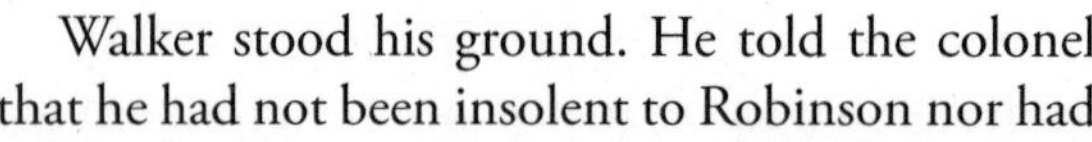

Walker stood his ground. He told the colonel that he had not been insolent to Robinson nor had he disobeyed him. The colonel asked for a witness and Sergeant Cochran, who had been present at the time of the incident, supported Walker. Colonel Henderson said he did not want to hear any more about the matter. He ordered Walker to apologize to Robinson and promise never to do such a thing again. He refused. He was then threatened with being gagged.[22]

The next day, he was again called before Henderson and threatened with gagging. Walker said he thought he should be able to speak on his own defense and should not be gagged. Henderson told him he had no right to think. He was then taken to the guard tent and ordered to wash clothes that belonged to some "miserable creatures" who had been confined for some time. Their skin was thickly covered by dirt and filth having had to lie in the dirt for months on end in a tropical climate, and they were swarming with lice. Two guards stood over Sam while he washed the "miserably dirty lousy clothes."[23]

On the third day, Henderson again threatened Walker with gagging, but then sent him to the guard tent, saying if he did not apologize to Robinson, he would be tied to a tree for two hours with a sign stating, "For insolence and disobedience to his commanding officer." After a two-hour tree-hug, Sam was released and immediately sought a fine-tooth comb and "combed out the cattle (lice) which had crawled from the heads of my miserable bedfellows."[24]

Although Walker claimed he was not writing to seek his discharge, it appears he had written to his parents, complaining of his dissatisfaction with the way he was being treated. They acted accordingly. The Adjutant General of the Army received the following:

Washington City, August 17th 1836

General Jones,
Sir; As my son Samuel H. Walker, a volunteer under Capt. Edward B. Robinson of the W. City Volunteers, complains very much of his treatment, and the possibility of his having nothing to do, wishes to get his discharge; Col. Henderson has informed him that I could get his discharge by making application to you; you will therefore confer a particular favour on his aged father by sending on to him his discharge, as soon as you conveniently can, and oblige very respectfully

Your obt. Servt.
Nathan Walker[25]

Brig. Gen. Roger ap Catesby Jones, Adjutant General, United States Army. (Photograph in the public domain)

To which Gen. Roger Jones,[26] Adjutant General of the U.S. Army replied:

Washington, August 18th 1836
Nathan Walker

Sir;
Your application for the discharge of your son S. H. Walker, a private in Captain Robinson's Company of Washington Volunteers, has been to the General in Chief, who instructs me to inform you that your request cannot be complied with.

I am Sir;
R. Jones.[27]

A second letter, sent by Attorney Alexander Keech, renewed the request, but through a different governmental authority:

Waverly [MD] Sept 2nd 1836
[Honb. Lewis Cass
Secretary of War
Washington]

Dear Sir,
This will be presented to you by my neighbor Mrs. Walker, who is anxious to effect the release her son, a minor, who volunteered in

> Capt. Robinson's company of Washington. Samuel Walker is in his twentieth year, left home contrary to his Father's wishes and commands and the old gentleman and family in every respect very unhappy. The old gentleman wishes him discharged upon the grounds of his being a minor and this fact, if necessary, can bear testimony.
>
> Yours very respectfully,
> Alex. Keech.

This letter bears the notation, "See letter Dated 19th August '36. Cannot be discharged."[28]

On August 1, Walker's company was transferred to the command of Maj. Greenleaf Dearborn,[29] whose detachment of the 2d Infantry was nearby. It was then Captain Robinson went into the village of Tallassee and came back very drunk and immediately got into an argument with another drunken soldier. An intoxicated Robinson ordered the drunken soldier to be placed in irons. Then the two men began to curse each other. Robinson then drew his sword and stabbed the shackled man in the chest. Thinking the man was mortally wounded and this drunken officer with a sword was a danger to all, eight or ten witnesses (including Walker) went to their tents for their muskets to disarm the captain. Walker had second thoughts and did not load his musket (thinking of the punishment he could get for such a serious violation of military law). His friends were loading their weapons when Sgt. George Cochran stopped them and was on his way to report the incident to Major Dearborn when he was spotted by Robinson. Although intoxicated, the captain had the presence of mind to call out to the major before the sergeant got to him. Robinson claimed his company was mutinying against him and the orderly sergeant was their leader. Dearborn ordered his detachment and Col. Alexander S. Brook's artillery regiment under arms to deal with this possible mutiny. Robinson successfully placed the blame for the entire incident on Sergeant Cochran, who ended up in confinement for two months.[30]

Walker was not alone in feeling Captain Robinson should be removed from command. On August 23, charges were filed against Robinson for "unofficerlike and ungentlemanly conduct" citing five violations including repeated drunkenness, the most public being when he was drilling the company and was so drunk his men could not understand his words. The charges were preferred by 1st Lt. William A. T. Maddox[31] with statements of several witnesses including two sergeants, two corporals, and eleven privates (including Walker). The charges and specifications were presented to Gen. Thomas Sidney Jesup,[32] who declined convening a court, giving the excuse of not having enough officers to hear the case and not wishing to have any of his officers broken.[33]

The Washington City Volunteers was attached to Capt. John Munroe's Company G, 4th U.S. Artillery Regiment, toward the end of September and encamped on the Hatchechubbee Swamp, about 30 miles from Fort Mitchell, Alabama (near the present Fort Benning, Georgia). Walker was impressed by Captain Munroe,[34] who was fair and rendered justice to his soldiers as well as his subordinate officers. Soon, the Washington Volunteers received orders to go to Fort Mitchell and prepare to march to Florida.

When Walker's company got word it was to be detached from Captain Munroe's company and marched to Florida (and possibly into combat) under Captain Robinson, a meeting of the men was called. Walker and four others were appointed to draw up a resolution. Walker recalled:

Gen. Thomas S. Jesup. (Photograph in the public domain)

> Our resolution contained in it a positive declaration that we would not march to Florida under Captain Robinson, but was accompanied with a very respectful petition to the Gen., stating our great objections to Captain Robinson, and the impositions he had practiced on us, and begging him at the same time to relieve us from the disagreeable necessity of being commanded by so odious a character.[35]

All but two of the 50/60 men in the company put their names to the resolution. Upon arriving at Fort Mitchell this petition was delivered to General Jesup in the hope he would do justice to the men. The general did not accept the petition in the intended spirit. Instead, Jesup saw the paper as a threat to good order and discipline and ordered Maj. Mann Page Lomax's command under arms to thwart potential insubordination. Walker and company were not deterred, so Jesup—seeing the determination of the aggrieved Washington men—decided a second look into the Robinson situation was in order. The end result was Robinson was suspended from command.[36] Upon gaining the justice he and the rest of his company had long wished for, Sam wrote his brother Jonathan Thomas with the news.

> Fort Mitchell, Alabama, Oct. 2, 1836
>
> Dear Brother.
> I received your letter which duly came to hand, and was happy to hear you were all well. You stated that you and Father was endeavoring to obtain my discharge. I was very glad you did not, as my grievances are all redressed. Since my last things has taken a very great change and I hope for the best. We left the Creek Stand about the last of Augt and marched to this place. We left here on the third day of Sept with one company of Arty under command of Brevet Major Munroe and marched about twenty five miles below here to scour the Hatchee Lustee Swamp. We remained there untill the 28 scouring the swamp

> and surrounding country viewing the distribution of the Indians which is immense. The hostile Indians have all given themselves up except a tribe called the Hitchitees [Hitchiti] which is supposed to be in Florida. The inhabitants is returning to their farms. We received orders to return here and prepare to march for Florida. We addressed a letter to Genl Jessup [Jesup] stating our dissatisfaction in respect to Capt Robinson. He is now arrested and Lt. Maddon [Maddox] has command of the company. He is a young officer who is respected by his men and also the officers of the army. I have not time to state particulars as we shall strike tents and march in one hour to the steam boat warf 12 miles below here and proceed down the Chatahoochee to Florida. You shall hear from me again when I get in Florida. My health and the company is all exceedingly good. Give my best respects to all inquiring friends and tell them I wish to see them again when I gain a crown of laurels.
>
> I remain your affectionate Brother.[37]

Walker's company was now attached to three companies of artillery under the command of Maj. William L. McClintock for the next three months.

Maddox's command was all too brief. The company, upon arriving at Tampa Bay on October 15, learned Robinson was reinstated but the company refused to recognize him as their commander. Jessup finally revisited the charges against Robinson and gave Robinson the choice of resigning or facing a court-martial. Robinson resigned. Maddox was expected to return to the command of the company, but was taken ill and left for treatment in New Orleans. He never returned. Sgt. Charles Irvine[38] was elected the new captain.

After Walker's company arrived in Florida, it was tasked with cutting wood for the steamboats as well as rebuilding Fort Alabama (later renamed Fort Foster after Col. William S. Foster, the officer who was superintending the rebuilding).

On December 25, the fort completed, General Jessup ordered Foster to Tampa Bay. According to Walker, the troops were presented an option. Those who chose to go to Tampa would be attached to the quartermaster's department and receive two dollars a day, while those who stayed at the fort would earn a dollar a day. All of the Washington volunteers chose to go to Tampa Bay. "I do not think," Walker wrote, "that our company would have taken this offer if there were any chance to have distinguished ourselves in battle." This comment is strange in that Walker remarked the general feeling among the men was they had enlisted for only six months.[39]

Perhaps the additional pay was meant to mollify those who complained about what they perceived as duplicity on the part of their mustering-in officer. His views on this matter and his plans after his enlistment expired were related to his brother Nathan.

March 5, 1837
Fort Dade Withlacoochee R[iver] Florida

Dear Brother
With great pleasure I write again hoping I may receive an answer as I have heard nothing from you since the 11th of September. In my last dated the 9th of Feb which was directed toward Father I stated I would write again when the Indians came in which was to be on the 18th. However there was but few came in on the day appointed. None of the chiefs except the negro chief Abraham came in until the 24th. They stated that they could not collect their chiefs and warriors together in so short a time. They agreed however to be in to day. They have been as good as their word for one time. A number of the chiefs came in to day and I understand the treaty is made with the exception of the time they are to leave the Territory. The [Indians?] say they do not wish to leave until next fall. And the General has no notion of granting them so long a time. However tomorrow [he] will decide. But it [illegible] doubtfull whither they will come to terms or not. It is thought by some that they will not and others think to contrary. As for my own part I shall believe it when I see it. Many of them have been drawing rations since the 18th of last month though it appears they would not suffer for anything but bread as they are every day fetching in deer wild turkeys etc enough to supply the wants of the Army which proved they are great huntsmen and capable of living where a white man would starve. And what makes me doubtful of their head chief Micanopy who's never been in camp yet and says he is coming in when the treaty is made. As for myself I think they are trying to play the gouge game but I shall stop thinking as the officers say Soldiers has no right to think. Our company is all employed in the guard as I stated in my last. Myself and the rest of the company are all in good health and I hope these few lines may find you the same. I long to hear from you and would rejoice to see you, but God knows when that may be. We have some hopes of being disbanded in the course of another month. However we ask no favours as our time will be out on the 1st of June at all events and if I were to return home I should not stay long as the country is too old for a young man. I have found by experience that new settled countries are the places for young men and I have come to a determination to purchase a small tract of land in Texas or somewhere else and settle myself. You can inform young men who wish to engage in enterprise that Texas is the place for them. Fifty dollars bounty horse and saddle to ride and twenty five dollars per month is offered to volunteers. The Mexicans are daily expected. I intend going to Texas but I shall go on my own footing after this and when I volunteer for six months again I will be certain it is not twelve however I do not regret it at last as it has taught me a lesson which I will never forget and will perhaps be

> of great benefit to [me.] You must give my love to all my inquiring friends and tell them I will see them if God spares me long enough. I remain your affectionate Brother
>
> Samuel H Walker
> Tampa Bay & Florida[40]

Here, for the first time in Walker's writings, the possibility of establishing himself in the infant Republic of Texas is mentioned.

General Jesup's actions in matters in which Walker was intimately involved aroused the young volunteer's indignation.[41] Not only had he allowed Robinson to stay in command until he was forced to do something, the general—who had been sent to put paid to the Seminoles' debt at the point of the bayonet—chose to entertain the natives rather than to beat them into submission. In Walker's view, food, tobacco, and even bread was given to the natives at the expense of the soldiers who were cut off from their tobacco and had their bread ration reduced to but a few ounces a day.

In addition, Walker's high sense of morality was offended by watching officers take squaws into their tents during the night. Many Black people in the area were known to be acting as pimps for the squaws. Later Walker, working as a carpenter, built double beds to accommodate these officers and their nocturnal visitors.[42]

On January 1, 1837, Walker was promoted from private to corporal and his allowance for clothing for one year was paid on December 31, 1836.

In April, Walker's company was informed by the quartermaster they would work for the remainder of their months of service at 15 cents a day rather than two dollars as they had been promised. Walker quit work and persuaded at least one other soldier to do so also. Lt. James H. Simpson, assistant quartermaster, came for Walker and his companion to put them in stocks. Walker appealed to his new captain, Charles Irvine, but to no avail. The captain told the two he would do what he could, but they should go with the officer. Walker and his friend were about to be put in stocks, when he complained. Simpson cursed him and threatened him with a thrashing if he did not shut up. Sam told him he would welcome the opportunity "to give him a fair trial" but the lieutenant did not take Walker up on his offer. The corporal and his friend were thus placed in stocks.

Captain Irvine then arrived and asked the lieutenant why his men were in stocks. Lieutenant Simpson said it was none of his business. Calling the lieutenant a "damn'd insignificant puppy," Irvine then went to see the quartermaster, Capt. Lorenzo Thomas. Thomas told Irvine he had a general order to pay the men only 15 cents extra duty pay per day and nothing could be done about it. Irvine threatened to go to General Jesup, but Thomas suddenly remembered seeing the general earlier and the latter had affirmed the extra allowance per day. Walker suspected this was nothing more than a scheme for the quartermaster to give the men only 15 cents a day and pocket the rest of the money.

On May 10, Samuel Walker brought his brother Jonathan up to date with his service and plans to meet with his brother Nathan in New Orleans:

> Tampa Bay E[ast] F[lorida] headquarters
> Army of the South, May 10, 1837
>
> Dear Brother
> I this day received your letter which gave me the greatest pleasure imaginable. I also received your letter of Jan 1st not however untill the 4th of April. When I wrote to you last there was considerable doubt whether the Indians would come in or not. It has been the case ever since untill a few days ago. News was received that [Lt. Levin] Powell [USN] was at Tuscaloosca with a considerable number of Indians on his way here. Micanopa [Miconopa], Cloud and Aligator are all kept at this Fort as hostages for the fulfilment of the treaty. A considerable quantity of shipping has been lying in the Bay for the last six weeks waiting for the Indians to embark for Arkansas but I think they may wait as much longer though there is no doubt at present of their intention to go but not untill they get ready. They have already brought in five or six hundred head of fine cattle and Powell has a great many more which is expected in a few days. This proves their intention of going to the west. You will perhaps think it a miraculous story when I tell you that upwards of forty thousand cattle have been slaughtered since the war commenced and a great many left yet. You may judge then what a man can do in this country. I should say it is the best place for all poor People. If Brother has given up the idea of going to the west I would advise him and all other poor people to move to the south especialy Mechanics. If you or Henry was either in this county in five years with economy and industry you might save more than you would in all your lifetime at the north. That is exactly my notion of the south. I would advise Charles to stick to his trade untill I see him again which will be in twelve months at most when I hope to be of some service to him and also my single Sisters. You can inform them that they are welcome to what trifles I have left behind as I shall not want for them anymore. I should be very happy to see you all again and through the persuation of my friends and other considerations I had almost determined to come home this summer and return in the fall but hearing from Nathan I have determined to remain. I expect to leave here in three weeks for New Orleans to meet Nathan. Our time expires in three weeks from today. You can direct letters to Neworleans hereafter. I have this day closed a letter to Nathan and promised him

> to be there as quick as posible. My health is extremely good and also the whole company. There is not a man in the hospital of our company which is fifty men in number, the largest company in Florida and I hope when you receive this you may all be the same. Give my love to my Parents and Sisters and likewise to all inquiring friends and tell the girls I hope they will not all get married before I return. I will write no more at present but remain your affectionate Brother.
>
> S H Walker[43]

The men of the Washington City Volunteers served out the remaining days of their enlistments uneventfully and were mustered out at Tampa Bay on May 31, 1837.

Sam would later note the army at that time was in poor shape. He said "the majority of the enlisted men in the service were worthless dregs of society from almost every European nation. … Very few were American except some outcast of society, [who] were accustomed to being cuffed or kicked by anyone in authority; they were used to be treated thusly therefore so a military officer … roughing them up was expected."[44]

Sam's observations, expressed in his pamphlet, about the role of an officer would reflect his own ideals and values when he later became an officer. He wrote "a man must be a good soldier, or he will not make a good officer to command soldiers." Capt. Sam Walker remembered the lessons he learned as an enlisted man in the Seminole War. A few years after the end of the Mexican–American War, George W. Myers, a former sergeant in Company C, U.S. Mounted Rifles, wrote of Sam Walker as an officer:

> Capt. Walker was a man universally beloved. … He was a father to us in his care, and one of the very best I have met with in my walks through life. Often would he be up two-thirds of the night, when we were on a scout, to see if his men were comfortably quartered, and the horses taken care of, and in the morning, he would be as fresh and vigorous as any of those who had slept undisturbed all the night.[45]

As a civilian returning home to Toaping Castle in 1840, Sam ventured into Washington City to visit his brother, Jonathan. There, he learned a veteran of the Washington City Volunteers had returned home to a good government job. Sam's nemesis, Captain Robinson—who had been so abusive to his soldiers—was now a mail guard for the U.S. Post Office. Sam Walker bristled at this gross injustice. He wanted everyone to know how badly this man had treated his men and then returned home to be rewarded by the federal government. The 12-page summary of Robinson's infamy was printed at his expense and handed out to any who would take it, including as many congressmen as could be contacted. Family tradition has it this was very embarrassing to several members of the Walker family who lived in the Washington area and had business dealings with many in the city. Some were very glad when he did return to Florida.[46]

CHAPTER 3

The Florida Civilian Years

To understand why Walker made the decisions he did later in life, one needs to understand his convictions on various topics. This chapter consists of Sam Walker's own letters expressing his thoughts on Texas, his desires to get married, on drinking, his belief in a Supreme Being, established religion, justice, the futility of war—but primarily his desire to prove himself on the field of battle, and on his desires to command men in the defense of settlers against the indigenous people.

Sam Walker wrote primarily and often to his oldest brother Jonathan Thomas; always addressed as Tom or Thomas among family members.[1] But it was his brother, Nathan, five years older and known for his extraordinary memory as well as his quest for adventure,[2] who wrote Thomas about the many opportunities in New Orleans. Business was so good; he wanted his entire family to join him.

New Orleans, March 20th 1837

> Dear Brother
> I am very glad to heare from you and all the families. Mr. Bowen says you were all well when he left. I have had the yellow fever about eighteen months ago but it is of no consequence. I was disabled about three weeks but did not feel alarmed. I layed in my bed and seen them get frightened to death three in two hours. I have enjoyed very good health ever since and think this to be as healthy as any City. I had declined ever writing to you, as I never knew when I should stop. I have been in Orleans ever since June following that I left home, and I am very well pleased with it and have been harde at worke ever since, and getting three dollars per day till the last few months I have been jobing it which is very good business and will pay five to six dollars per day. Business is geting so good that I shall make it my home. It is superior to any city that I have ever been in for mechanics. Thomas you had better sell what you have and come to orleans if you wish to make money and persuad my Brothers and sisters to come and Father and Mother I suppose it is no use to persuade, but if they knew how

Jonathan Thomas Walker. (Walker Family Archives)

easy it would be to live they would not hesitate a moment. Every Man would bring thirty five to forty dollars per-month and women twenty. This is true a statement as I can give with out flattery. I have several Jobs on hand that will pay me fifty dollars per week for about six weeks. I have not saved much till the last six months but what I have I intend to buy me a lot of ground which has been the greatest speculation I ever saw. Lots here twelve months ago bought for five hundred dollars cannot be bought for three thousand and still increasing. I have seen no persons I knew but Thomas Beall and William. I could write to you a deall more, but the Steam Boat Monmouth is to go at four Oclock which Mr Boen is gowing on. It is now Drawing near the time, and I mush bee in haste. You will send my love and best friendship to Father Mother and sisters and Brothers and likewise all the coulered folks and all inquiring friends. But I supose I have none by my bad action. I beg to be excused for a little while longer as I shall be feel myself able to face them. I could do it now but it would put where I started. I have nothing more at present but your affectionately

Nathan Walker[3]

Thomas wrote Sam about Nathan's good fortune in New Orleans. He changed his mind about going to Texas. The Native American troubles were ending and the South was on the verge of an economic boom with fortunes waiting to be made by skilled carpenters such as his brothers and himself. He saw the same waiting for him in Texas, but before leaving for the new republic, would see if Nathan's description of New Orleans offered him better opportunities. Walker arrived in New Orleans and spent four fruitless days in search of employment and, more importantly, Nathan. He went so far as to post a notice in the New Orleans *Daily Picayune*. His ad, which ran from June 14 to June 20 read, "If Mr. Nathan Walker is in this city, he will please call at the Western Exchange Coffee House, corner of Tchaitoulas and Natchez streets and much oblige his affectionate brother, S. H. Walker." Nathan soon saw the notice and arrived to greet his much-relieved brother. For the time being, Walker was content to stay in New Orleans; however, it was not the place that actually matched the description of the city that Nathan wrote of so glowingly. Florida, however, was still a land of opportunity. If Nathan could be persuaded to leave New Orleans and go back with him to Florida, chances of success were better. Good fortune would follow and a permanent settlement for their family in Florida was possible.

New Orleans, La, July 7th 1837

Dear Brother
I received your letter yesterday and was much pleased to hear from you. You stated in your letter that you wished me to give you a history of New Orleans. I will commence from the day of my arrival which was

on the 13th June. The first two or three days I spent in looking for Nathan and also a job without success. And on the fourth day when I was consulting myself about going to Texas, who should come in but Nathan. He had just got over a severe spell of the billious fever. He is now finally recovered and looks much the same as when you saw him. When he wrote to you, was very flatering as my kind of business was very brisk now it is quiet. This can vary. Every kind of business is stagnated except the rag manufactory that is very brisk. Every restaurant coffee house and exchange issue their own notes for charges. Some of the banks pay their bills to the amt. of five dollars. One of them a few days ago after being closed as long as his charter would allow opened and paid specie thirty minutes and closed again. You may swear that they will hold on to the specie. Their notes is now twenty five percent at discount and those who have them are glad to get shut of them on almost any terms. This however is not telling you what my views are of the place. My first views are that it is a very bad place for poor people at present though I have no doubt it was at one time as Nathan represented it. There are a great many very extensive buildings on hand but not much work done on them at present. There is a great many improvements in contemplation which will doubtless make it one of the greatest places in the country. The appearance of the city in many places is already very handsome and clearly the whole city is paved and the greatest trouble is to keep the streets clean to avoid sickness. Though I doubt not that if you were here with your little Family that you might do much better than in your present situation. Notwithstanding the present hard times I don't think they can last long. However I would not advise you to make a permanent residence in New Orleans. I would not do it myself. I would much rather be in the woods somewhere so that I could enjoy the fresh breezes and have a free range. I expect to remain here until next spring and then proceed up the Mississippi homeward and by that time I shall determine on my future residence. I should be happy if you were with me and Nathan. We are both boarding together and have both got work at $2.75 per day boarding $5.00 per week though we can make more at job work which we will work at for the future. I would advise you not to sell any of your property yet. I will endeavor to find out some handsome and healthful situation where you may make a permanent settlement, live independent and enjoy good health. I will write no more at present but remain your affectionate Brother.

S H Walker

PS Nathan has not received your letter but he will write shortly. We both join in sending our best love to you all particularly our kind

> Parents and to the [illegible] and tell them I am well at present though I have had a short spell of the bilious fever just by way of introduction to the place.[4]

It took a month for the brothers to finally realize New Orleans was not the place for them. Sam heard the army was hiring civilians to work in the quartermaster's department in Tampa Bay.

Pay was good and travel expenses would be covered by the army. He and Nathan took advantage of this. Even if the duration of the work was only for three months, the brothers had an eye toward a future in Florida.

> New Orleans, La, July 13, 1837
>
> Dear Brother
> Since my last my ideas are much changed about remaining here untill next spring. Finding times so hard here that I could not more than clear expenses I have this day made an agreement with the Quarter Master of the U S Army to return to Tampa Bay Florida to work as a carpenter for three months at two dolls. & seventy five cents per day & rations. Pay to commence from today and expenses paid to Tampa. This I considered much better than working here for the same wages and finding myself, besides losing half my time from the unfavourableness of the weather and the scarcity of work at present. Now I shall receive pay for every day Sundays included which will amount to eighty odd dollars per month and after paying all necessary expenses I can save seventy dollars per month. And more over I can demand the Specie which is a great consideration at present. I expect I shall remain there untill next spring. Nathan is going with me for the same considerations above stated. There is not much news here at present only the rag money is as plenty as ever and two more new banks in progress. God knows what will become of the working class if they continue to charter banks. There is about one half of them idle in this city and this is said to be the best at present of any city in the U S. This of course is a great distress which is occasioned only by the Banks. I hope in twelve months shall roll around they may all be sunk to eternity [illegible] there will not be so much speculation on the poor and we shall see our country prosper. You can inform the W C Volunteers who talk of coming out to the south that they had better go to Florida if they wish to get employment. Tell them that Mclean is here, Jewel has taken passage for Boston. Wharton I believe has gone up the river. None of them could get any work at any thing. And I do assure there is more loafers here than I ever expected to see at one place. Tom, I have always had a very favourable opinion of Florida though I have only seen the poorest part of it.

> I think any many would do well to go there. At present Government is paying high wages and when the Indians are removed it will be still better especially for mechanics as the plantations [illegible] to rebuild being all burnt by the Indians. When I get there again I will give you all the information posible concerning this country. I am persuaded you would do well to settle there. Nathan and myself will embark tomorrow evening for Tampa. You must write often and direct yours Tampa Bay C F. I shall be glad to hear from you at any time and also the folks in the old neighbourhood both Ladies and Gentlemen. Nathan and I send our best wishes & respects to all inquiring friends and particularly to our kind parents and tell them we will be home next June. I have nothing more at present but remain your affectionate Brother
>
> S H Walker[5]

Sam and Nathan went to Tampa Bay and completed their work for the army. Other accounts of this period in Walker's life report him getting his position through the influence of George Gordon Meade, who would 25 years later gain fame as the victor of the Battle of Gettysburg during the Civil War. There is no evidence showing Walker and Meade in the same place at the same time during either man's service during the Seminole War. Meade resigned his commission as a second lieutenant, U.S. Army while stationed at the Watertown Arsenal in Massachusetts on October 26, 1836. As a civilian, he worked as an assistant engineer on the construction of the Alabama, Florida, and Georgia Railroad from November 1836 to April 1837. Following this, Meade was employed by the War Department to assist in a survey of the mouth of the Sabine River boundary line between the United States and Texas, after which he worked on a survey of the delta of the Mississippi River.[6] During the Mexican–American War, Meade, having been reinstated as an officer in the army, was with Gen. Zachary Taylor's army at Point Isabel, Mexico. In a letter to his wife dated May 5, 1846, he told of the precarious situation in which the 7th Infantry Regiment, manning the fieldworks opposite Matamoros, found itself. Hearing heavy cannonading in the direction of the position held by the 7th, General Taylor took action. Meade wrote, "He [General Taylor], however despatched an express by a gallant Texan by the name of Walker, who being perfectly well acquainted with the country, said he could make his way into the work and bring us back the news."[7] Had he and Walker been friends or coworkers on any project in Florida in 1836 or 1837, Meade would certainly have mentioned it in this letter. It is clear Walker was a complete stranger to him in May 1846.

The Walker brothers were enjoying the success of the business endeavors and Sam was happy to let his family know it:

Iola Calhoun County West Florida February 16, 1837 [1838]

Dear Brother
I received your favour of the 25th Jan and was extremely happy to hear you were all well and still hope that these times may find you all enjoying the same good health and blessings which it has pleased the hands of Devine Providence to bestow upon you in former days.

I was sorry to hear the death of Thomas's youngest child as it must certainly have been a source of grief to its parents. Though they should console themselves by taking everything as the will of the Supreme Being.

You stated in your letter that you thought you had best remain where you are and possibly you may think very right though your thoughts are very different from mine on that point as the chances here are much greater to a sturdy industrious young man than what you can have there. Then I would advise you so long as you remain there to pay strict attention to your business and try if possible to acquire all general information you can relating to mechanisms as you will find it of great importance to you if you should ever remove to a new country like this.

I have concluded to leave here next summer and go about one hundred miles up the river to some of the water Mills and ship to Texas all the buildings we can finish during the summer months. Nathan will remain here and keep the Hotell and manage our business in this place. We have a steam saw mill here which we had at one time agreed to take a share in it by the constant solicitations of the present owners, neither of them being mechanicks themselves. They were very anxious to sell us a share in it but I have since declined taking it, though I have still got the managment of it and we are now paying upwards of three hundred dollars per anum for nine negroes to run it. She [i.e., the steam engine] runs two gangs of saws and one grist mill. We have put her in good time for running and she will cut from five to seven thousand feet per day. Notwithstanding it will be much better for us to go up the country to buy our lumber than it will be to get it here as we can get it there for $8 to $10 per me [In this context, "me" is most likely an abbreviation for 1000 feet of lumber since Roman numeral "M" represents 1000 and the "e" likely represents feet] and here it is $15 per me and besides it costs us twenty dollars per month for board here and one hundred miles up the river you can board for five dollars per month. So that you may judge what this difference will be besides the advantage of a healthful situation, the last account from Texas stated that lumber was selling for $80 per me and a vessel will sail it in four or five days so it cannot fail to be a profitable business as there is at present very few engaged in the trade. Should you think proper, you can have an interest in it if you can come out by the 15th of May or the first of June next and I am convinced you would never regret it. If Mother and Father would agree to let you bring out several of the Negros we can well afford to pay double what they have for them and still make it profitable to us. If they would consent to it, I would send you money to pay yours and their expenses out. We are now paying fifteen dollars per month for a girl fourteen years of age. We are all in good health. Nathan talks of taking his wife to see you some suitable opportunity though I am afraid the longer we stay here the less chance we will have of paying you a visit as our business is still increasing so much so it always demands our presence. I think you will be much pleased with Nathans Wife when you see her. She is industrious handsome and very agreable company. Her name was Annette Stone. She was born in Alabama and raised in Florida. I am in hopes I shall have the pleasure of giving you an invitation to my wedding within the next six or twelve months as I am determined to marry the first suitable partner I can make a bargain with. Though I have got her to look for, my business has always heretofore confined so closely that I have never yet spent a day for that purpose. Theres but very few immediately in the vicinity of our new Town though there is a great many wealthy young Ladies where I intend going next summer so that the chance will be much better to make a selection. You must write again soon and let me know what is going on in the old neighborhood and what is going on in Washington and know what is going on in congres or else send me the intelligence and I will endeavor to compensate you for it by the first suitable opportunity and let me know shortly what you intend doing. You will please accept our love to yourself and all the rest of them and tell them I often think of them and it would be great pleasure for me to see them again. Give my best respects to all inquiring friends and tell them to write to me as it would give me great pleasure to have a communication with any of my acquaintances. The railroad to this place will soon be completed, distance from St Joseph 28 miles. Several country roads will centre at this place and there is a good prospect of another railroad being connected with this to run entirely across the peninsula to Brunswick [Georgia] harbour on the atlantic. The object is to make this the great thorughfare from N Carolina Mobile Pensacola and Texas and the west Indies so as to avoid the necessity of going around the capes of Florida which is very dangerous and many vessels are lost every year. And this will in my opinion be a great place for a public house. Our house will accommodate 100 persons with lodgings and I am of opinion we shall make something handsome by our undertaking though there is a possibility of it being otherwise. Nothing more but I am Sir, with great respect your affectionate Brother

S H Walker[8]

When the brothers went to Tampa Bay, they inevitably met area businessmen. One was probably Col. Henry Dessex Stone who was once President of the Territorial Council of Florida and founded the Apalachicola River town of Iola in 1835. Stone and Walker shared a commonality of interest in the lumber business. Although Iola was over 300 miles to the north, sailing from St. Joseph on the coast to Tampa Bay, Colonel Stone and his daughter Anne apparently visited Tampa Bay where she met Nathan. On June 28, 1838, Nathan married Miss Anne Stone.[9]

A month later, in a brief letter to his brother Charles, Walker announced the marriage to his family and inquired about the cost of certain properties in the Washington area:

> Mr. Charles E Walker Washington City DC Sixth St in great haste
> Iola W Florida July 22 1838
>
> Dear Brother
> I write to inform you that I am in good health and hope these lines may find you all the same. Nathan was married on the 28th of June to Miss Anne Stone. She is a lady of considerable accomplishments and very amiable qualities. Nathan has since had a spell of the billious fever and has had the ague & fever. He is now able to get about and is fast recovering. I have not received any answer from you since I wrote to you though I do not lay it to your negligence as I expect they are now in the post Office at Apilachicola and I will send down by the first opportunity for them. I am in hopes you will come out next fall to see us and try the southern country a while. I want you write shortly and let me know the prices of 2 Negros as I wish to purchase a few for my own use as they are by far the most valuable property a man can own in this part of the country. Give my best respects to Father & Mother and all the rest of them and tell them they need not look for me home this season as I do not wish to travel until my income will pay my expenses, and that time I think will be some distance off. Nathan never says anything about returning home lately. I have nothing more to write at present but remain your affectionate Brother.
>
> SH Walker[10]

Sam, his brother Nathan, and Nathan's new wife, lived in Iola—the community founded by Anne's father three years previously.[11] Iola began to grow after the completion of a railroad, from the port town of St. Joseph 28 miles away, linking Iola to the Apalachicola River.[12]

The brothers Walker now embarked upon new ventures in the town of Iola, Florida; Nathan as a hotel keeper and Sam in the sawmilling business.

Sam, while choosing not to be part owner in a steam sawmill, did manage the operation in Iola and paid $300 a year for nine Black people who ran two gang saws and one grist mill. The sawmill cut from five to seven thousand feet of lumber per day, but he looked to the possibilities of leaving Nathan to keep the hotel and manage the sawmill, and the next summer going upriver one hundred miles where he could buy lumber at almost half the price than it cost to saw it himself. He then could ship it to Texas at a great profit.

The expanding economy of Florida demanded a safe, secure, and less time-consuming method of transporting raw materials from their sources and bringing finished products from the Gulf Coast ports to those towns and plantations that were springing up beyond the reach of steamboats. A railroad from St. Joseph to Iola was the answer. Walker was very optimistic railroads would bring increased business to his sawmill and his property eventually would become very valuable. The reason for the construction of the railroad was the competition between the two port towns of Apalachicola[13] and St. Joseph.[14] Both towns were interested in trade from the cotton growing regions in Florida, Alabama, and Georgia, served by the Apalachicola River and its tributaries—the Chattahoochee and Flint Rivers. Normally, the trade would travel by barge down the Apalachicola River to its mouth at Apalachicola. But the harbor there was shallow, only 8 feet in a constantly changing channel. However, St. Joseph had a harbor 17 feet deep—more than enough for any ocean-going vessel. With a better harbor than Apalachicola, St. Joseph planners hoped a railroad would serve the town best. They looked to Tennessee Bluff on the Apalachicola River (the site of the town of Iola). Nearly 30 miles from St. Joseph, a railroad would cut 70 miles from dangerous river navigation and provide a great advantage to the town.[15]

Sam wrote Charles, again extolling the opportunities in Florida, but also told of the illnesses that plagued him, Nathan, and his workers. Nevertheless, his confidence in the completion of the new railroad and his construction endeavors never dimmed.

> Iola, West Florida, Oct 21st 1838
> Mr. Charles E Walker, Washington City, DC, Sixth Street
>
> Dear Brother
>
> I received your letter which duly came to hand. But being unable to write from a short spell of the billious fever which I had at that time I did not write so soon as I should have done provided I had been in good health. Nathan and myself however are both in tolerable health at present though Nathan has had a long spell of it and has not been at work more than ten days and my other partner and all my hands have been sick with the Ague and Fever for several months past so that I have not made out as well as I anticipated. Our new town

has proved unhealthy this summer though it has been generally a very sickly season all through the south though we cannot complain much. We have had two deaths in the place only. One was principally intemperance the other was a coloured woman who died with fits. Our population is about one hundred. The Rail Road to St Josephs is nearly all ready for the iron which is daily expected from Liverpool and it is expected that the cars will run by Christmas. We are still progressing slowly with our hotell which we commenced last spring and I shall use every endeavor to have it fited out by the time the Rail Road is done. I am in great hopes that either your or Thomas will come out and see us this winter. As for my own part I shall not make any more promises when I shall visit you. Times are dull at present though we expect much better in a short time, as all the adjoining states are improving considerably. Give mine & Nathans best love & respect to Father & Mother & all the rest of them and tell them we often think about them & would be very glad to see them. And also give my respects to all inquiring friends. I want you to write shortly. Direct your letter to Iola W F. We have now got a front office at this place. You must let me know what has become of Bull Robinson as I have a particular wish to see him. I will write no more at present but still remain your most affectionate Brother.

S H Walker

To C. E. Walker
PS Nathan's wife is well and they live very agreably together. Either you or Thomas must not fail to come out this winter. I remain your, etc.[16]

In January 1839, Sam wrote his brother Charles again, inviting him to join him and Nathan, either as a partner in their construction business or to establish his own. Their business was expanding as was the town. Walker, a success at 22 years of age, was realizing his dream.

To Mr. Charles E Walker, Washington City, DC
Iola, Calhoun Coty, Florida, Jan 16th 1839

Dear Brother
I have not received any answer to my last letter which was written several months ago. At any rate so long ago I have forgotten the date and I have been going to the Post Office every arrival to inquire for a letter. I sometimes get a few Numbers of the Native American sometimes it is three or four weeks after publication. The reason is they are directed to St Josephs and remain sometime before I can get them. You will please have them directed to Iola for the future and I shall get them fast however as we have a Post Office here and receive the mail twice

Steamboat *Marion* on the Ocklawaha River—Iola, Florida. (Courtesy of Florida Memory)

a week. We are now keeping house and boarding our own hands and Nathans wife is Landlady. We have not got any of our own buildings finished yet though I expect to have them finished this season. I think if you could come out this winter it will be much to your advantage. I can promise you a permanent situation at seven or eight hundred dollars per annum or sell you an interest in our building or guarantee you work at $3 per day without a change for the worse which I don't think can be as it is the worst I ever experienced though there is some prospect of better. The Banks have commenced specie payments again though all kinds of produce are very high. But the principal reason is that there are many new settlers consequently the consumption is much greater than the production. I send you the prices of produce Labor etc as you may then be able to Judge for yourself. Corn $1 per bushel. Potatoes $1 per box. Beef 8 & 9 cents per lb. Pork $26 per bbl. Mackarel $16 per bbl. Negro men hire for three hundred dollars per Annum. Women from $130 to $180 per Annum. We are all well at present hope when you receive this it may find you the same.

Nathan and myself send our love and respects to you all and also all inquiring friends. Nothing more at present but still remain your affectionate Brother.

S H Walker[17]

Walker did not attend church services on a regular basis; however, it is clear from letters he wrote to his family he did believe in a higher power. The loss of his infant niece Martha Ellen (his brother Jonathan's youngest child) who died on June 19, 1838, just 17 days after her birth was, in his mind, the will of the Supreme Being. Walker's religious thought was to wrong no man intentionally and attend to his own business and, if the Almighty felt he was not doing the duty that he should toward God, the Almighty would, as a good master, provide some evidence of what he should be doing differently.

The letter Walker received from his brother Charles was the one that brought the sad news of the death of Thomas's child. However, Walker's response focused on the good economic times he and his brother Nathan were enjoying in Iola. So much so that Sam even offered to the pay passage from Maryland so Charles and his parents could visit. Nathan talked of taking his wife to see their parents in Maryland in his letter dated February 16, 1837, but business was still increasing and it was doubtful when that would happen. In April, Walker wrote his parents an extensive letter, letting them know he, Nathan, and his wife were in good health and he hoped to come home in the not too distant future. However, times were not good financially. The sawmill, with a few thousand feet of lumber and over $150 worth of his tools, burned in February—a major blow as his business was considerably indebted.

Mr. Nathan Walker
near Beltsville, Prince Georges County, Maryland
Iola, Calhoun County, West Florida, Apl 20th 1839

Dear Father & Mother
I take this opportunity of informing you that I am in good health & Nathan & Wife likewise. I have just received Charles letter of the 6th inst. and was glad to hear you all were yet in the land of the living and enjoying a reasonable share of health. I hope you will not think hard of my not writing to you often, as I have written to you before and have never received a scrip of writing with your signatures attached to it, so that I have sometimes been forced to doubt whether you would wish to hear from me or not. Though I often think of you and hope that the time is not far distant where circumstances will admit of my returning home to see you all once more this side of eternity, my circumstances at present render it rather difficult to return, as it is now about the hardest times that has been experienced in a long time in regard of money matters though the prospect is fair for a change and I hope the time is not far distant when we shall see things flourish again. We were amongst the first settlers of this place and you must judge of the many hardships and disadvantages which people have to undergo in settling a new Town in a new country. Though from the prospects, we were induced to purchase a Lot and commence building a public house which will, when complete, be worth about ten Thousand dollars or more so that it has kept us under a strain the most of the time to purchase material and provisions to enable us to advance with our improvements. We also had another misfortune which happened in February last which has made us fall short in our calculations. The Steam saw Mill which I spoke of some time ago took fire and burnt up in which we sustained a considerable loss as the concern was considerably indebted to us for work, besides burning about one hundred and fifty dollars worth of our best tools together with about four or five thousand feet of Juniper lumber—the logs of which we procured from the swamps at considerable expense and labor. It was worth about seventy five dollars per-thousand. We intended it for the inside finishing of our building on account of its durability and pleasant smell. Though we are glad it was no worse, as we had at one time agreed to buy the half of it though we had never entered into any obligation but agreed to wait untill we had put it in good order for work before we would sign any agreement. We succeeded in making her cut five & six thousand feet per day which pleased the owner so well that they didn't say any thing more about the trade and she only run about two weeks before she got burned. Though we have got our building considerably advanced and if no other misfortune happens we shall be able to complete it next fall if not sooner. We have

the most of the work that is going on though it is at present rather limited and for some time past. So that you may judge for yourselves what our situation is at present without any further particulars so that the expense and time of a trip home would throw us considerably behind and, though I need not say home, as I have got so that I already consider myself home. Though I have got so that I would give almost any thing in the world to see you again. Nathan has a handsome agreable wife and we all live very agreable together and business goes on very, very smooth. Nathan is fond of hunting and often supplies our table with abundance of wild game such as Turkey & deer and we have a big Turkey roasting now which I intend to do justice to as soon as I finish this letter. The river abounds with fish and we can have a mess almost at any time with a little exertion. The Railroad to this place is all completed ready for receiving the iron and one cargo of the iron has arrived and they will commence laying down in a short time. And it is thought by most of People this will be a place of great business next season as it will be the great thoroughfare from the northern cities to the great heart of the south to Mobile Pensacola and Texas. With these considerations I entertain no doubts but our property in this place will eventually be very valuable. Nathan has become rather sickly to do much hard work and is often laid up when he takes much severe exercise. He is to keep public house and my other partner and my self will continue to carry on the carpenters business pretty largely and I have also determined to take in another partner as I have found that a union of poor men in business is the only means which will enable them to compete with rich capitalists. I have just been making a calculation of what your negros would hire for if you had them out here. At the present rate they would hire for two thousand dollars per anum. They would be still more profitable on a farm at the present prices of cotton. And no negros that I have ever seen brought from the middle states out to Florida would wish to return even if they had their choice as negros generally speaking is treated much better here than they are in Maryland and Virginia. I would be very thankful to you when I return if you would let Nathan and myself have two or three to bring out when I come back to Florida as it would save us a great expense of hire and enable us to get along with much more ease. It may be posible that I shall be home by the last of Augt. or september. Nathan may perhaps return some time in 1840. He will bring his wife with him. I expect you will be much pleased with her. She is lively and fond of sport and civil amusement. A first rate seamstress & her disposition agrees very well with that of Nathan. I have come to the conclusion to get a Wife the first suitable companion I can select though I have not made any selection as yet. You will please write soon. Direct your letter as usual via Quincy as I expect to be in that section of country in about a month hence where I shall possibly remain most of the summer. Charles gave me a long discourse about religion in his letter—which I am thankful to him for as I know it came from his heart and it is my disposition always to thank people for this friendly admonition and advice although I may not view things as they do. I make no pretentions to religion and never expect to. I do unto all as I would have them do unto me and have as yet a clear conscious that I have never wronged no man except where I have done it to myself and if I ever did it was derogatory to my intentions. I went to church last sunday for the first time since I was in Neworleans. This was in St. Josephs thirty miles from this place. I heard a long discourse and explanation of holy writ from Father Gautier which had about the same effect that it usually does with me. He preached strong Hellfire and damnation to all who did not repent. And after he was done I compared his religion and mine together—and of the two, I think I am about as sure the kingdom of heaven as he is. He is a red hot Methodist and was at one time expelled from the church for being to fond of dark skin Ladies though I do not doubt that the pious old man has repented of that sin since his head has got grey and has been reinstated. As for my own part I never can believe in forcing any notion to think I could be born again. I think that religion does much good in one respect as it keeps people from vicious habits which the human mind is always incident to when it has no moral occupation. It is very true that I feel confident that there is a power which is far greater than that of man and also there seems to be a supreme ruler which every sensible man or woman looks up to with reverence though they may not make long Prayers and fastings. That much we know of a supreme being and that is the sum and substance of what we do know relative to a supreme being. And we know and all as that we are creatures in one respect like all others born to die. Now some people may argue about the intentions and will of the supreme power—though it would be useless for me to attempt any thing of the sort as I have read the bible and studied these things and have always found myself a long ways from any definite conclusion on such matters. I was always compeled to bring my whole study to this focus: 1st That whatever we could see we knowed. 2nd That whatever we have good and plain evidence of we can believe it. Everything else is imagination and it is a weak minded man or woman who would suffer themselves firmly to believe in the imaginations of the brain without proof or good circumstancial evidence. For instance, could I reprimand or chastise a servant for not fulfiling a duty or performing any thing that I wished him to do without my telling him. No I would be callus and unjust and cruel master. The same rule will apply to the supreme rules of the universe in relation to myself and all his creatures. I contend that whenever the Almighty and infinite being wishes me to seek him in any other way he will at least give me some circumstantial evidence of it and first cause me to believe it. At present I do all that I actualy think is required. I wrong no man intentionally and attend to my own business. We are told in the Scriptures that God created all things out of nothing and I have never heard any one contradict it though I have heard that it has been argued that every thing came by chance. I do not contradict this or that, but I earnestly ask the question for information and light on the subject. As I stated above I never could come to any definite conclusion on such matters. Therefore I would be very thankful to any one who could correct me in my delusion as I expect it will be termed by most of religious sects. The great and marvelous question I ask is from what spirit and will did the Almighty everlasting and infinite spirit of God spring from? The natural conclusion is that something must have sprung from chance. This is an idea that has for many years occupied a portion of my mind though I have never made it my business to ask the question before.

My Dear Parents I did not intend that part of my letter for you particularly nor did I contemplate writing about it when I commenced. I intended it partly in answer to Charles letter and all others whom it might concern, and would be glad to receive any communications on the subject. As reading and writing is my greatest amusement of evenings and sundays, you will please accept mine and Nathans love to yourselves and all the Family and tell them we often think of you all and sometimes our imaginations even places us in company with you. But alas, the imagination of man is false and delusive and we still find ourselves in the far distant and beautiful wilds of Florida. Give our best respects to all inquiring friends and tell them if any of them should be traveling towards Neworleans or Texas to give us a call. Nothing more at present but remain your most humble and affectionate Son.

SH Walker

PS Be sure and write soon. Direct your letter as follows
To Samuel H Walker
Iola, West Florida, via Quincy
Nathans wife sends her respects to you all.[18]

In the collection of Walker's letters, there is a gap from April 1839 until the end of the year. Nathan's health apparently grew worse as he died in November 1839. On November 18, a committee of citizens of Iola, with great respect for Nathan, sent a letter of condolence to Walker's father.[19] Jonathan responded and thanked the committee who sent the letter and inquired about Sam.[20]

Family friend and now-Florida resident by the name of Hudson showed Walker the letter received from his brother, pointing out the lack of letters from Sam to his family and the concern for his well-being. Sam's next letter, no doubt written under the pain of Nathan's death, has an edge to it not seen in any of his previous communications.

His brother Charles apparently belittled Sam's enthusiastic accounts of the success he and Nathan were enjoying in Florida and the opportunities awaiting him if he would only come and take advantage of them. Sam accused Thomas of having a lackadaisical attitude toward answering the letters he wrote him. Sam seemed to be bitter toward his family for seemingly not appreciating the efforts he and Nathan put into their businesses and the success they had found. If it was not for the death of Nathan, he would not have written to his family again. Nevertheless, he soon got over his ill feelings and again invited his family to visit him in Florida. Although written on December 29, 1839, the letter was not posted until January 10, 1840.

Iola, Calhoun Cty, Fla, Decr 29th 1839

Dear Brother—
I have seen your letter which was directed to Messers Hudson & Roach and should have written sooner if I had not thought that you would have received my letter which was written the 16th of Nov. which related all the particulars of my Brother's Death, &c. though it was not mailed until the 1st of Decr and I expected you to receive it by the 14th.

I also received Charles' letters of July 10th and Nov 25th both of which duly came to hand. The reason why I did not answer the former was because he received mine a month before he answered it, and then it was scribbled and crosslined with a pack of stuff which made it too contemptible to merit an answer. You stated that you had written several times without hearing from me but I think you are mistaken because I answered the last I received from you of which the receipt of was acknowledged by you. It was by Charles since that I have received all the letters he has written and he has never mentioned about your writing. And from your Carelessness generally towards us about writing I had determined never to write again and should not only on account of my Brother's death. It is true that I often think of you all, and visit the Post Office regularly for letters and have been disappointed very often. In some instances you have received two letters from me without writing and it is only wright that I should treat you all with the same justified contempt, however I do not feel disposed to encourage this feeling as it is a pleasure to me to hear from you, and also to write to you, and would be extremely glad to see you all once more though it is impossible for me to come home unless I could sell my property which I can not do at present without sacrificing it as the currency of the country is in a deplorable situation at present and property will not bring its value, however I do not feel much disposed to sell at present as the Town is improving and I think that property will greatly increase in value, and this is one of the best stands for a Public house in the southern country, there are about 16 steamboats plying the river during the boating season the most of which are laden and unladen at this place. The termination of the Rail Road and also the termination of three public roads for wagons and stages one from Marianna one from Tallahassee & one from Mt. Vernon all will be completed in 1840. The buildings which we have on hand is very suitable for a public house. It is large enough to accommodate about eighty or ninety lodgers. We have much sickness this season generally. It has been a very sickly [illegible] fall and consequently we are behind hand and necessarily compeled to work and pay our debts at present. Though it is healthy now and will continue so until Augt. Myself and sister Ann are well at present and hope these lines may find all the same. She has left our establishment and returned home to her parents where she must live very unhappy, as her Father is very dissipated and abusive and the wants of his family by no means too well supplied. Her parents, however are of respectable families and were once in good circumstances and reduced by his dissipation. I told my sister in law that she could have the same house which she formerly had but owing to her delicate situation she did not choose to accept it. I have advertised for letters of administration in order to settle his—Nathan's—debts and ac[coun]ts. And to place the residue which will probably be four or five hundred dollars in such a situation as may do his off spring and his distressed wife the most good. She expressed great desire to see you all and I should be extremely glad if you should come out this winter and I will return with you in the spring. You can at all events come if you only stay a few days and return if it was only for seeing a part of the world you live in and I think you will not regret your journey. You can come in about six or seven days by taking the present mail route to Norfolk N Orleans from Norfolk Va.

Before I close I have one particular request to make. It is this. I want you to have a small neat tombstone to adorn my Brother's grave with his name, age, birthplace, date of death, &c neatly engraved on it and send it by the first vessel for St. Josephs. You must remember me to them all and tell them I often think of them.

Nothing more now but still remain your affectionate Brother.

S.H.W.

PS You must be sure and write and let me know whether you will come out or not.[21]

Walker's intemperate comments in his December 1839 letter may be the result of the sudden collapse of Iola's economy and his having to hire himself out in order to make ends meet, even though he was barely recovered from an attack of typhoid fever. The machinations of what he called villainous railroad owners and their association with an Apalachicola business conglomerate in competition with Iola interests had brought ruin to Iola and St. Joseph. (Although Iola would ultimately recover, St. Joseph would not. The next year an epidemic of yellow fever would kill 80 percent of its population. Its railroad company fell into bankruptcy and storms would sweep away the once-thriving boomtown soon after.) Walker's once enthusiastic reports of prosperity and good times were replaced with grim tidings. Instead of encouraging family and friends to settle in Florida, he warned them away.

Iola, Fla, Jan 17th 1840

Dear Brother—
I received your letter of November 18th and was much pleased to hear you were all well and in good spirits from the anticipation of better times though when I contrast your situation with the distressed inhabitants of Florida I am compelled that you have cause to rejoice and return thanks to the divine Creator or the blessings bestowed upon you. I left here on the 6th of November sick and went to St Josephs and was confined to my rook about a week with the typhus fever. Having made an engagement previous to my going down I went to work as soon as I was able to stand up all day and soon recovered my health. Manuel[22] and myself both worked for the same employer, building a steam boat cabin. There is no house building going on at present neither in this place or St Josephs. I quit the job I was at work on, on account of the difficulty of getting money, and I had some difficulty in getting enough to pay my passage to Tallahassee. Manuel was necessarily compelled to continue in his present situation as he could not get the money due him. It will probably be several weeks before he will leave St Josephs. The business at this place and with St Joseph is broken up for the present by the Treachery and vilany of the President of and three or four leading men of the rail road company residing in Columbus Georgia by selling their interest and influence to the Apalachicola land company for the bribe of about one hundred thousand dollars in cash and about an equal amount in town property in Apalachicola city and this the citizens of Iola and St Josephs are ruined for the present by the viliany and faithlessness of men who have heretofore been considered among the first men of the state of Georgia. The best of our property now if sold at auction would not bring 12½ cts on the dollar of the original cost. I believe, however that it will terminate to an advantage in the end, as the Florida stockholders will use greater exertions, and the villainous act will rouse the indignation of every honest man engaged in commerce and I fancy that the time is not far distant when Iola and St Josephs with the superiority of its harbour and the many other advantages over Apalachicola will soon check

its growth, however we are all ruined for the present, and there is a good chance for speculators. I have advertised our property for sale, but have not had any offers for it.

My Brother Nathan's wife and child is well. If I return next summer I will take them on with me. She sends her respects to you all. Manuel also desires to be remembered by you all and sends his compliments to those young ladies across the way.

The news from the seat of war is favourable and some hopes are entertained that the Indians will be removed. The runaway Creek Indians are still in this vicinity and will probably commence their depredations when the leaves and foliage of the forest puts forth again. Our winter is over here and the buds are beginning to put forth. We have had two or three days cold enough to freeze a thin crust of ice on still water. I do not hear anything very favourable from Texas though the country is still rapidly increasing in its population. The currency is bad. Florida money is forty percent below par and some of it much more. The new bank that was started in St Josephs has suspended operations though it redeems what few notes it issues in specie. The bank was established under the charter of the old Magnolia Bank and it has been served for the liabilities of the old Bank though the suit will be decided in favour of the new Bank, and it would have been a great help to the citizens of this place had it not been for the conduct of those Gentlemen in Columbus has so paralised every thing at present that they will not discount or loan under any considerations.

I have found several odd fellows out here but I regret to say that I have found none who would reflect honor on the order and consequently I did not become very intimate with any of them except the Gentleman that I worked for in St Joseph and I did not approve of his conduct as he was entirely too fond of drinking parties &c which appear to be quite common though. I think I shall be able to give you something more interesting when I arrive in Tallahassee as the reports from there are very favourable though I would not advise any person to come to the south at present to find better times. I shall leave here tomorrow. I am thankful to you and P.H. Boss for the papers you have sent me. Please direct the next to Tallahassee. Give my compliments and respects to all inquiring friends and tell them I am well and wish them the same. I am your aft. Brother.

SHW

PS I should have written sooner but I am always apt to defer writing when I have nothing good to write. I hope this will be a sufficient apology. I will write when I get to Tallahassee more regular.[23]

There were no jobs for Walker and his friend Manuel Navarro in Tallahassee. With no hope for immediate employment, Walker decided to visit Maryland and his family.

Charleston, SC, Feb 24th 1840

> Dear Brother
> I take this opportunity to inform you that I am on my way to Maryland but shall probably remain here for several months, however there is no certainty and you must write to me as soon as secure this letter as I have not heard from you since you rote to Messers Hudson & Roach in Florida. I have written twice since Nathan's Death and secured no answer up to the 21s of Jan the time I left Iola Fla. All business is very dull in the south at present. I shall not write much at present as my object is to let you all know that I am on my way home and where to write to me I am very anxious to hear from you. When I left Iola I did not think of coming home so soon, but only my arrival in Tallahassee where we expected to get a profitable job for several months. I was disappointed. I then determined to come home and see you all once more. My sister in law was in good health when I left. Her confinement was expected in a short time. I have not heard from her since I left but shall write today to her. I am in good health and hope this may find you the same. Give my best respects to them all and tell Father and Mother that I will be home as soon as I can conveniently.
>
> Nothing more at present but I remain
>
> Your affectionate Brother S H Walker[24]

In his absence, or because of it, things were not going well for Walker's endeavors in Iola. John C. Taylor,[25] left in charge of Sam's businesses in Florida, was concerned about the economic situation. No lumber was forthcoming from suppliers, creditors would press for payment of bills, and concern that Walker would not return to Florida was mounting. Colonel Stone, Nathan's father-in-law, was interested in loaning money—likely from his sons, William S. and Lackland M. Stone who had opened a bank in St. Joseph—to allow the completion of the building Sam and Ann owned. Other associates in Iola were interested in buying his property. Knowing Sam was en route to Maryland, Taylor—not aware of where Walker was in his journey north—wrote to him in care of his brother Jonathan.

Iola Fla March 15th 1840

> Dear Sir
> I take the opportunity to write a few lines to you to let you know that I am well and all the rest of the family and hope you are the same. Anns child is born and grows fast. It is a girl. Three weeks old

next Wednesday. We received your letter March 9th and was glad to hear from you after an absence of about 10 weeks. We expected you was dead not hearing from you sooner. No doubt you heard of the murder of [illegible] wife and two children by Indians about the second of March. The Commerce [steamship] burst her boiler on her trip up the river and six men killed and wounded some others. I have not had any lumber from Alexander yet. I have seen him lately and he don't know when it will be here. I have had not much to do since you left. Write to me immediately and let me know if you are coming back or not for some thinks you are not. Lack and William Stone[26] has been here and established a bank in St Joseph. Colonel told me you could get money to finish the building if you was here. Moreover they talk of buting it. I heard last week that Kimbro and Smith wished to buy the House. Frank Arnow is preparing to make brick. I am going in with him if I can. I don't think it is best. If you don't wright as soon as you receive this, and give me some instructions, how shall proceed in case I am pushed by our creditors which no doubt I shall be as soon as they know you have gone home. It is more than likely that the houses will be attached. Snell has not got home yet and it is very dull here. Ed in Apalachicola to work for J. Davis. Our county is incorporated but it dont improve a bit. It is useless to write as I have no further particulars.

Respectfully Yours &c
J. C. Taylor

NB If Manuel goes to Providence he must see my father. He will find him at work for Church and Sweet if he will take so much upon himself. My Best Wishes to you both[27]

Two days later Taylor, assuming Walker had reached Washington, wrote again pleading with him to respond as he'd heard that he and Sam could be swindled out of their property. Nothing had been done on their building and Taylor feared the worst. He mentioned Lackland Stone stopping by and implying that the property would all belong to him shortly. Advising him never to return, Taylor suggested letting the creditors take his property to settle their debts.

Iola Fla March 17th 1840

Dear Sir
I take this opportunity to inform you that I am well and all of the family and hope that this may find you both the same way. A long time I delayed wrighting on account of not knowing how people were conducting about the affairs of the estate [the property owned jointly by Walker and his sister-in-law Ann Stone Walker], which is very hard

to do, but it is the impression of several men here that we are to be swindled out of the whole of the property, unless you can write and make it safe. Attachments are made on the estate but I understand Lack Stone stopped them for a while, but I think that it will all belong to him in a short time. Nothing has been done to the building since you left nor Alexander. He never sent a stick of lumber since you left. There is nothing doing in this place and the Indians are raising hell all about as, Harlin's family are kild by them, though this was wrote to you before. The most of the people from Iola have been out after them last week but found none. Ed Huld has gone to New York and if you take a fool's advice you will stay where you are and never return here again and let the property pay the debts. It is getting to be very sickly. I heard you wrote to Col. Stone, but I never heard wether you was well or most dead. If you will so good as to answer this as soon as you get it and give me some instructions how to do. If you can I will be very much obliged to you for it. It is useless for to think of returning before fall if you do come at all but you are a fool if you do come. I never will strike another lick on the building till I know that it is safe. Nothing more at present.

My best wishes to you both. I think I shall leave for good.

John C. Taylor[28]

Upon reaching Washington in mid-May, Walker immediately read Taylor's first letter. Dismayed and disgusted by what he read concerning the state of his affairs in Iola and Taylor's noncompliance with the instructions he gave him before he left Florida, he turned to his sister-in-law Ann, the only person he could trust, to determine the facts of the situation and report back to him.

Washington City, DC, May 18th 1840

Dear Sister in law

As I have not received any letters from those persons who I have written to concerning my business I take my pen again hoping you will oblige me so much as to give me what information you can about the prospects of the times and things in general as I cannot with any confidence write to those persons again whom I once depended on to give me information about what materially concerned me and I believe that the friendship and good feelings that was manifested towards me when I was with you no more occupies a portion of the minds of those persons whom I once considered to be my true friends, or my letters would not have been treated with such contempt though it may be possible that I may judge them wrong. If so, I shall be sorry for it. Myself and Manuel has very good health and I hope this may find you enjoying the same. My Father's death is dayly expected.

I have been out in the country with him for some time and intend going out again today. All the rest of them are well and send their respects to you and express a great anxiety to see you and the child and I have no doubt but you would be much pleased if you could visit them before next fall. One of my Brothers will come out with me. I did not write any direct answer to the letter I received from Taylor as I had previously given him directions how I wished him to proceed and I discovered from his letter that he was not disposed to follow my directions concerning the building or he would certainly have used some means to have got the lumber down rather than do nothing. If he has not done anything towards finishing the building, I authorize you to employ some good steady mechanics on the most reasonable terms you can to enclose the building and I will give them a satisfactory settlement when I come out next fall. I should be glad to sell my interest in it provided I get anything like the value of it as I am very anxious that my creditors should be paid up forthwith and I should judge they were getting rather uneasy. Nothing more but my respects to all inquiring friends, I remain

Yours most Truly
S H Walker[29]

Ann replied, saying many were threatening to sue to get the property that she and Sam and owned. Moreover, Taylor had completely neglected the building. She hoped he would soon return to put things in order.

Iola, Calhoun County, Fla
[May 24, 1840]
Mr. Saml H. Walker

Dear Brother.
I have neglected writing to you but now I take the opportunity of addressing you a few lines to inform you how the times is here at this time so far as I know. I am in tolerable health at this time and hope these few lines may find you enjoying the same blessing. I have the pleasure of informing you that I have a fine daughter which favours her father considerable and she is a fine child not as I think but everybody says so. Now I will proceed to tell you the business part of our city. The house is under Execution by Holliman and John D. Grag was going to sue on the lot but Stone has stopped it expecting you to come back, Every body talks of suing since you left. I am in hopes you will come back and disappoint some men that expect to sacrifice our property. Mr Taylor has done nothing since you left. He is not tended to your tolls. I think part of them is stole. They are in mighty bad order them that is left. I do not like his management since you

left but he does not stay here. He has been on the steamboat Levy. Now he is working up at the mill. I do not know how long he will stay but we get along without no words.

In speaking of my daughter I did not tell you her name but now I will. Her name is Florence Florida Walker. I have nothing more to say at present but be sure and write when you receive and tell me how you and the rest of the family are. Give my best Respects to the whole family and all relations.

I am your most affectionate Sister in law until death.

Ann M. Walker

P.S, The whole family send there Respects likewise[30]

Walker replied to Ann's letter with concern for her, his new niece, and those he left behind when he returned to Maryland. The upturn of Native American raids, including the murder of civilians, gave Walker hope to realize his dream of leading a contingent of horsemen to protect the lives and property of the settlers and to pursue and chastise the perpetrators. He asked his sister-in-law to encourage the writing of a petition, signed by all the citizens of the affected area, to be sent to Congress for relief and to approve the formation of a self-defense company. Walker, of course, suggested himself as the leader of that force.

Washington City, D.C. June 6th 1840
Mrs. Anne M. Walker

Dear sister in law
I received your letter and was happy to hear you were all well. We are all in good health and I hope this may find you the same. My Father has been very low in health again but is recovering again so that he is able to walk about.

I had some idea of trying to come out immediately but I cannot get ready before fall. I wish you would try to get my tools together and keep them for me as I am afraid I shall have none to work with if I depend on Taylor. I am sure from the way he writes he must be like a man frightened out of his wits. He told me if I would take a fool's advice I would never come back there again. You can tell him that I do not feel despised to take a fool's advice, and if I live and nothing happen you will see me in three months at most. I feel very anxious about your distressful situation on account of the Indians. I think it would be necessary for the people to send petition to Congress representing all their grievances stating all the particulars of Indian outrages on the inhabitants of that section of the country, and the disregard that has been paid to the peoples lives and property by the commanding officers of the Army with a petition of that sort depicting all the sufferings and hardships the people have to undergo and insufficiency of their crops to support them being driven every year by the Indians. They might obtain relief. It would be necessary to recommend some person whom the people can confide in to be commissioned to raise a large company of horsemen well equipped for the express purpose of protecting the citizens between Quincy and St Andrews Bay.[31] If they should place confidence enough in me to recommend me to Congress to fill that situation I think with the influence of my friends and acquaintances who have several with me, both in Florida and Alabama I could obtain the commission without any difficulty.[32] Your petition should be signed by both males and females generally from the whole neighbourhood between Quincy and St Josephs. You can shew the citizens of Iola this letter if you choose. I have written to Col. Stone on the same subject. Nothing more at present but remain your most affectionate Brother.

S H Walker

PS The Family sends their respects to you and say they would be very glad to see you and the little child. Give my respects to all the people, Yours &c.[33]

Ann Walker replied five weeks later, reporting natives were raiding, burning, and killing ever closer to Iola. She did not, however, mention the petition, which must have been a disappointment to him, referring to her brother-in-law in the familiar for the first time in her letters.

Calhoun County Iola July 11 1840

Dear Brother
I received your letter and was glad to hear you were all well. I have enjoyed very good health and my little Florida is five months old and never had a days sickness in her life. The people generally are sickly. Most of them have the chills and fever. There is no business doing here. Most of the people on account of health have gone to St Joseph. Taylor is keeping bar for Whipple so I am told. I have not seen him since I received your last letter I sent several times after him to get your tolls up together. He did not come. I took all I could find and put them in your chest. I do not expect you will find them all when you come home. He has let every person take them that chose. I hope Sam you will come home soon as you can. I think it would be much better for you. We have a new bank at St Joseph and I hope it will be of great advantage to the place. Most of the stock holders are very wealthy men from Alabama. The Indians are very troublesome. They are committing depredations in the east every day. About six weeks ago

they killed a man and wounded two others about five miles from here. [illegible] and burnt Thomas house in a mile of Graves. I have nothing more at present but remain your affectionate sister in law til death.

Ann M. Walker

Give my love to all the relations. Tell them I want to see all them. I think if my babe was weighed she would way thirty pounds. She is given up to be the first child there ever was seen. She can turn the grindstone and crawl enough to fall out of bed.[34]

Ann wrote again in September saying she hoped by winter things would be better for Iola and St. Joseph. Natives were continuing to plunder and murder, with local militia unwilling or afraid to engage them. Ann makes a very interesting comment concerning her relationship with Sam. She urged him to come home soon, saying she never knew how much she missed him until he left Iola.

Iola, Sept 3, 1840

Dear Brother
I received your letter yesterday and was happy to hear of you coming home so soon. You wrote to me to write all about the prosperity of St. Joseph & Iola. Today I will tell you all I know. The times at either place is very dull at this time. I expect it will be a great deal better next winter. There has been a great many strangers to visit St. Joseph & Iola and like very well if it was not for the Indians, and I think they were very right. If there is not something done with them soon they will take Florida. They have taken India Key and murdered a good many families in Monticello in the east and when soldiers find them, they are afraid to attack them, Captain Bowie's company came on a party of Indians on Pig Island and was afraid to attack them and retreated back to camps and left them. The people in Iola is very much frightened. They hear guns every knight over the river. Mr. Hudson speaks of leaving here on account of it. I am in hopes he will. It will be better for us. He has made a great deal of money by his house. If our house was finished if you were not disposed to keep it you could sell it for a good price. J. D. Gray is anxious to buy it, so I am told. I have nothing more at present only I want you to come home. I am not satisfied to stay here without you. I never knew how much I thought of you til since you left here. You must give my love to all the relations. Tell them I want to see them all. We are all well and I hope this will find you the same. Nothing more at present. I remain your affectionate sister in law

Ann M. Walker

The baby is well. She can sit alone. I think she is very smart. It may be because she is mine. I think so. You will be surprised when you see her. Give my respects to Manuel and excuse bad writing and a bad pen.[35]

On October 2, Walker arrived in Florida after a week's journey from Washington. His friend and traveling companion Manuel Navarro was taken with the fever coming through Georgia but had since recovered. He commented that the people of Georgia often cheered "Old Tip" [William Henry Harrison, the Whig candidate for presidency], and the Whig Party[36] seemed strong enough in middle Florida to make the territorial Governor, Robert R. Reid, a Democrat, uncomfortable.

Iola, Florida, October 20th 1840

Dear Brother
I arrived home on the 2nd, inst. Being one week after I left Washington, stopping one day in Charleston and one day in Augusta Ga. for the propose of striking [?] the Aligator here so you will perceived that it is only one side days travel from this to Washington. Manuel was taken with the fever coming through Georgia which continued on him until several days after we arrived home, though he has recovered his health aggin without taking any medicine. My health is remarkably good and our town is generally healthy. The inhabitants of Ga was very sickly, but not so much so as to make them forget Old Tip as the hussas for him were very frequent and from my observation through Georgia she may be set down as certain for the old Hero. Our [illegible] County has not made a political question as it was agreed upon by the leading men in the County from various reasons, but in nearly all other parts of the Territory the Whigs have triumphed, particularly in middle Florida so that our Loco Foco Governor will feel very uncomfortable, when he reflects on his past conduct. The war in Florida after five years duration with a few Seminole Indians has at last become a defensive war as it is called by giving up all the country to the Indians that they formerly occupied and pretending to protect the old frontier settlements but from what I can learn there is no active operations whatever as they are laying in their camp nearly the whole time and the Indians has them and roam all over through middle and West Florida and continue to butcher the inhabitants with impunity, The spars settlements through middle and West Florida is deserted entirely by the inhabitants and no protection is sent to them whatever the people are. Many of them breathing out a miserable existence in all the thin settled parts of the Country some of them being almost destitute of food and clothing and if the present executive should continue in power the most of this beautiful country would be given up to the savages is my humble opinion. I have been on two excursions since I arrived. I went over

on Pig Island where the Indians had been, in company with seventy four others all citizens but we had no means of carrying provisions for a long march, so we hd to return home after scouring the Island as there was very few of them who was willing to undertake a ten days march without some certainty of provisions. Our trailers assured me they would find them in ten days or less and having every confidence in them, I was willing to follow them and depend on the chance of wild game for my food but my party did not relish the idea. These two men who live in this county that can trail a single Indian in the pine woods they have volunteered their services to go with me as guides if I can raise an independent volunteer company and I have been trying but it is impossible to do it, as the most of those who are willing are four men and not able to equip themselves and besides it would seem almost as prudent for a man to stay and perish with his family as to forsake them and leave them entire [illegible] to the merciless savage who is now watching for an opportunity to quench his thirst for the blood of the helpless female and infant. But to give you a complete description of all these matters it would require a half dozen sheets of paper. I should have written sooner if I had come to any definite conclusion what I should do here. I have been advised not to sell my property yet. I expect to leave here in a short time for Tallahassee and I have been informed that business was very brisk there and also that there was a planter in the vicinity of Tallahassee who was waiting for us to come on and build him a dwelling house. I have several other prospects in view, and you shall hear from me again soon as I come to a definite conclusion. Nathan's wife and child is well and sends her respects to you all. She has a very lively, and interesting child. She is well grown and lively. our passages including fare cost about eighty five dollars or more each. If I can see my friend H. V. Snell, which I expect will be very shortly, I will make a remittance to you provided I am not disappointed. Give my best respects to all inquiring friends and to the ladies. Anyhow, I have been very much at a loss for ladies company since I left and you and my friend P. H. Boss will please to accept my thanks for the many newspapers you have sent me as my leisure time is spent to a better advantage in reading than I can spend it otherwise at present in this place. You can tell H. Davis that I think from what I have heard that he will do well to come out to Tallahassee. Nothing more at present, but remain your affectionate Brother

SHW.[37]

Iola's commercial lifeline was the port city of St. Joseph. However, Georgia railroads ultimately connected western Georgia with the port of Apalachicola, Florida.[38] Soon afterward, railroad construction spread to cities on the Atlantic coast and it was no longer profitable to ship cotton from the Gulf. By 1842, the northern Florida railroads were bankrupt and the next year St. Joseph was virtually a ghost town with many of the buildings dismantled.

Walker, finding no employment in Iola, decided to see if Tallahassee offered better prospects. However, he vowed he would never work for anyone unless he was paid before he started the job. Finding no immediate work at his profession, he took a job with the Tallahassee Railroad Company at $60 per month. His observations of the character of Tallahassee's citizenry are informative. The society there needed all the help it could get. Shootings and stabbings were common. This would be an example of the first lawless frontier area that Walker would encounter. It would not be his last. It is ironic Sam one day would become a Texas Ranger. There were, nevertheless, some families of quality and Sam made it his business to socialize with them, but felt himself out of place given his lack of money. There were also members of the Odd Fellows. Some good, some not. He was disappointed that the brotherly camaraderie espoused by that order was not accepted by more men. He firmly believed the tenets of the order, if adhered to, would make a better world. He also wrote of his outlook toward war. It was something that was in direct opposition to the Creator's wishes for mankind. There was, however, something he admired in military splendor.

Near Tallahassee, Florida, March 7th 1841
To Mr. J. T. Walker

Dear Brother
With extreme pleasure and with much gratification I received your letter of Feb. 3rd on Monday last, and should have answered it forthwith only for my having written to Cousin Samuel Hamilton and did not have it until I received yours.

I arrived in Tallahassee about the 18th of Jan and remained there about three weeks doing nothing at all in my business in consequence of my being determined not to labour on credit any more in Florida as I shall be happily disappointed if we ever get what is now owing to us, and I have accordingly reconciled myself to my unfortunate and base luck with the consolation of knowing that it is not by negligence or extravagant expenditures or any thing censurable on my part that has occasioned my failure in my youthful enterprise, as I feel convinced that the same exertions which I have made in Florida if attended with good luck would have placed me in a prosperous condition in almost any of the old states of the Union. However these things are essential and necessary occasionally to remind us of the fallacy of man in sacrificing things of more importance and more worthy of his nature, for the mere love of wealth such I must confess has been my case. In part I have been working for the last four years using all the endeavors that honesty would admit of for the sake of making what is generally termed a fortune while at the same time I have excluded myself from the enjoyments of good and virtuous society, though I am thankful that the want of it has learned me how to appreciate the value of it and I hope to profit by experience and dear bought wisdom. I am now employed by the Tallahassee Railroad at $60.00 per month and found Florida money at that, so you may judge what the times are at present without any further comment. I have the promise of some jobs and many assurances that I will do well if I wait till times get better. During the three weeks I was in Tallahassee I found a good many acquaintances amongst the gentlemen. I was also fortunate enough to have an invitation to pay a visit at about 12 miles in the country. The whole family was very agreeable and the young ladies quite handsome, and my visit was quite agreeable to me considering I felt somewhat out of my element in company with the wealthiest family in the Territory who live in princely style. However they were once poor themselves and as a remarkable instance their vanity has not increased with their wealth. This is the wealthiest part of the Territory and the people are quite intelligent. There is three churches in Tallahassee, one Presbyterian, one Episcopalian and one Methodist. The free Masons are numerous and have the grand lodge of the Territory at Tallahassee. The society is as good as could possibly be expected taking all things into consideration, though it is far from being as good as it ought to be at present. Shooting and cutting is very fashionable in settling quarrels and insults, and any man may with impunity shoot here if has a few friends who says it was justifiable. Hanging for downwright cold blooded murder is out of the question. They are sometimes condemned but suffice to escape before they are executed. Instead of getting better it has been getting worse. I occasionally find a stragling Odd Fellow by profession but none who I could claim as a Brother. There are some few in Tallahassee who I have not formed an acquaintance with as yet, but there are very few good Odd Fellows in Florida as the present state of society is by no means calculated to attach them to this country and after once understood the true principles of the order and imbibed a taste for morality and good society and I believe that the Odd Fellows society if the principles of it is properly carried out and acted up to will eventually effect a more noble object than all the religious societies combined and that is to create a union of Brotherhood and good feeling throughout the whole human race, and instead of raising Armies and equipping them at enormous expense to slay each other we should turn our attention to things more noble and perhaps be enabled to arrive at that perfection which would be more worthy of our race. It is true I must confess that delight in seeing the crash and

> the steady [illegible] I confide my fear [of Armies?] and have always felt an eagerness to be engaged in them, but if I was asked why I have such feelings the most wise answer that I could give would be that the events of human affairs as they now are require this disposition on our policy of our nation by rewarding our Military Heroes with the highest honour and applaud in their gist. This all seems right enough but when we come to more noble reflection and consider the [illegible] of our divine creator in the formation of man and the capacity he has given him to comprehend his will and wishes, we must at once see the importance of a unity of interests aside a Brotherly feeling throughout the world, and I believe the principles of Odd Fellowship is better calculated to effect it than any thing in existence. Mr. Navarro has not arrived from St Josephs. I am afraid he has not got pay for his work and is detained on that account. I hear from Nathan's wife & child last Sunday. They are all well. I am altogether undetermined bout returning home.
>
> We still have some hopes of St Josephs & Iola. A new Co. has been formed and the Apalachicolians has flew from this contract. Also some hopes of a Naval Depot at St Josephs Bay. I was in company with Mr. McHuew at Port Leon and spent several pleasant evenings with him.
>
> I am very sorry that I had not remained home with you all this past winter as I feel assured I should become equally as well off. You stated in your letter that your situation was preferable to have you judge very correctly at the present time. However, I still keep a looking ahead. Fortune may yet smile, and it is no use to fret about things that can't be helped. I have has some notion to go to Cuba. The money here would not be worth carrying to Md. Write again. Direct to Tallahassee. I was glad to receive the [illegible] of Brother PHB and return him my best wishes & his wife also hoping they may prosper and live happy and likewise all the Odd Fellows of my acquaintance and my love and best respects to all inquiring friends and relatives. Tell Brother Dun [?] that I could not consistency advise him to go to Texas.
>
> SHW.
>
> I have heard nothing from the seat of war lately. Col. Harney is highly spoken of for his measures of hanging.[39]

Six weeks later, Sam's situation had improved. He was still working for the Tallahassee Railroad Company, apparently a construction foreman, and was learning the profession of civil engineering by his relationship with the engineer in charge and through his own study of that skill through reading and study. His next letter to his brother, Jonathan Thomas, contained a detailed description of the new methods used in laying down the ties and track—an innovation for the railroad-building industry. Although enthusiastic about his new job, he was unsatisfied with his lot in life, yearning for the company of those in the higher rungs of society.

Near Tallahassee, Leon Coty, M Fla. April 20th 1841
To Mr. J T Walker

Dear Brother
I was in Tallahassee on the 11th inst and received your letter of the 29th March and was glad to hear from you and I hope this may find you in good health and prosperity. We also received by the same mail the confirmation of a verbal report received some days previous of President Harrison's death. The citizens of Tallahassee were crowded around the Post Office at a late hour waiting to hear the unwelcome news officially announced, and all seemed to hope that the verbal report might prove to be untrue, but after waiting several hours in suspense all doubts were dispelled by an official statement which was handed from the office and read in the street by candle light to the anxious crowd, and a silence immediately pervaded the whole crowd and their countenances plainly shewed how deeply they were effected. It is an event which has filled my heart with sorrow, and forms another proof of the instability of human greatness. He who but as yesterday was looked up to as a nations deliverer is now cold and lifeless mingling with the dust, but nothing can erase his memory from the minds of his countrymen, But him, who has deprived a nation of her favourite but I sincerely hope that his successor may be guided by his worthy examples and place our country in a better condition. The currency of our Territory is still on the decline. Since writing to you last about St. Joseph & Iola the prospects have changed amazingly and if I could believe all I hear respecting the arrangements making to carry out the grand scheme, I should say that it certainly would succeed, though I am doubtful whether I shall wait to see it or not as I have already undergone enough hardships in this country in hopes of future prosperity to put me out of practice, and you need not be surprised if I should return to Washington again in July or August. Mr Navarro has been over here with me about three weeks. He intends to remain here until the fall and then visit his native land and return to Washington City. We are both in the employment of the Tallahassee Rail Road Co. and Gov. R. H. Call who is acting President and the largest stock holder in the Company assures me that if I remain with them I shall never be in want of a hospitable job. I told the Governor a few days since that I had almost made up my mind to quit the country and return to Maryland but he insists on my remaining and by way of flattery tells me they cannot do without me. We are at present building a railroad on a new and improved plan which makes the most substantial road

in the US without being subject to decay more than timber in current use. The sawed rails is ten inches square bedded on broad caps and pinned down with large pins with a small ribband on top of it to receive the iron. It is built entirely above the surface and consequently the timber will last double as long with less expense in repairs than the usual mode of covering of it up to make it solid. We allso use a great deal of hewed timber also for railing though we only hew two sides of it with the tines averaging from eighteen inches to two foot in diameter from 35 to 65 feet long bedded on caps of seven feet apart with a ribband in the centre to receive the Iron. As I before stated this [torn from the letter] however is to be dispensed with as soon as the Company [?] get the T or H Iron. I make this statement thinking it may possibly prove useful to somebody [?] as I feel confident that it is the best and cheapest plan ever adopted in the US. With thirty hands and the most of them awkward negroes we have torn up a half [?] of a mile of the old road and entirely replaced it with an entire new road in one week only and taken a half days holiday on Saturday. A half mile per week we can do with ease, and you will bear in mind that a seven ton engine is run over this road four times a day at the rate of twenty odd miles an hour. From this you can perhaps form some idea how internal improvements advance in this country and from some estimate of the cost, also recollect that U Sam always gives the time and land for such improvements. Nathan's wife and child were well when Mr. Navarro left Iola. I go to Tallahassee to church occasionally though I spend most of my leisure time in reading and studying geometry, civil engineering &c as I am determined to spend my leisure moments to the best advantage. The chief Engineer and myself are on very intimate terms and he takes a great pleasure in giving all the instructions that I require of him. These advantages in some measure compensate me for my absence from good society though by no means satisfies my mind. I covet good society more than any thing else and I cannot long content myself without it. There is some talk about closing the war but very doubtfull. Our delegates Election takes place on the 1st Monday in May. The whigs have split and Col Downing will not be elected. Give my humble respects to all inquiring friends and relatives. Tell Charles I wish him success in all his worthy enterprises both matrimonial and professional.

Yours &c SHW

Mr Navarro desires to be remembered to you all.[40]

A month later, Sam replied to a letter he received from his sister-in-law. He wrote in general terms, saying only there was danger in Tallahassee from those who espoused violence and paid no heed to the teachings he listened to when he did go to church. He remarked upon his new friend among the better class of society in Tallahassee, but was eager for more and frequent company with the young women. His future was yet to be determined but his health remained a factor. Florida was an inhospitable place for white settlers.

Leon Coty Fla. May 24th 1841

Dear sister in law
I received your kind letter of the 7th inst. and was truly glad to hear of your good health and I hope this may still find you all enjoying same inestimable blessing. My health has been very good since I left you. Manuel had a very severe attack about a week ago, but he is able to work again. We are both at work for the Tallahassee Rail Road Company, and they seem so anxious for us to continue that. We shall remain with them all summer if we have good health. However, I shall endeavor to spare as much time as to visit you all in July or August, but if my health should be impaired by that time it is probable that I May go North. People are very sickly at present in Tallahassee & Port Leon, and are dieing very fast, and still they are not satisfied the dispensations of divine Providence. They seem determined to kill each other. Occurrences of this sort are too numerous and some of the too outrageous to mention particulars as the rehearsal of it would only put me in a bad humour. I have enjoyed myself quite as well as I could. Many Acquaintances amongst the gentlemen but very [few] amongst the Ladies, though I shall probably visit the Ladies much more for the future as it is impossible to enjoy myself in any situation except where I can visit the Ladies, I frequently go to Tallahassee to church, but I cannot tell you much about their good influence on the society as it is difficult to perceive any great good they effect, though society might possibly be a great deal worse, and we should always chose the best ever and endeavor to guard against the greater by religious influence and example. Since writing to you I have received several letters from Maryland. My friends & relatives are all well and send their respects to you. I hope little Florida will be able to run about and talk when I come over to see you all. From the assurances I have received I have concluded it would be greatly to my interest to remain in Florida as long as my health will admit of it, but should circumstances which may occur operate favourably on St Josephs & Iola I shall return. I still consider Calhoun Coty my home as long as I have any interest there. I have nothing more of importance to write but remain with great respect

your most sincere friend
Samuel H. Walker

PS give my respects to all my old acquaintances and tell them that I should be very happy to see or hear from them.

Yours &c.[41]

He wrote to his brother Jonathan in mid-June, still undecided as to his future. He had been offered a job with the railroad that paid a decent salary in specie, not the depreciated Florida currency, but was undecided as to whether he should accept it. He contemplated selling his property in Iola if the price was right. However, he believed the potential of St. Joseph becoming a major shipping port for Florida produce was excellent and thought the navy could establish a base there for receiving the abundance of quality timber from the interior. Nevertheless, he remained torn between staying in Florida and returning to Maryland. An incident with a disreputable character that might have cost him his life must have had an influence on his immediate plans.

Tallahassee, Fla, June 16th 1841

Dear Brother
I received your kind letter of May 14th in due time, but did not write sooner on account of my wavering disposition whether it would be best to take your advice and return home or remain in Florida and I am still undetermined about the matter though you may not be surprised if you should see me in August. I am at present about starting to St Josephs & Iola. All will depend on my success in disposing of my property & settling my business in some satisfactory manner to all parties concerned. I think the chance is better than it has been for some time. The Rail Road is about to change hands and arrangements are already made which will ultimately place St. Josephs in a very prosperous condition. It is possible that I may return here again, as I have a positive assurance of employment at $75 dolls specie per month payable the first of Jan. 1842 though the situation is by no means desirable, and one of such great exposure that I could scarcely expect to pass the summer with sickness, especially if I was working on credit as I am very apt to doubt mens ability to pay according to promise, though they may be honest. Florida money at present is only worth fifty cents on the dollar and very scarce at that. Our banking institutions in Florida are all calculated to injure our prosperity and demoralize the community. It is now seen and felt and acknowledged by the good citizens of each party. It is useless for me to enter into the details of the matter but suffice it to say that they are real and personal. Be sure and write. Direct your letter to Tallahassee as usual.

State banks with such power that our legislature cannot control them, and nothing now but the timely interference of the General

Government can save us from disgrace both home and abroad. Our citizens manifest some disposition to reform and if the General Government will do their duty, Florida will yet be one of the most important portions of the US, possessing as she does a tropical region sufficient to supply our citizens with all the fruits for which we have to be dependent on the Islands of the West Indies and for variety of production she will exceed any portion of the Globe and when we take into consideration her vast quantities of timber of the most valuable kind for our Navy and her beautiful Bays & harbours constituting more than one third of our whole sea coast, she should certainly attract the attention of all wise statesmen of this Confederacy, and in case of a war with any foreign power her situation at present would certainly be a most horrible one, though it could not be much worse than it is in this community at present though it has been checked in some measure by heavy fines and imprisonment, I was yesterday called to an account by a murdering villain whose character I exposed for the welfare of the community. The circumstance which I related occurred in Brunswick, Georgia, while I was on my way to Washington. He has been here for some months sponging on the community and being refused board any longer at the hotel he came down to take boarding at a private boarding house kept by a widow Lady whom I had always boarded with while in Tallahassee and I could not forbear speaking my sentiments about his conduct though the conversation was guarded on my part until he knew I was acquainted with the transaction and attempted to justify his conduct when I was compelled to speak the truth, and the frowns of indignations from the boarders to plainly told his company would not be desirable. He had an elder Brother with him who seemed disposed to justify him. In a few hours later afterwards I was standing in front of the Post office in company with several merchants & members of the Bar when he came up armed with Pistols & Bowie knife & commenced on me with the most desecrating oaths swearing he would cut me litteraly [in] pieces but not seizing weapons myself I commenced on him with my fists telling him I was not to be intimidated by the threats of a murderer. The bystanders then interfered and separated us and he them got out his pistol an attempted to shoot me but was prevented by my friends. I was likely commended by those present and the case will probably be brought before the Mayor of the City and he will likely be put in gaol as it will not be in his power to give security for his conduct or to pay the fine of two hundred dollars for having weapons, which is the present penalty. He gave a verbal challenge but I told him I did not consider him worthy of such notice.

June 17th 12 oclock. I have just been before the Mayor and have been fines the sum of fifty dollars and my adversary one hundred.

All the evidence declared I was certainly justifiable in striking but notwithstanding I was fined more as an example than otherwise. I paid the fine without murmer and highly commended the mayor for the course taken to preserve good order in the community stating that this was the course that might to have been taken long since. My adversary is now looked upon with that contempt which his conduct merits, and if I should judge from the expression of the citizens the course I have pursued has made me more popular twelve months [illegible] would have done otherwise. I shall leave here on Sunday for St Josephs & Iola. I shall return here in a few weeks if I do not determine home when I get to St Josephs, and when I think of the great difference in society here and that of M.D. I almost come to a positive determination to return and rove no more though it would be justifiable without a wife for me to be content. Give my best respects to all my friends & relations, the Misses Early particularly.

Yours in FLT [Friendship, Love, and Truth, the motto of the Order of Odd Fellows]

S H Walker[42]

Walker's next surviving letter was in response to an April 1840 communication received from a family friend, Zadoc McKnew, who had been in Florida at one time.[43] Walker quit his job with the Tallahassee Railroad over a dispute over his monthly salary being paid in Florida currency worth only half of the equivalent in specie. There was business news of St. Joseph to be told, he went on to describe the town as the most pleasant spot in Florida.[44] But for all its beauty and potential, it was not immune to the scourge of yellow fever.[45] He himself fell victim to the disease, but after subjecting himself to liberal doses of calomel[46] and the ministrations of his sister-in-law and other friends from Iola, he soon regained his health.[47]

New Town, 4 mls from Tallahassee, Fla, Aug 18 1841
Mr. McKnew.

Dear Sir
I received your communication from Apalachicola of Apr 27, and should have answered it sooner if it had been possible for me to have given you any information of importance. I will now state for your information that the negotiation that was pending when you left has all been settled in favor of St Josephs, by all of the Columbus merchants joining their influence with the middle Florida stockholders & property holders with those of St Josephs which will be capable of controlling about three fourths of the trade of Apalachicola River. A new Co. has been formed incorporated with banking priviledges under the Charter of the old central Bank of Fla. The stock has been

taken to the amount of 175,000$ dollars, and it seems as though they were determined to establish a good currency, though the people have been so completely gulled and swindled by Banks & Bank men in this Territory that it will be almost impossible to establish any institution that will be free from suspicion and doubt. I left the employment of the Rail Road Co. about two months ago in consequence of their paying me off in Fla. Currency without making any allowance for its depreciation from the time I commenced with them, which I considered very unjust and expressed myself accordingly in a written note addressed to the Board, which caused some ill feeling and I was reused by one of the gentlemen to withdraw the communication which I positively refused to do and seeing I was not to be daunted or frowned into submission he became perfectly friendly again and offered to pay me seventy five per month and found in specie or its equivalent if I would continue. I told him that I should go to St Josephs & Iola and if I could not do better I might possibly return provided they would insure me the situation and the proposition was agreed to. I left Tallahassee just seven weeks ago and stopped about ten or twelve days in Iola and the neighbourhood and then went to St Josephs on the 2nd of July and remained one week. A considerable number of people had already arrived from Tallahassee & Apalachicola to spend a pleasant summer and a great many more expected in a few days, and from my appearance St Josephs bid fair to be the most enchanting and desirable that the southern clime could boast of. The long wharf which extends out into the Bay was promenaded by hosts of persons both young and old, and the sails of the pleasure boats might be seen indifferent directions by the glimmering light of the moon beams, with the enchanting music which usually accompany those excursions all conspired to render the scene most beautiful, that the imaginative mind devoted to pleasure would fancy, and I imagine there were if any who contemplated the great contrast that was about to take place on the shores of the beautiful Bay of St Josephs, but also how changeable and uncertain are the pleasures of this vain and troublesome world, behold in less than a fortnight from the time I have described the destroyer had stretched forth his right hand and about forty including some of the best and most useful of our citizens have fallen victims to his grasp and those whose circumstances enabled them to move with there friends and families precipitously fled in all directions into the interior of the country. While the disease does not seem to be quite so infectious as on the gulf a good many was taken with it after they had left and in most cases it has proved fatal. There had been several deaths previous to my going to St Josephs and some had pronounced one case Black Vomit but all was accounted for by the devoted citizens of the place whose confidence was implicit in the health of St Joseph by ascribing it to intemperance, imprudence, severe exposure, &c. In the course of the week that I remained there was a great many taken sick though the deaths were few. On the evening before I left a girl died in the same hotell here I stoped and some had at last it the yellow fever. There were also several other cases in the same house. Though. I had no fear of taking any disease prudence would have dictated to me to remove to another house if I had known it. About two days before I left my eyes & skin began to turn a little yellow. This I calculated to remove without any difficulty by a dose of calomel & oil whenever the symptoms should increase. On the morning after I left St Josephs on the 11th about two miles and a half above Iola at the present residence of my Brother's wife & child I was taken with a light pain in the head and judging from the yellowness of my eyes and skin I concluded that I should have a severe spell and on which would require extraordinary measures. I accordingly mixed about twenty grains of calomel and swallowed it. My fever soon began to come on and before the middle of the afternoon my senses had entirely left me, and I continued for about three days in a complete state of insensibility and a part of the time that I could not speak. They continued to give me calomel & oil a plenty, and some of my friends from Iola came up and gave me a bath and afterwards rubed me and bathed me in warm water which brought to a state of sensibility. My [fever] began to abate some and I continued taking medicine until it subsided. I very soon regained my health. I arrived in Tallahassee last Sunday. I am, at present engaged in fitting up a summer residence 4 miles from Tallahassee immediately on the rail road in a poor piny woods hill which it is thought will prove very healthy. There is about one dozen temporary buildings going up. We find good water at thirty five feet deep. The health of Florida so far has been worse than any previous year and as the decomposition of vegetable matter takes place it is natural to suppose that it will be a great deal worse, and from what I have seen this summer it has convinced me of the folly of a man's attempting to summer it in this country especially a northern man, though I do believe it is much worse then the neighbouring states. It is a pleasant country to spend the winter but a very disagreeable summer residence.[48]

The rest of the letter has been lost to history.

During the summer of 1841, St. Joseph was hard hit by yellow fever brought into port by sailing ships from the Greater Antilles. Thirty-seven deaths were reported between the middle of June and July 30. Many very important residents would die and by August the town was virtually abandoned. Then in September, a powerful storm hit and virtually swept away what was left of the town. St. Joseph would never recover.[49]

Shortly after writing to McKnew, Walker wrote to another friend. James H. Boss was a brother Odd Fellow and member of the Grand Lodge in Washington. In this letter, Walker described his near-death bout with yellow fever and the continued rampages of the yet to be pacified natives, and their acts of murder, arson, and pillaging that federal troops could not prevent. He and his friend Navarro returned to work for the railroad, supervising construction gangs made up of Black men, saying it was easy work. He and Navarro supervised from the shade of trees while their workers labored under the blistering sun. He also railed against the banks and bankers, arch villains in his opinion, who worked only to the detriment of Floridians. Florida remained a rough country. There were few of the social comforts he grew accustomed to in Washington, especially those he enjoyed with brother Odd Fellows.

Leon County Florida near Tallahassee, Aug. 22, 1841
To Mr. James H. Boss[50]

Dear Friend
I take the present opportunity of writing a few lines to inform you that I am in good health &c., & I hope this may find you the same. The mortality has been very great in Florida this summer and the decomposition of vegetable matter if a dry fall will render it much greater. Already has the summons been issued from on high, for many of my acquaintances and I amongst them have almost been past hope, but through the will of a divine Providence I have as it were been snatched from the yawning jaws of death, and in a few days restored to perfect health. My friend Navarro is with me and is also in good health and often expresses his intention of returning to Washington to renew his old acquaintances and enjoy the pleasures and heretofore of good society &c. Since writing to my Brother in June I have been to St Josephs & Iola but owing to the unknown and wholly unexpected epidemic at St Josephs which so suddenly changed the aspect of affairs, I concluded to return to this part of Florida, and from the pressing solicitations of my former employers I have accepted the situation in part that I formerly with an increase is salary. The hands employed on our works here have this far been comparatively healthy, and the remainder of our work for the being located through a pine woods we do not apprehend much sickness the most of our hands being of the African race or descent rather well insured to summer heat. And as for myself and Navarro, we are not required to work ourselves but only to look around and see that others do it in a proper manner, and the shade of a majestic pine tree very frequently protects us from the scorching sun. At present the times throughout the Territory are very dull, although the corn & cotton crops bid fair to relieve the country of much embarrassment as it is the greatest ever known. The corn

is ripe and the cotton is looking very pretty. The weather at present is much more pleasant and seasonable than it was in May & June. The most of the country has been favoured with copious showers of rain ever since the first of June, though it is a remarkable fact that St Josephs City had up to the 10th of July been nearly two months without any rain sufficient to wet the sand and ten miles from the City there was rain almost every day for a fortnight. The same might be said of Apalachicola and Tallahassee. Together with the prevalence of the east wing in the latter part of June & the early part of July has by the most of June been pronounced the cause of so much sickness as it has been much more fatal in the cities than the country.

I would like to give you a good deal of satisfactory news and converse freely with you, but the fact is this. You must content your self with a few unsatisfactory statements, for if I were to undertake to write about all of my observations of customs, the scenes of the country, which you nor I ever thought of until I have seen them and give you a full detail it would take me a great while longer than I have to spare at present for I can assure you that a down East sharper would find himself very deficient in shrewdness, as the Yankee terms it, in this land of humbugs and bankridden country. Indian depradations are so common again gain that with us it is almost considered unimportant news and when you ask the news, if you do not ask respectfully for Indian news nothing will be probably said about it. At present they are scattered through the middle & west Florida in small parties and scarcely a week passes without some mischief. A few days ago they shot the miller and afterward robbed & burned the Grist Mill of T. P. Charles about twelve of fifteen mls. from Tallahassee and about two mls from an encampment of soldiers. A few weeks ago they murdered a Family in ten mls of Marianna. In a thick settlement another depradation was commited on the Apalachicola River. One more killed and another wounded, both the express and male [mail] Rider have within a few miles of Tallahassee both been killed & severall others fired on and some wounded making their escape. A few days ago a party of deer hunters from Quincy and in pursuit of a deer fell in with and killed three Indians and about twelve or fifteen more warriors making their appearance and firing on them, being only four in number compelled to retreat wounding Mr. Gilarease in the shoulder. Four or five wagons have also been taken during the summer belonging to citizens and their negroes tried and was beat to death, and is not half that I could enumerate, and I fear from the present prospect that we will hear of many more. I have seen one scout of regulars since I came over here and they had no commissioned officer with them and so long as West Point officers are depended on we shall hear [illegible] news for a long time as you seldom ever hear of them in the proper place. Our currency is improving very rapidly as you can now buy a hundred dollars in specie for a hundred and fifty in Florida money. It has been as much as sixty one per cent below par. That has been one reason I did not return home this summer. It was with difficulty that I could travel to St Josephs on the money I heretofore received by paying the difference by two for one in the settlement of my accounts. This state of things has been occasioned by the combined viliany of the debtors of the Banks who have bought themselves rich with the bill of those Banks while in good respect and have since been buying it up at depreciation which will enable them to pay their debts with half or less. They have from time to time had the courts put off to prevent the Banks from getting executions against them. The capital of these Banks of all remember is raised by the sale of Territorial faith bonds sold in Europe, which has involved the Territory, and placed it rather a curious situation, as the most of citizens in Florida seem determined never to pay the interest, as the most of them think that we are not accountable because we are under the supervision and care of the Genl Government and they have been wrong in sanctioning any law of our Legislative council, which opinion I have always had since I knew anything about Legislation. The election will this Fall be placed on that issue. I will close my observations on these matters for the present. Navarro and myself both think of returning next spring and I shall also bring my Brother's wife and child with me if nothing prevents us. You will please present mine & Navarro's respects to all our friends and acquaintances and tell Charles I am in hopes he will not marry before me or at any rate before I return. If he does, however, I wish him every success and all the happiness imagination can present. I also take pleasure in congratulating him as an Odd Fellow. I have not seen so much pleasure with any new acquaintances as those I formed in Washington and my anxiety to join a band of Brothers and once more enjoy the pleasures of virtuous and good society keeps me ever thinking and talking about the citizens & the City of Washington. Inform my parents that I may have not been thoughtless about their health then I desire to be remembered by them. Present our respects to the Central Lodge and tell them that although we have been in a country where there are few Brothers to greet us we are not [illegible] of the moral influence of such societies and beg leave to urge them on in their noble cause and to give them the assurance of our high regard FLT. Please write and let me all [illegible] going on. Nothing more. Yours very respectfully in FLT.

Samuel H Walker

PS The report from East [illegible] closing of the war. Verbal reports says that the Indians have again butchered and killed about 70 more of our soldiers. It wants confirmation. I am much indebted to you for

> your trouble in forwarding my papers. You will please send me some numbers of the Odd Fellows magazine or something of the sort & some reports. I want to see the progress.[51]

Walker's last surviving letter from Florida was written to his sister-in-law Ann. He had not mentioned moving to Texas since his letter to his brother Jonathan in July 1837, but it remained in his mind. It became his exit card, only to be played when his situation in Florida became untenable. Over the course of fall and winter 1841, things went from bad to worse. Unable to contend with his business losses, and unwilling to return to Maryland as a failure, he came to a decision. He wrote of his unquenchable desire for "chivalric immortal fame"—illusive in Florida, but Texas offered a chance of seizing it.

> Tallahassee, Jan 22nd 1842
>
> Dear Sister
> I have just been conversing with Capt. Arnow, and it gave me great pleasure to hear from you and also little Florida and the Family generally and I must apologize to you for so much of delay about writing. The reason why I did not write, I was waiting to receive information from home, which I have not until about three weeks ago. Since that time I have been almost without any settled determination, though I can look around me and see none but those of friends who are almost ready to return the Right hand of fellowship toward me, but that undistinguishable love of chivalric immortal fame still clings to my heart, and though the passionate fondness of my friends & relatives often affect my feelings, the love of Fame still urges me on. And this amidst all those contending passions this body cannot rest content. Though Heaven forbid that I should ever mistake the path of true glory, forgetting the true and proper elements of a great man in the pursuit of that honourable distinction. My Brother Thomas desires to be remembered to you. He is very much troubled with a disease which renders his breathing difficult, being something like Asthma. He has lost his youngest child. Charles & sister Jane is both married. My Poor old father is still alive, but his faculties are reduced to that of a newborn infant, thus plainly amplifying the old adage once a man, twice a child. My Brother still advises me to return home but to return without wealth or Fame too hard; therefore be not surprised if my next communication to you should be written in Texas as I shall probably leave in a short time. My health has been very good ever since I left you. Manuel is well and sends his respects to you. I shall write again when I am ready to leave.
>
> Yours in Friendship; Love, and Truth until death.
> S H Walker[52]

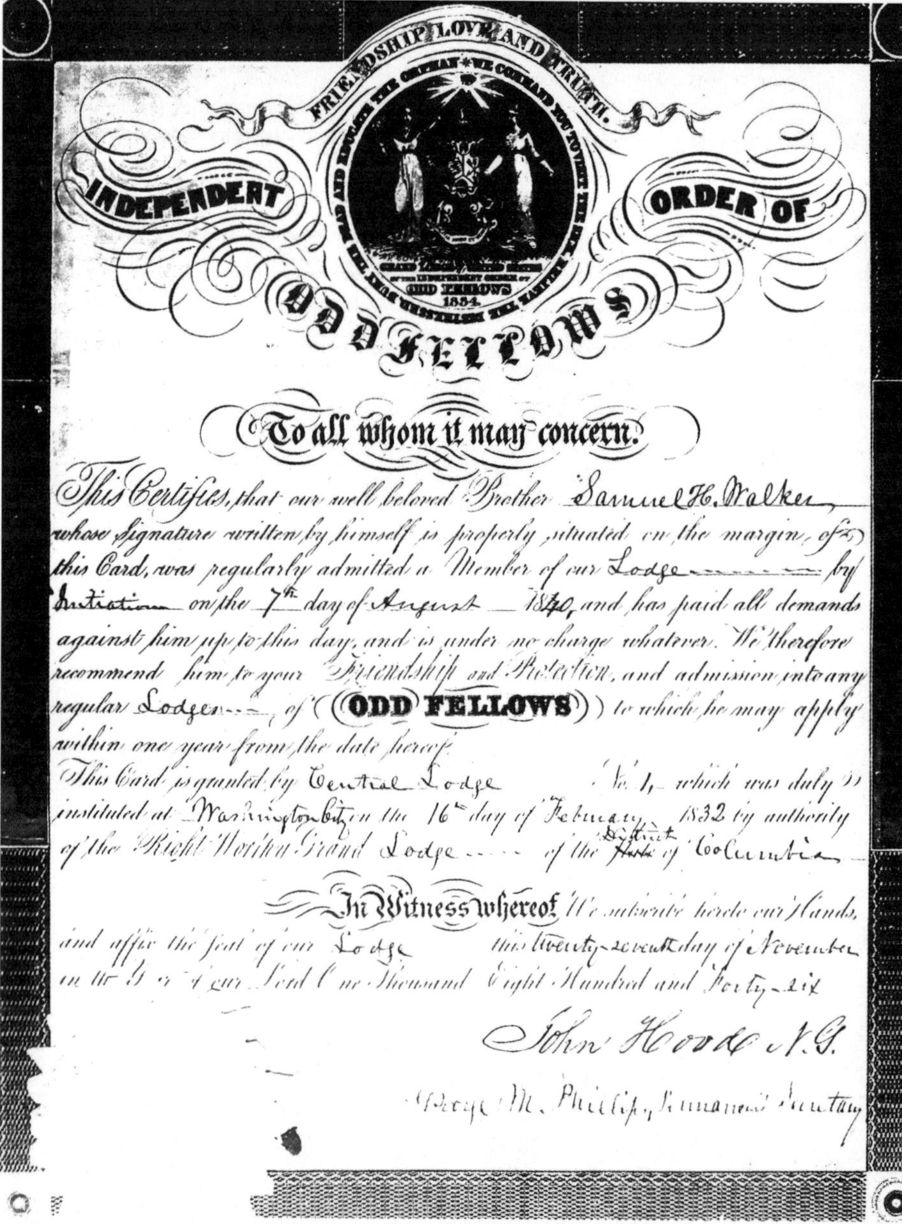

FRIENDSHIP LOVE AND TRUTH.

INDEPENDENT ORDER OF ODD FELLOWS

To all whom it may concern.

This Certifies, that our well beloved Brother Samuel H. Walker whose Signature written by himself is properly situated on the margin of this Card, was regularly admitted a Member of our Lodge by Initiation on the 7th day of August 1840, and has paid all demands against him up to this day, and is under no charge whatever. We therefore recommend him to your Friendship and Protection, and admission into any regular Lodge of (ODD FELLOWS) to which he may apply within one year from the date hereof.

This Card is granted by Central Lodge No. 1, which was duly instituted at Washington City on the 16th day of February 1832 by authority of the Right Worthy Grand Lodge of the District of Columbia

In Witness whereof We subscribe hereto our Hands, and affix the Seal of our Lodge this twenty-seventh day of November in the Year of our Lord One Thousand Eight Hundred and Forty-six

John Hood N.G.

George M. Phillips, Permanent Secretary

Odd Fellows membership certificate of Samuel H. Walker. The certificate of Samuel H. Walker as a member of the Independent Order of Odd Fellows, an international organization that promotes the ethic of reciprocity and charity, by implied inspiration of Judeo-Christian ethics. (Walker Papers, Texas State Archives)

CHAPTER 4

The Long Ordeal, 1842–43

Given his problems with conforming to army discipline, Sam Walker's service as a 12-month volunteer to fight in the Second Seminole War was less than a rewarding experience. He did, however, learn lessons that he carried with him when he took up residence in Florida, and subsequently migrated to Texas in February 1842. Foremost among them was fighting to preserve a way of life was necessary.

When the Republic of Texas declared its independence from Mexico on March 2, 1836, its entrance upon the world stage was fragile at best. Her victory at the battle of San Jacinto on April 21, 1836, and the subsequent agreement between the defeated President of Mexico, Gen. Antonio Lopez de Santa Anna, and Interim President of Texas David G. Burnet on May 14, 1836—known as the Treaty of Velasco—did not, in the long run, result in a de facto recognition of Texas as an independent nation by Mexico. Article 4 of the treaty stated:

> That the President Santa Anna, in his official character as chief of the Mexican nation, and the Generals Don Vicente Filisola, Don Jose Urea, Don Joaquin Ramires y Sesma, and Don Antonio Gaona, as Chiefs of Armies, do solemnly acknowledge, sanction, and ratify, the full, entire, and perfect Independence of the Republic of Texas, with such boundaries as are hereafter set forth and agreed upon for the same. And they do solemnly and respectively pledge themselves, with all their personal and official attributes, to procure without delay, the final and complete ratification and confirmation of this agreement, and all the parts thereof, by the proper and legitimate Government of Mexico, by the incorporation of the same into a solemn and perpetual Treaty of amity and commerce to be negotiated with that Government, at the city of Mexico, by Ministers Plenipotentiary to be deputed by the Government of Texas for this high purpose.[1]

However, there was no attempt on the part of Santa Anna or his generals to fulfill their obligation to use their influence to gain the ratification of a final treaty between Mexico and Texas. To the contrary, Santa Anna was deposed as president and sent into exile in disgrace. The Mexican congress denied the legality of the treaty, stating it was signed by Santa Anna under duress, and for the next several years used means, fair and foul, to reclaim the breakaway province.

Texians Working on the Road at Tacubaya. Sketch by Charles McLaughlin, one of the Mier prisoners. (From *Journal of the Texian Expedition Against Mier* by General Thomas J. Green, published by Harper and Brothers, New York, 1845)

The ink on the Treaty of Velasco was barely dry when, on May 20, 1836, the Mexican congress voted to continue the war against the rebellious Texians. Gen. José de Urrea was ordered to take command of the Mexican forces at Matamoros on June 5. As soon as orders came from Mexico City, he and his troops were to advance into Texas.

Gen. José de Urrea. (www.texasonline.org; photograph in the public domain)

Rumors and reports abounded; four thousand Mexican troops were concentrated at Matamoros; an expedition of similar numbers was fitting out at Veracruz for a landing on the Texas coast; and thousands more were gathering to invade Texas at other points. General Urrea was reported to have enlisted the support of various Native American leaders who promised to add eight thousand warriors to his ranks.

Panic seized the government of Texas. On June 20, Acting President Burnet issued a proclamation calling for every male citizen between the ages of 16 and 50 to prepare themselves for immediate service. Urgent appeals for volunteers from the United States went out. The perilous situation caused Maj. Gen. Edmund P. Gaines, USA, commanding the Army of the Southwestern Frontier of the United States at Fort Jesup, Louisiana, to send the 4th U.S. Infantry Regiment from that post (with the permission of the Texas government) to Nacogdoches, Texas, on 11 July, ostensibly to look into Native American outrages. Six additional companies of infantry and three of dragoons were later sent from Fort Towson, Native American territory.

David G. Burnet. (Photograph in the public domain)

However, by mid-July, reports of a different character began arriving in Texas. Thomas Toby, purchasing agent for Texas in New Orleans, wrote Burnet on July 12, 1836, giving his appraisals of the possible invasion of Texas—the troops under General de Urrea at Matamoros were in a wretched condition, so much so that there was no possibility of an invasion for at least two or three months.[2] The *Telegraph and Texas Register* of August 9, 1836, published a report from one Peter Suzeman who stated many of de Urrea's troops were deserting the ranks or refusing the march into Texas. It soon became apparent there was little money to purchase supplies for de Urrea's proposed campaign or to pay his unenthusiastic troops. By the end of August, the threat had subsided.

Gen. Edmund P. Gaines. (National Archives photograph 528719)

During the emergency, Texas had mustered some 2,500 troops, mostly volunteers from the United States, to counter the Mexican threat. With no immediate need to defend Texas from invasion, some thought these troops, now idle but nevertheless eager to fight, should be used in a preemptive strike against the Mexicans to, as Texas Gen. Felix Huston stated in a letter to Sam Houston, make the Mexicans pay for their scorched-earth policy in Texas and "make her feel the desolation of war."[3]

He said he could do it in a month with the forces in hand. Houston wanted no part of it. In his opinion, nothing would be gained from it. Such adventures were discouraged by the most influential citizens of Texas and faded from the scene by October.

The area between the Nueces River and the Rio Grande, sparsely populated, but nevertheless important to both parties, remained a bone of contention and would remain so until the end of the Mexican–American War. The boundaries between Texas and Mexico were delineated by Article 5:

> That the following be, and the same are hereby established and made the lines of demarcation between the two Republics of Mexico and of Texas, to wit: The line shall commence at the estuary or mouth of the Rio Grande, on the western bank thereof, and shall pursue the same bank up the said river, to the point where the river assumes the name of the Rio Bravo del Norte, from which point it shall proceed on the said western bank to the head waters, or source of said river, it being understood that the terms Rio Grande and Rio Bravo del Norte, apply to and designate one and the same stream. From the source of said river, the principal head branch being taken to ascertain that source, a due north line shall be run until it shall intersect the boundary line established and described in the Treaty negotiated by and between the Government of Spain and the Government of the United States of the North; which line was subsequently transferred to, and adopted in the Treaty of limits made between the Government of Mexico and that of the United States; and from this point of intersection the line shall be the same as was made and established in and by the several Treaties above mentioned, to continue to the mouth or outlet of the Sabine river, and from thence to the Gulf of Mexico.[4]

The disputed area became a hotbed for armed gangs of Texians, some claiming the right of restitution for property lost during the War of Independence, while others simply saw an opportunity to ply their murderous business against defenseless civilians. Both raided and robbed Mexican merchants and traders who were crossing this no-man's-land. The Mexicans, more often than not commanded by army officers, raided across the Rio Grande, doing the same to Texian traders. Moreover, the Mexicans armed and encouraged natives, mainly those of the Cherokee and Tonkawa tribes, to attack and murder Texian settlers. The Comanche—the largest and most warlike of the Native American tribes—fought both Mexicans and Texians, regarding both as interlopers.

Twenty-five-year-old Sam Walker's arrival in Texas came at a difficult time for the young republic. The Mexican congress did not recognize Santa Anna's surrender of the area to the Anglos and on occasion would make a military incursion into Texas. Just as the British and natives threatened the early eastern frontier after the Revolutionary War, Mexican and natives endangered the Texas southern border.

While six years had passed since Santa Anna's humiliating defeat at San Jacinto, he had not been able to stabilize the resources of his huge country to organize a full-fledged invasion to retake Texas. To rally national pride and divert attention from his country's disastrous economic affairs, he authorized these smaller strikes northward into Texas.[5]

As a mobile defense force to deal with minor incursions, Texians had their Rangers, but on one occasion, a large group of Texians journeyed into Mexico themselves to react to these invasions of their republic. An expedition to Santa Fe (then Old Mexico) was launched on June 19, 1841, under the auspices of Texas President Mirabeau Lamar.

Mirabeau B. Lamar. (Photograph in the public domain)

It was his effort to firmly establish Texas authority in those regions specified in Article 5, above. To that goal, a commercial and military expedition was formed consisting of 21 wagons filled with merchandise and 320 soldiers, including a company of artillery. Poorly prepared and without certain knowledge of the best route to take, the expedition met with disaster. The Texians finally arrived in New Mexico in mid-September and were met by some 1,500 Mexican troops. In no condition to resist, the Texians surrendered. Although promised a safe escort back to the border of Texas as recognized by the Mexicans, the Texians were subsequently treated as bandits and forced to march some 2,000 miles to Mexico City where they languished under harsh conditions in Perote Prison until June 13, 1842.

Samuel C. Reid, Jr., a private in Capt. Benjamin McCulloch's Company of Texas Rangers, wrote of a conversation Walker had with him and a few fellow Rangers. According to Reid, Walker said "he came to Texas in January 1842 and went out with General Johnson on the frontier. He there joined an expedition against the natives who had murdered a family near Clark Owen's camp and carried off two children. The raiders were pursued and a skirmish took place on San Antonio River, in which they were defeated and the children retaken."[6]

Samuel H. Walker's Memorandum Book

This portion is taken from Walker's "Memorandum Book," kept during the Mier Expedition, his subsequent capture and imprisonment, and ending with his escape. His account is in italics. Clarifications relative to Walker's entries (taken from the published collections of other Mier Expedition members) and Walker's personal letters are in roman type. Walker's entries have been transcribed as he wrote them with name corrections, additions, and some punctuation corrections made for the ease of the reader. As will be seen, Walker frequently misspelled words, used phonetics when it came to the names of Mexican cities and towns, while paying little attention to grammar and punctuation. Other accounts of the events written by other members of the Mier Expedition that provide additional details of events mentioned by Walker are interspersed throughout in italics, as are editorial comments, and a few of Walker's letters written during this period. Walker loaned this "memorandum" to Gen. Thomas J. Green—one of the Mier Expedition and a fellow prisoner—sometime in 1844 when Green was writing his version of events, which was published as *Journal of the Texian Expedition Against Mier* in 1845. Green never returned it to Walker and it made its way with Green's papers to the Southern Historical Collection of the University of North Carolina.

Walker's account begins with the events leading up to and including the battle of Mier. A microfilm copy of the memorandum book was provided to the author by the Southern Historical Collection with permission to use it in this work. His entries are in italics.

On the 6th of March 1842 Gen Bascus [Rafáel Vásquez][7] *entered and took possession of [San Antonio de] Bexar with about 700 Troops*[8] *without resistance having induced the Texians, whose force was small, to believe that his force was the advance guard of a large invading army.*

News of the Mexican capture of Bexar spread quickly and calls for the militia to be activated followed. Rumors spread even faster. A general call to arms was issued by now President Houston on 10 March, ordering all who were "subject to military duty … to be in readiness to repair to the scene of action at the call of the authorities of the country." On the 11th, Houston wrote to Commo. Edwin Moore,[9] Texas Navy, to make his ships ready for action. Houston ended his missive with the words, "Make haste." Agents were sent to the United States to get volunteers and material assistance. The troops and volunteers assembled at the frontier awaiting orders.

The Texians, about 3,000 in number, soon rallied to the frontier to meet the supposed invading force, but we were much disappointed as it proved only to be a marauding party authorized by the government of Mexico, their stay was short and their retreat hasty. Their inroad however was marked with pillage & plunder taking with them about $30,000 worth of goods.

Walker was among those who answered the call.[10] He enlisted in Jesse Billingsley's company at Bastrop.

Galveston, Texas, March 10th 1842

Dear Sister
I write to inform you that I am in good health and hope this may find yourself and child enjoying the same blessing and also your Father's

family and neighbors. I have been here three weeks & thus far I am much pleased. I have not much time to write about particulars as we are now making preparations to meet the Mexicans on the frontier. I have many other communications to write, but I will endeavor to give you more satisfactory information hereafter. I will write again to your cousin Dick in a few days or send him some files of papers from which he may glean the spirit of the times. Since I arrived I have made a good many acquaintances and enjoyed myself quite as well as I could. Expected society is very good indeed. The cause of Temperance & religion flourish here as well as any place I have ever been in. One hundred & eighty persons took the total abstinence pledge in two nights. The Ladies of course are doing their part in the great cause. Give my compliments to Col. L[ackland]. M. Stone & Family & all inquiring friends and tell them I should be glad to hear from them and they shall hear from me as often as circumstances will admit. Direct your letters to Galveston as I can have them forwarded to me on the frontier.

Thursday night 10 oclock.

Since writing the above information has been received from various sources too creditable to doubt any longer of an actual invasion by a large force of Mexicans and there will no doubt be some hard fighting and this war will be carried to Mexico. Nothing more at present but

Remain Yours Very Respectfully
SH Walker[11]

The most of the Texians were anxious to pursue the enemy across the Riogrande, but discontent occasioned by Sam Houston endeavoring to place Gen Somerville[12] [Alexander Somervell, 1796–1854, was appointed brigadier general by Houston on 18 November 1839] in command because he was the militia Genl. of the western district, while the volunteers would not acknowledge Houston's right to appoint a commander of Somerville's ability to command an invading force. [Somervell's force was officially titled the Southwestern Army of Operations] The expedition was given up and the Texians returned to their homes with loud curses against Sam Houston, but scarcely had they reached their homes when Sam Houston's celebrated reply to Santa Anna made its appearance. It was written in the language of a statesman and a patriot and of course pleased the people and made them

Gen. Alexander Somervell. (Photograph in the public domain)

satisfied to wait untill an expedition could be got up under the sanction & patronage of the executive.

Houston's letter was in response to the attempt of James Hamilton, former financial agent under President Mirabeau Lamar, to bribe Santa Anna and other agents of the Mexican government to enter into a treaty of peace with Texas; $5,200,000 was the amount Hamilton guaranteed. Santa Anna regarded Hamilton's clumsy attempt as "an insult and an infamy unworthy of a gentleman," and Mexico would continue the war until she planted her eagle standard on the banks of the Sabine.[13] The reply Walker referred to read, "In the war which will be conducted by Texas against Mexico, ... we will march across the Rio Grande, and, believe me, Sir, ere the banner of Mexico shall triumphantly float upon the banks of the Sabine, the Texian standard of the single star borne by the Anglo-Saxon race, shall display its bright folds in Liberty's triumph, on the isthmus of Darien."[14]

The call was made to the many friends of Texas in the US, and many of them in a short time landed in Texas ready armed & equiped for active service, but in return for their patriotism they received very cool & disrespectful treatment from Sam Houston and eventually returned without compensation or thanks for their services fully convinced that the immortal hero of San Jacinto was more smoke than fire, because he had complained in the first place that congress had not given him the authority to use the public lands which were the principle resources of the Government. Meanwhile he called congress together and after they had given him the authority while they supposed he wanted he vetoed the bill on the grounds that it was unconstitutional and some future aspirant might use such authority to the destruction of the liberties of his country. Congress then passed a bill giving him authority to authorize volunteer expeditions into the enemy's country and commissioned such officers as should be duly elected by the organized companies at the sulpher springs on the Cibola the place of rendezvous. He accordingly published his proclamation that it had not become generally known before another report was in circulation that the executive of the US had requested a cessation of hostilities and would endeavour to use her influence to make an amicable settlement of the difficulties between the two countries, and it was reported that Sam Houston intended to recall the navy[15] *and neither would he allow the expedition which he had authorized to cross the riogrande, but he denied having made any such insinuation and expressed a wish that the people would turn out, cross the riogrande and chastise the enemy for their depredations on Bexar. The people however have lost all confidence in any thing being done under Houston's management and therefore would not turn out in sufficient numbers to make a campaign. On the 7th of July Gen. Canalles [Antonio Canales Rosillo]*[16] *with one piece of artillery 500 cavalry & 200 infantry attacked about 100 volunteers principally from the US, on the Bank of the Neuaces [Nueces] river at a place called Lapatitlan [Lipanantitlán]. They made several charges but were easily repelled by the volunteers, who had not a man hurt. Much credit is due to Capt. [Ewen] Cameron*[17] *in this affair.*

The enemy left 4 men on the field besides some 8 or 10 wounded which they took off it. So happened however that Gen Canalles claimed a decisive victory from the following circumstances.

The volunteers have heard so many reports of mexicans that they at last got so they would not believe any such reports. Houston has neglected to feed them and for several days previous they have been without food the consequence was they have become reckless & careless and when they were informed on the evening of the 6th of July of the approach of the enemy it was with some difficulty that Gen. [James] Davis[18] *the commander could prevail on the Texians to take the precaution to move to a more advantageous position leaving their camp equipage and every thing in the old camp intending to return early in the morning. The night was passed a few hundred yards off and at day light on the 7th as the volunteers were returning to their former camp they found it surrounded by the enemy who opened a fire on them with their field piece. The Texians fell back to their chosen position where they had spent the night leaving their banners and camp equipage in the hands of the enemy which enabled Canalles to palm his deception on the people of his country that he had gained a decisive victory over 500 Texians. Thus ended the Campaign of Canalles whose victory was celebrated throughout all Mexico.*

Antonio Canales Rosillo. (Photograph in the public domain)

On July 6, Gen. James Davis, in pursuit of Canales, camped at the Nueces River to await reinforcements. He had 192 men under his command while the Mexicans outnumbered them by a ratio of five to one. Davis wisely decided to abandon his campsite in the face of superior numbers and take a position that offered better protection. At dawn of the 7th, the Mexicans advanced—hoping to take the Texians by surprise—they bombarded the camp and launched their attack, but the surprise was theirs. The camp was empty. Canales reordered his men and assaulted Davis's new position. The Texians delivered a hot fire that brought the charge to a halt. When the commander of the Mexican cavalry refused Canales's order to press the attack, he was compelled to withdraw. Canales, however, reported killing 22 Texians and wounding several, and drove them from the field. He did not take up the pursuit due to the landing of two hundred Texians at the Rincon de la Cerda. Davis reported killing and wounding 30 of the Mexicans.

On the 11th of Sept Gen. [Adrián] Woll[19] entered and took possession of Bexar after a slight resistance. Court was sitting and the Texians in Bexar had some warning of his approach but were disposed to believe that it was another robing party like that commanded by Bascus. They accordingly sent commissioners to meet him and inquire of him whether he came as a Robber or a warrior under the authority of his government. If the former the Mexican citizens of Bexar expressed a determination to defend the place in concert with the Texians about sixty in number of the latter. They desired the commissioners to say that he would meet with no resistance but instead of letting the commissioners return he detained them, and entered the Town at day break in the morning of the 11th with 700 cavalry 600 infantry & 2 pieces of Artillery. Although he was a little surprised when a fire from about 53 Texians killed 6 & wounded 23 of his men killing the Generals horse from under him and also several others of his staff, and after withdrawing from the square & cannonading a short time he sent a flag and officers to treat the Texians as prisoners of war if they would surrender. Amongst them was several of the Santa Fee Prisoners who were named and were also assured they should be treated as prisoners of war. These prisoners were in a short time sent off to Mexico.

Gen. Adrián Woll. (Photograph in the public domain)

To avenge the repulse of Canales, on July 10 Santa Anna made it known to the Mexican Congress he intended to invade Texas. He had, on June 5, ordered Gen. Mariano Arista, commander of the Army of the North, to instruct Gen. Adrián Woll to ready his division for another attack on San Antonio. On August 17, the (Houston) *Telegraph and Texas Register* printed a letter dated July 2 reporting Woll on the Rio Grande with twelve hundred men and scouting parties that had made their way almost to Bexar. Famed Texas Ranger William A. A. (Bigfoot) Wallace[20] told Capt. John C. Hays[21] he had seen about a dozen strange Mexicans in San Antonio. Woll's force consisted of 957 officers and enlisted men; 12 wagons of corn; 150 loads of provisions; 50 or more head of cattle; two pieces of artillery and an artillery train, 919 horses; and 213 mules. The Mexicans began their march on August 31. On the 11th, the city was surrounded. Inside San Antonio, two companies of defenders under the overall command of Captain Hays; one hundred loyal Mexicans under the command of Salvador Flores; and about 75 Texians led by Chauncey Johnson, were roused from their beds to meet the enemy. The Mexicans advanced through the city in a dense fog and were fired upon by Flores and Johnson killing one and wounding 24. Momentarily confused by the firing, the Mexicans recovered and opened fire with small arms and artillery. Outgunned and outnumbered, the defenders sent four commissioners; William E. Jones, Samuel A. Maverick, George Van Ness, and C. W. Peterson, under a white flag to surrender. Johnson's men and those of Flores who had not run away were taken prisoner along with several important townsmen and citizens, 52 in all. Hays and his Rangers were not in the city when it was captured.

Capt. John Coffee Hays. (Photograph in the public domain)

The news reached the Colorado on the 14th and the Texians again supposed this to be the vanguard of a large invading army. On the 18th of Sept Col [Matthew] Caldwell[22] *took a position on the Salado within 5ms [miles] of Bexar with 202 men.*

He sent Capt Hays with fifty horsemen to the suburbs of the Town to draw out the enemy which succeeded. Hays rejoined Caldwell on the Salado pursued by the whole force joined by about 200 Bexar Mexicans. The fight continued untill about four oclock with very trifling loss to the Texians and considerable loss to the enemy, at this time.

Col. Matthew Caldwell. (Photograph in the public domain)

Zachariah N. Morrell,[23] self-described as a "Canebrake preacher and Indian fighter," took part in the battle of the Salado, and put his recollections to paper.

> About the first of September, as it was not considered safe to move our families back to Gonzales, I took my wagon, attended by my son, and went to gather our corn on the Guadalupe.
>
> The corn was gathered, and just as we were starting back with a load to Colorado, Colonel Matthew Caldwell rode up with an express from San Antonio, as follows:—
>
> Colonel:—General Woll has arrived at San Antonio with thirteen hundred men. The court,—judge, jury, lawyers,—and many citizens in attendance, are prisoners in the hands of the Mexicans, I made my escape, and came round under the mountains to Seguin.
>
> John W. Smith.[24]
>
> Colonel Caldwell said, "Something must be done quick, and you must go with me." My excuses were rendered,—I was in very feeble health, was a cripple, was riding a wild, untrained, borrowed horse, and was badly needed at home. He urged me to accompany him, stating that I could be of great service to him in controlling the young men who would be with him.

Zachariah N. Morrell. (Photograph in the public domain)

My patriotism was appealed to, and remembering the sentiment … that I expected "to rise or fall with Texas," my consent was given to go on another perilous expedition … My son started on alone with his load of corn to the Colorado, fifty miles [distant]. Although an Indian country was between him and home, I did not apprehend danger, as men in companies would soon be on the road from the east towards the scene of action.

We gathered what ammunition we could at Gonzales, and left for Seguin, with instruction that recruits coming from the east should follow our trail. At Seguin I obtained ten ears of com, had it parched and ground, and mixed with it two pounds of sugar. This we called cold flour.

Recruits were coming in all night, and on Tuesday morning we marched on within twenty miles of San Antonio. Colonel Caldwell was in command, by common consent. A call was made for ten of the best horses and lightest riders, to go and meet Jack Hays that night on the Salado. He had notified us, by express, that he was there watching the enemy, and needed reinforcements.

The number called for was soon obtained,—the writer among them, on his fine, untrained, borrowed horse. A charge, with some instructions, was given us, and a short while before day we arrived at the spot where we were ordered to go. A keen whistle was given, and readily responded to by Hays. Wednesday morning came and found us thirteen strong, with nothing but cold flour to eat, and a limited supply of that. Our ration consisted of a spoonful for each, mixed with water. A detail was made to stay at camp, another to go down on the east side of San Antonio, and another under Jack Hays to head the San Antonio River, and go entirely round in the rear of the city, to ascertain if any reinforcements were coming in from Mexico. Hays was discovered during the day and driven back, making no discovery himself as to reinforcements. Thursday morning came, and with only a spoonful of cold flour for each, another effort was made to get the number and intention of the enemy. Caldwell still remained at his camp twenty miles east of the city, expecting the Mexicans to march on Gonzales. Hays was repulsed, as on the day before, and failed to get in the enemy's rear. The writer and part of the company went down the Salado, and discovered what we supposed to be the trail of two or three hundred cavalry, going in the direction of Gonzales. On our return we met Hays with his company, driving in some horses. Very soon, about forty Mexicans made their appearance in pursuit. We retreated until they were drawn from the timber, when, under the order of our gallant leader, we wheeled, and forty Mexicans failed to stand the charge of thirteen Texans. No damage, that we know of, was done to either party.

Friday morning, a mutiny rose in our little camp, in consequence of the condition of our commissary department. Plenty of deer and turkeys were in sight all the time, and we were all hunters; but our leader thought it best to fire no guns, and keep our position concealed from the enemy. From Monday till Friday, on a little cold flour, measured out by the spoonful, made us feel very lean; and now that the flour was all out, our men began to swear vengeance on the game at all hazards. Captain Hays insisted that I should make them a speech. I remembered the old saying, "Never try to influence a man against his inclination when he is hungry," but as my captain insisted, and as I was under orders, I determined to try. To have approached these men with a long face, and taxed their patience with a long speech on patriotism, would have been sheer nonsense. So I mounted my horse and rode out in front, with as cheerful a face as I could command, and spoke as follows:—

"Boys, when I left Colonel Caldwell's camp, I felt like I was forty years old. When I had starved one day, I felt like I was thirty-five. After that, on two spoonfuls a day, I felt like I was twenty-five; and this morning, when our cold flour and coffee are both out, I feel like I was only twenty-one years old, and ready for action. Our situation this morning is critical,—the Mexicans, we fear, have gone toward Gonzales; secrecy surely is the best policy; and we ought to report the situation, if possible, to Colonel Caldwell to-night."

An agreement was soon entered into, that we get information, report that evening, and get some game for supper.

In a few minutes we were off, and soon met Henry McCulloch[25] with thirteen men, swelling our number to twenty-seven. Here we learned that Caldwell had discovered the enemy's trail below, and that the Mexican cavalry had retreated back to the city. The families on the Guadalupe were safe for the evening. Here was fresh beef hanging to the saddles of McCulloch's party. The company was organized on the spot, with Jack Hays captain, and Henry McCulloch lieutenant, and the young captain, with his first command, led us to the nearest water. We refreshed ourselves with this delicious beef and a good night's rest. We were camped within five miles of the city.

Image thought to be that of Henry E. McCulloch. (Cowans Auctions)

Before day Saturday morning, Captain Hays detailed three men, and myself as the fourth, to go in sight of the city before daylight. He took three men with him, and made the third attempt to go round the city, and was successful, bringing off with him a Mexican spy as a prisoner. Lieutenant McCulloch watched both roads leading to Seguin and Gonzales. My associates and I remained secreted near the powder-house. … We rode twenty miles in about two hours, and reported to Colonel Caldwell. …

Hays and McCulloch both preceded us to Caldwell's camp, and as some anxiety was felt for our safety we were welcomed with many cheers. The two captured Mexicans told the same story. With these statements, coming from the front and rear of the city, Saturday morning, ten o'clock, revealed to Col. Caldwell and his men the strength of the enemy. General Woll crossed the Rio Grande with thirteen hundred men, and picked up afterwards three hundred "Greezers" and Indians. Our entire force, ordered into line, numbered two hundred and two men; General Woll's Mexican force was sixteen hundred.

Saturday night we were marched to the Salado, and camped near midnight within six miles of San Antonio. Here we had much the advantage in the ground, if attacked, and during the night a council of war was held. The council decided that it would not be prudent to attack the enemy in these fortifications; but if he could be decoyed out to our own chosen ground, we could tie our horses back in the timber, out of range of his guns, and from behind the natural embankment make a successful battle, although the enemy numbered eight to our one.

Sunday morning about sunrise Captain Hays and Lieutenant McCulloch were placed in charge of thirty-eight men, to approach San Antonio and lead the enemy out. Out of two hundred and two horses only thirty-eight were found, by a committee appointed to examine them, fit for the expedition. My untrained, borrowed horse and his rider was selected to go on the trip. We reached a point a half mile from the old powder-house, and about a mile from the city, between nine and ten o'clock, Sunday morning. … Captain Hays and Lieutenant McCulloch, attended with six men, left us, with orders to be ready for any emergency. They went down close to the Alamo, and bantered the enemy for a fight; supposing that forty or fifty mounted men would be sent out, whom our captain intended to engage in battle. Contrary to this expectation, four or five hundred cavalry turned out in hot pursuit. Hays soon approached with the command, "Mount!" We moved off briskly through the timber, and as the Mexicans went round an open way, we were about half a mile ahead when we reached the prairie. They had about fifty American horses, in fine condition, captured from the citizens and members of the court, and our horses were considerably worn with the labor of the past seven days. During the first four miles we kept out of their reach without much difficulty. Two miles lay stretched between us and our camp, and soon Lieutenant McCulloch, in charge of the rear guard, pressed close on our heels. Hats, blankets, and overcoats were scattered along our track. No time then to pick anything up. The race was an earnest one; the Mexicans, toward the last, began to fire at our rear guard, doing no damage. We reached the camp, and, when formed into line, every man was present, unhurt.

The cavalry that had pursued us passed round to our rear on the prairie. About a half hour intervened, during which time we refreshed ourselves and horses with water. Captain Jack Hays, our intrepid leader, five feet ten inches high, weighing one hundred and sixty pounds, his black eyes flashing decision of character, from beneath at full forehead, and crowned with beautiful jet black hair, was soon mounted on his dark by war-horse and on the warpath. Under our chosen leader, we sallied out and skirmished with the enemy at long range, killing a number of Mexicans, and getting two of our men severely wounded. In a short time they retired, and we fell back to the main command.

Between two and three o'clock in the evening, General Woll appeared with all his infantry, cavalry and artillery spread out on the prairie in our rear, and between us and our homes. As we stood in line under the brow of the hill, the brave Caldwell informed us that he could never surrender to General Woll; that he had just returned from the Santa Fe expedition, and that it would be certain death to be taken in arms the second time. He urged us to make up our minds to fight it out, and even if it required a hand-to-hand combat, the white flag would not be raised. Closing this earnest address, he invited me to make a speech to the men. As well as my memory serves me I spoke as follows:—

"Gentlemen,—We are now going into battle against fearful odds,—eight to one,—and with artillery all on the enemy's side. The artillery can't harm us under this bank. We have nothing to fear as long as we can prevent them from coming to a hand-to-hand fight. Keep cool; let us not shoot as they advance on us till we can see the whites of their eyes; and be sure to shoot every man that has an officer's hat or sword. This will prevent them from coming into close quarters. Let us shoot low, and my impression before God is, that we shall win this fight."

Just as this time the cannon fired, and the grape shot struck the tops of the trees. The Mexicans now advanced upon us, under a splendid puff of music, the ornaments, guns, spears and swords glistening in plain view. Captain Hays' attention, as they drew near, was directed to the fact that they were intending to flank us above, and pour a raking fire down our line. Accordingly, ten men, with double-barrel shot-guns, were detached, and stationed above to prevent it. Some of the Mexican infantry were within thirty feet of us before a gun was fired. At the first fire the whole of them fell to the ground. My first impression was that they were all killed. Soon, however, all that were able rose to their feet, but showed no disposition to advance further upon our line. Not a sword nor officer's hat made its appearance after we had been fighting five minutes. The ground on which we stood was of such a character that we could step back two or three paces and stand straight up to load our guns. The battle lasted but a little while. General Woll was at his cannon on the top of the hill, looking on; his artillery was of no use, being right in the rear of his infantry, and our men sheltered by the embankment. He could see his men falling while the Texans were entirely out of sight. The horn sounded a retreat, and the Mexicans ran away in great confusion. It was with great difficulty that the Texans were prevented from pursuing.

Andrew J. Sowell. (Photograph in the public domain)

The Mexicans moved off towards San Antonio about sunset, and spent the night carrying in and burying their dead in the city. A large number was killed, the exact estimate it was impossible for us to make. Caldwell lost only one man killed; no prisoners; three wounded.[26]

Andrew J. Sowell,[27] who also took part in the battle of the Salado, wrote the following:

Creed Taylor. (Photograph in the public domain)

> Mathew Caldwell was in command of the force, which amounted to about 200 men. Caldwell advanced to the Salado, and took up a strong position on this creek, about seven miles northeast of San Antonio. … Captain Jack Hays then advanced with about fifty men to San Antonio, and drew the Mexicans out. In his (Captain J. C. Hays') company, H. E. McCulloch was first lieutenant, and C. B. Acklin orderly sergeant. They were chased back from within half a mile of the Alamo, by 400 cavalry, to the Salado. McCulloch covered the retreat with ten picked men, and they had a lively time. The names of the ten men are as follows: William Polk, Green McCoy, Stuart Foley, C. B. Acklin, Cloy Davis, Creed Taylor, Josiah Taylor, Pipkin Taylor, Rufus Taylor, and James Taylor. The Mexicans made a desperate effort to cut Hays off, by passing up on his right flank. McCulloch kept between him and the Mexicans, sending couriers every half mile or so urging him to put for the timber, and finally when the timber was reached, McCulloch had only one man with him, Creed Taylor. These two were targets for the Mexicans for the last half mile, and at from 100 to 200 paces, there must have been from 100 to 200 shots fired at them on the run, but fortunately not a ball struck man or horse; but Creed Taylor was wounded in the battle which followed on the creek.
>
> The men in camp had killed some beef cattle and were engaged in cooking and eating when Hays and McCulloch dashed in, closely pursued by the Mexican cavalry. Every man was soon at his post and ready for action. The whole Mexican army then advanced from San Antonio, and crossing the creek, took up a position on the hillside, east of Caldwell's position. There they planted a battery and opened fire on the Texans, but without effect; for Caldwell's men were protected by the creek bank, behind which they were formed. The only danger they had to guard against was the falling limbs which the cannon shots tore off from the large pecan trees over their heads. Seeing he could not dislodge them with artillery, the Mexican commander ordered a charge. The Texans as yet had not fired a shot. The cannons ceased, bugles sounded, and the rush of tramping feet was heard in the flat, as the Mexicans advanced to the charge.
>
> Caldwell gave orders for half the men to reserve their fire, while those in front were to step back after a discharge and reload, while those with loaded rifles were to man the bank. The Mexicans had to advance very close before they could see the Texans; and then firing their escopetes [escopetas/muskets], they fell back before the deadly fire of the rifles. A loud, keen yell went up from the Texans as the Mexicans broke and dashed back in disordered squads out

James W. Taylor. (James Worsham collection)

of range, leaving quite a number killed and wounded behind them. They rallied again on the crest of the ridge and formed, and the officers were seen riding to and fro among them. The Texans elated with their success had no fears of the final issue, although greatly outnumbered. They continued to whoop and yell at the Mexicans, and some resumed their repast of beef, bread and strong coffee, which had been interrupted by the advance of the Mexican army. The Mexican cavalry kept dashing about and prancing around, but kept out of range. Finally, they stopped on the hill some distance up the creek. Green McCoy noticing this, came to Andrew Sowell and proposed to him that they would lead their horses up the creek a short distance, tie them so that they would be at hand in case of need, and then slip within rifle shot of the Mexican cavalry, get a good shot each, and then fall back to their horses, and make their escape in case they were pursued. Andrew agreed to this readily, and they left the camp, keeping out of sight of the Mexicans until they went far enough, and then tied their horses to a mesquite tree. They could see part of the cavalry through the bushes, not far off, and bending low, started to slip within range. They had taken but a few steps when they were started by a low, keen whistle near them, and hastily looking around, saw a company of Mexican infantry in fifty paces of them, where they had been concealed in the high grass, and had just risen up and whistled to them like a hunter would to a deer, to make it stop until he could shoot it. They saw the Mexicans were fixing to fire, and sprang towards their horses and bent low for a few seconds and received the first fire. The bark and mesquite beans fell on their hats which were cut off by the bullets, but neither one of them was touched, and drawing their knives, quick as lightning almost, cut their ropes and mounted the terrified horses, which had begun to rear and plunge about. They were young, active and good riders, or else they would never have been able to mount under the circumstances. They received the second fire from the Mexicans as they bent low in their saddles and dashed off. The balls cut the air around them, but still they were unhurt. Andrew ventured one look behind as they started, and some of the Mexicans were so near that he said he could see halfway down the barrels of the big-mouthed escopetes as the Mexicans presented them to fire. They dashed into camp just as the Mexicans were again advancing to charge; but as before, they could not stand the unerring aim of the riflemen, and were again driven back with great loss.

General Cordova[28] whom Burleson fought at Mill creek, was killed in the charge. He had taken refuge behind a small mesquite in the retreat, to avoid a discharge, and was killed when he attempted to leave it. Cordova was a noted man in Mexico, and on receipt of the news of his death, the bells were rung in Monterrey, and an ode was published to his memory at Saltillo. The Texans, as yet, had not lost a man, and had but few wounded. The Mexicans invariably overshot them, knocking over more coffeepots, which were in the rear, than Texans. Calvin Turner received a glancing shot in the head, and fell; his brother, William, who was near, vainly endeavoring to force a tight ball down his rifle, dropped it, and ran to him, and assisted him to regain his feet, and he soon recovered. The Mexicans, who had been freely supplied with mescal from San Antonio, and being now pretty much under the influence of it, somewhat lost their terror of the Texas rifles, and once more advanced to the charge, yelling like Indians. They threw away their hats and came down the hill bareheaded, and with their dark skins and black hair, very much resembled a host of savages. They made no halt when fired on, but came on like demons, firing their escopetes in the very faces of Caldwell's men, at not more than fifteen paces, and for a few moments the cracking of rifles and the yells of the combatants were terrific. But drunk or sober, they could not stand such a deadly fire at short range, and again fled out of reach, followed by scattering shots and loud yells. …

During the progress of the fight, the Texans noticed that the Mexicans moved their artillery, also the cavalry, and a portion of the infantry, and presently they heard cannon shots in the prairie some distance to the east of them. Boom after boom came ringing across the prairie, and the Texans were satisfied that some brave band of men had encountered the Mexicans in trying to join them. But they dared not move from their position for here was the only place

> where they could successfully fight Wall's army, with his superior force, flanked by large bodies of cavalry, and supported with artillery, which was between them and the brave men who were at this time selling their lives so dearly.[29]

Capt [Nicholas] Dawson[30] imprudently advanced in the open prairie with 53 men, and making a stand rather than retreat. The cannon was brought to bear on him. 33 of his men killed 18 wounded & taken prisoners two only making their escape. They made consid[erable] slaughter however amongst the enemy. Dawson after finding he had got in a situation from which he could not extricate himself hoisted a white flag and as he asked for quarter but was refused and many of them died fighting hand to hand with the enemy. The reason given by the Mexicans for refusing quarter [to] these brave men was that Caldwell had refused to receive a white flag from them, which was a poor reason as they never ceased firing when they sent their flag to Capt Caldwell and besides it was to demand a surrender.

The following account of the Dawson Massacre is an excerpt from the book *History of Texas from 1685 to 1892* (St. Louis: L. E. Daniel, 1893) by John Henry Brown, who joined Caldwell's force on September 17.[31]

> While the battle was going on as before described, a company of fifty-three volunteer citizens, all but two or three of whom were from Fayette County, under command of Capt. Nicholas Dawson, was approaching from the east to reinforce Caldwell. When on the prairie about a mile and a half distant and within hearing of the guns, they discovered a body of Mexican cavalry directly in front and approaching them. The enemy's cavalry had been unemployed during the fight on the creek. They numbered four hundred men, and, on the discovery of Dawson's approach, had been sent by General Woll to engage him. For a mile or so around the country was almost level, but much higher, and out of view from the battlefield on the creek. Dawson took position in a small grove of mesquite trees, covering from one to two acres of ground, dismounted and prepared for action. The enemy advanced in a compact mass to within a point just beyond rifle shot, then divided into two parties, passing to the right and left of Dawson's position, thereby revealing the presence of a cannon, which at once opened fire with grape and canister. A very few moments revealed the fact that the Texians were at the mercy of this gun. Men and horses rapidly fell. The fire of Dawson's men proved to be totally ineffective at such a distance. When more than half their number had fallen it became evident that death or surrender was inevitable. Efforts were then made to surrender. Several signals to that effect were hoisted, when a rush was made by the enemy into the grove. As the Texians surrendered their arms in numerous cases they were cut down, and, had it not been for Col. Carrasco and a few other honorable officers, every man would have been slain. In this moment of confusion, two men escaped, one of whom was [Henry] Gonzalvo Woods of Fayette, who surrendered to a Mexican, who attempted to pierce him with his lance. Woods, already wounded in three places, seized the lance, jerked the Mexican to the ground, drove the lance through his heart, mounted the Mexican's horse and made his escape. The other was Alsey S. Miller of Gonzales, who, at the same moment, mounted a horse near by (his own having been killed) and attempted to escape by flight, but was pursued by Antonio Perez and a few other renegade Mexicans, formerly from San Antonio, who were mutually acquainted. Miller's horse rapidly failed, but the fine horse of Edward T. Manton escaped from the grove and came galloping by. Miller mounted this horse and outran his pursuers. The result was that, of the fifty-three men, forty-one were left dead on the ground, two escaped and ten were

taken prisoners, four of whom were wounded, Norman B. Woods receiving wounds from which he died afterwards in the prison of Perote. Among the ten prisoners were: Nat W. Faison, Edward T. Manton, Norman B. Woods,—James, Joseph Shaw, Joseph C. Robinson, Wm. Trimble, J. E. Kornegy, Richard Barclay, and Allen H. Morrell. Among the slain were: Capt. Nicholas Dawson, the venerable Zadock Woods (father of the two brothers named), aged nearly eighty years, a mulatto man belonging to Samuel A. Maverick, Jerome Alexander,—Cummings,—Farris, and David Berry, over seventy years of age. The dead were stripped of every particle of clothing and left on the field. About sundown General Woll, rejoined by the cavalry and their ten prisoners, retired to San Antonio—employing about sixty carts in bearing away most of his wounded, and some of his dead. This engagement was wholly unknown to Caldwell and his. men until early next day, but one or two persons reported to Col. Caldwell that they had heard artillery in the direction of this tragic scene. The night being dark and stormy, with a continual downpour of rain, nothing could be done until morning.[32]

Cicero Rufus Perry. (Courtesy of John McWilliams)

Cicero Rufus Perry also had a first-person account of the last stages of the bloody affair.

Capt. Jesse Billingsley. (James Worsham collection)

I am myself a Texas veteran and very likely the only man living who can give a correct account of where Captain Billingsley and his men were at the time of Dawson's massacre, which took place two miles east of the Salado. Returning from an Indian campaign with Captain Burleson's command to the town of Bastrop in 1842, we learned that General Waul had taken San Antonio and that Captain Billingsley of whose company my father, William M. Perry, was a member, with his men had left Bastrop a few hours before we reached there.

Captain Burleson lived about ten miles from Bastrop and went home and I myself being the only one able to get a fresh horse immediately followed Billingsley's Company, overtaking them at the Alligator waterhole on Cedar creek in Bastrop county, and was by Billingsley placed in the advance, and without meeting with any opposition, reached Seguin a few hours before I reached there. After I left Seguin with a Tonkaway Indian, I heard the sound of a cannon and went back to report this fact to Captain Billingsley. He ordered Sam Walker, afterward a captain, and who was killed in the Mexican war; a man by the name of Flint, myself and the Tonkaway Indian, to go on and learn what was happening. We four reached the top of a hill and from there could see the battleground, just in time to see that Dawson had raised the white flag. We saw then Alsey Miller ran out; saw him get another horse, and hallooed at him.

Miller, however, did not come to us, because, as he afterward told me, he believed us to be Indians. Captain Billingsley and his men at that time were at least three miles from the battleground, did not know what was going on and what had happened until I reported to him the facts. He repaired to the battleground, and there met Walker, who had been sent by me to find Caldwell, and who had found him and returned with four of his men to the battleground before we reached there, and we all buried the dead. That night, we went into Caldwell's camp, and next day took up the march in pursuit of the Mexicans, nothing occurring until we overtook them at the head of the Hondo. Mr. Moore in his letter also states that Sam Lenkey was wounded with Captain Hays when fighting on the Hondo they captured a cannon and tried to hold it. This is also a mistake. Sam Lenkey was wounded by the rear guard of the Mexicans before we reached the head of the Hondo. The men wounded with Captain Hays when the cannon was taken were A. Gibson of Gonzales, Judge Hemphill and one Harel of Austin, Travis county, Texas.

Alsey S. Miller. (Photograph in the public domain)

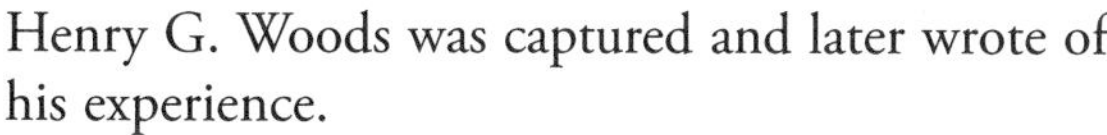

Henry G. Woods was captured and later wrote of his experience.

Molena Del Rey—July 5th, 1843

As I have never described to you my sufferings after leaving you, I will now give you a short description of them. I was shot across the hip at the time that Captain Dawson ran out with the white flag. It was Carascoes order for his soldiers to disarm us then put us to death. We were released from this order by General Woll. I was left on the ground as dead until they came to stripping us and tearing the clothes off of me I had recovered enough to ask for quarters, which was granted by a sargent who kept off the soldiers with his sword. I had received five wounds with the sword. Four on the head and one on the left side, which nearly proved fatal. I was carried into Bexar that night and the next morning left for Precedio Rio Grande in an open wagon. Here I was separated from the rest of the boys that were not wounded and have never seen them yet. I remained in Precedio one month, until I was entirely recovered and from there was marched to San Fernando forty miles west of this place.

Henry Gonzalvo Woods and wife. (Photograph in the public domain)

From losing the handkerchief off of my head I took a severe cold which settled in my wounds which caused me to keep my bed for about two months. From this place I was removed to Saltillo where I

> remained some fifteen or twenty days in a state of delerium. Here Milvern had a great deal of trouble with me, my being entirely helpless. At this place Mier prisoners overtaken me and we went on together four days march to the Salado where the boys stampeded. Myself not being able to go with them I prevailed on Milvern and Richard Keen to stay with me and assist me in getting along. We came on to San Louis Potosi where I remained in the hospital about two months. Milvern and the rest of the boys went on to Perote.[33]

On the same evening Capt Billingsly's [Jesse Billingsley[34]] Company [of which Walker was a member[35]] arrived just in time to witness the closing scene of the action with 75 men but deeming it imprudent to advance on the enemy and fell back a few miles to await reinforcements. I had in the meanwhile reconnoitered the enemy and allso gained some idea of Caldwells position, in which I learned to appreciate the value of good stock. My horse was well tried and as I afterward learned he was from Maryland my native land which made me value him still higher. At twilight I returned to the Company & volunteers being called for to enter Caldwells Company by night if possible to learn his situation. I started in company with another gentleman whose name I do not recollect. The moon shown bright and I told him I should take the precaution to keep down the hollow untill I reached the timber on the Salado as a man on horseback could be seen for several miles so clear was the atmosphere. We had not proceeded very far before he objected to [the] course I had taken through precaution & insisted on my taking a more direct route which I at last consented to telling him that I was as willing to risk the consequences as he could. He soon proceeded to return saying he thought it dangerous & fruitless which I would not consent to. He accordingly left alone. I proceeded on taking the precaution to lead my horse to see the enemy first as I could see much further in the open Prairie. I soon succeeded in finding Dawsons battle ground and took a hasty view of the dead bodies which were horribly mangled & stripped naked.

John Henry Brown was sent to investigate the sound of cannon heard during the day and found what had happened to Dawson and his men:

> During the night Captains Jesse Billingsly and W. J. Wallace of Bastrop, each commanding a company (including men from La Grange, in all one hundred men), and Major James S. Mayfield[36] commanding the whole, arrived in camp. Among them was Samuel H. Walker on his first campaign in Texas. When morning came Col. Caldwell dispatched John Henry Brown, Wm. Burnham, Griffith Jones, and Dr. Caleb S. Brown, and one other to investigate the reported sound of the cannon, the first named and a young Mexican named Chico being the only persons who claimed to have heard the guns in that direction. They speedily arrived at the scene, guided thereto by the wounded horses around the grove. They counted in the grove forty dead bodies entirely naked, so mutilated with cannon shot, sabre wounds and lances as to be unrecognizable. The heads of several were nearly severed from their bodies. The cold rain of the previous night had cleansed them of blood and given the bodies a marble-like appearance. It was simply a horrible sight. The forty-first man, whose name was Cuminings,

from the Lavaca settlement, having run about four hundred yards before he was killed, was not found until afterwards.[37]

Preacher Morrell also visited the ghastly battlefield.

I learned that my son, A. H. Morrell, was in the company defeated the evening before in our hearing. Was he dead? Was he a prisoner in the hands of our cruel oppressors? were questions that revolved through my mind all night long. Three men volunteered to go with me to the "Mesquit battle-ground," and at daylight we were in our saddles. My colonel and captain cautioned me to be careful, as the enemy would certainly keep out spies; but the time for caution and fear with me had about passed. At sunrise we were on the fatal spot, examining carefully for the lost son, while two of my colleagues stood guard. Thirty-five dead bodies of friends lay scattered and terribly mangled among the little cluster of bushes on the broad prairie. I recognized the body of nearly every one. Here were twelve men, heads of families, their wives widows, and their children orphans; and here, too, lay dead the bodies of promising sons of my neighbors. The body of my son could not be found. The place was so horrible that two of the men with me rode away. One remained on guard while I continued my examination. A number of bodies were turned over before I could recognize them. One or two of my neighbors' sons were so badly mangled that I could not recognize them at all. Supposing that one of these might be my son, I examined their feet for a scar that he had carried from childhood. By this time I was satisfied that he had either escaped or was among the prisoners. I then drew a pencil from my pocket, and took down the names of the dead, so that I might make a correct report to the bereaved. Judge Hemphill accompanied me to San Antonio, to look after news from my boy, while the main army crossed the river above, and went directly in pursuit of General Woll. We visited Mrs. Jakes and the English minister's wife, Mrs. Elliot, who had a list of the prisoners' names. My son, A. H. Morrell, was certainly among them. The Mexicans had robbed them of their clothing; my son, on his arrival in San Antonio, was in his shirt-sleeves. Mrs. Elliot took a green blanket-coat off of her son, and put it on mine. This coat, he afterwards said, was the means of saving his life. My son was reported by these ladies as carrying a wound from a lance in the engagement, though not serious. After he surrendered, two Mexicans pursued him with lances. As a lance was hurled at him, he dodged it, but as it passed it glanced his left arm, near the shoulder. He only saved his life by running in this defenseless condition round the horse of the Mexican colonel, Corasco, who drew his sword and drove his pursuers from him.[38]

I took the trail again and went in search of Caldwells camp and to my Joyful surprise I found the enemy had withdrawn. I found Caldwell preparing to fall back to await reinforcements. I informed [him] of the force under Capt Billingsly which altered his determinations. I returned & conducted our company which had by this time been joined by another company from Austin and Col Mayfield as commander of the Battallion to Caldwells Company. Caldwell held his position untill about 8 oclock on the morning of the 20th during which time he received no further reinforcements and the enemy commenced their retreat. We pursued them with about 300 men, crossed the Madina River & encamped about 12 oclock at night. On the morning of the 21st we recrossed the River and continued up the East bank taking several prisoners & killing one of their spies. We learned that the enemy was at the upper ford and would not move untill next morning. About 12 oclock we crossed the River for the purpose of procuring an advantageous position to rest & grase our horses. At 2 PM we were reinforced by 100 men. We again took the East Bank of the River and marched toward the enemy coming near them about 8 oclock PM. A halt was called & Capt Hays of the spie company with several of his chosen men were sent to spie out & ascertain the position of the enemy. He returned after crossing the River & thoroughly reconnoitering the enemies camp and reported their position favorable for an immediate attack. It was however deferred. At day break we received intelligence of another reinforcement of a hundred men which would be able to join us by 8 AM. We waited untill they came up. Our force now amounted to 500 men, and we took up the march in pursuit of the enemy but found they had made a hasty retreat. About 1 PM Capt Hays came up with & received a few shots from the rear guard of the enemy in which Capt Lucky [Samuel H. Luckie] was shot through the body. Our field officers formed the men but instead of advancing immediately one hour was spent in useless delay the commander effecting to believe that the attack would be made by the enemy. He at last started to the supposed position of the enemy but found they were retreating as fast as possible. About 5 oclock PM we came up with them again & Capt Hays was ordered to bring on the engagement by an attack on the rear guard of the enemy with the assurance from Col Mayfield & Caldwell that he should be immediately supported. Col Caldwell instructed Col Mayfield to select a hundred of the best mounted & equipped men in the 2nd Battallion which he commanded to support Capt Hays in the charge. Col Mayfield unfortunately halted the Battallion but before he could execute the order it was countermanded by an order to move on with the whole Battallion. Meanwhile Capt Hays was ordered to make an immediate attack on their rear which was promptly executed. He succeeded in driving their field pieces with trifling loss but finding he could not be supported in time by the main body he immediately fell back with two men wounded & two horses killed. Col Mayfield with the 2nd Battallion was ordered to dismount, tie their horses and recommence the action. Col John H. Moore with the first Battallion was ordered to act as a horse guard & reserve while the 2nd Battallion brought on [the] engagement.

The 2nd Battallion was anxious for the conflict notwithstanding they disapproved of half our force being held back as a reserve, but notwithstanding our anxiety & the earnest solicitations of Capt Hays to make the attack, we were ordered to countermarch and fall back to our Horses after we had approached nearly in rifle shot of the enemy & were only observed from them by the musquet [mesquite] undergrowth on the bank of the Aroyohundy [Arroyo Hunde] a creek which did not run though it had plenty of large holes of good water.

Col. John H. Moore. (Photograph in the public domain)

John Holland Jenkins and wife. (Elgin Depot Museum. Photograph in the public domain)

John Holland Jenkins, a private in Jesse Gillespie's company, later wrote his account of the situation:

> We were now certain that a fight was at hand, and already hearts beat fast and eyes brightened in prospect of action and danger. There seemed to be a strange want of discipline or system or harmony among the officers, who could not agree as to the proper line of policy, and stood discussing and debating questions, while the soldiers were all the time growing more perplexed and impatient.
>
> Captain Billingsley, understanding the situation, and knowing the value of prompt action called out to the soldiers, "Boys, do you want to fight?" A loud "Yes" was the instant reply. "Then, follow me!" he called, and marched on at the head of a considerable force. We were already approaching very near the Mexican infantry, and were drawn up in line of battle, in two minutes the charge would have been made and the fight commenced. But at this juncture superior authority interfered. Colonel Caldwell galloped up and called out to Billingsley, "Where are you going?"
>
> "To fight," was the answer.
>
> "Countermarch those men back to ranks!" Caldwell commanded, and we were forced to take our places back in the standing army, all worried and disgusted with what seemed to us a cowardly hesitation and a disgraceful and confused proceeding without motive or design. Nearly 600 men standing almost in sight of an invading army, whose guards would sometimes slip in near enough to throw bullets into our midst. There we stood till dark, suffering for water and tantalized almost to madness by the delay and want of harmony among our leaders.[39]

About 8 oclock PM we proceeded up the creek to get water [and] were fired on from the opposite side of the creek by the picquet [picket] guard of the enemy. The bullets whistled close to our heads without doing any damage and we proceeded on without thinking them worthy of sufficient notice to return the compliment. We encamped about 1 ½ miles above the enemy. Col Caldwell still effecting to believe he would be attacked by the enemy but he laid down to sleep however without sending out any spie to watch the movements of the enemy. Capt Hays by his own continued exertion & allso his company were so much fatigued and allso having lost confidence in Col Caldwell that they would not voluntarily undertake this service. At 12 oclock a proposition originated amongst the men for about 50 men to go down the creek drive in the enemies outpost & bring on a skirmish engagement. Col Caldwell could not be found in the camp to sanction the proposition. Col Mayfield however took the responsibility. About 30 men arose from their slumbers to participate in this service but a majority of them determining it too daring an adventure for so small a number of men to undertake only twelve could be found willing to go. They proceeded down the creek and soon ascertained that the enemy had again retreated. (Jenkins recollected Walker had raised fifteen or twenty men who went to investigate. They found no sign of the Mexicans.) This fact was communicated in camp and many of the men were up and saddling their Horses. Col Caldwell was at length roused but still pretended to believe that we would be attacked in the morning. Col Mayfield was now requested by several of his friends to take command and pursue the enemy as it was evident that Caldwell did not mean to fight them, but Col Mayfield was unwilling to take this responsibility and after some time spent in useless delay the men were ordered restake their Horses and await till morning. The sun had risen on the morning of the 23rd. Before the men were ordered to get up make coffee and prepare for a start. At 8 AM the Battallions were formed and Col Caldwell made a speech to justify himself in returning in which he represented the probability of the enemy being reinforced allso stated that we had no provision, and allso represented the enemy as being very superior to us and that they were commanded by an able & experienced General and he therefore thought it prudent to return. Col Mayfield sanctioned what had been said by Caldwell and to the great disappointment of his friends allso recommended that we should all return.

This unexpected address from Mayfield acted like an electrick shock. One voice called out for a vote on the question but the motion was not seconded and all was silent for a half hour. When we had proceeded several miles homeward when curses loud & deep were heaped upon the fichal [fickle] officers and much discontent manifested, The enemies Drums had been heard at day break and abundance of cattle were in sight. We afterwards learned that the enemy had left the greatest portion of their baggage their ammunition—wagons and one piece of Artillery. The officers of the enemy have since acknowledged that their men were panick stricken, and nothing but our own cowardice prevented us from taking them all prisoners. On the same day we returned we were met by an express informing us that Gen [Edward] Burleson[40] *was on his way with 200 men to join us though it did not influence our officers to recommence the pursuit. Thus a very important advantage was lost for the want of more resolute & determined officers. On the 24th we returned to Bexar. On the 25th a meeting of the troops was called at the Alamo by Gen Burleson and it was recommended by him and all of the officers that the troops should return home and meet again at Bexar on the 25th of October and immediately take up the line of march for the Riogrande as this would give the people time to prepare them selves for an effective campaign. A number of men with no business to call them home remained in the vicinity of Bexar. We next learned that Sam Houston had ordered out the 1st and 2nd classes of malitia which prevented Gen Burleson from making any farther exertion to raise a force to cary on the campaign. The rivers were in the mean while very high which occasioned great delay. The Malitia from Montgomery Coty under Col Bennet [Joseph L. Bennett] were the first who arrived in any large number though several hundred volunteers had arrived in small parties. The malitia under Bennet soon manifested a strong disposition to return home and eventually done so after eating &*

destroying much of the subsistence necessary to cary on the campaign. Before the troops could be organized for the campaign Sam Houston gave it as his opinion that it was unconstitutional to order the malitia across the Riogrande, yet Somerville was forced upon them as a commander with discretionatory authority to cross the River. The volunteers had little faith in Somerville, but rather than the campaign should fall through again they cheerfully consented to go under his command by his pledging himself to cross the River.

Joseph D. McCutchan had a dim view of Somervell's ability, which was shared by many:

> And worst of all—what was most trying to our forbearance and blasting to our hopes—we were reduced to the necessity, for the sake of order, and through obedience to the laws and authorities of our country, of submitting ourselves to the Command if Brigadier General A. Summerville, in whom not one of us could place any confidence. We believed that he might be brave, but his very looks and deportment combined to prove him no general, I say that we lacked confidence in the commander placed over us; and whether we were justified in entertaining this contemptable opinion of his military abilities, his after conduct, and the sequel to the campaign will prove.[41]

Early in Nov. our force amounted to about 1000 men at which time they moved westward and encamped on the Leon & Madina untill about the 28th of Nov. at which time we took up the line of march. [Capt. Jack Hays and his company were not officially part of the expedition and no complete record of the men survived. However, since Ben McCulloch was Hays's lieutenant and Walker has been named as being under McCulloch's orders on at least one occasion, it is likely this was Walker's first time serving with Jack Hays.] Our force however by unnecessary delay had decreased to about 750 men. We had been waiting for the artillery to arrive from Gonzales and after we had got it a council of war decided on changing the point of destination and leaving the field piece behind. The determination was to strike the River at Loredo cross & proceed downward as far as prudent. On the second night we encamped at Novarros Ranch on the Tusiosa. On the 3rd day our troubles commenced. We had a rain and post oak country to travel through. We had not proceeded far untill it became impossible to ride and many of our best Horses were bogged and it was with difficulty we could find firm ground only enough to encamp on. We were three days in this situation losing a number of our packs. On the 3rd day we struck old Loredo Road and our traveling was much improved. The Nueces was high but we crossed it without much delay. Capt Hays was sent ahead to gain information. He succeeded in catching two Mexicans spies and gained all necessary information. Previous to our entering the place he informed Gen Somerville of his success and the main body hurried on as fast as possible. As the service in which Capt Hays had been engaged was very laborious and fatiguing to his men & Horses and supposing one of the prisoners to be severely wounded he determined to await the arrival of Gen Somerville but through the carelessness of Allsbury who was on guard the wounded prisoner made his escape and gave information of our approach which gave the soldiers at Loredo time to make their escape or disguise themselves so that we could not distinguish them from the citizens. On the 7th of decr at night Col Cooke [William G. Cooke][42] was sent with some picked men to procure the boats at the ford to effect a crossing with 150 men to take Col Bravos with about 150 regular Soldiers on the opposite side of the River.

Col. William G. Cooke. (library.uta.edu. Photograph in the public domain)

Two men of the spie company were sent up to find the boats with instructions to drop down below the Town. They succeeded in finding a large Cannoe which would cary 25 men but having no paddles they concluded to let it remain where it was. As the water was much more favourable for crossing at this point than what it was below they returned & reported to Col Cooke who returned and reported to Gen Somerville. After much time spent useless Col Cooke was ordered to take the boat & cross 150 men before day for the purpose of taking the fort on the opposite side which was reported to be manned by 80 regulars and 20 rancheros. Col Cooke showed no disposition to perform this duty and deferred it untill it was too late. At daylight we surrounded the Town & took Town & the Alcalde was informed of our mission & we received possession of it without resistance. We marched & encamped about 1 league from Town. The men were hungry & no grass for their Horses and no assurance that their wants should be supplied by a requisition. No guard was placed to prevent the men from going into Town. The consequence was that many of the men were in the Town and some of them commenced plundering by taking such things as was necessary to their actual wants. The men were then informed by the officers that a requisition had been made on the Town but it was now too late. Pillage had commenced and it was difficult to check it immediately. In the evening we moved our camp below Town to get grazing for our horses. Here Dubois of Camerons co. was killed accidently. On the 9th it was ascertained that some of the men had taken articles that they were not entitled to by the Rules of War. Much dissatisfaction prevailed inconsequence as the great majority of the men were disposed to war with the enemy on the most magnanimous principles of civilized warfare. The Captains of Companies were ordered to see that all property taken by their respective companies should be delivered up to the qr master which was as far as practicable complied with & the things thus taken were delivered to the Alcalde of the Town, It is due to Capt Hays & Camerons Companies to say they did not participate at all in this plunder. On the Morning of the 9th we left Loredo and after traveling untill 9 or 10 oclock at night through a thick chapperell. We encamped without water. Much discontent prevailed in consequence of not crossing the River at Loredo. About 10 oclock on the 10th we found water and halted to grase our horses. Gen Somerville here formed the men and stated o them that if they would pledge them selves not to molest any private property and be submissive to orders all the men with the exception of 50 who returned home pledged themselves to do so. While Somerville proceeded down the River and crossed opposite Gouara a few troops amounting to several hundred showed themselves under Canalles but disappeared as soon as about 30 of our men showed themselves on the west bank. On the next morning the 14th we finished crossing the whole force. Commissioners came out to inform us they would surrender the Town and fill any requisition we might make, They offered quarters in the Town which the officers did not choose to accept although the weather was very bad. We encamped near the Town and after having our requisition partly complied with which was very insufficient. On the following day we returned to the Bank of the River. Much dissatisfaction prevailed amongst the men inconsequence of Somerville not making a larger requisition and allso of his not enforcing the one he had made. On the same night our troops commenced crossing the River. On the next morning 10 men of the spie company was sent in Town to demand an immediate fulfilment of the requisition. The authorities of the Town expressed a great willingness to do so but made many excuses and continued to bring in our supplies very slowly, so much so that it was evident that they intended to detain us as long as possible so much so that it rather provoked Gen Somerville & on the next morning Capt Hays with his Company and a part of Capt [Samuel] Bogarts was ordered to Town to state to the Alcalde that as he had shown no disposition to comply with the first requisition according to agreement, and he therefore made a demand on them for 5000 dollars which if not complied with in a very short time that he would march his men into the Town and ransack it. Capt Hays was instructed to wait two hours and return. In this time they raised 380 dollars which Capt Hays would not receive and returned to camp. The Alcalde however insisted on taking the money to Gen Somerville in person who had the main body of his men crossed to the east Bank of the River and when he was informed of the amount of money they had raised he told him to go to Hell with it. On the same night we all crossed the River. The next day Gen Somerville ordered the flat-Boats sunk which were taken from Gouaro. This order however was not complied with as there were many of the men on foot who wanted the boats to down the river and allso to assist in crossing at Mier. Gen Somerville took up the line of march homeward with about 300 men & about 300 proceeded down the River electing Col [William S.] Fisher[43] *as commander. [Actually, Somervell's contingent numbered 189 rank and file.]*[44] *The Boats were under the direction of Gen [Thomas Jefferson] Green*[45] *manned by about 60 men.*

Thomas J. Green. (Photograph in the public domain)

The fleet consisted of four flat Boats and as many Canoes, Their business was to destroy all the boats

The expedition descending the Rio Grande. Sketch by Charles McLaughlin, one of the prisoners. (tsl.texas.gov. From *Journal of the Texian Expedition Against Mier* by General Thomas J. Green, published by Harper and Brothers, New York, 1845)

which they could take with them and procure supplies wherever practicable. We encamped together every night. On the 22nd 8 men [including Walker] under Maccllоug [Benjamin McCulloch][46] *crossed the River for the purpose of spieing out the Town of Mier.*

We reconnoitered and entered the Town & the Alcalde was informed of our mission & we returned to camp with information that Gen [Pedro de] Ampudia was hourly expected in Mier with a large force. [On December 22, the 308 Texans reached a point on the east bank of the Rio Grande opposite Mier, and Ben McCulloch's spy company was sent to reconnoiter the town. They found that Mexican troops were assembling along the river, advised Fisher against crossing, and abandoned the expedition when their advice was not heeded. Walker remained. Lt. John R. Baker of Ewen Cameron's Company then took command of the spy company.[47] *Walker then joined Cameron's company.*[48]*]*

Benjamin McCulloch. (James Worsham collection)

Col Fisher however crossed the River with this men the next morning the 23rd Decr and marched to the Town and entered without opposition. Our requisition was made out and the Alcalde expressed a willing ness to comply with our requisition and commenced collecting his stores but it was evident that he intended to prolong the time as much as possible. We waited untill late in the afternoon when Col Fisher left Town taking the Alcalde along to insure the fulfillment of the requisition which his inferior officers promised to deliver on the Bank of the River down below our camp. Note: J Yookum [Jesse Yocum] killed accidentally on our return to camp. On the 24th we marched down the River to the place where the provision was to be delivered but encamped before we reached it. Had [Gideon K.] Lewis & [Allen S.] Holderman taken prisoner.

At dusk, Lewis was captured within 200 yards of the camp by a notorious robber called Agatoné. He was bound, gagged, and almost suffocated. He would later join his surrendered comrades.

James L. Truehart, one of the prisoners taken at Bexar and who marched to Perote Castle with the men captured at Mier, related the following:

> On the 25th, however, Captain Baker and his spy company on the west side captured a Mexican, who informed the commander that after the requisition had been started in compliance with the Alcalde's order the troops of General Ampudia and Canales had arrived and stopped them; that they numbered about 700 men, two field-pieces, and had taken a position upon the west bank of the river two miles below to prevent the Texians further progress down. Upon receipt of this information a council of war was held when it was unanimously agreed to cross the river and fight. By 4 o'clock all was crossed and ready for march when a brisk fire was heard in the direction of the enemy's position. "In a few minutes, a courier arrived from Capt. Baker, stating two of his most efficient spies had been captured, Samuel H. Walker of Galveston, and Patrick Lusk of Washington."[49]

On the 25th we learned that Gen Ampudia & Canalles was encamped on the River below and were waiting our approach. We immediately determined on crossing the River and giving them Battle leaving about forty men to guard the Horses which all with the exception of about 15 to act as spies or scouts, Myself 4 other of my messmates [George Lord, Patrick Lusk, John McMullen from Captain Cameron's company, and one other] were chosen to perform this service. Capt [John R.] Baker [Sheriff of Refugio County, succeeded to the command of the spy company after Ben McCulloch abandoned the expedition on December 22] being in command of the scout. We had not proceeded far before we discovered several of their spies. Four of us immediately pursued them depending on our horses in case of danger. Being ahead I soon found myself in close gun shot of about 50 well-mounted men. I brought my piece to bear upon them but finding I could have no support from my comrades I determined to reserve my fire untill the last resort.

My two messmates & one other the scout were all that was in sight. Of course a hasty retreat was necessary being then in close pursued by the cavalry under a continual of scopits [escopetas—the escopeta was a blunderbuss-looking weapon with a powerful kick]. One of my messmates [Patrick Lusk] was taken prisoner while in the act of mounting his horse his girt having broke which caused him to dismount. I should have made a safe retreat had not my other messmate who was ahead of me taken the wrong trail which

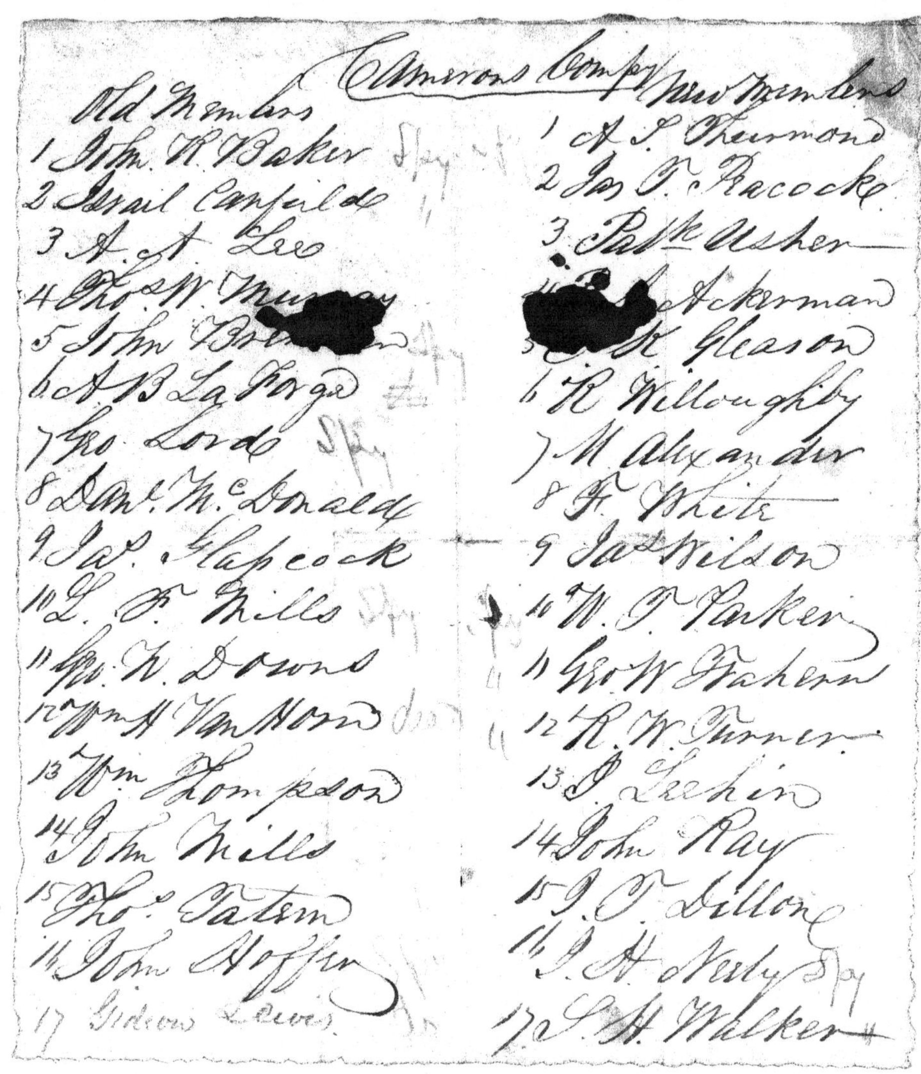

Camerons Compy

Old Members	New Members
1 John R. Baker	1 A. S. Thurmond
2 Israel Canfield	2 Jas. P. Peacock
3 A. A. Lee	3 Patk Usher
4 Thos W. Mu[illegible]	4 [illegible] Ackerman
5 John Br[illegible]	5 [illegible] R. Gleason
6 A. B. La Forge	6 R. Willoughby
7 Geo. Lord	7 M. Alexander
8 Danl. McDonald	8 F. White
9 Jas. Glascock	9 Jas. Wilson
10 L. F. Mills	10 W. P. Parker
11 Geo. R. Downs	11 Geo W. Graham
12 Wm H. Van Horn	12 R. W. Turner
13 Wm Thompson	13 [illegible]
14 John Mills	14 John Ray
15 Thos. Tatum	15 J. O. Dillon
16 John Hoffer	16 J. H. Neely
17 Gideon Lewis	17 S. H. Walker

Capt. Ewin Cameron's company roll. (Texas State Archives)

led us into a labour surrounded by a high bulrush fence from which it was impossible to escape with our horses. We accordingly dismounted my two companions making their escape by climbing over the brush fence which I might have done. Allso had I not been too anxious to give them a shot. When I raised my gun they were in thirty feet of me. I then discovered I had lost both caps of my gun, and before I could recap it a half dozen of them had seized me. They tied my arms. One of them took me behind him and hurried me off to Town. I was taken before Ampudia who informed me that I must tell him the truth, If not I would be shot. I decided to tell him that his threat would make no difference in my answers to him, that I was a prisoner and he could dispose of me as he thought proper. I was asked by the interpreter if I was not a spie. I told him I was not a spie but he insisted otherwise untill I stated that a spie was one who tried to obtain important information by palming himself on the enemy as a friend. Nothing more was said on that subject. I was now asked many questions relative to Col Fishers movements & intentions, about Gen Rush [Thomas J. Rusk] & Burlesons division and allso Gen Somerville. To all of these questions I gave evasive replies except as regards the disposition of our men to fight. To which I told him they have been waiting for some time to get a fight and were not willing to go home without it that they were resolved on death or victory. I now discovered my messmate [Lusk] who had been taken and we were both conducted to a small prison adjoining the Alcaldes office where we found Lewis & Holderman who had been taken the day before. We were locked up and before we had finished relating each others adventures when a volley of musquetry which was answered by a volley of rifles. The bullets whistled about our door. The sentinels deserted their post and ran in the house, but soon returned to tie us so tight with our arms behind us that we were in much pain. Not forgetting to rifle our pockets for the small change, the guard deserted this place and retreated to the opposite side of the Square. The fire of musquetry & cannon was kept up with out intermission, with an occasional report from a rifle. We waited with much anxiety till daylight, when the dread sound of the rifles silenced many of the muskets and at length silenced the Artillery. The officers had their horses saddled, servants holding them near the gate of the back yard open evidently for the purpose of retreating, At 2 or 3 PM the firing ceased. Bewsly [David H. Beasley], Keen [Richard Keene] & Dr Sinicson [John J. Sinnickson] were brought in as prisoners and we were soon informed by Gen Ampudia that Gen Fisher & Greene had surrendered to him.

Sinnickson has been somewhat vilified for his interactions between General Ampudia and Colonel Fisher. The following is his lengthy letter to Thomas J. Green, giving his version of the events that led up to the surrender of the Texians:

> When I was taken prisoner (at the Battle of Mier), I was immediately conveyed to General Ampudia, the commander-in-chief of the Mexican army then there, who, after interrogating me, through the medium of an interpreter, respecting the numbers of the Texian force, and the name of their commanding officer, ordered that I should bear a flag to Colonel Fisher, demanding an immediate surrender. Perceiving that I gave no reply, and evinced no disposition to obey such an order, he said that it was useless for me to refuse, as I should be compelled to do it. He seized me by the shoulder, while Colonel Carasco laid hold upon the other, and forced me to the corner of a street leading in the direction of our troops, dictating at the time the following message to me, to be delivered to the Texian commander, viz.: "Say to Colonel Fisher that he must surrender with his whole force in five minutes, or I will cause them all to be put to the sword, and give no quarter—to

accomplish this, I have 1700 regular troops, and look every moment for a re-enforcement of 800—and that, if he will cause his troops to lay down their arms, and surrender in that time, their lives shall be spared, and they shall be treated with all the humanity and deference due them as prisoners of war; and, furthermore, I will exercise my influence with the supreme government to prevent their being marched to the city of Mexico, but to have them retained east of the mountains until they are released or exchanged."

Accompanied by a Mexican soldier, as I entered our lines I discovered Colonel Fisher, who, when he perceived me, advanced a short distance to a low stone wall. When we met, I informed him that I had been compelled to bear a flag with a verbal message to him, and while relating the purport of it, the incessant discharge of musketry prevented him from hearing; motioning for me to remain silent, he gave orders for the firing to cease. So soon as it had discontinued, he turned to me and inquired, "What does this flag mean?" I then repeated what has been stated above. After concluding, I watched closely and eagerly for a reply. Without saying a word, he cast his eyes upon the ground as if undetermined, and endeavouring to decide upon what course he should pursue. Meditating in this position for a brief period, he at length came to some conclusion, when he leaped the wall and advanced to the position occupied by Cameron and Ryan's companies particularly, without taking any farther notice of me, either by word or sign. I instantly followed to await his instructions. He called together a council of his officers, at which time the Mexican officers took the opportunity to venture within our lines. What occurred from this time you had an opportunity of becoming as well acquainted with as myself. The preceding, sir, is a brief statement of facts, as they transpired between the colonel and myself. I do not wish to increase the length of this paper so as to become wearisome to the reader, yet I cannot conclude without mentioning some circumstances relative to this matter that, I trust, will enable the reader to arrive at a just and impartial opinion. I presume it is well known that during an action, when an order is given by an officer to his inferiors in rank, and the obedience of which is necessary in securing the safety and success of a body of men, that a disobedience most frequently is considered as a direct violation of the regulations of the military code, and renders the offender liable to the severest punishment that can be inflicted upon him, instantaneously, and that without the convening of a military court. Had I voluntarily disobeyed any order that Colonel Fisher states he gave me, why did he not enforce upon me the penalty as the results of its violation! He held a pistol in his hand at the time, and would have been held justifiable in making immediate use of it upon me. Again: Does it not appear improbable that he should have commanded me to return with the flag without having any knowledge of the object for which it was sent, as he could know nothing of its errand excepting from conjecture? He had as much right to suppose, as otherwise, that the enemy wished to enter into some terms with him for their own safety, as well as that of their wounded, and the town with its inhabitants; for he is well aware that a commander will always, whenever within his power, after he is defeated, make the best stipulations he can with his victor. You will recollect I had an interview with the colonel in the morning of Friday, the 30th December, a short time previous to our men being marched off to Matamoras. In the conversation I then held with him, he never intimated, in the slightest degree, that he had given me such an order, but, on the contrary, when the subject of my bearing the flag was introduced, he assured me that himself nor any other person had or could attach any censure to me for the course I was compelled to pursue. Moreover, I do most positively assert, that during my imprisonment I had frequent conversations with the men, as well as the officers, in relation to our capitulation, and not one of them ever mentioned to me of having heard of such an order being given, or ever passed a word of condemnation upon me for my conduct during any period of that engagement. Having already extended this communication to a much greater length than I intended, I shall add nothing more than a sincere desire that your publication may have an extensive circulation, and that it may be written both justly and impartially.

Most respectfully yours,
John J. Sinnickson.[50]

The fight on Monday morning December 26, and its consequences were described by Israel Canfield,[51] first sergeant of Capt. Ewen Cameron's company. Canfield's diary entries were generally one continuous sentence with slight regard for grammar or punctuation. Some of the latter has been added for the convenience of the reader.

Israel Canfield. (James Worsham collection)

At daylight the firing became general on both sides, the Enemy being posted on top of the houses (the roofs of which were flat with the outer walls some three feet higher that the roof) with nothing but their heads exposed, yet our riflemen scarsly ever missed the mark, about 8 oclock A.M. it Commenced raining and Continued about one hour during which time the Cannon of the Enemy were twice cleared. Several request being made to Col. F for permission to Charge and spike the same, the answer Was "spare your

> ammunition" Col F was inactive during the morning. Altho the enemy made three desperate charges, they were repelled at the instance of Capt. Ewen Cameron & other with several killed & wounded. On our post, although we had such numbers (about 2600) to contend with, our men were generally firm during the morning feeling confident they would be able to sustain themselves against such odds. Our loss at this time was eleven [possibly twelve] killed Viz Louis, [Joseph] Barry, [William H.] Hannon, [R. P.] Bassett, [William A.] Jackson, [John] Dixon, [William J.] Hopson, [Alvin E.] White, [Isaac S.] Towers, [James] Austin, John E. Jones Joseph Berry & [J. C.?] Cronican [probably Michael Cronican, who was with the camp guard and escaped capture] and Twenty Two wounded two or three considered dangerous, While the loss on the part of the enemy was 650 killed and 200 wounded. About 1 oclock P.M. a Doctr. [J.J.] Sinnickson (who had been taken prisoner in the morning approached us bearing a "White Flag:" and as fortune would have it reached us in safety altho a hundred Rifles were raised to shoot down the bearer 'till it was ascertained to be borne by one of our own men) at the moment demanding of Col F on the name of Genl. At the immediate surrender of his command with a continued statement that Genl. A had received a reinforcement of 800 Infantry, which was generally supposed was false. To this demand Col. Fisher finally acceded after a deliberation of about one hour during which time many of our men became panic struck, while others shed tears that so disgraceful a surrender was about to be made. Under all the circumstances owing to the discussion of our band Col. F. might possibly be warranted in pursueing the course he did:—as there were so few timed ones in our ranks, on the arrival of the "White Flag" that any disposition to surrender could have been quelled by disposing of not more than 3 or 4. As a proof of this, many of the Mexican officers stated that had we not shown a disposition to accede to their terms the town (Mier) would have been left to our disposal as their loss was too severe to have continued the action—but we (227 in number) being all reported as surrendered as per written stipulations! … Viz that we should be "retained on the frontier and treated as prisoners of War."[52]

We were then untied and in a short time joined our unfortunate companions who had been induced to surrender as prisoners of war. From them we learned that the entering of the Town on the part of Green & Fisher was a very gallant affair, but after Col Fisher became satisfied of the force he had to contend with which amounted to about 3000 men he became low spirited and gave his men no encouragement, but on the contrary when a white flag was brought in by Doct Sinicson who had been left a short distance from Town with 10 men to take care of [Joseph] Berry who had his leg broke by a fall on the rocks and was taken prisoner. [He was subsequently murdered by one Captain Elduret.] It is said that Fisher shewed a great want of firmness and after holding an interview with the enemy he returned to his men with representations well calculated to cause a division in our ranks, telling the men that he was acquainted with Col Huraset and knew him to be a Gentleman of his word and he had such & such assurances from him which the men might rely upon. He told his men that all who was in favour of surrendering should march to the Public Square and surrender their arms. This created great confusion and resulted in the surrender of the whole. Our loss was 11 killed and 22 wounded. 263 men crossed the River. About 40 odd were left as camp guards with the Horses. [Whitfield] Chalk & Sinclair [Caleb St. Clair] made their escape from Mier by concealing themselves in a bake oven at night, [Both men had been on the Santa Fe expedition of June–September 1841 that ended in the surrender of the entire party. After being promised safe conduct to the border, the Mexicans reneged and, after a close vote of the Mexican officers as to whether they should be shot, were marched some 2,000 miles to Mexico City and imprisoned in Perote Castle. (The Castle of San Carlos de Perote was constructed between 1700 and 1773.) The survivors were released in June 1842.] The loss of the enemy was between 6 and 700 killed or wounded the most of the wounds being fatal as the Texians had nothing to shoot at but their heads as they stuck them above the ramparts on the Houses.

Canfield recorded the comments made by their Mexican captors with regard to their dead "the idea of 9/10th of the Killed, being shot in the head seems strange to them."

Walker's account now takes the form of a daily diary:

On the morning of the 27 of Decr a guard with several of our men were sent to cross the River to inform our camp guard of our surrender and to demand the same of them, but to our great joy we learned that they would not surrender.

Strangely, Walker does not mention what took place on the afternoon of the 27th. According to several of the Mier prisoners, a council of Ampudia's officers was held to determine their fate. An hour passed with the men formed up in a back yard surrounded by a high wall and under guard. Despite Ampudia's assurances the Texians would be well treated, the rest of the Mexican officers determined they should be shot. The single dissenter was General Ampudia. His vote outweighed the others and the Texians were marched from the yard.

On the 29th a large force of cavalry pursued them but we were happy to see them return without success.

The experiences of the camp guard were related by George B. Erath:

> It was not an hour before rifles and musketry were heard and, soon after, the noise of Mexican cannon. It seems that with but faint opposition they were allowed to march to the center of the town, and to take possession of a block on the square where they maintained themselves all night. The Mexican cannon and the guns on our side we heard at intervals all night. During the morning the firing increased. Two men, one on foot and one on horseback, came into camp. They had not been together during the night, and neither could give much information. One described the Mexican force as very large.
>
> We watered and fed the horses; there were over three hundred captured ones to be looked after, but corn was plentiful.

George B. Erath. (Photograph in the public domain)

About ten o'clock I and George Hancock, late a resident of Austin, went to a high bluff up the river about half a mile from camp. We could see the smoke of firearms and masses of Mexicans outside of the town moving about, but nothing more definite. The rain was less and the clouds higher. For some ten minutes about twelve we heard exceedingly heavy firing, the rifles predominating. The Mexicans then seemed to cease firing, and in a little while there was no more on either side. A considerable smoke arose. We imagined our side had perhaps carried the day, went back to camp to report, and there waited till three o'clock for news. Then we two went down the river to a higher bluff still nearer town, but could see nothing, and returned to camp. The outlook was gloomy.

Buckman, a lieutenant [4th Sgt. Oliver Buckman], with whom I had been frequently associated in frontier service, was captain of the guard. He urged me to take command, but I refused as the guard was a mixture from companies of men from all over the Republic and unknown to me. When he next asked my advice, I said to remain in camp till after night, move off in the dark a mile or so, but return in the morning. They would perhaps have followed this advice, but Captain Bonnell [George W. Bonnell], who had been more or less in Texas service but who at this time had no command, was one of those who could not believe that disaster really might overtake Texans; he declared that he thought there could be no danger in remaining, that our men were not whipped but only delayed by some accident. However, all except Bonnell and four or five with him prepared to leave at a moment's notice.

The rain had ceased and, although it was a cloudy night, the moon gave a little light. Some time after dark we distinctly heard the words: "Bring over the boat, bring over the boat!" coming from over the river. Buckman and several of us ran down to the river, but no reply came to our challenge. Some said we had imagined the call. Bonnell declared he had been listening intently and had not heard it. Just then the words came again and Bonnell did hear. But still we could get no other words to our questioning. Bonnell returned to his belief that we had heard nothing. Buckman said he had heard enough, and thought it time to leave camp. He called for all who wanted to go with him, and mustered about twenty, each having from one to two extra horses; one man went off leading five with their heads and tails tied together.

Probably 22 or 23 of us still remained in camp. I prepared to go, and there were thirteen with me. Each had a lead horse with saddle, saddle bags, baggage, and provisions, but in general the horses were those of our messmates who had gone into Mier. I brought home to his family the horse of Wiley Jones, who started out with me. The rain had again commenced. After going about a mile and a half, hardly knowing where, as we had left the river, we heard the sound of a gun some distance off. It was after midnight; we camped. At daylight we mounted again to start back to the river, but halted for a council to determine which way the river lay. The rain had ceased, but it was very cloudy. We were at an open place on a trail. One of the men, Pierce [John G. Pierson] from Washington County, being well mounted, volunteered to go back and look about the camp we had left to find out if those remaining there were still safe and if any more news had been heard from Mier. I lent him my pistol, and he started, accompanied by another of the party whose name I cannot remember. We were to wait for them till nine o'clock; then, if they had not returned, to go on without them. At nine the men became anxious to go on. I went back to hunt Pierce, knowing that the men would not go far without me. I had not gone over three hundred yards before I heard talking in the brush on my left. I turned thither and found about a dozen of the men we had left in camp the night before, and with them two of my messmates escaped out of Mier, Chalk, and St. Clair. We all returned to my party of men, and delayed for Chalk and St. Clair to eat something; they had been long without food. By that time Pierce and his companion had got back. They reported that they had found the camp deserted by all except Bonnell and Hick [Milton Hicks], who were at the river bank talking to Mexicans on the other side; the Mexicans had with them one of our men [Capt. Samuel C. Lyon] a prisoner, to explain the situation.

Chalk and St. Clair told me that about the time the firing ceased at noon the day before the Mexicans sent a flag of truce to our men, offering to allow them to capitulate, and promising to treat them as prisoners of war—not to march them to Mexico City, but to keep them in the valley of the Rio Grande—subject, however, to ratification by the government and Santa Anna. Our men were divided as to what they should do. Half of them were tired of fighting; ten or twelve had been killed [actually eleven] and fifteen to twenty were wounded. The others declared they would not surrender and wanted to fight their way out. The leaders of the latter called for a hundred men, but did not get the response expected; they called for fifty, but got only about half that number; then they gave up. The Mexicans talked flatteringly; among other things they declared that they would not keep them long, as peace negotiations were then on foot. This was news; the Texans knew nothing of such negotiations.

St. Clair was one of those who wanted to fight his way out, and he determined to escape somehow. He induced Chalk to hide with him behind a bunch of cane stacked in a corner of a room where they with others were confined. After nightfall they slipped out of the town. In jumping a wall St. Clair sprained his ankle and was badly lamed. He had already lost one boot; it had been pulled off by a Mexican as he got over a fence going into Mier. They finally reached our camp on the river at daylight. The men took a boat over to them, and I then all the men in camp, except Bonnell and Hicks left, each with two horses. They came up with us as I have already described.

We learned later that Bonnell and Hicks, after talking with Mexicans across the river, returned to camp and also started off with two horses apiece, but missed our trail, got lost in a chaparral thicket, remained lost till late the next day, and then struck our trail again. In the meantime, the Mexicans must have passed beyond them in pursuit; for a hundred men had been crossed over to our camp in our boats. These men mounted our remaining horses and set out in pursuit of Bonnell, Hicks, and the rest of us. They must have been nearly up with us the first night after we all got together and went on; but they then turned back, found Bonnell and Hicks, who had at last struck our trail, behind them. They carried the two men back and, while busy plundering our camp, sent Bonnell under guard into a boat. Hicks was told to push the boat from shore and to jump in. He obeyed, pushing the boat from shore, but jumped in the other direction and made for the bank of the river. Guns were fired after him but he escaped, and he, without; so much as a pocketknife for a weapon, walked all the way to Victoria, swimming streams and sustaining life in a manner hard to conjecture. It is supposed the Mexican guard, exasperated at Hicks' escape, shot Bonnell in cold blood, as that was the last heard of him.

We had a very good open route during the first day, but in attempting to travel at night, got retarded, and at ten o'clock found ourselves at the same place that we had been at dark. We proceeded at daylight and that evening arrived at a watering spot known as the Palo Blanco, on a trail leading to San Patricio. The place was only sixty miles from Mier.

Buckman and his party, who were ahead of us, also got lost on their way from the Rio Grande, and we fell in with them in a few days, but did not remain with them. After we reached and crossed the Nueces we separated into small parties, the better to find game, which was scarce except for wild horse. Chalk, St. Clair, and a young man named Oldham [William Oldham] remained with me, and we four were the first to arrive at the San Antonio River, at Goliad, then unoccupied.[53]

[29th, continued] The Guard sent to camp to get our camp equipage blankets &c left nearly every thing of any value so that many of the men were left entirely without covering and suffered much in consequence.

On the 31st started for Metamoras. Marched 8 leagues to Comargo. Encamped for the night in the suburbs of the Town having left 23 men in Mier. 21 wounded one Doctor & interpreter.

Sunday 1st Jan. Crossed the St John River & entered the Town of Comargo amidst a great parade & triumph of the citizens displaying handkerchiefs & banners to the honor & glory of Canalles and Ampudia. We remained in quartells untill the 2nd. Marched 10 miles and encamped at a rancho herded in a cow pen.

Tuesday 3rd. Made an early start. Marched 21 miles over a much better section of the country than any we had yet seen, and encamped at Las Rinoso in a sheep pen.

Wednesday 4th. Took up the line of march for New Rinoso 18 miles distant. We arrived at foot of the hill on which the Town was situated about 2 oclock PM and was halted a short time and ordered to march two & two. As we approached the firing of guns & fire crackers commenced and lasted for an hour when we were marched under a great many triumphal arches which were decorated by the shawls handkerchiefs & petticoats of the Ladies. As we entered the square about thirty children dressed in fantastic stile were dancing to the music of the Bells. We were gazed on by the inhabitants with great astonishment. Their much triumph effected the feelings of our men very differently. Some of them laughed at their insignificance. Others occasionally give a yell as the muskets & fire crackers went off while others again could scarcely contain themselves with indignation and rage. After the parade was over we were marched to a large unfinished brick building where we remained untill the 6th. Left McDade sick. Marched to a church to witness the ceremony of mass which was completed by firing cannons & we marched 25 miles after a late start. Encamped in a coral [corral].

Sat 7th. Marched 18 miles and encamped in a corall for the night.

Sun. 8th. Marched 13 miles over a low musquet [mesquite] country and some prairie admirably adapted to the cultivation of sugar though there is not a great deal cultivated. We encamped at a large ranch called Warloupe [Guadalupe el Carnicero].

On Monday 9th. we started early for Metamoras 3 leagues distant. Here the mexicans endeavoured to make a grand a display as possible. The road for some distance out of Town was crowded with men women & children greeting their husbands & sweethearts, but many of them were disappointed as their sweethearts & husbands had experienced the effects of Texian Rifles at Mier. [Canfield called it "accidentally or rather Bullet-dentally."] The main avenue leading to the square was decorated with triumphal arches and crowded with all sorts sizes colours some of them hissing at us as we passed. We saw a good many foreigners who appeared much interested in our situation. We were much admired for our bravery by some of the mexican officers. Our comforts were greatly increased by the donations of clothing & blankets sent in to our prisoners by the foreigners and our thanks & Gratitude is particularly due to Mr. Isaac D. Marks the US Counsel, and a Mr. J. R. Thatsell [J. P. Schatzell] who advanced a large sum to different individuals. He formerly resided in Kentucy.

John Rufus Alexander, another prisoner, was more specific.

> Major [William] Oldham[54] sent for an Englishman, then a resident of Matamoras, and whom he had known in Kentucky. This generous acquaintance came promptly, and he loaned Major Oldham $100 and advanced to the prisoners the sum of $2,000. In addition to this he gave as a free gift $5 to each man that chanced to be from Kentucky.[55]
>
> Here we had the priviledge of writing home and some of the men embraced this opportunity. A consultation was held by the mexican officers relative to our being ironed which was as we learned strongly insisted upon by Canalles stating that he would not guard us without. This was protested against by Fisher & Greene, & Gen Ampudia at length decided that we should not be ironed but determined on sending our staff officers ahead of us as a precautionary measure to prevent us from attempting our escape being told that if any attempt was made they would be held responsible.

John Rufus Alexander. (Houston Wade, *Notes and Fragments of the Mier Expedition*, LaGrange, TX: LaGrange Journal, 1936)

On the 12th Green, Fisher, Murray [Thomas Murry, Adjutant], [Surgeon William M.] Shepperd, Capt Lions [Samuel C. Lyon] & D. Henry [Daniel Drake Henri] interpreter left for Mexico [City] via Monterrey.

Saturday 14th. We left Matamoros for Mexico [City] via Monterrey, Saltillio & San Louis Potosi. We Marched 12 miles & encamped for the night. Our guard was about 500 with one piece of Artillery commanded by Canalles. We did not have strong hopes of whiping our guard, and making our escape home.

While at Matamoros, General Ampudia turned the command of the prisoners over to Col. Antonio Canales, known among Texians as a man without character, a traitor, who harbored a deep hatred for them. Canales insisted the prisoners be manacled, but as a parting gesture to the Texans, Ampudia overruled him. A new guard was assigned to the prisoners. These new men, sensing Canales's contempt for the Texians, behaved accordingly. The prisoners were subjected to physical abuse; fists, feet, and the point of the bayonet.

Joseph D. McCutchan, a Mier prisoner, wrote of his comrades:

> They were placed under the conduct of Gen. Canales, who, at first. Refused to answer for their safekeeping unless Ampudia would permit him to take them in irons. But the latter, being possessed of a glimmering spark of generosity would not grant his request; and the former, mean traitorous, and dastardly as he was, dared not disobey.[56]

William Preston Stapp, another prisoner, described Canales and the new guard in these most unflattering terms:

> This guard consisted of five hundred men, (four hundred infantry and one hundred cavalry, with a field piece,) all new levies, and with none of the discipline and soldierly bearing of those from whose custody they had taken us. It is an old and most correct observation, that the rawer the recruit, the more insolent and brutal is he in his intercourse with all under him or in his power. Not a dog of this guard who did not scowl upon us with all the cowardly malice of bigoted hate, and practise every annoyance toward us that his mingled sense of discipline and apprehensions from ourselves, brought within the scope of impunity. The character of Canales we were familiar with before, and knew that every severity he could exercise on the way, that would fall short of exciting us to open resistance, would be certain to be inflicted. We were, therefore, not wholly unprepared for the inconveniences and petty tyrannies we endured from him and his felon recruits. One security from him we relied on, and that was his fear. This he openly manifested before setting out, in refusing to take charge of us, unless we were all first ironed. To so brutal a proposition Ampudia opposed his prompt and decided opposition; and the sneaking poltroon recompensed himself for his baffled cruelty by maintaining, through his subalterns, the most irksome police over us, himself never venturing nearer our lines during the march than a hundred yards. To such excess did he carry his caution, that frequently on the march, when it was necessary for him to pass from the rear to the front of the division, his circuit.[57]

William A. A. "Bigfoot" Wallace said of Canales and his guards:

> The officer in command of our guard was well known to many of us by reputation as a cruel, cowardly tyrant, and we knew very well we had no favors to expect from him, or from the ignorant, undisciplined recruits of which his force was composed.[58]

Canfield's recollection was somewhat different. An escape was planned for the change of the guard.

> Reached the pass Lacata on the "San Whan." Distance 20 mile. Here every thing was arrainged to charge the guard at day light, but owing to the fact that Capt. C. K. Reese would not take the position allotted to him by Capt. Cameron the attack was necessarily abandoned. It was supposed also that information had been given our enemy, as fires were placed aside the 2 pieces of artillery and sentinels with firebrands continually in hand.[59]

Sunday 22nd. Crossed the River at St John & marched twelve miles & encamped at palmetto Ranch, We were put in a stone fort made as a barrier against the Camanches.

23rd. Marched and passed a large ranch at 3 miles. At 12 ms. At 12 oclock came to a village called Mantaca. Encamped in a coral.

24th. Marched 24 miles crossing a small creek early in the morning and encamped in a coral.

25th. At 5 miles came to Capisaro on the River of the same name a branch of the St John. Crossed the River and inclined upwards. The mountains present themselves. Crossed a creek at 21 miles, Encamped in a coral for the night.

William A. A. "Big Foot" Wallace, ca, 1872. (James Worsham collection)

26th. Marched 15 miles to Padaet. Crossed a small stream close to the Town. This is a pretty place of about 5000 inhabitants in a very pretty little valley, As usual we were marched in triumph under triumphal arches.

27th. Moved to a better situation. Friend Bullock gave us Tobacco,

28th Saturday. Bad roads from a great deal of rain. Marched for Monterey and encamped at 15 miles. A large Rancho that is several Sugar farms in this neighborhood. The land is situated as to be irrigated by the River.

Sunday 29. Marched 6 miles. Passed Warloupe [Guadalupe] & Mission the first city of the mountains and in the State of New Leon. Monterey is situated between 2 mountains and on a branch of the San Whon [Juan]. The highest peak is called Camanche Saddle and is about 1500 feet. Less parade over us here than elsewhere.

Monday 30–Tuesday 31–February 1st. Remained in the prison at this place.

Feb 2d. At 12 oclock left Monterey for Saltillio and encamped at a ranch 12 miles distant. San Catherine.

On February 2nd, the much-despised General Canales was replaced by Lt. Col. Manuel R. Barragan, who, initially was much favored by the prisoners for his humane treatment. A new guard came with Barragan—100 cavalrymen and the same number of infantrymen. These were mainly raw recruits, many swept up from the prisons of Monterrey.

3d. Marched 25 ms to a ranch Rengeona. This here we intended to attack the guard take their arms make our escape to Texas. The guard as we anticipated having been much reduced, but they received some warning which put them on their guard which prevented it. We supposed that Capt Reese had informed the Commander.

Canfield and others, however, were fairly certain Reese was in collaboration with the enemy.

> We had determined on charging upon our guard at or just before day but on making an examination at day light we found the position of the enemy so changed. We were satisfied they had information of our intention; many were of the opinion that C. K. Reese informed the Col. As he, Reese, with one or two others were endeavouring to make individual escape. Consequently, were opposed to a general charge. Had we overpowered the guard at this point we could have reached the Rio Grande in between two & three days.[60]

4th. Marched 27 ms and camped. Our course Due west inclining up the River or valley of Monterey between the rugged ledges of mountains.

Sunday 5th. Marched 12 ms to the City of Saltillio. This Town is situated on the waters of the River St John in a pretty little vally surrounded by rocky dreary looking mountains without vegetation.

6th. Remained in prison. We have overtook our officers and 5 of Wolls prisoners. Amongst them was Vanessee [George Van Ness], who was taken as an interpreter to go on with our officers who continued to go a head of us. Here we received a donation of tobacco from a liberal Frenchman,

7th. Took up the line of march for San Louis Potosi, Marched 24 miles & camped at the Ranch were Dimmits men made their escape from the guard, and Dimmit killed himself by poison to prevent being killed by the enemy who treated him very brutally. The name of the Ranch is Guas Neuava [Agua Nueva] which is in english New water.

Philip Dimmitt, a pioneer Texas trader, merchant, and major figure in the Texas Revolution, having brought the first supplies and reinforcements to Houston's victorious army after the battle of San Jacinto. After the revolution Dimmitt began building a trading post near the site of present Calallen. On 4 July 1841, Dimmitt and some comrades were taken prisoner by Mexican troops. He and his comrades, together with 19 other Texians, were put in irons and marched to Monterrey in August 1841, enroute to prison in Mexico City. At Saltillo the Texians tried to escape by drugging their guards with alcohol laced with morphine. Eighteen escaped, but eleven were overtaken and shot, and the others were pursued into the mountains. Dimmitt, separately confined and unable to escape, overheard that he would be shot if the fugitives did not surrender. Facing either execution or interminable imprisonment, he chose to take his own life by morphine overdose, remarking, "I do not fear death but dread the idea of ending my life in a loathsome dungeon. Tell them I prefer a Roman's death to the ignominy of perpetual imprisonment, and that my last wish is for my country's welfare."[61]

Wednesday 8th. Marched 24 ms and came to water at a tank or artificial lake at 12 ms farther. Encamped at a large Ranch called San Salvadore. The water being very brackish being drawn from a deep well by means of a wheel worked by a mule with buckets on a large belt in which the water is drawn up.

Thursday 9th. Marched 33 ms to a large Ranch [St. Salvador]. Encamped in a coral. Here the water is allso brackish and the country very poor & barren almost destitute of vegetation.

Friday 10th. Marched 20 ms and encamped at a large Ranch called the Salado. Here we again overtook our officers and had some little intercourse with them. They did not advise us much in regard to our attack on the guard but told us to use our own judgement. We had been arguing & agitating the subject for some time but could not get the men unanimous although more favourable opportunities have passed than the present both for attack and retreat but the men appear now to be more desperate and determined at all hazards to strike a blow which might once more regain their liberty.

Canfield wrote:

> During our march this day several of us came to the Conclusion We had gone far enough, if not too far, into the country, and were determined not to be driven this way through the

> country, if to be avoided. After our arrival at Camp the names of all those who were willing to go into a charge were taken, the number amounting to between 60 & 70 out of our 200. All who intended to take part in the coming contest agreed upon Capt. Ewen Cameron as the leader. He did think of attempting the charge at night, but deferred it 'till morning owing to the fact that the same Reese before mentioned was endevouring to dissuade the men from joining our party 'till Cameron stepped up to him and remarked in his mother tongue, "You shall not talk any more about this."[62]

[Friday 10th, continued] Col Barragans treatment to us had not been very harsh untill the last two days when his conduct bid fair to be rather cruel towards us for the future as he had given the Soldiers liberty to whip us and several of our men had already experienced their cruelty. It now appears from the report of the Captains that a majority of the men was in favour of making an attempt to regain our liberty. The next day [February 11] the attack was agreed upon that the signal should be given when the commander came into the yard to order us up to draw our rations and prepare for the march as was his usual custom. He came in early in the morning discovered our excitement & retired immediately before the word was given but not withstanding this important advantage of taking the commander was lost. There were some who were determined and urged the attack with a great deal of zeal.

John Rufus Alexander recollected having been initially opposed to any breakout due to the condition of the men and the long distance to Texas they would have to cover; however, he told his companions Dr. Richard Brenham and Willis Copeland "but if the break is made, I will be among the first on the charge, and I believe I can go as far as any man." Alexander continued:

> Copeland said the guards were a gang of hoodlums and they would run over them. Brenham, who had been on the Santa Fe expedition and held prisoner of the Mexicans at Perote Castle, was sure if he was recognized when they got to Mexico City, he would face immediate execution. The break will be made this morning [and] if I have to make it alone and singled handed; I would rather die fighting like a man, here, than to be lot out and shot like a felon at Perote.
>
> Before taps there was the usual amount of merriment among the boys, and it appeared to me that the spirit of fun and repartee ran with greater exuberance than on any former occasion, even to the extent that it attracted notice on the part of some of our guards, and one of the petty officers came in and asked Captain Cameron the cause of the general good humor. He was told that it was in view of the near approach of St. Valentine's, our Saint's day, which we always celebrated with great rejoicing and hilarity, since it never failed to bring good fortune.[63]

The morning found the prisoners, many who had passed the night without sleep but ready for the break, eagerly awaiting the word from Captain Cameron. Colonel Barragan, as usual, came from his quarters to call the prisoners to their breakfast. It was the plan to take him as a hostage but he seemed to sense something amiss and unexpectedly turned on his heel and went back. The men drew their rations of rice and waited. Alexander described that morning:

> Few of us gave heed to the chill of the morning air. The murkey dawn announced the approach of a great crisis, and it found the men ready, eager and waiting for the signal. There was no unusual movement observable among the men; there was a total absence of that spirit of levity and good-natured badinage that had prevailed the evening before; a silence that presaged the coming of a great event in our lives prevailed; the men stood in groups, or sauntered in apparent listlessness about the narrow confines of our prison as dumb, submissive cattle, waiting the coming of the pound manter to dole out the morning provender. Men looked into each others faces with inquiring eyes and read decision in every countenance and grim determination in every eye. Our shackles were to be broken, the grave had less terrors than the dungeons of Perote, our backs were to be turned towards Santa Anna's boasted capital, and our faces toward home, Texas, and liberty. What greater incentive to nerve men to daring deeds? I saw men grasp each other's hands in silence, as if in greeting, encouragement congratulation, or a final farewell, each, seemingly, realizing that the minute hand of time was swiftly approaching the stroke of doom, or the chime of freedom for over 200 brave men. It was a scene fit to arouse the war gods of antiquity, and to command the admiration of the world. The Spartans at Thermopylae were led by tried and experienced officers and in their hands swords, spears and lances; the immortals who went down in the Alamo stood behind walls of masonry while their unerring eyes glanced along the gleaming barrels of the deadly rifles. The Captives of Mier, cold, hungry, their emaciated forms clad in rags that fluttered in responsive salute to the mountains' chilling breath; these stood in expectant silence awaiting the signal to spring upon a vigilant, heavily-armed foe. Weapons? Bare hands, more deft in the arts of peace than implements of warfare Armor? Rugged breasts that never quaked with fear, always turned to the enemy, and faces that never blanched in the presence of danger.[64]

[Saturday 11th, continued] It now appeared to be the last chance and many of us were determined not to let it pass. Our commander after much persuasion gave the word of attack in a very cool & deliberate manner by pulling off his hat telling his men to come on and taking the musquet from the sentinel on the left of the door while I took the one on the right.

Alexander remembered the incident.

> All eyes were fixed upon Sam Walker and Captain [William] Ryon as they carelessly advanced towards the doorway leading into the compartment occupied by the guards. Captain Ryon, after looking through the gateway turned and said something to those who stood near, and the word was whispered around, "Too late; the Red Caps are underarms!" Ryon and Walker still stood in the doorway as if waiting, while Capt. Cameron stood a few steps in their rear. … Suddenly Capt. Cameron threw off his hat and pushing up his sleeves, his face aflame with a strange light shouted, "Now is your time! Come on boys!" [Other Mier prisoners recalled Cameron shouting, "Now Boys! We go it!"] With Walker at his side, these two were the first two to rush through the gateway, each grappling with a sentinel whom they disarmed and knocked down.[65]

Ewen Cameron. (Texas State Archives)

Capt. William Ryon. (Texas State Archives)

[Saturday 11th, continued] The rush was now as great as the seize [size] of the door would admit of. About 150 infantry were stationed in the yard adjoining the one we were in. And notwithstanding the warning they had of our intentions to attack and the precaution to prevent it. We had about 5 minutes, and the Soldiers begging for quarter which was readily granted not killing any more of them than was actually necessary to rescue their arms from them without incurring great loss ourselves but the most difficult part of the victory was yet to gain. The Cavalry was encamped outside and a part of the infantry was allso stationed through which we had to pass before we could get to the horsemen. A few of us however charged out under their fire into the street driving them at the point of the bayonet. Being only 5 or 6 we were compelled to retire to the yard to procure ammunition. This delay on or part to procure ammunition increased the confidence of the enemy who now began to pour their fire in at the door while our men were crowded it.

Here Lyons and Brenham were both shot dead and Haggerty mortally wounded & Baker severely wounded.

Brenham's death was reported differently. Brenham and Patrick Lyons, also a Santa Fe prisoner, led the charge and were killed as they made it through the outer gate. Lyons was shot dead. Brenham, according to Captain O'Phelan, killed three Mexicans with a bayonet and was rushing toward a fourth when that soldier dropped his rifle to the ground "and the gun fell toward the Doctor, who rushed upon it inadvertently, and the bayonet passed directly through his body."[66]

[Saturday 11th, continued] Had the first charge been sustained without waiting to get ammunition we would not incurred this loss. As soon however as Cameron had succeeded procuring ammunition after his return from the first charge out of the main entry he immediately made the second and we were soon in the street with the enemy fleeing before us. Some of them however retreated to another yard surrounded by a high wall and some of them still kept up a brisk fire. Here Fitzgerald was mortally wounded. We charged up to the door of the yard to which they had retired where we exchanged a number of shots and John Stansbury was shot in the eye while in the act of firing his piece. The order was now given to cease firing. I was now on the opposite side of the door where Stansbury was shot, and endeavoured to make the mexicans cease firing allso by calling to them in their language, but the Soldier who had shot Stansbury as if he were elated with success continued to load without seeming to notice me at all. I took a deliberate aim and the gen-

Texian charge upon the guards, and victory of Salado. Sketch by Charles McLaughlin, one of the prisoners. (tsl.texas.gov. From *Journal of the Texian Expedition Against Mier* by General Thomas J. Green, published by Harper and Brothers, New York, 1845)

tleman tumbled from his position without ceremony. I now discovered by the whizzing of the balls that we were exposed to a cross fire from some port holes in an offset in the corner of the wall for defense against the Indians. Myself and one of my comrades ran down to it and jabbing a rock in the hole the firing entirely ceased. About 40 or 50 of the Cavalry with the Commander made their escape. All the rest fell into our hands as prisoners though we did not detain them or exact any conditions on them nor take any thing but what we were entitled to by the rules of war. We got about 70 horses & mules & saddles about 1400 dollars of Public money, ammunition provision Arms &c. Our officers [who] had been marched off about 15 minutes before the action commenced under the charge of Capt Romano were halted when the firing commenced and which halted. Capt Romano received an order from Col Barragan to execute them. They replied to him that they were at his disposal. He told them they were in the hands of a gentleman and in a short time ordered them to mount and I have since learned traveled them 75 ms without resting only sufficient time to get fresh horses. In the action we had two men Brenham & Lions a scotchman killed dead one man by the name of [Lorenzo] Rice killed dead in the horse trough in the yard where we slept & two others mortally wounded since dead. [Capt. Archibald] Fitzgerald [John] Haggerty [Higgerson] & four others [Capt. John] Baker and [George] W Trahem [Trahern] & [John A.] Stansbury [Stansberry] severely wounded. [Thomas] Hancock & [John] Harvey slightly wounded in the yard where we slept while not taking any part in the action. We were very unfortunate in losing Fitzgerald & allso

Hancock who was too much effected at the time to go with us supposing a stab which he received to have reached the hollow though it proved otherwise. On these two men we depended as guides as they had a better knowledge of the country over which we intended to pass than anyone else we had along. Before proceeding farther I must stop to make some remarks about Capt [Charles K.] Reese whose conduct has been much censured by his comrades. In the first place he is said to have acted childish at Mier when the white flag was brought in By Doct Scinicson crying & telling him he has saved his life. In the next place he is guilty if inconsistency such as advocating an attack on the guard on our way to Matamoros while our guard was five to one, and while on our march to Monterey with a much less guard and every one entertaining hopes to escape he went so far as to bribe the guard to let him escape but had not sufficient nerve to go after he succeeded in getting the consent of the soldiers who guarded him went he went after water. At Monterey he again intended to make his escape if he could have persuaded others to have gone with him notwithstanding he knew there would be an opportunity of all of us making our escape and we all felt confident of the same and an attempt in him to escape would have been a great barrier to our success and the second night from Monterey when we had positively determined on the attack he now disapproved of the attack although we could have reached the Riogrande in three days and not have lost a man in the attack and besides he was engaged in consultation with the Commander early in the morning the infantry was put under arms much earlier than usual and prevented an attack from being made. In the course of the day one of our Lieutenants J[ohn M.] Shipman was informed of our intentions. We have since judged that it was Capt Reese gave information. Capt Reese was now opposed to our break and continued in the confidence of Barragan and was treated with much more attention than many other officers amongst us. When we arrived at the Salado Capt Reese was angry with those who advocated an attack and made himself noisy & clamorous in opposing it. At night he was out in company with Barragan and again the guard was doubled and precautions taken to prevent it. Capt Reese declared he would take no part in it and persuaded a number of others to remain neutral. After the fight was over he came out and made preparation to go with us but determined to send his Brother Wm Reese with Barragan to Mexico after we had spent about two hours in preparing to march and several of our interpreters had conversed with Barragan in which they learned from him that Capt Reese had told him that he could prevent an attack and after being mounted on a good Horse & musket which himself & Brother both secured he went over with it as a peace offering to the enemy and never more returned to do it is due however to say for the credit of Wm Reese that he fought Bravely although his Brother forbid him. In relation to the 1st charge however it is confuted by Doct Sinicson who clears him of any want of manly behavior in the affair at Mier. Dr Sinicson however is liable to censure and perhaps very justly so as has since acknowledged that it was his opinion that the enemy was whipped when he came in with the white flag and did not express his opinion to the Texians which would in all probability have made the most timid willing to have fought on instead of surrendering. His reason for not doing so is that some unforeseen event might have changed the anticipated assault or rather might possibly have given the battle in favour of the mexicans and in that event the Texians all put to the swords as the Mexican officers threatened in case they did not surrender which he says might have been a charge of infamy against him hereafter by making representations which were not so.

But I must now return to the Salado. About 10 AM we took up the line of march homeward including the wounded & sick. We left 18 men at the Salado. We marched 53 ms and stopped at San Salvadore and bought corn & fed our horses & proceeded on. At 65 ms slept about two hours before day. We were dogged behind by the Cavalry that escaped at the Salado thought they manifested little disposition to come very close to us.

Sunday 12th. Marched early in the morning leaving the Saltillio Road at 10 oclock. Struck the Zacatecas Road at about 10 ms and took the left hand to a ranch in sight for the purpose of obtaining water. We found the Tank was close to the house which was defended by a few Regular Troops who hoisted a red flag and commenced a fire on us at about 200 yds. Our commander having determined not to be detained by an engagement that he could avoid. Our men however shewed great coolness as they filed right. They marched deliberately off under the fire of the fort while the bullets were whizzing about our heads. No other man as I discovered dodging his head except the reverend Parson Case. We had no damage only a few horses wounded. We directed our course northward to a trail we discovered leading over the mountain which was very rough in descending however we were fortunate enough to find a hole of water the greatest treat we could have had at this time having about 20 hours without any. It was truly a godsend and just about as much as would give us a drink round. Here we discovered a party of Mexicans dogging us, and the two Sergeants left us and went to Saltillio and proceeded on. At about 6ms came to a Ranch where we got water for our horses. We found them in arms but did not molest them except to inquire the Camago Road and proceeded on with what without any intention however of taking it but more for the purpose of deceiving them than otherwise about the road we intended to take. We continued our course west and after descending a mountain into a deep valley. About 3 oclock at night we laid down to rest placing a guard out and took a mexican spie who rode into our camp. Here Jack Sweeezy [Sweizy] was left asleep or deserted us.

The following is Canfield's account of the aftermath of the successful break:

> Preparations were now being made to take up the line of countermarch as soon as possible by securing Horses provisions, &c &c which was accomplished by 9 oclock A.M. having obtained from their supplies an abundance of bread stuff, sugar, &c with 150 or 160 muskets & Escopetas 4000 rounds of ammunition (cartridges) 90 Horses & Mules and $1400 in specie which was taken for the purpose of satisfying the Citizens for such articles as we received from them on our way home. Being now formed and homeward bound, the aforesaid Capt. Reese and some 15 others left us and joined a small party of Mexican Cavalry about ¼ of a mile distance, we all anxious to reach our adopted country and he with the others willingly embracing the lousy Mexicans with some little trouble. I am able to give the names of these "birds." Viz

> Capt C. K. Reese, Richd. Keen, D[aniel] Davis, G[eorge] W. Bush, A[ndrew] B, Hannah, D[aniel] R. Hallowell, C[harles] Clark, D F Barney, (T[homas] Hancock Wounded in the charge) (Harrold [Milvern Harrell] attending a man [Norman] Woods at the time) [Simon] Glenn, Wm. Reese brother of Capt. R, and S Saunders [Leonidas Saunders] since dead ... Our march continued without intermission for 48 miles where we fed our Horses paying the Ranchero for the corn from our "Military Chest."[67]

According to Joseph M. Nance in his book, *Dare-Devils All*, those named by Canfield refused to take part in the insurrection. Captain Reese changed his mind once the fighting started and did join in the charge. Nevertheless, all but Harrell—who was taking care of the wounded Norman Woods and Thomas Hancock—went with the escapees, but soon changed their minds and gave themselves up to a squad of Mexican cavalry commanded by a Captain Posas.[68]

March [February] 13th. We started early taking the prisoner with us our course west. At 8 ms came to water, and proceeded on and struck the Montclova Road. Here a friend came to us and gave us directions & advice which we ought to have followed but for want of confidence in him we did not do so. The prisoner we had taken was to act as pilot. At 12 oclock crossed a small creek and came to a ranch and sent John Brennan the interpreter and our mexican to buy some corn & beef. The Mexican was detained and John Brennan told to leave or he would be fired on. We passed in gunshot of the Ranch not molesting any thing. A woman then came out and inquired if any of Jordans men was with us and being told there was she said if they would vouch for the good behavior of the rest that we could be accommodated at the Ranch with what we wanted though we would not return and continued our course, and was soon overtaken by the proprietor of the Ranch who expressed some regret that he had been mistaken in our intentions, and shewed us a good place some short distance from the Road to graze and rest our horses.

[Samuel W. Jordon,[69] commanding a force of Texian volunteers with the rank of colonel, joined the forces of the short-lived Republic of the Rio Grande and fought against the Centralists who were attempting to crush the separatists. Following the Battle of Saltillo, 25 October 1840, in which the Texians were betrayed by their allies, Jordan led his men in a fighting retreat back to Texas. Their withdrawal brought them to the Monclova Road where they encountered the ranchero and his family.]

At sunset we again took up the line of march and left the road at 8 oclock to sleep. Were fired on by a small party of Mexicans.

John Rufus Alexander recalled the incident.

> The next day we came to another military post, and as we approached, the occupants opened a brisk fire upon us from a distance of at least 500 Yards, "Convicts, said Patrick Mahan [Maher, who drew a black bean and was executed at Salado, March 25, 1943], just out of the penitentiary, and the officers want them to get used to the sound of their own guns, which are as safe at one end as at the other, and little harm in either." We did not return their fire but passed on.[70]

We then proceeded on. Our commander [Cameron] was now influenced to leave the Road entirely and take the mountains contrary to his instructions and his own judgment and as well as I can learn by officers and men who attached much of prudence as being the better part of valour, and opposed the break at Salado and done little towards fighting once it was begun. We continued our march a few miles & encamped for the night placing out a guard.

Joseph McCutchan described Cameron's plight.

> On the twelfth, they, misjudging their policy, left the road and took to the mountains. To this Cameron was bitterly opposed, but it appeared to be the general wish of the men and he consented. In that he was to blame, for he should have assumed the entire command, as he had been chosen for that purpose, but he was too much given to acceding to the propositions of his men. Still Captain Cameron cannot be censured; he must not be answerable for the acts of others. There were two (perhaps more) of the captains who went to Cameron telling him that if he did not leave the road that they would draw off their companies and leave the command. Here Cameron was placed in a delicate and critical position; he saw that he must either go directly contrary to his own will, or that he must see a band of brave men, already *too* small for the undertaking bursted asunder and cast apart in an enemy's country, where distruction would soon overtake them. Here were two very great evils presented to his view, and he finally concluded to give the reign to his men in preference to seeing the[m] disunite. Of the two evils he chose the least. No man can be found who would not have acted the same way under similar circumstances.[71]

Feb 14th. Directed our course through the mountains. Traveled hard and made but little progress the country being too rough for our horses. Found no water. Being much fatigued we encamped for the night in a very deep ravine. Having passed a shepherd with a large flock of sheep in the morning and allso learned that we would find no water the direction we were going which ought to have been sufficient warning to have induced us to return to the Road.

March [February] 15th. Some of our men found water about a mile & a half from camp. We now determined on leaving our horses and taking it on foot, We proceeded to kill the fattest and best of our horses & mules & jerk the meat for our subsistence and cut up the saddles flaps to make sandals to protect our feet from the rocks & thorns. The scene here was awfully grand so much so that language can not fully describe it, It presented a mass of destruction and a set of men reduced to the necessity of eating mules and horse flesh apparently in fine spirits & willing to endure any hardships & make any sacrifice to regain their liberty.

John Rufus Alexander had the following regarding difficulty in navigating the unknown mountain passage and the slaughter of the horses.

> Having passed one of these declivities of six feet perpendicular fall, we came to one of at least fifteen feet, forming a barrier that forbade all hope of further advance with our horses. The six-foot wall was just behind us, at our feet was a fifteen-foot precipice; we could neither advance nor retrace our steps; we could only kill our faithful horses. It was a sad, heart-rending ordeal, and touched the most obdurate heart. These patient animals had borne us thus far,

Texians killing their horses in the Mountains for Sustenance. Sketch by Charles McLaughlin, one of the prisoners. (tsl.texas.gov. From *Journal of the Texian Expedition Against Mier* by General Thomas J. Green, published by Harper and Brothers, New York, 1845)

> and even now, while we were planning their destruction in their famished condition, their gentle lustrious eyes were turned upon us appealingly for relief. But there was no alternative; we also were threatened with starvation, and the sacrifice had to be made. The die was cast, the horses were slaughtered, and some of the men drank their warm blood in order to relieve their consuming thirst.[72]

At 3 oclock we proceeded on. Our water having given out so that the men could not fill their gourds. At 10 oclock we encamped for the night in a deep ravine having left Esty [Edward E. Este], [John] Fitzgerald & Isam [Zed Island] & several others that joined us in the morning before we started.

16th. Continued our course north. No water leaving [William H.] Miller & Pilly [Michael Robert Pilley] at camp. At 12 oclock left Parson [Capt. John Goodloe Pierson].

[Thomas W.] Cox, Miller & [?] Davis who gave out & could not keep up. Came to a road or trail on our course and continued on it till night. At about 14 ms farther on we here began to use the Palmetto as a substitute for water.

Friday 17th. Marched early in the morning. Our course west of north. At about 8 ms Mark Rogers is unable to keep up. [Allen S.] Holderman and [Levi] Williams remained with him. About 12 oclock discovered some Mexican spies in a large valley. Our course now northward across it. Rogers Holderman & Williams again overtake us while stopping to rest. We proceeded on and encamped about 9 oclock without water. A number of men however continued on changing their course eastward in search of water.

Saturday 18. No signal from any of our water hunters. Continued our course across the valley, Much dissatisfaction prevailed in regard to the course most likely to find water. Some were for going east and some west and some for continuing our course north thinking we might find water in the west valley. The men however were all unable to travel and halted to rest. Capt Cameron with about 50 men continued on a short distance bearing more to the west and allso stopped to rest during the heat of the day. Being undetermined what course to take, several small parties having already left in search of water and the main body scattered for several miles over the valley with their blankets spread on the thorn bushes to protect them from the sun. The groans of the men were now distressing even to those of the greatest fortitude & perseverance. Some of them had been drinking their urine several days. Some of them eating or chewing nigrohead & prickly pear to raise a moisture in their mouths while others were scratching up the cold dirt & gravel from the shade of the bushes and applying it to their breasts & stomachs to cool their fevers. At 6 oclock PM discovered a large smoke to the right. At first supposed it to be a signal made by some of our water hunters who had gone in that direction. Sent a messenger to Col Cameron to inform him. A large number of the men threw down their muskets unable to cary them farther and late in the evening started for the smoke. It was now impossible to keep 20 men together as some would stop to get juice from the magaya and others compelled to stop every 15 or 20 minutes to rest. I was with a party of the men. When we came close enough to the fire to ascertain that it was a camp of Mexican Cavalry. It was now about 8 oclock at night. We passed them and continued on to where we expected water. Found several small parties [that] had preceded us. At several leagues we passed another camp. Leaving it to our right and continuing in the trail that the Horsemen had made leading to a large gap or pass in the mountain. At day break we came close to the pass and heard a sentinel hail which proved to be one of the parties who had preceeded us. Our party scattered and friend and messmate John McMullin [McMullen] continued in company with me.[73]

John McMullen (1824–?), was born in Baltimore, Maryland, and immigrated to Texas in 1839. In 1842, he volunteered for the Somervell expedition, perhaps in company with Samuel H. Walker. He is likely the same John McMullen who served as a Texas Ranger under Capt. John C. Hays. He served as fourth corporal of Capt. Zaccheus Wilson's company of Col. Joseph L. Bennett's First Regiment, South Western Army. McMullen was one of the command who refused to heed Somervell's order to disband and return to San Antonio, but remained with the rump of the army under Col. William S. Fisher. When Fisher reorganized the army, McMullen became a private in Capt. Ewen Cameron's Company A. He was captured at Mier and marched to Perote Prison, but according to fellow prisoner Joseph D. McCutchan, McMullen was among "those who have money" and thus was able to board at his own expense. McMullen was released from captivity on September 16, 1844. McMullen enlisted as a private in Capt. John C Hays's Company, Texas Rangers, on February 12, 1845; and was discharged and reenlisted a number of times. On September 28—the same day as Walker—he was mustered into federal service as a private in Capt. Robert A. Gillespie's Company I of Col. John C. Hays's First Regiment, Texas Mounted Rifles, in which he served until March 28, 1846. (Courtesy of John McWilliams)

Bearing a little to the right and still approaching the pass we stopped a short time after perceiving the pass was guarded and rested at the same time consulting on what course should pursue. We concluded that the only alternative was surrender as we could not survive longer without water. We had one musket between us and we throwed that away and walked into the camp and were met by some of the Rancheros who told us to give them our money and they would take care of it for us, that if we did not the Regulars would take it from us. This however I did not do as I had always taken the precaution to hide what little I had in the waistband of my pantaloons knowing well that the first thing a Mexican thought of when they took a prisoner was to rob him of all he had and allso that if I gave it up I should not see it again. In a few minutes another party of our men were brought in and a few had allso preceeded us. There was now about 50 in each camp and continued to come in two or three together all day. The mexicans seemed to have some pity for us and used great caution in giving us no water or in all probability a number of the men would have killed themselves had they been allowed free access to drink want they wanted. In the evening Capt Cameron with about 60 men were brought in having the most of them surrendered the night before at the first camp of mexicans on the conditions they should be treated as prisoners of war. We were all tied two & two with rawhide strings and the officers separated from us. This being the 19th. We remained here untill the 22nd and took up the line of march for Saltillio 134 of us in number having surrendered. They gave us plenty of raw beef & corn but very little wood to cook it and being tied so that we could only use one hand. It was very troublesome to do our cooking. On the 23rd being the second day from the pass in the mountain. Came to a Ranch where we found Dr [William F.] McMath, Holderman & Tawny [John Taney] on the 24th.

25th. Remained at the Ranch. During the time about 20 more of our men were brought in. [Prisoner Thomas W. Bell claimed the total number of those captured was 177.][74] The nights were very cold and many of the men suffered a great deal as they nearly naked and the Mexicans had taken the blankets from them. They allso took all the money from them they could find so that many of them were left entirely destitute of almost every thing.

On Sunday 26th marched 20 ms and encamped at a Ranch in a cow pen our number 160. Some of the sick were permitted to ride Burrows or Jack Asses.

27th. Some of our boys were struck several times for untieing the Raw hide strings and severely threatened if they done so again. Marched 24 ms and encamped at San Antonios Ranch. Here the rawhides were exchanged for hand cuffs of Iron. They continued to guard us very closely not allowing us to stand up in camp lest we might charge them. Our boys however seemed determined to bear up and keep a stiff upper lip under all circumstances and on this occasion were more lively than usual receiving their irons with smiles and promising to remunerate the mexicans for their kindness the first opportunity. The evenings ceremony was followed by singing and telling stories which attracted the attention of the officers and Ladies of the Ranch who were much amused as astonished at the unusual fortitude of our men under such circumstances.

28th. Marched 20 ms and encamped at an old camping ground. Have water.

March 1st. Started early for the Town. 16 miles. Got no water untill we reached the suburbs of the Town where we were permitted for the first time to wash our faces which were thickly covered with dirt. We were then halted and remained for several hours waiting for the Governor and allso for preparations to receive him which were making in the City. We entered the City with a band of music with a great parade and firing of crackers. We were marched to the square where a speech was delivered with loud cheers. We at length marched to our quarters which were very lousy. This day we got nothing to eat.

Not mentioned by Walker was the order sent by Gen. Nicholás Bravo—interim President of Mexico—to execute all of the prisoners, which was received by Gen. Francisco Mejía, Governor of Nueva León on March 1. Mejía declined to obey the order and was subsequently removed from office. U.S. Minister to Mexico, Waddy Thompson—upon learning of the order—protested to the Mexican minister of foreign affairs, warning if the order was carried out, Mexico would find itself at war with "a much more powerful enemy than Texas." Santa Anna returned to Mexico City on March 5, and found a new order was about to be sent to Saltillo ordering only one in ten should be shot. He promptly sent an order to shoot all the Texians. However, under pressure from the ministers of the United States, Great Britain, and France, he rescinded the order and put in its place orders for the decimation of the prisoners.

Canfield later wrote of Mejía "recollect this ye Texians, there are not many officers under Santa Anna who would dare to disobey an order; yet Maher [Mejía] was only complying with the terms of our capitulation."[75]

Thomas Bell recalled the events of March 1, and the entrance of the prisoners and their escort:

> Thousands of people were on the ground to witness this triumphal entry and to express their joy at the glorious success of a gallant Mexican army, of one thousand in number, just returning with the branching laurels of the recapture of one hundred and seventy-seven Texans. But it was not entirely to witness the triumphal entry that so many people were summoned together on this occasion, but to witness the execution that was to have taken place here, according to the first order of Santa Anna.[76]

March 2. We got breakfast at 10 oclock.

3rd. [Robert G.] Walters & [James N.] Torry were brought in and ironed and allso the two seargeants who had been in Town for several days.

Sat 4th. Remained in prison.

Sun 5th. 9 more of our boys were brought in. Sweizey had allso been brought in.

Waddy Thompson. (npg.si.edu)

Mon 6th. Received a donation of tobacco from a citizen which was very thankfully received.

7th. Remained in prison.

8th. Mr. [Peter A.] Ackerman was brought in having got with 60 miles of Riogrande before he was taken.

9th. Petitioned to the Governor for more rations and in addition to the one meal a day. We got coffee in the evening. Brian [Barney W. Bryant] died from the effects of cold contracted from sleeping without a blanket. He was a young man of Amiable modest unassuming disposition and a good soldier.

10th & 11th. Nothing important occurred except a comet had been discovered some nights ago which excited considerable uneasiness amongst the Mexicans.

11th. Nothing of importance occurred.

Sunday 12th. Visited by some Americans who were watched closely and not allowed to converse with us.

Stapp recalled the visit differently:

> Several American wagoners of Zacatecas called to see us on the 12th, who informed us, with less sensibility than they would probably have displayed in recounting the loss of a horse, that an order had arrived directing every tenth man of us to be shot.[77]

Allso visited by six Lipan Indians who were allso watched closely and not allowed to converse with us. The object of their visit we did not learn but some of the men were inclined to believe they were merely desirous of knowing our condition, as they expressed great surprise at seeing so many American prisoners. There were five of the sick baptized by a catholic Priest, and were afterward treated with considerable attention by some of the Citizens though we did give them much praise for the Christianity as they visited Brian a few days previous to his death and because he would not consent to bé baptized. They refused to do any thing for him when good attention might have saved his life. Those who were baptized were considerably censured by some of their comrades. In the meanwhile learned that an order had been sent to shoot every 10th man for the break at the Salado but the Citizens & Governor had refused to execute the order and petitions were sent on to procure our release which they hoped would be granted as they agreed that our conduct at the Salàdo was magnanimous & brave and allso our retreat and when they learned all the particulars that they could our Commander Capt Cameron was treated with more than usual kindness by Americans declaring they loved him and admired him for his Bravery & magnamity.

Monday 13th, 14th, 15th, 16th, 17th, Nothing of importance occurred.

Saturday 18. Joe Watts [Watkins] & [E. D.] Wright were brought in found near Montclova having laid to die for want of water. They were taken to a little own called quartro Sinicas when they were very kindly treated after being first robbed of every thing they had. They informed us of the death of [A. J.] Lewis of Brazoria who died for want of water. They allso learned that two of our men had passed Montclova and would probably reach Texas.

List of names of the men who were and were not taken after the attack at the Salado.

R [Perry D.] Randolph from drinking too much [illegible] [Died at Benado, 25 February]

[Alexander John] Lewis allso for the want of water. [Lost in the mountains]

[William T.] Morehead—supposed to be dead. [Escaped to Texas]

[William D.] Cody—do—do. [Lost in the mountains]

[William] Mitchell—do—do. [Died from drinking too much water at Benado, 25 February]

Maj. [William] Oldham—supposed to have reached home. [He did, in April 1843]

[George] Anderson [Reached Texas in April 1843]

[James H.] Calvert [Recaptured near the Rio Grande]

[John L. D.] Blackburn [Escaped to Texas]

[Thomas Washington] Cox [Escaped to Texas]

Toofred [Unknown]

[Capt. Claudius] Buster [Recaptured near the Rio Grande]

[Sanford] Rice [Lost in the mountains]

List of those killed and wounded & left behind at the Salado.

D[r. Richard F.] Brenham—killed in the second charge at the main entrance of the front yard

[John] Lyons—fell by his side.

[Capt. Archibald] Fitzgerald—mortally wounded while charging the enemy into a back yard where they had retreated.

Rice—killed in a house through the yard where we slept.

Haggerty—mortally wounded at the main entrance to the front yard.

Baker—severely wounded at the same place.

Stansbury—severely wounded while firing at the door of the back yard.

W. Trahern—severely wounded in the hand in the first charge.

Hancock—slightly wounded in the charge.

Harvey—wounded in the eye while standing in the yard where we slept.

Wood—unable to travel from his wounds received at the Salado. At Dawsons massacre.

Herold—nephew of the above who stayed to take care of him.

Caldwell—unable to travel from fever.

Two of the wounded W. Trahern and Hervey continued with us untill we were taken in the mountains.

List of names of those who shewed no disposition to regain the liberty.

Capt Reese

Lieut Clarke

Richard Greene

Hannah

Hallowell
Bush
Saunders
Daniel Barney
Wm Reese—though a youth fought Bravely but was [illegible] to remain by his Brother.

Total Killed & left at the Salado—21. Total not retaken & died in the mountains—14. Total that were retaken and surrendered—177. Total including 5 of Wolls prisoners and joined us at Saltillio—214.

Gen Greene & Fishers party including vanesse [Van Ness] who was allso taken at Sanantonio by Gen Woll and joined that at Saltillio was 7 and up to the present date 176.

On the 19th and 20th an examination of our interpreters took place in relation to the break at the Salado. It was for the purpose of finding the Ring leaders and the particulars allso of Col Barragans conduct in the action.

On the 21st the Cavalry arrived from Sanlouis Potosi [San Luis Potosi] to guard us on our way to the City of Mexico.

On the 22 took up the line of march under command of Col Orteese [Juan Ortiz] accompanied by a company of infantry. We marched 8 leagues to newwater Ranch.

23rd. Marched 14 leagues and encamped at Sansalvadore Ranch. There our handcuffs were examined and all the sick men who had loose were again ironed. We begun to suspect that some thing was wrong yet we hoped otherwise.

24th. Marched 11 leagues and encamped for the night.

25th. Marched early and arrived at the Salado about 2 oclock. 20 ms. Soon after we arrived we received the melancholy intelligence that every 10th man was to be shot. We were ordered to form the officers in front when the following order was read. That for the offense committed that [took] place on the 11th of Feb that the expense by Government of Mexico had decreed that every 10th man should be shot. We were Ironed and of course bound to submit as we could not make effectual resistance. We at once determined to bear it like men & soldiers. Had we known it or anticipated it we should have made another attack on the Guard at Saltillio but it is now too late. We are now closely ironed two together and the Soldiers with their guns presented. The only way we could shew our bravery was to bear it with resignation & fortitude. Our fate was destined by drawing beans from a covered mug. A white bean signified exemption from the execution. A black bean Death. The number to be executed was the same now is one of awful grandeur which surpasses description. A manly gloom and a look of firmness pervaded the countenances of all the Texians and it was difficult to distinguish by their countenances while the drawing was going on who had drawn the black beans while some of the Mexican officers who were present shed tears as though they were much grieved to witness such a scene of horror and a disgrace to their country. The names of those unfortunate men are as follows. Capt Wm. Eastland, T[homas]. L. Jones, Jas. M. Ogden John S Cash, Patrick Mahan, Henry N. Whaling, Robt. Dunham, W[illiam] Rowan, James D. Cocke, Robert Harris, James N. Torry,

Texians drawing the black beans at Solado. Sketch by Charles McLaughlin, one of the prisoners. (tsl.texas.gov. From *Journal of the Texian Expedition Against Mier* by General Thomas J. Green, published by Harper and Brothers, New York, 1845)

J[oseph] N. M. Thompson, C[hristopher] M. Roberts, James Turnbull, E[dward] Esty, M[artin] C. Wing, Jas. L. Shepherd.

The latter could not be found on the morning after the massacre. They all died with firmness telling us in their farewell embraces that they desired their murder to be remembered and revenged by their countrymen and some of them allso telling the Mexican officers that it was coldblooded murder and their countries should revenge their death and as a small a matter as the mexicans may think it the blood of these men may yet cost them the blood of thousands as circumstances will make it more lasting than the murders of Fannin which will be remembered by future generations. The deed was a dark one and needed the shades of night to execute it in. The victims after writing a few hasty lines and making some requests of their friends, were blindfolded & their hands tied behind them and led out just at dusk divided into two parties. A wall of 10 or 12 feet in height obscure them view except those who were permitted to see it, and very few had any desire to witness it. The firing commenced and lasted about 5 minutes when the groans of the murdered ceased having shot some of them 10 or fifteen times and that in the most brutal manner shooting their heads and faces. Instances of shooting them dead through the hearts as some of them requested. At an interval or 10 or 14 minutes the firing recommenced and ceased in about 5 minutes as before. Several of the officers who came in and asked a number of our men if we were contented. This I thought a strange question to ask men in our situation.

Shooting of the decimated Texians at Solado. Sketch by Charles McLaughlin, one of the prisoners. (tsl.texas.gov. From *Journal of the Texian Expedition Against Mier* by General Thomas J. Green, published by Harper and Brothers, New York, 1845)

Capt. Charles Keller Reese, commander of Company F, distinguished himself at the battle of Mier by taking an active role in the fighting, staunchly opposing surrender, and advocating an escape plan before the prisoners were marched south into the interior of Mexico. However, he was suspected of warning the Mexican officers of the February 10 escape plans. There has never been any concrete evidence he did so, but the suspicion tarnished his reputation. He wrote the following account of the infamous "bean drawing" a few weeks after the release of the Mier prisoners in September 1844:

> A number of Mexican officers made their appearance upon the opposite side of a low wall, between five and six feet in height, among them was Col. Comingo Huerta, (one of Santa's fit instruments always ready to obey his master's will, however barbarous and mean it might prove rather than resign his commission) who had preceded us from Saltillo for the purpose of which was as follows:
>
> That it was the order of the executive of the government of Mexico, that we should be marched to the Rancho Salado, at which place we killed several Mexican soldiers and succeeded in effecting our escape, and then by lottery we should be decimated and every tenth man be shot. As we had received not the slightest information to the moments of the reading of the order of what was to take place, we were much surprised. Preparations were made immediately for the purpose by counting out 159 white and 17 black beans as we numbered 176 men. These were placed in an earthen jar, over the mouth of this a handkerchief was placed and it stood up a low wall previously mentioned. The muster roll of the men was then provided and their names called by the interpreter, as each man heard his name he advanced to the jar and took from thence a bean, did it prove to be black the hand-cuff that fastened him to his companion was

taken off and he was passed into the courtyard, where all the troops were stationed under arms, the drawing continued until 17 men were designated. During this scene which was sufficient to test the fortitude of the men, they were perfectly composed, and apparently indifferent as to the results when they went to the jar to decide whether it was life or death to them. There was no shout of gladness or marked change of the countenance by those that fortune favored, and those more unfortunate appeared to exhibit the same composure; there were several Mexican officers much affected by the scene they were witnessing, there is but little doubt would have rejoiced could it have been countermanded. The drawn men with the interpreter were placed in a private room, where those of their fellow prisoners with whom they wished to see were permitted to visit them. Pen, ink and paper was allowed them for the purpose of writing to their relatives and friends. They spoke of the fate that awaited them with the utmost coolness and indifference, and expressed a willingness to die provided the balance of their companions would be saved, as they firmly believed that more would be victims to the relentless vindictiveness of the executive, none were seen to shed a tear, nor heard lamenting their fate, but appeared calm and resigned.

They requested to see Quarter Master, F[enton] M. Gibson[78] and Capt. Ryan, they were permitted to visit them. To the former, Powan and Torry said, "Gibson you see us for the last time. We die for our country. To our friends we look for revenge, our nerves are unshaken." Capt. Eastland then spoke, "Say to my friends that I addressed you and hour previous to my arraignment before my God. For my country I have offered all my earthly aspirations and for it I now lay down my life. I never have feared death, nor do I now. For my unjustifiable execution I wish no revenge, but die in full confidence of the Christian faith." Cocke's dying words were as laconic as strange, "Tell my friends," said he, "I die with grace." Then did these men in the hour of their manhood meet their bloody fate, displaying to their executioners the dauntless spirit that liberty inspires.

About half past six o'clock in the evening the Lieut, and 30 soldiers, who accompanied us from Saltillo, entered the room, who pinioned their arms behind them, and bandaged their eyes. Nine were led out, and marched to the wall on the east side of the square we were in; they were ordered to sit on a log, and in that position barbarously murdered; the eight remaining were taken to the same place and shared the same fate. Whilst this transaction was passing we were separated from them by only a narrow wall and forced to become the unwilling listeners of the scattered firing and groans of our dying companions. In order to complete the execution some of the men were shot 7 and 8 times, and Henry Whaling received 15 shots before life was extinct. They requested as a favor from the officer who attended the executions, that he would command the soldiers to place the muzzles of their guns to their breasts and fire, this undoubtedly was not done from the fact of their having shot so frequently.[79]

The last glimpse of the slain filled writer Stapp's pen with venom:

The next morning as we left the shambles of the Salado, we caught a mournful blood, lay where they had fallen; whilst their rigid countenances, pallid and distorted with agony, appealed in death for retribution on their slayers. And many were the vows of vengeance registered that moment against their cowardly assassins. … At the ranch we parted company with the infantry, who returned to Saltillio; the infamous miscreants having only been brought thus far to perform the butcher's work agreed upon. They were the identical heroes whom, with naked hands, we had disarmed and routed the morning of our break at this place, and who, smarting under a sense of their disgrace, had petitioned for the brutal employment just dispatched.

Stapp ended with a plea. "Should a Texian army ever penetrate to Saltillo, let the memory of this transaction claim the amplest expiation."[80]

When news of the murdered Texians reached New Orleans, Charles DeMorese, editor of the *Daily Picayune*, wrote:

> Their death has revealed the vindictive impulses of the Mexican villain who rules that nation; and another augmentation has been made to the hecatombs of the murdered patriots who have been perfidiously slain by his orders, after the fairest promises of honorable treatment upon capitulation. … All this could not have been, had the miscreant despot been swung by the neck, as he should have been, when captured at San Jacinto.[81]

We marched 7 leagues and encamped in a coral. The water here is good the first in four days.

27th. Marched six leagues and came to a ranch where there was a beautiful running water the first running water we found in 45 leagues the first few Ranchos on the Road being supplied by wells as I have already described. The country from here to Saltillio is very poor and would afford very little supplies for an army. These wells might allso be filled up and easily destroyed by a retiring force. At 2 leagues further we encamped at the St John [San Juan de Vanegas] Hacienda.

28th. Four of our men were baptized. [John P.] Wyatt, [Richard] Brown, [W.] Miller & Isam [Zed Island].

The conversions were much protested by their fellow prisoners. Stapp wrote, "The Converts, however seemed extremely sanctimonious and devout after the ceremony."[82]

After the ceremony we marched 18 ms and campt for the night at San Christopher for the night. Here the country is more thickly settled & though very poor the inhabitants seem to have on hand a surplus sufficient to feed an army.

Wednesday 29th. Marched 30 ms and encamped at a large Hacienda warloupa [Guadalupe de Carnicero]. Passed several large Haciendas on the road.

30th. Marched 20 miles to Lagoona [Laguna] Saco a large Ranch owned by a Frenchman who divided his wardrobe with us giving us shirts &c which we stood very much in need of, Samuel McClellan [McClelland] died here from the effects of Pleurisy.

31st. Marched 15 ms. Watered at a large Tank. Here a mule throwed Willson. At 30 ms came to the Banio a small Town on a small Brook and campt for the night.

Apr 1st. Here we rested and was permitted to go a bathing though many of them could not get their shirts [off] on account of our handcuffs. This a small place apparently about 100 acres or 200 acres of fertile land with fruit trees and vegetation of various descriptions surrounded by barren hills covered with rock yet there is a population of several thousand souls. The most remarkable growth I have ever seen for hedging or fencing is the orange which grows here in great abundance. The prickly pear allso grows to most incredible height from 12 to 15 feet in height.

Sunday 2nd. Again took up the line of march an came to a small Town called Gedediunda [Hedionda] and camped for the night. This something like Bana.

3rd. Marched 20 ms & came to another small Town Lahocas [Las Vocas] and camped for the night.

4th. Received a donation of cigars from the Ladies of the Town, Marched 20 ms and camped.

5th. Marched leagues into San Louis Petosi. Marched through the Public square which presents a very respectable appearance and from thence to our quarters. Here we found Capt Baker, Stansbury, Wood [Norman Woods] & Caldwell [Thomas Colville] who had been left in the Hospital.

6th. The handcuffs were taken off.

7th. 14 men were taken to the Hospital. [James J. Blanton, Benjamin Z. Boone, Philip F Bowman, Charles Hill (died soon afterward), Allen S. Holderman [died soon afterward], James H. Michen, John Mills, David Overton, Peter Rockefellow (died soon afterward), John A. Stansberry, William P. Stapp, Thomas S. Tatum, Levi Williams, and William Wynn.]

8th. E G Caughman [Elkin G. Caufman] & [Robert] Beard died in the hospital. Here we were better fed than usual.

9th. Remained in prison.

10th. We were told here that Fisher had sold us at Mier and recd. a part of the money in San Louis. Did not credit the report. Were treated with great coolness by the most of the foreigners in consequence of false reports which had been circulated about us. A german merchant however was very generous & kind to our officers and some of the men giving them clothes &c.

9th remained in prison. Nothing important occurred. Col Orteese [Ortiz] is again to take charge of us with a part of the same Cavalry and escort us to Caratero [Querétaro].

Of Colonel Ortiz, Stapp was very generous with praise:

> Colonel Ortiz, though a rigid martinet, and inflexible in all that appertained to the interests of the service, manifested the greatest kindness and benevolence to us in everything that he considered compatible with his duties. Whilst on the march, we had occasion to remark the delicacy of his humanity in guarding us from every insult from the people or the soldiers, refraining from all painful exhibitions of us in towns and haciendas through which we passed, and enforcing the most comfortable quarters and rations to be procured.[83]

Thomas Bell, although in agreement with Stapp's assessment of Ortiz's benevolent treatment toward the prisoners, stated: "but his kindness did not reach so far as to give them enough to eat during those long and wearied marches."[84]

Monday 10th. Left San Louis for Carataro leaving 14 men behind in the hospital. Williams, P. Mills, Hill, Blantin, Overton, Rockyfello, Stepp, Boon, John Stansbury, P. Macmiecham & Winn. From San Louis we were joined by about fifty pressed volunteers [and, according to Stapp, 300 convicts]. Marched 5 leagues and camped for the night at a small Town called Warloupa [Guadalupe de Carcinero]. San Louis is a pretty valley though it is badly watered being supplied entirely wells from which the most of the land in cultivation is watered. The valley however is badly cultivated and every thing seems to be on the decline.

11th. Marched 21 ms to a small Town called Eliguel Francisco [Francisco de Bayou].

12th. Marched 15 ms to a small Town called Hacienda Akral [Jaral].

13th. Marched 27 ms Sanfillipe [San Felipe].

14th. Marched 6 leagues and encamped at a poor ranch. [Hacienda Comadré].

15th. Marched 18 ms to a small Town. Doloris [Dolores Hidalgo] a pretty place with a fine church. At this place a memorable battle was fought between the mexicans and Spaniards [Father Miguel Hidalgo y Costilla began the Mexican Revolution of 1810 at this place].

16th. Marched 24 ms to San Miguel [San Miguel el Grande]. This is a large town and situated on the side of a mountain well watered by springs from the mountain. Through the politeness of our commander Col Orteese [Ortiz] about 20 of us were taken all through the Town which is remarkable for its churches. Two of them we visited and were much pleased. They were extensive. One of them presented a very rich & gorgeous display of fine quilt work with a large gallery of fine Paintings attached to it. The other was more neatly finished and finely decorated and had the appearance of being lately finished though it could not have been executed by Mexicans as their genious for mechanisms as at rather a low ebb.. We allso visited a place of resort for the fashionable Ladies & gentlemen of the City. It was a yard forming a half circle and surrounded by beautiful shade trees with a beautiful fountain of water in the middle or center. We found a number of fashionable Ladies & Gentlemen setting round though there was no conversation between them as the Ladies & Gentlemen did not mix as usual with the mexicans or English & French on such occasions. A large number of the common class followed us but did not presume to enter amongst the Lords of Fashion but kept a respectful distance and looked on at us untill we reached our quarters. We were quite a ragged set and I felt rather bashful at being seen by Ladies of fashion & taste.

17th. Marched 24 ms to Santa rosa a large Hacienda [de la Santa Rosa].

18th. Marched 15 ms to Carettaro [Querétaro] a large Town watered by a reservoy [reservoir] or conducter built at considerable expense being built on pillars & arches 40 or 50 feet high across a valley several miles in length.

19th. Marched 12 ms to a Hacienda called xxxx.

20th Marched 24 ms to a small Town St John Derio [San Juan del Río]. Here we overtook Adjt [Maj. Thomas W.] Murray who had been left sick by Fishers party.

21st. Marched 42 ms and camped at a large Hacienda [de Río Seco] a stage stand. Here we conversed with an American who was on his way to Mexico and lived in Carettero.

22nd. Marched 24 miles. Encamped upstairs in very dirty quarters [in Hacienda Todia].

23rd. Marched 4 leagues to Toula [Tula] a small Town and quartered in an old convent. Here we were joined by more volunteers together with those who had joined us at different places on the road numbered about 300. Here we were turned over to another officer from the City of Mexico who informed us that we had nothing to fear that Packingham the English Minister [Sir Richard Packenham] had requested him to treat us well and he intended to do so.

24th. Marched 8 leagues to the Town of Uewatoka [Huehuetoka] & were treated very bad on the road. At night we were locked up in close quartells which was remonstrated against but without effect. At 8 oclock Capt Cameron was called out from us and told he was to be shot. Thermon [Alfred A. Thurmond] was also taken out as interpreter but was not allowed to return.

Captain Reese wrote of Cameron's execution:

> Between 8 and 9 o'clock in the night an officer came to the door and inquired for Capt. Cameron, and also the interpreter, Shumard; they arose and went to the door, he requested them to follow; they were ordered to a room and a paper presented to Shumard to interpret to Cameron. The purport of it was, "That in order to complete the former order for the execution of the Salado which had only been partially executed, Capt. E. Cameron should be shot."
>
> Pen, ink and paper were allowed him, and he addressed a letter to the British Minister calling his attention to the cruelty of the Mexican government in putting their prisoners of war to death. He spoke frequently of the injustice of the order and pronounced it a cold-blooded murder, and that he had been looking for it daily on his journey to the city.
>
> On the morning of the 25th of April, about 10 o'clock, he was taken out and shot.[85]

Murder of Captain Ewen Cameron. Sketch by Charles McLaughlin, one of the prisoners. (tsl.texas.gov. From *Journal of the Texian Expedition Against Mier* by General Thomas J. Green, published by Harper and Brothers, New York, 1845)

Joseph D. McCutchan wrote the details of Cameron's execution:

> The following is told by a Mexican who saw it. "They lead him out, and wished to blindfold and tie him; he refused, saying that he feared not death, and would die as a man and a soldier should die, free and unfettered. Then they shot him, but not to kill, only to cripple. After wounding, they tied, blindfolded, and shot him as if he had been a dog! But he received his death bravely, without a murmur or shudder. Thus died your leader."[86]

Another version, written some dozen years after the murder of Cameron, lays the cause at the feet of a bitter enemy:

> The survivors were marched thence to the city of Mexico. Arriving at Huehuetoca, within eighteen miles of the capital, they were met by an order from Santa Anna directing Captain Ewing [*sic*] Cameron to be shot. The command was promptly executed the next morning; and Cameron, in dying, left to the world an example of heroic fortitude in the manner in which he met his fate. He had passed the ordeal on the 25th of March, and drew a white bean. After thus trifling with his life, it seemed to be a refinement of cruelty to order his execution, almost within sight of the capital of a nation that would at least wish the world to believe it civilized. The warrant for his death was procured through the influence of Canales. When the federal army was encamped on the Nueces, previous to the campaign of 1840, Cameron lost his horse, but afterward found him in the possession of a Mexican. The former seized his property, and the Mexican resisted, calling upon his countrymen to assist him. Canales, hearing the altercation, ordered Cameron to deliver up the horse, which he refused to do, and, drawing his pistol, declared in broad Scotch that he would shoot the first man who laid hands on his property. Shortly afterward, Canales had him tried by a court-martial (of which Captain Thomas Pratt was judge-advocate), for disobedience of orders. The court, looking upon the affair as an attempt of Canales and the Mexican to rob the prisoner, acquitted him. From that moment the vengeance of Canales pursued him; and in 1843, when the one had got into favor with Santa Anna, and the other was a captive in chains, the order for his execution was solicited and obtained.[87]

25th. Were joined by another old grey headed officer and some 10 or 12 more soldiers. We secured our days pay for rations $1 to four men. This old officer was very kind and obliging to the men in changing their money. So much so that it attracted my attention. I saw him smile and pat several men on the cheek like a young Lady would her lover and take their money and run off to get it changed. I now began to think he had been sent to execute some black deed and we soon learned that he had been sent to execute Cameron.

His name I have not learned. We marched 5 leagues and halting to rest were overtaken by the old officer and soon learned that our beloved & Lamented Capt Cameron had been shot. [Alfred S.] Thurmon[d] was allowed to rejoin us. At 9 leagues we camped at a small Town called Tampautla [Tampanlta].

26th. Marched 9 ms to Mexico and confined in Santiago. We here found Dr Sinicson, [David] Allen, Judge [Patrick] Usher, [D. H.] Gattis, [John] Day, [John] Harvey, seller [William H. Sellers], Gilbert Brush, J Hill, and Jas C Wilson. [George Bibb] Crittenden[88] [released upon the appeal of former U.S. Congressman and Senator Henry Clay] left for home. These men who had been left wounded & sick at Mier & Matamoras.

27th, 28th, 29th, 30th. Nothing of importance. Visited by some foreigners and presented with a few clothes which are very acceptable.

1st, 2nd, 3rd, 4th, 5th. Nothing of importance. Through the foreign ministers have been furnished with a statement of the murder of the 17 men at the Salado and allso that of Cameron. [This statement, dated April 27, 1843, was sent to the American, British, French, and German ministers in Mexico.]

Albert Sidney Johnston. (Texas State Archives)

On May 4, however, Walker wrote an interesting letter to Gen. Albert Sidney Johnston, former commander in chief of the Army of Texas and secretary of war, then residing in Kentucky.

Prison Santiago City of Mexico May 4th 1843
Gen A Sidney Johnson

Dear General
Myself & comrades are in a tight place at last, from which we will not likely be released until Texas strikes some decisive blow on the Riogrande and takes some of the officers and principal citizens of this Government to exchange for us. Two thousand men can with security penetrate as far as Monterey, return and hold possession of Matamoras until Mexico would be glad to acknowledge the independence of Texas. I feel confident that one thousand Texians can take possession of Matamoras against all the troops East of the Mountains, as my experience teaches me to believe we can whip them against almost any odds, we learn that Santa Anna has sent propositions to Texas to bring her back under the Government of Mexico but we all here unanimously scorn the idea of such a thing and would rather run the risk of dieing with old age in prison than Texas should listen to any such a proposition. Our most sincere wish is that the Texians will reply to all propositions coming from them by the dread sound of the Rifle. The Ministers here believe are doing all they can for us. We have called upon them to demand our release on the grounds that they have again violated the laws of nations in shooting of Cameron and the seventeen men at the Salado. What success they will have I cant venture to predict. It was through their interference that prevented Santa Anna from having us all shot. Santa Anna rules the country single handed. It is thought by many that the country is again on the eve of revolution. How true it is hard to say but certain it is that the country is in a miserable condition and every thing on the decline. I have been much disappointed in the country. I have not been able to see much

of Santa Anna's boast [of] wealth & great resources. The country is Generally poor rock & barren or rather dry and unseasonable. grass very scarce. So much so that we have not eat a good piece of Beef in the country. Texas is worth a dozen such countries as this as they both now stand. The fact is that this country would not [illegible] any other people so [illegible] as the servile race that now holds it. To give you all the particulars relative to our engagements, our captures &c would occupy much more space & time than the present will admit of, but I will assure you that we have whipped them at Mier, and the fault of surrendering was mainly attributed to the officers particularly the commander at the Salado. about forty leagues from Saltillio on the road to this City we attacked a guard of supervision members charging them through a narrow doorway under great disadvantages they being beforehand apprised of our intention it is supposed by Capt Reese of Brazoria whose conduct has been very dishonourable but notwithstanding we whipped them in about 15 minutes taking about 180 stand of Arms & prisoners the remainder making their escape by flight. Our loss was five killed & five wounded. The enemies loss was the same killed but many more wounded. We killed as few of them as possible & generously gave them all their liberty & taking nothing but Horses, Arms, Ammunition, provision & such things as we had a right by the rules of war. We started our journey home and would have reached Texas in safety had we not unfortunately left the road contrary to our instructions and taken the mountains where we could find not water or make very little progress on our course homeward. The consequence was that the most of us surrendered on the 8th & 9th days not without the word of the Mexican officers that we should still be treated as prisoners of war. At the time we surrendered we were much debilitated most of the men had been drinking their own urine for several days. being five or six days without water several of our men died and there is nine more yet unheard of by us but we hope they have reached Texas. After our surrender we were taken to camp tied with raw hides two together and a few days ironed with handcuffs and marched to Saltillio where we remained twenty days and again commenced our march to this City. When we arrived at the Salado we were formed and the following order read that for the offence committed at this place on the 11th of Feb the supreme Government of Mexico have decreed that every tenth man should be shot. We were all ironed and of course4 compelled to submit. our fate was decided by drawing beans from covered mug. A white bean signified exemption from the execution. A black bean signified death. Our number being 176 men, seventeen was the number to be shot. Our comrades met their fate like brave men. Not a tear was shed by those doomed to die, all meeting their fate like brave Patriots telling us un their last embraces to give their love & best wishes to their countrymen in Texas, that is was for their glory and the independence of Texas they fought, and fail not to revenge the death of their countrymen thus murdered in cold blood. Cocke of Galveston wrote an interesting letter to the US Minister before he was executed which is very interesting. After this awful scene we were told no farther atonement would be required but to our great misfortune when within twelve leagues of this place we were locked up in close rooms almost approaching suffocation, Capt Cameron was taken out and shot, stating that it was to fulfill the order of shooting every tenth man, but it was evident that it was only because his reputation was that of a brave & good man. These things have been represented to the ministers and I understand that the B minister is much displeased. It is reported we are to be put to work but we have determined unanimously to resist it. If you could render me any assistance it will be very acceptable as I am anxious to make my escape in which case I should be glad to join you in an expedition to the Riogrande. Had you have been in Texas last Fall you would have been unanimously proclaimed commander in chief and I flatter myself that a brilliant campaign would have been the result. Nothing more but allow me to congratulate you & accept this assurance of [the rest of the writing is illegible].

SH Walker[89]

Saturday 6th. All hands except a few sick at the hospital chained two & two with heavy chains the size of a large log chain weighing from 12 to 15 lbs and learned that we are to be put to work. We have already passed resolutions declaring we would not work for the Tyrant Santa Ana but the committee who drew up the resolution and signed it strange to say are with one exception sick. We are advised by friends not to be stubborn in this matter. We reconsider the matter appoint another committee to address the US Minister

Mier prisoners. (Courtesy of Fort Bend Museum)

asking his advice. This evening receive a large contribution of hats shoes & clothing principally from the French who are always friend to the Americans. Leathers have also been brought in to make garatches [sandals]. Our commandant is much displeased because we would not receive them as we did not want any thing from the government. He tells us that we shall have them and a full suit of striped Lincy [linsey-woolsey] besides or 1000 lashes.

On this date, Walker wrote a letter to his sister-in-law Ann Walker, describing what had transpired since his last letter of March 10, 1842:

In Prison Santiago City of Mexico May 6th 1843
To Mrs Ann M Walker

Dear Sister
I write to inform you I am in good health, hoping this may find you the same. when I shall return I don't know as my experience thus far has only increased my anxiety & ambition to fight the mexicans. I have witnessed the murder of 18 of my comrades in cold blood and I am determined to revenge their death if I have an opportunity. In Decr last I crossed the Riogrande under Gen Somerville with 600 men. Gen. Somerville thought proper to return after taking two small Towns and accordingly done so without getting a fight a large number of the men not being in a situation to return being without horses or provision and not wishing to return without a fight. 300 in number proceeded down the river to Mier crossed and took possession of the Town on the 23rd Decr but disdaining to take what we were given there without fighting for it we retired without molesting any thing to our camp taking the Alcalde as security for the fulfilment of the requisition we had made on the 25th. we learned that a Mexican force was in the vicinity. we crossed to give them battle with 257 [other sources state 261] men leaving the balance on the east Bank of the river to guard the Horses. the force of the enemy was about three thousand with two pieces of Artilery having taken possession of the strongly built Town of Mier. not with-standing this great advantage in numbers & position the Texians gallantly entered the town under a heavy fire about 7 o clock and after maintaining the conflict for about 18 hours killing & wounding about three times their number surrendered only through their own bad management or rather for the want of a more determined resolute Commander. from Mier we were marched to Matamoros under a strong guard. from thence we took up the line of march for this City, where 40 leagues from Saltillo at a Hacienda called the Salado. on the 11th of Feb about 8 oclock in the morning we attacked a guard of superior number. in fifteen minutes the victory was ours. we took about 180 stands of Arms & prisoners,

about 70 horses & mules, the remainder making their escape by flight. we commenced our march homeward and would have reached Texas had we not unfortunately left the roads and took the mountains where we could find no water or make very little headway on our course. the consequence was that we surrendered ourselves again as prisoners of war, the men being nearly all famished for water having been five or six days without water. under these sircumstances you need not be surprised to learn that we surrendered ourselves to the Mexicans who were guarding the only water we could get for a long time with two pieces of Artilary, and our men were so weak that few of them were able to carry their muskits. the Mexican officers however promised our commander Capt Cameron that we should be treated as prisoners of war before surrendering, but not withstanding our situation and their promises we were tied two & two with rawhides and in [a] few days these were exchanged for irons which we continued to weare about forty days. we were marched to Saltillo where we remained 20 days and again started for this City. when we arrived at the Salado, we were all formed and told that for the offence committed at that place on the 11th of Feb that the supreme government of Mexico had decreed that every tenth man should be shot being prisoners of war we have to submit. our fate was decided by every man drawing a bean from a covered mug, a white bean signifying exemption from the execution a black bean Death, and seventeen of our comrades were executed accordingly our number being one hundred & seventy six. amongst them was William Rowan from Apilachicola, Fla & PL Shepherd of Jackson City Ala who escaped with both arms [broke?] the night after he was shot and made his way back to Saltillo where he was again taken & executed. they all however met their fate like brave & gallant soldiers who were willing to die for their countries sake.it may be truly said that they met death with a manly firmness that added much to the honour & glory of their country. their last request was that their countrymen might avenge their death, which we have sworn to do, after this unhallowed scene of cold blooded murder we were told that no further atonement would be required But to when within twelve leagues of this City our much esteemed & gallant commander Capt Cameron whom we had chosen after our break at the Salado was taken out & shot for the avowed purpose of filling the order to shoot every tenth man but it was evidently [to] get him out of the way lest they might have cause to fear him hereafter on the frontier of Texas. these things have been represented to the foreign ministers and they [are?] now interesting themselves in our behalf, which will probably protect us from future outrag[e]s, but how long our imprisonment will last I kow [know] not. we have been told we would be put in chains and put to work but we intend to resist all impositions not legally imposed

> on prisoners of war. this country is now on the eve of revolution. Santa Anna rules the country single handed. I am not much pleased with Mexico as the country is generally very poor. Texas is worth a dozen such countries with all of Santa Anna's boasted wealth and great resources. I have not heard from home since I arrived in Texas, but I am now writing to my correspondents. you must give my best wishes to all inquiring friends and tell them I desire to be remembered by them, nothing more. So I remain most sincere & devoted friend
>
> SH Walker[90]

Sunday 7th. Our men make quite a respectable appearance being dressed in the clothes that their friends has given them and we are again visited by a number of foreigners. Our Bill of fare since we have been here is a cake of course bread and a little corn flour gruel for breakfast about 3 oz of poor beef with soup and a cake of course bread for supper beans half cooked and a small cake of bread. These rations will keep soul and body together but never fatten.

Mon 8th. Received a full suit of [red and green] striped woolen cloth, hat & garatches in the bargain. Ordered to put them on immediately and prepare to march for Tackabayou [Tacubaya]. We soon marched out under a guard of Cavalry and arrived with some shovels &c. We were marched some distance into the City and halted for a short time when we received some 25 or 30 crobars and a large copper kettle to pack. We were now complete for service and marched to Tackabayoou 2 leagues from the City. About 1 oclock we arrived in Town and after marching & counter marching for some time passing near the Presidents Palace we [were] driven into a small room where we could not lay down. In an hour we were again taken out and marched about 7 leagues to an old church and again forced into another room too small to lay down.

On May 8, prisoner Richard A. Barkley, member of Capt. Nicholas Dawson's company prior to the Woll invasion, was captured at Salado and was one of the fifteen spared execution. He wrote of the treatment he and his fellow prisoners were forced to endure.

> How different it is now. We are made to work nearly every day and made to pack as mutch as possibly can—to add to our misery a large body of calvary has binn stationed (here). We have had their filth to carry out every morning … our food guets worse. We guet in the morning, nearly 3 oz bread about a half pint corn meal, coffee. We then work until twelve o clock then guet a small quantity of potatoes, badly sprouted, and a small piece of bread. Our supper is the same as in the morning. … In the evening we let out at six or seven oclock. I made an attempt to make my excape but was stopped by my fellow prisoners. They thought it would act to their harm. The Mexicans point me out and say that I am the worst one in the castle.—I have worn hobbels two weeks. Binn beat with their spades and muskets. Calaboosed and (every means to) cow me that they can think of … You need not rite me any more for I shall make my excape. There is no hopes of release—General Thompson tells us it is his opinion that he thinks we will be released in June, I think not.[91]

9th. We were ordered to put on our uniform to go and see the President taking our tools along. About 10 oclock we arrived at the Palace. 20 men were taken and put to work paving close to the Palace. All the rest were allowed to sit in the shade untill dinner and were then marched down to the foot of the street in [illegible] shady groove. The Ladies presented us with cigars. We spent the evening here and returned to our quarters.

10th. Remained in prison. Nothing of importance occurred.

11th. Moved to better quarters nearer the Palace [an abandoned powder mill known as Molino del Ray]. Faired rather rough day. Compelled to pack all our provision cooking utensils tools bedding &c. When we arrived at our quarters we were much fatigued. Every man had a load as much as he could cleverly wag with. Journey [Henry Journey] a sick man was whipped for not carrying the load they gave him.

12th. At work this day. I was struck by a criminal Peon who was placed over us for an overseer without cause. I returned the compliment over the head with a shovel and choked him in the bargain for which I was afterwards severely beaten by a drunken soldier and the same overseer. I was allso compelled to cary three times as much sand as usual.

Sunday 14th. In prison.

15th. I am unable to work. The men were at work as usual.

16th. The same as yesterday except the overseers have not whipped any of the men since Saturday. 17th. At work as usual.

18th. The same.

19th. At work all except the sick. The fair is rather rough and a good deal of Possoming. 20th. As usual.

Sunday 21st. In prison. Visited by Mr. Pratt & several others of the Americans and other Foreigners who visit us on all convenient occasions.

Mon 22. J[ohn] Shipman died at 3 oclock in the morning. At 4 PM Buried with a shroud and coffin.

23rd. As usual. All at work that are able. A good many puny and some not able to work.

24th. Nothing important. A dinner given by the Ladies of Tackabayou.

25th. 5 more Mier prisoners who were left wounded arrived. This is Feast day and the men are not required to work. Seven of the sick left at San Louis & Carettaro have allso arrived some days ago and John Blantin [Blanton] died the night after he arrived. Middleton died in the 6th.

26th. Nothing important.

27th. Nothing of importance.

Sunday 28. Nothing of importance.

Mon 29th. At work as usual.

On this date, Walker wrote to his brother Jonathan, giving him an account of his prison life and his hopes for the future.

In Prison near the City of Mexico May 29th 1843
To JT Walker

Dear Brother
Since writing to you myself & comrades have been ironed two together with chains weighing from 12 to 15 lbs and put to work in front of Santa Annas residence improving the street at a small Town two leagues from the City of Mexico called Tackabayoug. we have been treated rather rough on several occasions, by the criminals placed over us as overseers, I had the misfortune myself to be struck by one of them about two weeks ago and returning him the compliment with a blow over the head with a spade and a severe choking I was afterwards pretty severly beaten by a drunken soldier, which bye the bye has done some good as we have not been ill used since and have not worked but a half day since, I reported their conduct to the officers and told them if I was ill treated by their overseers or soldiers again I should kill the one that done it, if I died for it the next minute, but the fact is we are chiefly indebted to the US and British Ministers for all the good treatment we receive for our attak on the guard Santa Anna ordered as all shot through their timely interference it was prevented and only one tenth was shot Santa Anna then sentenced us to ten years imprisonment and hard Labour on the Acapulka road from here to the Pacific this was allso prevented by the remonstrance of the ministers, the British Minister I am informed has made an application for our release probably on the grounds that Mexico has already violated the rules of civilised warfare in our treatment, it is now rumoured that we will be released on Santa Annas Birthday the 13th of June thoug we fear to believe it as it is almost too good to be true, though we live in hopes and keep up our spirits pretty well, and I believe that the Mexicans are pretty well satisfied that it is Impossible to break the spirits of the Americans by ill treatment or any punishment they can inflict, and I think that ere another spring rolls round that Mexico will be glad to acknowledge the Independence of Texas notwithstanding their great anxgiety to regain Texas which is worth more than all the balance of her extensive territory, mexico has some very pretty valleys yet there is many inconveniences which renders it a very poor country for our use, there is a great sercity of water and timber and the land produces very light crops except where it can be irrigated, this is the handsomest valley I have seen in the country though the buildings and every thing seems to be rapidly decaying and no improvement going on, a large standing Army without the means to pay their Soldiers, the people pay little attention to the improvement of the arts & sciences and every thing except military discipline is neglected Their army in yacatan has all been captured by the yacatans, and their navy

is badly maned and will all so be taken by the Texians & Tucatains, the country is in a lamentable condition and cannot long exist under the present circumstances, we have been treated with consider able attention by the Resident Foreigners of the City they have given us consider quantity of clothes which were greatly needed, the mexican government has given us a suit of striped wollen which we received much against our will though we were compelled to receive them and wear them, Texas is too poor to do any thing for us and our chance of leaving the country if we are liberated will be very small, and besides the yellow fever is raging at vera cruz, so that I shall probably remain here until September before I can get away unless I can meet with some friends liberal enough to assist me I hope you will endeavor to send me some money as soon as possible as I have a great aversion to the people and would like to get back to Texas as soon as possible, I shall probably get some land in Texas for my services. Texas is most a beautiful country and I hope that she will become a state of the US. The people of Texas are in favour of being united to the states and I think it would be a valuable acquisition to the US, and one which no man would object to who has seen Texas, To give you an account of the beauties and ail the advantages of Texas would occupy such time & space But allow me to assure you that it is a country in which a farmer or stock grazer can soon acquire wealth with a very small capital, and there is no local causes for sickness and I think the country is generally healthy, the metallic wealth of Texas is also thought to be very great, there is several mines which were worked in the good many years ago, which the Mexicans say were very rich, the mines of this country are worked very little at present, from duty of 12 per cent emposed on them by the Government, from what I can see in the papers you are likely to have a number of candidates for the next Presidency my wish is that Mr Clay will be elected, though I trust that party spirit never gets so high as to make people lose sight of the true interest of the country by embroiling themselves in civil wars, the evil effects of which I have seen enough in this country, war in any way should be avoided if possible, more especially a civil war, yet it is my misfortune to be a warrior engaged in a war which I cannot with honour to myself or in justice to my murdered comrades on the Salado and my beloved Captain … abandon until the independence of Texas is acknowledged and Mexico humbled. I was amongst the foremost at the Salado and urged my comrades to make an attempt for our liberty, and when they were condemned to die for the offense, I promised to revenge their deaths which promise I feel bound (?) to fulfill if my Maker spares me long enough to do, so this act of cold blooded murder will make an indelible impression on the minds on all true hearted Texicans which will never be forgotten the ages to come, this act of cruelty & bloodshed has made a ... (?) which time cannot obliterate and as little as the Mexicans think of it, it may yet cost them the blood of Thousands and their downfall as a nation. I am anxious to hear from you and all my friends & relatives and hope will write soon and let me know all the news, and also let me know when Navarro is, if he is in Washington give my respects to him. I have not heard from him since I have been in Texas. I have not heard from my sister-in-law in Florida for 12 months or more. Give my best respects & compliments to all my friends and relations and tell them I desire to be remembered by them and hope once more to embrace them & enjoy the pleasure of their company and tell them a few stories about Texas & Mexico. Nothing more but remain your affectionate Brother. In Friendship, Love & Truth

SH Walker[92]

Tuesday 30th. About ½ of the men at work as usual packing sand. Santa Ana leaves Tackabayou on a visit of seven or eight days some six or 8 leagues distant. We allso learned that an account was published in the Mexican papers of an engagement Texian and Mexican fleets near Campeachy [Campeche] which lasted 11 hours and the Texian fleet it stated took refuge in the Bay of Campeachy. [On 30 April 1843, the sail-powered Texas Navy defeated the steam-driven Mexican Navy. This battle is engraved on Colt Navy revolver cylinders.]

31st. About one third of the men are at work to day packing sand and all the rest sick or rather much indisposed. 5 sent to the Hospital rather against their wishes today. The best and largest rations of meat for dinner we have had in this City, although at best, is but poor and small.

Prisoner Bell described the daily menu:

A large kettle appeared every morning at six o'clock, filled with "tola" [atole: a thick, hearty, maize-based hot drink native to Mexico and Central America, where it is consumed as a breakfast drink] of which every man received nearly one pint, and this was to suffice until dinner, when a few ounces of lean boiled beef and five ounces of bread made up the meal. At night they had still another change of diet, which was boiled beans.[93]

And the work the prisoners undertook:

This officer [in charge of the work party] spoke a little English and was well acquainted with the French language; but he was soon found too mild and easy tempered, to suit the task he had now undertaken; for under his supervision not as much work was done by the Texans, consisting of nearly one hundred and fifty in number, as could easily have been done by ten industrious laborers; he was therefore superseded in a few weeks by another. But he now selected a party of ten men and set them to work on trial, while the remainder seated themselves under the boughs of a spreading ash, to enjoy the shade, thinking this an easy berth, and if the Mexican Government called this work, they were willing to perform it on these easy terms;

> but this like all other terrestrial enjoyments, had to come to an end, for all were invited (as gentlemen commonly are) to take part in the labors of the day. The greater part, with sack on their backs were marched about half a mile and ordered to fill them with sand and stones, did thus for several months succeeding this, a chain gang might be seen, consisting of about sixty in number, in double file with a chain uniting each file, daily trudging the same road with a slow and even pace; laden with these materials, and a file of Mexican soldiers with a lieutenant or sergeant at their head, on each side of these gentlemen and apparently inseparably connected with them; for as one of these parties moved the other invariably moved with them, and when one stopped the other halted also. But while this was going forward others were employed in digging up the ground with heavy iron crow bars, while thers leveled it with wooden shovels and laid a pavement of stones. Various other employments were followed here, such as culling stones and beating the sand and stones until a road was graded.
>
> And it was now very evident that a road was intended to be made; but for what distance was the question, and some ilk having been afloat that the Texan prisoners were sentenced for life to work on a road that led to the western coast of Mexico, they did not know but this was its beginning; but this turned out as they afterwards learned by experience to be only a quarter of a mile in length. Down a gently descending slope, from the residence of Santa Anna, towards the capitol city which was in view of this place.[94]

June Thursday 1st. About 2/3 of the men at work the remainder indisposed. Some sent to the Hospital.

Friday 2. The same as yesterday.

Sat 3rd. As yesterday pretty much. My companion P[eter] M Maxwell cut loose and was sent to the Hospital having worked a day in three weeks. Only complaint Rheumatism. This is a very good complaint to go to the Hospital with, as the patient is generally allowed enough to eat. In all other cases of starvation is resorted to although the patient may be debilitated in constitution and require nourishing food there is little chance of getting it, Consequently the men although unable to pack sand will stick to it a long time rather than go to the Hospital. Those who have been to the Hospital inform us that the patients are stripped perfectly naked as the enter the establishment and are compelled to lay in bed the whole time they remain. Have corn meal gruel to eat in small quantities and after undergoing a severe operation of Salts & oil and several greasings which is resorted to. In almost all cases the patient either dies or regains his appetite in which case he has to report himself well. He is then sent to prison where there is a great many convicts called the Acasardo. After remaining here a few days he is fed as usual with beef soup &c and in a few days sent out to this place to be put to work as soon he is able. This is an old establishment erected for the manufactory of powder some 80 or 100 years ago. The walls are falling down and all the timber decaying about the houses and no improvement going on to prevent it from falling down.

Sunday 4th. Nothing important. No visitors to see us to day.

5th. Nothing important. This feast day. The men are ordered out to work and sent in again at noon.

Tuesday 6th. Feast day but the men are all at work notwithstanding except those that are indisposed. I am again cut loose from John McMullin [McMullen] my old companion and chained Mr Vandyke [Wilson M. Van Dyke] who is rather unwell.

Wednesday 8th. At work as yesterday. Santa Anna returns to Tackabayou. We are allso visited by several Foreigners who informs us that the Mexican Government are withdrawing all their forces destined to act against Yucatan to put down about 3000 Indians who were in arms against the Government in south Mexico.

The pro-federalists of Yucatan broke from Mexico on March 16, 1841. Negotiations with Santa Anna's government that would lead to the dissolution of the Republic of the Yucatan and its return to Mexican authority failed and in August 1842, an invasion fleet was sent to subdue the rebels. Britain supported the Mexicans providing warships and sailors, while France and Texas supported the Yucatan. Before the Yucatan formally declared its independence (scheduled for October 1841), agents were sent to Texas to gain support for its cause. Col. Martín Peraza met with Texas President Mirabeau B. Lamar in Galveston in September and an agreement was signed on September 17, wherein the Republic of Texas would send three or more ships to prevent Santa Anna's forces from invading Yucatan by sea and other considerations. In return, Yucatan agreed to pay Texas $8,000 per month to defray the expenses incurred.

We allso learn farther particulars of the Mexican account of the Naval action with Com. Moore. They report both of their war steamers much injured and allso Co. Moores flag ship which they say ran into the shallow water so they could not fallow her and after the engagement the Steam Ship Warloupe [Guadalupe] ran into the bay of Campeachy to get water and the most of her crew captured while getting water by the Yucatans.

Commodore Edwin W. Moore, chief of the Texas Navy, put to sea under orders from President Lamar dated September 18, to wit, he was to assist the Yucatan until its government said it was no longer needed or was recalled. However, Lamar's presidency ended on December 13, 1841, and his successor was Sam Houston—a stringent opponent of the Yucatan agreement—and he recalled Moore's ships on the fifteenth, stating he did not want to interfere with Mexico's internal affairs. However, Houston's order was not received by Moore until March 10, 1842, and by this time the Texian ships *San Antonio*, *Austin*, and *San Bernard* were either on station at Sisal, Yucatan or en route.

Commodore Edwin Moore, Texas Navy. (Private collection)

When all three ships had arrived, Moore was greeted by a vacillating Yucatan government. It now regretted the agreement and was in the process of negotiating a return to Mexican authority. Moore then withdrew his ships from Yucatan waters;

San Antonio to New Orleans, and *Austin* and *San Bernard* to blockade Veracruz. In mid-April 1842 Houston ordered Moore and his ships back to Galveston.

Houston was persistent in his efforts to scuttle the Texas Navy. He vetoed an appropriation bill to fund the outfitting of Moore's ships and, more importantly, to provide back pay due to the officers and seamen—who had only received pay three times in the previous two years. His veto overridden, by legal trickery—hypothecation—Houston pledged a draft for $18,812 against the Republic of Texas as security rather than an exchange for cash, which made it impossible for Moore to cash the draft for the discounted amount of $9,000 in New Orleans that would have been used to pay his officers and men.

Houston did authorize Moore to use his ships to blockade Mexican seaports and to place them under contribution—pay Moore not to bombard them—using the money received to repair and outfit his ships. No funds were provided by Houston.

While Moore was doing his best to secure the means to carry out his orders, the British sold two modern paddle-wheel steamers to the Mexicans. One, *Guadalupe*, was the first iron-hulled warship ever launched and carried two 68-pounder Paixhan guns that fired explosive shells. When delivered, her complement was entirely British—officers, seamen, and Marines. The other ship, *Montezuma,* was larger than *Guadalupe* and carried four Paixhan guns, two 68-pounders and two 32-pounders. *Guadalupe* arrived at Veracruz at the end of August, and *Montezuma* a few weeks later. In the opinion of many Texians, these ships were intended to be the vanguard of a Mexican invasion, reinforced by the news of General Woll's raid on San Antonio, September 11, 1842, the day after Houston had lifted the blockade of Mexican ports. Although the threat of invasion ruled the day in Austin, the only means of preventing seaborne supply and reinforcements to the invaders was the navy. In spite of the obvious, the Texas Congress passed a bill to sell the remaining ships of the navy, which Houston signed into law on January 16, 1843, and sent commissioners to New Orleans to take possession of the ships.

In the meantime, Moore had, as agent of Texas, signed a new contract with Yucatan agents then in that city and accepted several thousand dollars expense money. He raised several thousand dollars from other sources and his ships had full complements of experienced seamen and Marines and were ready for sea. James Morgan, one of the commissioners, was convinced the Mexicans were preparing an invasion force at the Yucatan city of Campeche and would be carried aboard transports guarded by the two British-built warships. He felt it his duty to contravene Houston's order to seize Moore's ships, stating, "I concluded to stretch my authority as Commissioner, a little, and authorize Com. Moore to go ahead: believing we could visit the Coast of Yucatan & accomplish every object we had in view, in 20 or 30 days at the fatherist." This is in view of Houston's March 23, 1843, proclamation suspending Moore from command, asking all nations to seize Moore and his ships if he sailed without authority.

Moore did sail, and with Morgan aboard his ship, in two actions forced the Mexican fleet—heavily damaged—to withdraw from engagements off Campeche on 13 and 16 May.

Houston branded Moore as a pirate and upon the latter's return to Texas, he faced a legal entanglement that resulted in his being brought before a court-martial in June 1844. After a 10-week trial, Moore was acquitted of the most serious charges—treason, murder, embezzlement, contempt—but found guilty on four counts of disobedience of orders. The court found extenuating circumstances in that they were conditional or impossible orders. No sentence was given.

It is allso anticipated that the difficulty between Texas and Mexico will be settled between this and fall. It is probable that this opinion exists under the supposition that Texas will accede to the propositions made by Santa Anna. This however is a delusional hope as Texas cannot with honour to herself stop short of any thing but Total independence which she has both the ability & force to maintain against any such government as Mexico. We allso learn that the new constitution for the government of the Mexican Republic will be presented to Santa Anna for his approval next week and it is said that it is draughted by creatures of his own choice. Under these circumstances he will approve of it and it is anticipated a revolution or civil war will follow.

Thurs. 8th. Nothing very important. Since we have been here many reports about being released on the 13th of June the present month. All are in great hopes it may be true but fear to believe it too confidently as the Mexicans so seldom tell the truth that our general rule is always to anticipate just the reverse of what they say. In this case however we have waived the general rule and the most of the men have a good deal of confidence in the reports.

Friday 9th. Today I volunteer to work in hopes of improving health though my partner Vandyke is taken with a fever and we lay in the shade in the afternoon. 22 of the men return from the Hospital.

Sat 10th. 14 men sent to the Hospital and all the rest who came yesterday chained. I am again cut loose & chained to my old messmate P[atrick] H. Lusk The men at work today say they have a great many officers overseeing them to day, and they worked harder than usual, and nearly completed the job which is a piece of road about 150 ft long and 30 wide. Any six of us with a horse & cart with our own management could have done the same labour in 10 days whereas it has employed from 75 to 120 men 26 days &½ under the superintendence of both civil & military officers. One of the colonels treated the men to a loaf of bread and a glass of liquor.

Sunday 11th. In prison. Nothing important.

Monday 12th. The men are at work repairing to road in the worst places. Hopes of liberty are getting faint.

Tuesday 13th. This Santa Annas birth day. He issues an order to release all political prisoners but we have not yet ascertained whether we are included or not.

Wednesday 14th. The men are taken to work on the road again and are visited by our old friend the Frenchman who is confident Santa Annas order does not include us and nearly all of us are without any hope of liberty untill the existing difficulties between Texas & Mexico are settled.

Thursday, 15th. This the national feast day of Mexico and we are not at work.

Friday 16th. At work on the road between Tackabayou and the City of Mexico filling up the mud holes &c.

Sat 17th. [John] Owens died after a very short illness of about 48 hours, At work as yesterday. Santa Anna is expected to return from the City. We are formed and wait some time after 5 oclock for him to pass without seeing him. We then marched to our quarters. We allso heard again we were to be liberated very shortly.

Sunday 18th. In prison. We receive letters from Perote. We are told by the commandant that the reason we have not been released was because the Texians have been doing a good deal of mischief about Santafee. I have hopes this may be true.

On this day, prisoner Barkley wrote:

> Castle of Perote June 18, 1843
>
> My friends:
> I can at last give you a true list of our case- The long looked for 15th of June has passed, no liberty. It is hard but what I really expected, yet the greater part is very much disappointed. Our friend Gen. Thompson has binn disappointed also. On last evening we received a letter from Gen. Tho[mp]son. He says plainly there is no chance for us any time soon- I shall resort to the project that I last spoke of in a letter of the 8 May. I sent it by Phelps—We are all well; far better than could be hoped for in such a climate.

And sometime later:

> [Our] chan[c]es were then examined again riveted and ourselves [examined] with as mutch contempt as they possably could contrive or invent a way to show their authority. This somewhat surprised me as on looking around what did I see—a company of soldiers skulked in a corner house with loaded guns and a can [on] … another company in the like manner with muskets on sight ready to fire on a parsel of us. Armed men from the [tops] of the surrounding houses not … to face a free but timid men that shrink from it near at hand sitting with … prisoner … I would say that we are to see [hard times] When we shall guet out of this snap God only knows. My only hope is an exchange of prisoners … things grows daily more gloomy … they treat us worse every day. They have us in their charge [when things] takes

> place to their disadvantage they contrive in some way to punish us that is as inicent as a child unburned ... To illustrate if the Governor or mayor of this place guets mad at anybody they reak their vengance on us, a pore helpless set of convecks as they call us. They say we are not prisoners of war.[95]

Monday 19th. Robert Smith died. 22 men came from the Hospital. At work again at the old place near the Presidents Palace breaking up the work which we have done several times over already and a part of us packing rock & stone from the bayou a half mile distant.

Tuesday 20th. At work as yesterday. Heavy rain ½ past 4 oclock. All hands very wet. Received information again that we will be liberated shortly.

Wednesday 21st. Misty and light rain in the morning. Go to work at 10 oclock. Major Murray came from the Hospital. Morris allso.

Thursday 22nd. We have a new guard. At work as usual.

Friday 23rd. Another new guard. At work as yesterday. Nothing else important.

Sat 24th. At work as usual. Nothing of importance. The guard continues to be changed daily.

Sun 25th. In prison to day. Visited by two foreigners who furnished us with some papers Spanish & American. We see that Santa Anna has again declared that no prisoners will be taken in their war with Texas in consequence of the late expedition against Sana Fee & Moore in the gulph. Dr Mcmath addressed a letter to Santa Anna on the subject of our rations.

Monday 26th. At work as usual. Nothing important.

Tuesday 27th. Nothing important in the way of news. Colville died of damp cholic with the chains on him.

Wednesday 28th. Colville was buried at the expense of the B[ritish] Consul. Reports say that Yucatan has come to terms and Com Moore is likely allso to be taken.

Thursday 29th. This is a feast day. No work.

Friday 30th. At work. Nothing important.

Sat 1st July. Nothing important.

Sunday 2. Was visited by a number of foreigners who gave us twelve dollars.

Monday 3rd. At work as usual. Addressed a letter to Santa Anna requesting the priviledge of celebrating the anniversary of the Independence of the U.S. which priviledge is granted.

July 4th. We remained in our prison and celebrated the anniversary U S of America. Resolutions & toasts were regularly drawn up suitable to the occasion. The Star Spangled Banner was sung and a spirited address was given by Judge Gibson. The Mexican officers of the guard were invited to attend and some of them became highly insulted by Judge Gibsons remarks and gestures which they partly understood. The Americans in the City have a grand celebration commencing late in the evening and two of them try to get permission for some of our officers to join them but without success.

Wednesday 5th. Visited by W[addy] Thompson US M[inster]. He informs us that Sam Houston has published his proclamation recalling all the Texian forces, for a cessation of arms.[96] *At work as usual.*

Thursday 6th. Nothing important.

Friday 7th. Nothing important. At work as usual. The British Minister sends us word that we may expect to be released in the present month. Our commander is allso changed and some hopes of better living for the future. 57 men return from the Hospital. The men generally speaking are in high spirits.

Sat 8th. Nothing important more than the confirmation of yesterdays report that Santa Ana has agreed to the armistice and great hopes are entertained of our release in a short time. John Hill a boy of sixteen set at liberty by Santa Anna.[97]

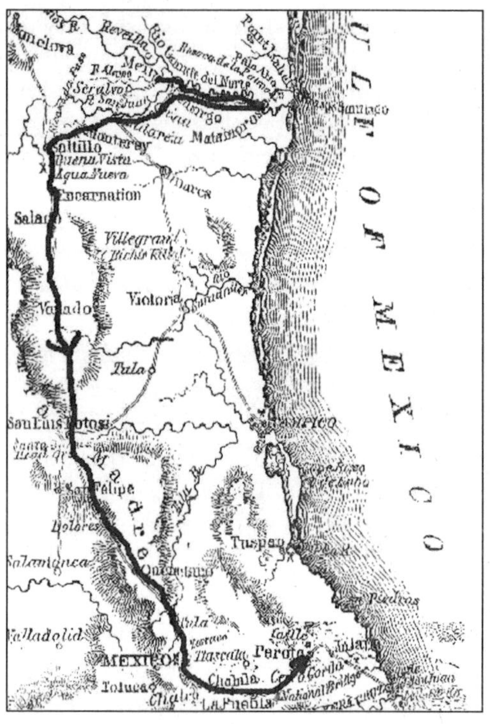

Route of the Somervell/Mier Expedition prisoners. (James Worsham collection)

Sunday 9th. Some change in our rations. Great parade & new arrangements made for conducting the work on the street of Tacubayou. All the interpreters and officers are unchained and appointed to different squads are held responsible for the labours of the others, and if they do their duty and make the men work themselves, they are to be put to work themselves. To day we are visited by several foreigners. No other important information.

Monday 10th. Instead of packing ourselves we have booros [burros] furnished us. The criminal overseers are not allowed to whip the men and we do a great deal more work than usual.

Tuesday 11th. Every thing goes on pretty smoothly. The men are in better health from a change in diet but are still dissatisfied as the quantity is insufficient to satisfy the cravings of hunger.

Wednesday 12th. Every thing went on pretty much as yesterday. We are informed that Santa Anna says he will release us as soon as we finish a certain piece of road which is now 300 yards long, We have little confidence in this assurance or we would finish it in a very short time.

Thursday 13th. At work as yesterday. Nothing else important.

Friday 14th. We learn by report that 4 of the 16 prisoners that made their escape from Perote Castle was retaken and shot on the coast.

Sat 15th. Every thing went on pretty much as yesterday. We learn that the Texians have actually arrived in Santa fee and sixteen hundred government troops have been sent to meet them. Nothing else important.

Sun 16th. For the first time I am permitted to have my irons taken off in consequence of the interposition of Judge Gibson who assured the Colonel that I was a good hand to work. The report of the four prisoners who were lately retaken being shot is contradicted. Judge Gibson [William] Ryon & Wm Moore have leave to go to the City to day. They conversed with W. Thompson and learned that the rumor was actually cited that Sam Houston denounced us.

McCutchan was of the same opinion. Upon hearing the rumor, he stated:

> We have been disowned by our government it is said! Can this be true? What? Disowned and thrown upon the mercy of our enemies—a mercy that would or will, result in the death of all who are in the power of Santa Anna. For he is a man to whose bosom the sentiment of mercy is an entire stranger; in whose heart justice can never dwell.[98]

In a letter dated January 24, 1843, Sam Houston wrote to Capt. Charles Elliot, British chargé d'affaires to Texas, he stated, in part, "It is true the men went without orders; and so far as that was concerned, the Government of Texas was not responsible; and the men thereby placed themselves out of the protection of the rules of war. This is granted." Houston went on to state, "But the Mexican officers, by proposing terms of capitulation to the men, relieved them from the responsibility which they had incurred; and the moment that the men had surrendered in accordance with the proposals of capitulation, they became prisoners of war, and were entitled to all immunities as such."[99] However, the media and political enemies of Houston seized upon the first portion, claiming Houston insinuated the prisoners were "Banditi," thus the opinion of Walker and his fellow prisoners was formed. There was truth to this insinuation.

Mr. Elliot, on seeing in the opposition papers the charge against the president that he had endeavored to produce a prejudice against the prisoners in the eyes of Santa Anna, wrote him as follows:

> I forwarded to Mr. Pakenham, in a private letter, what you said to me on the subject. In my understanding, your position was, that these prisoners were entitled to the benefit of their capitulation, though you could not, of course, deny that the movement across the Rio Grande had been made on their own responsibility; and I concluded your purpose in saying this was, to free yourself from the imputation of using the language of aversion to an irregular and incursionary character of warfare in your communications to foreign governments, and of sanctioning it in your orders to the officers of the republic.[100]

It is clear that Eliott recognized Houston's statement for what it was—a clumsy attempt to deflect accusations that he, in fact, had not authorized an incursion of

Mexican territory when that portion of his orders to General Somervell—relative to the recruiting of troops for the expedition specifically stated not to recruit any soldier unwilling to cross the Rio Grande—sanctioned it. Walker would later personally confront Houston on this matter after he escaped and returned to Texas.

Monday 17th. At work as usual. Nothing of importance.

Tuesday 18. As yesterday at work.

Wednesday 19th. James S. White is put in double irons because he not go out to work in consequence of his being severly affected with the rheumatic pains. He is allso put in close & solitary confinement in a damp and filthy room. A. Hill allso received.

Thursday 20th. At work as usual. Nothing else important.

Friday 21st. Pretty much as yesterday.

Saturday 22nd. Nothing important.

Sunday 23rd. In prison. A number of men are unchained and we learn that all of them are to be unchained between now and next Wednesday. Wm Beard died this morning at 6 oclock. His brother died at San Louis Potosi. They were both brave soldiers unassuming in their manners and much beloved by their comrades.

Monday 24th. At work. Nothing of particular importance.

Tuesday 25th. Nothing important.

Wednesday 26th. At work. Nothing important.

Thursday 27. Carter Seargent died at the Hospital. Nothing else important.

Friday 28th. At work on the street as yesterday. Nothing important.

Sat 29th. At work as usual.

Sunday 30th. Nothing very important except W. Copeland having made his escape from prison last night is not yet discovered by the Mexicans, and having contemplated doing the same thing myself as soon as I received money sufficient myself and friend Jas C Willson and James Mcgattis [D. H. Gattis] came to the conclusion that if we deferred it any longer untill they discovered Copeland had made his escape which they certainly would do the next morning, our chance for the future would be very small as we all expected to be rechained on Monday morning and not allowed to step out of doors after sunset. With these considerations we determined on trying to make our escape. Willson and myself on this evening had the pleasure of a walk in the park of the military academy which is about two leagues from the City and is closely connected to our prison yard.

One of the greatest curiosities we saw was the secret passage which it is said Montazuma had to the City. However the most interesting part of our walk to me was to ascertain the walls for the purpose of getting out. We passed the sentinels at the doors early in the night and scaled the walls about 8 oclock splitting our blankets and tieing them together for the purpose of letting ourselves down with. We passed through the City. About 11 oclock we [Walker, Wilson, and Gattis] climbed over the two gates on the Warloupa [Guadalupe] road and walked very brisk. When we arrived at the village of Warloupa we found a soldier on post at the gate. We turned to the right side. Proceeded inside the ditch about one mile or less but finding our crossing place we were compelled to swim it. At day break we left the road. On the morning of 31st July we stowed ourselves away under a bunch of bushes to spend the day in secret repose, but we were much disappointed as we happened to be in a place where all the shepherd boys of the Town came along and we were near being discovered several times. At length we determined to move our position so we started across the mountain. When nearly sunset we were discovered by two Mexicans who were gathering Augh meal [auguamiel] from the megay [mauguay]. They enquired our business &c and then told us to go with them to the Town and shew our Passports. This we objected to but they insisted and we could only get clear of them by giving them one dollar which was all we had and promised them 25 more. They agreed and not to say any thing about us, but we thought it best to lay close untill night. We then commenced our march and crossed the mountain close by fearing the road in the pass might be guarded. We marched about six leagues, and halted at day break near a small Town.

August 1st. We lay close all day in the best hiding place we could find but we were a little surprised about sunset when four Mexicans with sharp sticks [bayonets] as the Texian called them and marched us off to Town to see the Alcalde. He asked us for our passports, which we could not produce. He told us he would send us back to Mexico to see the Prefect. We told him we would like to have some supper. He referred us to the Fonda. We told him we had no money. Upon close examination however we found we had one Picayune [a small denomination coin] left, which we all supped on. We were then taken up Town and shut up in an old gaol which was allso used as a school house. They locked us up and contrary to our expectations they left no sentinel at the door. We laid down about one hour untill every thing got still. We then to be assured there was no one about raped several times at the door and called for water. No person answered. I then began to try and pick the lock with a pair of old scissors but could not succeed. I then began to examine the hinges of the door which was of the old stile though very substantial though. I thought by the aide of the leavers we had used which were used for bushes I could succeed in making an opening large enough to get out of it and I continued operations and in one hour we succeeded in getting out. We marched rapidly untill day break Wednesday morning and hid ourselves on the top of a hill close to a small Town and remained untill night not undiscovered as the shepherd boys were all around us and one of them discovered us but we soon moved our position where we remained untill night and took the road and after traveling some three or four leagues we found out we were in the elongated vally. We climbed the mountains and at day break Thursday we halted and hid in the bushes on the side of a mountain and remained till night. We then took the trail which led us to a small hut where we inquired the road. In about an hour after this we met two mexicans who appeared to be much alarmed crying out to know what nation we were but would not come near enough receive an answer. We continued our march on the road. In about 3/4 of an hour they returned and demanded us to halt but would not come nearer than long rifle shot distance. They wanted us to go back to the Town. This we objected to telling them we had our passports which we supposed would be good, that we worked in the mines at Mineral Del Monte, that we were already two days behind our time and as for going back we could think of it. Willson pulled out an old song ballad of when shall we three meet again and endevoured to get them to look at it but could not get near enough to shew it to them. They agreed however to go with us to the next ranch where they could a light and examine it. He told them it made no material difference about a light as he could interpret it to them by moon light as it [was] written in English. They proceeded on however untill we came to a ranch. We all steped in with the boldness and self importance of Englishmen, and our companion J. C. Willson took out his song ballad again and told them what it was a passport written in English for all three of us. The told him to translate it. He commenced and translated a pretty good passport out of the song ballad. They said it was bueno and then apologized for detaining us stating that they thought we were bad men. We told them that we did not blame them atall that their regulations were essentially necessary and they had only done their duty. We proceeded on laughing very hearty at the hoax we had played on them. At day break Friday 5th. We were close to Mineral delmonte but could not get in before day light. As our friend J. C. Willson had become so weak from debility of constitution and starvation since we left he could not walk a half a mile without lying down to rest, so we started up the mountain to lay by during the day. We saw several shepherds in the course of the day and they all wanted to know what we were doing there. We told them that we were mineralogists, and were hunting small specimens of ore &c for the English mining company. That appeared perfectly satisfactory. In the course of the day we satisfied ourselves of the position of the Town and succeeded in getting in about 8 oclock at night. Here we found friends who had done considerable for us.

Sat 6th. Remained at Mineral del Norte untill 7 oclock at night and took up the line of march for tampico leaving our friend Willson behind too unwell to travel. We marched through a town called grandee laid down near the road and slept till day light Sunday 6th and renewed our march. Passed through Zaquatapan [Zacualtapan] 13 leagues. Slept by the road side untill Monday morning 7th. We are in a hilly though a very beautiful country covered with timber of various descriptions. The little valleys all thickly settled and hillsides steep that a man might break his neck by a misstep covered with fine crops of corn. We marched 13 leagues and slept near Potipcan. Awaked near day Tuesday 8th by a heavy rain and resumed our march through mud and mire, Marched about 12 leagues and camped in an Indian village 3 leagues from Pesca.

Tuesday 9th Marched 13 leagues to a small Town called Tontiuca [Tantoyuca] and slept for the night. Here we were required to shew our passports which were pronounced good.

Thursday 10th. Marched 18 leagues to Oslewauma [Ozuluama] and slept near the road side,

Friday 11th. Marched 12 leagues and slept at a house.

Sat 12. Marched 6 leagues to Tampico old Town and from thence to Tampico water in a canoe and after walking round for some time we found the US Consul and took lodgings at the house of a Frenchman.

Sunday 13th. Remained at the house of the Frenchman indoors. At night we were visited by Mr C. [Franklin E. Chase] US [Consul at Tampico] and afterwards introduced to Mr W. and went to his house and took lodgings where we remained untill 4 oclock Monday 14th and started up the river with Mr. L. [Lynch] to await the departure of a vessel. Here we remained untill Sept 2nd to work some to pay our board and pass off the time more agreeable,

Sept 3rd. I embarked on board of the schooner Richard St Johns Capt Everson master. My friend Gattis embarked on board of the schooner Brassos bound for New York. I soon found another comrade on the Richard St Johns. Dalrimple [John Dalrymple] one of the Perote prisoners who had made his escape about the last of June. He shipped as cook and I shipped as Seaman. Our vessel being a good sailer and easily managed we arrived at the Balise and crossed the bar on the 9th against head winds nearly all the way. At a little past sunset we were taken in tow by the Texian Steamer Sarah Barnes from Galveston.

Walker was gone from prison but not forgotten.

To Samuel H. Walker
Care of Genl Sidney S. [*sic*] Johnston

Washington, Bexar
Texas
Courtesy of Mr. B. Hill
Castle of Perote Mexico Octr 18, 1843.

Dear Friend.
After your exit from Tucabaya I was closely questioned about my red headed companion or the man that was chained to me. I told them that I had seen the ascension of a Baloon on that night and that I believed that you were in it bound (for) Texas, my story was believed as they think there is nothing impossible to a Texan. I think they made much search for you. Dougherty made his escape a few days after you and we lurnt that he was safe. We left Mexico (City) on the 12th September and arrived here on the 22d. We passed through Puebla one of the finest cities in the Republic.

What is the Texas doing that they don't get us out of this scrape. Does our Congressmen take up all their time passing laws regulating roads & canals or custom house duties. What that they cannot give one moment's thought or kind look towards their suffering countrymen in the castle of Perote. Now is the time for the Texans to take down that Rio Grande country. Take & snatch to let them make prisoners of, the A the priests, the Alacaldos, the rich Rancheros and I will be bound that an exchange. 200 Texans with stout hearts and strong arms can effect this with very little expense. Their is at present no troops on that frontier. I understand that they have all been called to Vera Cruz either on their way to Campechy, or expecting the English. Doyle the English minister has had a Rupture with cork leg. It was something about an old English Lack that was taken from us at Mier. We had taken it from the cronkaway Indians on the Rio Grand, this .... George Jack was displayed in a military ball room in Mexico and so the fuss began. Santa Anna passed here a few days ago with several thousand troops. He is now at Japala. What his intentions are no one knows. He is as dark as midnight.

We are all here now with the exception of 22 we left in Mexico sick. We have understood since we left Mexico tat Willis & Irvine have died. Capt Pierson was at the point of death, but is probably dead before this. We buried van horn to day and there is several others laying very sick. The climate here does not seem to agree with us as it is very cold summer & winter. All our hopes about liberation has fled. It seems Texas will do nothing for us. If I had a pair of wings I would fly off. it is I am bound to wait for Pokeotiempo. This is perhaps one of the strangest fortifications in the world. It contains 26 acres of ground and will quarter so said 20,000 troops. Altho badly treated the boys are often in good spirits and it really amusing to see some of them in their present Guarb strutting about with their rags and a smile on their countenance, barefooted. Bareheaded and nearly naked does not seem to quell their spirits. Whenever they can go to the Sienda it is laughable to see them drink toasts to the one star Republic. You would think that they were in Bishops coffee house. We are fed as usual. Pan basso carne de Tauris and I will assure you that I am really tired of it. I have not the heart burn continually from such fare and to cap the climax we have all turned religious. We have hyme singing in our prison every night. Brother W sings the Texas hyme and we are Join in chorus. This is the way we spend our evenings. Our days are spent in a game of chuchaluck or talking over camp news. We often fight the battle of Mier over & over again. Old Col. W. is still here cherishing the same kind feelings for the whole Mexican nation that he did when you left. Doct Shepherd, Judge Gibson, Col. Fisher Ryan are all in good spirits (the vain old Rickety Major M we left in Mexico muncho malo with the Hystericks alias muncho muscal. I am thinking that he is a gone case. That epistle that you & myself wrote for him to Petersburg VA have you seen it published O God. What licks) Whenever you find yourself … at the Tremont I wish that you would … leg of a Turkey for me or a small piece of … and I shall duly appreciate the kind … I want you also inhale a small quantity of the air of Liberty for me as I have almost forgot the sweets of it. Do not take so much of your time with the Ladies. Spare a little of it for my benefit. I want some good news from Texas as we have had a sufficiency of bad (McMullin and Lusk are in good health and we all long to see you. Gov Ball of Florida wrote you a letter which McMullin opened that authorizes … To draw on Gen Thompson for $100. M has wrote you on the subject. Write me on Receipt of this. My kind regards to the … McLane … & all friends) It is now 11 o clock and this black heathen at the door hollowing sentinel alert & quin viva. So I will close this epistle for I am out of sorts. With that fellow.

Your Friend Truly
P. M. Maxwell

Direct your letters care of T.M. Diamond Vera Cruz.
Brother Jeff has obtained his liberty and is about to leave a blue streak behind him for Texas.

James C. Wilson provided his account of the escape, which was published in the November 18, 1843, issue of the *Northern Standard*:

ESCAPE FROM THE PRISON OF TACUBAYA

The following is the narrative by Capt. Wilson one of the Texan prisoners, detailing the escape of himself and two others from one of the Mexican dungeons in which they were incarcerated: We effected our escape from the prison of Tacubaya, near the residence of Santa Anna, on the night of the 30th July. It was attended, with considerable difficulty, as we had to climb over the wall in view of two sentinels, and the night was by no means so dark as we could have wished it. We let ourselves down by means of our blankets, which were torn in strips and twisted into the form of a rope.

We had to keep very much on the alert in passing through the city of Mexico in order to avoid the sentinels who are posted in front or the numerous quartels in every part of the city. By morning we had got six leagues from Mexico, and as it was unsafe to travel in the day. we left the road, and, secreted ourselves in the mountain, passed the day in alternate repose and watching—two of us sleeping while one kept watch. About sunset we were discovered by two Mexicans, who happened to visit that part of the mountain for the purpose of gathering the juice of a plant called the mauguay, from which a kind of fermented liquor, called pulkey, is made. They attempted to take us to a village at about the distance of a league; but by giving them to understand that we were determined to resist, and that, if it were necessary, we would kill them rather than be taken, and giving them what money we had, amounting to little over a dollar, we persuaded them to allow us to proceed. That night we made a march of about ten leagues, and spent the next day as we had done the previous one: but, notwithstanding our vigilance, we did not escape observation, and we were preparing to resume our journey, six men, well armed with lances, surrounded the little thicket where we were concealed, and,

> pointing their lances at our breasts, ordered us to get up and accompany them. Resistance would have been worse than vain, so we were taken before the Alcalde, who committed us to prison, with the pleasing information we should be sent to Mexico next morning. But we could not wait so long. Finding that they placed no guard on the prison door, we set to work, and digging up the pavement near the door we succeeded in getting out a kind of metal cup, in which the lower hinge of the door turned, and with a plank and a piece of oak that we found in the prison, we forced the door from its post sufficiently wide to allow a man to pass out, and in less than an hour and a half after our confinement we were again upon the road. That night I suffered severely, as I was very unwell; in fact, I had a severe attack of pleurisy when I left Mexico, and by this time I bad become so weak that it was with the utmost difficulty I could get along.
>
> For a day and night, we met with no person who was disposed to molest us, but on the second night after our escape from the village prison we were again arrested by a party of mounted rancheros, who tried to take us back to a town about three leagues distant. This we flatly refused, and they accompanied us to a rancho which lay on the side of the road we were going. I told the fellow who seemed to have the command of the party, that I had a passport, and forthwith produced a half a sheet of paper, upon which one of my fellow prisoners had written some ballad song. Of course, it was written in English, and the man could not read it, but ordered me to translate it. I pretended to read from the paper something purporting to be a translation of my passport, and the fellow, thinking it was all right, suffered us to depart in peace.
>
> We had left the prison without any other provisions than five small, coarse biscuits, which we ate during the first day, and by the remaining time (five days and nights) we had no other sustenance than a few prickly pears which we found in the mountains. By the time we reached Real del Monte my illness had increased to such a degree that I could not go one hundred yards without lying down. My own respirations sounded in my ears so that I could not hear anything else, and had it not been for the kindness I experienced from the English residents there, and the skillful treatment of an excellent physician, I must have died, as it was, I was not in a situation to travel for six weeks, during which time I experienced the most unremitting care and kindness from my generous entertainers. Here I obtained a passport, a good horse, and sufficient money to defray my expenses to the coast.

Several weeks after his return to Texas, Walker saw Sam Houston on a street in the city that bore his name. Walker confronted Houston and, according to an exchange recorded in Joseph Milton Nance's *Dare-Devils All*, charged him with being responsible for the decimation of the Mier men because of statements to Elliot (British chargé d'affaires at Galveston). Houston denied making such statements and asked Walker for the source of his charge. When told that Waddy Thompson had revealed the news, Houston requested that "the charges be put in writing." Walker wasted no time.

> Galveston, Octr 28th 1843
> To His Excellency President Sam Houston
>
> Respected Sir—in compliance with your request I take this occasion to state to you the substance of Gen Waddie Thompsons conversation with Capt Ryon and Judge Gibson, in relation to the letter of Capt Elliot to the British Minister at Mexico, which letter was said to have been written circumstances he could not interpose in our behalf. Gen Thompson then informed the British Minister that all such

statements were false, and he was prepared to prove them so, at the same time requested him to send the letter containing the information. Mr Doyle then replied to Gen Thompson that there was a letter containing the information in his possession addressed to his predecessor Mr Packenham but he was not authorized to expose the contents of it. Gen Thompson without delay addressed him again on the subject, and demanded of him as a duty which he owed to the cause of humanity if nothing else the expose of the letter containing such information and also his interposition on our behalf. *Gen Thompson also produced your proclamation authorizing volunteers to cross the Riogrande and retaliate on the enemy* [emphasis by the author]. He was also in possession of the fact that you required a pledge from young men in Houston that they would cross the Riogrande, before you would let them have arms. With these proofs of our being under the authority and sanction of our executive the B Minister consented to use his influence in our behalf and informed Gen Thompson that the letter in question was written by your instructions to Capt Elliot B. Chargey to Texas to Mr. Packenham B Minister to Mexico instructing him to say to Santa Anna that we "had entered the Mexican Territory without your authority and contrary to your wishes, but notwithstanding you desired it as a personal favour of Santa Anna that he should treat us with leniency." There, sir, were the statements of Gen Thompson related to my me by Judge Gibson and Capt Rion, and to convince them more fully of the facts he shewed them all the correspondence on the subject between him and the British Minister. These statements were corroborated by many reports in Mexico which was a source of mortification to our feelings, and from the high office and respectability of Gen Thompson are believed to be true by many of my unfortunate comrades and others. As your Excellency denied the truth of these statements and accused Gen Thompson of falsehood in our conversation the other day the issue of truth or falsehood is between you. Each will have his believers. I would greatly prefer to believe with your Excellency that such reports are without foundation in Truth, because you must admit that if true the Mier prisoners would not have much cause to love you as a private or support you and a political man. If they are untrue Gen Thompson would justly sink in the estimation of every honest man and prove to the world that high and honorable office will not prevent men from lieing. As one of the prisoners who suffered from the report, whether true or false, I wish only to be satisfied myself but to satisfy all who doubt. Will your Excellency have the kindness to introduce me to Capt Elliot that I may hear his denial in your presence of any authority from you to make the statements said to be contained in his dispatch to Mr Packenham referred to by Gen Thompson, the substance of which is stated above. Allso his denial that your Excellency had ever used in the presence of Capt Elliot such expressions relative to the Mier prisoners as would make Capt. Elliot deem it his duty and proper to inform Mr Packenham and through him Santa Anna that the Mier prisoners had crossed the Riogrande without the authority of the Government of Texas &c. I trust your Excellency in justice to yourself and to gratify me as well as my fellow prisoners will comply with my request. I shall be at all times ready to accompany you and as Capt Elliot is in Town I hope your Excellency will at your earliest leisure procure me the opportunity of having an introduction to Capt Elliot by yourself in person. I remain

Sam Houston. (James Worsham collection)

Yours respectfully,
SH Walker[101]

In support of Walker's claim that the Texas volunteers were acting under the authorization given by President Houston, the following excerpt from the orders he gave to General Somervell on October 3, 1842, is presented: *You will receive no troops into your command but such as will march across the Rio Grande under your orders if required by you so to do [emphasis added by the author].*[102] The same phrasing was used in Special Orders Number 52 dated October 13, 1842, given to Somervell by Morgan C. Hamilton, Acting Secretary of War and Marine.[103] (Full text in Appendix III.)

Houston did not respond to Walker's letter. When he later met Walker, he extended his hand. Walker ignored Houston's proffered hand. Houston called out to him, "I am very sorry you are indisposed, Mr. Walker."[104]

His fellow prisoner Tom Green, having heard of his exchange with Houston, asked for a copy of the letter sent to the president. Walker was quick to respond.

Nov 9th 1843
To Gen Thomas P Green

Sir—Your note of yesterday was handed to me requesting a copy of my letter to Prest Houston and his answer concerning the Mier Prisoners and feeling all the [illegible] the whole truth of that bloody tragedy and the cause which [illegible] should be known, [illegible] in furnishing you with a copy of said letter which was written at his request to me to state in writing what Gen Thompson said relative to him or rather second hand communication to Santa Anna

Walker to Green re. Sam Houston letter. (Southern Historical Collection. University of North Carolina, Chapel Hill, North Carolina)

> & on perusing my letter you will perceive my statements of Gen Thompson some conversation was accompanied with a request &c and Gen Houston's only reply was that he would not be justified in calling for a private correspondence as it would be an insult to her B.M. Minister.
>
> I remain with respect your friend and fellow soldier.
> SH Walker

With the dispatch of the copy of his October 28, 1843, letter to Green, Walker apparently let the matter drop; however, Green took up the attack on Houston with letters to newspapers and persons intimately involved in bringing Houston's abandonment of the Mier prisoners. See Appendix III.

Survivors of the Mier Expedition pose for a group photograph at a reunion. Standing (left to right): Unknown, Big Foot Wallace, Unknown, James C. Armstrong. Seated (left to right): Caleb Sinclair, Unknown, William Kinchen Davis, Unknown, Creed Taylor, Richard Brown. (Courtesy of Fort Bend Museum)

Walker's Mier Pension

On December 26, 1845, Sam Walker applied for a pension from the Republic of Texas for his Mier imprisonment. His friend Texas Ranger Maj. John C. Hays served as his attorney. He applied for "all such sums of money appropriated by an Act of Congress of said Republic passed … for the relief of the Texian Prisoners in Mexico, the proportional part of said appropriation due me."

Interestingly, there are two documents, both signed by Walker. Apparently, he did not read the first as it described him as a prisoner at the Castle of Perote. The second document has this same phrase but there is a line through it, plus it is "X"ed out. For some reason even during his lifetime—even before he was stationed at Perote during the Mexican–American War—his imprisonment in Mexico had associated him with the Castle of Perote.

William Kinchen Davis poses in chains at the reunion to symbolize the treatment he and his fellow prisoners suffered at the hands of the Mexican Army. (Courtesy of Fort Bend Museum)

In the second corrected document Walker dictated, that he was "conveyed as far as Tucobayo in said Govt [Mexico] at which place … [he made his] escape." He further stated he returned home to the Texas Republic and was not paid for his time in prison, although the Texas Legislature authorized $15,000 for the relief of the Mier prisoners on February 5, 1844.[105]

CHAPTER 5

The Rangers of Texas

Samuel Hamilton Walker's name will always be associated with the Texas Rangers. While the new Texas Republic started many new traditions, the Texas Rangers was a continuation of a defense organization that had been around for a long time. The unique heritage of Rangers in America began a century before America declared its independence. This tradition continued through the Texas Rangers.

The First Rangers in Anglo America[1]

Rangers were first organized in the late 1600s[2] along the colonial Maryland frontier. One of their most well-known commanders was Col. Ninian Beall who had a chance meeting with Sam's ancestor Charles Walker Sr. in the late 1690s.[3]

Based on the English Muster Law of 1572, in which citizen-soldiers were formed to be called on in emergencies, Rangers served a most important need with the continuous Native American threat.[4]

Armed and mounted at their own expense—but paid a salary by the colony—these border sentinels continually patrolled—on horseback—the fringe areas of white civilization, constantly vigilant for hostile natives. They were the early warning system for Native American raids. If such a threat was discovered in time, the Rangers would have an opportunity for a preemptive strike on the raiders. If the knowledge of the Native American raid was after the fact, the Rangers were prepared to carry the war back to the enemy with a determined hunt of the raiders or a retaliation raid on the natives' own settlement.

Col. Ninian Beall. (The *Georgetown Metropolitan*)

Small patrols of Rangers were first organized as early as 1676 in Sam Walker's home state of Maryland and in 1682 in Virginia. In 1716, the Carolinas formed Ranger companies, and as late as 1739, Georgia began the Ranger system.[5]

George Catlin. Comanche Feats of Horsemanship, 1834–35. (Smithsonian American Art Museum, gift of Mrs. Joseph Harrison, Jr., 1985.66.487)

Rogers's Rangers and Other Ranger Units in the Colonies

Robert Rogers. (Courtesy of Gary Zaboly)

The most famous of the colonial Rangers, however, came from the northern colonies, with the French and Indian War serving as the impetus for the legendary Rogers's Rangers. Organized by Robert Rogers of New Hampshire in 1756, these Rangers admirably served the British Army in America as both scouts and raiders.

Traveling by whaleboat on the Lakes George and Champlain, then on foot through the dense New England wilderness, these fighting men were resourceful, effective, and determined.[6] Wearing green duffel hunting shirts and Scotch Balmoral Bonnets, others wearing buckskin hunting shirts and leggings, they were described by clergyman as "a body of irregulars, who have a … cutthroat, savage appearance."[7]

Many of Robert Rogers's "Rules for Ranging" service of the 18th century can be easily compared to the unconventional tactics used by 19th-century Texians.

While Rogers's Rangers were very effective in what they did, there was one drawback in the use of frontier backwoodsmen. Just as with the early Texas Rangers, these extremely independent men could become unruly and hard to control. Rogers seemed to be the one man who could control his Rangers as Hays later did with his.[8]

While Rogers is the most famous of the early Rangers, he was not the first in the history of Colonial America. That distinction belongs to Benjamin Church.

Benjamin Church (*ca.* 1639–January 17, 1718) was the captain of the first Ranger force in America. In 1676, Church was commissioned by Josiah Winslow, the Governor of the Plymouth Colony, to form the first Ranger company for King Philip's War. He later commanded the company to raid Acadia during King William's and Queen Anne's wars in the early 1700s.

Church designed his forces to emulate Native American practices of warfare. Toward this end, he worked to adopt Native American techniques of small, flexible forces that used the woods and ground for cover, rather than mounting frontal attacks

Harrison Bird, "Rogers's Rangers." (MUIA plate 97, *Military Collector & Historian*, 7, no. 1 [Spring 1955]: 19–20. Courtesy of the Company of Military Historians)

in military formation. Church developed a special full-time unit that combined European colonists—selected for their frontier skills—with friendly natives, in order to carry out offensive strikes against hostiles and French in difficult terrain. His memoirs, *Entertaining Passages relating to Philip's War*, were published in 1716 and are considered to constitute the first American military manual.

John Lovewell (1691–1725) of Nashua, New Hampshire, became the most famous Ranger of the early 18th century. He led three expeditions against the Abenaki, the last being known as "Lovewell's Fight," in which he was killed. Lovewell's Fight marked the end of hostilities between the English and the Abenakis of Maine. This conflict was a turning point. So important was the battle to western Maine, New Hampshire, and even Massachusetts colonists, it has been celebrated in song and story, and its importance was not eclipsed until the American Revolution. More than one hundred years later Henry Wadsworth Longfellow (poem, "The Battle of Lovells Pond"), Nathaniel Hawthorne (story, "Roger Malvin's Burial") and Henry David Thoreau all wrote about Lovewell's Fight.

Virginia raised units of Rangers during the French and Indian War, 1755–63.

> A sum of money not to exceed two thousand pounds, to be laid out for and in the raising and maintaining three companies of men, consisting of fifty men each, with their officers, to be

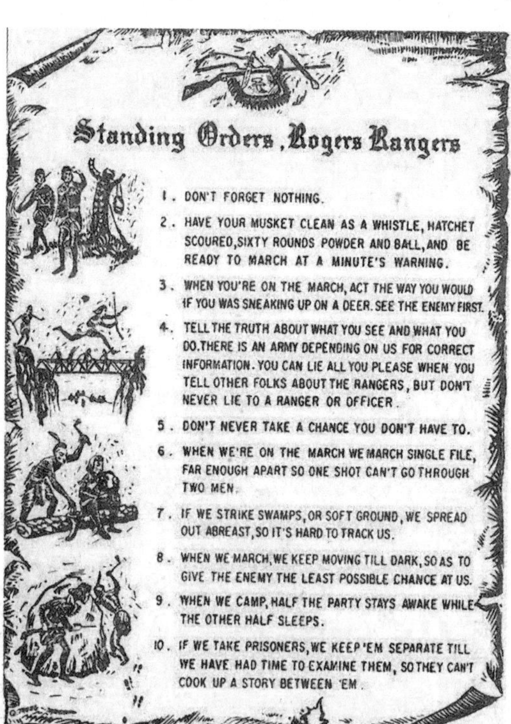

Standing Orders, Rogers Rangers

1. DON'T FORGET NOTHING.
2. HAVE YOUR MUSKET CLEAN AS A WHISTLE, HATCHET SCOURED, SIXTY ROUNDS POWDER AND BALL, AND BE READY TO MARCH AT A MINUTE'S WARNING.
3. WHEN YOU'RE ON THE MARCH, ACT THE WAY YOU WOULD IF YOU WAS SNEAKING UP ON A DEER. SEE THE ENEMY FIRST.
4. TELL THE TRUTH ABOUT WHAT YOU SEE AND WHAT YOU DO. THERE IS AN ARMY DEPENDING ON US FOR CORRECT INFORMATION. YOU CAN LIE ALL YOU PLEASE WHEN YOU TELL OTHER FOLKS ABOUT THE RANGERS, BUT DON'T NEVER LIE TO A RANGER OR OFFICER.
5. DON'T NEVER TAKE A CHANCE YOU DON'T HAVE TO.
6. WHEN WE'RE ON THE MARCH WE MARCH SINGLE FILE, FAR ENOUGH APART SO ONE SHOT CAN'T GO THROUGH TWO MEN.
7. IF WE STRIKE SWAMPS, OR SOFT GROUND, WE SPREAD OUT ABREAST, SO IT'S HARD TO TRACK US.
8. WHEN WE MARCH, WE KEEP MOVING TILL DARK, SO AS TO GIVE THE ENEMY THE LEAST POSSIBLE CHANCE AT US.
9. WHEN WE CAMP, HALF THE PARTY STAYS AWAKE WHILE THE OTHER HALF SLEEPS.
10. IF WE TAKE PRISONERS, WE KEEP 'EM SEPARATE TILL WE HAVE HAD TIME TO EXAMINE THEM, SO THEY CAN'T COOK UP A STORY BETWEEN 'EM.

Rangers' Standing Orders. (Print in the public domain)

Capt. Benjamin Church. (New York Public Library)

> employed as rangers, for the protection of the subjects in the frontiers of this colony, as the governor shall direct from time to time, and shall not be sent out of this colony, nor incorporated with the soldiers now in his majesty's service, or made subject to martial law.
>
> *Laws of Virginia, May 1755*

> WHEREAS it is judged necessary in this time of open war, that a number of forces should be raised and kept on foot, for vindicating the honor of his majesty's crown, and for the safety and defence of this dominion, amounting to fifteen hundred and seventy-two men, including three companies of rangers, to consist of one hundred men each.
>
> *Laws of Virginia, April 1757*

They did not fare well.

> February 18–March 13, 1756. After her return from captivity in November of 1755, Mary Ingles provided her husband, Capt. William Ingles, with intelligence about Shawnee villages along the Ohio. In December of 1755, Captain Ingles approached Governor Dinwiddie about conducting a raid against two of these villages near present day Portsmouth, Ohio. Maj. Andrew Lewis was designated to lead the expedition of approximately 200–300 men from the Virginia Regiment and Militia Rangers along with approximately 80–130 Cherokees. Captain Hogg was ordered to provide and lead forty men from his Company. A draft of sixty men from Capt. William Preston's and Capt. John Smith's Ranger Companies, to be commanded by Captain Smith was ordered to participate. Captain Overton and Capt. Obadiah Woodson were to provide forty men each and serve as company commanders. Captain Pearis commanded the Cherokees. Capt. Robert Breckinridge, was ordered to take his companies as well. Capts. Archibald Alexander, John Montgomery, and Dunlap commanded volunteer companies of indeterminate size. Capt. David Stuart served as commissary. Capt. William Ingles, the instigator if not, perhaps, the planner of the mission, joined the expedition as well. The main body of the expedition departed Fort Frederick (vicinity Salem, Virginia) on February 18, 1756. The expedition with the exception of Captain Hogg's men who were behind the main body, reached the north Fork of the Holston River by February 23. By February 26, the expedition was at the head of the Clinch River and at the head of Sandy Creek by the 28th which they followed towards the Ohio River until desertion and insubordination caused the expedition to turn around on 13 March.
>
> April 18, 1756. Capt. John Mercer and sixty men garrisoning Fort Edward were ambushed while in pursuit of hostile Indians near Fort Edward. Captain Mercer and fifty-four men were killed in the Battle of Great Cacapon.[9]

In colonial Pennsylvania, the idea of fighting at all was called into question. This colony had a Quaker pacifist-controlled legislature[10] during the French and Indian War, therefore the Rangers that were privately raised to defend the colony from Native American attack were paid privately and acted independently, and without government support as "volunteer militia." In 1755, five hundred Rangers were recruited. These frontier Rangers were to scout all the way west to the Ohio and north to Iroquois country.[11] The hardly pacifist British government later sent regular soldiers to Pennsylvania to help with the Native American problem. Only after the end of the war in 1763 did the Quakers lose power in the legislature.[12]

Gorham's Rangers, formed in 1744 as an auxiliary unit of the Massachusetts provincial army, was an amphibious strike force that patrolled the coasts, inlets, bays, and rivers of the Canadian Maritimes in modified whaleboats. Initially manned by Native Americans from southeastern Massachusetts and commanded by British colonial officers, by its final deployments in the early 1760s, Gorham's Rangers had become a unit of mostly Anglo-Americans and recent Scots and Irish immigrants who, nonetheless, continued to employ the tactics the unit's original Native American members had pioneered. For Native American members of the company the cost had been dear; combat fatalities, disease, debilitating wounds and injuries, and years of brutal captivity in French or indigenous communities in Canada were common fates.[13]

In the Revolutionary War against the British, American companies of Rifle Rangers were organized as early as 1775 in the Continental Army.[14] These frontiersmen

Frederick Ray, *Gorham's Rangers*. (MUIA plate 170, *Military Collector & Historian*, 12, no. 1 [Spring 1960]: 14–16. Courtesy of the Company of Military Historians)

with their long rifles were uncannily accurate at fantastically long range[15] and were dreaded by the British as the "much feared riflemen."[16]

On 15 September 1777, beating orders were issued to Maj. John Butler, authorizing him to enlist eight companies of Rangers; each to have a captain, a lieutenant, three sergeants, three corporals and fifty privates. Two of the companies were to be formed of "people speaking the Indian language and acquainted with their customs and manner of making war," the men to get four shillings (New York currency) a

Eric I. Manders, *Butler's Rangers, 1778–1784.* (MUIA plate 196, Military Collector & Historian, 12, no. 1 [Winter 1961]: 118. Courtesy of the Company of Military Historians)

day. The men of the remaining companies, "to be composed of people acquainted with the woods, in consideration of the fateague they are liable to undergo," were to receive two shillings a day. The Rangers were used principally for commando-like raids along the frontiers, concentrating on the grainfields of northern New York.

As a body or in detachments, they took part in almost all the major actions of the Hudson–Delaware–Susquehanna border. Parties from Fort Niagara kept the Pittsburgh–Wheeling sector active, while another detachment at Detroit operated on the Ohio as far south as Kentucky.[17]

The Third South Carolina Regiment (Rangers) 1775–80, was established by the South Carolina Provincial Congress in June 1775 as Mounted Riflemen who used horses for transportation but dismounted to fight on foot. It consisted of a lieutenant colonel commandant, a major, nine captains, 18 lieutenants, a surgeon, a paymaster, an adjutant, and a quartermaster, and with each of its nine companies having two sergeants, a drummer, and 50 privates. The regiment was placed on the Continental Establishment in September 1776 as Mounted Riflemen, and in October its complement increased to 600 men in 12 companies, with the commanding officer, the major, and the senior captain all being promoted one grade.

The regiment was recruited in the back country and on the frontiers, and normally served in multi-company detachments. When first raised, the men were to provide their own rifles, powder horns and shot pouches, tomahawks, horses, provisions, and forage, or to be so provided by the public with the cost taken from their pay. However, higher pay and a clothing allowance were soon authorized and their rations were to be furnished.[18]

After the first war with England, an independent America still had the Native American menace lingering on and Rangers were still needed as scouts for the army in the War of 1812 and afterwards on the Native American frontiers in both the Northwest[19] and the South.[20]

Darby Erd, *The Third South Carolina Regiment (Rangers) 1775–1780.* (MUIA plate 494, Military Collector & Historian, 32, no. 2 [Summer 1980]: 73. Courtesy of the Company of Military Historians)

The Mounted Ranger

The first Anglo colonial mounted Ranger had been replaced by Rangers who served on foot. In America's combat with the Native American east of the Mississippi River in the dense, mountainous wilderness of the eastern seaboard, the mounted soldier was of little significance. Against the Native American, the superior armed and organized American Army—without a permanent mounted force—had comparatively little trouble subduing the primitively armed and loosely organized, unmounted Native American east of the Mississippi River.

As the American frontier advanced westward, settlers and soldiers found a different terrain. Forest thinned and the ground was more level. And the opposition to settlement had adapted to warfare very successfully. In 1832, the army took action to form another mounted force. The Battalion of Mounted Rangers was organized and spread from Fort Gibson on the Arkansas River north to Michigan.[21] These Rangers still fought as infantry—the horses only gave them extra range. In March 1833, Congress finally created the 1st Regiment of Mounted Dragoons while disbanding the Rangers.[22] With a new uniform, a new weapon (the percussion carbine), and the determination to fight as real cavalry, this was America's first permanent cavalry arm for the army. Secretary of War, Joel Poinsett, then sent four company-grade officers to the internationally famous Calvary School of Saumur in France: William Eustis and Henry S. Turner, 1839–41; William Hardee and Lloyd J. Beall, 1840–42. They were sent to learn cavalry theory and to translate the French manual on cavalry tactics into English.[23]

As the frontier moved westward, however, the American military found the mounted Native American was to be a deadly opponent indeed. It was not merely because the Native American had the horse, but it was the kind of horse he had and how he used it that made him so dangerous. The story of these horses is an interesting one and has a rather interesting legacy.

For seven centuries, the Spaniard fought to rid his country of the African Moorish invaders. When he finally succeeded in the late 15th century, he drove the Moors out of Spain but kept behind part of their culture. Of particular interest in this study is the Moor's Afro-Arabian breed of horse.[24] It was short, shaggy, and apparently ill-proportioned, but could live entirely off grass and endure long periods of time without water. The Spaniards of the high, timberless plains of Salamanca especially found the Moorish horse most adaptable to their region.[25]

As the Spanish empire extended into the New World, conquistadores came to what was later to be the state of Texas. They brought with them their Moorish-bred horses—ancestors of the breed known as mustangs—to help them begin settlement of the new land. To care for these horses, the Spaniards used captive natives as slaves. In the process of teaching them their work, the Spaniards also taught them horsemanship. It was not long before some natives escaped, taking with them both a new skill and a new weapon.[26]

It was the Apache who first learned the deadly art of mounted attack. In the first half of the 17th century, they used it to develop a stumbling block to Anglo-American expansion for the next two centuries. Yet it was not the Apache who became the greatest danger on horseback in Southwestern America.

The Comanche[27]

The horse had affected natives other than the Apache, but none were influenced as much as the Comanche. For the Comanche, the horse changed their entire lifestyle, and soon their culture began to revolve around the horse. By the end of the 17th century the Comanche had replaced the Eastern Apache as the power in the area later to be Texas, and it was no idle expression that the Comanche were soon known as the "Lords of the Southern Plains."[28]

Completely mobile, the mounted Comanche struck with lightning-like speed—their primary goal being to steal more horses. They had adapted Spanish horsemanship to their own needs, closely copying the Spanish riding equipment with crude but effective replicas of the Spanish bit, bridle, and saddle with wood and buffalo hide.

They even had an additional refinement of a leather loop attached to the saddle by which a warrior could drop over on one side of the horse and, protected from his enemy by the horse, fire an arrow under the horse's neck. Comanche also adapted the Spanish custom of mounting from the right side of the horse—a habit the Spanish had acquired from the Moors.[29]

It was ironic these masters of the saddle came to power when they did, for within the same decades that they had gained their powerful position, the colonial mounted Rangers in the Eastern seaboard colonies were first organized. Over a century and a half later, the Texas Mounted Rangers not only were greatly influenced in their mounted combat by the Comanche, but also eventually used this same skill to virtually put an end to the Comanche power.

Rangers in Texas

After the War of 1812, the land to the west of the Mississippi River—opened to American expansion by the Louisiana Purchase—looked inviting indeed. Southerners in particular were considering moving westward to replace the land that had been depleted of its fertility by continuous planting of cotton. Due west, however, was Texas; still a part of Spanish Mexico and not American property. Nevertheless, it lay in the path of the relentless American push to the Pacific; therefore, it was only a matter of time before the Mexican, like the Native American, would find himself pushed aside by westward-advancing Americans. Cotton exports were a serious matter in the overall American economy and many supported its expanded area of cultivation. By 1850, two-thirds of America's exports were cotton.

The first Texas colony was not organized by a native Southerner, but by Connecticut-born Moses Austin. Having moved to Louisiana in 1796 (while the territory was still under Spanish rule), Austin used the fact that he had once been a subject of the Spanish crown to favorably influence Spanish officials when he applied for permission from the government to begin a colony in Spanish Texas. In 1820, he did receive permission; however, before he was able to organize his colony completely and move them to Texas, Moses Austin suddenly died.

Austin's son Stephen, however, took over the work of preparing the 300 families to journey to Texas. A revolution in 1821 gained Mexico independence from Spain, and during the same year, independent Mexico issued grants of land to sixteen American colonizers. Stephen Austin was one of the first.

Settling the colony was a different matter from founding it. Raiding natives plagued them, and although they were spared from Comanche attacks (Austin's small colony was outside the territory claimed by the Comanche), smaller tribes proved to be deadly nuisances. In 1823, Austin himself is reported to have hired 10 men to serve as mounted Rangers to help defend his colony from the Karankawa, the Tonkawa, the Waco, and the Tahuacano.[30] By 1826, the growing colony had organized a more permanent Ranger force with 20 to 30 men serving full time as Rangers.[31] This was the first recorded formation of Rangers in Texas.

The next obstacle to the peaceful settlement of the entire group of Texas colonies came from the changing attitude of the Mexican government. In the Colonization Act of April 6, 1830, Mexican authorities forbade further colonization of Texas and ordered the occupation of the land by Mexican troops to enforce the new law.[32] It was difficult, however, to keep Americans out of such a large and sparsely settled area. The law proved to be even more of a failure as the Mexican troops in Texas increasingly became a source of friction between the colonists and the government. Instead of helping the problem they had made it worse.

The Mexican authorities had already had their patience tried by the colonists. They had come to a new land with an alien religion, language, and culture, and continued wholeheartedly in all three—in spite of continual pressure from the Mexican government for them to conform to Mexican ways. It also took little imagination to see the Americans soon outnumbering native Mexicans, creating a new American territory, and ultimately being annexed to the United States. This seemed especially likely, considering the unpopularity in the United States Congress for the 1819 Adams–Onis Treaty between the United States and Spain that placed Texas within the Mexican border. Therefore, the Mexican government tried every measure in its power to discourage further American settlement.

In 1835, Mexican President Santa Anna—whom the Texicans at first trusted as a good, democratic leader—suddenly replaced the federal system of government with a centralized one and set himself up as dictator. All civil government in Texas was suspended and it was soon obvious that military rule would be next. Friction of this nature quickly burst into flame. After a few armed clashes resulting in early Texican victories, the colonists declared their independence and formed their own government.

Mexican reaction came before the Texicans were entirely ready and with a ferocity which they did not expect. Warned that Santa Anna with a large force was headed northward, Cols. William Travis and James Bowie with 180 other Americans fortified the Alamo mission at San Antonio de Bexar. They prepared to hold off Santa Anna's army as long as possible to give the Texas Army to the north more time to organize. For the last week of February 1836, and into the first week of March, the Alamo defenders held their fort. Santa Anna's masses of men and weapons, however, eventually claimed their victims. When the Alamo was attacked on March 6, Santa Anna ordered that no prisoners be taken. All American defenders were killed when the Alamo was taken and their bodies were thrown unceremoniously onto a large bonfire for cremation.

Meanwhile, within two weeks of the fall of the Alamo, Col. James W. Fannin and 350 Texicans—who at first tried to aid the Alamo defenders—were surrounded and captured by Gen. José de Urrea of Santa Anna's command near Goliad. Santa Anna ordered all of these prisoners executed. All, save a handful who escaped, were shot on March 27, 1836. These atrocities hung heavily in the minds of the Texicans, many of whom had lost close relatives at the Alamo or Goliad. In the "law by vengeance" of a lawless frontier, if a Comanche war party wiped out a settlement, the obligation was for a counterraid to settle the score. The deeds of Santa Anna were a great blow to many Texicans and burned in their memories, leaving an insatiable demand for vengeance. As mentioned in the previous account of Sam Walker's experiences during the Mier imprisonment, Sam had a personal reason for vengeance with the loss of his fellow prisoners who were executed by Santa Anna's orders.

The end of Santa Anna's invasion of the new republic came as a surprise. The Texican Army under Gen. Sam Houston caught Santa Anna off guard at San Jacinto and not only defeated the Mexican Army but also captured Santa Anna himself. Although Santa Anna signed a document recognizing the new republic; the Mexican government continued to claim it was not obligated to abide by a captured president's actions. Nevertheless, Mexican authorities made no immediate reaction against the Texians, and during the Mexicans' inaction, the Republic of Texas (that had already been functioning since the latter part of 1835) continued to become better organized and established.

This new land presented an opportunity. It also presented a serious problem for settlers. Texas was huge. It was a vast new land with very few people at this time. This was a great opportunity for some to own and develop land. For others it was an opportunity to prey on these few people in this early frontier time for they surely brought valuables and livestock with them. And for the native Americans, it was still a time to defend their home from the invading white man.

With this triangle for trouble, the inhabitants of this land needed a government to bring some kind of order and life and property protection. The new Texas Republic felt it did the best it could by proving mobile Rangers to be constantly on the lookout for trouble and then taking care of it when discovered.

The Earliest Texas Rangers

In her 2012 PhD dissertation, "Tejano Rangers: The Development and Evolution of Ranging Tradition, 1540–1880," Aminta Inelda Perez wrote, "As early as the 1540s, almost three hundred years before Austin arrived in Texas, mounted Spanish subjects on the frontiers of northern New Spain ranged, scouted, pursued, and waged offensive war against Chichimeca enemies. These methods were employed and accepted actions on the hostile frontier, and were also the characteristics Texans so highly revered in Ranger traditional lore."[33]

This study is definitely worth considering as the mounted tactics first used by the Moors against the Spanish were eventually adapted by the Spanish through the centuries of warfare to reconquer Spain. The Moor's leather shield was adapted very successfully by the Spanish and later by the Comanche. And the more fluid mounted fighting style was definitely passed down from the Spanish to the Native Americans as well as the colonists of New Spain. This Spanish Ranger system probably had a strong influence in the forming of the Texas Rangers. The Spanish Rangers had to adapt to the now mounted Native American who had used the horses brought to the New World by the first Spaniards. They used them very effectively against the first invader of the New World. The Texas Rangers would also adapt themselves to fight a very effective foe, finally succeeding with the advantage of the repeating revolver.

But the first continual organizational form of the first Rangers in Texas was Anglo, dating back to the 1600s in Maryland, and not the techniques taught by the early Hispanic rancheros.

The Anglo Ranger system was used by the early Austin colony. As mentioned, Austin himself is reported to have hired 10 men to serve as mounted Rangers to help defend his colony in 1823. Rangers had a definite place in the new republic. One of the first actions taken by the General Council of the new government dealt with the lawlessness and the Native American problem. On November 21, 1835, it authorized the creation of three Ranger companies of 56 men with Robert McAlpin Williamson elected as major.[34] These early Rangers, originally only 169 men, were enlisted for one year with pay of $1.25 per day and were under orders to have at least 100 rounds of powder and ball ammunition with them at all times.[35]

Texas Ranger. (James Worsham collection)

As historian Walter Prescott Webb wrote: "The Rangers were an irregular body; they were mounted; they furnished their own horses and arms; they had no surgeon, no flag, none of the paraphernalia of the regular service. They were distinct from the regular army [of Texas] and also from the militia." They were, above all, constabulary.

At no time did the Texas Rangers have a uniform of any description. Their dress was according to individual dictates.[36]

These relatively few Rangers were spread thin over the Texas Republic. To supplement their work, volunteer "Minute Men" were organized in the late 1830s in various areas. Sometimes commanded by former Rangers, these volunteers, according to a contemporary,

> Kept a good horse, saddle, bridle, and arms and a supply of coffee, salt, sugar, and other provisions, ready to start at a minute's warning in the pursuit of marauding Indians. At a

Randy Steffen, *Texas Rangers, 1839*. (*MUIA* plate 150, Military Collector & Historian, 10. no. 3 [Fall 1958]: 79. Courtesy of the Company of Military Historians)

> certain signal given by the cathedral bell, the men were off, in buckskin clothes and blankets, responding promptly to the call. They were organized to follow the Indian to their mountain fastness and destroy their villages, if they failed to kill the Indians.

In the meantime, to increase the number of Rangers, their number was raised from three to several companies and their enlistment was shortened from one year to three months.[37] Those who served as Rangers in the early days, for even the short enlistment, faced great danger. These early Rangers were young and many were inexperienced (their average age about 22) therefore many paid with their lives during their early encounters with the fierce Comanche, who by now were very much on the warpath against the Texicans. Often the casualty rate for the Rangers ran as high as 50 percent.[38]

According to a visitor to Texas in 1858, this is what he was told about the Rangers:

> Any one, having obtained from the government a commission to form a ranging-company, advertised a rendezvous where all wishing to join should be on hand at a specified time, where they were inspected by the enlisting officer. The men furnished their own horses (American or large mustangs), saddles, pistols, and knives—the state providing only rifles. The pay was $25 per month. The recruiting officer was only provisionally captain, the corps, when organized for service, choosing its own leaders. Rations of hard bread and pork, or, sometimes fresh beef, flour, rice, sugar, coffee, were served out once in four days, with a bushel of corn and hay for the horse. If sent on a separate scout where rations could not be taken, the party subsisted on game.
>
> They carried no tents, and seldom employed baggage-wagons. … They … lay, rolled in their blankets, wherever they pleased, within the lines of sentinels.
>
> … (In one situation the Rangers) returned to post … were issued a pint of moldy corn and a right smart chunk of bacon. … One man took the corn and broke it as fine as he could between two flat stones, and then with some fat, fried from the bacon, mixed a cake, which he baked, wrapped in green leaves, by a bed of ashes and coals in a hole in the ground. (One man commented) I never had eaten anything in memory of which was more delicious.[39]

The Comanche and Texas

The deadly Comanche, once friends of the Texicans, became their mortal enemy. The southern bands remained friendly for a while, but the northern band joined the Kiowas and on May 19, 1836, made one of the most destructive raids of the Texas frontier at Parker's Fort in the present Limestone country in northwest Texas. In the same year, Texas President David G. Burnet, who had lived with the Comanche and understood something about them, sent Maj. Alexander LeGrand to try to negotiate a peace treaty with the northern bands. Chief Traveling Wolf replied to LeGrand that so long as he could see the whites continuing to take the Comanche's land from him, the Comanche would fight.[40]

On November 1, 1837, the Texas House Committee on Indian Affairs recommended that offensive action be taken against the Comanche. They specified the northern band, but Texans regarded all Comanche as being hostile. President

Council House Fight. (James T. de Shields, *Border Wars of Texas* [...], Austin: State House Press, 1912)

Houston (in office 1836–38 and 1841–44) was also friendly toward Native Americans and urged a system of trade with the Comanche to help in making peace. Congress, however, was now more concerned with public defense than with trade with the Comanche.

On February 4, 1838, a party of 150 Comanche warriors met with Texians at San Antonio and offered to settle on a peace treaty if a definite boundary agreement could be made—specifically, the Comanche wanted the country north of the Guadalupe Mountains. This land was too rich for the Texians to give to the Comanche, so the peace conference ended.

A circumstance that doubly insured war between the Texians and the Comanche was Texas President Mirabeau B. Lamar's term in office from 1838–41. Using the power of his position, he urged not only aggression toward but actual extermination of the indigenous people who stood in the way of Texas progress.

Texians continued to occupy Comanche land, but the act that began large-scale hostilities was another abortive peace conference in San Antonio on March 19, 1840. Sixty-five Comanche warriors had come to San Antonio to discuss the return of white prisoners. Once inside the Council House, they were told that four or five chiefs were to be held prisoners until all white prisoners taken by their tribe were returned. The Comanche objected, a scuffle broke out and their fight for freedom resulted in a massacre—35 were killed, including 3 women and 2 children. From that day on, whenever a Ranger encountered a Comanche raiding party, it was usually either victory or death.

The Ranger and His Equipment

The Rangers who survived these desperate encounters with the Comanche became wiser and deadlier from the experience. From many battles with the Comanche, the Ranger—in a fight for survival—became extremely skillful as both a marksman and a rider. From the Mexican environment, the early Rangers developed their "uniform." It usually consisted of a sombrero; a colorful serape over a buckskin shirt and pants; high, soft boots worn on the outside of their trousers; and large Mexican roweled spurs. They were usually armed with Bowie knives, rifles, shotguns, flintlock "horse pistols" (percussion by the 1840s), and as many Rangers as could acquire them were carrying the deadly Colt revolving pistol after the mid-1840s.[41]

During their many encounters with the natives, a fight to the death was often the result. This was especially so when they clashed with their other enemy—Mexican bandits. To find one of the Mexicans who dared prey on Texians either alone or in small groups, the Texians often saw an opportunity to exact vengeance. Former Ranger Charles Wilkins Webber made the observation that any Ranger who brought in a Mexican prisoner alive was accused of having the "vice of mercy."[42] Toward the Mexican civilian the Rangers may later have been civil and even kind, but to the bandit he often was brutal in punishment—not only for the unfortunate Mexican's own deed, but also for those of his comrades who had killed Texicans at the Alamo and Goliad.

Not all Rangers had this characteristic. John "Jack" Coffee Hays, the most famous of the early Texas Rangers (in both the republic and early statehood years), was not a man of vengeance. Born in middle Tennessee in 1817 and orphaned at an early age, Hays (a nephew of General Andrew Jackson of Tennessee) learned surveying and, at the age of fifteen began practicing his trade in the Native American-populated Mississippi territory. The quick wit and cool courage that later aided him to survive such dangerous times, served him well when he journeyed to Texas and joined the Texas Rangers in December 1836.[43]

Jack Hays. (Texas Ranger Hall of Fame)

Hays became the dominant figure of the Rangers for more than a decade and had a direct and strong influence on his close friend, Sam Walker, whose later experience with Mexicans during his imprisonment blossomed into a full-fledged hatred for them.

Although only 19, Hays was exposed to the Texians' feeling for vengeance when—soon after he enlisted for a year with the Rangers—he helped bury the remains of Colonel Fannin's 350 men murdered at Goliad. On Christmas Day,

1836, Hays was reported to have helped inter the ashes of the Alamo defenders.[44] Nevertheless, although extremely deadly in combat, Hays never seemed to have obtained the obsession with reprisal that many of his men later demonstrated.

As he continued with the Rangers, Hays was soon promoted to sergeant. In spring 1840, he became captain of a Ranger company formed in San Antonio. For the next few years, he served as a Ranger, and for a while worked as a surveyor, still remaining "on call" with the Minute Men.[45] On his surveying trips, he often spent many days alone on the frontier in Native American territory. The Native American admired him for his bravery and independence. One of them, a Lipan Apache chief, Flacco, commented: "Me and Red Wing not afraid to go to hell together. Captain Jack heap brave; not afraid to go to hell by himself."[46]

Hays had already developed many skills that kept him alive on the frontier, and from the Native American he learned more. From the Delaware and Lipan Apache—both enemies of the Comanche—he learned trailing. This involved not only the discovery of "sign" but also the determination of relentlessly keeping on the trail. Hays never forgot what he learned from the indigenous people. Accompanying Delawares chasing raiding Comanche, Hays—on foot—forced himself to keep up the pace as they trailed their enemy day and night for two days before catching them. They kept up a swinging, never tiring trot … for hour after hour. They stopped only briefly to eat or sleep. They stopped shortly at a spring to drink and eat a few bites of cold, dried meat. Then they resumed the pace. Discovering their foe in the dark, the Delawares and Hays slept briefly—then attacked. This was a special lesson for him as he learned from the natives to continue on their mission in spite of fatigue, hunger, or loss of sleep.[47] (In the meantime, Sam Walker, too, was learning these lessons of overcoming fatigue, sleeplessness and hunger as a prisoner of the Mexicans.) These skills of self-discipline along with horseback riding and shooting made the Texas Rangers comparable to the expert cavalry of the Comanche.

From Flacco, a young headman of the Lipan Apache, Hays learned of the Comanche "open field" fighting (the Apache used ambush attacks). An admirer of Hays, Flacco rode with Hays for nearly a year until killed by a Mexican bandit.[48] In later years, Hays emphasized to his men the lessons learned from the Native American—to use their skills automatically; indifferent to weather, fatigue, or surprise.[49]

A good horse, a good weapon, and skill in using both of them was the primary prerequisite for the early Rangers. Hays is reported to have demonstrated the required shooting ability himself, by using a revolver to shoot off the head of a crowing rooster at 30 paces.[50]

The Ranger's sombrero was eventually replaced by their trademark slouched hat. It shaded him from the intense sun; its more durable broad brim protecting not only his face but the back of his neck, too. This also held true during heavy rains.

His buckskin clothes were soft, tough, and insect-proof. Although the appearance and smell of his clothes—after being worn for a month—may have been shocking to polite society, to the Ranger it was a necessary evil. The same held true for his beard and long hair—extended expeditions into waterless areas made both of these an obvious result.

High greased boots or leggings were worn because of the thorn-filled chaparral country that could tear clothes to shreds.[51] Cowboys of later years adapted leather leggings for chaparral country and called them, appropriately, "chaps."

The Ranger's weapons also were chosen on the basis of effectiveness. The Bowie knife had already been demonstrated as an excellent fighting tool by its namesake—knife fighter Jim Bowie. In the days of single-shot firearms, moisture-vulnerable black gunpowder, and misfires, many fights which were begun with guns were finished with the reliable Bowie knife.

Some Rangers carried shotguns for the obvious close-range advantage in mounted combat, but most carried short rifles that had both range and accuracy. Misnomered as "plains rifles," these short-barreled large-bore weapons were, in fact, "plainly finished rifles."[52] Usually .40- to .50-caliber, these weapons were made for hard service, with no fancy decorations of the long woodland "Kentucky rifle." Although he usually carried his rifle in a saddle scabbard, in enemy country the Ranger rode with his rifle across the fork of his saddle, swung from a short leather sling on the saddle horn, ready for instant action.[53]

Swung from the left shoulder on a wide leather strap was the Ranger's powder horn and bullet pouch. The horn was scraped thin so that by holding it up to the sun, a Ranger could see in an instant exactly how much powder he had. It was plugged with a hardwood peg that would not swell when wet. Under the horn was tied a powder measure—usually a section of cane. In a fight, however, the Ranger would have time only to guess the measure of powder in his hand. Accurate powder measurement for long shots was not important in the heat of close combat. Also, beneath the horn was hung a pouch for rifle balls and buckskin patches.[54]

The early Ranger carried single-shot pistols in his saddle and belt holsters; however, eventually the growing favorite was the Colt five-shot revolver. Rangers first began carrying Colts as early as 1839,[55] and by the time of the Mexican–American War, they had become the Rangers' trademark and part of their unorthodox "uniform." The function of rifles and revolvers together is illustrated in the following observation: "when the enemy's line is broken by the rapid volleys of their rifles, they then 'pitch in promiscuously,' and finish the work with the 'five-shooter' delivering their fire right and left as they dash along at full speed."[56] A more detailed examination of the Ranger and the revolver is presented later in this study.

The Ranger's horse was his prize possession because if a Ranger was not well-mounted, he could not expect to live very long in the highly mobile war of the plains.

Many learned from the Comanche and the ranchero to choose a good mustang. As author J. Frank Dobie observed:

> During the era of frontier wars, critics constantly asked, "Why cannot our cavalry on picked, grain-fed horses overhaul Indians on their scrub ponies?" Texas rangers on cowponies of Spanish blood overtook them where grain-fed cavalry horses fell behind. In a phrase applied to some men, these ponies, whether ridden by Indian, cowboy, or ranger, would do to ride the river with. They would stay—stay till hell froze over and a little while on the ice.[57]

Almost as important as a good horse was a good saddle. One contemporary observer, Lt. Col. George T. Denison, Jr., an American officer in the Mexican–American War, wrote:

> Texas saddles combined the best qualities of the Mexican and Comanche saddle … Essential parts are a wooden tree frame with a large horn in front, braced together without the use of iron, covered nicely with raw hide and iron fixtures or rings attaching the stirrup-leathers and girths … The saddle when fully rigged, was little more than a bare tree … Under the tree … a cloth of horse-hair, which was preferable as chafing or scalding of the back was less common with that than any other contrivance … a wooden stirrup was used with a leather covering in front.
>
> Anything to be carried was readily attached to the saddle before or behind by means of buckskin thongs … Mounted on his horse, with a saddle made of wood, raw hide, and very little iron, with a blanket, a canteen gourd tied to the horse, a rifle, and a revolver, the Texan ranger was the most formidable horseman in the world … He had to be killed or disabled before he was unhorsed, and himself, his horse, and his saddle seemed to be one being. At a full gallop he could pick up anything from the ground, and you never saw him bobbing up and down but he maintained his seat apparently without the slightest effort.[58]

James W. Nichols, wife, and daughter. (Photograph in the public domain)

The Ranger carried both his bedding and provisions on his saddle. Behind him was tied a blanket and his "wallet"—a leather bag filled with extra ammunition, a little salt, parched corn, jerky (dried meat), coffee, and tobacco. A spoon of buffalo horn and a cup could also be attached to the saddle by thongs.[59]

Ranger James Wilson Nichols told of preparing penolie for such times:

> It is corn parched brown and ground into a coarse meal and mixed with brown sugar. We rangers … seldom ever stopped to cook, and when we began to feel hungry and came to water, [we] take our tin cup half full of water and stir some penolie into it. It keeps off hunger.[60]

Near the saddle horn was tied the Ranger's braided rawhide lariat and horsehair staking rope. The staking rope, about 35 feet long, had one end tied beneath the headstall of the bridle, encircling the horse's nose. One Ranger explained why:

> If we were to fight dismounted, the captain would order the men to foot, some swinging off on the run, reins flying loose, staking ropes tied with slip knots were jerked free with their left hands. If held by the reins most horses shy from a gun. Hence, as his feet hit the ground, the ranger flipped the free end of the rope around his hips, drew it into a slip knot and gave his attention to the Indians. If the horse ran on the end of the rope, the nose hitch ordinarily kept him from dragging the rider, who in an emergency could pull the loose end of the slip knot and set the mount free. If the company retreated, the ranger gathered up the rope as he ran back to the horse, swung into the saddle and tucked the coils into his belt as he rode.[61]

Training for Hays's Rangers

To a young Texian who desired to join the Rangers, Hays requested him to prove himself and his horse by performing the following feat. Pointing to two trees 300 yards away, Hays told him to "jump your horse into a run, pull your pistols and put a ball into the first tree as you pass it, circle your running horse beyond the second tree and shoot into its trunk on your way back."[62]

Within a few years of their organization, the Rangers had developed such skill as horsemen and marksmen that it is enlightening to examine an account of a contest of riding and shooting ability among the Rangers and riders who had a reputation of being the best horsemen in Texas. At San Antonio in 1843, through a chance meeting, a riding competition was held among Mexican rancheros (descendants of the early Spanish settlers), about 50 Comanche warriors (in town negotiating a treaty), and a company of Texas Rangers. John Crittenden Duval, who was there, observed:

> The Rangers were mounted on their horses, and "dressed in buckskin hunting shirts, leggings, slouched hats, with pistols and bowie knives stuck in their belts … The Comanche warriors were decked out in their savage finery of paints, feathers, and beads … The Mexican rancheros with their steeple crown, broad brim sombreros, showy scarfs and slashed trousers … rode fiery mustangs."[63]

Duval recalled that for one event a board with a bull's eye painted on it was placed on the ground. The first contestant—a Comanche warrior—rode toward it at a full gallop and as he passed, two arrows were sent quivering into the board. The Rangers and rancheros were next, and using their pistols, all left bullet holes in the board as they rode past—many placing them in the bull's eye.

The next feat had the same objective, only this time the riders were to swing over on the far side of the horse as he passed the board and fire under the horse's neck. Their accuracy proved hardly impaired.[64] The winners of the prizes—mounted pistols, bowie knives, and blankets—were: First prize, Ranger John McMullen; second prize, a Comanche warrior, Long Quirt; third prize, Ranger Henry L. Kinney; and fourth prize, Senor Don Rafael.[65]

In the next contest of fighting skills between the Ranger and the Comanche, they competed not for prizes but for their lives on the field of battle. In years to come, the same would be true for all three—ranchero, Ranger, and Comanche warrior—who would be at each other's throats in the deadly triangular war that raged during what is known to Americans as the War with Mexico.

Sam Walker, after recovering from his time as a Mexican prisoner, learned from such training with the Rangers. To become a skilled Ranger, for him as well as any Ranger at this time, was a serious goal as it meant the difference between life or death. In combat they faced the Comanche, the extremely skilled "Horse People."

The Comanche Ethos

In appearance, the copper-complexioned Comanche had thin lips, black hair and eyes, an aquiline nose, and were of low or medium stature, but well-proportioned. They wore buckskin moccasins, breechcloths, and leggings—in cold weather, a buffalo robe—but into battle they wore only breechcloth and moccasins. They wanted to be light in the saddle and never carried anything heavy or useless when they went to war on horseback.[66]

With the muskets and pistols of the day, a bullet would ricochet off the convex surface of the shield or would be absorbed by the tough but resilient leather-covered padding. The Comanche would test a new shield himself with both arrow and bullet at fifty yards. If it failed to turn away or absorb both projectiles, it was discarded.

The greatest of the Comanche's weapons was his horse. Most warriors had learned to ride their ponies by the time they had learned to walk. Carefully and lovingly taught by his grandfather (his father was usually gone on raids) to ride, shoot, and hunt, the Comanche male—by the time he was old enough to become a warrior—had a goal of being an expert in all three arts.[67]

The Comanche's mustang, both his means and incentive for war, was valued very highly by its owner. Often loved even more than the warrior's wife, it was nearly regarded as murder to kill a man's horse. However, spare horses taken on raiding parties, laden with leather boxes of dried meat, served as fresh mounts—and in the event of scarcity of food, were to be eaten.[68]

To the Comanche, the ultimate act of bravery was to get close enough to touch an armed enemy—to "count coup" on him—and live to brag about it. Honor, to the Comanche, was a sacred thing; and in cases of vengeance raids, counting coup was forgotten. Death was the only way to resolve the problem—be it an attack on another Native American for stealing horses or humans, or on another tribe for a mass attack on the Comanche. Torturing a prisoner was preferred, if the situation allowed it; as the Comanche felt in that way, he could appease the Great Spirit and show his power over his enemy.[69]

A very religious person, the Comanche was a very dangerous fighter. A firm believer in the Great Spirit, he felt that the will of this Supreme Being was made known to him through visions or dreams. The Comanche sought these visions through days of fasting and self-laceration. Whatever ideas or dreams that he could recall from this period of self-abuse and hardship were interpreted by the Comanche himself, as the "Will of the Great Spirit." However, he interpreted it that he felt duty-bound to do it. In this way, many suicidal and seemingly insane attacks on the whites were attempted after the receiver of the "vision" had revealed the Will of the Great Spirit.[70]

In the case of a vengeance raid, preparation was made by the whole village. A war or vengeance dance—very similar to a college pep rally—was held. War songs and even love songs by the young warriors, who would soon be separated from their lovers, were sung around a blazing campfire. Dancing almost to exhaustion, the young warriors would stop for a while to listen to inspiring stories from older warriors who spoke of the raiding days of their youth.[71]

Before the night was over, the elders of the tribe would brief the leaders of the raid with a map drawn in the sand. They were told not only of the land into which they were going, but also if the tribe were to move while they were gone, where the tribe would be located in days to come. The Comanche, whose whole culture was centered on the horse, could and did move frequently.[72]

In the actual raid, a surprise attack and rout of the enemy was the goal. If the foe stood his ground, the Comanche would form a giant circle of riders—not around the enemy but tangent to him. As a warrior approached the part of the circle near the enemy, he would swing over on the side of the horse away from the adversary and shoot under the horse's neck. If the horse was wounded or lost its footing, the warrior could hit the ground on his feet and use his shield that he had strapped to his back to protect himself. Otherwise, he would continue to ride the circle, notching another arrow on the side of the circle away from the enemy.[73]

If the enemy tried a counterattack, the center section of the Comanche battle formation would fall back while the two flanks would move to surround the enemy in a pincer movement. Hays appreciated this action in particular and sometimes copied it.[74]

One morale factor the Comanche possessed when he went into battle was that if wounded or killed, his body would not be left to the enemy. Riding two abreast, two warriors would swoop down and retrieve a wounded comrade or as a last resort use their lassos to remove a body from the field of battle.[75]

In any fight with the Texans, the additional incentive was a passion for revenge. Although the Comanche remained at peace with the United States, they hated the Texans with a bitter loathing. The Republic of Texas had followed a policy toward its indigenous people that made the deceptive and often harsh treatment by the U.S. appear benevolent in comparison. Long after Texas became a state, the Comanche still made the distinction between Americans and Texans.[76]

Rangers played a very special role in the early history of Texas as well as the present. Rangers have a long and proud legacy in the nation and a tradition of over a century and a half in Texas. The history of the Rangers is worthy of understanding and appreciating. Texas would not be what it is today without men like Sam Walker and the Texas Rangers who stood by their beliefs no matter what the odds and endured to create an honorable heritage of determined men who would "keep on coming" against injustice—no matter what.

CHAPTER 6

The Battle of Walker Creek, June 8, 1844

The clash between mounted Rangers and their Comanche enemy that day in 1844 changed Texas frontier history from that time onward. These masters of the saddle swarmed around each other across the hot west Texas hill country. Being and beast as one, shouting, shooting Texas Rangers and whooping Comanche warriors desperately fought. They fired at each other from but a few paces apart. In a life or death combat they swept across the prairie, the quick soon left the dead strewn in their wake.

Rangers and their opponents collided and then regrouped to attack again. With months of horseback and weapons training, these experienced riders all strained with the intensity of an animal fighting for its life. They rode expertly and as experienced marksmen sent deadly projectiles at each other in close combat. Rangers were wounded by arrow and lance; when it was all over with, one was dead and three seriously injured. According to their captain, Jack Hays, his 15 men all had arrows grazing their saddles, rifles stocks, hats, and clothing. But the Comanche numbered 70 or more. The Rangers survived because for the first time they were all armed with repeating firearms. They fired their continual unseen bullets from the small but serious revolvers that relentlessly found their marks. They left 23 Comanche dead and 30 seriously wounded as the new Colt Paterson revolvers did their job

When the encounter began, the Comanche used the white man's single-shot muzzle loaders for their first shots but quickly resorted to their primitive but deadly repeating weapons, their bows. The Rangers also used their long-range single-shot rifles at first but soon shocked their enemy as all had the deadly close-range technology of their new repeating pistols. Usually such a fight ended with many more white men to bury than red. That day the results changed.

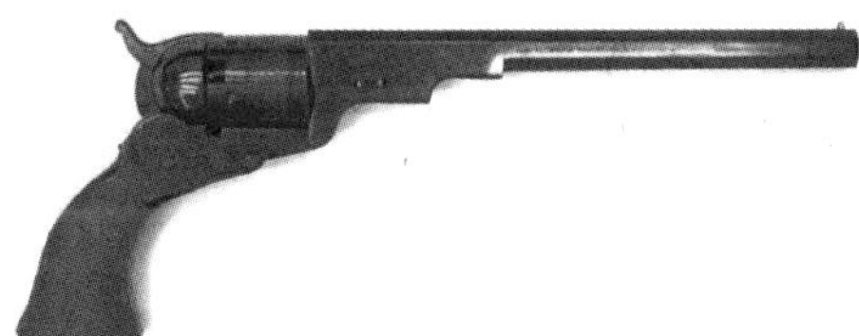
The Colt five-shot Paterson revolver. (Photograph in the public domain)

The battle of Walker Creek in early June 1844 was a watershed in the history of the continual conflict between the settlers of Texas and the

Walker Creek. (richardluce.com. Courtesy of Richard Luce)

former residents. The Comanche were the reigning experts in mounted combat. While their opponents, the Rangers, were very, very good in the saddle, prior to this battle the Texians had one major weakness. They depended on single-shot pistols and rifles as their main weapons. The Native Americans used bows and lances with which they were both deadly and superior. They were more effective because the muzzle loading pistols and rifles the Rangers used took nearly a minute to reload. After the Rangers' first fire, with their weapons empty, they were severely vulnerable to a mounted attack with arrows.

On that day in June the balance shifted in favor of the Rangers from that time forward. It happened because of the use of an invention produced in Paterson, New Jersey, that was a game-changer for the Rangers of Texas. It was the Colt Paterson five-shot revolver. This new technology had a major impact. But in itself it did not make the difference in battle. It was a catalyst combined with the preparation, training, and experience that would make the difference. Prior to that day in June, the Comanche nearly always had the advantage.[1]

The Lords of the Southern Plains

To appreciate the serious skill of the Native American enemy that the Rangers fought that day, the Comanche need to be considered. These Horse People armed themselves with a bow, a lance, and sometimes a rifle, and for protection carried their special round, convex leather shield. Their bow was accurate up to 50 yards and had a range of 300 yards. At 10 to 15 yards, a warrior could drive an arrow through a buffalo. The Comanche was extremely deadly with his bow; many could loose two arrows accurately in quick succession at a full gallop, as demonstrated at the riding contest with the Rangers at San Antonio in 1843. Most arrow heads were metal; many from metal barrel hoops. The points were shaped and then heated red hot and dropped into water to harden. All war arrows were barbed, some had only one barb; for when pulled upon by a victim, the barb would catch in the flesh and turn the flint or iron arrowhead crosswise in the wound, making removal possible only by cutting the point out.

According to research at the Comanche National Museum and Cultural Center in Lawton, Oklahoma, the short buffalo bow was usually about 4 feet long. It was made of Osage orange or bois d'arc wood with a sinew bowstring. Many times, the Comanche bow had a tuft of horsehair attached to the top of the bow and was painted with decorative pigments. It was powerful enough to shoot an arrow through a bale of hay. The arrows were usually made of dogwood and fletched with the feathers of the red-tailed hawk. These feathers were tied at the top and bottom with sinew usually softened by chewing. The quiver and bow cover were made of animal pelts with a baulkman retrieving handle attached to a cup that was first inserted in the quiver so it could be pulled up to retrieve arrows if necessary. The Comanche hunted buffalo with a lance as well as a bow. Usually 6 to 8 feet long, the lance could be very effective in mounted combat.

Comanche hunting buffalo by George Catlin. (Smithsonian American Art Museum, gift of Mrs. Joseph Harrison, Jr., 1985.66.564)

The Comanche's shield also made him an enigma to the early frontiersmen. It was round, roughly two and a half feet in diameter, with a convex surface. Made from the thick shoulder hide of the buffalo bull, it was steamed to contract and thicken it. Two or more layers were stretched on a wooden frame with a space of about an inch between them that was stuffed with feathers or paper. Settlers were puzzled at the Comanches stealing their books when they knew that the Native American could not read. They did not realize at first that the paper was for their shields. Yet what really perplexed them were the shields themselves—they could not be pierced by low-veloctiy musket balls.

It may be argued that the Comanche shield could be a protection for the Colt Paterson pistol. Yet, the accuracy of the Rangers, the close contact that Hays reported, and the aggressiveness of both Ranger and Comanche made the use of the shield difficult.

The Comanche's prowess on their ponies in mounted warfare was legendary. As the Comanche swarmed around the Rangers, they shot their arrows many times, protected by their own horse's bodies. Artist George Catlin witnessed and drew a depiction of the young warriors demonstrating this special skill. He thus described it:

> Amongst their feats of riding, ...—a stratagem of war, learned and practiced by every young man in the tribe; by which he is able to drop his body upon the side of his horse at the instant he is passing, effectually screened from his enemies' weapons as he lays in a horizontal position behind the body of his horse, with his heel hanging over the horses' back; by which he has the power of throwing himself up again, and changing to the other side of the horse if necessary. In this wonderful condition, he will hang whilst his horse is at fullest speed, carrying with him his bow and his shield, and also his long lance of fourteen feet in length, all or either of which he will wield upon his enemy as he passes; rising and throwing his arrows over the horse's back, or with equal ease and equal success under the horse's neck.[2]

The Rangers' Training

The Rangers also spent many hours in training on horseback. On a galloping horse they learned to keep their focus, aim and control with single-shot rifles and pistols. Ranger James Nichols wrote in great detail from his own training under Hays:

> Those not on scout were every day practicing horsemanship and marksmanship. We put up a post about the size of a common man, then put up another about 40 yards further on. We would first run our horses full speed and discharge our rifles at the first post, draw our pistols and fire at the second. At first there some wild shooting but we had not practiced two months until there was not many that would not put his balls in the center of the posts.
>
> Then we drew a ring about the size of a man's head and soon every man could put both his balls in the circle. We would practice this a while, then try riding like the Comanche Indians. After practicing three or four months we became so perfect that we would run our horses half or full speed and pick up a hat, a coat, or rope or even a silver dollar, stand up on the saddle, throw ourselves on the side of our horses with only a foot and a hand to be seen, and shoot our pistols under the horses neck, rise up and reverse, etc.

Hays summed it up rather well when he told his Rangers, "Boys, keep up your practicing shooting on horseback. It beats the Indians at their own game." At the battle of Walker Creek, they did.

How the Rangers Got Their Revolvers

These two mounted warrior clans, the Rangers and the Comanche, had much in common in their skills and training. It was just that up until this time, the Comanche had better weapons for fighting on horseback. But they came from two very different backgrounds. Two extreme cultures clashed at Walker Creek and following the story to its beginnings involves going from one extreme environment to another—from the dry prairie to the wet wind of seagoing sailing vessels, the Rangers' victory at Walker Creek never would have happened had it not been for the Texas Navy. How the Rangers were to finally get enough revolvers to arm a whole company made this eventful day possible and is a story within itself. It involved deals for a new invention, stubborn Texas political leaders, and a just as determined Texas Navy commodore.

As early as 1839, the President of the Republic of Texas, Mirabeau B. Lamar, was interested in Colt's repeating carbines to arm his soldiers. At the same time, Commodore of the Texas Navy Edwin W. Moore specifically wanted 180 carbines and 180 belt pistols (revolvers). These were to be belt pistols with 8-inch barrels with accompanying cap primers for each pistol. According to documents in the Texas State Archives, the Republic of Texas Navy ordered a total of 250 belt pistols, 80 carbines and 100 rifles. The army's carbines never were ordered nor were any ordered for the Rangers. Eventually, however, the Rangers would end up with the navy's pistols.

The Colt Paterson Revolver: Pros and Cons

The reason the army did not get Colt weapons earlier was the negative report of Texas Colonel of Ordnance George W. Hockley to the Texas Secretary of War, Albert Sidney Johnston. Upon test firing some of Colt's weapons, Hockley concluded in a report written March 28, 1839:

> Such percussion weapons (as compared to flintlocks) misfired very frequently; ... the barrels (with rapid firing) is heated so that a soldier could not hold it. ... a quantity of dirt (fouling) remained in the chambers after firing ... the length of time for reloading ... and the whole formation too complicated for use in the field.

What criteria Hockley used and how many shots the revolvers were fired in this evaluation is unknown. At Walker Creek, Hays needed the Paterson revolvers only to perform 10 shots—five shots and then another five from a preloaded cylinder. Knowing how to use these new revolvers was just as important as the technology they provided the user. Lack of familiarization with the Paterson Colt could lead to disaster. Captain G. T. Howard of the 1st Regiment of Texas Infantry wrote the Paterson revolver could be dependable with disciplined soldiers who understood how to care for weapons. In unskilled hands they were sometimes known as "Colt's Patent Wheel of Misfortune."

In addition, the earlier Paterson, that the Rangers first used, had a problem with the barrel wedge that held the barrel on the frame. If, during reloading, this was lost in the heat of battle, the cylinder could move forward just enough so that the hammer could not make contact with the caps to fire the weapon. Or the barrel could just fall off. The wedges of the older model Patersons, such as those Texas Navy were issued, did not have a spring to keep the barrel wedge from falling out. One Ranger, Andrew Erskine, reportedly had the barrel of his Paterson fall off without his noticing it and resulted in an interesting hand-to-hand encounter with a Comanche who had a broken bow. If either of these problems of the older Paterson happened at Walker Creek, it would explain why the Rangers did not fire all the shots that they potentially could have.

While the navy Paterson revolver had its faults, it also had strengths. It had added accuracy from 9-inch barrels. The original request was for 8-inch barrels but Colt historian Bill Edwards reports that, "A notation on the (Colt) records indicates that eight-inch barrels were not in stock, and that the nine-inch sizes, the common length found today, were supplied."

In spite of Hockley's negative evaluation, for the most part, these weapons worked and worked well. Commodore Moore would later testify to their reliability in the hands of those who knew how to take care of them. Repeating firearms—and especially repeating pistols—were perfect for sailors to repel borders from an enemy ship drawn up alongside. The first shipment of carbines and pistols ordered August 3, 1839, was issued to the Texas Navy in November 1839. Later the navy would receive 250 pistols. Samuel Colt was very pleased; while his sales were not as numerous as he wished, he hoped it would lead to continuing orders for Colt repeating weapons. The Texas Army later received Colt's pistols and carbines but the Rangers were the only Texas military arm not to directly receive the Paterson Colt. But once they had them, the Rangers' use of the Colt Paterson pistols, primarily from the Texas Navy, would make the Colt revolver famous.

Colt wrote that Texas was to be praised for the supplying its military with his new repeating weapons. Texas, surrounded by enemies on all sides with but a few soldiers to call to her defense, has sought to judiciously multiply her means, by placing in the hands of the soldiery the most efficient weapons so as to equalize her army to her enemy—not by men … but in the arms they carry.

The Texas Navy

Texas President Lamar supported Commodore Edwin Ward Moore in his plans to arm and recruit for his small fleet. Yet he was soon powerless to help Moore.

In the fall of 1841, Sam Houston became president; Lamar constitutionally could not seek a consecutive term. Houston opposed the Texas Navy as he wished to concentrate on annexation of Texas to the United States and feared a Texas Navy would help provoke war with Mexico. Lamar in one of his last acts of office arranged to protect the navy by "renting" it out to Yucatan which opposed the current Mexican government. In the meantime, Houston's government could not and did not pay the navy's officers and sailors. Houston considered the navy a waste of money so desperately needed by his government. Operation cost for its fleet cost the republic $200,000 per year.

Finally, in January 1843, the navy was ordered to be sold. By the time representatives of the republic arrived to prepare for such a sale, much had happened. When the representatives of the Texas Republic arrived for this task later in 1843, Commodore Moore was able to convince the commissioners to have second thoughts. He persuaded them to consider the navy was needed to defend the Texas coast from Mexico. Moore showed them a top-class fleet outfitted with the support of Yucatan silver. It had already fought the Mexicans in a great naval victory. On behalf of Yucatan—not Texas—it fought the Mexican fleet in May 1843.

Moore's *sailing* ships had indeed defeated steam warships. Heavily outgunned, disadvantaged by sail against steam, the Texian fleet scored an amazing victory. The Texians lost 5 killed and 22 wounded. The Mexicans lost a total of 47 killed and 64 wounded on one ship alone; 40 killed and wounded on another. What made the victory even more unusual was the main vessel in the Mexican fleet was the 1,100-ton English-made 200-foot-long *Guadelupe*, at the time the world's largest iron steam ship which was mounted with two monstrous Paixhan swivel guns that fired 68-pound exploding shells. Moore's flagship, the wooden sailing vessel *Austin* was only 125 feet long, displaced 500 tons, but had mounted twenty 24 pound Columbiads.

The Mexican commodore was court-martialed for being defeated by a smaller, less powerful fleet. It was a major naval victory, yet it would lead not to the official support of the navy by the Texas Republic but instead to its demise.

Moore returned home a hero to Texians for defending their shores but a villain to Sam Houston. The Texas President tried and failed to convict Moore of piracy. Moore would never again command the Texas fleet in battle. The fleet was finally placed for sale on November 22, 1843, at the port of Galveston. No one bid, so the Texas government was forced to buy it. The Texas Navy was then beached and left to rot.[3] The pistols Moore had ordered no longer were owned by the navy. Ironically the Paterson pistols purchased by Moore for the navy to use at sea would then make a great impact on land warfare.

Two events in Texas history are memorialized on the cylinders of Colt revolvers: the battle of Walker Creek on the Walker Colt of 1847; and Moore's naval victory, the battle of Campeche, on the Colt navy revolver of 1851.

The Rangers Get Colts

In early 1844, President Sam Houston informed Capt. John C. Hays, commander of the Texas Rangers, that the defunct Texas Navy had a number of the Colt Paterson revolvers. He suggested Hays appeal to the Texas Secretary of War Albert S. Johnson to get some pistols for his Rangers. Hays did so and the request was granted, and he headed for Galveston to pick up the revolvers. On February 2, William Bollaert—on the newly built steamboat *Vista*—wrote in his diary that he crossed Red Fish Bar at daylight with Major Hays on board who was going to Island (Galveston) to purchase arms, etc., out of appropriations made.

Hays brought the new shipment of pistols to San Antonio where his Rangers got at least one each with an extra cylinder.

Commodore Moore wrote, "The Colt's pistols used by the Texas Rangers before annexation, were all supplied from the (Texas) navy after they had been in constant use for upwards of four years, and I know that some of these arms that have been in constant use for nine years and are still good." Moore also reported that with his sailors armed with Colts repeating firearms, they "could fire nine hundred and sixty balls in one minute and forty seconds."

Not all the Rangers' Colts came from the Texas Navy. While the bulk of them from the navy were delivered by Hays himself, there is a letter in the Texas Archives documenting the fact that, as early as 1839, the Texas Army ordered 50 belt pistols and that in March 1840 there were five cases of Colt weapons ready to be shipped to Austin. It is possible that a few of these pistols made their way to the Rangers as early as 1842. Of the various models of the early Paterson Colt revolvers that came to the Texas Republic, there is one that can be documented back to Jack Hays's Rangers. This pistol and holster belonged to Texas Ranger William M. Lowe. He was issued this five-shot .36-caliber pistol with a 7.5-inch barrel revolver in Austin by Captain Hays himself in 1842—perhaps a revolver from the Texas Army acquisition.

Hays brought his men the Paterson No. 5 Holster pistol with the 9-inch barrel in the spring of 1844. When these revolvers from the navy got into the hands of a whole company of 15 Rangers for the first time, they made a major difference.

Truth More Fascinating than Myths and Legends

On June 8, 1844, a company of Texas Rangers armed with repeaters made a major difference in Texas frontier history at Walker Creek near Sisterdale, Texas. It was dramatically demonstrated that the mounted Native American warrior no longer was the superior threat on horseback to the settlers of Texas. Because of Colt's repeating pistol—the five-shot Paterson revolver, the white man was no longer was limited to single-shot pistols and rifles to defend himself against the Native American with multiple arrows.

Walker, who would later work with Colt to design the monster four and one-half pound Walker Colt revolver was there at this particular fight and nearly paid for his part of the battle with his life.

On that June day, a small band of Texas Rangers were armed with the new-to-them Colt revolvers that Hays had brought from Galveston. They would encounter a Comanche war party four times their size. This enemy, in addition to outnumbering the Rangers, also were known for their expert horsemanship and skilled use of the bow with rapidly shot arrows. This landmark frontier event has been told and embellished so much through the decades, that it is hard to tell half-truths from the truth or even factual events attached to the wrong time and place.

There were at least four accounts of this encounter that were written days after the June 8 event. The first was Hays's Report written at San Antonio on June 16:

Report of the Battle of Walker's Creek fought by Capt. J. C. Hays in June, 1844

San Antonio, June 16, 1844
Hon. Secretary of War and Marine,

Sir.—On the first of this month, I left camp, which was near this place, with fifteen men, for the purpose of scouting the country, and, if possible, to ascertain what tribe of Indians were committing so many depredations, I proceeded a north course, as far as between the Perdenales and Llano. After scouting that country and wishing to go no further, on account of the negotiations that were going on, I concluded to return; although I. saw sufficient sign of Indians to have induced me to proceed farther up the country. But having an eye single to my instructions, I deemed it prudent to return.

When on Walker's creek, about fifty miles above Seguin, when encamped, a party of Indians made their appearance, numbering about ten, and endeavored to draw me out. I immediately ordered my men to saddle, and prepare to fight; for could have no doubt but that their intentions were hostile.

After being mounted, I proceeded slowly towards them—they, at the same time, using every art and stratagem, to throw me off. My guard, and induce me to give chase to them. They, however, did not succeed in their design.

I then fell into the timber and moved up the creek about a quarter of a mile, when I discovered their number to be between sixty and seventy. After ascertaining that they could not decoy or lead me astray, they came out boldly, formed themselves, and dared us to the fight. I then ordered a charge; and, after discharging our rifles, closed in with them, hand to hand, with my five-shooting pistols, which did good execution. Had it not been for them, I doubt what the consequences would have been. I cannot recommend those arms too highly.

The fight, which was a moving one, continued to the distance of about three miles—being desperately contested by both parties. After the third round from the five-shooters, the Indians gave way; but, whenever pressed severely, making the most desperate charges and efforts to defeat me.

I however, charged their ranks; and, with a courage that is rarely displayed, my men succeeded in routing and putting them to flight—killing twenty dead on the ground, and wounding, at the lowest estimate, twenty or thirty more.

The second day after the fight, (having remained where the fight took place, on account of my wounded), a party of four made their appearance. I immediately ordered six men to give chase to them; thinking at the same time that they had embodied and presumed to give me another fight. My men, at the word, mounted their horses, and pursued them about a mile when they came upon them and killed three of them—the fourth having evinced a disposition to escape, if possible, from the first.

My loss was, one killed (Peter Fohr) and three badly wounded, but not mortally, and one slightly. Two were wounded with lances and two with arrows.

The party consisted of Camanches, Wacoes and Mexicans. I will, here take occasion to say, that my men evinced no dismay; but on the contrary, would dare them to come to the charge.

Your obedient serv't
John C. Hays
Commanding S. W. Frontier.

Recapitulation

Loss of Mexicans and Indians killed on the ground, 23.—Wounded, most of them badly, 30. My loss was, killed, 1—Peter Fohr. Wounded badly, 3, S. H. Walker, R. A. Gillespie and W. B. Lee. Wounded slightly, 1, Andrew Erskine.

J. C. Hays,
Com. S.W. Fron.[4]

The second account was written by Mary Maverick on June 21 in her diary after Hays visited her in La Grange, Texas, shortly after the event. Mrs. Maverick said she wrote the account the day of Hays' visit:

> Remarkable Indian Fight. On June 20th, 1844, Major Jack Hays came to see me and gave me the particulars of a noted encounter he had had with the Indians only twelve days before he called on me. The fight took place on June 8th. Hays, with fourteen men, was scouting on the Guadalupe about fifty miles above Seguin, [it must have been between the present sites of Sisterdale and Comfort in Kendall County]. Whilst some of the Rangers were cutting a bee tree, the spies galloped up with the news that a very large party of Comanches were close upon them. At once the Rangers mounted and made ready—by this time the Indians had formed

in admirable order on the level top of a hill nearby. The Rangers following their leader, spurred forward in full charge, and, when they reached the foot of the hill which was steep and somewhat overhanging, they found they were no longer in sight of the enemy. Taking advantage of this, Hays led his men half around the base of the hill, still out of sight, and dashed up at a point not expected. The Comanches had dismounted, and were kneeling down with guns and arrows fixed for a deadly aim. Strange to say, Hays was close upon them before they discovered his stratagem, and before they could mount their horses, the Rangers were in their midst—shooting them right and left, with their new revolving pistols. But the Indians were numerous, some sixty-five or seventy warriors, and were led by two especially brave and daring chiefs. The chiefs rallied their forces and closed completely around the Rangers and fought with great daring, but the astonishing "six-shooters" [actually, the Colt revolving pistol was a five-shooter] did the work—the Indians speedily became demoralized and they broke and fled, leaving twenty-three of their comrades dead on the battle-field This was opportune, for the loads were exhausted in the six-shooters of the Rangers, and they immediately took advantage of the enemy's flight to reload their vigorous little weapons. The Indians, finding they were not pursued, paused and reformed for battle. The Rangers charged now with the same result. The fight lasted nearly an hour, the Indians fighting stubbornly and retiring slowly and still forty strong- A chief then made a great talk to his followers, rising in his stirrups and gesticulating—he rode up and down their lines and got them to make another desperate stand. The Rangers were reduced now to eleven fighting men, and Hays called out: "Any man who has a load, kill that chief." Ad Gillespie[5] answered: "I'll do it," dismounted, aimed carefully with his trusty yager, and shot the chief dead, when a panic seized the Indians, and they fled in the utmost confusion.

Andrew Erskine. (Photograph in the public domain)

Peter Fohr was killed, and four of the Rangers wounded and many arrows passed through their hats and clothing, for several thousand arrows were fired into their midst.

I wrote the memorandum of the fight just after Major Hays had related it—I was much struck with the odds in the numbers of the opposing forces,—fifteen against sixty-five or seventy, and with Hays remark that "more than thirty Indians were killed."

Hays modestly gave the credit of the victory to the wonderful marksmanship of every Ranger, and the total surprise to the Indians, caused by the new six shooters, which they had never seen or heard of before.

Colonel Hays's closing remarks were that:

> We were right glad they fled, for we were nearly used up with the fatigue of a long day's march that day and the exertions on the battle-field, and we were almost out of ammunition. The Indians made a magnificent fight under the circumstances. They seemed to be a band of selected braves in full war-paint, and were led by several chiefs, showing that they were marching down upon the settlements, where they would have divided into parties commanded each by a chief, and great would have been the mischief done by such a number of savages.[6]

Then there was the third account, the June 23 Houston newspaper interview with the Ranger Commander Capt. Jack Hays at Washington on the Brazos on June 22:

PARTICULARS OF HAYS' FIGHT WITH THE INDIANS

Mary Maverick. (Photograph in the public domain)

Washington, June 23d, 1844
To the Editor of the Star:

Sir:—Captain Hays arrived in town on yesterday, and from him I have learned the details of the late action between the Texians (fifteen in number) commanded by himself, and a large body of Indians. He had been up on the Pierdenalis to ascertain whether there was any encampment of Indians in that section, and was returning after an unsuccessful search, then being encamped about four miles east of the Pinto trace at a point nearly equidistant from Bexar, Gouzaids and Austin, the guard stationed in his rear to watch out for his trail, discovered ten Indians following it, and immediately reported the fact to Hays. They we seen about the same time by the Indians who fell back into some brush with scattering timber intermixed. The Texians saddled up and advanced toward their place of concealment, when three or four Indians made their appearance and as if for the first time perceiving the white men, fled with great precipitation and apparent alarm. Hays, however, was too old an "Indian fighter" to be caught by such traps, and made no effort at pursuit. As soon as the Indians saw that his stratagem was of no avail, they came out of the timber, and displayed their whole force in line, some 75 in number. Greatly superior as was this force, Hays determined to attack them. His men were highly disciplined, of tried courage, horses well broke, and the average number of shots to each man, about eight. The face of the country in that section is broken and rocky, with a growth of scrubby live oaks and black jacks, with some undergrowth of brush. A short distance in the rear of the Indians, was a steel hill, from the summit of which stretched a prairie plane, its sides rocky and covered with brushwood, as above described. The Texians advanced slowly, the Indians falling back until they crowned the hill, where they dismounted, formed in line, and secure in strength of their position, called to Hays as he approached, "Charge, Charge." When the Texians reached the foot of the hill, from the nature of the ground they were concealed from the view of the Indians. At that point Hays wheeled his little band at full speed, some two or three hundred yards, around the base of the hill, ascended it, at the same place, gained the level ground above, and made his appearance at full charge on the flank of the Indians, in the direction in which they little expected to see him. They at once leaped on the horses and before they were well prepared to receive him, he was in their midst. The Indians gave way when the shock of the charge struck them, but wheeling it on each flank, they charged the Texians with wild yells, secure their prey, since on their bravest warriors. The pursuit had now been pressed for nearly two miles. The Texians had loaded their arms in detail, whilst the others hung on the rear of the enemy. The Indians had made their last rally, reduced in numbers to about thirty-five, were driven back with great loss, when the voice of their chief again rose high, exhorting them to turn once more, whilst he dashed backwards and forwards amongst his men to bring them back to the charge, The Texians has exhausted all their shots. Hays called out to know which had a loaded gun. (Robert Addison) Gillespie rode forward and answered he was charged "Dismount and shoot that Chief" was the order. At a distance of thirty steps the ball did its office, madly dashing a few yards, the gallant Indian fell to rise no more and in wild affright at the loss of their leader, the others scattered in every direction in the brushwood.

Thus ended a fight, unparalled in the history of this country for the gallantry displayed on both sides, in it close and deadly struggle, and the triumphant success of the gallant captain of the West, at the head of his brave followers. I scarcely know which to admire most, the skill and courage of the officer who command[ed], on that occasion, or his modesty when giving the details which are here narrated. Concealing his own deeds, he did ample justice to his comrades, and at the close of this narrative "blushed" to find himself "famous." As a brave man, he was before celebrated; as a skillful and able officer he now holds that rank to which he is justly entitled, and well does he deserve the praise and admiration of his countrymen.

The result of this contest is well worthy of the attention of our frontier men who are constantly engaged in conflicts with our Indian foe, as evincing the advantages resulting from discipline and obedience to officers. The only security to the men in this instance, against such overpowering numbers was in keeping a serried front, and giving mutual assistance; and had they been scattered by too great eagerness, or undue timidity, all must have perished save those, the speed of whose horses might have saved them.

Hays brings the pleasing intelligence that the wounded men are all doing well and fast recovering. He computes the loss of the Indians at one half their numbers killed and wounded. Twenty-three were counted, dead on the field, No shot was fired at a distance of more than eight or ten paces, except the last, and no more than one hundred and fifty shots fired in all. You can well imagine the execution that must have done at such a distance by arms in the hands of men who are in the constant and daily use of them. It was a glorious fight and triumphantly ended.

I have given you the above account as received from Capt. Hays and although the language is not his still there is no embellishment of the facts. I have stated what he said and have no doubt of the truth of every word of it. I have written it as a proper need of praise for an action which has, in my opinion, no parallel in the history of our country or any other.[7]

Interestingly, Hays omits the name of the Comanche chief, Yellow Wolf, from the names of the killed and wounded, and omits mention of the firepower of the Colt five-shot pistol that gave him the victory in this account.

This fourth version of the battle was compiled by author James Kimmins Greer and used in his biography of Jack Hays. Greer gave his own testimony as to its accuracy. Hays's associates and other contemporaries have been used as collaborators in telling his story, which is shaped from his papers and other bibliographical sources. Condensation has been necessary at most points; nearly every paragraph could be elongated from the material collected. Objectivity has been sought; stock depictions have not always been accepted; no testimony has been suppressed.

Hays led his company northward over the routes he formerly had followed and found Indians. This time he discovered none. After three weeks of riding, he turned back toward home.

When they came to Sisters Creek, two miles above where it empties into the Guadalupe, a scout discovered a bee tree. San Antonio was fifty miles away, and as men and horses had earned a rest, Hays permitted Kit Acklin and John Coleman to rob the bee tree. Thirty feet above the ground, the men paused occasionally as they chopped. After a time, Coleman glanced back over their trail and gasped with astonishment: twenty-five Indians were sitting quietly on horseback three hundred yards away watching the bee robbers.

"Indians!" Coleman yelled, pointing and beginning to descend. Acklin was stepping on his friend's fingers in his haste to get to his horse. Hays and the others were tightening girths and examining their guns preparatory to mounting. Soon all were climbing the slope which they had descended.

The Comanches, legs crossed in front of them, still sat on their horses. There was one sure way to ascertain whether the calm impudence was designed. "Come on, boys!" Hays shouted, sending his horse into a run. Since the Indians never changed their positions, Hays became more wary as he charged. Suddenly within sixty yards from the line of warriors Hays halted his men as he plowed his mount's forefeet through the sod. Behind the row of braves, just appearing over the opposite side of the hill, were two other lines of warriors. Hays motioned his boys to some timber off to one side. Each man held a revolver in his hand. When the Rangers wheeled for the timber, the first row of braves charged, their war whoops ringing across the prairie to terrify the white men. With Hays in the rear and his guns silent, his men rode swiftly without panic. The last two lines of warriors rapidly dashed off the hill and fanned far to both sides.

As the Texans came within fifty yards of the timber, a shower of arrows and shrill whoops met them from an unseen group within. Hays spurred through the center of his racing line, crashed hard into the brush, and fired. An Indian sprang erect and fell, with the horse's shoulder striking the corpse. Indians scampered to get away from the horses and the spitting guns. No attempt was made to follow them as they rushed twenty strong for their mounts behind the thicket. Hays and his men wheeled, dismounted, and gave their horses' reins—five animals to a man to hold.

The three parties of Indians united and charged the thicket. When Hays shouted "Now!" bullets thudded into warriors and their gaily decorated horses. The line of riders divided, thundered by on each side of the thicket, and circled to safety. Beyond rifle range the chiefs re-formed their men. When the long line trotted forward, the rifles of the palefaces began to speak. Because this had been expected there was no confusion. The red men were galloping now, and as chiefs shrilled their war cries, braves rode recklessly at the grove. The line parted, and horsemen raced in a semicircle to unite for a charge before the white men could reload.

Comanche Attack by George Catlin. (Smithsonian American Art Museum, gift of Mrs. Joseph Harrison, Jr., 1985.66.496)

With deadly lances poised in their hands, back they came whooping and shooting arrows and rifles. But right in the faces of their paralyzing war horses the white men rose and stood with a smoking stick thundering from both hands. Braves and horses went down hard, dying as they fell and rolled. The charging line halved at the thicket, and the survivors galloped on. Here and there warriors swooped up behind their shields as many wounded and dead as possible. Then the chiefs led a slow withdrawal to a prairie height for council. Watching their gestures, Hays saw that they were whipped. He decided to take the initiative and inflict more punishment.

When the Rangers charged, the Comanches showered them with arrows. Three men were hit and reeled in their saddles; whereupon a companion caught each man to prevent him from falling. In the terrific attack, Hays and nine comrades pierced the line of warriors, then broke back through the line. Braves tumbled to the ground. Their wounded horses screamed, reared, and stampeded, but the Comanches continued to fight. Hays motioned to the three Rangers who were supporting their friends to lead a retreat, while he and the others hurriedly spread out to protect them. The Indians followed, keeping as much as possible behind their shields, shooting their arrows, and riding zigzag to avoid the white men's aim.

When near the timber, Sam Walker shot an Indian who was trying to get close enough to thrust him with his spear. In the encounter, Walker's back was turned a second, and another warrior drove a lance through him. John Carlin saw the brave make his thrust and shot him through the head just as another Ranger spurred forward, jerked the lance out, and assisted Walker to the thicket. Seconds later, Ad Gillespie stopped an arrow and fell from his horse at the edge of the grove.

The Comanche war chief galloped forward to stab his lance through Gillespie, but as the chief poised, Ad sent a bullet through the red man's brain. Two dismounted Rangers dashed to Gillespie and pulled him into the brush. Indians galloped toward the three, but Hays and the others drove them back. Warriors crowded forward in an attempt to rescue their chief's body. The odds were seven to one in a desperate conflict over the corpse. Other Indians galloped up and joined in the struggle. There was danger of the Rangers' being surrounded and overcome by sheer numbers.

Hays ordered his men to leave the body and retire into the thicket, where the five wounded Rangers lay. Firing as he moved backward behind his men, the Major watched the braves pick up their chief's body, place it in front of a mounted Indian, circle their horses about the fallen leader, and gallop off. Three Rangers sat down within the thicket and pulled arrows from each other's bodies.

As the Indians moved rapidly away, chanting loud lamentations, Hays remounted. "Follow me!" he shouted, and seven men streamed out behind him across the prairie. When within range Hays began firing. The Comanches fought back only halfheartedly as the Rangers unhorsed a number of them. In trying to carry away their dead and wounded, they could neither travel fast nor offer other than a haphazard rear-guard resistance. The Rangers followed them until darkness began to make targets uncertain.

Back at the thicket, the eight Rangers were found to be seriously injured. At least half of the red men must have been killed. On his return to San Antonio, Walker for several months was a slow convalescent. Hays unhesitatingly gave the revolvers the credit for their survival.[8]

Also documented at Washington on the Brazos on June 25 was when Hays signed a receipt for $1,325 for pay for his Rangers and $460.29 to pay for their provisions.

Hays sent Joshua Threadgill back to San Antonio with a letter to Capt. Ben McCulloch to send reinforcements. Twelve Rangers with medical supplies were dispatched to help Hays.

The next day the Hays's camp was attacked by a small group of natives. Hays wrote "A party of four Indians made their appearance. I immediately ordered six men to give chase to them … killing three of them." In Hays's letter to McCulloch dated June 9, he reported none of his Rangers had been killed, but two—Walker and Gillespie—were serious lanced.

Veteran Ranger Irishman Peter Fohr, who had served under Hays since 1841, made a fatal mistake. Fohr saw a wounded Comanche go into a thicket and, although warned by Hays, went in after him. The dying warrior, reportedly with wounds from four rifle balls (one of which apparently had broken his leg) still was able to put an arrow entirely through Fohr with the feather end seen on one side of his chest and the point protruding on the other side. Ranger Peter Fohr would die of this arrow wound two days later. Andrew Erskine was slightly wounded by an arrow and W. B. Lee was more seriously injured also by an arrow.

Of Hays's 15 men, one-third—a total of five Rangers—had been wounded. One would die in two days and Hays had grave concerns about Sam Walker's chance of survival. In fact, Hays mentioned three times in his letters and report that he did not think Sam Walker would live. Gillespie was seriously wounded as well.

The Rangers identified as being in this battle are: Jack Hays, Sam Walker, Ad Gillespie, Rufus Perry, Kit Acklin, Mike Chevalier, Josiah Taylor, Pipkin Taylor, Peter Fohr, W. B. Lee, Andrew Erskine, Joshua Threadgill, A. Coleman, John Carolan, James Dunn, and Frank Paschal.[9]

Perry recalled that 21 horses and saddles were captured—many with the shields, bows and quivers attached.

Ad Gillespie and Sam Walker were nursed back to health in San Antonio by Mrs. William B. Jacques, the wife of a leading merchant. Walker spent several months recuperating from this injury and not only took his scars from the battle with him, but his lessons learned about the importance of the revolver for mounted combat. But the Paterson revolver he used needed to be more powerful, needed more range, needed a trigger guard and needed another shot. Walker himself, with Sam Colt, would design the huge Walker Colt revolver that would have these changes. It was the first army-issued revolver—the most powerful issued revolver and the first of the legendary Colt six-gun series.

The Rangers' victory at Walker Creek, with their new repeating Colt revolvers, would definitely enhance the Rangers' fame as mounted fighters. This reputation would follow Rangers to Mexico during the Mexican–American War. There, with the next generation Colt revolvers, the 4.5-pound Walker Colt revolver (co-designed by former Texas Ranger Sam Walker and at the time of the design of Colt's new six-shooter, captain, Regiment of Mounted Riflemen), the Rangers were a force to be reckoned with. Armed with this pistol, the Rangers would be a major factor in the Mexican–American War as they used their new repeating pistols to put down the menace of Mexican guerrillas. These bandits used the war as an excuse to prey not only on the U.S. Army but their own people. They were a thorn in the side of the army as guerrillas often stalled or delayed the moving of troops and supplies across Mexico from Veracruz to Mexico City.

This road to success all began on one day. That day, June 8, 1844—at the battle of Walker Creek—was the day the Texas frontier changed forever.[10]

Location of the Battle Site

The exact site for the running battle of Walker Creek is not known. There are two possibilities for the site.

The first is the map included in Kenneth F. Neighbours, "The Battle of Walker Creek," *West Texas Historical Association Yearbook*, 41 (October 1965): 120, gives some idea where the battle may have occurred.

Neighbours made a personal visit to the site where he believes the battle occurred near Sisterdale, Texas. He talked with area residents who spoke of an oral tradition of where the battle happened as well as the location of the bee tree.

Based on the map, he includes the aerial photograph was located in the Texas State Archives in his work. It was taken in the spring of 1945—almost exactly 100 years after the battle.

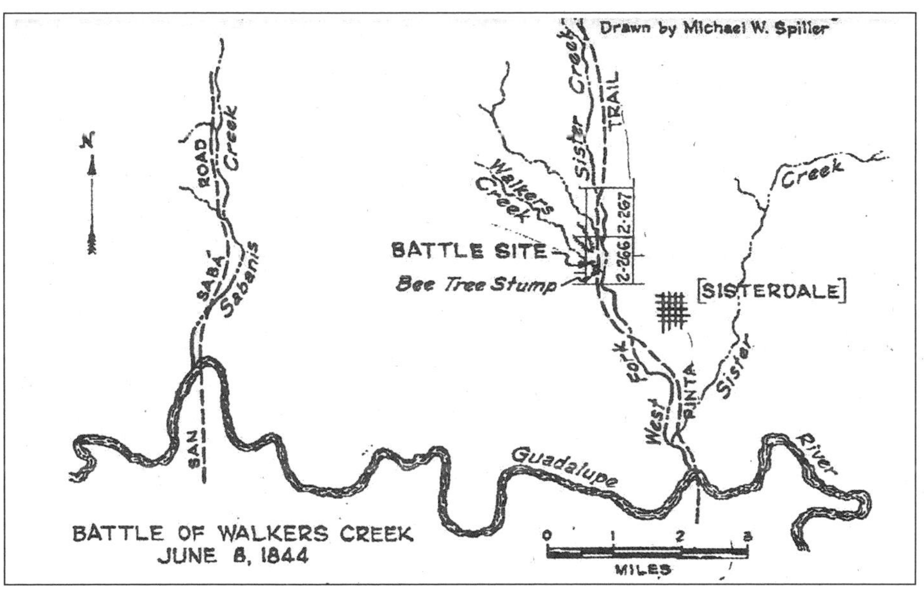

"The Battle of Walkers Creek." (West Texas Historical Association Yearbook)

Aerial photo taken April 25, 1945, Kendall County. (ASCS, Frame 5–58)

The second site is based on two newspaper accounts.

Upon receiving a letter from Hays, written the day after the battle, requesting more Rangers, Ben McCulloch wrote to Thomas Green on June 9, 1844:

> Dear Sir:
> Mr. Threadgill has just reached town with news that the Hays [party] has had a warm fight with the Indians, the particulars I give you.
>
> Hays left here nine days since, with a small party of his company, for the purpose of seeing if there was any large encampment [of] Indians in the mountains near this place. He went to Predernalis and not seeing any Indian signs started back to this place; within five miles of the Guadalupe river on the "Pinto Trail" he encamped. We were cutting a bee tree, when Mr. Coleman, who was on post, discovered that some Indians coming in on Hays' trail—The horses were saddled in double quick time, and the men were ready for action. In the meantime, the Indians conceal themselves behind some timber, leaving out one horse, which our boys could see, for bait. After Hays had advance within a few hundred yards to the horse, about 20 Indians displayed themselves on the Prairie—flourishing

their lances and bantering Hays for a fight—leaving 20 or 30 more in ambush for the purpose no doubt of a flanking our boys in case having their stratagem succeeded.

But after firing a few shots at a distance, the Indians, after having failed in their ruse de guerre, retire to a body of timber not far distant. Hays pursued them, and here they showed only a part of their force, again Hays made a movement to take possession of a part of the timber, but upon coming near, discovered that the main body of the Indians had possession of it, and were strongly lodged. Hays then ordered a charge, which was gallantly made by our brave boys: the fight was now a hand-to-hand one—they took it rough and tumble.

While our boys were engaged with those in front, a part of the Indians charged them in flank. Our boys fought so gallantly, that the Indians soon fled, after sustaining a loss of 20 or 30 killed and wounded.

Samuel Walker and Robert A. Gillespie were wounded with the lance: the former dangerously—supposed to be mortally, while the latter, Mr. Gillespie, slightly wounded. They were both in front, and both distinguished themselves.

Hays' party only consisted of fifteen men, while the Indians numbered fifty or more. After defeating the Indians, Hays pursued them some distance.

Your friend
Ben M'Culloch.[11]

CHAPTER 7

Matamoros to Monterrey: Early Ranger Wartime Service, 1844–46

Walker became a veteran Ranger with continuous service under John C. Hays. According to the official Texas Ranger Rolls, Sam Walker served in Captain Hays's company from early 1844 through late summer 1845. He was wounded at least twice during that time. During his first enlistment, February 25 to June 26, 1844, he was seriously wounded by a Comanche lance on June 8, at the battle of Walker Creek. Upon his recovery, or near recovery, he enlisted in Bexar County to serve from June 27 to August 27, 1844. His third enlistment, also in Bexar County, was for only two months—August 28 to October 28, 1844.

His next enlistment lasted from October 29 to December 29, 1844. It was during this enlistment Walker suffered his second wound. Ranger William Oury reported Sam pursued a renegade Cherokee in a running fight near Corpus Christi in the winter of 1844:

> A fugitive from justice, who had taken refuge among the Comanches. ... Several shots at close quarters were interchanged, the Indian's horse was killed, Walker's spirited mustang was wounded, became unmanageable and threw him, and as he was rising from his fall he was shot by the Indian with an arrow through the shoulder, then fired the last load remaining in his pistol, and dispatched the troublesome antagonist.[1]

William Oury. (Cornelius Smith, Jr., *William Sander Oury, History Maker of the Southwest*)

Perhaps his latest wound delayed his enlistment since it did not begin until February 12 in San Antonio and it lasted until May 11, 1845. His sixth enlistment under Hays in 1845 was from May 12 in San Antonio to August 12, 1845.[2] Walker then enlisted in Capt. Robert A. Gillespie's company of Mounted Rangers, on September 28, 1845. In addition to his normal duties as a Ranger, Walker also recruited men for Gillespie's company.[3] He was discharged on March 28, 1846.

Lieutenant Colonel Samuel H. Walker. (Photograph in the public domain)

On August 26, 1845—shortly after leaving his last Ranger service under Hays—Walker wrote his first letter to his sister-in-law Ann since he was wounded on June 8, 1844.

San Antonio De Bexar
August 26, 1845

Dear sister
I take the present opportunity of communicating a few lines by Mr. Smith who has been here for some time he gave me information respecting you and your little girl, your mother's family etc., which afforded me much satisfaction and afforded me much pleasure to congratulate you on the prospect of your future happiness.

I wrote to you soon after my escape from prison but I have heard nothing from you until I saw [illegible] Smith since I have been in Texas, I have been nearly all the time in active service. I have been twice wounded and suffered a great deal while prisoner in Mexico but my constitution as yet unimpaired in my health is very good.[4] I shall remain in the service until the final settlement of all our difficulties with the Mexicans. If circumstances will then admit of it I will visit Florida our frontier Rangers are about to be reorganized and augmented in force to be mustered in the US service to the amount of near 400 men to be commanded by our Gallant leader John C Hays who have served continuously since I have been in the Republic all of us who know him best have implicit confidence in him and look forward to the coming events which are giving us a better opportunity with the pleasing anticipations as to the result, it is useless for me to enter into particulars about anything that has been transpired.

Suffice it to say that I am much pleased with the country and immigrants may now come to the country without making any speculations respecting its fate they can settle in peace and security anywhere between the rivers Nueces and Sabine notwithstanding Mexico is making her coastal threats of war and devastation because we are just as certain to defeat them and scatter their forces as any thing can possibly be which has not already transpired, for further participation in general information and I must refer you to Mr. Smith who will return to this place and bring any communications which my friends have to make give my best respects and kind wishes to your mother in the family and be assured that my friendship for you and all have not been worn out by absence.

Yours Very Respectfully
SH Walker

PS I've heard nothing from my relations in Maryland or the D C for a long time. I received a letter from my relative Samuel Hamilton about fourteen months ago expressing his disappointment in the most decided terms in relation to the part I have taken in the war with another country, and wound up by giving me what he no doubt considered a great deal of good advice by telling me by all means returned to my native land and no longer to seek fame and glory in a foreign country, I replied to him and told him that I would continue with the colonists until the peace and independence of Texas was fully consummated, since then I have received nothing from him or any of my relatives nor shall I ever travel them with my communication began until they choose to open the correspondence and make an apology for their indifference and except my aged mother who I shall write the now which my hand it's the, this is the first letter I have written since last summer when I was badly wounded with a lance and they have all taken it for granted that I am dead I am and unable to determine.

SH[W][5]

Prior to the start of the War with Mexico, Hays and Walker had gone to meet with the Texas governor to gain permission to organize a Ranger Regiment when the war began. They received permission to do so, and both visited several Texas towns giving speeches and visiting with former Rangers.

Anticipating military conflict between the United States and Mexico, on the day he was appointed U.S. Senator from Texas and three months before the declaration of war passed in the U.S. Congress on 13 May 1846, Sam Houston asked his most experienced field commanders, Maj. John C. Hays and Capt. Benjamin McCulloch, for recommendations of deserving Texans to be nominated for positions in the U.S. Army. He received a reply that same day.

Austin, 21st Feby 1846
To Genl Sam Houston

Sir
In accordance with your request, you will see subjoined the names of those gentlemen whom we have thought qualified to receive commissions for office from the War Department of the United States, together with the office hey should receive.

We have depended entirely on you to induce the President of the United States to raise a Corps of Rangers in Texas and upon your influence in procuring the men commissions for the gentlemen we have recommended. Your position in Texas together with your intimate knowledge of the military men and affairs of Texas will entitle your opinion to more respect than that of any other man in this country and consequently we have relied mainly upon you.

It would be gratifying to us, and we believe it would be acceptable to the whole country, that these gentlemen should receive their appointments in the order as they are named as they are men fully competent to fill these offices, as their services and (most of them) their sufferings have entitled them to a preference over those who have not continued in service.

Accept our thanks for the confidence you have reposed in us, and also the [con]gratulations for your success and best wishes for your continued prosperity.

from Yr. obt. Srvts.
John C. Hays
Ben McCulloch

For Captains
Robert A. Gillespie
Christopher B. Acklin
Samuel H. Walker
Michael Chevallier

1st Lieutenants
John McMullin
William Wallace
William Hurbert
Gouverner H. Nelson

2nd Lieutenants
R. L. Woolfork
Alfred Thurman
John Adams
Thomas Lyons
Fielding Alston

P.S. Of the above we would particularly recommend Capt. R. A. Gillespie to your especial notice as his claims are superior to those of any other man we know.[6]

Of those on this list, only Samuel H. Walker, then a private in Captain Gillespie's company, Texas Mounted Rangers, would receive a commission in the U.S. Army. There is no record of any other man being nominated or placed before the Senate for confirmation. Walker's name was third among the ten nominated for the post of captain of the Mounted Riflemen.[7]

While Walker and Hays were in San Antonio, something life-changing happened to both men. Hays met Susan Calvert whom he would later marry. Walker met Mary Chalmers whom he almost married. Walker's letters often said that he preferred the company of the ladies. Apparently, he had found one he enjoyed being with very much. However, another Ranger enjoyed her company also. It was to his advantage that Walker was already a friend of Mary's father, Dr. John Gordon Chalmers, who trained as a doctor in Scotland, and helped establish the Democratic Party in Texas. A leading figure in the Texas Republic, he served as secretary of the treasury and later helped draft the resolution approving the annexation of Texas to the United States. In 1845, he became editor and publisher of the Austin *New Era*. Chalmers and Walker were close enough that Chalmers looked up his brother when he visited Washington City. Chalmers wrote Walker on May 4, 1846, that he was in Washington City and had visited Jonathan Thomas:

> La Grange
> To S Walker Esquire
> Army of occupation May 4, 1846
>
> Dear Walker
> I have nothing to communicate worth your special interest in this section of the country except to assure you of the heartfelt sympathy of myself and others of your friends hereabouts in your present one in public estimation. Without a single its exception save an occasional Houston man, the whole community exalts in your achievements deep-rooted and you will place yourself in a condition to a what a honorable man but which. Behoove and the guarded against the atrocities for jealousy of the young Texans and your success is sure
>
> I met your brother frequently in Washington city and was much pleased with his modesty and most excellent good sense, promised him to scold you for obstinacy in not writing home. The family are daily and hourly thinking of you the fear of a vagabond life in Texas one not unreasonable or so many young men have been lost they must avail yourself of such opportunity as may occur to your conscience to write me of your doings and things in general. I'll shall be pleased to hear from you at any time the family joins with me in sending their best wishes and regards to you
>
> your friend
> John Chalmers[8]

According to the biographer of another contemporary "for some time preceding the Mexican War, Tom Green and Sam Walker had been contending for the hand of one of the prettiest girls in La Grange (Texas), Mary Wallace Chalmers, the oldest daughter of Austin newspaper editor Dr. John Chalmers." In the end, he was "Unlucky Walker" in love. The other Ranger got the girl. Green married Mary on January 31, 1847.[9]

While Hays and Walker had been recruiting Rangers for the Ranger Regiment approved by the Governor of Texas; he had also watched the unfolding hostilities closely.

On July 25, 1845, the steamship *Alabama* unloaded U.S. troops on St. Joseph's Island. Gen. Zachary Taylor, commanding U.S. forces, remained there for nine months trying to come to a peaceable understanding with Mexico concerning the annexation of Texas by the United States. Texas held the land down to the Nueces River but claimed the land as far as the Rio Grande. Mexico grudgingly recognized only the Nueces as the Texas border.

Gen. Zachary Taylor. (Photograph in the public domain)

On March 8, 1846, Taylor—under orders from Washington—marched his 3,000-man army across the Nueces River, 200 miles south to the Rio Grande. To the Mexicans, this was an invasion of their country; to the state of Texas, he was advancing to the Texan southern border to defend that part of the United States from a potential foreign invader.

By April 1, Taylor was across the river from Matamoros, Mexico, in what is today Brownsville, Texas. He was supplied from ships and transports at Point Isabel, twenty miles away.

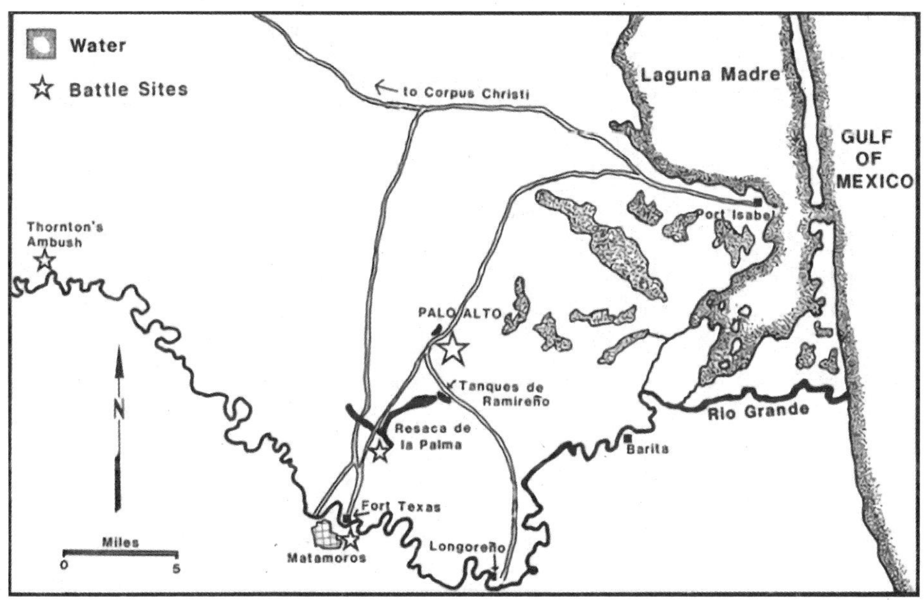

Point Isabel and environs. (www.nps.gov)

In April, Mexican Gen. Mariano Arista was ordered to open hostilities with the United States and advanced into the disputed territory claimed by both Mexico and Texas.

Gen. Mariano Arista. (Image in the public domain)

Taylor's base was Fort Texas (later Fort Brown), built on a peninsular bluff beside a bend in the Rio Grande, directly across from the Mexican artillery positions on the other side of the river in Matamoros. It was a large six-sided star with earthen walls. The fort had been garrisoned with 500 soldiers and had an 800-yard perimeter with six bastions, walls more than nine feet high, a parapet of 15 feet, and the whole surrounded by a ditch 15 feet deep and 20 feet wide. Armament included four guns that fired 18-pound projectiles. The 7th Infantry Regiment with Company I of the 2d Artillery and Company E, 3d Artillery, commanded by Maj. Jacob Brown, garrisoned the fort.[10]

Realizing his supply depot would soon be in danger of capture by a Mexican force that was becoming continually larger, General Taylor decided to take preventative action. Leaving a 500-man force at Fort Texas, on May 1, Taylor directed most of his army to Point Isabel to protect his growing depot of supplies and a likely target for a Mexican attack. With the departure of the main portion of his forces from the Fort Texas area, the Mexican forces threatened the fort by opening a bombardment.

The Texas Rangers

The Texas Rangers participated, as historian Walter Prescott Webb describes them, as a "recognized and famous separate arm of the (U.S.) service."[11] Rangers were originally organized to protect Texas's scattered inhabitants from natives and Mexicans. It was to be a temporary force as the republic could not afford a permanent one. On February 1, 1845, the Texas Congress authorized Capt. John C. Hays to organize and command five detachments of 10–30 men each for the protection of the frontier.[12]

These Rangers had learned from the Alamo; the massacre of Fannin's men at Goliad; another massacre known to history by the name of its ill-fated commander Nicholas Dawson; and the treatment of the Mier prisoners to expect no mercy from the Mexicans, and that one of their breed should never surrender.

The Rangers trained by Major Hays were self-reliant and resourceful, frequently extracting themselves from difficulties, not by fighting, but by quick thinking. They knew how to make a great show with a small force, how to deceive, retreat, and how to strike unexpectedly with the fury of the tiger. … They gave quarter—sometimes—but never asked and never expected it. … In short, they made wonderful spies, scouts, fighters, but otherwise mighty poor soldiers.[13]

Captain Walker's Rangers

The Texians in the Sante Fe campaign, Mier invasion, and other spontaneous reactions to the Mexican threat to the Texas Republic, had proved themselves to be eager to fight for their new republic. Now with statehood, they were equally willing to take on the Mexicans again, but as part of the U.S. Army.

Walker—who had volunteered as a teenager to fight in the Seminole War and upon coming to Texas quickly volunteered for service with volunteer units, the Mier Expedition and the Texas Rangers—was ready to join the fray. Foremost in his mind was the brutality of his eight-month Mier imprisonment and the execution by the Mexicans of some of some of his close friends.

One newspaper writer reported the details remembered by one of Walker's Rangers:

> I was informed by Capt. Walker upon his arrival at Point Isabel, that he had come down merely as a looker on, with the intention of acting as a private in a company. … He used every exertion to get Gen. Taylor to order down Maj Hays' company from San Antonio, but without success. A few Texans came down directly after the army, insisting upon his (Walker) asking permission of Gen. Taylor to raise a company; he did so and was refused.[14]

On April 10, 1846, Col. Truman Cross, General Taylor's chief quartermaster, failed to return from a reconnaissance. Search parties were dispatched. One, under the command of Lt. Theodoric H. Porter of the 4th Infantry, was ambushed on April 18 and Porter killed. Cross's body was later found but the death of Porter, the son of the U.S. Navy's Commo. David Porter, had an impact on his longtime friend Taylor. Porter's party was ambushed because it was on foot and unfamiliar with the ground it had to cover. General Taylor realized he needed mounted troops who knew how to scout in the Texas terrain. Taylor, writing to the adjutant general stated, "I shall authorize the raising off two companies of Texan mounted men for service in this quarter, particularly for the purpose of keeping open our communications with Point Isabel and relieving the regular Cavalry of a portion of their duties which are now oppressive." And so, Taylor rescinded his earlier refusal and Walker was appointed to the rank of captain and got permission to raise a company.[15] On April 21, newly minted Capt. Samuel H. Walker and the first 23 of ultimately 97 men were mustered into

Col. Truman Cross. Cowan's Auctions. (Photograph in the public domain)

U.S. service under the militia laws as Captain Walker's Mounted Ranger company. At the same time, General Taylor verbally authorized him to recruit as many privates and noncommissioned officers within the limits prescribed by law.[16]

Word traveled through Texas, and Walker, slowly but surely, filled his Ranger company. Old friends: three veterans of the battle of Walker Creek—Joshua Threadgill, Josiah Taylor, and Pipkin Taylor—were in his company; two fellow Mier prisoners—George Washington Trahern and Gideon K. Lewis—who were with him in Captain Cameron's company; and veteran Ranger Creed Taylor also joined.[17]

Texas Ranger Gideon "Legs" Lewis. (Photograph in the public domain)

Trahern recalled meeting up with Walker. "Walker had a few men with him, and a good many hangers-on following the army, and by that means he raised about thirty-five men. He wanted to recruit and raise a spy company—and we joined."[18] Another veteran was Cpl. Moffett E. Trimble who had been a sergeant in Capt. Jesse Bean's company of U.S. Rangers out of Fort Gibson, Oklahoma, in the 1830s.[19]

One new Ranger later observed that while many of the new recruits were inexperienced, some brought with them important skills. Trahan, one of Walker's men, demonstrated his ability to ride at a full gallop, lean from the saddle and pick up three coins. He explained to his Eastern-trained cavalry counter parts, that in addition to continual practice the Texans had special saddles that enabled them to stay in the saddle during a fight and had heavy bits to control their horses to with one hand at a full gallop.[20]

On April 20, 1846, among the arms and ammunition issued by the U.S. Army to Captain Walker's company of Mounted Rangers were:

8 Carbines, Halls
400 musket percussion caps
300 Carbine Buck and Ball Cartridges
32 Pistols Colts patent
32 screwdrivers Colt's patent
32 Flasks Colt's patent
23 percussion priming boxes Colt's patent
23 Bullet molds Colt's patent

6	Rifles, North's
2	Arms Chests
10	Cartridge Boxes, Carbine
7	[powder] flasks

James Francis Blair. (Courtesy of John McWilliams)

Walker also drew axes, shovels, blankets, tents, and 40 pounds of lead. Later he drew eight bridles, eight martingales, and a surcingle—a wide strap that runs over the back and under the belly of a horse, used to keep a blanket or other equipment in place.[21]

Walker was ordered to take his new Ranger company and "pitch his camp half way between the point and Matamoros," which he did. One unnamed Texas volunteer in the 7th Infantry who came through the area later that summer wrote:

> The country about Matamoros and Pt Isabell being the valley of the Rio Grande is a rich and fertile Perairie country—no timber but muskeet and chapparal and Prickly Pear of which this country abounds the soil of a dark chocolate color—covered with the most delightful muskeet grass ... weather extremely hot—too hot for a lizard to live and do well—musquitoes intolerable at night.[22]

One of Walker's men wrote: "We were mustered into service on the 21st of April, 1846, numbering about twenty-five men; we then received orders to build a picket fence around his encampment, as protection against surprise, in five days we had this completed." The camp at Lagoon (small lake) Iran Pelon was about 15 miles from Point Isabel, it was "in an enclosure where some butchers had formerly kept their cattle."[23]

Apparently, Walker had time to grow a beard. A contemporary portrayed him thus: "His hair and whiskers are red; his complexion not naturally dark is much tanned from exposure. His stature is somewhat beneath the medium height. ... He appeared to one well informed on most subjects and tolerably well educated."[24] He was "stooped with a sloughing gait, thin face, and small red whiskers."[25] From quartermaster receipts we also know at least how he was dressed. Captain Walker drew, "One hickory shirt [a long-sleeved pullover shirt,[26] opening to mid-chest] & one pair of drawers and One pair Kinky Jeans [drop-front] pantaloons in late April."[27] In all probability he wore a buckskin jacket also as did almost all the Rangers of this era.

Walker's camp was then established and equipped. On his return to camp on April 27, accompanied by only one Ranger, Walker was attacked by mounted Mexicans with rifles from a timbered area. He tried to draw them closer so he could effectively use his Colt's revolvers.[28] Unable to get them to follow him, Walker made his way to camp and "immediately prepared to evacuate it" acting on Taylor's order to do so if threatened by a large force of the enemy. This large force of cavalry was a serious threat to Walker's men. But before he abandoned his camp, he needed more information for General Taylor.

Walker first sent out Lt. Joseph P. Wells with seven men, to the Little Colarou, in search of Col. Antonio Canales (Mexican cavalry), who he supposed was there with a party of Rancheros. Walker then took 14 men and "went in search of the main body of the enemy, intending to reconnoiter them, and give them a fight or run, as might be thought most prudent."

During the nights of the 27th and 28th of April, the force at Point Isabel expected to be attacked, and every disposition was made accordingly. The masters of vessels in port were called on for their crews, and about five hundred men were furnished with arms. Small parties of Texians had previously arrived, among them was Captain Walker of the Rangers who was destined to occupy a prominent place in the stirring events that followed. Major (John) Munroe expressed himself able to hold out with his reinforcements against any number of Mexicans that chose to attack him. At this time several teams that had started for Fort Brown, were compelled to return; and Captain Walker, with a number of men, who had, on the 28th, gone out to reconnoiter, were driven back to Point Isabel, suffering great loss. He stated that midway between Point Isabel and the camp, an overwhelming Mexican force suddenly appeared, and many of his men (who were just enlisted) had scattered in confusion, and he was compelled to retreat. He was followed by the Mexicans until within a short distance of the point, where he arrived with only two of his command; seven afterwards came in. Captain Walker estimated the force he met at fifteen hundred, and thought many of the enemy fell in his engagement with them.[29] At least this was what was reported in period media, which was absolutely false. Former Ranger William Oury and now a private in Walker's company wrote a different, and more accurate account of the mission.

> I was mustered into the U.S. Service at San Antonio, Texas, shortly after the annexation of Texas to the Union. I was placed under the command of Captain R. A. Gillespie. General Taylor, who was at Corpus Christi with his command, had said that our company should take the field at the first appearance of war. Sam Walker, who was also with our company, had gone down with our Captain from San Antonio to Corpus Christi, and remained there to obtain permission to raise a small company of scouts. This body was to accompany the army on its march from Corpus Christi to the Rio Grande. Learning from Taylor that Captain Gillespie's company would not be called to the front, but instead would remain in Texas to protect settlers from Indian forays, Walker wrote to Gillespie, and requested that the latter send Sy Taylor, Jim Taylor, "Shap" Woolfolk and myself down to Corpus to help him. This was readily agreed to, and we set out the same evening for the army, which by then had gone on to Fort Brown. We were welcomed by our old companions, arriving just before the Mexicans commenced bombardment of the fort. General Taylor, with the greater part of the army, had gone down the coast to Point Isabel to see to the landing of supplies and troops. General Arista took advantage of our divided condition to cross the Rio Grande and throw his whole force between Fort Brown and Point Isabel, thus cutting our small army in two.
>
> Several attempts were made by Major Brown to communicate with General Taylor, but the Mexican lancers were scouring the whole plains, and every party making the attempt was driven

back to the fort. In this emergency, Walker went to Brown and told him that if he would allow him to mount his men upon the pick of his artillery horses, he would engage to deliver any despatches he might desire to send to Taylor. The Major agreed at once, and at dusk Walker with 14 men started upon a most perilous journey. I was one of the 14 men. Every pathway was watched by Mexican cavalry. They saw us leave the fort at dark, and their vigilance redoubled. Finding it impossible to go by any of the regular paths, Walker resolved to cut a new one. With hatchet and Bowie knife, through the thorniest thicket it has ever been my bad luck to encounter, we cut our way for six hours. The night was so dark, too, that one could not see the hand before the face, and we had not even a star to guide us. There you have one of the gloomiest pictures that might be painted.

Fortunately, we had a man equal to the task. Sy Taylor, born on the Texas frontier, and possessed of an instinct equal to that of the most acute animal, led us through. Under his guidance, a path was hewn through the jungle, and at dawn we emerged upon the prairie to the astonishment of the Mexicans; they had cavalry pickets stretched along almost the whole front of the thicket. Luckily for us, there was no picket in our immediate front, and we had just time to mount and fly over the prairie with about 500 lancers in full chase. We were pursued all the way to Point Isabel, where our guns gave us protection. We were received with the wildest demonstrations of joy by General Taylor and his whole command. The distance from the fort was about 23 miles, and every report of cannon during the bombardment there had been heard at Point Isabel. The General and his command were kept in continual uneasiness for the fate of the garrison until our arrival. The general, when told that the stars and stripes were still saucily flying over Fort Brown could scarcely contain himself, and at once resolved to take up the line of march for the fort on the next morning.

No one can describe the joy with which this news was hailed by the whole his command, had said that our company should take the field at the first appearance of war. Sam Walker, who was also with our company, had gone down with our Captain from San Antonio to Corpus Christi, and remained there to obtain permission to raise a small company of scouts. This body was to accompany the army on its march from Corpus Christi to the Rio Grande. Learning from Taylor that Captain Gillespie's company would not be called to the front, but instead would remain in Texas to protect settlers from Indian forays, Walker wrote to Gillespie, and requested that the latter send Sy Taylor, Jim Taylor, "Shap" Woolfolk and myself down to Corpus to help him. This was readily agreed to, and we set out the same evening for the army, which by then had gone on to Fort Brown. We were welcomed by our old companions, arriving just before the Mexicans commenced bombardment of the fort. General Taylor, with the greater part of the army, had gone down the coast to Point Isabel to see to the landing of supplies and troops. General Arista took advantage of our divided condition to cross the Rio Grande and throw his whole force between Fort Brown and Point Isabel, thus cutting our small army in two.[30]

When Walker left his camp at Lagoon Iran Pelon, he told the 15 men he left there to keep a good watch. He also told them "to sleep in a ravine close by and not in the fortification. This way they could not be surprised."[31] They, however, stayed in the fortification but did keep watch that night. But with daylight, they fell asleep.[32] Another account stated that a picket guard was kept some distance from the camp at night but came in at daybreak. The Mexicans had approached the picket in large force and followed them into camp. The attack occurred just at dawn.[33]

Walker arrived about 9 a.m. April 28 to find his camp in disarray. Indeed, six men were dead, four taken as prisoners, and five escaped.[34] The Mexicans were still in the nearby thicket and Walker knew that with only 13 Rangers with him he did not have enough men to attack them there. However, if he could get them to leave the timber and follow his Rangers out on the prairie, he could have "got them scattered so as to have done them some injury."[35] Even though the Rangers rode slowly just out of rifle range, the Mexicans could not be lured out. They stayed at the timber line. Walker returned with his men to Taylor's camp realizing he could do nothing with Mexican patrols in the area. He came back to bury his fallen comrades the next day.

One newspaper reported what had happened during the attack on Walker's men. The article said that Maj. Don Rafael Quintero, with his cavalry patrol of about 100 men, bragged about their attack on the small camp of Texas Rangers. The Mexican commander claimed "only one of his men was wounded with a rifle ball in the left arm."[36] The small band of Rangers were not so lucky—six Rangers killed and four captured. The mutilation of the bodies was witnessed by one of those concealed in the bushes and stayed hidden until the Mexicans left.[37] One report claims that one was lariated around the neck and dragged to death.[38] According to the *Commercial Bulletin of New Orleans*, there may have been some truth in this account. The newspaper reported, "The bodies of five have been found but owing to the shocking manner the Mexican mutilated them, Captain Walker recognized only two, McClister and Radcliffe; however, it was not McClister. He had been taken prisoner."[39]

The *Corpus Christi Gazette* reported the Rangers deaths in its obituary page on April 30,1846. "Edward RADCLIFF, the sergeant in command, and privates McCLIESTER, REISE, VAN REED, HALBERT, HASTINGS, ROBINSON and HARRIS. HASTINGS had merely camped with them for the night."[40] Walker reported 15 in the camp and six killed. Of the above number those killed in action were 1st Sgt. Edward S. Radcliffe and Pvts. H. H. Hastings, J. Robinson, and E. Harris. Two others killed were Pvts. Joseph Prostoski and William Waters. The other four mentioned in the article as dead were prisoners of war.

One who did escape was Mier veteran George W. Trahern who recalled:

> We didn't apprehend any danger, and they attacked us and we just jumped for our guns. We hadn't pulled off our clothes, just our boots and shoes. … and we fought them there, and found they were so heavy and strong against us we just broke through this laguna … and went on the other side into the brush there. … I had my five-shooter with me,[41] and I went out and got in the thicket. I laid beside an old log and some little brush … two fellows came right as close to me as that door … two Mexican rancheros got off and threw their saddles off and picketed their horses and sat there about two hours … let their horses graze and got up and saddled up. They never saw me. I had my pistol cocked, though, ready for them.[42]

He hid, thinking he was the only survivor, but later making his way back to the main force found out that four others had escaped.

Walker returned in the afternoon of April 29. That night he buried his dead and left for Taylor's camp. He sent his men ahead to Taylor's camp as "the enemy being in full force between the two points."[43] Walker and another Ranger rode back together.

Captain Walker returning from his April 29, 1846, expedition. The artist has erroneously drawn Walker wearing a U.S. Army uniform. (Drawing in the public domain)

Arriving at General Taylor's camp, Walker reported the loss of weapons and accoutrements after the attack on his men as:

12	Colt's pistols
28	flasks
12	bullet molds
12	percussion cap boxes
6	Dragoon Carbines
6	Cartridge boxes
3	Arms chests
3	Rifles, North

He reported:

> The above arms were in the possession and care of 15 men of my company whom I left in Camp at Lagoon Juan Pelon on the night of the 27th of April 1846 and that in the attack of the Mexicans on our Camp on the following day, all these arms (above) were lost & captured.[44]

General Taylor included Walker's unfortunate circumstances in his report to the adjutant general.

> I regret to be under the necessity of reporting that the camp of Captain Walker's company of rangers, between the point and Matamoros, was surprised on the morning of the 28th inst. By a party of Ranchero cavalry; five rangers are known to have been killed and five others are missing. The enemy sustained some slight loss but of what extent is not known. The officer of the company and about half its strength were absent on detached service at the time the surprise occurred. Had the men who were left obeyed the instructions of the Captain, a tried frontier soldier, they would never have met such a disaster for men and officers have spirit enough, but lack guidance, which a little active service will soon teach them.[45]

On May 1, Lieutenant Wells—Walker's second-in-command—went out with a small party to reconnoiter and returned the next day. He reported contact with small patrols which his men defeated or drove back to their main camp. On May 2, Taylor and his army reached Point Isabel; Walker and Wells led a patrol of 18 men to attack the enemy's picket guard that Wells had discovered the night before. Eight miles out they encountered Mexican scouts. Walker planned to attack them and divided his men to cut off their retreat, but they escaped in the growing darkness and low palmetto bushes. Walker located the enemy camp at Palo Alto (where Taylor had been the night before) and he and his men rode entirely around the enemy camp and even sent one dismounted Ranger close enough to get more specific intelligence. Returning, Walker and his men were between the Mexican camp and their 45 to 50 picket guards. They encountered a group of six of the enemy and killed five. However, at the first shot, five of his men deserted (three Germans, one Englishman, and one American). The Englishman would stay with the Mexicans.[46] To counter the charge that he had 17 Irishmen desert his company, several weeks later Walker wrote a public announcement as to the nationality of his deserters:

> No Irishmen Deserted
>
> To all whom it may concern:—I hereby certify that no Irishmen deserted me in my engagement or skirmish with the Mexicans during the Campaign on the Rio Grande; and for public information, I will state that the deserters on the night of 2nd May, when an attack was made on the enemy, were one Englishman, two Americans, and three Germans, who all speak good English. One of the Americans gave such an excuse for running that his horse was lame.
>
> S. H. Walker.
> Lt. Col. Texas Rangers.[47]

On May 3, Taylor was alarmed by the ominous sound of cannon fire coming from the direction of Fort Texas. The general had become increasingly concerned about the safety of the men left behind at the fort across the river from Matamoros. Although there were 500 men manning this post, he realized Mexican forces were daily growing stronger. Walker was ordered by Taylor to carry a communication to the commander at Fort Texas and get an update of the condition of the fort and the men stationed there. As Walker's horses were "very much worn down," he could only find Lieutenant Wells and four men who had mounts able to go with him.

Capt. Charles A. May. (Photograph in the public domain)

Walker and his men, under the command of Capt. Charles A. May left about 3 o'clock that afternoon of May 4.

The enemy had been firing on the fort since daybreak. Following General Taylor's orders, Captain May halted in the chaparral about seven miles from the fort. May then ordered Walker and his Rangers to advance to the fort and if any enemy were found they had permission to fire on them to let the fort know that an effort was being made to communicate with them. When Walker reached the fort around 2 or 3 in the morning, he was hailed by the sentinel at the fort and Walker answered, "Captain Walker and friend from Frontone (Point Isabel)." Walker's voice was recognized and he and his Rangers were told to advance toward the fort. A soldier from the fort let a ladder down into the ditch and then up the other side where Walker and his Rangers waited. Walker entered the fort directly and the Rangers led their horses around to the fort's entry.[48]

At daybreak, May was discovered and his men forced to retreat. When Walker returned to the rendezvous at sunrise, May was not there. But two hundred mounted Mexicans were spread out and were waiting. He and his men fired on small groups of the enemy but their number was growing. Seeing no use in skirmishing with the enemy, Walker and his men fought their way through the Mexicans and safely returned to Fort Texas.[49]

According to Robert N. Pruyn who was at Fort Texas, "Capt. Walker of the Texas Rangers, with five men all covered with sweat and dust of the road, galloped up to the fort and told of cutting their way through."[50]

Interestingly, a civilian construction engineer was serving with General Taylor's Troops at Point Isabel, and took notice of Captain Walker. He was aware of Taylor's concern for Fort Texas, and it was apparent to the engineer. Knowing Taylor could not weaken his own force:

> He, however, despatched an express by a gallant Texan by the name of Walker who, being perfectly well acquainted with the country, said he could make his way into the work and bring us back the news. This bold fellow left on the after of the third and had not returned at 8 A.M. to-day. In the meantime, one or two others had started out at the same time, for the same purpose, but returned, stating the country was filled with Mexicans, and it was impossible to get through them. Fears were openly expressed for Walker, when about nine this morning he made his appearance, having been in the fort and brought an official report from Major Brown, its commanding officer.

The engineer's name was George Gordon Meade, he of Gettysburg fame.

The official report by Major Brown given to Walker at the fort read:

Capt. George Meade. (James Worsham collection)

Head-Quarters, Fort Texas,
May 4, 1846.

Sir: I have the honor to report that on the morning of the 3rd instant the enemy's batteries opened on us at 5 o'clock. The firing commenced at the small sand bag fort, and was continued with seven guns. Our batteries were immediately manned, and a strong fire kept upon it from our batteries of eighteen and six-pounders until the firing ceased from it; this battery ceased firing in thirty minutes after our batteries opened upon it, two of the guns of the enemy supposed to have been dismounted.

The enemy then commenced firing from the lower fort and mortar battery. One mortar only observed, which was removed from the sand-bag fort, from whence the first shell was thrown; this fire was kept up briskly; and although the shot were generally well aimed, they did us no harm.

After this removal of the guns of the enemy from the sand-bag fort, I ordered a deliberate fire from Captain Lowd's battery on their guns and the town, ordering the consulate flags to be respected. My men were sent to work at 7 o'clock on the unfinished curtain and gateway, which was completed at 9 p.m. Although the fire of the enemy was kept up with little cessation until half-past 7, there was but one casualty, a sergeant of company "B, 7th Infantry," killed. At half-past 9, I ordered Captain Lowd to throw hot shot into the town; the attempt was made, but the shot could not be sufficiently heated to effect my object, to fire the town.

Finding that our six-pounders effected little the enemy's guns, owing to the distance, and wishing to husband our men and means, I ordered the fire to cease and the guns posted to repel an assault from the rear. The enemy's fire was then concentrated on Captain Lowd's battery, but doing no harm, although the embrasures were frequently struck. Our 18-pounders were fired deliberately and effectually until about 10 o'clock, when, finding that the enemy could do us no harm, I ordered the firing to cease, as it was impossible to silence the enemy's mortar, and from this we were only in danger; at this time, 10 o'clock,

> the enemy's fire was suspended temporarily, but recommenced, and continued at intervals until 12 o'clock at night. It is believed that during this period the enemy fired twelve or fifteen shot. Between two and three o'clock this morning Captain Walker came in, and left here about 4; shortly after reveillé he returned. At 5 o'clock this morning the firing was recommenced by the enemy, continued for about twelve or fifteen shots, and kept up at long intervals; one shell at 11 o'clock, one at 12, one howitz and shell at 5—all ineffectual. We are constantly on the alert, and I cannot speak too highly of the efficiency of the officers and men of my command. Our defences are continued daily, and, when necessity requires, at night.
>
> I am, sir, respectfully, your most obedient servant,
> J. BROWN,
> Major 7th Infantry, commanding.[51]

Walker and his men remained in the fort waiting for darkness. Changing their exhausted mounts for fresh artillery horses, the captain and his men, accompanied by William A. Caldwell as a guide, left the fort at dusk (7 p.m.). By taking bypaths through the chaparral, they made some progress but the fort was entirely surrounded and they eventually were found and fired upon in the growing darkness. But their enemy then suddenly raced away. Walker's men spurred their horses as fast as they could to escape. Soon they would hear heavy musket fire as the Mexican fired into the chaparral where the Texans had been.

The guide did well and, with difficulty, they worked their way through thick chaparral and then swam across a lagoon as wide as the Rio Grande. At 2 o'clock that morning they reached the prairie. It was cloudy and there were no landmarks. Experienced frontiersman Ranger Creed Taylor then became the guide. They stopped briefly to rest their horses, and reached Point Isabel about 8 a.m. on May 5.[52] There Walker gave Brown's report to General Taylor and told him he felt the fort was in no danger of being captured.

When Walker and his Rangers returned from his mission to Fort Texas, there was double rejoicing. First, Fort Texas was not in real danger, and second, that the Rangers were not captured after all. Walker was very popular and the news of his "capture" had "spread gloom over all the camp."[53] The newspapers soon heard of Walker's daring ride through Mexican lines and their reports of his first "heroic" acts of the war made him a national hero.

On May 7, Captain Walker with 28 of his men—now well-mounted—scouted for Taylor's army. While Taylor had moved his main army but six miles, the Rangers had scoured the countryside as far as Palo Alto and reported sighting none of the enemy. Then he and his men slept and the next morning at daybreak left for their old campsite where he had hidden forage for his horses.

In the meantime, some of the Rangers, including the "Taylor Boys" came in contact with enemy spies and gave chase and even dismounted one.[54] This was all reported to General Taylor on the main road about six or eight miles away heading back toward Fort Brown.

Walker then sent all but seven of his best mounted back to the main command. He then proceeded to Palo Alto where he discovered several small parties of the enemy. This he reported and returned to drive in all of their scouts. According to the Ranger reporting these incidents, "It was now evident that a fight would take place, as the enemy's forces were in sight and rapidly advancing."[55]

An interesting phenomenon corresponded with America's first foreign war. The technology of printing had advanced to the degree that newspapers could be printed with the steam powered rotary printing press quickly and cheaply. This meant that the upper class were not the only newspaper readers. The "Penny Press" not only kept a very large number of Americans updated on the events of the day, it also spread stories about the war developing in Mexico. Sam Walker was one of the first examples of a widespread following of admirers.

This was evidenced by plays on Broadway, one such was *Campaign on the Rio Grande or Triumphs in Mexico*—written by Walter M. Leman, author of several "national dramas" on Revolutionary and Native American themes—with the country's new heroes, General Taylor, Captain May, and Captain Walker, heading the cast. It opened in Philadelphia at the end of May 1846 to a long run.[56]

When he later accepted a captain's commission in the new regiment of mounted riflemen and went East to recruit his men, wherever he went while recruiting, he "created a sensation."[57] Wherever he went in the fall of 1847, he was mobbed by crowds. In Philadelphia, a crowd of several hundred gathered around his hotel to see him. When he did appear, he was greeted by hearty cheers.[58] When he went to New York to buy weapons for his mounted rifle company, the Ironton, Ohio, *Spirit of the Times* called him the "leader of the gallant Texas Rangers."[59] Another New York play, *The Texan Rangers* was popular in February 1848 with Walker as the main character.[60]

Walker, as perceived by *Brother Jonathan's Almanac*. (Image in the public domain)

Walker's adventures were treated in music with a quickstep by Charles Grobe. He was portrayed in buckskin, fur hat and long rifle like the image of Daniel Boone in *Brother Jonathan's Almanac* (Philadelphia, 1847).[61]

In the *Rough and Ready Almanac*, Walker, Hays and McCulloch are pictured as supermen. In the second edition, the Texas Rangers are featured almost exclusively borrowing heavily from Samuel C. Reid's *Scouting Expeditions of McCulloch's Texas Rangers* (1859).[62] In 1847, George Lippard wrote a fictionalized account, *Legends of Mexico* in which Sam Walker was described as "erect as an Indian, a fine specimen of an iron man."[63] And in Emerson Bennett's romantic novel *Clara Moreland; or Adventures in the Far South-West* (1853), Texas Rangers under Sam Walker become the "heroic deliverers of Clara and her father from their Mexican captors."[64] Residents of New Orleans went one step further.

New Orleans, May 15, 1846.

> Dear Saunders.
> A number of our citizens, desirous of showing their appreciation of the gallant services of Capt. Walker of the Texas Rangers, and being informed that he has lost his horse in the daring enterprises he is undertaken for the safety of the American Army upon the Rio Grand, beg to present him such a steed as they hope will be suitable for the work he has in hand.
>
> He is a Bay gelding five years old last spring, about 15 hands 2 inches high, of great substance and vigor. …
>
> We could have procured for him a more showy horse, but none better horse and bottom and speed. The qualities he possesses in a remarkable degree, …
>
> The horse is called Tornado from the circumstances of his being born the day of the great tornado in Natchez. He's acclimated and of unquestionable blood. Present him to the Capt. Walker as a token of esteem in which his valor and prowess are held this side of the Sabine River.[65]

In addition, some officers in Taylor's command took up a collection and presented him with $1,000 cash.[66]

The *New Orleans Bee* reported:

> Captain Walker is here [at Matamoros] with his men. He rode by our quarters yesterday on Tornado, the horse sent from New Orleans to him. Tornado seems as fond of his backer as the backer does of him, and they were the observed of all observers. Walker's men say he has but one fault and that is too brave for his discretion.[67]

Not only did his fame spread, he had developed a following.[68]

> SWORD FOR CAPT. WALKER. A very elegant and serviceable sword, with an appropriate inscription, was purchased from the subscription raised at Bravos Exchange, New Orleans, for the brave and daring Capt. Walker, and despatched to him in the care of Gen. Smith.[69]

In September 1846, the St. Louis *Weekly Reveille*, reported a new steamboat—the *Sam Walker*—"arrived Sunday evening from the Ohio River. … She was built at Jeffersonville."[70]

Palo Alto and Resaca de la Palma

Ulysses S. Grant. (Smithsonian Institution)

The observations made by Ulysses S. Grant during the Mexican–American War were recounted in his memoirs. His first was that he was "a young second lieutenant who had never heard a hostile gun before, I felt sorry that I had enlisted."[71]

He then gave the following eyewitness account:

> On the 7th of March [May] the wagons were all loaded and General Taylor started on his return, with his army reinforced at Point Isabel, but still less than three thousand strong [2,200], to relieve the garrison on the Rio Grande. The road from Point Isabel to Matamoros is over an open, rolling, treeless prairie, until the timber that borders the bank of the Rio Grande is reached. This river, like the Mississippi, flows through a rich alluvial valley in the most meandering manner, running towards all points of the compass at times within a few miles. Formerly the river ran by Resaca de la Palma, some four or five miles east of the present channel. The old bed of the river at Resaca had become filled at places, leaving a succession of little lakes. The timber that had formerly grown upon both banks, and for a considerable distance out, was still standing. This timber was struck six or eight miles out from the besieged garrison, at a point known as Palo Alto—"Tall trees" or "woods."
>
> Early in the forenoon of the 8th of May as Palo Alto was approached, an army, certainly outnumbering our little force, was seen, drawn up in line of battle just in front of the timber. Their bayonets and spearheads glistened in the sunlight formidably. The force was composed largely of cavalry armed with lances. Where we were the grass was tall, reaching nearly to the shoulders of the men, very stiff, and each stock was pointed at the top, and hard and almost as sharp as a darning needle. General Taylor halted his army before the head of column came in range of the artillery of the Mexicans. He then formed a line of battle, facing the enemy. His artillery, two batteries and two eighteen-pounder iron guns, drawn by oxen, were placed in position at intervals along the line. A battalion was thrown to the rear, commanded by Lieutenant-Colonel Childs, of the artillery, as reserves. These preparations completed, orders were given for a platoon of each company to stack arms and go to a stream off to the right of the command, to fill their canteens and also those of the rest of their respective companies. When the men were all back in their places in line, the command to advance was given.
>
> As I looked down that long line of about three thousand armed men, advancing towards a larger force also armed, I thought what a fearful responsibility General Taylor must feel, commanding such a host and so far away from friends. The Mexicans immediately opened fire upon us, first with artillery and then with infantry. At first their shots did not reach us, and the advance was continued. As we got nearer, the cannon balls commenced going through the ranks. They hurt no one, however, during this advance, because they would strike the ground long before they reached our line, and ricocheted through the tall grass so slowly that the men would see them and open ranks and let them pass. When we got to a point where the artillery could be used with effect, a halt was called, and the battle opened on both sides. The infantry under General Taylor was armed with flint-lock muskets, and paper cartridges charged with powder, buck-shot and ball. At the distance of a few hundred yards a man might fire at you all day without your finding it out. The artillery was generally six-pounder brass guns throwing only solid shot; but General Taylor had with him three or four twelve-pounder howitzers throwing shell,

Battle of Palo Alto. (Print in the public domain)

besides his eighteen-pounders before spoken of, that had a long range. This made a powerful armament. The Mexicans were armed about as we were so far as their infantry was concerned, but their artillery only fired solid shot. We had greatly the advantage in this arm. The artillery was advanced a rod or two in front of the line, and opened fire. The infantry stood at order arms as spectators, watching the effect of our shots upon the enemy, and watching his shots so as to step out of their way. It could be seen that the eighteen-pounders and the howitzers did a great deal of execution. On our side there was little or no loss while we occupied this position. During the battle Major Ringgold, an accomplished and brave artillery officer, was mortally wounded, and Lieutenant Luther, also of the artillery, was struck.

A regiment of Mexican lancers, commanded by Gen. (Anastasio) Torrejon, moved towards our right, as it was supposed to gain possession of our train. The 3d and 5th Regiments of Infantry, with a portion of Ringgold's battery, under the command of Lieut. (Randolph) Ridgley, were ordered to check this movement, and turn the left flank of the enemy. They, however, still keeping up an irregular fire, continued to steadily advance toward our right and front, so as to outflank our line, if possible. Upon their near approach, the 5th (Infantry Regiment) was thrown into square, with Captain Walker and twenty mounted men on its right. Ridgely having dashed forward, unlimbered his battery, and commenced rapid discharges of grape and canister upon the enemy's artillery, causing it to retreat; but the lancers, fifteen hundred strong, continued steadily to advance, in spite of all opposition, until the 5th poured into them from the front of the square a fire so deadly, that the front of the cavalry recoiled; great numbers fell dead, and those in the rear, without pressing forward on to the bayonets ready to receive them, broke into confusion.[72]

During the day several advances were made, and just at dusk it became evident that the Mexicans were falling back. We again advanced, and occupied at the close of the battle substantially the ground held by the enemy at the beginning. In this last move there was a brisk fire upon our troops, and some execution was done. One cannon-ball passed through our ranks, not far from me. It took off the head of an enlisted man, and the under jaw of Captain Page

Texas Rangers at the Battle of Palo Alto. (Print in the public domain)

of my regiment, while the splinters from the musket of the killed soldier, and his brains and bones, knocked down two or three others, including one officer, Lieutenant Wallen,—hurting them more or less. Our casualties for the day were nine killed and forty-seven wounded.

At the break of day on the 9th, the army under Taylor was ready to renew the battle; but an advance showed that the enemy had entirely left our front during the night. The chaparral before us was impenetrable except where there were roads or trails, with occasionally clear or bare spots of small dimensions. A body of men penetrating it might easily be ambushed. It was better to have a few men caught in this way than the whole army, yet it was necessary that the garrison at the river should be relieved. To get to them the chaparral had to be passed. Thus I assume General Taylor reasoned.

He halted the army not far in advance of the ground occupied by the Mexicans the day before, and selected Captain C. F. Smith, of the artillery, and Captain McCall, of my company, to take one hundred and fifty picked men each and find where the enemy had gone. This left me in command of the company, an honor and responsibility I thought very great. Smith and McCall found no obstruction in the way of their advance until they came up to the succession of ponds, before described, at Resaca.

The Mexicans had passed them and formed their lines on the opposite bank. This position they had strengthened a little by throwing up dead trees and brush in their front, and by placing artillery to cover the approaches and open places. Smith and McCall deployed on each side of the road as well as they could, and engaged the enemy at long range. Word was sent back, and the advance of the whole army was at once commenced. As we came up, we were deployed in like manner. I was with the right wing, and led my company through the thicket wherever a

> penetrable place could be found, taking advantage of any clear spot that would carry me towards the enemy. At last, I got pretty close up without knowing it.
>
> The balls commenced to whistle very thick overhead, cutting the limbs of the chaparral right and left. We could not see the enemy, so I ordered my men to lie down, an order that did not have to be enforced. We kept our position until it became evident that the enemy were not firing at us, and then withdrew to find better ground to advance upon. By this time some progress had been made on our left. A section of artillery had been captured by the cavalry, and some prisoners had been taken. The Mexicans were giving way all along the line, and many of them had, no doubt, left early. I at last found a clear space separating two ponds.
>
> There seemed to be a few men in front and I charged upon them with my company. There was no resistance, and we captured a Mexican colonel, who had been wounded, and a few men. Just as I was sending them to the rear with a guard of two or three men, a private came from the front bringing back one of our officers, who had been badly wounded in advance of where I was. The ground had been charged over before. My exploit was equal to that of the soldier who boasted that he had cut off the leg of one of the enemy. When asked why he did not cut off his head, he replied: "Someone had done that before." This left no doubt in my mind but that the battle of Resaca de la Palma would have been won, just as it was, if I had not been there. There was no further resistance.[73]

All of the skirmishes and battles that took place before May 13, were actions taken before a formal declaration of war by the U.S. Congress. On that date, war was actually declared.

On May 17, after a parley with General Ampudia in which the Mexican, faced with an overwhelming force commanded by General Taylor, asked for an armistice. It was denied. The U.S. forces awoke on the morning of the 18th to find the enemy

Remember Your Regiment, U.S. Army in Action Series. Captain Mays's 2d Dragoons charge at Resaca in the Mexican–American War in 1846. (Image in the public domain)

gone. Walker was ordered into the city to ascertain the number and position of the enemy, if near the river. There was nothing to report. However, General Arista, who had relieved Ampudia, was reported to command four to five thousand troops and was heading for a collision with Taylor's force.[74]

General Pedro Ampudia. (Photograph in the public domain)

Grant remembered:

> The evening of the 9th the army was encamped on its old ground near the Fort, and the garrison was relieved. The siege had lasted a number of days, but the casualties were few in number. Major Jacob Brown, of the 7th infantry, the commanding officer, had been killed, and in his honor the fort was named. Since then a town of considerable importance had sprung up on the ground occupied by the fort and troops, which has also taken his name.
>
> The battles of Palo Alto and Resaca de la Palma seemed to us engaged, as pretty important affairs; but we had only a faint conception of their magnitude until they were fought over in the North by the Press and the reports came back to us. At the same time, or about the same time, we learned that war existed between the United States and Mexico, by the acts of the latter country. On learning this fact General Taylor transferred our camps to the south or west bank of the river, and Matamoros was occupied. We then became the "Army of Invasion."[75]

Immediately upon taking possession of Matamoros, U.S. troops were distributed so as to occupy the upper and lower suburbs of the town—a small guard only being stationed in the city itself. Col. David Twiggs's command was stationed above the city along the banks of the river—his own headquarters occupying a romantic spot directly on its brink. Gen. William J. Worth's command was located in the bend of the river below, having a fine view from his tent, and Lt. Col. William G. Belknap's view was of the surrounding country. Directly opposite Colonel Belknap's, were a few torn tents, and a number of wiry-looking horses. They marked the headquarters of Captain Walker of the Rangers.[76]

Reinforcements having arrived during the month of August; General Taylor then planned to direct his forces against the enemy. His army marched toward a pass in the Sierra Madre Mountains, at Monterrey, through which the main road runs to the City of Mexico. Monterrey was built on a plain two thousand feet above tide water, where the air is bracing and the situation healthy.

Grant continued:

> On the 19th of August the army started for Monterey, leaving a small garrison at Matamoros. The troops, with the exception of the artillery, cavalry, and the brigade to which I belonged, were moved up the river to Camargo on steamers. As there were but two or three of these, the boats

had to make a number of trips before the last of the troops were up. Those who marched did so by the south side of the river. Lieutenant-Colonel [John] Garland, of the 4th infantry, was the brigade commander, and on this occasion commanded the entire marching force. One day out convinced him that marching by day in that latitude, in the month of August, was not a beneficial sanitary measure, particularly for Northern men. The order of marching was changed and night marches were substituted with the best results.[77]

Ranger Regiments

Walker's Rangers identified the enemy's location and provided an estimate of his strength. This intelligence allowed Taylor to commit forces to reestablish his lines of communication, leading to the successful battles of Palo Alto and Resaca de Palma. The Rangers' activities and presence clearly aided General Taylor, and as he recognized the value of these unorthodox Texans, he would continue to utilize their unique talents and capabilities in the future.[78]

Taylor openly admitted the reason he had to call for more Texas horsemen. He wrote: "Owing to the peculiar nature of the country and our deficiency in the proper light troops, I have been kept ignorant, to a great degree, of his [the enemy's] movements."[79]

Taylor authorized the governor of Texas to organize two regiments of Texas volunteer cavalry;[80] one of these regiments was later assigned to Maj. John C. Hays, at that time in command of a Ranger company in San Antonio. Hays's regiment—1st Regiment, Texas Mounted Riflemen Volunteers—would come in as companies were recruited and formed.

Shortly after his latest victory, Taylor received a second Ranger company. Under the command of Capt. John T. Price, this company of Rangers were soon encamped near Walker's company, close to Fort Brown on the Rio Grande.[81] On May 23, Capt. Ben McCulloch and his Rangers arrived. General Taylor now could use their services to scout the retreating Mexican Army and discover the best route to attack them.[82]

Capt. James Gillespie. (Photograph in the public domain, www.sonsofdewittcolony.org)

McCulloch was joined in July by Capt. James A. Gillespie's Ranger company, while Walker's company was discharged on July 16.[83] It was primarily McCulloch's, Price's (he mustered out of service on June 25), and now Gillespie's Rangers who were responsible for scouts for General Taylor, prior to the battle of Monterrey.

McCulloch was sent to follow the retreating enemy. Returning from his scout, McCulloch reported first—the route from Matamoros was not a practical one. There was very little water to be had on the way and the better route would probably be via Comargo and Serralvo. Second, General Arista had moved most of his troops from Linares to Monterrey, and General Canales was recruiting rancheros not far from the road to Monterrey.[84]

Capt. Benjamin McCulloch. (Courtesy of John McWilliams)

Hays's Regiment of Rangers and the U.S. Mounted Rifles

Walker with his Ranger company served as scouts for the U.S. Army while Hays recruited Rangers in Texas.[85] After their three-month enlistments had expired, Walker and his men joined Hays and his Ranger Regiment for another three-month enlistment.[86]

Hays's Regiment, Texas Mounted Volunteers (Texas Rangers). (MUIA plate 167, Military Collector & Historian, 11, no. 4 [Winter 1959]: 117. Courtesy of the Company of Military Historians)

Painting thought to depict Walker after his election to lieutenant colonel. (Image in the public domain)

It came as no surprise that on June 24, the men of the 1st Regiment of Texas Mounted Rifle Volunteers, inevitably known as Hays's Texas Rangers, elected Jack Hays as their colonel and Sam Walker as their lieutenant colonel, which he accepted.

However, on May 22, the United States Senate had received President Polk's nominations for the new regiment's senior officers—the newly approved (May 19) 1st Mounted Rifle Regiment in the U.S. Army. Walker was the third of six captains so nominated.[87] His appointment was confirmed and he was commissioned captain to rank from May 27, 1846.

There was much criticism that the new regiment was being filled by the Democrat president with members of his party. Doctor Chalmers, Walker's friend and organizer of the Democratic Party in Texas, may have influenced the president as Walker was a Whig and supporter of Henry Clay for president. However, Walker and Chalmers shared an intense dislike of one man in Texas politics—Sam Houston—and that may have been enough to encourage Chalmers.

Walker was unaware of his Regular Army commission until the end of June. He promptly wrote his acceptance of his commission:

> Head Quarters
> Army of Occupation
> Matamoros, June 30th, 1846
> To the
> Hon. R. Jones
> Adjt Genl.
>
> Sir;
> I have the honour to acknowledge the receipt of your communication of June 1st also the communication from the Hon. W.L. Marcy, Secretary of War informing me of my appointment as Captain in the Regiment of Mounted Riflemen. You will please inform the Department that I will accept the appointment, hoping at the same time that I may not be ordered from my present position until the War with Mexico has assumed such an appearance as to have no hope of active service.
>
> I remain Sir
> Respectfully,
> Your Obt. Servt.
> S.H. Walker Captn.
> Mounted Riflemen[88]

Walker penned a second letter to Adjutant General Jones on June 30, this one more detailed as to his situation:

Head Quarters
Army of Invasion
Matamoros, June 30th 1846
To The Hon.
R. Jones' Adjt Genl.

Sir,
I have the honor to acknowledge the receipt of your communication of June 2nd in which you seem to have anticipated my wishes. Having participated in the late short and glorious campaign in the Rio Grande under a Commander whose determination and bravery has won my esteem and confidence, I am extremely desirous of remaining with him as long as he may need my services.

As to my chances of success in raising Recruits for the service, they are not very flattering at present. I believe however that I can succeed in getting a few good men such as the Regulations require, and as soon as six months Volunteers are mustered out of service, I may succeed in raising a sufficient number to fill up my Company. I fear that few, if any of the men who have served with credit to themselves and[89] the Country in the service of Texas can be induced to enter the service of the U.S. Those Democratic Republicans principles which have always been triumphant amongst the American people in the civil affairs of life, prevails to some extent also in Military affairs all intelligent men acknowledge the necessity of discipline, strict obedience to orders &c yet there are few men of intelligence and character who are willing to allow their sons to enter the ranks of an Army even in times of War where there is little chance of rising according to their merits. The Regulations also which prohibit anything like intimacy and social intercourse between the officers and their soldiers when not on duty is another objection to the regular service which is repeatedly urged by the Citizens of my adopted State. You may rest assured however that I will do all I can with honor to myself to promote the interests of the service and bring such men into the ranks of my Company as will o themselves and their Country credit.

I remain Sir, Respectfully
Your Obt Servt,
S.H. Walker Captain
Mounted Riflemen[90]

In addition to composing letters to Adjutant General Jones, Walker finally made good his promise to his friend Chalmers that he would write to his brother Jonathan:

Matamoros July 1, 1846
Head Quarters
Army of Invasion

Dear Brother
I received your communication by the politeness of Dr. Chalmers, who has taken the liberty to scold me for not writing to you. You also demand an apology of me which I of course would be very glad to make since you inform me that you have written some three or four letters which I have never received. I suppose you were of the same opinion of some others that my case was a hopeless one, and because I have not been fortunate in making money it was by my own imprudence. … I should be glad to hear from you frequently. You will have no difficulty in communicating with me and I shall be with the Army or in advance with my Regiment of Mounted riflemen Texas volunteers and the communication will be kept up regularly if the Mexicans should continue the war's end and make a stand at Monterey as I anticipate you will hear from me again if not you may see me about Christmas. Give my respects and best wishes to my mother and sisters and inquiring friends and tell them I am well.

Yours respectfully
SH Walker

PS you can direct your letters to Lieut Colonel SH Walker of the first Regiment of Texan mounted riflemen.[91]

Soon after, Walker received a letter from W. B. Jaques, whose family nursed him back to health after his wounding at Walker Creek:

I feel certain that you are yet to have a dreadful Battle with the Mexicans and it will be on or at Monturay [Monterrey]. The result of which I have no doubt, but at the same time many must fall on both sides and I fear some of my friends may be numbered among them but I trust and hope that you and McMullen and Hays may be spared among the brave. The Madam feels quite uneasy for you … and she hopes her prayers may be herd but she fears that we will never see you in San Antonio again.[92]

Monterrey

While Taylor's army was settling in at Camargo, Hays took 30 Rangers and went there to make his report. In his absence, Lieutenant Colonel Walker had been in command of the regiment since August 6.

Head Quarters 1st Regt
Texas Mounted Riflemen
(ca.) August 27, 1846

Regimental Orders
The Lieut. Col. Comdg. finds himself under the disagreeable necessity of issuing the following orders for the better security and protection of the Camp also the reputation of the Regt and the state we represent in the field.

Viz that any soldier found sleeping on his post or found guilty of pilfering or plundering or any disgraceful transaction while this Regt is on detached service shall forthwith be dishonorably discharged from the Regiment without any regard to their safety and ordered forthwith to leave the camp and not make his appearance again in our lines under the penalty of being shot. His name to be published in the Picayune his place of residence & place of nativity also.

It is due to all good soldiers in the Regt that the above shall be strictly enforced, It is expected that all officers & soldiers desirous of promoting the welfare & reputation of the Regt will cooperate with me in carrying out the above orders should it be hereafter necessary.

Yours very respectfully,
C. I. Harper, Adjt
Per orders of S H Walker Lieut Col
Comdg the Regiment[93]

In July, Taylor moved to Camargo, about a hundred miles up the Rio Grande and on August 19 he began to move toward Monterrey. Walker went with an expedition to spy out this Mexican fortification. Upon returning, Walker reported the Mexican forces seemed to be more interested in preparing Monterrey for defense than giving battle to Taylor's approaching army.[94] Walker's observations indicated, "There is no probability of an opposition being made to the advance of the American troops between Camargo and Monterrey, and from what could be collected, the Mexican force concentrated at the latter point is extremely insignificant."[95] Nothing regarding the reported approach of (General) Parades with the army of reserve, of an authentic nature had been ascertained.

From mid-August to September 17, the regiment—less McCulloch's and Gillespie's companies—was covering the eastern flank of the army as it advanced. Taylor's plan was to attack Monterrey from both the east and west.

James Buckner "Buck" Barry, one of the Rangers, recalled that eight Ranger companies were ordered to scout the land before Taylor to confirm that the Mexican Army was concentrating in Monterrey. Upon reporting to the general, the Rangers led the advance of the American forces.

Ranger Buck Barry later wrote:

> Saturday evening … we arrived in sight of the city of Monterey, which was in a bend of the San Juan River, a tributary of the Rio Grande. The Sierra mountains were to the south and west while to the north were the woods. It was there at the Black Fort that the Mexicans opened fire on us with shell and round shot.[96]

James Buckner "Buck" Barry. (Photograph in the public domain)

Hays's Rangers were ordered to scout out the upper section of the city down to the Saltillo Road. It was dark when they reached their destination and the Rangers dismounted to rest and wait for daybreak. Some soon were asleep with their horses unsaddled to let them cool. This was their condition at sunrise when a regiment of Mexican lancers suddenly appeared forming a line 200 yards away. It was a tense time as Ranger Barry commented "each (lancer) had the Mexican flag waving from his lance, making the most beautiful spectacle of mounted men I expected to see. Although everything was silent, these little flags told us in plain language they were after our blood."[97]

Hays acted quickly to buy his unprepared men time. Speaking excellent Spanish, he rode out toward the enemy regiment alone, saber in hand, and challenged the Mexican colonel to meet him halfway for a saber fight.

Ranger Barry commented:

> Hays knew no more about saber fighting than I did. … Soon the Mexican commander advanced waving his saber, while his horse seemed to dance rather than prance. Within a few feet of the Mexican, Hays pulled a pistol and shot him dead from his horse. With that the lancers charged "like mad hornets." Hays galloped back to his men shouting for them to dismount and take shelter behind our horses.[98]

Outraged, the Mexicans charged riding through the Texans, regrouped and charged again. Barry was most impressed by the ferocity of the attack. He said he would never call a Mexican a coward again. "They left many of their dead among us. We had but one man killed but many wounded. They would have ruined us if we had not dismounted. We killed about eighty."[99]

Barry added the Rangers could have fought even more effectively if they had better weapons than the single-shot pistols they carried at the time. The enemy charged and regrouped so quickly the men hardly had time to reload.

One newspaper reported an attack by lancers on the Rangers, perhaps the above event, during which Walker was reported to have lost his horse, but it was later reported Tornado was merely disabled for the time being hit by a scopet (musket) ball.[100] On September 21, another account reported the enemy charged the Rangers at a gallop. "Four rangers were badly lanced and the splendid horse which the people of Louisiana sent Walker was run through the neck. He will get over it, though. The Texans emptied several of their saddles for them."[101]

As Taylor's strategy continued to unfold, General Worth with two thousand men circled around the city and cut off the Saltillo Road and the plan was to attack from the west. Once in position they were to join Hays' regiment. By noon on September 21, Worth's force reached the Saltillo Road. The first wave against the city from this direction involved four companies of artillery (fighting as infantry) and six companies of dismounted Rangers. By nightfall they were storming Federation Hill.

At 3 a.m. the next morning, September 22, two hundred Rangers were roused from their blankets and—commanded by Hays—joined an equal number of Regulars and reached the foot of the hill.

"The command consisted of three companies of the artillery battalion under Capt. J. R. Vinton, acting major … Capt. J. B. Scott, Lieuts. Bradford and G.W. Ayres; three companies of the 8th Infantry under Capt. R. B. Screven, commanded by Lieuts. James Longstreet, T. J. Montgomery, and E. B. Holloway; and seven companies of the Texas Rangers under Col. Hays and Lieut. Col. Walker, commanded by Capts. R. A. Gillespie, Benjamin McCulloch, Thomas Green, C. B. Acklin, Jas. Gillespie, C. C. Herbert, and Ballows, the whole under the command of Lieut. Col. Thos. Childs, who had been assigned to lead this storming party numbering in all 465 men besides the officers.

Independence Hill, between seven and eight hundred feet high, is not only the most inaccessible height from its almost perpendicular ascent."[102]

Hays reported, "We reached the foot of the hill … undiscovered … the command was divided. Col. [Thomas] Childs and myself taking the right, Col. Walker and Maj. [John Rogers] Vinton the left. … In this order we ascended the hill."[103]

One of Ben McCulloch's scouts, Samuel C. Reid, Jr., watched the ascent and wrote his description of the fight at the top:

> Forward pressed the men, invigorated by the fresh morning air, until they arrived within a hundred yards of the crest of the hill, when a crash of musketry from the enemy's skirmishers announced that they were discovered. An incessant random fire was poured down upon the stormers, the day having yet hardly dawned, but not a shot was returned—not a word uttered. The two columns steadily advanced, climbing over projecting crags by means of the fissures in the rocks, or clinging to the stunted, thorny bushes which had imbedded themselves among them, until they were within about twenty yards of the top, when a shout and yell rose on the stilly air, amid the rattling

Col. Thomas Childs *ca.* 1846. (Photograph in the public domain)

> of a volley of musketry from the regulars, and the whistling of the rifle balls of the Texians, which appalled the enemy, and drove them back from the brow of the slope. Then came the deadly struggle. Panting and breathless, men and officers strove to gain the height, contending with the rocky steep as well as with the enemy—peal after peal, and shout and cry, rang wildly forth for victory—onward they rushed, braving the storm of hail until they gained the brow, and with a loud huzza bore back the foe, while the mist now left the mountain's top for the sunbeam's warmer glow, to shine upon the triumphant colors of our victorious troops.[104]

Walker's close friend Lt. Robert A. Gillespie was the first man to reach the summit; however, he was mortally wounded in the stomach. As he lay bleeding from his wound, he passed his sword to Lt. G. H. Nelson and said, "Boys, place me behind that ledge and rock … and give me my revolver. I will do some execution on them before I die." Gillespie passed away the following day. He was buried near where he was fatally shot.[105]

Private Barry remembered: "Our regiment, led by Lieutenant Colonel Walker, followed up the retreating rear of [the demoralized defenders] right to the walls of the castle."[106]

Capture of the Independence Hill, Samuel E. Chamberlain. (Courtesy of San Jacinto Museum of History)

The Mexicans fled to the Bishop's Palace and were quite content to wait for the Americans to charge into their lances and bayonets. Hays did not want to oblige the enemy.

According to Ranger Lt. Walter P. Lane:

Walter P. Lane. (San Jacinto Museum of History)

> Captain Vinton came over, and I heard Colonel Hays advise him of a plan to try and draw the Mexicans out of the Palace, and it was at once approved. … Part of the force [Hays's] were to be concealed on the right of the ridge, and the balance [under Walker] were to take position on the left side … all to be hidden over the steep sides of the ridge … the Mexicans could be seen forming by battalions in front of the Palace.
>
> Capt. Albert G. Blanchard's company, 2d Louisiana Volunteers, now advanced and fired. When the enemy advanced, they [Blanchard's] retreated hastily back to our line, as had been arranged. The lancers rode boldly up the slope, followed by their infantry, eager to make an easy conquest. When they were close upon us, … Vinton's men and Blanchard's company formed a line across the ridge, and the two flanking parties [Hays's and Walker's] closed the gap completely across the ridge [behind the attacking enemy].[107]

Reid's narrative continued:

Albert G. Blanchard. (Photograph in the public domain)

> The critical moment was at hand. Large reinforcements of cavalry and infantry were seen ascending the road from the city to the Bishop's Palace, and everything indicated that some strong movement was about to take place. Don Francisco Berra, general commanding, finding no other resource left, determined to save the Palace by making a desperate effort to drive us from the summit. Orders were given for Blanchard's company to fall back on the alignment, while the Texas Rangers kept their covered position on each side of the slope of the mountain. This movement, apparently retrograde, was soon after followed by one from the enemy, which realized the very hopes that Capt. Vinton had so warmly cherished. Battalions of infantry formed in front of the Palace, their crowded ranks and glistening bayonets presenting a bold and fearless front, while squadrons of light-horsemen, with lances bright and fluttering flags, and heavy cavalry, with escopetas and broadswords gleaming in the sun, richly contrasting with the gaudy Mexican uniforms, made a most imposing sight. Their bugle notes now echoed forth the charge. Onward they came, in proud array, prepared for desperate strife—nearer and nearer they approached, their troopers dashing up the slope with fierce and savage air, until the clang of their arms rang wildly on the ear—then, when within twenty yards of our position, the appointed signal being given, out rushed our gallant troops and formed a serried line of bayonets which suddenly rose before the enemy, like an apparition, to oppose their progress. Most bravely were they met; one volley from that long line, with a deadly fire from the Texians, made them reel and stagger back aghast, while above the battle-cry was heard the hoarse command to "charge." On, on, rushed our men, with shouts of triumph, driving the

> retreating enemy, horse and foot, who fled in confusion down the ridge, past the Palace, and even to the bottom of the hill, into the streets of the city. The victory was won—the Palace ours; and long, long did the cheers of the victors swell on the air, which made the valley below ring with the triumph of our arms.[108]

By noon, the first fort was taken.

Texas Rangers in Combat in the Courtyard of the Bishop's Palace, Samuel E. Chamberlain. (Courtesy of San Jacinto Museum of History)

Storming of the Bishop's Palace and raising the Stars and Stripes, Samuel E. Chamberlain. (Courtesy of San Jacinto Museum of History)

Desperate Fight Inside the Bishop's Palace, Samuel E. Chamberlain. (Courtesy of San Jacinto Museum of History)

An officer from the 3d Artillery was one of the first to enter and cut down the enemy's flag. Soon Walker and another Ranger cut down the blue and yellow signal flags.[109]

Sam Chamberlain, who wrote of his wartime experience in *My Confessions; Recollections of a Rogue*, commented on the appearance the Mexican Army:

> I was surprised at the fine soldier-like appearance they presented: all clothed in blue uniforms of coarse cloth. With red facings, white belts well pipeclayed, the brasses well-polished. The arm of the infantry was the "Tower Musket, Brown Bess."[110]

On September 23, Hays's Regiment entered the town. He led a column of Rangers on the right prong of the attack down the Calle de Monterrey while Walker led the left column down Calle de Iturbide toward the enemy's batteries. Every house and block had to be taken individually.

Some walls were three and four feet thick, many with embrasures for one or more cannon to rake the street with grapeshot. The walls of many gardens and roofs sandbagged with a concentration of enemy troops prepared to shower the invader with a "hurricane of [lead] balls."[111]

The troops used picks, crowbars, and bayonets to tunnel through walls and ladders to scale the walls. Many of the enemy fired from housetops from behind sandbag barriers some four feet high. Both sides also used artillery with round shot and grapeshot at very close range.

Street fighting in the Calle de Iturbide, Samuel E. Chamberlain. (Courtesy of San Jacinto Museum of History)

Fight in the Calle de Iturbide, Church of Santa Maria, Samuel E. Chamberlain. (Courtesy of Anne S. K. Brown Collection, Brown University)

Hays advanced on the riverside of the city while Childs and Walker were marching parallel on the land side. Hays easily entered the main plaza but Walker's troops had to fight their way through heavy barricades, all the while taking fire from the rooftops of buildings that ran along both sides of the street.

The Rangers, as a team, selected a house and under covering fire battered down the door, cleared the house from bottom to top, and then took up firing positions on the roof. Their Colt five-shooters, for those who had them, proved to be most valuable in close-up street fighting. In addition, the Rangers, upon piercing an adobe wall, would place a mortar shell in the small hole and make a larger one for entry.

As Walker's men advanced, a column of Mexican infantry with fixed bayonets charged around the corner of a church. Walker and the 20 Rangers with him were able to make all their shots count before quickly withdrawing. Soon they were joined by two 6-pounders from George McCall's battery that arrived just in time to begin canister fire. The numerous iron shot forced the withdrawal of the enemy column.

Dashing around the corner of the church in pursuit of the enemy, Walker's men found the street barricaded. They scrambled over them under intense gunfire. Soon they would seek any cover they could. Walker and about 20 of his men huddled in a large doorway that was suddenly splintered by a volley fire from within. Three of Walker's men fell. Rangers with axes soon came up and began dividing the door. But another volley brought down one axe-wielding Ranger with a shattered arm. Soon the Rangers burst inside while 10 of the enemy tried in vain to escape.

Pickaxes, crowbars and 6-pounder shells were then put to work, while the best shots went to the roof. Breaking through the walls with pickaxes and artillery shells, the Rangers found food abandoned by the fleeing enemy. One surprise on the other side of the wall was the interior of a liquor store. To prevent the obvious temptation to thirsty Rangers, the men were told that the liquor was poisoned. This gave the Rangers a reason for taking enemy soldiers alive. Yet failing to find a convenient enemy soldier, they chose a Dutch artilleryman who spoke little English, and offered him plenty to drink. When he survived to become very drunk, the Rangers finished what the Dutchman did not drink.[112]

As the Rangers ran across the street, bullets ricocheted around them. Inside one building they felt the building shake as American artillerymen fired bags of musket balls and canister down the street from two 6-pounders—one on the roof and one in the street. Among the swarm of blue American uniforms, the Rangers, wearing buckskin hunting jackets such as the ones worn by a frontiersman in the republic era, could usually be distinguished.[113] House after house was taken, many times with the blasting open of holes into a roof and entering rooms full of terrified civilians.[114]

As night began to fall, Ranger forces under Walker and Hays were within one block of the main plaza. While most of the U.S. forces—including Hays's Rangers—were ordered to withdraw in preparation for an artillery barrage, Walker and his men did not get the word and stayed while American artillery shelled the square. About an hour after sunset, Walker and about 50 of his men gained the Post Office and governor's house.

Grand Plaza of Monterrey as seen from the top of the Post Office, Samuel E. Chamberlain. The figure of the man wearing a buckskin jacket in the right foreground may be Lieutenant Colonel Walker. (Courtesy of San Jacinto Museum of History)

There in the Post Office, Walker caught a little rest in Gen. Pedro de Ampudia's bed. As brief as it may have been, it was sweet. This was the man who captured him at Mier. One Ranger, a survivor of the Mier Expedition, who was among those who fought his way through the city was Ranger William A. Wallace, known to friend and foe alike as "Bigfoot." His brother and cousin had been murdered at Goliad. He vowed vengeance. He reportedly said the storming of Monterrey allowed him to take "full toll" out of the Mexicans for the killing of his brother and cousin.[115]

What quiet there was, was shattered by American 9-inch mortars, followed by enemy artillery fire from the Black Fort, a strong point in the city commanded by Col. José López Uraga, and whose defenders included the infamous—in the eyes of the Americans—"San Patricio" Battery, made up of deserters from U.S. forces.

At daylight, Walker's men opened a murderous fire with their rifles. During the night several Rangers had crossed the street and picked a hole through the wall of the house on the opposite corner. When the Texans broke through the wall, a company of Mexican infantry rushed to escape through the front door, only to be shot by the deadly fire of Walker's men from the Post Office.[116]

But then there was a Mexican bugle call and a white flag that signaled for a parley. The Mexicans had enough; a ceasefire followed and the battle was over by noon September 24. General Taylor negotiated a two-month armistice, much to the disgust of the Texans, who felt they were within reach of a clear-cut victory.

Here are the terms of capitulation:

> "ARTICLE 1. As the legitimate result of operations before this place and the present position of the contending armies. It is agreed that the city, the fortifications, cannon, the munitions of war, and all other public property, with the under-mentioned exceptions, be surrendered to the commanding general of the United States forces now at Monterrey.
>
> "Article 2. That the Mexican forces be allowed to retain the following arms, to wit: The commissioned officers, their side arms; the cavalry, their arms and accoutrements; the artillery, one field battery, not to exceed six pieces, with twenty-one rounds of ammunition.
>
> "Article 3. That the Mexican armed forces retire within seven days from this date beyond the line formed by the pass of the Rinconada, the city of Linares, and San Fernando de Pusos.
>
> "Article 4. That the citadel of Monterrey be evacuated by the Mexican and occupied by the American forces to-morrow morning at 10 o'clock.
>
> "Article 5. To avoid collisions, and for mutual convenience, that the troops of the United States will not occupy the city until the Mexican forces have withdrawn, except for hospital and storage purposes.
>
> "Article 6. That the forces of the United States will not advance beyond the line specified in the third article before the expiration of eight weeks, or until the orders of the respective governments can be received.
>
> "Article 7. That the public property to be delivered shall be turned over and received by officers appointed by the commanding generals of the two armies.
>
> "Article 8. That all doubts as to the meaning of any of the preceding articles shall be solved by an equitable construction, and on principles of liberality to the retiring army.
>
> "Article 9. That the Mexican flag, when struck at the citadel, may be saluted by its own battery."[117]

Criticism was heaped upon Taylor, including a verbal blast from President James K. Polk, who insisted that the U.S. Army had no authority to negotiate truces, only to "kill the enemy." In addition, his terms of armistice—which allowed Ampudia's forces to retreat with battle honors and most of their heavy weapons—were seen as foolish and shortsighted, not to mention the thousands of Mexican troops that lived to fight another day. John R. Kenly, a captain in the Washington–Maryland Battalion had this to say when he recalled his feelings when he watched the Mexicans as they marched out of the city:

Col. John R. Kenly. (Irish Railroad Workers Museum)

> I saw enough of the Mexican troops when they marched out, to satisfy me that they only lacked one daring leader to have made their escape or a successful defense. They went out sullenly, defiantly, and their attitude was such as to create a well-founded apprehension that a collision would occur between them and our troops who lined the roadside. This behavior increased the feeling against the capitulation; and when it became known that the administration had manifested its disapproval, its opponents largely outnumbered its defenders.[118]

Cathedral at Monterrey. Army resting in foreground, Samuel E. Chamberlain. Sam Walker's Texans at the surrender of Monterrey. (Courtesy of San Jacinto Museum of History)

Among the disapprovers were the majority of those serving in the 1st Texas Mounted Rifles. Given the history of Mexican perfidy and butchering of prisoners of war, the Texans understood that this might be the last opportunity to avenge the murders perpetrated upon fathers, uncles, brothers, sons, cousins, and friends at the Alamo, Goliad, and the Dawson Massacre, not to mention the 18 Mier prisoners who were murdered to satisfy but another example of Santa Anna's blood lust.

Hays's regimental losses were 6 killed, 15 wounded, and 2 missing. The most grievous loss was Capt. Robert A. "Ad" Gillespie—the friend and comrade-in-arms in many exploits while serving with both Hays and Walker in Texas.

On September 30, the service of the two Texas mounted volunteer regiments expired. The curtain would soon be going up on the second act of the War with Mexico and the part Samuel H. Walker would play in it.

CHAPTER 8

The Walker Colt Revolver

After the battle of Monterrey in the fall of 1846 and the preparations for the hostilities in the spring of 1847 at Veracruz, training for the second half of the war continued unabated. One man's preparation—that of former Texas Ranger Sam Walker—resulted in the development of a new weapon for the army that was to have far-reaching effects. Walker's assistance in the design of a new Colt revolver helped begin a new era of mounted combat for the U.S. Army. The cavalry's use of the revolver played a major role in the American Civil War and the wars with the mounted natives of the plains.

The Colt revolver's first proving ground was Texas. It was ironic that both Texas and the Colt revolver should be linked from the beginning—at first by coincidence and later with definite consequence. The Texas War of Independence and the weapon later used to tame the wild new land, had landmark beginnings within a few days of each other.

During the same fateful week that the Alamo was besieged in late February 1836, Samuel Colt received his first American patent for his revolving pistol.[1]

Samuel Colt. (Photograph in the public domain)

By the summer of 1836, Colt had begun manufacturing his revolving rifles and pistols in Paterson, New Jersey. Selling weapons in peacetime, however, was a difficult task; but Colt felt he could get the start he needed if he could sell his revolvers to the government. A trial of his firearms for army ordnance officers in 1837 met with failure. According to the army, Colt's revolvers were rejected because "their advantages are counterbalanced by complexity of construction and consequent greater liability to derangement and accident."[2] In a letter dated June 1, 1840, Colt admitted, "The arms submitted in 1837 …

Capt. Samuel H. Walker, Regiment of Mounted Riflemen. (Courtesy of John McWilliams)

were the first arms ever made on my principle, and were got up in a great hurry ... consequently the arms were imperfect and easily gotten out of order."[3]

Although Colt's haste in preparing his samples for the test had prejudiced the Army Ordnance Department against his revolving weapons, certain individual army officers were favorably impressed. Gen. Thomas S. Jessup, on duty in Florida during the Seminole War, wrote the Ordnance Department on September 16, 1837, and requested that it send him two of Colt's small pocket revolvers.[4] Seeing the possibilities of promoting his weapons in a combat zone, Colt went to Florida personally in February 1838. After a special demonstration for General Jessup, Colt was able to sell all the Colt weapons he had brought with him—50 rifles and 25 pistols. During the next few years, Colt did some business with field commanders, but he wisely made sure that certain prominent officers received gifts of special presentation revolvers.[5]

Meanwhile, Colt began to realize that traders heading west were buying as many Paterson Colts as they could afford and were selling them at considerably inflated prices.[6]

On April 29, 1839, Texas Secretary of the Navy Department Memucan Hunt and Armory Officer Col. George W. Hockley placed an order with Colt's representative, John Fuller, for 180 revolving carbines and 180 revolving pistols for the Texas Navy.[7]

These pistols were the large .36-caliber Paterson No. 5 holster model. Completely out of stock of the standard 8-inch barrel, Colt substituted 9-inchers instead.[8] This model, delivered to Texas in 1840, was without the permanently attached loading lever underneath the barrel that was common in later models.

The Texas sale did little to help Colt financially who, at the time, was only a year away from bankruptcy. After six years of manufacture and the production of 5,000 to 6,000 revolvers, Colt was forced to close his business in 1842. Two years later, however, the sale of the revolvers to the Texas Navy did, although indirectly, actually help to reestablish Colt in the arms business—permanently. In 1844, the Texas Navy was beached and its revolvers were turned over to the Texas Rangers. These frontier fighters, already familiar with Colt revolvers, were firmly convinced of their effectiveness and were delighted to be fully armed with them. Soon the Rangers would prove the Colt revolver to be a superior cavalry weapon.

They did not have to wait many months to put their newfound firepower into action. Ranger Sam Walker, a participant in the action described below, wrote Colt:

New York City Nov. 30th 1846
Mr Sam' Colt

Sir,
In compliance with your request I take great pleasure in giving you my opinion of your revolving patent arms.

The pistols which you made for the Texas Navy have been in use by the Rangers for three years, and I can say with confidence that it is the only good improvement that I have seen. The Texans who have learned their value by practical experience, their confidence in them is unbounded, so much so that they are willing to engage four times their number. In the Summer of 1844 Col. J. C. Hays with 15 men fought about 80 Camanche Indians, boldly attacking them upon their own ground, killing & wounding about half their number. Up to this time these daring Indians had always supposed themselves superior to us, man to man, on horse—at that time they were threatening a descent upon our Frontier Settlements—the result of this engagement was such as to intimidate them and enable us to treat with them. Several other Skirmishes have been equally satisfactory, and I can safely say that you deserve a large share of the credit for our success. Without your Pistols we would not have had the confidence to have undertaken such daring adventures. Was it necessary I could give you many instances of the most satisfactory results.

With improvements I think they can be rendered the most perfect weapon in the World for light mounted troops which is the only efficient troops that can be placed upon our extensive Frontier to keep the various warlike tribes of Indians & marauding Mexicans in subjection. The people throughout Texas are anxious to procure your pistols & I doubt not you would find sale for a large number at this time.

Yours very respy
S H Walker, Capt.,
Mounted Riflemen U.S.A.[9]

Meanwhile in the East, the U.S. Navy, which had bought 60 rifled revolving carbines from Colt in July 1841, were again interested in making an order. On August 28, 1845, navy officials wrote Colt and requested 100 more carbines and 100 revolvers.

Although Colt had been out of business for over a year, his former treasurer, John Ehlers, was able to obtain the remaining stock of arms and parts, and tried to comply with at least part of the navy's request. Of the revolvers (the latest .36-caliber Paterson No. 5 holster model with the new attached loading levers), Ehlers was able to supply only 50 to the navy.[10]

Less than a year later, these same late-modeled Patersons were apparently in the possession of the U.S. Army as they prepared for the invasion of Mexico. On April 20, 1846, Capt. Samuel Walker and his company of Texas Rangers were issued 32 of these Colts.[11] From his experience with these newer Paterson models and his work with the older Paterson from the Texas Navy, he was soon in an excellent position to evaluate the effectiveness of both models in combat.

In May 1846, Walker was offered a commission in the new cavalry unit of the American Army—the U.S. Mounted Rifles. He declined until he finished his enlistment with the 1st Texas Mounted Rangers in September.

Samuel Colt, always with an eye toward promoting his business, took notice of Walker's declination, and throwing caution to the wind, decided if not Walker, why not me? He wrote a letter to Levi D. Slamm, a shipmate from his days as a cabin boy in the U.S. Navy and, since November 30, 1846, a purser in the navy.

> Believing you may have it in your power to favour my views & that you will act with promptness, I have taken the liberty to enclose to you a letter addressed to the President of the United States & I wish you to show it to General Rusk & Mr Hanagin of the U.S. Senate & should they think favourable of the aplication, & it is a fact that captain Walker has declined accepting the nomination of Captain in the new regiment of Riflemen—I beg you to present my case to them, & if possible induce one or boath of them to call with you upon the President with the letter & present my clames in a proper light.[12]

The letter Colt wished Slamm to deliver to President James K. Polk is reproduced in its entirety, revealing his total lack of understanding as to the desired military background for applicants seeking commissions, and his abysmal spelling which, by itself, would have been reason enough to deny him an appointment.

> Sir.
> Lerning through the medium of the press that a vacancy exists in the new rifle regament caused by the non acceptance by Capt Walker of Captency I desire to offer myself as a candidate for the commission offered to him, & in doing so I beg leave to state that I am governed with a desire to make myself useful in the service of my cuntry to my abillity to perform the deautes which may be alotted to me. I will endever to give ample evidence if time will be allowed for that purpus & I sincearly hope that the vacancy may not be filed until the opertunaty is offered me to do so—
>
> My clame upon the government for this apointment is based upon the fact that I have spent the last ten years of my life with out profit in perfecting millitary inventions—The repeting Rifles Carbenes & Pistols The Submarine Battery for fortifying harbours & Rivers the Waterproof cartridges & other like inventions bearing my name give some evidence of my abellity to make my self useful in the millitary service & especilay so in a service like that contemplated for the regiment of Riflemen in question wher rules & formes must give way in a great mesure to emergencys in service not common & for which there is but little or no darter to govern—
>
> To repeat I am a candidate for the apointment in question & if there is a probabillity of my aplication being favourably received I will adopt such meens as will strengthen my clame & make an early visate to Washington on this business—
>
> With the hope of hearing from you on this subject at your earliest convenience.[13]

After Walker's discharge from the Rangers, he received his orders dated October 1, which instructed him to "repair to Washington for orders."[14] Before leaving, Walker made sure he had the New York addresses of rifle maker Daniel Fish and pistol manufacturer Samuel Colt.[15]

Col. William A. Thornton. (www.kancoll.org)

On his trip from Texas to the East Coast, Walker found himself to be somewhat of a celebrity. He discovered that he, as well as the Texas Rangers, had become national heroes to the public. The press had publicized his daring rides for General Taylor early in the war, and the paper-novels and the theater had continued the publicity.

Jack Hays traveled with Walker to Washington and stopping in New Orleans, they learned their fame preceded them.[16] One newspaper reported that as they walked through the streets, they "attracted crowds at their heels. Capt W stoops with a slouching gait, thin face, and small red whiskers."[17] Walker's two known civilian daguerreotypes show him clean shaven as do the two of him in his mounted rifles uniform. Apparently, while in the field with the Rangers and later with the Mounted Riflemen (as shown by other descriptions), he let his beard grow.

Col. George Talcott. (https://goordnance.army.mil/history/chiefs/talcott.html)

Meanwhile, even before Walker reached Washington City, there was evidence that he was not the only one looking for more Colt revolvers—others from Texas were also looking for these. On November 18, 1846, the Chief of Ordnance Lt. Col. George Talcott wrote Capt. W. A. Thornton:

> It is very probable that a large number (say nearly 1000) of Colts pistols, Rifle calibre, may be called for by the Regiment of Mounted men to be raised in Texas. I have no idea that such a number can be obtained and would much rather furnish arms of ordinary patterns, but it will be well for you to inquire what number of the above arms—rifle calibre, could be had by the 1st day of December at latest, and inform me at once.[18]

Apparently, Texas volunteers would be requesting more Colt revolvers to supplement those that had previously been issued by the Texas Republic to the Texas Rangers. There were very few Colt revolvers available for Texas Rangers or Mounted Riflemen.

Washington City

By late November, Walker was back home in Maryland. He apparently visited his brother Jonathan Thomas in Washington City and while he was there, he signed and received his commission as captain of Mounted Riflemen.

He also dropped in on the president; in 1846 anybody could stop by and see the president. On Thursday, November 26, 1846, President Polk wrote in his diary:

> This being a day of Thanksgiving set by the authorities of the City, I directed that public offices should be closed. Capt. Walker of the Texas Rangers, whom I had appointed a captain in the mounted Rifle Regiment, called to pay his respect[s]. He had been in the City several days and made apology for not having called earlier.[19]

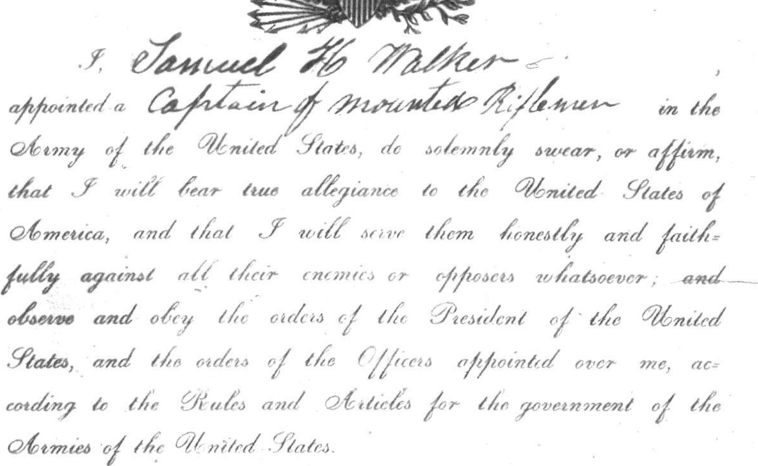

I, Samuel H Walker appointed a Captain of mounted Riflemen in the Army of the United States, do solemnly swear, or affirm, that I will bear true allegiance to the United States of America, and that I will serve them honestly and faithfully against all their enemies or opposers whatsoever; and observe and obey the orders of the President of the United States, and the orders of the Officers appointed over me, according to the Rules and Articles for the government of the Armies of the United States.

Sworn to and subscribed before me, at Washington D.C this 26th day of November 1846

Samuel H Walker
Capt mounted Riflemen

Thomas C. Donn
Justice of the Peace

Walker's commission as "Captain of Mounted Riflemen." (Walker Papers, Texas State Archives)

Maybe it was a thank you or a wise political move for a Whig to have a face-to-face meeting with a Democrat president. It was probably a good idea as he would soon see the president again. His next priority was a source for handguns for his new company of riflemen.

President James Knox Polk. (Library of Congress)

On his way to New York to find a way to arm his new command, Walker was besieged in a Philadelphia hotel by several hundred people who were eager to see "Samuel Walker—the Texas Ranger." When he finally appeared, they greeted him "with hearty cheers."[20] Later in New York, where he was looking for arms makers Colt and Fish, he was hailed by the Ironton, Ohio, *Spirit of the Times* as a "leader of the gallant Texas Rangers."[21]

Walker had in his pocket the note with the names and addresses of gun makers in New York: Daniel Fish, Cooper, Blunt and Simms, a Colt representative, and Simpson.[22] According to historian William Edwards's research: "Fish was in no position to make rifles for Texas, and Blunt and Simms on Chatham Street were … most in the business of importing and limited production of handmade arms."[23] Of the remaining gunsmiths listed in the New York Directory, Colt seemed to be the only remaining choice who had ever made any pistols in quantity. And it was Colt revolvers that had impressed Walker in the first place and Colt had already written Walker about an endorsement of his pistols.

Samuel H. Walker *ca.* 1844. (Photograph in the public domain)

Walker wrote Colt on November 30 to suggest with "improvements" his pistols would be the "most perfect arm in the world for light mounted troops."[24] Colt explained that while he no longer had a factory (his Paterson, New Jersey, operation was bankrupt and had been liquidated), he still had his patent. With an army contract he could subcontract more revolvers. It did not take Colt long to contact Walker. Colt saw an opportunity to work with Walker for their mutual benefit. Although bankrupt, apparently before his first meeting with Walker, he boldly wrote:[25]

> I have heard so much of Colonel Hayse and your exployeys with the Arms of my invention that I have long desired to know you personally & get from you a true narrative of the various instances where my arms proved of more than ordinary utility …

... It has occurred to me that if you think sufficiently well of my arms to earge the President & Secy of War to allow your company to be thus armed you can get them the arms are very much Improved since we first commenced there manufacture & I have no doubt that hints which I may get from you & others having experience in there use in the field that they can be made the most complete thing in the world.[26]

December 1846

Soon, the inventor (who was looking for a way to resume manufacture of his revolvers) met with the former Ranger who was looking for revolvers. Walker and Colt met for the first time in New York and on December 1, Colt wrote formal estimates of a manufacture of 1,000 revolvers to be redesigned from the former Paterson model under the direction of Walker. Colt's offer was to make 1,000 pistols for $25 each.[27]

Colt met with Walker the next day to discuss his trip to Washington. Colt urged him to avoid Chief of the Ordnance Department Talcott—Colt revolvers were a dead issue with him—but to bank on his popularity to get an interview with the president. To aid him in his presentation, on December 1, Colt wrote a letter to Col. John Mason of Washington asking him to loan him one of his Colt revolvers if Walker needed a pistol to show the president.[28] He would also check with John. H. Offley, Chief Clerk in the War Office.[29] Apparently it was finally decided to make a prototype from scratch in January.

At this meeting with Colt, Walker also probably discussed some more of his ideas about design changes. The next day Colt wrote him:

> If you find ... the President is disposed to incurage the use of my pistols by our light troops & will autherise you to contract for a supply, you shall have them on your own terms and of a patern embracing all the alterations and mprovements sirgested by you & I will use the Greatest possible dispatch in furnishing a full supply.[30]

Colt had already alienated himself from the War Department for his too-aggressive approach in promoting his pistols and watching them fail upon trials. On the other hand, Walker, the Texas Ranger, was well known nationally for his heroic actions in the first months of the war and was welcome throughout the nation. On his journey from New York to Washington, he was again thronged in Philadelphia by several hundred people eager to see him. A popular stage play featured Walker as the lead character.[31]

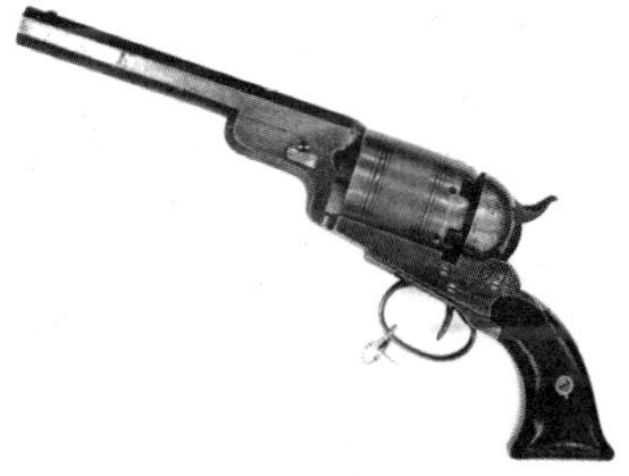

Experimental Walker Colt. (Springfield Armory National Historic Site)

Not only was Walker popular, his friend and former commanding officer, Texas Ranger Col. John C. Hays, was a former Tennessee neighbor of President Polk. He was also a grandson of Rachel

Jackson's favorite sister and therefore grandnephew of Andrew Jackson. Walker's fame would have an ear at the White House. In addition, he was a close friend of Dr. John Gordon Chalmers who founded the Democratic Party in Texas. In fact, as indicated earlier, he was almost Chalmers's son-in-law.

It is, however, ironic that Walker had been given a commission in the Mounted Riflemen from an administration notorious for approving Democratic appointees. In a letter four years earlier, Walker advocated support of Whig presidential candidate Henry Clay.[32] Two weeks after leaving the president's office, Walker was even invited to the December 29, 1846, Third Annual Ball of the Young Men's Henry Clay Association. Walker responded, stating that he had no time to attend. He wisely wrote, "Besides these are political considerations connected with the war between the two great parties of the country which preclude me at this time from participating with you in any thing that was not National in its character."[33]

The Contract

To get a contract, Walker went directly to the president. On December 7, 1846, Walker met with President Polk and Secretary of War William L. Marcy. On the same day, the following message was sent to Colt from his old enemy in the Ordnance Department, Col. George Talcott: "At the instance of Capt. Walker, the Secretary of War desires you to furnish one thousand revolving pistols … at twenty-five dollars each in accordance with your letter to the Captain."[34] Walker immediately wrote to Colt announcing the contract.

> Washington City D C
> December 7th 1846
> To Saml Colt
>
> Sir
> I hasten to inform you that the Ordnance Dept have agreed to order one Thousand pistols, Doubts were entertained of yr ability to furnish them in three months, I hope you will use every exertion to complete them within that time, And I doubt not you will receive orders for at least two thousand more in a very Short time, In case you should not however do not let it prevent you from making at least that number as I feel confident that you can sell that number in New Orleans & Texas at a rate that will pay well I thought it best to be content with one thousand for the present in a few days when the bustle & confusion is over here I will try for two thousand more by the time those are completed they will need no farther recommendation from me as they will recommend themselves by practical result in the hands of such men as will use them you have nothing to fear in regard to their Success and allso of their being brought into general use by our Mounted

light troops which are indispensable to the protection of our vast & extensive Frontier I think you would do well to turn your attention entirely to the manufacture of those arms feeling perfectly satisfied that you will be well rewarded

Yrs Very Respectfully
S H Walker Capt
U.S. Rifles[35]

Eli Whitney, Jr. (Photograph in the public domain)

Colt, who had a patent but no company, now had a promised contract. The next day, December 8, Colt wrote Eli Whitney, Jr., about subcontracting the manufacture of the pistols.[36] Rifle maker Edwin Wesson also received a similar request in a letter written on December 16.[37] Six days later Colt wrote Wesson that he and Captain Walker would be visiting him to discuss the manufacturing of the pistols. In a follow-up letter Colt wrote that he regretted missing meeting Edwin Wesson and had apparently met Daniel Wesson instead. He had left a sample of his large pistol with Daniel so he could get an estimate for making 1,000 barrels for his pistols.[38]

With things seemingly moving toward successful arrangements with those who Colt had chosen to make the pistols, the contract was composed and signed by Colt and Walker.

Memorandum of an agreement made this 4th day of January 1847 between Samuel Colt (inventor of Colt's Patent Repeating Pistols) and Samuel H. Walker. Capt. U. S. Rifles, and acting by authority of and direction of the Secretary of War, for the immediate construction of 1000 or a larger number if hereafter determined by the Secretary of War, of said Colts patent Repeating Pistols, made to correspond with the model recently got up by said Colt and Walker and being as follows, viz,

The barrels to be nine inches long and Rifles made of the best hammered Cast Steel and of a bore suited to carrying round balls, fifty to the pound with strength sufficient to firing an elongated ball weighing thirty-two to the pound.

The cylinders to be made of hammered cast steel with chambers for six charges each, and of a length, size, and strength, sufficient to be charged with an elongated ball 32 to the pound.

The lockwork with the exception of the hammer to be made of the best cast or double sheet steel and the parts sufficiently uniform to be interchanged, with slight or no refitting.

The Hammer and lockframe to be of the best Gun iron and case hardened.

The stock to be of sound black walnut, bound and secured by a strong strop of [brass or] iron.

The Pistols answering to the above specification to be maid [*sic*] with the least possible delay, [and turned in to the Government in lots of not less than one hundred] and to be paid for at the rate of [not less than] $25 each on delivery,—[the whole to inspected and approved by Capt. Walker] in New York in passels or lots of 100 each. The first hundred of said arms to be completed, if possible, in three months from the date this contract is confirmed by the Secretary of War, and all the remainder as soon thereafter as possible, and not under any circumstances to exceed five or six months if the arms can possibly be completed by the dividing up of the work [of] or the employing of two sets of hands to work night and day.

In addition to the arms, it is agreed between the parties that there shall be furnished one entire set of springs for every 10 pistols, one entire lockwork, one spring vice extra set of cones and screws for every 25 pistols [One Bullet mould] for every 10 Pistols to cast one elongated ball. One do to every 50 Pistols to cast six elongated balls at one casting.

One Powder Flask, one screw driver, one nipple wrench, and one lever for driving home the balls for each pair of Pistol. For the whole including the additional sixth chamber in the cylinder and all the above mentioned extra fixings, [a fair] a price, not exceeding Three to be allowed on each Pistol in addition to the Contract price.

The above contract subject to the approval of the Secy of War.
Saml Colt
S H Walker Capt
Mted Riflemen U S Army[39]

Walker wrote Colt further explanatory letters over the next few weeks.

Washington Jan 6th 1847

Sir
Your contract has been approved by the Secretary of war—with the proviso that the Arms be subject to the inspection of Capt Thornton or any other officer he may choose to designate, I hope you will not make any objection As I am fully satisfied that they will stand any test that may be required of them—They can not of course restrict you to small fractions or require any thing of you that is not in the agreement—a copy of the original will be sent you without delay, I trust you will use every exertion to complete them you can rest assured that there will be no difficulty about the inspection of the arms—I shall use every exertion to procure you a larger order, I wish you would use great exertion to complete me a pair—as I know they will recommend themselves better than I can by argument I spoke freely to the Secretary on the subject and think him favourably disposed toward your Arms—send me the wooden Model as soon as practicable—you shall hear from me again as soon as I have any thing of interest to communicate.

Very Respectfully
Your Obt Servant
Capt S H Walker
USA[40]

Washington Jan 13th 1847

Dear Colt
I received all three of your letters—and am surprised to find by the last that you have not recd a copy of the Contract. I will attend to it forth with, And am now making every exertion to have the order increased

I have just sent a communication to the chairman of the committee on military affairs—I wish it may be possible for you to get me a pair of the pistols complete. As I know practical demonstration is the best argument in favour of any thing, I shall leave here in a week or ten days and shall stop a few days in Baltimore try if possible to have me one pair complete & I will be more certain to secure the order for a large number And do not delay a moment upon any consideration as you may rely with certainty upon me; even if Dept should try to put you to inconvenience about the matter, I will write again as soon as I have any thing of interest

Respectfully your obt Servant
Capt S H Walker[41]

Washington Jan 24th 1847

Dear Colt
I received your letter of the 18th I have called upon Houston & Rusk and they will do all that can be done my memorial in regard to the adoption of these arms &c is now before the military committee of the house—all seem favourable to my recommendation and I shall do all that can be done to accomplish all you desire—I defered writing hoping I might be able to effect something of some importance—but I feared you might get out of patience I authorise you to make any change in the construction of the loader or leever you may think desirable—I cannot consent to using the round ball untill I can see the other properly tested—I contemplate leaving here in a short time say first of Feb—and do not think it advisable to ask permission to remain any longer to superintend the Pistols as I might loose all the influence I have by so doing—as they might suppose I was anxious to rest upon my Laurels—I deem it of great importance to have a pair of these Pistols to exhibit here before leaving—The fact is that they all want to see the identical thing a description will not satisfy them of its great utility—all that can will be done however—and I wish you would make extraordinary exertion to send a pair or two before I leave Washington—as soon as I can succeed in procuring any thing like an assurance from Col Talcot I will let you know all about it—I am now on the recruiting service and have just as much as I can attend to and I fear I cannot give the matter as much attention as requisit—there will be an article published in a day or two on this subject if I am not mistaken.

Very Respectfully
Your obt Servant
Capt S H Walker[42]

Washington D C
January 30th 47
Saml Colt

Dear Sir
I received your letter of 23 inst & having just answered the one of previous date and being much pressed with public duty as recruiting officer—I have not written as soon as I should have done—I cannot see how I am likely to have any success with Talcot in relation to his arrangement with Whitney—I have lost no opportunity in recommending your arms and have succeeding in attracting public attention to them, but every body wishes to see them and you may rest assured that the best argument now is a pair of them complete so as to exhibit them here—Tibbatts of the House is extremely anxious to see a sample of them—I shall leave on Monday for Baltimore & stop four or five days, and if you can get the pair complete I will return here with them expressly to exhibit them to the Military committee who have the matter now under consideration and much depends on their recommendation Houston & Rusk will give the highest recommendation to these arms & you may have no fears about their adopted for general use by all the U S Cavalry if you can only get some of them complete nine men of Ten in this City do not know what Colts Pistol is and although I have explained the difference between yours & the six Barrel "Pop Gun" that is in such general use a thousand times they are still ignorant on the subject—As regards the lever to load with you must of course be governed by circumstances; if you cannot use the conical ball without the lever being attached to the barrel, you must of course adopt it without any hesitation—

The Powder Flask I think had better be plain with a single charge without any other aparatus attached to it—as the Pouch which will be carried on the belt will do to cary every thing necessary—I will endeavor to arrange every thing satisfactory to you before I leave. I shall stop long enough in the west somewhere to select my horse and you my rest assured that there is nothing shall be left undone that I can do to forward your interests. I enclose the Copy of correspondence between yourself and Talbot & hope you will not attribute my not writing more promptly to any indifference on the subject—as I am much pressed I assure you I wish you to continue to communicate freely on the subject as I shall be glad to hear from you—and shall expect to see you in Baltimore next week as I do not believe it would be prudent for me to ask permission to come on at this time so you must not expect it unless things take a very favourable turn—Tibbitts desired me to order a pair of your Pistolls Houston Rusk Caughman & many others are desirous of getting a pair with as little delay as possible and all you have to do is to manufacture them I want 100 pair at least to supply the immediate wants of my intimate friends in Texas & New Orleans and will undertake to dispose of that number for you and forward you the money as soon as I receive them any place I may be in Mexico.

Respectfully your Obt Servant
Capt S H Walker
Mtd Riflemen
USA[43]

On February 5, Colt again wrote and asked Wesson to make several conical bullet molds for Colt's new pistols; this would include the cherries so that Colt could make the molds.[44] Walker continued to make suggestions as the design of the weapon.

Washington D C
Feb 6th 1847

Dear Sir
I have received both your communications, and must reply in great haste, I leave this evening for Baltimore where I will be likely to remain about one week at which time I hope you will get the models complete and have an opportunity of exhibiting of them here I cannot do any thing more in the matter till I get them—I am not getting any holsters made, I expect to stop long enough in Louisville or Cincinatti ohio, to select my horses and hope you will get a sufficient number of the Pistols done to arm my company before I leave New Orleans, I doubt very much the propriety of your making any parts of the mounting of Brass as it is differently agreed upon in our specifications I cannot authorise any change in the material, I can do no more to procure additional orders than what I have done; the President & Secretary are, they say, both disposed to give me what I recommend and refer the matter to Congress & they will not act without seeing a proper specimen of the arms recommended, But I repeat the assurances that I have allways given that your arms would be in great demand And I have not the least doubt that 5000 Five Thousand of your Pistols could be sold in a very short time, but it is useless for me to waste any more time in argument with a set of asses to convince them of the importance of getting your arms I flatter myself that the best argument I can use will be in the field, But I will make another desperate effort if you will get the moddells and meet me in Baltimore next week say next Thursday & I will come on to this place with you and do my best

Yours Very Respectfully
Capt S H Walker

P. S. you will find me at Fort McHenrie Balt Md I have not yet reed the Pistol you sent perhaps Ill get it by next arrival

Yours &c[45]

Baltimore
Feb 8th 1847

Dear Sir
I received your communication directed to me at this place I have no time to write much at present, but hope you will do all that can be done to get the pair of Pistols finished, and send them to me as quick as possible, I am now satisfied I shall stop at Newport Kentucky several weeks to select my horses & drill the men I have recruited, I shall expect you to do all that man can do to get enough Pistols completed before I leave to arm my company you can communicate freely with me, and should you have any difficulty with the ordnance Department I will slip over and attend to it, I have just received communications from Gen Jesup approving of my saddle and equipments and allso giving me the priviledge of selecting my horses in Cincinatti or Louisville if you will get the Pistols ready in time for the next engagement I have no fears for the result you will have your arms recommended in such a way as to place their great superiority beyond any question, I do think it almost impossible for me to come to Newhaven before leaving for Newport but shall expect to see you here before I leave.

Yours very
Respectfully
Capt S H Walker

PS I am so much pressed with public duties on the recruiting service that I have not time to turn around.[46]

Washington D C
February 19, 1847

Sir
In reply to your enquiries in relation to the Pistol Guards, which you are now manufacturing for the Government, I have to say that I have no objection to their being made of Brass, as you propose as I believe when all things taken into consideration, they are the best, I have also consulted with Col Talcott of the ordnance Department and he also thinks it preferable to any other quality of mounting, & so far as my authority extends, you have the priviledge of borrowing thus far from the original contract—The principle Lever however for loading

must be made of Iron or steel, you will number the pistols according to Companies, by pairs, numbering each part alike from 1 up 220, provided the law passes, authorising the increase as anticipated to that number, you will also stamp them by letters in then-alphabetical order, stamping the letter C., on the first two hundred and twenty as the letter of my company, should the law not pass you will be authorised to number them as high as 76—,

The powder flasks you propose to furnish to carry balls also—I do not approve of, as I prefer it plain & substantial suited for a narrow lether strap say & inch in width and of very strong hinges [ ]to screw it & to hold about 3/4 of a pound more or less, and of much stronger material than the sample you have shown—In regard to the sights you must make the hind sight much finer and the front sight, of German Silver, and of different shape altogether from the model furnished, say half inch in length 1/8 of an inch at bottom tapering to 1/16 about this shape [ ] these general principles I wish you to observe, but as a matter of course—slight alterations are admissable which you may find necessary by practicing with the Arms—I approve of your substitute for Spring vice by connecting it with cone screw, & screw Drivers, and 1 Powder flask and other fixtures to each pair, and not to each as stated in the contract as it was not intended by me to have more than one to each pair, but they must be made more substantial, & have better fixtures to screw than your sample—The handle of pistol is rather short & not quite full enough, and must be increased a little in length and thickness if it can be done without much delay

I am sir
Very Respectfully
Your Obt Servt
S H. Walker Capt
Mtd Riflemen

P. S. Direct your letters to me at New Port Kentucky and let me know as early as possible what your earliest moment is that you can complete the arms for my company

Yours &C[47]

Recruiting Rendesvous
Baltimore MD 24 Feb/47

Dear Colt
I have just received your note on the subject of getting up a device, I have not a moment at present, perfectly bored to death with Mothers & Fathers about minors &c I send you a copy of a letter to Tailcot,

which I have just found, I leave tomorrow for Newport stoping six or seven days on the way to recrut

S H W[48]

Newport Barracks Ky
March 6th 1847

Dear Colt
I arrived here to day all safe and sound this is a very pretty place but at present very much crowded with recruits I have a fine set of young men and all I want now is the arms, I hope you will rush things as rapidly as possible and get me enough completed for my company before I am ordered to leave, write and let me know the earliest possible moment you can get them ready, there is nothing now not even a Female that gives me so many thoughts I have not had time yet to get up the Drawing you requested and you must not stop now to trouble yourself about any thing of the kind if I can find any body however that is good at drawing I will send it to you, be sure and write and let me know the earliest moment you can furnish the 220 pistols give my compliments to Whitney and tell him he has my best wishes I remain

Yours Very Respectfully
S H Walker
Captain[49]

Newport Barracks Ky
March 19th 1847

Dear Colt
My hopes are all on the my dear fellow and I trust I shall hear something from you in a few days that will be interesting, do for heavens Sake rush things as rapidly as possible and send me some of the Pistolls immediately I want to commence drilling my men on horse back with them I have now 120 men with me and will enlist 180 more to take out with me, every thing now is depending on you, let me hear from you immediately if not sooner and let me know when they will be forthcoming, find out how things are likely to work in relation to inspection &c and let me know all about it," Could you not get Mr Whitney to turn all his force upon them and turn them out immediately if you will only manage to get them turned of rapidly and forward me enough to arm my detachment before leaving, "you shall wear the brightest Laurel of our first victory and the Glory shall all be thine," yours in haste

SH Walker
Capt M. R.
Rctg officer

Bank having no time to get a N. york draft I send this to Mr Willard by Mr. Edwards 27 wall st.[50]

Newport Barracks Ky
March 24th 1847

Dear Colt
I received your letter in answer to mine of the 6th, The news from the army is of such a nature as to induce me to believe that I will be ordered of in a short time I have been fearful that some thing would occur before I could get the pistols, and I now write to request you to send them to me as rapidly as you can posibly turn them of if it is only 20 at a time the smallest number would be desirable, dam the odds about all inspection send them to me and I will inspect them, and make it all right If possible get Whitney to turn all his force on them and send them out immediately, every thing now depends on action all of old rough and readys communications are cut of and you may rest assured that orders will reach me in a few days to leave so you must move heaven and earth to get the Pistols ready, I will write to the New Secretary of War and endevour to save you any trouble with the Ordnance Department," be sure and write immediately upon receipt of this and let me hear from you," If I should be compelled to leave you must not delay forwarding of these Pistols box them up and send them by the most direct route you can it will never do for me to go into another engagement without some of these Pistols I have now got 127 men and could recruit as many as I wanted if I only had the arms for them You may rest assured that the material I have will give a good account of themselves if they get a chance to use your arms and I have no doubt they will, and I doubt not you will use extraordinary exertion to have me supplied with them before I leave, it is useless for me to give you any accounts of the various rumours here as you will of course hear them all before you receive this communication

Yours in haste
S H Walker
Capt M.R.

PS I will advise you of my point of destination and direct you which way to send those arms so as to reach me without delay when I get orders to leave here, You must try and distribute your work in such a way as to get them done as early as possible," if you can make any possible arrangement to get them all done in half the time of your contract it is better for you to do it because this promtness would secure a contract hereafter that would enable you to make some thing to compensate you.

Respectfully
your obt Servt in haste S H Walker
Capt M R[51]

Newport Barracks Ky
26th March 1847

Dear Colt
As I anticipated my orders came immediately after my last communication to repair with as little delay as possible to the seat of war, I have protested in very strong terms against being sent to the field without horses or equipments making the recruits serve as foot soldiers when those under my command have all been enlisted for mounted service, I shall obey the order at least by going where I am ordered provided they do not countermand it, which I think posible by the time I reach Neworleans, I have written to the President protesting in very strong terms against sending me into the field under such circumstances I had commenced the purchase of Horses here by authority from the Qr Master Gen USA, And notwithstanding this authority which was granted me in January It is regreted by the Adgt Gen that I should have taken any steps for the selection of horses without Authority from the proper Department Such things is by no means very agreable as the language used in my opinion amounts to a censure though I cannot believe it the intention of the Adgt Gen to wound my feelings, and attribute it all to their having too much to attend to and not giveing the subject that consideration which it merited, I have used up a little ink however on the ocasion which you may hear from hereafter, do not hesitate to send forward the Pistols I think it probable that I may stop some time in Neworleans, I shall leave here on the first day of April and will reach Neworleans on or before the 10th at which place I expect to hear from you and think that I may wait there long enough to get some of the Pistols if you will hurry.

Yours in great haste
S H Walker
Capt M R[52]

On Board Steamer Albertros
10 oclock P M 1st Apl 1847

Dear Colt
We are now on our way to the seat of War I have a fine set of young men that will give a good account of themselves as soon as they have an opportunity," you must try your D—st to send me those Pistols they are determined to get us into the field any how I have purchased

nearly enough horses to mount my company," and my equipments will be nearly ready or ready to be shiped at this time," our departure from Newport Barracks was rendered very pleasant by the very flattering testimony the people particularly the Ladies who waved their handkerchiefs to us untill the Steamer had taken us entirely out of sight, they of course expect to hear a good account of us and I am in great hopes of receiving some of your Pistols very soon so that I may not disappoint them write to me again on receipt of this and let me hear what I may rely on in regard to the Pistols I will write to you again in Neworleans, and if it is probable that I may get Pistols in a very short time it is possible I may wait for them, as I know our army is in want of Mounted troops and it is likely that Gen Cadwalader will take measures to have us mounted, my boys are in fine spirits and all my sick improving yours most Truly

S H Walker
Capt M.R.[53]

Neworleans Barracks La
18th April 1847

Dear Colt
I have received both your letters 31st March and 3rd of April and have only time to say that I agree with you in your views, and fear that some delay may occur, I have written to Col Talcot and requested him to have them forwarded direct to Vera Cruz with inspection promising to take upon myself all responsibility and to pay all expenses of transportation &c of any that may be rejected, this is all that I can do and if there is likely to be any difficulty about it and you can possibly do it I want you to send them any how, direct to Vera Cruz to my order and I will make all necessary arrangements to satisfy you in a very short time, I shall leave here about the 24th for Vera Cruz and if you will be in haste I will succeed in getting these arms in time for the Big fandango at the City Puebla or Mexico, I have 160 men and am still recruiting for the Regiment and have choice material, Holsters to suit the revolvers were made in Washington with the Saddles and ought to be on their way out before this time I shall take my horses with me and shall want nothing but the Pistols to go immediately in to the interior of Mexico, where you will soon hear some account of us that we think will please you, Hays has been on to Washington and is now in Texas raising a Regt of Texans Rangers he has the promise of all the Pistols except those for my Company They could not be in better hands and I would rather he should have them than any person else except my own Regiment, And I have no doubt that my Colonel will make some exertion to try and prevent

this disposition of these arms, I have no time to write more as I have just as much duty to attend to now as any other Six officers in the Service only one commissioned officer with me and him on the sick list," the health of my Recruits is generally good, though I have lost two men since I left Baltimore from the effects of Measles which we have had pretty extensively

Your Friend
S H Walker
Capt M. R.[54]

Neworleans City La
21st April 1847

Dear Colt
I have just received your letter of the 12 Apl I shall stay here at least a week longer and then go by steam-packet to Vera Cruz I am still recruiting men and will continue to do so up to the time of my departure from this place as you will receive my letter written some few days ago informing you of my communication to Col Talcot I have but little to write except to urge my request that you will send the arms forward as soon as they are complete without waiting any time for inspection if the Department does not send some person to inspect them and receive them as soon as they are ready I will have to depend upon your exertions entirely to forward them to Vera Cruz or do with out them, I think by making some arrangement to ship them on some steamer that is going direct to Vera Cruz I would be able to get them in a very short time after my arrival at that place say by the 12th of May provided the Boxes and every thing is ready to pack them as soon as finished all of which I hope you will attend to, and be sure and send me a good and large Supply of the best Caps that can be procured as I fear Col Talcot will never think of it although I have made a requisition on him for all such things the Holsters were made in Washington

Yours in haste
S H Walker
Capt M R[55]

Neworleans La
28th Apl 1847

Dear Colt
I have received your letter of the 18th inst having written to you a few days ago I have nothing more to write than merely to reexpress

my hope that you will make some arrangement to forward my Pistols direct to Vera Cruz as I shall be compelled to leave here as soon as I can get my Saddles and Bridles which will be about the first day of May and I shall be compelled to go direct to Jalappa and will have the Pistols forwarded to me as soon as they reach Vera Cruz, I can not tell you any thing about the marking of the Pistols yet as Hays has the Promise of them and there is no telling what changes may take place," I hope you have made the alteration in the Britch that I suggested as the handle is very imperfect being so short that a suitable grip cannot be taken to enable you to hold it steady enough to shoot with much accuracy, believing my saddles would not be sent from Washington in time I have got another full set making here which will be complete in a few days which I am now waiting for, I shall give orders here for a full set of Holsters allso which will be sent to Vera Cruz as soon as your Pistols can reach me, I learn that our whole Regt is ordered to be remounted, and I have no doubt that an additional number of the Pistols will be required as soon as you can manufacture them, be sure and make the alteration I suggested in the Handle, and do not make them hard on the trigger I have had a great many applications for these Pistols from Gentlemen of high standing but told them that it would be impossible to get them untill you had first supplied the Government according to your Contract which would be in about three months you can sell a great many at this place I am still recruiting and shall take about 180 recruits with me for the Regt all of good material so that you will put your Arms in pretty good hands as I think they will be apt scholars, Try and procure a good supply of Percussion Caps of the right sort and send them with the Pistols

Your Friend
SH Walker
Capt M.R.[56]

However, Colt would select Eli Whitney, Jr. to make the revolvers.[57] Samuel Colt asked if he could make 1,000 revolvers for him in three months. By this time Whitney was so well-equipped that even though he'd never made pistols before, he confidently replied "I can make them. … no Factory has machinery as complete as mine." He added, however, "The 1000 cannot be made in 3 months by Any Factory."[58]

Colt supplied a model and some machinery from his defunct factory in Paterson, New Jersey, and in only six months the 1,000 revolvers were finished.

Ironically this innovation in American technology would be made from English Steel.[59] Colt had used Sheffield steel as it had fewer flaws and by being more uniform, the machine operations would not have to make corrections in the manufacture of the pistol parts.[60]

Crucible steel used at the Whitney Armory through much of its ninety years came from Sheffield, England. It was bent into springs; it was hammered into ramrods and bayonets in the forging shop. In the 1840s Eli Whitney, Jr. adopted the use of steel for gun barrels earlier than did the Springfield Armory. In the 1840s Eli Whitney, Jr. was among the first to shift from wrought iron to crucible steel in the manufacture of barrels for his guns, and from the 1850s onwards successfully applied the little-understood technique of malleable iron castings to the production of pistol frames and rifle fittings.[61]

Rifles

Apparently, Walker approached Edwin Wesson also about making rifles for his company of Mounted Riflemen (while Colt also approached him to make the pistols). Wesson replied to a letter Walker wrote him on December 11.

I should think that rifles suitable for the service you mentioned might be afforded for from 30 to 40 Dolls. Each. Should wish a particular description before setting an exact price—The time required to get them out would depend on the quantity required—Should I get a large contract, I could shape my business to turn them out with more dispatch. …

I have just recd an application from Mr. Colt to make 1,000 of his repeating pistols—I have business with the patent office in Washington & think I will see you there the last part of next week, if agreeable.[62]

On January 18, 1847, Walker did indeed order a rifle for himself (and one for his brother Jonathan) from Edwin Wesson.[63] It weighed 8 pounds and was .44 caliber (the same caliber as the Walker revolver).[64]

Evidently, the word was out about Walker's plan to arm his men with Wesson's rifles and Colt's revolvers. The following was published in a New Jersey newspaper on January 20:

Captain S. H. Walker will leave Washington on the first of February for the scene of war via Baltimore and Pittsburg—he is ordered to recruit 50 young men to take out with him for a new regiment of riflemen commanded by the gallant Persifer F. Smith now in the field who is loved and respected—Captain Walker has succeeded in procuring 1,000 of Colt's large revolving pistols for this regiment of which he is endeavoring to give each man a PAIR—he is also desirous of Clarke's patent rifle[65] which is said to be the most deadly weapon in the world—Walker has been five years on the Texas frontiers under Jack Hays, and the equipment for the US light cavalry is similar to that of Rangers in all their fights with the Indians and Mexicans.[66]

A February 7 letter from Walker to Edwin Wesson indicated Wesson would probably be making 1,000 rifles for Walker's regiment, hopefully funded by the State of Maryland.[67] This contract never happened but Wesson had made preparation to make them by buying the steel for the anticipated contract. Daniel and Edwin Wesson had overextended themselves financially by the purchase of the steel for the 1,000 rifles and ended up being forced to make a temporary partnership with Thomas Smith (a gunsmith at Harpers Ferry, Virginia—no relation to Horace Smith of the later Smith & Wesson partnership).[68] The only Wesson rifles sold to Walker were two, one for him and one for his brother Jonathan Thomas.

Pistol Production

Whitney wrote Colt on December 14, asking if the pistol parts were to be made "strictly uniform" (interchangeable) as was John Hall's rifle of a decade earlier.[69] There was neither time for making gauges, as did Hall, nor using them. According to one study, as Whitney workmen shaped each revolver individually (each Walker revolver was, therefore, unique within itself) the workmen used an average of two and one-half quality English files per revolver.[70] While the goal of the Walker revolvers would be to be uniform enough that they could be interchanged with "slight or no refitting,"[71] they would hardly be interchangeable.

Interchangeable parts were a milestone for American industry and first accomplished by John Hall at Harper Ferry's Armory a decade earlier. While Eli Whitney Sr.'s name has been associated with interchangeable parts, he did not make interchangeable parts for his arms—although he championed the process.[72]

On December 16, Colt wrote Walker's brother Jonathan Thomas that he was trying to get in touch with him. He wrote Jonathan that "it would be better to have the order for the Pistols to come through your Brother's hands ... to give him control of their construction." He said that this would speed things along rather than the production of the pistols being "subject to the whims & caprices of an old officer in the ordnance department."[73] Walker would get his pistols through a federal government contract but not his rifles.

January 1847

Colt and Walker did meet to work out the details because on January 4, 1847,[74] they signed the contract for the pistols. According to the agreement, the new revolvers (issued in pairs)[75] would have 9-inch barrels,[76] a .44-caliber bore, and a six-chamber cylinder. All 1,000 were to be delivered within six months.[77]

It was easy for Walker to listen enthusiastically to the manufacturer of the pistols that had saved his life in many a fight. But the bankrupt pistol producer's overenthusiasm was promising Walker what Walker wanted to hear so that a contract could be signed.

The problem was that Colt had to start from scratch with someone else actually making the revolvers. It was hard under wartime stress as well as Walker's personal pressure to get everyone working together.

Even bigger was the problem of pompous bureaucrats with a mindset that was never to be bothered with facts. They had the power which they abused. While Walker would rather face screeching Comanche "Lords of the Southern Plains" or disciplined attacks by Mexican lancers, many of the wartime leaders in Washington could not be counted upon to fund any weapon he could use or had time to use. They took their time when they wanted to, no matter how many lives it would cost.

Yet Walker needed the pistols and Colt needed to get back in the gun making business so the two got down to details in doing what they could do.

The Walker Colt Revolver

Walker and Colt agreed that if a contract could be worked out with the army, the primary design change would be in the size and caliber of the pistol. The former Ranger knew from experience that he needed greater impact and stopping power than the old .36-caliber Paterson, which used only 22 grains of black gunpowder for each round. For the new revolver, Walker wanted a handgun that would fire a .44-caliber bullet from a chamber that could hold up to 50 grains of powder.

.44 Caliber

Walker specifically mentioned to Colt when he first discussed the production of the new pistols in a letter written on December 1, 1846, that he wanted a revolver that could shoot "50 balls [round as opposed to cylindrical] to the pound & adopted to carry an elongated ball of greater weight [32 balls to the pound]."[78] This was later reflected in the final contract for a pistol that shot a .44-caliber bullet. Molds were provided for of round lead ball and .44 "elongated bullet." The Paterson Walker had fired a .36 round ball. The size of the projectile and the shape were of his insistence.

Six Shots and 9-inch Barrel

The former Ranger had two very good reasons for wanting a larger pistol with a 9-inch barrel (as specifically called for in the contract of January 4) that fired a conical bullet. The power and penetration he wanted, was partially because of his experience with the Comanche. He remembered their bulletproof war shield, but more emblazoned in his memory was his recollection of not being able to stop all the Comanche that swarmed about him in that well-known clash of the 16 Rangers and the 80 Comanche in June 1844. On Walker's back and chest were the scars from that time just two years earlier when he had been severely lanced through the body by a Comanche warrior.[79] The next time he came in conflict with a Comanche, he wanted as much of an advantage as possible. Stopping power and an extra shot meant a great deal to this veteran of mounted combat.

The Mexican encounters also had a part in his desire for the more powerful weapon. Extra power meant extra range, and the Rangers knew all too well the frustration of being held at bay by Mexican cavalry with their escopetas. These carbines were small but had more range than the usual short-barreled rifles and the Rangers' revolvers.[80] With more range, the new Colt revolver was designed to give the user the advantage in combat.

Trigger Guard

Walker also mentioned to Colt the problem of the Paterson's trigger—a folding lever that sprung out only when the weapon was cocked. In the confusion of battle, this presented a definite problem. Walker suggested a more conventional trigger with a trigger guard. This and other ideas would be worked out later; his main concern about design was that the new revolver be the rugged, powerful cavalry arm that he felt was needed for mounted combat.

Colt would contract a competitor—master gunsmith Orison Blunt, owner of the Metropolitan Arms Company—to make a prototype of the newly designed Colt revolver and he would present it to Colt in January. It had an iron trigger guard but no attached loading lever.[81]

Attached Loading Lever

Soon Colt had to change his plan for a separate loading lever because of complications in loading the conical bullet. On January 23, he wrote Walker:

> I have been bothered to deth in endevering to lode the cillinders with the conical ball by means of the old fashioned leaver and have abandoned it as a bad job. There must be a leaver attached to the barrel upon a new plan which will work purpindicular otherwise you can never get your balls strate into the cilinder.[82]

Walker wrote back on January 30, as regards the lever to load "if you cannot use the conical ball without the lever being attached to the barrel, you must adapt it without hesitation."[83]

Walker had good reason to welcome this change. The separate loading lever that was used on the earlier Paterson, while quicker to manufacture in this pressing circumstance, had a major flaw. To load a revolver with it, the weapon had to be broken down into three parts—any of which, if lost, would make the pistol useless. On horseback and in the heat of battle, dropping a loose pistol part was more than a possibility.

Brass Trigger Guard and Brass Powder Flasks

A week later, Colt was writing about the trigger guard, requesting Walker's permission to use brass instead of iron. Walker accepted this change; however, there were other suggestions (such as Colt's idea of a special powder flask that held both powder and ball) to which Walker objected. On February 19, Walker wrote:

> The Powder Flask you propose ... I do not approve of, as I prefer it plain & substantial suitable for a narrow leather strap ... & to hold 3/4 of a lb more or less and of a much stronger material than the sample you have shewn—In regard to the sights you must make the hind sight much finer and the front sights of German silver and of different shape altogether from the model

> furnished … say half inch in length 1/8 of an inch at the bottom tapering to 1/16 about this shape. … The Handles … is rather short and not quite full enough and must be increased in length and thickness if it can be done without much delay.[84]

The Cylinder

When it came to making the "hammered cast steel"[85] cylinders for the Walker Colt (United States Model 1847), the end result was striking. First the cylinder was not blued but shiny silver "in the white." Some have speculated that Colt was in a rush to get the pistols produced and others thought that he was hesitant to heat treat the cylinders for bluing that could weaken the walls of the cylinders that would be withstanding considerable pressure with up to 50-grain loads.

The second special treatment of these cylinders was the engraved depiction of the famous Colt revolver victory at the battle of Walker Creek. Sixteen Texas Rangers—all armed for the first time with Colt Paterson revolvers—defeated a force of nearly 80 Comanche.

To commemorate this landmark event, Colt had employed bank note engraver W. L. Ormsby to do the engraving. Ormsby had already done work for Colt, engraving his 1839 Paterson Shotgun. Walker wrote Colt on March 6, 1847, that he had not had time to "get up the Drawing" Colt had request and that he would if he could find anyone good at drawing, he would let Colt know. But he urged Colt not to let the lack of a drawing slow down the pistol production.[86]

Ormsby was very good at making high quality copies of existing art works in steel.[87] When Walker was unable to furnish a drawing of the famous battle between Texas Rangers and Comanche, Ormsby sought what had already been drawn and went to a very authoritative source for depicting the Comanche warrior on horseback in battle. He found copies of the works of nationally famous artist George Catlin. When Ormsby discussed with Colt seeking Catlin drawings, Colt easily accommodated him. Colt and Catlin were good friends and the drawings were readily acquired. Ormsby copied very closely the drawn from life work of this experienced artist.[88]

While there was no way to distinguish a mounted Texas Ranger who had no uniform, Ormsby knew that the engraving was on a pistol cylinder to be used by Captain Walker's new mounted command, the U.S. Regiment of Mounted Rifles (RMR). So, the Rangers were shown in the uniform of the RMR, down to military saddles and horse gear including saddle holster for the new Walker Colts. On close examination, the Rangers/RMR figures are riding like U.S. Cavalry and upright in the saddle while the Rangers had learned to fire from the behind the mounts just as well as the Native American enemy.[89]

While Walker did not send a drawing for the cylinder, there is an indication that he mentioned that he rode a dark-colored horse and Hays rode a light-colored

Catlin. Cylinder engraving of the battle of Walker Creek. (James Worsham collection)

horse, as Ormsby specifically engraved one horse as light and the other as dark.[90] Many Colt historians consider the rider of the dark horse to be Sam Walker.[91]

On a strip of mild steel, Ormsby engraved his scene with a sharp hardened steel tool. After Ormsby's signature on the engraving are the letters "sc" which shows the pride Ormsby had in this work. It means "he sculpted it" from the Latin sculpsit—often used on bank note engravings. Ormsby only signed his work on the Walker cylinder this way and not on later Colt cylinders.[92]

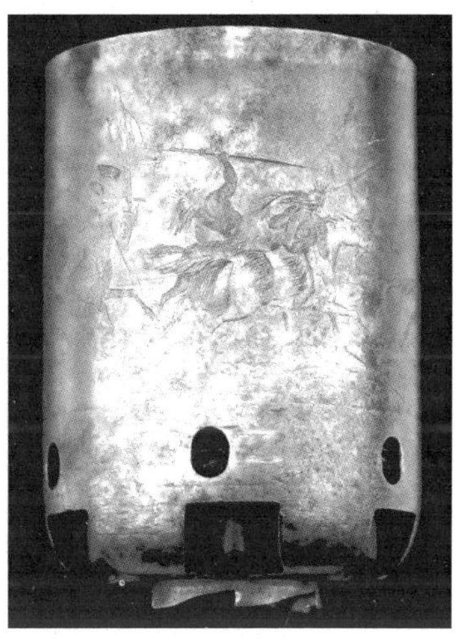

Detail of engraved cylinder. (James Worsham collection)

The engraving was then case hardened and then an annealed softened steel roller was passed across the engraved scene several times under great pressure. This roller was then hardened and under equally great pressure, rolled on the fresh unblued polished, unbored revolver cylinder.[93]

On March 22, Colt paid $200 for "Dies for Cillenders."[94] In the finishing schedule at Whitneyville after George Whiting polished the cylinders, "Lazel & son & helper" rolled on the figures.[95]

To Be Issued in Pairs

The single-shot flintlock pistol, currently the standard issue for mounted troops, was issued in pairs. When this issue was brought to light early on about whether the pistols would have one powder flask per pistol or one per pair was resolved; one flask per pair was approved by the War Department.

Later, Colt asked about holsters that were usually issued in pairs and hung balanced on the saddle.[96] To Colt this was insurance that if that many holsters were made, it would be a safe bet he would have to make more than the 1,000 pistols of the contract. When Walker said the pistols would be in two holsters, Colt wrote, "I am pretty safe in making 1600 (revolvers) on the order for 1000 even if the department do not extend the order at once."[97]

Not only did Walker plan to issue pairs of revolvers for their saddle holsters, he insisted the serial numbers reflected this. While Sam was only authorized 76 men for his company, Sam was planning on a new law expanding the company from 76 to 110 men. He foresaw and even planned on it as he expanded the number of men he recruited from 120 that he took to Newport Barracks for their initial training to nearly 200 that he brought to Mexico.

He wrote Colt on February 19 "you will number the pistols according to Companies, by pairs, numbering each … from 1 up to 220, provided the law passes authorizing the increase as anticipated to that number … should the law not pass … number them as high as 76."[98]

Colt was able to get Thomas Warner "one of the most gifted mechanics to serve at Springfield Armory" to make all the tools needed to make the pistols. Warner would get $1.25 a pistol for this service and Colt would get to keep the tools.[99] He was also able, with Walker's help, to get Whitney a three-month extension on the Whitney contract to make rifles for the army.[100]

In the meantime, Colt was having enough problems; Whitney was not able to manufacture the revolvers as fast as were needed, even though Colt had workmen on the job until midnight every night. Colt sublet the making of the barrels and cylinders to Slate & Brown of Hartford. He later regretted it; for in April of that year he wrote of the "backwardness of their work."[101]

Holsters Made Specifically for the Walker Colt

It is evident that the Walker Colt would require a holster specifically designed and made for this pistol and it alone. J. C. Shackleford and Company of Cincinnati, Ohio, manufactured the holsters and requested Colt to send a wooden model of the Walker Colt upon which a substantial, form-fitted holster could be made.

The holsters would be slapped and pummeled against a horse when loaded with the heavy Walker Colt pistols. On a cantering horse, and when coupled with very wet or very dry weather, one can understand the stresses the holsters were designed to take. The leather is also thick bridle leather (⅛ inch) and is about the thickness of the leather skirts found on the typical Civil War McClellan saddle. The leather of the yoke is doubled over and slotted for the martingale (breast) straps. The holsters were attached to the saddle by using a 1-inch-wide strap that buckled onto the martingale strap. The strap was slotted through the yoke between the holsters and a separate strap encircled each holster body below the cover button, and that looped strap was sewn together after it was threaded through the strap slot. This saddle holster attachment was a very secure way to keep the holsters from flopping when the horse was running. A single 1-inch-wide strap was slotted through both holsters and over the central yoke between the holsters with its ends punched with holes for a buckle on each end of the martingale/breast strap. This then allowed the strap to secure the holsters against the pommel inside of the saddle seat to either end of the martingale with buckles—a simple, clever, and very secure way to fasten the holsters to both the horse and saddle.

The dimensions provide a sense of just how big the Walker Colt is.

Overall dimensions (inches)	
Overall holsters end to end	41
Length of yoke between holsters	13
Holster body	
Body dimension	14
Holster opening length	4½
Holster opening width	2
Holster depth from top to plug insert	12¾
Length of the brass end cap	2½
Diameter of the cap	1¾
Length of the bubble at base of cap	½
Thickness of the leather	⅛[102]

Given the delays involved with just about everything required to get his company ready for battle, it is unlikely Walker had a pair of the newly designed holsters for his pistols when he was killed.

Walker Colt with holsters side by side. (Courtesy of John Thillmann)

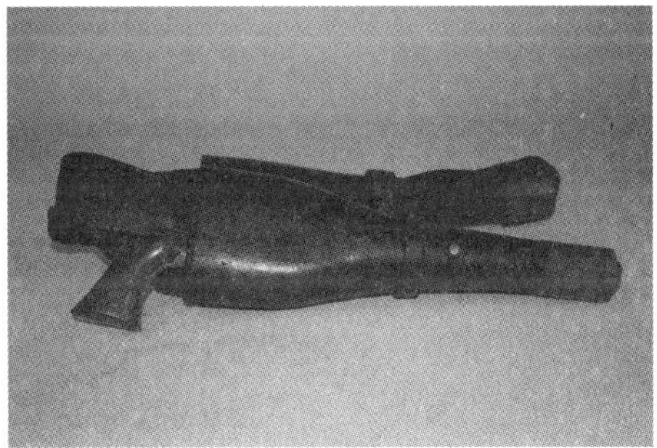

Perfect fit of the Walker Colt in the holster. (Courtesy of John Thillmann)

Arming Young Men for War

Walker, who had been on recruiting duty at Fort McHenry, Maryland, since early February, left for Newport, Kentucky, on February 25 and arrived on March 6 with 120 men. While he had obtained his horses in Louisville and Cincinnati, Colt had not been able to complete the revolvers and received an urgent letter from Walker pleading "for hevens Sake rush things … send me some of the Pistolls immediately. I want to commence drilling my men on horseback."[103] In a letter written near the end of March, he again wrote asking that the revolvers be sent even if only 20 at a time.[104] Yet to further frustrate both Colt and Walker, the army itself would cause delays "with the regulations of the Ordnance Department in making gauges … for the inspection."[105]

On April 1, Walker left Newport Barracks, Kentucky, for New Orleans by the steamer *Albatross*. He arrived there on April 10.[106] To Walker's chagrin, he was informed by the Ordnance Department on April 2 that 1,008 sabers and 608 flintlock pistols would be issued to his regiment of mounted riflemen.[107] These would be their weapons for training until the Colts were delivered. Colt notified Secretary of War Marcy of Walker's request of shipping the revolvers in small amounts as they were completed, rather than the whole 1,000 pistols at once. The Ordnance Department replied to Colt on April 26 that they would have an inspector in New Haven where Whitney was manufacturing the revolvers so that they could be shipped as soon as tested. On May 29, Whitney wrote Talcott that within a week or so he could deliver 200 revolvers;[108] but it was not until June 26 that Captain Thornton of the Ordnance Department had completed the inspection of 220 of the revolvers and they were ready for shipping.[109]

Colt announced on July 6 that he had completed all 1,000 revolvers, but it was not until July 8 that even his first shipment of the 220 pistols (which had been tested three weeks earlier) were shipped from the Ordnance Department to Mexico.[110] These first Walker Colts were sent to Veracruz, Mexico, to Ordnance Lt. Josiah Gorgas, who had orders to issue to Walker as many pistols as he needed to arm his company.

Ironically after Walker's death, the bulk (394) of the Walker revolvers sent to Mexico (including the first group for Walker's Company C), were signed over to Col. John Hays, commander of the 1st Regiment of Texas Mounted Rifle Volunteers, unofficially known as Hays' Texas Rangers. On October 19, 1847, Hays was issued 214 Walker Colt revolvers. Then on October 26, Hays received 180. Finally on November 19, Lieutenant Claiborne, now commanding Walker's Company C, was issued 100 Walker Colts—yet by this time the Walker Colts stamped Company C were long gone and Claiborne got revolvers that were a mix of pistols marked "Co A" and "Co B."[111]

The delivery of the remaining 500 Walker Colts is a mystery. They were not issued in Mexico; they apparently never reached the Veracruz Ordnance Department. The 2d Regiment of Dragoons in Texas and the federalized Texas Rangers would receive some—the exact number is undocumented—of these from the Baton Rouge Arsenal.[112]

Colt sent "presentation" Walker Colts to numerous high-ranking military personnel, who gladly received them. The following is one recipient's letter of thanks and delight:

> Mr. Samuel Colt
>
> Dr. Sir,
> It affords me pleasure to acknowledge the receipt of a fine six shooter (revolver pistol) by the hands of Lt. McDonald, for which you will please accept my thanks.
>
> I think I can say as much for and about this formidable weapon as any one now living except Col. J.C. Hays of Texas (Poor Walker is no more.) I have seen them tested in several severe and bloody conflicts, where a few men armed with your revolver were equal to five and in several instances ten times their numbers. No weapon is equal to it in close quarters. One man is always equal to three or more. I know the use of it well and would recommend that all mounted forces be armed with your six shooters.
>
> With great respect
> I am sir your obt servt,
> (signed) Joseph Lane[113]

Ironically, while Colt would earn a fortune in pistol production, his only cash profit on the manufacture of the Walker Colt revolver was only about $2,000.[114] According to the Colt Manufacturing Company "by the end of 1861 the factory was running at full capacity with over one thousand employees and annual profits exceeded a quarter of a million dollars." At the time of his death in 1862, Colt had produced over 400,000 firearms and had a fortune worth 15 million dollars.[115]

Sam Walker's Legacy

Sam Walker's greatest legacy is the Walker Colt revolver—the first Colt six-gun. The experience reflected in the advanced design of this new weapon did not happen overnight. Sam served for more than four years of hard fighting in the Texas Rangers as a private, captain, and lieutenant colonel. From his Ranger experience with the Colt five-shot Paterson, Walker sought to improve its design into a hard-hitting, repeating handgun for mounted combat. As a captain in the new Regiment of Mounted Riflemen, he wanted his men to be as well-equipped as he could make them. With the eye of an engineer, "mechanic" Walker considered several new ways of using his knowledge, and persistence to draw the equipment he needed from the War Department.

He set several precedents during the process.

First, to get more Colt revolvers, he had to rescue Sam Colt from bankruptcy and helped him restart his revolver business. This provided Colt with the opportunity to establish almost a monopoly in the revolver business from 1851 until 1856. Colt revolvers became an American classic. Historian Walter Webb even states that the use of Colt revolvers was one of the major factors Americans used in adapting themselves for the conquest of the frontier on the Great Plains.[116] Also, Walker's legacy to the military was the codesigning of the first six-shot revolver to ever be issued to the American military. When the enemy had one or perhaps two shots available, a dozen shots from two Colt revolvers made a real difference.

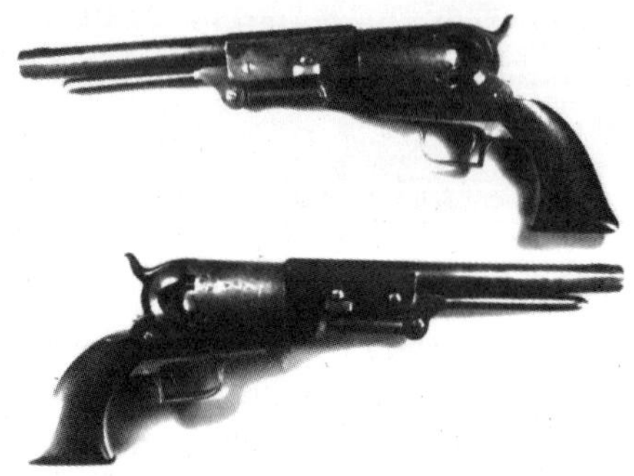
Captain Samuel H. Walker's personal .44-caliber pistols. (James Worsham collection)

Second, Sam Walker would have a major impact on the struggling E. Wesson Company. Walker almost involved Edwin Wesson, older brother of Daniel, one of the founders of Smith & Wesson revolvers, in arming his Mounted Riflemen Company with Wesson rifles—one of the most accurate rifles in America at the time. But Walker did not get a government contract for Wesson rifles. Sam Colt, who did have a government contract for pistols, did consider Edwin Wesson making revolvers for him. Had Colt not chosen Eli Whitney, Jr. to make his revolvers, the famous revolver competitors might never have materialized. There might have been a Colt & Wesson Firearms Manufacturing Company rather than the Smith & Wesson Company so well known today.

Ironically, because Edwin and Daniel Wesson believed Sam Walker would be able to acquire a contract from either the State of Maryland or the federal government for rifles, they purchased the steel they needed for the assumed contract of 1,000 rifles. To make these 1,000 rifles, a temporary partnership of Edwin Wesson, D. B. Wesson and Thomas Smith (a gunsmith at Harpers Ferry, Virginia—no relation to Horace Smith of the later Smith & Wesson partnership) was formed.[117]

Third, Walker kept his company mounted when almost all of the Mounted Riflemen were dismounted. He personally purchased their horses and even tried to have them equipped with floats for crossing rivers. He also requested and got new model saddles that did not hurt horse's backs. He wanted his company to be as well-equipped as he could make it.

One contemporary writer wrote of Sam Walker:

> He was the fast friend of improvements in the art of war, and his experience and keen perception led him to adopt the best of arms and equipments that could be had. Old customs and old-fashioned arms, unwieldy and ineffective, found no favor with him, so long as radical improvements were within reach.[118]

CHAPTER 9

Capt. Samuel H. Walker, Regiment of Mounted Riflemen

Captain Walker was assigned command of Company C, RMR. The regiment was formed just after the war with Mexico began and would have an impact on the war and on American military history. Considered the origin of the Army's 3d Cavalry Regiment, the Mounted Riflemen had an interesting heritage.

The Regiment of Mounted Riflemen

Throughout the U.S. Army's first half-century of existence, it had no permanent cavalry. The leaders of the new country recalled all too well the "Old Country" use of mounted troops by monarchs as tools of oppression. Congress, controlling purse strings, also saw the cost of cavalry as too rich for the new nation.[1] Disbanded in 1789, dragoons were called back into service in 1794 for Gen. Anthony Wayne's campaign against the natives. Dissolved in 1800, in service again during the War of 1812, and then disbanded in 1815, the mounted troops of the United States Army led an uncertain existence.

Yet as the frontier advanced westward, conflict with mounted natives made the need for a permanent cavalry pressing. In 1828, Gen. Alexander Macomb wrote the secretary of war:

> It has suggested itself by the nature of the country which opens upon the plains toward the Mexican frontier and towards the Rocky Mountains, that the efficiency of such regiments which occupy the posts … could be greatly augmented by providing the means of mounting the light companies and giving the character and effect of rangers or mounted chasseurs.[2]

On May 5, 1829, four companies of the 6th Infantry Regiment under Maj. Bennet Riley were frustrated trying to guard a supply train on the Santa Fe Trail from attacks of a mounted enemy. Major Riley wrote:

> Think what our feelings must have been to see them going off with our cattle and team horses, when if we had been mounted, we could have beaten them to pieces; but we were obliged to content ourselves with whipping them from our camp.[3]

2d Lt. George H. Gordon, Mounted Riflemen. Note spread-eagle cap device. (Photograph in the public domain)

As emigration to Oregon brought more and more settlers to the Oregon Trail and more danger of hostile attack, Secretary of War Joel Poinsett was an advocate for a mounted protective force. He also recommended a chain of posts along the trail to provide for their defense. In 1845, President James K. Polk called for a force of mounted riflemen to protect the emigrants.[4] Congress quickly passed the mounted riflemen bill. On May 19, 1845, President Polk signed the bill into law to form the Regiment of Mounted Riflemen to protect emigrants en route to Oregon. The Bill appropriated $75,000 for mounting and equipping, and $3,000 for each station established along the Oregon route.[5]

Maj. Edwin V. Sumner. (National Park Service)

The appointment of officers appeared political, with a major portion coming from the south and west. Whig Gen. Winfield Scott, commenting on the commissions for the newly authorized regiment of Mounted Riflemen, said "the proposed Riflemen are intended by western men to give commissions … to western democrats." No eastern man, West Point or Whig "would obtain a place."[6]

A Regular Army dragoon officer, Maj. Edwin V. Sumner,[7] was assigned by General Scott as their training commander.

According to one military historian, who was very critical of political appointments in the military, there were problems when political appointees were given officer positions. There were interesting results as:

> Consistent with army administration by politicians, men of experience or education for the profession were placed in the lower grades … companies would go to drill with full complements of officers, and return under the command of brevet second lieutenants, all the seniors having been relieved in the order of rank by the stern old major for inefficiency.

One who served with it later said, "The officers were all gentlemen, brave and generous to a fault, strict disciplinarians, and looked well after the wants of their men, but the most cantankerous lot I ever met."[8]

The "Kangaroo Regiment"

It was a reflection of the above criticism that the regiment was called for a time the "Kangaroo Regiment" because it was "strongest in its hind quarters."[9] However in retrospect, according to one young RMR officer, Sumner (who was called "Ole Bull") "acted so rigorously and impartially to all, that most excellent drill, discipline

... brought the Rifles ... to great efficiency."[10] The newly appointed colonel of the regiment, Persifor Smith, a graduate of Princeton who practiced law in New Orleans, was also an experienced soldier from the Florida War who was respected by his men.[11]

Persifor Smith. (Photograph in the public domain)

There were 10 companies which were authorized to have three officers and 114 enlisted men each. In spite of the accusations of incompetent political appointees, 17 of the captains and lieutenants were graduates of the U.S. Military Academy, and later during the Civil War, 11 would serve as generals.

The recruits of the newly formed regiment had been sent to Jefferson Barracks, Missouri, where companies A, B, D, E, G, H, I, and K were organized. In the fall of 1846, at dress parade, it was announced while the regiment had been organized for service in Oregon, the regiment was now directed to leave for the war in Mexico.

Proposals for Arming the Regiment

The arms developed for this regiment set precedents and made military history. The search for upgrading weapons for the new regiment began. Persifor Smith of Louisiana, who had been appointed colonel of the regiment, was asked by Brig. Gen. Roger Jones, Adjutant General of the Army on June 2, 1846, what arms and equipment he needed for his regiment.

Colonel Smith's Proposed Rifles

Smith, showing his conservative outlook upon change, answered on June 26:

> I am from experience, averse to the use of those Rifles which load at the breech, but would urge that they have percussion locks—loading at the breech certainly facilitates loading on horseback, but the excellence of the Rifle is in its accuracy, which is lost in firing from the saddle.[12]

One would say his last comments applied equally to both percussion and breech-loading weapons, but loading at the breech, especially on horseback, would be faster in circumstances when a trooper's life depended upon how quickly he could get off his next shot.

Colonel Smith's Proposed Knives and Sabers

> I know of no improvement to make on the present Dragoon Sabre. ...

> The arms I suggested were a short, percussive lock rifle avoiding the revolving & repeating barrels, a hunting knife—& a Sabre. In conversation since with several intelligent officers of the Texas Mounted troops, they urge the value of the repeating pistol of Colt particularly in a contest with the mounted Indians ... they attach great importance to the possession of this pistol.[13]

One of these officers of the Texas Mounted troops was Texas Ranger Lt. Col. Samuel Walker who was appointed a captain of the Regiment of Mounted Riflemen to rank from September 9, 1846. Smith wrote that he had discussed the question of arming the regiment with Walker and wrote on October 2 that:

> His views as to the armament & equipment of the regiment are entitled to great weight, he has had great experience in the kind of service expected from the Regiment. He joins me in condemning the present dragoon saddle[14] as do all the officers of that arm. The Attakapas & Texas Saddle is far preferable both for the horse and rider.[15]

In the same letter, he lists what he thinks are required and specifically asks for a revolving pistol of Colt's patent with the same caliber as the rifle.

> A dragoon sabre (if altered, to be shortened a little) and a hunting knife. He requests the rifle be "made to sling on the shoulder & to the saddle, the pistol in the holster & waist belt, the sabre slung to a shoulder belt & the hunting knife always in the waist belt. The rifle & pistol to use the same percussion cap & cartridge."[16]

On 19 December, Adjutant General Jones wrote to Walker regarding the acquisition of pistols for his company: "In compliance with the instructions of the Secretary of War, you will proceed to New York to superintend the preparation of suitable models for the pistols for the mounted rifle regiment."[17]

Reality: A Dismounted Mounted Regiment

Fighting on horseback was the goal of the new mounted unit. Only the two RMR companies that arrived in Mexico months after the regiment first entered the theater of operations would be mounted: Company I, Capt. Charles Frederick Ruff[18] commanding, was delayed in arriving at Jefferson Barracks for training; and Company C, Capt. Samuel Walker commanding, had been recruiting for his company in the East and would not arrive with it until the spring of 1847. The horses for the regiment were prepared for shipment from New Orleans to Mexico, but the Quartermaster Department had no experience in shipping horses. Some of the horses were shipped on the decks of schooners, over which a frame of

Capt. Charles Frederick Ruff. (Friends of Mount Moriah Cemetery. Photograph in the public domain)

boards was constructed on which bales of hay were placed. However, storms at sea cost the regiment almost all of its horses. Of the 700 horses shipped only about 250 were saved.[19] These were turned over to the 2d Dragoons and most of the Mounted Riflemen fought dismounted.[20]

Walker's Proposed Saddles

Earlier that year, Walker planned in detail for mounted combat for his company. On February 11, 1847, Walker wrote Assistant Quartermaster Col. Henry Stanton requesting permission to have the saddles for his company made in Washington.

> I respectfully request that you will contract with Mr. Campbell of Washington who will understand precisely what I want and what is suited to the service, and can have such [saddle] trees manufactured as will suit in every particular. The importance of a tree is very great and would require a week's attention, at least to make any Mechanic understand the principles to be observed in their construction.[21]

Among Walker's papers is a proposal to make saddles for him at a cost of between $32 and $34.50. It is uncertain whether this manufacturer did or did not get a contract, but the prices are an example of what the market was getting at the time.[22] Unfortunately, if Walker submitted drawings of his proposed saddle, they have been lost to history.

Walker's Proposed Colt's Revolvers

As indicated by the previous chapter, Walker's name will always be linked with Samuel Colt's first six-shot revolver—the Walker Colt. Walker used his fighting experience to codesign this huge handgun.

Walker's Proposed Rifles

Walker's previous, less than satisfactory, experience with a mixture of Hall's carbines and North's patent rifles made him desirous of getting the best available rifle for his company. He made no secret in his interest in the Clarke's patent rifle made by Edwin Wesson for his company. He wrote to Wesson on December 11 requesting the cost per rifle if he was to get the contract. Wesson responded the cost would be between 30 and 40 dollars each. Walker then wrote to Secretary of War Marcy on December 22, requesting authorization to order the rifles. It was published in the *Washington Weekly Union*, January 23, 1847, that Walker was "desirous of procuring Clarke's patent rifle, which is said to be the deadliest weapon in the world."[23] On February 11, Walker, not having a response to his December 22 letter, wrote to Secretary of War Marcy directly requesting permission to contract (probably with Edwin Wesson) to make 100 rifles for his company.[24] On February 18, Walker wrote again about rifles, this time to Ordnance Department Col. George Talcott:

Clarke rifle. (www.rockislandauction.com)

> There being no rifles furnished by the government that are suitable for mounted troops and there being none in the armories of the U States that Are suitable for mounted troops, and this being a species of Troops whose efficiency much of our future success must depend both from the nature of the country & the character of the enemy renders the arm of this service indispensable.
>
> I … recommend to your Department the adoption of an arm especially adapted to that service. The Rifle now in use being entirely too long & heavy which renders it cumbersome to the Troops. I would also respectfully suggest that this Rifle [should fire a bullet of the caliber of] … 50 round balls to the pound or a half oz. conical ball which is preferable, not exceeding 2 ft in length of barrel, and not to exceed 8 lbs in weight, to have a false muzzle and globe sights in addition to plain of cast steel barrel with a slight increase of twist and the best … workmanship. The cast steel will be but little additional expense and will last twice as long as the common barrel, all of which I respectfully submit for your consideration.[25]

When Walker wrote Edwin Wesson to discuss the manufacture of rifles for his company on December 16, 1846, he probably had Clarke's design in mind. Alvan Clarke, of Cambridge, Massachusetts, had an 1840 patent for a false muzzle design for a rifle and granted to Edwin Wesson of Northboro, Massachusetts—one of the leading American rifle makers—the sole right to make and sell rifles with a false muzzle on a royalty basis. The object of a false muzzle is to serve as a funnel to ensure the exact seating of the bullet—especially conical bullets—as it is pushed down the barrel with the ramrod.[26] All of Wesson's rifles were cut with gain twist rifling[27] which, with globe sights, gave the rifles extreme accuracy for ranges up to 200 to 600 yards. The globe sights meant the front sight was extremely fine and used with a peep rear sight, with a proper rest, could render some spectacular long-distance shooting.[28] According to one owner of an Edwin Wesson rifle, at 350 yards a good marksman could hit a target the size of his hat 8 times out of 10.[29]

Recruiting

Arms and equipment are critical to a new military organization, but not quite as much as putting cash into the pockets of the recruits to cover their expenses not covered by the government. Ever watchful for the needs of his men, Walker contacted the adjutant general on this subject and other matters:

> I request that you will issue the necessary orders to the Commissary Department to have the recruits I have enlisted supplied with funds necessary for their subsistence. I have thought it advisable to allow them the priviledge of making their own arrangements board while here as most of them would greatly prefer it. [An abstract of expenditures for the month of January

showed he spent $3 for postage; 46 premiums for furnishing recruits; rent of rendezvous $57; stationery $4; and commutation for quarters $85.16. Nothing for expenses for recruits.]

I am somewhat at a loss which are laid down to govern to know whether in my particular case the regulations which are laid down to govern recruiting officers should be strictly adhered to in regard to supplies &c, as the recruits I have enlisted are expected to leave immediately for the field. I am desirous that some special instructions should be given me so as to enable me to proceed forthwith to the field with the recruits I have enlisted or may enlist on the route to Mexico, and to procure the necessary supplies and transportation for their speedy departure. Should it be desirable I can without difficulty enlist a sufficient number of men on my way to Mexico to fill up the Mounted Riflemen U.S.A. to one thousand men as I am almost overwhelmed with communications from young men who are anxious to join our Regt. You will please make my views known to the Hon Secy of War and should it meet his views I would suggest the importance of sending with me an assistant commissary of subsistence, and an assistant Qr Master with authority to purchase the horses & equipments, and to make all the necessary arrangements for transportation &c. With such arrangements I am fully convinced I could enlist a sufficient number of intelligent & respectable young men to fill up the Rifle Regt with great dispatch as I do not think it would be necessary to stop but very few days in any one place to effect this this object. And I am extremely anxious to return to the field with as little delay as possible & render myself of service to my country. I trust you will appreciate my motives & take the necessary steps to forward me in my wishes & should my views meet with the approbation of the Department I would also suggest that the officers appointed as assistant Commissary and Qr Master should be active & energetic your men, well acquainted with their duty so as to transact the business entrusted to them without delay.[30]

It appears Walker enjoyed recruiting but the business side of commanding a company, not so much. It is not surprising that no assistant commissary or assistant quartermaster were made available to him. It was the same result when Walker requested the transfer of a recently discharged sergeant who was assisting another recruiting officer to his rendezvous in Baltimore. Perhaps recruiting was starting to lose its luster. Nevertheless, on February 9, Walker wrote Jones reporting he had enlisted the number of men ordered and should he continue, and if so, to what number.

As early as February 8, Captain Walker planned to stop at Newport Barracks, Kentucky, on the Ohio River across from Cincinnati, Ohio, for several weeks to drill his men and select his horses.[31] Apparently, Walker's company of Mounted Riflemen was still scheduled to serve with General Taylor in northern Mexico as Jesup himself suggested sending the horses through Texas to reach the seat of the war.

When Walker tried to recruit men for his Ranger company when the war started, he had no problems finding enough men—he recruited 94 during the three-month time frame he commanded his company. However, this time he had a problem with too many recruits. The word had spread that the well-known "Texan Ranger Samuel Walker" was recruiting for a mounted company to serve in the war. He began receiving letters from young men or their parents seeking a place under his command. This from one whose desire to go to war was based on Walker's fame and the writer was not too embarrassed to say so.

Having understood that you were about to organize a corps of "Mounted Riflemen" for the Volunteer Service during the existing war and having an ardent desire to enlist under a brave officer, in a station where I might distinguish myself, I have taken this mode of informing you that Fame

> having recommended you to me as the most worthy, that a young soldier under you could have the desired post, I would ask you will and assistance in becoming if not an officer of some degree, as a private under your command. My family are among the first in Kentucky, my native state my age 22 height 5′11″ and what Kentuckian in is not a good horseman I am at present meeting an enervating life as clerk in the house of Pollard Hopkins and company in the city to whose care you will please [page torn] your reply with which I hope you will favor me Begging you [page torn] me for this troubling you I remain dear Sir with respect due [page torn] honored a Soldier.
>
> Yours Sincerely
> James J Tarleton[32]

The army was also concerned, not about the number, but of the age of these young men. On February 13, 1847, Walker wrote Adj. Gen. Roger Jones, assuring him that if any of his recruits were underage, he had written permission of their parents for their enlistment.[33]

Regarding the number of recruits he was allowed, he had the following to report to Adjutant General Jones:

> Having recruited twenty five men I can obtain the requisite number on the route I am desirous of obtaining orders to proceed with them enroute to Mexico via Balt[imore] & Wheeling with the priviledge of stopping long enough on the way to select my horses at some suitable point in the West that may be designated by the Qr Master Genl who I have communications with on the subject. I expect to hear from him in few days. I apprehend there will be no difficulty in procuring a sufficient number of men to fill the companies of our Regt to one hundred each. I am desirous of obtaining authority to increase my company to that number as I can do so with the best material without any difficulty or delay.
>
> I have conversed with several members of Congress on that subject and they are of the opinion that the Law authorizing the increase of the Dragoons to the number of one hundred men also contemplated that same number in the Rifles. The men that I have enlisted are a superior class of men and if I could promise them all that apply to be under my command, I could continue to enlist the same class of men.[34]

On the 16th, Jones instructed the quartermasters department to immediately send the following to Newport Barracks for Capt. S. H. Walker:

250 wool jackets
500 wool overalls
500 flannel shirts
250 blankets
500 pairs of stockings
250 pairs of drawers
500 pairs bootees, various sizes
250 forage caps do
250 leather stocks
250 greatcoats with straps complete
250 haversacks[35]

Plans to March Through Texas

On February 18, Walker again commented to General Jones he was still planning on marching his company through Texas with their horses as "recommended by

General Jesup."[36] Walker apparently was optimistic about how much General Taylor needed his company. Below is Walker's dream request, perhaps feeling that all they could say was no and he might get some of what he asked for. He wrote Capt. W. G. Freeman of the Adjutant General's Office in Washington in mid-February that he "requires for the good of the service":

> 300 horses and full sets of equipment
> 300 Rifles Clarke's Patent not exceeding 8 lbs in wt.
> 300 suits of clothing complete including blankets
> 60 Pack horses or Mules & equipment for Packing for the transportation from Newport … Request orders to march through Texas to join my Regt as early as possible.[37]

Later, on March 6, Walker wrote about the tents and pack saddles he wanted for his company:

> The pack saddles should be made of the same pattern as the one which I exhibited in Washington; five men to each. The tents should be one to each five men and constructed as to require one pole in the centre and large enough to hold the saddles and equipments of five men. The pole should have a hinge in the centre, so as to double up, and there should not be more than ten tugs to the tents, with a very small opening for the door, of size only sufficient to allow one man to pass with a saddle without inconvenience.[38]

Walker had another interesting additional suggestion for his equipment list. As he still planned to bring his men on horseback through Texas to northern Mexico to join General Taylor, he wrote: "In anticipation of an order to march his Detachment of Recruits through Texas" and "knowing the probability of being detained by high water in many places"; Walker made a unique request for cavalry equipment.

Walker's Proposed Amphibious Cavalry

He wrote the assistant quartermaster general at Baltimore on February 23:

> I would beg leave respectfully to recommend a sufficient number of small floats be furnished me of suitable Capacity to cross the baggage of the Detachment without delay in case of high water. I would also recommend a few horse floats conveniently arranged as to be carried without inconvenience to the Horse or Rider to enable a Vidette to plunge into a River at any convenient point while making a reconnaissance of an enemy and crossing without danger of losing his arms or horse.[39]

Newport Barracks, Kentucky

A Boston newspaper dated February 10 reported the

> DEPARTURE OF CAPT. WALKER AND THE MOUNTED RIFLEMEN… last Saturday at 3pm Captain Walker and his recruits for the rifle regiment departed DC in a special train of cars for Baltimore—left the depot amid cheers of a large concourse of people Prince George's County contributed largely to the formation of the company, no less than twenty men.[40]

Walker's Company of Mounted Riflemen, enlisted in Washington City and Baltimore[41] and numbering 110 picked men, left Baltimore on February 26th at 7:15 a.m. by the B&O Railroad for Cumberland, Wheeling, and ultimately to Newport, Kentucky,[42] where they "are to be equipped and mounted and then to the seat of war."[43]

At six in the evening, the train arrived in Cumberland, Maryland. The next morning, Saturday, March 24, six stage loads of young, mounted riflemen recruits headed for training; Captain Walker left the next morning. At four o'clock on Monday morning, March 26, the company arrived at Wheeling, (West) Virginia. There, they boarded the steamboat *Monongahela* and at midnight started down the Ohio River, arriving eight days later at Cincinnati on March 3.[44]

Walker stopped to recruit for six or seven days on the way.[45] He had spent the last three days of February in Baltimore and the following 10 days en route to Newport, Kentucky. He reported upon arriving at Newport Barracks, Kentucky, on March 6 that he stopped to recruit in Cumberland, Maryland, and Wheeling, Virginia, but even though there were a number of applications, the applicants were of such a "low order" he did not wish to have them in his company. Knowing the dismounted state of the regiment, Walker still planned to have his men mounted. Thus, he requested funds to buy horses—funds that had not arrived when he got to Newport Barracks.

The recruiting party and small number of recruits arrived March 6, but as men began to arrive in numbers, Walker was faced with a problem of too many men and too little space. "This is a very pretty place but at present very crowded with recruits," he wrote. "I have a fine set of young men and all I need now is arms."[46]

Crowded was an understatement. There was a total of four hundred recruits crowded into a space meant for one hundred fifty men. Walker would prefer to be

The City of Cincinnati, Ohio. (Print in the public domain)

"encamped somewhere in the country" but he had no tents or equipment. While the commander at Newport suggested taking the men to Jefferson Barracks where the former companies of the regiment trained, Walker did not want any further delays. He had the invoice for two hundred and fifty suits of clothing for his men so the uniforms were en route to Newport Barracks.[47]

George Myers. (Rees-Jones Collection)

Before arriving at Newport Barracks on Monday March 3, some men visited Cincinnati, the well-known river city. Recruit George Myers wrote:

> On board the steamer *Monongahela* … in charge of Lieut Fannistock [Simon Snyder Fahnestock]. I paid a visit over to Cincinnati. It is a beautiful place no wonder. they may call it the queen city of the west. … and it is astounding what amount of business is done there. Steam boats plying up and down the river all the time and then always ten or twenty at the wharfs loading at the same time. It is a lovely sight to behold from the barracks immediately opposite particularly at night, for it is lit by gas and the reflection on the river makes it one of the most imposing sights I ever beheld.[48]

Myers also said his company drilled three times a day. Their fare was "coffee in a tin cup and bread, at dinner bean soup, piece of fat pork and bread." Then he adds in his diary that on Thursday, March 6, Captain Walker arrived.[49]

On Tuesday, March 9, Myers crossed the river in a small boat to visit the circus (at the invitation of the manager) in Cincinnati, returning at two o'clock in the morning and "went to bed with four or five dollars in my purse, was robbed of purse and money between 2 o'clock and daylight." He would later write, "You cannot lay anything down and turn your back before it is picked up and that is the last you will see of it."

Horses for Company C

On January 28, 1847, Quartermaster General Thomas S. Jesup wrote to Walker regarding the loss of the horses destined for his regiment and other matters:

> Captain:
> In reply to your communication of the 19th instant. I have to say that the Equipments you may prefer, and your order to be made for your Company will be approved of; you are also authorized to select and purchase horses for your company in the quarters you mention, Cincinnati or Louisville, for the payment of which horses

> and equipments, funds will be placed by Col. Henry Stanton in the hands of the Qr Master at Newport Ky opposite Cincinnati.
>
> Most of the horses recently shipped from this place for your regiment have been lost at sea. It would therefore be advisable for you to make some arrangement sending through Texas by land to Matamoras, the horses you purchase for your company.[50]

Capt. Charles F. Ruff[51] was commanding officer of Company I of the Mounted Riflemen and was also planning to join General Taylor as Walker was preparing himself to do so.[52] Ruff and Walker were the last to recruit their companies and join the regiment. As mentioned, these would be the only two mounted companies of the Riflemen.

Since learning of the RMR fighting dismounted in Mexico, one of Walker's first orders of business at Newport Barracks was to get mounts for his men. Uniforms would come in time but if Walker did not act, his men would end up fighting on foot like the rest of the regiment. With authorization by General Jessup, Walker set to work. Walker purchased horses on March 10, 1847. The contract was with G. R. Gilmore and F. Egbert of Cincinnati, Ohio, for "a number of horses not to exceed fifty," to be delivered to Walker in Cincinnati. The animals were to be sorrels, bays, and "dark dapple greys"; not more than 15 and not less than 11 and a half hands high; between 3 and 7 years of age; "of fine form and appearance, and in every way fit for Cavalry service"; the sum of $90 to be paid for each animal.[53]

On March 10 and 11, the company were drilled as cavalry by Lt. John G. Walker and Corporal Woods. That Sunday, "Capt. Walker with his company attended divine service at Christ Church in Cincinnati."[54]

Walker wrote Colonel Stanton, Assistant Quartermaster General on April 2, 1847, stating he had contracted for the purchase of 80 horses and needed the colonel to send $7,200 to Newport Barracks to pay for them. He also requested that the saddles and bridles that were being made for him in Washington be sent to him "as soon as they are delivered."[55]

The number of horses needed depended on how many men were authorized for the company. Walker may have needed to buy more. On March 11, Walker had written requesting information on the passage of the law to increase the number of the company size of the RMR. Currently it was limited to 76 soldiers and he had hoped it would be increased to 110 (as indicated by his directions to Colt about the serial numbers of the Colt revolvers currently being made for the regiment).[56]

Company C Grows

On March 1, Walker submitted his enlistment forms for the month of February along with his muster roll. He also advised the adjutant general of his recruiting situation:

> My recruiting office in this place was closed Saturday night and I shall open an office in Uniontown today, nearly all the recruits enlisted have been sent forward with as little delay as practicable in accordance with your instructions under the command of Lieut. Fahnestock who has been directed by me to proceed with them to Newport Kentucky. I shall push forward as rapidly as I can, stopping a day at Uniontown and one day in Wheeling, believing it will not be necessary to stop longer than one day in each place as they have been notified of the time of my arrival and advised to be ready if any should wish to enlist. I hope that something definite may be understood in regard to the increase of our regt, as the possibility of the men being placed in the Dragoon Corps has prevented many from joining our regt being very much more popular than the Dragoons. I am also very desirous of knowing as early as practicable whether I can select horses for the whole number of the recruits I am ordered to enlist, the uncertainty pf the disposition to be made of the recruits is a great drawback. I have no authority as yet to select for any but my own company. I hope you will try and have the orders issued to select horses for the whole number of the recruits.[57]

Walker reported his arrival at Newport Barracks, Kentucky, on March 6:

> I have the honor to report my arrival at this place to day with my recruiting party and a small number of recruits that I listed on the route from Baltimore, having sent forward as directed by you the detachment under Lieut. Fahnestock, which arrived safely at this place on the fourth inst. My stay at Cumberland and Wheeling was shorter than anticipated as there was not sufficient encouragement to justify me in my own mind in remaining longer, making only nine recruits on the way. There were a number of applicants but of such a low order that I did not think them worth their transportation to Mexico.
>
> I would also respectfully inform you that there has been no funds placed at the disposition of the Quarter Master at this place to purchase horses for my company in accordance with instructions from General Jesup in a communication to me dated January 28 for a copy of which I refer you to the As Qr Master General Col. Staunton. It is highly important that I should get my horses without delay that I may have the opportunity of training and drilling them and making my men familiar with their duty before starting for the field.
>
> I have received the invoice of 250 suits of clothing which have been forwarded but not received.
>
> The situation of the recruits at this time is very disagreeable, there being upwards of four hundred recruits here and not more than sufficient room for one hundred and fifty and I have no doubt the present condition if affairs will have a tendency to create discontent and deter all such men from enlisting as would be likely to do credit to the service. I would greatly prefer being encamped some place in the country if we had tents and camp equipage. The commander here has suggested the propriety of our being ordered to Jefferson Barracks where there are good stables and quarters; but I would rather not move again till we secure our horses, arms. And equipments and are prepared in every respect for field service.
>
> Lieut. [John G.] Walker has reported to me and is now on duty with my detachment, but I believe he is a good deal like myself in his knowledge of tactics and the routine of garrison duty.[58]

Walker's many requests for action in the matter of the horses for his company finally bore fruit, but it was not quite ripe. If 50 horses were all the government would allow, 30 of Walker's men would be unmounted. Still waiting for official word from Washington on the status of the long-awaited arms, equipment, horses, etc., Walker wrote to Jones again:

I beg to reiterate respectfully, what I have before stated, that the recruiting service is falling off in consequence of the uncertainty of the disposition to be made of the recruits.

I am as yet uninformed as to the law authorizing the increase of our Regt of Mounted Riflemen. Something definite on this subject would be desirable as I find it impossible to enlist such men as I think worth the transportation to Mexico without assuring them that they shall be in the Mtd Rifles and give them some reason to believe that they shall have immediate active service as mounted men. Since it is known through the country that portion of the Regt in Mexico is serving on foot no man will enlist without seeing something to [illegible] him to believe that everything will be furnished him before he is sent to the field. Another thing which renders the recruiting service rather dull is that my recruits are crowded in a place where there is not room sufficient for their number thereby rendering their situation very disagreeable and which is well calculated to disgust them with the service.

The funds not having yet arrived for the purchase of horses to facilitate my departure to the field, I have determined to commence making my selection of horses and the purchase of them conditionally, hoping the funds may soon arrive. By the time I can select my horses, I believe horse equipment and pistols will ready, at which time I hope to receive orders to repair without delay to the field. I am at a loss to know what to do for rifles as there are none in the US Armories that were colt made for mounted men and are therefore unfit for our purposes. For this reason, I am disposed to adopt the sabre in addition to the Colt's revolving pistol. Knowing that the US Rifle such as are furnished would be rather an encumbrance than a useful weapon in such service as will be expected of me in the field.

I could raise five hundred very superior men in a short time if I was authorized to tell them they should be under my command during the war as all young men who are suitable for this particular service and of such character as would entitle them to the confidence of their commander when on detached service prefer going under some person of experience. The war fever in this part of the country seems to be abating. Several persons recruiting in Cincinnati for the ten regts with rather dull prospects and it will for the future require the greatest exertions on the part of the recruiting officers, and every care to provide for the comfort of the recruits, to secure such class of men as are calculated to insure success to our arms in an enemies country.

As soon as I can secure my horses and equipments and get my present number of recruits uniforms I can succeed in recruiting as many more as desirable provided they can be supplied with similar equipments without delay, and I think it desirable to secure as many troops if this description is possible, as there are but very few that I

> have seen organizing or the last ten Regts that are worth transportation to Mexico. Judging from what I have seen of them, the only good which we could hope to derive from sending such men would be to rid the country of such refuse of society.[59]

On March 18, General Jones sent word that the quartermaster general and colonel of ordnance were being notified to take action on Walker's many requests. Walker's question regarding an increase in the number of men in his company was answered in the affirmative but would remain at 80 (76) until he[60] was informed by the proper authority to add more men in line with what other regiments had done. He was then ordered to take his company and join his regimental headquarters upon receipt of these instructions.

Meanwhile, Walker's company was expanding but measles had disabled or killed many young recruits. Additionally, two recruits were dismissed on March 11, as they enlisted without parental permission, and another deserted soon after arrival at Newport Barracks; many men were sick with measles. On March 19, 20 men in the garrison had colds or dysentery.[61] On the 24th, Myers wrote that 10 to 12 of his company were down with the measles. He was sure that his fellow horse soldiers caught the disease from the infantry. On that same day, Walker received orders to "start for Mexico."[62] While he had horses purchased and the men finally in uniform by March 22, the company still did not have their promised pistols. He wrote Colt: "Send me some of the Pistols immediately I want to commence drilling my men on horseback with them I now have 120 men and will enlist 180 more to take out with me. … move heaven and earth to get the Pistols ready."[63]

By March 19, Walker had 120 recruits; on the 24th, he had 127.[64] To clear up any misunderstanding, on March 24 he emphasized that he was purchasing horses only for his company—not for the regiment. In the meantime, many of his men were very sick with the measles.[65]

The *Niles National Register* had the following to report regarding recruits—not at Newport Barracks—but at Jefferson Barracks, where conditions were apparently superior. The Regiment of Mounted Riflemen are thus described by a correspondent of the *Buffalo Commercial Advertiser*, writing from Jefferson Barracks, Mo. 24th, Nov. 1846:

> There are now at this point about five hundred men of the regiment who were enlisted in the short space of four months. Of these, all of nine-tenths are Americans, enlisted in the states of Ohio, Indiana, Illinois, Kentucky, and Tennessee. Very few were enlisted in the northern and eastern states. Two companies of the regiment were organized in September, and one is already serving in Mexico. These are commanded by Capts. Mason and Walker.
>
> I will venture to say that a finer body of men were never enlisted in this country. They are strong, athletic fellows, who appear capable of enduring and hardships. A good proportion of them are over six feet in height, and not a few will go six foot four "in their stockings." They have been well as cavalry tactics, and should occasion require they can act as trailleurs, or light infantry.[66]

By March 24, Walker, having had his fill with General Jones putting him off, finally played what he believed was his trump card—the January 27 letter of authorization from Gen. Thomas S. Jesup:

> Sir.
> I have the honor to acknowledge the receipt of your communication of March 19th in reply to mine of the 11th in which you seem to regret that I should have taken any steps for the selection of horses for the Regt, without instructions from the proper Dept.
>
> In Reply, I have only to say that the selection of horses has thus far, only been for my Company and not for the Regt; for this I have authority from General Jesup to whom I was referred by Col Stanton more than a month since, by which you will perceive that I am fully authorized to purchase such horses and equipments as I recommended, and I cannot doubt for a moment, but that you will, approve of the course I have pursued and I shall by all means expect the department to make good all contracts for the purchase of horses that I have made by authority from the head of that Depmt.
>
> Besides this the Recruits under my command have all been enlisted for the mounted service. They are just such men as are suited for that service and it would be regarded as a breach of faith on the part of government agents to send them to the field without horses, which I cannot acquiesce in. I must also respectfully express my regret that I cannot be allowed the privilege of increasing my company to 100 men as allowed by law, having understood from you that I could have this privilege, provided the law passed, authorizing it.
>
> In reference to your order to repair to the Seat of War, I must return you my thanks for this opportunity of winning new laurels for the present; however, it will be almost impracticable as many of the men are very sick with the Measles, and I cannot believe it is your desire or intention for me, to go into an Enemies Country, without arms and Equipments. I shall therefore wait with much anxiety for the arrival of such arms and Equipments as the Deprt will furnish. Should I be mistaken however in my interpretation of your order, and it is determined to send us to the field without any thing to fight with, and regardless of all the foregoing considerations, you will please inform me without delay, that I may not be in further suspense in regard to your real wishes.[67]

However, the ultimate trump card was in the hands of President Polk who, given the orders for the immediate movement of his company to Mexico, canceled any contracts dealing with horses.

On March 27, Walker reported that despite the action of the president, his horses had been contracted for and he hoped his saddles and equipment that were to be made in Washington would be forwarded to him. He requested 80 pistols and sabers for his immediate use until his Colt revolvers arrived. He now had 133 recruits.[68]

Off to the Seat of War

During the three weeks of drilling his company at Newport Barracks, he did get horses and uniforms for his men. The latter were delivered on March 22. On March 29, George Myers was promoted sergeant.[69] Walker would have no Colt revolvers and did not know if he could keep only 76 of these recruits in his company. Nevertheless, on April 1, Company C was off to war, and Lt. Col. John Erving so notified General Jones.

> General;
> I have the honor to inform you that in pursuance of your instructions to him, Captain Walker with 1st Lieut. J. G. Walker and 150 recruits for the Regiment of M[ounted] Riflemen left the depot at Newport, KY this afternoon for Mexico.[70]

On board the steamer *Albatross*, departing Newport Barracks at 5 p.m. on that first day of April, Walker wrote he had purchased nearly enough horses to mount his company and "my boys in fine spirits and the sick are improving."[71]

Writing at 10 p.m. that night:

> We are now on our way to the seat of War. I have a fine set of young men that will give a good account of themselves as soon as they have opportunity …, our departure from Newport Barracks was rendered very pleasant by the very flattering testimony the people especially the Ladies who waved their handkerchiefs to us until the Steamer was taken us entirely out of sight.[72]

On April 3, as the steamer headed down the Ohio and past the home of Gen. Joseph Lane on Indiana's north Ohio riverbank, the men gave the general six cheers. Entering the Mississippi River on Sunday, April 4, "a negro man on one of the islands shouted out at the top of his voice hurra for Capt. Walker now the Mexicans will catch hell."[73] Heading for Jackson Barracks just below New Orleans, they passed Covington; Claysville; Lawrenceburg; Madison, Kentucky; and Jeffersonville, Indiana. Walker and his men were probably welcomed along the way. One Pennsylvania soldier leaving Newport Barracks a few months earlier, wrote:

Civil War image of John George Walker. (Photograph in the public domain)

> Whenever our boat arrived at any town the little cannon [on board the steamer] would be fired off, which caused the people to rush to the river line and when they saw the boat was loaded with Uncle Sam's soldiers, would give cheers.[74]

On April 5, another man was taken by measles.[75] The next day, a soldier named Buckholder deserted. The company was glad to see him leave as he was considered a "very bad man" who in combat, as Myers put it, "would have put all our lives in danger." Captain Walker, nevertheless, offered a reward of 40 dollars for his capture.[76]

A letter from General Jones regarding Walker's trump card letter was sent to the captain with a slight apology for past delays, etc.:

> Your letter of the 24th ultimo enclosing a copy of General Jesup's letter of the 28th of January last, conferring upon you authority for the purchase of horses, equipments, &c, for your company, has been received.
>
> It is proper to state to you, that if this formal written authority from the Quarter Master General had been known by me, I should not have in my letter of the 18th ultimo to you at' Newport, Ky., expressed regret at the preliminary steps you reported as having been taken by you at that place for the selection of horses &c.
>
> Your letter of the 27th of March reporting that you had received instructions from the Ordnance Department on the subject of your arms, and that your clothing had been received, obviates some of the difficulties stated in your previous letter of the 24th March upon the subject of those supplies. With respect to the full complement of your company (100 men), which you had hoped to recruit, it is only necessary to remark that the state of the service in Mexico will not justify the withholding from the field any company of the Army which can muster as many as 60 privates the residue must be obtained from time to time according to the circumstances of the service.[77]

And another regarding current matters and future problems:

> Your letter of the 1st inst, reporting your departure; from Newport Barracks, has been received.
>
> As the state of the service on the Rio Grande and in the direction of Monterey has materially changed since General Cadwalader left Washington, I think it more than probable that there will be no necessity for detaining your detachment at Point Isabel; and I hope therefore you may be permitted to join your Regiment agreeably to the instructions of the 18th of March. It is always preferable that recruits should join their companies rather than to remain in separate detachments, where their instruction must be less perfect.
>
> As far as I can judge, I should think it advisable that you take with you the fifty horses you have procured for your company and which you report were sent to New Orleans; for I have no doubt that some, if not all the companies of your Regiment will be required to be mounted as soon as practicable.
>
> I must repeat the request that your correspondence hereafter with respect to horses and arms for your company, may be with the Quarter Master General and Colonel of Ordnance, to whom this branch of the service belongs.
>
> I am glad to see that you-take with you 150 good recruits, and as you commenced Recruiting for your own company, unless otherwise directed by superior authority, you are authorized to fill it up to 80 privates—the residue to be assigned to other companies of the Regiment by the Commanding Officer.[78]

On April 8, the men received their equipment at Baton Rouge Arsenal and visited the nearby home of General Taylor. Capt. Charles F. Ruff,[79] commander of the only other mounted company of the RMR, Company I, drew weapons for his company at this time also. Walker's company was met by several ladies including General Taylor's daughter. As they were departing, Myers said he could see the general's daughter[80] shed tears as Walker's Company C, now armed and trained, left for the seat of war.[81]

Walker and his men arrived at New Orleans on April 9, and embarked for Veracruz on May 3, aboard the steamer *Mary Kingsland*. They arrived at Veracruz six days later.[82]

The Steamboat War

According to an army quartermaster study, the Mexican–American War would be the first steamboat war:

> In handling the transportation problem, the Quartermaster's Department successfully utilized steamboats for carrying troops and supplies up the Missouri to Fort Leavenworth and down the Ohio and the Mississippi to New Orleans. It bought light-draft Mississippi River steamboats for the run up the Rio Grande to Camargo, and though these vessels were, in Lieutenant George Gordon Meade's words, "mere shells," never built to ply the ocean, it performed the notable feat of sending most of them from New Orleans six hundred miles over a "tempestuous sea" to Point Isabel. Steamships as well as sailing vessels moved men and supplies from New York and other Atlantic ports to the Gulf. For all these reasons the Mexican War has been called "the first steamboat war."[83]

This is one of the reasons the Mounted Rifles, as a regiment, wasn't mounted. They lost most of their horses when they were shipped by rivercraft on the ocean. Also, it was the reason why, earlier in the war, General Taylor had stayed at Point Isabel where he could be supplied by ship at the coast. After Taylor advanced into northern Mexico, he established another depot three hundred miles up the shallow Rio Grande at Camargo, which could be supplied only by river steamboat.

Unfortunately, during the second half of the war, while ships still brought supplies to the coast, there were no rivers for the steamboats, and supplies had to be sent overland from Veracruz to the main army approaching Mexico City. These roads were infested with guerrillas and Walker's Mounted Riflemen were sorely needed as guards, scouts, and a mobile assault force against the deadly irregulars. They would be based at the only main fortress, Perote, between Scott's army inland and Veracruz.

Still No Revolvers

Walker was most concerned about the delay in shipping his revolvers. He wrote Colt "you must try your D—st to send me those pistols, they are determined to get us in the field any how I have purchased nearly enough horses to mount my company, my equipment is will nearly be ready or ready to be shipped at this time."

On April 2, Walker again wrote Colonel Stanton, requesting the saddles and bridles being made for him in Washington be sent to him "as soon as they are delivered."[84]

Uniforms

In their new uniforms, Company C had left for "the seat of war." According to regulations the Mounted Rifles were issued ankle-high boots, and dark blue wool trousers with reinforced seats with a stripe of black cloth down the seam edged with yellow cord. The jacket was blue wool with a stand-up collar with yellow worsted binding, one row of 10 buttons down the front. The jacket was short, down to the waist only. The buttons were gilt for the officers and brass for the enlisted men. They had a spread eagle with a shield in the center and the letter "R" in the center. The officer's forage caps were blue wool with a yellow band across the middle with a gold embroidered spread eagle with the letter "R" in silver on the shield. The enlisted men's forage cap bore the company letter, i.e., "A," "B," or "C," etc. The caps had a patent leather visor. The waistbelts were of patent leather for the officers and were 1 and a half inches wide. The belt buckle had the letter "R" in old English characters, totally enclosed by a wreath of laurel leaves. Officers also wore a crimson sash under the belt. There was also a summer issue white cotton jacket cut in the same pattern and white trousers.[85] As shown by the portraits of Walker in uniform, he wore the winged epaulets on his shoulders as indicated by the 1846 description of the RMR uniform.[86]

Other Clothing and Equipment

This was the entire listing of the clothing issued Walker's men: 250 wool jackets, 500 wool overalls, 250 cotton shirts, 500 flannel shirts, 250 blankets, 500 pairs of stockings, 250 pairs of drawers, 500 pairs of bootees, 250 forage caps, 250 leather stocks, 250 great coats, with straps, and 250 haversacks.[87]

Change of Orders

There is at least the indication that Walker saw his company as an independent detachment, able to function with the flexibility he did as a Ranger when he served under General Taylor at Point Isabel during April–June, 1846. Perhaps he still envisioned this former duty when he told Capt. R. H. K. Whitely at the Baton Rouge Arsenal on April 3, "his command would not join the balance of the Regt, but would proceed to the Army under Genl Taylor, be independent, and must be equipped according to the service they would perform."[88] This is confirmed by later communications that were delayed reaching Walker. The change Adj. Gen. Jones refers to: "the state of the service on the Rio Grande has changed … and it was more than probable there will be no necessity for detaining your detachment at Point Isabel." Walker would then probably be ordered to join the regiment rather than be on detached duty as he had first understood.[89] Walker got his change of orders two weeks later; he wrote his brother Jonathan on April 18 that he was preparing to take his company to Veracruz.[90]

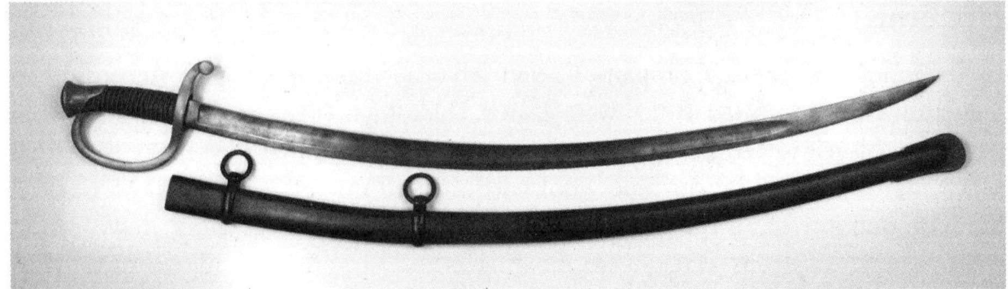

M1840 Ames enlisted horse artillery saber with scabbard. (*Original Light Artillery Saber with Scabbard, Model 1840, American Civil War Sword,* Shutterstock, 2125073495)

Sabers

Obviously, the Mounted Riflemen under Walker received sabers. One hundred were issued to his men on May 11, 1847, at Veracruz.[91] However, when supplies were issued to both Walker's and Ruff's[92] companies (on April 3, 1847, at the Baton Rouge Arsenal), an order was issued by Bvt. Maj. Gen. George M. Brooke that if the arsenal did not have on hand a sufficient number of dragoon sabers, then horse artillery sabers could be issued in their place. While both Ruff's and Walker's requisitions were filed, only Ruff's could be located. It indicated his company was issued 76 new pattern sabers[93] on April 8, 1847, at the Baton Rouge Arsenal.[94]

While requisitions for Walker's company could not be located for this time period, it is probable that his company may have been issued some horse artillery sabers. Apparently, this item seemed to be in demand by officers as the war progressed as indicated by a letter from Lt. Col. George Talcott to Capt. W. A. Thornton at the New York Depot on October 30, 1847. He wrote:

> As regards to the issue of Horse Artillery Sabers to officers, you must be governed by the very words—"if the state of the public supplies will permit." I am under the impression that our supplies of that arm are very limited and will not permit a general issue to officers. In a few weeks we shall have a supply from Europe when all who need them can be furnished.[95]

It is therefore probable that at least some artillery swords were issued Walker's company and perhaps used by some of his officers. One hundred "cavalry sabers" were sequentially issued to Company C.

Mississippi Rifles

The regiment was armed with the Harpers Ferry Rifle (known also as the Mississippi Rifle).[96] It was first issued to the dismounted Riflemen without bayonets at General Taylor's supply depot at Point Isabel. Musket bayonets, however, were secured. Since the shank of the musket bayonet was too small, the bayonet was attached to a wooden plug that was forced into the muzzle when the bayonet was to be used.

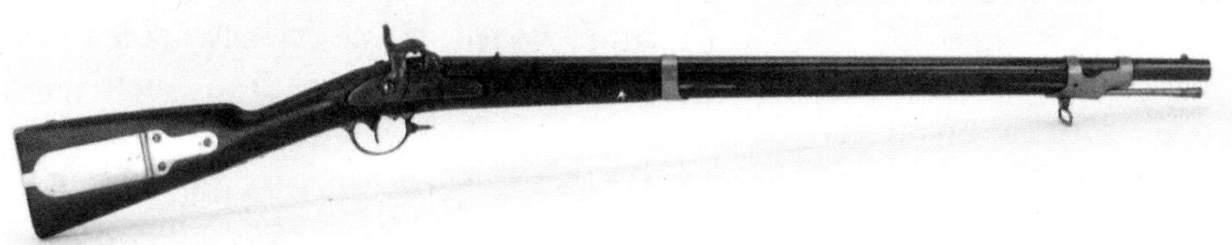

M1841 Mississippi Rifle. (Photograph in the public domain)

However, the plug broke easily. Therefore, blacksmiths had to stretch the shank and adapt the bayonet to fit the rifle. But it rested on the front sight and made it unusable when the bayonet was fixed in position.[97]

When he was issued his rifle on April 23, George Myers was eager to try it out. He killed a 6-foot alligator and then hit a bull's eye at 100 yards before an admiring company of spectators.[98] Walker and Ruff's companies were issued the percussion Mississippi Rifle (without the bayonet as they were mounted troops) and flintlock dragoon pistols.[99] Walker's men were issued 99 pairs of holsters and housings, 14 rifle pouches, 15 powder flasks, 20 percussion rifles, 100 cavalry sabers, and 5,400 percussion rifle cartridges on May 11 at Veracruz.[100]

Walker in Mexico with his Company

Captain Walker and his command had arrived at New Orleans on April 9 and embarked for Veracruz at 10 o'clock in the evening of May 3, aboard the steamer *Mary Kingsland*. Most of the company were seasick. George Myers observed the captain and lieutenant were "heaving up with all their might." Myers was not sick, claiming medicinal prevention with a bottle of good brandy.[101]

Myers and two or three others were in charge of "horse police," feeding and watering the 100 horses on board.[102]

Captain Walker arrived at Veracruz on May 8,[103] accompanied by 182 men with horses and equipment,[104] and bid farewell to the *Mary Kingsland*:[105] "horses, over one hundred in number, suffered nothing from the voyage, and were ready for service immediately." According to Myers, "We commenced landing our horses by throwing them overboard from the deck of the vessel. … They had to be hauled ashore by being tied astern of a boat and rowed nearly ashore. When they were set adrift and have to swim [to shore]."[106]

Guerrillas in Mexico

The army needed mounted patrols to protect Scott's soldiers as they traveled the main road from Veracruz to Mexico City. Forty years earlier when Napoleon invaded Spain, he was bogged down by small bands of Spanish peasants. They struck his army in hundreds of pinprick attacks. The end result was Napoleon was forced to keep a much larger force in Spain than he wished. He desperately needed more troops elsewhere but the small wars prevented him from sparing them. Interestingly, the involvement by the guerrillas in occupied Spain gave Mexico and other Latin American countries the opportunity to seek their own independence without concern of the mother country stopping them. Now with an invading army within Mexico itself, the Spanish heritage of guerrilla warfare was called upon.

In spite of their becoming a deadly nuisance, they were not the type of guerrillas that Napoleon fought. According to one historian: "The guerrillas robbed the people, seized funds belonging to the state, pillaged even churches."[107] Under the law designed for this service, a Mexican citizen could organize a band of volunteers. Goods captured from the enemy could be divided among the captors.[108]

Sgt. George Myers wrote in his diary: "Gen. Le Vega was robbed on the road from Jallappa to Perote of $25,000 and all his valuables by his own countrymen." He spoke of the area near Perote abounding with "a gang of rancheros who do nothing but plunder and murder and prevent the farmers around from bringing in their produce to the [Perote Fort] Castle for sale"[109] As part of his assignment with the Mounted Riflemen he wrote on June 2, 1847 "we went on a scout for robbers and murderers who killed two Mexicans and robbed them of all they had."[110]

Historian Justin Smith said it was a common practice of these mounted guerrillas to mutilate wounded prisoners (such as Walker's Rangers at Matamoras). They used their lasso to drag victims to death and had the rule to take no prisoners.[111] The guerrillas failed to affect the general course of the war. Secretary of War Marcy instructed Scott that—because of the ruthless, outlaw nature of the guerrillas who preyed on even their own people—he should deal with them in the "utmost allowable severity."[112] Polk selected Hays's Texas Rangers to deal with the guerrillas.[113] In doing so, not only did the Rangers come close to capturing Santa Anna himself, they (with their new Walker pistols) became a terror to the guerrillas. To them, they were known as the Texas Devils—*Los Diablos Tejanos.*

After Santa Anna's army was crushed, the guerrillas still remained a serious danger. On February 25, 1848, with some 250 Rangers under Hays and 130 dragoons fighting house-to-house at Zacualtipán, as the Rangers did at Monterrey, Hays's men would shatter guerrilla power[114] in this final battle of the war.

Company C in Mexico

One newspaper article reported that the mounted rifles were encamped four miles outside of Veracruz and that for two nights a band of about 200 Mexicans had been prowling about the camp; the second night they had aroused the men twice by venturing too close. Sam had had enough and "started out to give battle" with his recruits, the resulting skirmish ended with four of the Mexicans killed. It was upon returning to camp that Walker learned of the attack on the dragoons left to guard government stores at Santa Fe about ten miles away. Six dragoons were killed and only one escaped.[115]

Another article noted that on May 12:

> A small party of dragoons were surprised at Santa Fe, a small village about 14 miles from Vera Cruz, by a band of Mexican robbers or guerrillas. There were eleven dragoons in the party, and all but the sentinels were asleep. The Mexicans rushed upon them and his gun having misfired, he was unable to give the alarm, A scuffle ensued, in which the sentinel was killed and the Mexicans rushed upon the rest of the party. Of these, ten in number but one escaped unharmed. Six of the other were killed and three wounded. As soon as the news was brought to Vera Cruz by the dragoon who escaped, Capt. Walker of the Rifles was ordered out with his command in pursuit of the marauding party.[116]

George Myers wrote in his diary that on the morning of May 14, an express arrived regarding the attack at Santa Fe. "Our Captain ordered us to saddle up with all dispatch. ... each one of us drew our ammunition & saber and started for the scene of action."[117]

The *American Eagle* in Veracruz gave more details of the attack:

> The article states that 70 dragoons under Col. Harney's command left Jalapa for Vera Cruz under command of Lieut. Hill in search of more horses for the dragoons. "On arriving at Santa Fe, nine of the men were left behind, in consequence of illness on their part and fatigue on the part of their horses." After the main force of dragoons left, a large party of Mexicans attacked the nine "literally cutting them to pieces." One was killed and a five mutilated so badly that they would probably die. "The hand was cut off above the wrist—the abdomen of another cut ... to allow the bowels to protrude. Another had saber cuts on the head, penetrating the skull—and the arms and bodies of others are literally hacked and mangled."[118]

Whether the *Eagle* exaggerated the event or not, the fact that such details were later printed indicated that these were some of the stories circulated that perhaps reached Captain Walker. One of Walker's men commented that it was "an awful sight to see the dead and wounded ... and [Walker's men] left to seek revenge for our comrades."[119] What the Mexicans did is uncertain, yet Walker's treatment of his captives is a matter of record.

Walker soon brought his company into action. While Company C would later become well-drilled and proved themselves a well-disciplined, hard-fighting cavalry unit, when they arrived in Mexico, they were not yet so prepared.

On May 15, in a report to Colonel Wilson at Veracruz, Walker described what newspapers would call the "Santa Fe Incident."

Upon Walker's arrival at Santa Fe, he found the Mexicans had left before they could set fire to the store houses and at 5 p.m., Walker—with 82 men of his detachment of recruits and 36 of the 2d Dragoons—pursued them. Capturing two prisoners, Myers wrote "our Captain tied a rope around their necks and placed them on a mustang and told them that if they did not lead us to where the band of ranchero robbers were, he would hang them to the first tree he came to. It had the desired affect."[120]

When Walker located the apparent headquarters of the guerrillas, at 8 o'clock the next morning he saw the enemy on the hills above the ranchero where they had been encamped. Walker chose not to pursue them as "the heat was considerable and would have killed many of my unacclimated horses to have run them down."[121] His recruits were also unaccustomed to actual combat; one accidentally wounded another recruit.

At first light, on the trail and investigating a small shanty, a man in Company C named Russell was inside the shanty and one of Walker's men saw someone inside the building and drew his pistol and fired through the cracks in the wall, wounding Russell in the hip. C. T. Richardson writes: "If you think Captain Walker was not mad, you made a mistake."[122]

However, some of Walker's scouts on foot did capture several prisoners who had stolen articles from the American dead. Walker turned the captives over to the dragoons with orders to execute all but the youngest for their brutal murders of the sick dragoons.

Apparently, there was criticism in the press. Walker later wrote his brother:

> I see by the papers that some malicious scribbler who has been perhaps educated at public expense writing from Jalapa, has been laboring to injure my reputation in regards to the affair in the low country As you have not recd. my former letters it may be gratifying to you to know that my conduct was highly approved by Gen Scott and it may be satisfactory to my friends to know something about the circumstances connected with the affair not that I care one straw about the opinions of those who scribble for their reputation as many in the field do.

Walker then gave his report of the event:

> On or about the 15th of May a party of sick men of the 2nd Dragoons were attacked and butchered by the Mexicans at Santa Fe near Vera Cruz, I was ordered out after their from the camp near Vera Cruz and pursued them to their headquarters my men killed several of them in pursuit and we took the Alcalde[123] and … prisoners at the village and in the pursuit of the main party after satisfying myself fully that they were guilty of cruelty and barbarity of the party of sick dragoons having found in their possession several articles which I knew to be the equipment of Dragoons and were recognized by the comrades of the deceased. I turned them over to a Sergeant of Dragoons and told him as they had participated in massacring his sick comrades that I should entrust the execution of them to him and his comrades. He being the highest officer I had with me, I told him he might dispose of them as he thought proper provided he did not let them go, the youngest of them was released and the balance were shot while I marched out to meet the enemy who had returned to (the) heights that surround the valley, after reading my official report and conversing with me on the subject Gen Scott told me that I had done right[124] and commended me very highly for my promptness in carrying out the spirit of the Proclamation which contemplates protection to those who remained at home and severe punishment to those who violate the Rules of civilians warfare, you can scarcely imagine the disappointment when the result of my interview was known among certain individuals in the army almost every one was certain I would be arrested having received account so fit which were much exaggerated. The correspondent who has endeavored to make an unfavorable impression on the public minds has been most maliciously he says I took six Lancers on my way up which I had shot in cold blood.

Walker was joined by Captain Ruff's company of Rifles and perhaps another dragoon company to escort a large wagon train enroute to "*Jallappa*" (Xalapa), 62 miles northwest of Veracruz.[125]

Walker wrote:

> And although I had a large amt of Specie in the Train of 180 waggons guarded by three companies they [the Mexicans] never ventured an engagement or to do anything more than to fire a few shots at our rear late one evening without venturing to make anything like a stand and took to their hiding in the bushes before our troops could get near enough to think it worth while to fire on them on the occasion Capt Ruff's company of Mtd Riflemen[126] was in the rear the largest force which they have collected ... between this and the Coast and my opinion is that I could if permitted to do so keep the roads open to Vera Cruz with my company.[127]

Along the route of this large wagon train, George Myers commented on visiting Santa Anna's country home—or what was left of it after many American soldiers had pillaged it. Myers even acquired a "fine tortoise shell comb ... worth thirty dollars."[128]

At Xalapa, they met up with General Scott and his army, which was on its way to Mexico City. There, Walker and his men joined the rest of Company C, temporarily commanded by Lt. Thomas Claiborne.[129]

Claiborne and his detachment met their captain for the first time. Claiborne recalled Walker "a rather short, slender, spare, slouchy man, with reddish hair, a small reddish beard,[130] mild blue eyes and a quiet, kindly manner."[131] Walker arrived at Xalapa, Mexico, on May 21, 1847, bringing with him fresh recruits and mounts to join the original Company C. Also, he brought with him the Grimsley saddles[132] that the army now issued to the Mounted Riflemen—a great improvement over the Ringgold saddle previously issued.

Lt. Thomas Claiborne. (Southern Historical Collection. University of North Carolina)

Walker now took command of Company C.[133] He brought so many recruits with him that only some would be able to stay under his command. Among those he brought with him, Claiborne remembered, many were from prominent Maryland families.[134] He wrote: "The secretary of war gave him a carte blanche to purchase his horses and equipment."

Claiborne recollected his first meeting with Captain Walker on a "wet and chilly day" in May 1847. Claiborne watched him arrive in Mexico with 250 recruits. Captain Walker made quite an impression on a mounted unit that had no horses with his "patent leather saddles,

... adorned with long goose-necked pommels and high cantles, covered wooden stirrups and broad flaps for the legs to stand against. The soldier seemed to stand up when in the saddle; the horses were excellent."[135] Walker led his horse soldiers mounted on the handsome bay gelding Tornado that had been given to him by a collection by some appreciative citizens of New Orleans.

The original Company C, RMR, was organized on September 1, 1846; Samuel H. Walker was officially listed as the commanding officer, but on detached duty. Apparently, the company was originally recruited from the East Coast, perhaps the Maryland area, since it sailed from Baltimore for Mexico on September 5 and arrived at Camargo, Mexico, on October 13. The company was joined by Capt. Benjamin S. Roberts,[136] the acting commanding officer, who had arrived from Jefferson Barracks with 26 recruits on October 6.[137]

Company C left Camargo on November 13 and arrived at Monterrey on November 24, 1846, with three officers and 58 enlisted men. By December, the company was down to three officers and 48 enlisted men (and no horses). In January, at Tampico, Mexico, it was down to 45 enlisted men and required 31 recruits to bring it up to full strength.

Companies C and F left Villa Grande, Mexico, on January 1, 1847, and arrived at Victoria, Mexico, on January 4, and left on January 14, arriving in Tampico, Mexico, on January 23. Company C boarded the schooner *Enterprise* in February, bound for Lobos Island. Company C still needed 31 recruits and still had no horses. Captain Roberts was joined by Capt. George McLane and 2d Lt. Dabney H. Maury on the *Enterprise*.

On March 3, the regiment sailed from Lobos Island and anchored off Anton Lizardo on the 5th. It landed from the anchorage under Sacrificious Island, on the night off the 9th and took position in line before Veracruz on March 13, 1847.

In April, Company C reported three officers and 57 enlisted men for duty with 10 men wounded in action. Captain McLane and Lieutenant Maury reported sick, therefore, Lieutenant Claiborne had been acting commanding officer since April 16, relieving Captain Roberts, who was ultimately transferred to Company A.[138] Still no horses for Company C. The Regiment (except Company I) marched from Veracruz on April 8, 1847; arrived at Plan del Río April 12; engaged the enemy at Cerro Gordo on April 17 and 18, pursued enemy to Encerro; and arrived at Xalapa on April 19.

May 1847

Walker, en route to Mexico, reported to Jones:

> I have the honor to acknowledge the receipt of your letter of April 7th directing me to proceed to Vera Cruz according to previous instructions, I shall leave this place this evening with one hundred and eighty two able bodied men and horses and equipments for my company, although not entirely complete and such as desirable in every respect,

I hope at least to be able to give a god account of our seleves in the next engagement and regret very much our unavoidable detention at this place [New Orleans].

In reply to your "repeated request" and so forth, I have only to say that the proper department was addressed by me and if my communications had been promptly attended to I would have been in Mexico some time since.

I called your attention to these subjects mostly for the purpose of letting you know that it was from no negligence on my part that I was not able to move with that promptness which was expected of me.[139]

Walker Officially Takes Command of Company C, Regiment of Mounted Riflemen in Mexico

In May, with 2 officers and 70 enlisted men, the company was joined by Walker with 60 recruits who were added to the muster roll of Company C. An additional 31 were, disappointingly for them, transferred to other companies in the regiment. Finally, the company had horses. Walker arrived with 45 serviceable horses with an additional 43 which were considered unserviceable. Walker officially assumed command at Xalapa, Mexico, on May 21, 1847.[140]

On to Perote

The company marched from Xalapa on Sunday, May 24. It proceeded through the narrow pass at La Hoya for 8 miles to Las Vegas. Finally, it reached Castle Perote on May 26, 1847, where it was garrisoned with the troops of the 1st Pennsylvania Volunteers. Interestingly, his fame as a "Texan Ranger" went before him and it was thought the 2d Dragoons remained at Perote until Walker's "mounted Texan Rangers arrived from Vera Cruz."[141]

Walker's Riflemen were put to work quickly, guarding a wagon train out of Xalapa on May 27.[142] The company was to remain at Perote by order of General Scott for the purpose of scouting and freeing the vicinity of numerous bands of marauders, who daily robbed and plundered American citizens traveling the road.[143]

Historian Robert Utley explained the situation:

> Scott's biggest challenge lay not in fighting hard-contested battles but in keeping his army supplied. The National Road, linking the port of Vera Cruz with Mexico City, wound its way for 250 miles across three mountain ranges, from the tropics to the great central plateau Mexico. Guerillas and lancers infested the entire length, and only heavily guarded trains could get through. The surrender of Mexico City did not end the affliction, for Santa Anna took his army to the countryside to join with the guerillas and continue the war.[144]

Castle de Perote

The former Mexican fortress of Perote had 72 mounted guns, but after the panic occasioned by the American victory at Cerro Gordo, the castle surrendered without firing a shot.

Perote casements. (Pxthrere.com)

One soldier in Lane's Brigade described the castle thus, "The castle of Perote is a splendid work, though it looks odd enough to see such an immense fortification situated alone on an extensive plain … It stands about a mile from town … the castle covers an area of over twenty acres, … it is of stone, strongly built."

Company C was quartered inside the fort and the horses stabled in the casemates which were ill ventilated and caused health problems for the horses. The old Spanish Castle Perote is further described as being square with a bastion at each corner surrounded by a 30-foot moat. Inside the castle was a center court, five hundred feet square for military drills and parades. The quarters, however, were cramped as Scott had left his sick and wounded there while he advanced deeper into the Mexican interior. Each day 12 to 17 soldiers died, and their bodies were brought outside the fort and buried by prisoners of war. The countryside was swarming with guerrillas and each night the drawbridge was raised.

While the countryside seemed threatening, the climate was appealing to Walker. "The scenery and climate in this valley was lovely beyond description you can find any climate you desire here within one day's ride from perpetual snow to continual summer or autumn." Because of the altitude at Perote (8,602 feet), it was chilly even in the summer and Walker's men and horses suffered from the cold especially at night, but he appreciated the natural beauty around him.

> This morning as the day broke upon us on our march we witnessed one of the most lovely scenes that the eye of man ever beheld. We were in full view of the snow capped Orizaba[145] while its base was surrounded by banks of clouds The sun rose behind us and cast its beams upon all the ragged peaks that towered above the clouds … Almost any man would suppose that a country so much favored by climate and soil … to impress the mind with the greatness of Him who Runs the universe.[146]

Parade ground, Perote. (Print in the public domain)

Col. Francis M. Wynkoop

Col. Francis M. Wynkoop. (www.findagrave.com. Photograph in the public domain)

General Scott had appointed Col. Francis M. Wynkoop as governor of Perote, and Lt. Col. Samuel Black as troop commander. Wynkoop enjoyed this independence. A former newspaper editor, he had commanded a regiment of militia in Schuylkill County, Pennsylvania. He even went directly to President Polk to request his militia be sent to Mexico. Eventually, he would enlist as a private in one of the companies volunteering for Mexico, but it was not long before he was elected colonel of the 1st Pennsylvania Volunteers at Pittsburgh. It did not hurt that Wynkoop also had married the daughter of George Decatur Twiggs, nephew of Gen. David Twiggs.

Wynkoop was only 27 years old, three years younger than Walker, and had limited battle experience. Walker—a battle hardened, Comanche-fighting Texas Ranger as well as a former lieutenant colonel, 1st Regiment of Texas Mounted Rifle Volunteers at the battle of Monterrey—would have a difficult time dealing with Wynkoop's inexperience and arrogance. But he was also a soldier and Wynkoop was his commanding officer. It is ironic that Walker had been so concerned about the role of a bad officer after his experiences in the Seminole War that he wrote a 12-page pamphlet on the matter (see Appendix I). And now, as an officer himself, he had to deal with another officer with whom he had problems. The potential for conflict was definitely there.

Ironically, Walker had two nicknames while serving with the Rangers. He would be wounded so many times in his career as a Texas Ranger, his nickname was "Unlucky Walker." He was also known as "Mad Walker" for his focused determination on attacking the enemy.[147] He was unlucky in his assignment to Perote but the madness would be there when the fighting started. In addition, there was the tension of the several daily deaths in the hospital and very uncomfortable quarters in the former prison.

The garrison at Perote consisted of companies of the 1st and 2d Pennsylvania Regiments, as well as any major force on its way to Mexico City. For the four months Walker was stationed there, it was mostly companies B, E, F and H of the 1st Pennsylvania Regiment, Walker's Company C of the Mounted Riflemen, and companies of the 3d Artillery Battery. Colonel Wynkoop also commanded the hospital under Dr. John Reynolds. Many more wounded and sick were left there as more troops joined Scott's main army, which was advancing on Mexico City.[148]

According to a later analysis there were about 300 patients at Perote with the average death rate at four per day, but it could be as high as 12. A majority of the deaths were from diseases caught on the march, mostly diarrhea and dysentery.[149] Of the 100,000 American soldiers who came to Mexico to fight, 1,500 were killed in action; 10,000 died of disease.[150] While most of the dead were buried at Perote, Sergeant Myers recalled Edwin Hammond of Anne Arundel County (Maryland) who was "very much respected of the company" died of dysentery and his body was sent home. "Capt. Walker ordered the remains of young Hammond put in a coffin and boxed up and sent it to the U. States via train that comes from Puebla on to Vera Cruz."[151]

Walker's Fame

Capt. Samuel H. Walker was still known as "the celebrated Texan Ranger."[152] On June 5, Gen. José Joaquin de Herrera, who claimed to have been the commander of Perote when "Texas troops, including Samuel H. Walker, were imprisoned and confined" there, actually led a tour[153] (obviously without Walker present) and showed the Americans where the Rangers were imprisoned. He even continued the myth that Walker had buried a dime under a flagpole he was forced to erect when he was a prisoner at Perote; pledging to return and dig it up when an American flag flew over Perote.[154] This story spread as fact even with Walker actually in residence at Perote.

Someone apparently asked Walker about his imprisonment by the Mexicans because he told the story of his hardships and of prisoners bribing a blacksmith to make blackened lead links of chains so that chains could be removed when back in their cells.

June 1847

On June 6, the Riflemen were a part of a raid on Tepegahualco (a town 10 miles from Perote on the road to Puebla), a sort of headquarters for guerrillas in the area. No guerrillas were found but military clothing, arms, and ammunition were.[155] On the afternoon of June 8, one of Walker's men was buried near the castle. Lieutenant Claiborne read from the Bible and spoke of the man as a "gallant soldier, true Christian and faithful companion." It was reported his death came "from exposure and cold contracted while out skirmishing and in pursuit of guerrillas." His brother, in the same company, placed a small board with his name painted on it over the grave, as there was no time to have a headstone carved for it.[156]

At Perote, the Riflemen drilled. According to the monthly field returns (in Walker's words):

> Discipline of the Company is very good, being tolerably well drilled in Sabre, Pistol and Rifle[157] exercises and in the School of the Platoon and Squadron mounted. Deaths frequent, no decrease of sickness. Bad quarters and the energies of the men are weakened and destroyed for want of more excitement and active service; being composed of a class of Men, who anticipated nothing but active Service and are unfit for the dull routine of Garrison duty.[158]

Having settled in, Walker brought his brother up to date:

> Perote Mexico
> 6 June 1847
>
> Dear Brother
> I arrived at Vera Cruz on the 8th of May. I have been actively engaged ever since my arrival. I have succeeded in capturing a few those who had been guilty of many acts of the barbarity towards every unfortunate man who fell in their hands, I of course took some summary measures with them and I doubt not you have heard many exaggerated the stories about the affair and the course I pursued however it was approved and appalauded by Commander in Chief and I have been left here for that purpose of freeing this part of the country from the hands of marauders that infest it, we have not been able to get a fight out of

them yet that is worthy of mention, we have just returned now from a scout where we expected to get a fight and were disappointed, but we started this morning at 2 AM marching 21 miles and returned my recruits considerable fatigued. Day before yesterday we captured under the directions of Governor Wynkoop 19 prisoners who are now at work on police duty in the castle among them is one alcade, a few days since we entered the town called Altotongo consisting of about 1500 inhabitants with a thickly settled surrounding country, and the people were said to be very warlike and we were persuaded not to go with so small a force but we were in search of a party of robbers inhumanely butchered some of their own countrymen and we pushed on rode into town rather unceremoniously. A few of them got their arms but took a good care not to use them, we could get no clue to detect any of them after taking a late dinner with them and offering them to be peace and protection to all who might desire and were ... To this place the same night at a late hour and the scenery and a climate in this valley was lovely beyond description. You could have any climate as a matter here within one days ride from precipices with snow to continual summer or autumn. This place is never sufficiently warm to produce persperation Our horses are shivering with cold at most every morning in the stables and it is frequently necessary to cover them with blankets, yet vegetation grows finely and the market abounds with almost every variety of fruits. This morning as the day broke upon us and our march the witnessed one of the most lovely scenes that the eye of man has ever beheld we were in full view of snow covered Orizaba while its base was surrounded by banks of clouds. The sun rose behind us and cast its beams upon all the ragged peaks that towered above the clouds was such an unusual brightness that and it gave an air of grandeur to the scene which language like my own cannot describe, in reflecting I am often in amazement and wonder that the remarkable contrast between the country and the inhabitants. Almost any man would suppose that a country so much favored by climate and soil and so many objects to relieve the eye and to impress the mind with the greatness of him who rules the universe, would at least bring forth a race of men who had some manly and noble feelings about them, but alas for them that fate is final there seems to be no redemption for them as they seemed every day to be less regardless of their honor even personal or national they seem only to pride themselves in their obstinacy and hatreds to those who would aid them and extend the hand of friendship to them whenever they may feel disposed to accept it, " enough of this" General Scott it is said will be in the city of Mexico to celebrate this 4th of July, I hope I shall be with him, my only consolation in being left here was the hope of getting my pistols, but I think that doubtful and I must be contented to continue and this inglorious service with such arms as I have got I have been frequently tempted already to lay aside the rifle as it is entirely too heavy to be of much use to mounted men, I received a letter from Colt on the 3rd of May in which he says he a delay of two weeks in consequence of a freshlet which carries their water wheel and he expects me to wait in Vera Cruz to get the pistols so you may judge wants the prospects are, found out that my saddles would not be sent to me and I had a set of botched saddles made in New Orleans which have hurt a good many of my horses backs. I am in hopes those I had made in Washington will be sent out so that I may get them all about the time I get the pistols as I intended to throw these aside as soon as I can get those made by Campbell, I shall send soon to Vera Cruz for them and try and go with my company for them rather than not getting them. The entire Depot at Jalapa will be broken up in a few days and everything moved to this place. General Scott intends to concentrate all of his available forces for the next fight which will be I supposed in this city of Mexico he will not weaken his forces to establish Depots but to depend upon the resources of the country. The priests in the country are heading guerrilla parties and we are now double price for everything we consume. There is a abundance of provisions and the present year's crop is very promising the finances of the country is rapidly improving all under our liberal sisters, the dispatches sent out to General Scott were captured by the Mexicans through the imprudence and folly of the bearer who as killed with them on this person. If I only had my revolving pistols I could soon clear the road from all those bands between this and Vera Cruz. Give my respects and best wishes to all my friends and relatives, the young men under my command they behave well, at present however many of them are laboring under the effects of change from a southern to a temperate climate of which makes many of them unfit for immediate service

Yours … brother
SH Walker[159]

One soldier at Perote wrote that on the morning of June 10:

> While walking around the ramparts, I heard the clattering of horses' hoofs and the rattling of scabbards; it was Capt. Walker's company going on drill; they dashed out on the road, back of the Castle, on a level piece of ground, there they drilled for over an hour. They were under the command of Lieut. Thomas Claiborn. [Walker's second in command] Lieut. Claiborn is a tall, slim noble looking officer, a splendid horseman, of very good discipline, and takes great pains in drilling his company.[160]

Claiborne wrote that the sword exercise from horseback was done so vigorously that all of Company C became good swordsmen and some of them, expert. He commented that Walker studied the tactics and he instructed his men accordingly.

Rifle practice was done on the palisade opposite the right bastion to the flank of the rear bastion some one hundred and eighty yards. The young lieutenant noted that the bullets scooped out quite a hole in the side of the bastion.

Claiborne understood he was unpopular with the men because he enforced a certain command. He had been warned by the surgeon not to let his men sit on the ground without something underneath them. He had been told that as "the earth is a strong conductor and the lower bowel very sensitive, and the heat drawn off so rapidly as to congest it, hence the rise of diarrhea and dysentery."[161]

On June 11, Colonel Wynkoop moved six companies of the Pennsylvania Regiment from the fortress Perote into the town of Perote; on June 18, he moved them back into the fort "because of increasing rumors that the Mexicans planned an attack."[162] On June 12, Walker buried another one of his men, a Pennsylvanian. Many of the Pennsylvania Volunteers attended the funeral. Walker's men were mounted and fully equipped to honor their fallen comrade.[163]

Company C continued its scouting and on June 16, discovering a deserted guerrilla headquarters, brought back 40 to 50 mustangs. Walker reported a large force of guerrillas between Perote and Veracruz awaiting a large wagon train soon to leave Veracruz. Walker's scouts that night were on the road as picket guards.[164]

Blankets a Necessity for Man and Beast

Walker was also concerned with the care of his men and wrote directly to the commanding Gen. Winfield Scott on June 16. He wanted to call the general's attention to the sick at the hospital who were dying four to twelve daily. "Two of my best men have already died and I have the painful reflection of believing that they might have lived had they been provided with suitable bedding and a clean hospital," Sgt. George Myers wrote, "We have a great number down with the dysentery. In fact, every one of us has had it more or less."[165]

Walker had already made complaints to the surgeon who said he had "neither the means in his hands or the discretion to purchase … the necessary Hospital furniture and conveniences for the sick." Walker then complained why he thought there had been no help for the hospital. He plainly noted that the inactivity was caused more by "a fear of responsibility than necessary" and that "at least straw mattresses for the sick could have made their suffering more endurable." Since his arrival, the nights had been cold enough for a well man to need two blankets to keep warm at night, but the sick in the hospital had but one blanket each—their entire bedding. And all slept on beds of stone. Walker then reported that when he first came to Perote, he had made a request for his men to be issued "bed sacks" and straw mattresses for the whole garrison.

Walker wrote "this place is never sufficiently warm to produce perspiration. Our horses are shivering with cold at most every morning in the stables and it is frequently necessary to cover them with blankets."[166] But Colonel Wynkoop, although he agreed with Walker upon the need[167] "does not feel himself authorized to approve officially of such requisitions, without instructions from the commanding general."

Walker told the general that he had, on his own, done what he could to make his own men "more comfortable." He then added that while he had been actively employed at Perote he would "greatly prefer to be with you [General Scott] in your advance upon the city of Mexico as I am particularly anxious to visit my old stamping ground Tacubayou and renew the acquaintance of my distinguished friends Santa Anna and Ampudia."

Mexico City would not only be an objective of military conquest for Captain Walker, it had a very special meaning to him. He then adds in his letter, "It would be gratifying to me to have an opportunity of riding occasionally through Tacubayou over these streets which I helped to pave."

He expressed his wish for his command to join Scott but in character of a good soldier concluded that "any position that you might place us as we are ready to be used in any way that the interest of the service and our country may require."

Two of the enlisted men of the Pennsylvania Regiment, Sgt. Thomas Barclay and Pvt. Richard Coulter, kept diaries which were combined in one publication. The two made comments on both Walker and Wynkoop. Since Walker's men usually went on missions for a mounted troop, it would be hard for infantry soldier to have too many firsthand observations and perhaps read criticism in the newspapers about Walker's Santa Fe experience. Nevertheless, Sergeant Barclay, wrote:

> Capt. Walker has an inveterate hatred against the Mexicans and when he has the power he carries on the war according to his own peculiar feelings. I do not think this is good policy to permit the gallant captain to thus exasperate the whole people, for every man of common sense knows we should conciliate as well as fight.[168]

This likely refers directly to the story that Walker had killed six Mexican civilians in cold blood.

Wynkoop was criticized for trying to impress "the brass" and "pushing the men too hard" and seemed slow to act on soldiers who plundered. He was also criticized for not seeing to his men's needs and forcing them to camp where wood was scarce and water "very bad, dirty and stinking." The conclusion of Walker with regard to the camp conditions was, "This is a specimen of Col Wynkoop's discretion."[169]

Niles National Register reported on June 19:

> A train of 200 wagons arrived yesterday afternoon from Vera Cruz, and proceeded this morning in company with Gen. Twiggs's division towards Puebla and the city of Mexico. Captain Walker's gallant band of mounted men accompanied the train, and during the journey had two skirmishes with a superior force of Mexican lancers or robbers.
>
> The last took place at Santa Fe, at an early hour in the morning of Wednesday last, which resulted in the complete rout of the enemy, over 200 in number, who had 10 killed and many wounded. Our men had several wounded but none dangerously. The 2nd Dragoons, who were

> first attached by the lancers, while reposing in slumber, had six killed and eleven wounded. Walker, in person, pursued the wretches, as far and well as the darkness of the occasion would admit, captured six prisoners, who were handed over to the dragoons, and almost instantly shot dead. Captain Walker has 180 men, only 100 of which are mounted. They are a fine body, and their gallant commander is now "the lion of Japala."[170]

Undoubtedly, this was the source that Walker had executed six prisoners in cold blood.

La Hoya Pass

On June 19, having learned that about one thousand Guerrillas had taken possession of a strong pass called La Hoya, about 22 miles from Perote and about 12 from Xalapa, for the purpose of disputing the passage with Gen. George Cadwalader and Colonel Childs,[171] who had evacuated Xalapa, had a large train and considerable amount of specie, which it seems the Mexicans had strong hopes of capturing. The enemy had already attacked this rather large party that was advancing toward Scott's army in the interior. They had "captured a considerable amt of Public Property & stores from Col McIntosh who formed a portion of Gen's command."[172]

Colonel Wynkoop took five companies of the Volunteers, and Walker's company, and planned to attack the waiting enemy from the rear before daylight. Walker had learned of the location of the enemy's advance scouts[173] and with his mounted men, left the road in hopes of separating the smaller force with an attack. Failing to find them, he returned to the road and discovered the Volunteers had advanced up the road ahead of him. Upon hearing shots ahead, Walker and his men advanced; the foot soldiers parted for the horsemen. Wynkoop sent an order to Walker to advance on the firing but to be careful of Wynkoop's scouts some 200 yards ahead. Walker told Wynkoop that he would "take a few men on foot and make a close reconnaissance [of the enemy's] position" before he ventured to make a charge in the dark on horseback. Wynkoop made no reply.

Walker advanced with some of his men on foot. "To my surprise I had not advanced more than 100 yards in the Pass from his [Wynkoop's] infantry before I was hailed by the Enemies Piquet which I answered in the same language and received a second challenge." There were no American soldiers ahead of him as he understood from Wynkoop but the enemy. They had about the same force as Walker had and were about 50 yards ahead formed up across the road.

He decided that it was better to be shot at from the front than being fired on while withdrawing. Walker ordered a pistol charge and for the men to ride through the enemy's line. One witness recalled when the order "Ready! Charge!" was given "off they went with about fifty men with the awfulness rattling and cracking with the horses' feet and the jangling of swords and scabbards and yelling."[174] The Mexicans were stunned by the unexpected action and scattered, firing over the heads of Walker's men.

It would be a fateful night for Walker. It would be the last time he would ride his beautiful bay gelding Tornado into battle. It was a pitch-dark night at 3 o'clock in the morning.[175] Leading the charge in columns of four, Walker with his sword[176] in hand crashed into a more formidable foe than the enemy—a picket fence. As they galloped down the road, they suddenly came upon a large fire at an elbow in the road. It blinded Walker and his men to the turn in the road and they rode at full speed into the fence, injuring some of them and costing them several horses lost in the dark. The first two sets of fours quickly rolled over, unhorsed. Apparently, there was some gunfire in the dark as Walker thought his horse shot and lost in the melee.[177] There was no way he could search for him in enemy territory.

One soldier recalled, "The Captain says that when his horse stumbled and fell, he thought that he was wounded, and being anxious to be with his men he left his horse lay and followed, running after his company until the charge was accomplished."[178]

Walker hurt his hand[179] and damaged his sword.[180] And, he wrote "my round top [uniform blue] Hat lost in the bargain … I mounted myself again by dismounting David [Walker's slave who had accompanied him from Maryland] who was fortunately in the rear … who by the way is very fond of these expeditions. At dawn of day I was in search of my horses in hopes of finding some of them in the adjoining fields."[181] A few stragglers of the enemy were spotted and fired upon and in a "few minutes more between fifty & seventy of the enemy made their appearance on our Right," but Walker then received orders from Col. Thomas Childs to withdraw.[182] In his letter to his brother about the event—he was not just mildly upset and embarrassed over his encounter with the fence, loss of his horse, injured hand, and damaged sword—Colonel Childs and Colonel Wynkoop are classified as cowards more than once.[183]

After withdrawing briefly, Walker set out on a new course of action. While Wynkoop's men rested after their 25-mile march, Walker ordered "the head of my column to the left into a stack of barley which is very good food for horses and was asked by the Col where I was going I told him I was going to refresh my men & horses before retreating any further." Walker "turned into the barley and slipped his bridle"[184] there in the rear of the retiring infantry. Wynkoop directed his Adjutant Lt. A. H. Goff to order Walker to move on. Walker took his time. Then the order was repeated. Walker ordered "Boots and Saddles" for his bugler and the company mounted.

As there was no water in the area, Sam then requested permission to take his company to water. "This left me a good excuse to leave this cowardly wretch[185] and I ordered my command to a gallop for a mile in the direction of the enemy to a stream of water. After watering my horses I moved up into the mountains on a narrow road in the direction of the enemy who had shown himself."[186]

Sergeant Myers wrote Walker ordered every other man to dismount and take his rifle and scour the surrounding hills. A prisoner was taken and upon the threat of being hanged at the first tree they came to; he confessed that a large force of lancers was at the pass to cut off Cadwaladar's approaching wagon train.[187]

Lt. Thomas Claiborne, Walker's second-in-command, remembered Wynkoop sending word recalling Walker but the captain disregarded the order, and with "forty-seven men and three officers in column of twos with a small party of flankers advanced through a small village, continued at a walk, down a sloping hill, the road turned to the right at a little farm divided by a narrow lane walled with stone into two fields … to the left past a clearing a rude log house with an open shed on its left."[188]

As they approached the cabin, they could see a most suspicious group of armed Mexicans. Walker's men fired upon them and "in an instant the place was alive with guerrillas who rushed yelling into the open field" toward Sam and his company. Walker led his men to the stone fence beside the log house. Dismounted, they used the breast-high stone wall as cover. Walker personally went to each horse and took the sabers from the saddles and distributed them to his men. Apparently, he felt as if hand-to-hand fighting would be the result of the encounter. The horses were then placed in the house and shed.

In his journal, Sgt. Myers wrote:

> Our Capt. ordered that the horses should be tied behind the houses & the men to take their stantz behind the wall & let them have it. I assure you we did just about do the thing right. There were not more than thirty five or forty of us & between six to eight hundred of the Mongrels for all that we [repulsed] them with severe loss.[189]

Lieutenant Claiborne later wrote a detailed account of the event:

> Our men opened fire with great effect: the [Guerrilla] Chief in a red cloak was seen leading some of his men to our left. Corporal Goslin, … mounted his horse and dashed by the enemy already enveloping our left and carried to Wynkoop the tiding of our situation. … It would of done you good to see them come up to the man every one trying to out do the other & our brave Captain not caring anything about himself (he was heard to say don't give up on 'em boys but give them hell.) but with saber in hand he was constantly going from one end of the line to the other encouraging us to take good aim & not to waste our ammunition & every time that he would see one fall he would appear to be exalted & when he saw them about to retreating he hollered out, see boys they are worsening.[190]

In his report, Walker praised Claiborne for doing good service with his rifle. Claiborne said that he was in excellent practice with his Harpers Ferry rifle and seeing four men at the back lines—one of them "conspicuous for a wonderful hat"—took a rifle from one of the men holding the horses, and rested it on the corner of the house and fired. The men began to run, and another Rifleman handed Claiborne his rifle, and Claiborne dropped one of the men. A third rifle was passed to him and at 200 yards his shot broke the thigh of another one of these four.[191] Claiborne then noticed a party of about 30 enemy soldiers about 50 yards from their right flank, approaching the company's position behind the stone wall. Walker ordered Claiborne to take six men and drive them off.

Taking a dragoon pistol in each hand, Claiborne advanced with his men. Halfway to the enemy, Claiborne saw the enemy level their escopetas at him. He threw himself flat and they shot over him, and he lay still as if dead. As he heard no more firing from their direction, he slowly rose up and then ran back to the cabin. Major Brooks, with the cavalry from Cadwaladar's Brigade, now came on the scene.

Walker's men had nearly exhausted their ammunition. Some had bullet holes in their clothes. Fortunately, only one of their horses was slightly wounded. At least 60 of the enemy lay dead on the field when Wynkoop's men arrived and drove off the Mexicans.

The enemy withdrawing, General Cadwaladar's force arrived on the right and Colonel Wynkoop—following the firing—came from the left. Walker's men then proceeded after the enemy, dismounted, and followed a path off the road locating a party of the enemy and opening fire. Their return fire came from above to their right and left.[192]

The guerrillas estimated at being at least five hundred strong seemed confident of wiping out the small band of Riflemen. Claiborne wrote the fight lasted 40 minutes while Wynkoop, in his report, said it only lasted 10 minutes when he came with reinforcements.[193]

Walker reported to his brother that the enemy was already withdrawing when Wynkoop's men and Cadwaladar's force arrived:

> A few minutes after the enemy were defeated Gen Cadwallader's forces came up and the Penn Volunteers under Wynkoop on the other side and joined in the pursuit. A heavy firing was kept up at 1 mile distant from the retreating for which you know was only a waste of ammunition without doing any good. My company was joined by two companies of the 2nd Dragoons under Capts Blake & Hardee and in pursuing the enemy for about five miles as rapidly as we could owing to the nature of the ground the enemy at this time came to position for making another stand and done so at a place where it was impractical for us to approach them on horse back so we accordingly dismounted in company with the dragoons and fought them at long shot for half an hour our men killing a few of them without receiving any injury to ourselves.[194]

The guerrillas were defeated but they still presented a threat at this narrow pass which had to be used by future supply trains. General Cadwalader made a decision to burn areas that were suspected to have supported the guerrillas.

One soldier captured several small black guerrilla flags with skull and cross bones, and the words "No Quarter" on them. Arriving at Las Vegas, they found the town deserted; it was plain that it was fortified at one end and, although deserted, was prepared to be used to fight the Americans.[195]

A newspaper reported the follow-up operation by Wynkoop:

> They [Wynkoop's force] drove the enemy for several miles back from the road, and burnt every rancho in their route, leaving desolate the whole country over which they passed. On our reaching Las Vegas, a pretty and flourishing little town, it was found that the dwellings were entirely deserted by the Mexicans, and was satisfactorily ascertained that they had identified themselves with the guerrillas. With the consent of the commanding general, the torch was applied to the buildings, and in a few moments the entire town was one universal scene of conflagration.

Every building in it, numbering between eighty and one hundred, was destroyed by fire- the only one that was spared being the neat little Catholic church that adorned the town. Its solitary appearance among the smouldering ruins of the town, created sensations better imagined than described; and the example set in this instance, it is greatly to be hoped, will have the effect of restraining the enemy in future in their murderous course warfare.[196]

Wynkoop sent his after-action report of the battle at La Hoya to army headquarters. At this point in his association with the Mounted Riflemen, he freely praised Walker and his company—something that would not last.

I have the honor to report the following to the Commander-in-Chief.

On the 15th of June a courier reported with letters from Head Quarters stating that Alvarez was on the road between this place and Puebla.

At the same time hearing of a force of about five hundred in our immediate vicinity, I sent Capt. Walker to seize and bring down to the Castle 30 fine mustang horses which were secured at San Antonio and which I thought might be seized and used against us.

The next day I learnt from a Mexican courier that a force of fifteen hundred men were stationed at La Hoya with determination of attacking Genl. Cadwaladar and train.

Ascertaining afterwards that this information as correct and also learning the period at which Gen. C would arrive at La Hoya, I sent a courier to Jalapa telling Genl Cadwaladar I would meet him at the pass in the rear of the army on Sunday morning early.

At 10 o'clock on Saturday evening I left the Castle and moved down the National road with Walker's Rifles and five companies of my own regiment, B, C, F, H And K, in all about 250 men. We reached the enemy's pickets about a mile beyond Las Vegas and drove them in before daybreak killing one of them.

In the charge, Capt. Walker, who was in advance encountered a fence which threw his men, injuring some of them severely and in the melee, he lost his own horse and the horses of eight of his men. The accident I consider unavoidable and think that no blame can accrue to the Captain for the consequences.

At about seven o'clock finding a party of the enemy's horsemen occupying the hills around us, I sent out skirmishers who succeeded in driving them off, killing five of them. We then halted to rest the men having walked a distance of 25 miles. Captain Walker requested permission to ride on in order to get some food for his horses a short distance in advance and had been absent but ten minutes when he was hotly engaged with the enemy. I hurried up with my command and found him fighting about 500 in a deep valley beyond Las Vegas. Upon the approach of the infantry the Mexicans broke and I turned the battalion rapidly so as to cut off their retreat. I followed them for several miles fighting them upon every favorable piece of ground upon which they rallied and killing a number. All this time Genl Cadwaladar with Col. Childs were engaged in hastening them, a most complete route was the consequence. As near as I can estimate the loss on the part of the enemy was at least 50 them killed, among the killed was an officer who was shot through the body by my orderly. It is but just to state to the Commander in Chief that the officers and men behaves themselves bravely and well. They went into the fight cheerfully ignorant that Genl Cadawaladar's force was at hand and was desperately determined to drive the enemy off the ground alone. Major Bowman, who was in charge of my infantry distinguished himself by his coolness and courage was among the last to quit the pursuit, Capt. Walker and his company deserve the greatest share of the honor of the fight. Before the arrival of the infantry he held his position with 30 rifles against 500 of the enemy and had killed a number of them.

I am further happy to state that none of my command were wounded. All of which I have the honor most respectfully to submit to the General in Chief.[197]

And here is Walker's report of the same fight:

> Sir: When ordered forward by you at three o'clock, a. m., on the 20th I understood from you that you had a picket about two hundred yards in advance. In this I was disappointed. I had not advanced more than one hundred yards before I was hailed by the enemy, who appeared about forty in number. I could not return or delay a moment to reconnoitre, as I intended, without subjecting my command and yours also to a raking fire, and I immediately ordered the charge. The enemy were completely routed, and fled in such haste and confusion that no man was wounded; but unfortunately we found a curve in the road while we supposed it to be straight, and a number of us were unhorsed by the falling of our horses over a fence which was not seen until we were on it. In this affair I lost 7 public horses, which probably fell into the hands of the enemy—one of them so badly wounded as to render him valueless. I lost also my private horse. Richardson, musician, and Raborg, interpreter, were slightly injured by the fall of their horses.
>
> On the same day about 9, a. m., after leaving you for the purpose of watering my horses, I resolved to drive off the party who had made their appearance on the hills on our right early in the morning. I dismounted one half of my men and threw them out on the right and left. Several of their stragglers were killed and the balance made a rapid retreat before we approached near enough to engage them. I then returned to the village of Las Vegas, having also taken two prisoners whom I released, both being elderly men.
>
> About 11 o'clock, a. m., while advancing upon La Hoya, with your permission to feel the enemy and ascertain their position &c, I heard the firing of artillery at the pass. I dismounted some of my men and threw them out on each side of the road to avoid an ambuscade. When about two miles from the pass, we saw about fifty of the enemy on our left, I sent forward a few men on foot for the purpose of bringing on an engagement. It soon became apparent that the enemy either had a very considerable force, or that they had feared the consequence of allowing us the opportunity of attacking them in rear, and they had almost entirely withdrawn from the pass.
>
> In a very few minutes after the first shot was fired, my skirmishers were pressed by such overwhelming numbers as to force them to retire within distance of support; and, to give them a more defensible position, I then ordered my horses all to be tied under cover of an old farm house. I then ordered my men under cover of a stone fence and extended them sufficiently to the left to prevent the enemy from flanking. Being emboldened by their success in driving back my skirmishers, they rushed towards us in considerable numbers, confident of victory, with shouts of triumph, which were returned by shouts of defiance from my men. The moment was critical, many of my men had never been under fire of an enemy before, and nothing but my confidence in their heroic valor and coolness would have induced me to have remained in my position. At this moment I ordered the men to take their sabres from the fronts of their saddles, which were secured in that way for the purpose of secret movements by night, and prepare to use them when it came to close quarters. The coolness and gallantry of my men and the deadly crack of their rifles soon convinced them that it was better to retire.
>
> There could not have been less than three hundred Mexicans in the engagement, besides about three hundred more who were close by to support them, and might very properly be included in the number of the attacking party. I suppose their loss as near as I could judge in this affair, was at least forty killed and wounded. My whole number of men was fifty one, which included several that were injured in the fall of their horses in the charge the night previous, and a corporal and two privates, 2d dragoons. The action was warmly contested, and lasted about thirty minutes. I had one horse killed, and one man, private Huguenen, who volunteered his services, belonging to (F) company of the rifles, having been left sick in hospital, slightly wounded.

My officers and men behaved with great gallantry and such daring bravery, that it was with reluctance that some of them seemed to obey my orders to take cover behind the rocks from the shower of bullets which for some time filled the air above their heads. Where all behaved so nobly, it is difficult to make distinction. Among the many, however, who have gained my esteem for their good conduct, I cannot omit to mention the names of Serg't Thomas Sloan, of England; Sergeant Edward Harris, of Virginia; both of whom were wounded in former engagements—also Sergeant Henry Haugh, of Baltimore, Maryland. Corporal Gosling, of Maryland, who was also wounded at Cerro Gordo, is entitled to the distinction of being called the bravest of the bravest also, Corporals Joseph E. Mericken, of Maryland, and Samuel Hescock, of Maine; also, Privates Thomas H. Tilghman, of Maryland; James M. DeBaufre, of Maryland; Isaac P. Darlington, of Maryland; William Glanding, of Maryland; Thaddeus S. Bell, of Virginia; Francis G. Waltermyer, of Maryland; and also, Richard M. Bradford, of Baltimore, Maryland, who was always among the foremost, and the last to retire from pursuit of the enemy. All of these I recommend to the favorable consideration of the commander-in-chief of the American forces, and the War Department, and request that they may be rewarded for their gallantry. I will notify the War Department, and request that they may be rewarded for their gallantry. Many of them are gentlemen of education, and worthy of commissions in the service of the United States, and, I cannot too strongly recommend them for promotion to higher stations. And I must, also, take occasion to regret that sickness should have prevented so many of my most gallant spirits from participating with me in this affair. I must not omit to mention that Lieutenant Charles L. Denman, who was by my side, and behaved gallantly in the charge, was in the engagement and behaved well, and continued in pursuit to the last point, deserves much credit for his perseverance, energy, and bravery. Although on the sick report and suffering severely for some weeks past, he would not remain behind.

Lieutenant Thomas Claiborne took a rifle and used it with considerable effect on the enemy. Surgeon Lamar, also deserves my thanks for volunteering his professional services, and remaining with us in the pursuit. I must also mention Lieutenant Goff, 1st Pennsylvania regiment, who was with us, and took the news of our engagement to you.[198]

General Cadwaladar had this to say about his men and the battle: The Pennsylvanians and Captain Walker's men were engaged in a brisk exchange with the enemy when, "The advance of the 2d brigade under Colonel Childs drove the enemy in confusion for more than two miles."

Maj. Gen. George Cadwalader. (Library of Congress)

Walker's men were satisfied to see the Mexicans quit the field and rest, except for Claiborne and a handful of Riflemen who ran after the retreating for a hundred yards or so, firing as they ran; Cadwaladar's men drove the enemy for 2 miles; while Wynkoop's soldiers chased the Mexicans for "several miles." Perhaps some exaggeration was in play.

On the 24th and the 27th, Wynkoop, accompanied by Walker's mounted men, seized quantities of Mexican Army corn and barley.[199]

On June 29, a Mexican spy led Walker and his men to a large assembly of guerrillas. According to George Ballentine—an Englishman serving in the American Army—Walker's Riflemen: "Routed them in the utmost confusion; his dragoons cutting down a great many with their sabers. Arriving at the deserted village where the guerrillas were reported to have originated, the village was burned. Walker's duty was to hunt out and route bands of guerrillas who infest the area and his men rarely brought back prisoners."[200]

Ballentine told an interesting, but totally fabricated, story about Walker. Ballentine wrote that Walker was so vengeful against the Mexicans because they had captured his father and two brothers, and taken them to the prison at Perote where they had to draw beans to determine who would be executed. According to this story, Walker's father and brother were executed. Ironically Sam's father did die (of old age) in December 1842, the month before Sam was captured at Mier.[201]

While the English soldier garbled the stories he had heard about Captain Walker, Sergeant Myers saw the real Walker. Throughout his diary, Myers's devotion to Captain Walker and Company C never wavered. He described his commander as "brave," "much esteemed," and "gallant" with "nothing daunted." The Mexicans were as "afraid of us as the Devil is of Holy water"; "The Mexicans call us Capt. Walker's Devils. They do not like us at all. I assure you there is no love lost between us."[202]

Sergeant Myers reported one of Company C's early July patrols encountered a large wagon train of about 3,000 troops under the command of Gen. Franklin Pierce. Interestingly, this was also an encounter with the other mounted company of the RMR: Captain Ruff's Company I, reinforced by a force of mounted Mexican lancers employed by the U.S. Army. Myers reported that Ruff's company had killed 40 to 50 of the enemy in the encounter. One of the men told the story that during the fight, as one of the men was biting his paper cartridge, a musket ball passed under his ear and through his mouth. The soldier finished his loading and killed the man who wounded him. He was expected to recover. The mail also came with this wagon train carrying a letter for Myers informing him of his father's death.[203]

July 1847

In his memoirs, Claiborne detailed the account of Colonel Wynkoop's poor judgment during the next month. In July, Maj. F. T. Lally of the 9th Infantry, continually harassed by guerrillas, was able to fight his way to Xalapa from Veracruz with a large detachment of men. He sent for aid from Colonel Wynkoop at Perote. Wynkoop, with four companies of his infantry, Walker's company, and several pieces of artillery, was able to pass through La Hoya Pass without incident. Upon arriving at Xalapa, the first thing Wynkoop did was to get drunk and threaten to burn some of the buildings and destroy others with artillery if hundreds of arms—which he claimed the guerrilla had stored in the town—were not turned over. Emilio Carau, a man

Claiborne had met in his earlier visit to Xalapa, was the head of the town council and pleaded first with Claiborne and then with Wynkoop but to no avail. Walker refused Wynkoop's direct order and was placed under arrest.[204] Fortunately, as negotiations continued, Wynkoop sobered up enough to release Walker from arrest.

Wynkoop and Walker's men arrived back at Perote safely. But the friction between the two would flare up again. From this point on, Walker and Wynkoop seemed on a collision course.

On July 29, a false report was circulated that the Mexicans had killed Walker.[205] And interestingly, his reputation as a Texas Ranger was now associated with his men, and his Company C of the Mounted Riflemen were often referred to as Walker's Texas Rangers.[206]

August 1847

In mid-August, Claiborne (who remembered it as on July 4) wrote that he and Walker climbed "el Cofre de Perote." Both Walker and Myers recorded the date as August 16. Claiborne said that he and Captain Walker[207] resolved to place the flag of the United States atop the giant mountain that rose above Perote.[208] It was said to be 13,780 feet above sea level and visible for miles. On horseback, Walker, Claiborne, Myers, and two dozen others of Company C and Company H, Pennsylvania Volunteers, rode until the way was impassable by horse, then on foot for 2 miles.[209] They carried a U.S. flag and climbed past the tree line. They finally reached the base of the huge rock outcropping. Walker wrote his brother: "The Coffre, the summit peak, is a rock about 250 yds in length about 100 yds in width. At its base about 250 feet high nearly perpendicular."[210] The monstrous boulder seemed shaped like a huge chest. Walker wrote that they finally found a large crack ("a rift from top to bottom") up which they climbed by "pressing our bodies, aided by feet and hands." In time they stood on the top of the Cofre. They could see as far as the Gulf, and some 40 miles away the lofty snow-covered peak of Orizaba. The flagstaff they brought with them was planted and the flag was raised. Claiborne speculated that this was the highest point on which any flag had been placed up until that time.

Present-day view of el Cofre de Perote. (James Worsham collection)

Although Walker did not drink, apparently, he did join in a celebration. He wrote:

> They put up a flag staff [raised the flag] and toasted the Stars and Stripes. [They] fired a national salute sang the star spangled banner in the most lofty strain drank to the President of the US and our Flag and our Country amidst loud cheers and then ended the ceremony. The Star Spangled Banner now waves on the summit peak of the Coffre.[211]

Walker added that the climbers from his company and Company H of the Pennsylvania Volunteers went up to the top as a special challenge. Wynkoop and a group of officers visited the area 10 days earlier and pronounced such a feat as impossible.

On August 16, Sergeant Myers recorded:

> This day we started for the nob on the top of the mountain to put a flag there. The mountain is fifteen miles from the base to the top and very steep. We had to walk nearly all the way up when within two miles of the nob we fastened our horses. The nob is a solid mass of rock on the top of the mountain between two and three hundred feet high. We had a ladder to ascend the rock with but we found it was not necessary as we found a crevice in the rock which we found means to ascend which was a rather dangerous undertaking but we were determined to plant our flag on the top. I myself made the staff and ladder. The staff was 20 feet high. We succeeded in planting our staff securely & in a few minutes after we let float to the breeze of heaven the glorious stars & stripes of our country far above the clouds which were floating hundreds of feet below us. We sang the Star Spangled Banner and christened the peak as Walker's Peak. We also saluted the flag with 30 shots from our rifles and the echo was grand in the extreme for it would echo from mountain to mountain until it was lost in the distance.[212]

September 1847

In late August, Walker started a letter to his brother.

> By the permission of Col Wynkoop my company to my great mortification was allowed to pillage the town of Coetepa a village 9 miles from Jalappa, headquarters of the guerrillas. This man is labouring under a charge of cowardice for his infamous conduct at La Hoya is perfectly desperate in his feelings and determined to do something desperate regard. …
>
> He is determined to remove that impression or destroy my reputation by having my name associated with him in these disgraceful affairs.[213]

Wynkoop had ordered Walker to prepare to go with him to attack a village some 40 miles away where the guerrillas were rumored to have their quarters. Walker came to Claiborne (who was not among those going on the mission) and told him that he suspected Wynkoop was using the guerrilla threat as an excuse to plunder helpless villages. Walker told Claiborne that if that was the case, he would again resist Wynkoop and would probably be under arrest when he returned.

Thus, this was indeed the case and Wynkoop ordered the American forces to charge into the village where the sacking began. Walker, however, ordered his men to have nothing to do with such conduct. "High words ensued with Wynkoop, during which Walker denounced him as a coward." Walker was placed under arrest and the whole party returned to the castle. His letter to his brother continued:

> Sept 5th. On yesterday I returned from an expedition which was gotten up by Col Comdg for the purpose of pillaging the Town of Hollacingo I took measures to prevent it and succeeded in preventing it for which I was ordered under arrest by Col Wynkoop I told him I would not obey his arrest until I returned my company to the Castle without further strain upon my Reputation that I was fully satisfied that his object was to pillage—the disgrace of which he hopes to … upon me; I told him that I desired no such reputation as would be gained by charging at full speed into a defenseless town to frighten women & children with drawn sabres and in violation of Gen Scott's orders which was to treat unoffending inhabitants who are not found in arms with civility and above all things to respect private property.[214]

Sergeant Myers commented:

> It was astonishing to see with what coolness our captain acted under the circumstances while the abuses were being heaped upon him saying that he was not fit to command a company that he could not understand an order that was given to him & Our Captain told him Sir I am not allowed to draw my sabre or my pistol but Sir you are a damned coward & left him.[215]

It was ironic that Walker's imprisonment by the Mexicans following his capture during the Mier Expedition was linked by an oft-repeated legend stating that after Walker was captured at Mier he was imprisoned at Perote. During his captivity he buried a dime under a flagpole and stated he would someday return with a victorious American army and reclaim it. This never happened. Walker himself, when applying for a pension from the Texas Republic for his Mier imprisonment, personally had the statement that he was imprisoned at Perote stricken from the record. Thus was the Mier myth so strong within Walker's own lifetime. However, while Walker was never a prisoner of the Mexicans at Perote, he was arrested there and was a prisoner of Colonel Wynkoop.

During Walker's arrest, Claiborne was given command of the company. In his memoirs Claiborne wrote that Walker drew up charges and specifications against Wynkoop and sent them to Gen. Franklin Pierce[216] to be forwarded to General Scott.

Charges against Col. Wynkoop

Xerox copies of these charges and specifications came to hand from a private collector.[217] They were witnessed by six captains and four lieutenants of the Pennsylvania Volunteers as well as Surg. John T. Lamar and Asst. Surg. Thomas Bunting[218] and two lieutenants (including Claiborne) of the Riflemen.

The charges against Francis M. Wynkoop of the 1st Pennsylvania Volunteers, Commanding the Department of Perote, were:

> Cowardice—On the morning of June 20, 1847 at La Hoya Pass did, "Shamefully retreat for the distance of about two and a half miles with the command of three hundred effective men immediately upon the appearance of between fifty and seventy of the Enemy to the extreme mortification of the men and officers under his command."

> Also, he was accused of "raising false alarms and causing unnecessary excitement in his Garrison and thus destroying all confidence that should exist between Troops and their commander." On July 3, 1847 Colonel Wynkoop did "assert most positively, that, he saw a force of three hundred men near the Castle of Perote, and further that most positively there was about one hundred infantry and one hundred mounted men which proved to be false entirely and without foundation as they could not be seen by any person and no footprint could be seen on any roads or in any of the fields and the Plains where he asserted he saw them."

This could indicate that Wynkoop may have been drinking too much, as implied by other previous events.[219]

> "Partially and unjustifiable interference in the distribution of Quarters to the Troops in the Garrison" was charged against him. The document cites the Wynkoop assigned three of the officers to rooms on the second floor of the Castle to the noncommissioned officers and privates of Company A, 3d Artillery and did refuse to allow the quartermaster to appropriate them either for the benefit of the sick and even soldiers fit for duty.

Specifically, Walker's charges (with Claiborne's approval) detailed that Wynkoop issued an order to remove one of Walker's sick from Claiborne's quarters. The soldier was so ill that he soon died.

Wynkoop was further charged with "disregarding all reports of the Officer of the Day" who reported, from time to time, the inefficiency of the Police of the Garrison as well as other abuses and that he neglected to take "such measures as were necessary to promote the health of the troops and provide for the comforts of the sick under his command."

These charges were received at General Scott's headquarters and were labeled, apparently by Scott's aide, as "Charges and Specifications against Col. F. M. Wynkoop Pa Vol, Gov Depart Perote by S H Walker Capt. Co C, Rifle Regt." Then in a note, (signed by Winfield Scott), "So much of the within as relates to the Hospital at Perote, referred to D. Lawson, Surgeon General."[220] No further action was taken.

Conditions at Perote

In his memoirs, Claiborne recalled that the fortress at Perote had two 300-feet-deep wells and several cisterns as well as a spout in the moat from which poured water from the mountains.[221] But there were "no efforts at real sanitation; the two wells were permitted to be used as a cesspool and became a horrid deposit; the gray vermin invaded everywhere; the place took on such a degree of infection that it could be plainly noticed more than a mile to leeward." Those who were well, refused to carry out the dead for burial, and Walker had to raid a guerrilla-stronghold area to bring back prisoners to bury the dead.[222]

Captured guerrillas would have more than one use for the Riflemen: "The gallant Captain Walker has commenced his work of retaliation on the guerrillas. On the morning of the 8th inst. [June 8] he started with his command from Perote on an expedition some distance into the interior. During the expedition he succeeded in capturing nineteen guerrillas[223] and an alcade—he has, employed them in cleaning the streets and sinks."[224]

October 1847

On the morning of October 4, Gen. Joseph Lane arrived at Perote with reinforcements bound for Puebla, then under threat of attack. General Lane ordered Walker released from arrest and placed him in command of all mounted men. Lane had received word that Gen. Santa Anna was rumored to be going toward Puebla with several thousand cavalry and some artillery. Lane was to proceed to Puebla and support Col. Thomas F. Childs's forces there.

General Lane was well liked by his men. Sergeant Myers said: "Every officer & soldier … (knew) his good qualities towards them. He is one of the pleasantest Gen. I ever saw in all my life. Any man can approach him with ease to himself & be as much at home as if it was one of his comrades."[225] General Lane brought a pair of Colt's new pistols with him, and when he arrived at Perote—where Walker was stationed—he personally gave them to the captain.

In a letter to his brother Jonathan Thomas, he mentioned how delighted he was with them and how effective the new Walker Colts were. He wrote: "They are as effective as the common rifle at one hundred yards and superior to a musket at two hundred yards."[226] Although he did not mention it, along in the case with the two presentation pistols was a special Walker powder flask. The presentation Walker flasks had an image of two crossed Walker Colts embossed on them.[227]

But Walker would have had only an afternoon and evening to try his new pistols. He was so excited about his new revolvers that he wrote his brother at 10 p.m. that night (October 4) about his marvelous new pistols; he even misdated his letter October 5, as indicated by his writing that General Lane was leaving the next day.[228] General Lane brought Captain Walker his pistols to him sometime after his arrival at Perote at 11 a.m., October 4,[229] but the next day at 9 a.m.,[230] it would be Sam Walker who would be leaving—in command of all General Lane's mounted men.

Gen. Joseph Lane. (Photograph in the public domain)

The following is a transcription of Walker's last letter:

Castle of Perote
October 5th 1847
10 P. M.

Dear Brother
I write in haste to inform you that I leave here tomorrow under command of General Lane in command of three other companies of Cavalry with the expectation of fighting Gen. Santa Anna at the pass of Pinon about fifty miles from this place. He is said to have a force of eight thousand men. But I must confess that I have some doubts about his meeting us voluntarily our force being upwards of three thousand men. We will move light with as few wagons as possible.

A rumour has just reached us that Santa Anna has just left his position on the main road and gone to the City of Orizaba. In this event I think Gen. Lane will follow him untill he either fights or disperses his force, if we pass him he will probably pass down on the Orizaba Road to Vera Cruz and make some demonstrations against Vera Cruz or some other point on the line of our operation. Santa Anna seems determined not to make peace and seems disposed to continue the war under all circumstances. I look upon this determination as one of the most fortunate events that could transpire. As it will leave us the alternative of taking military possession of the country; which will finally result in the Annexation of Mexico and open a new and extensive field for the display of American genius and enterprise. I think Santa Anna's race is nearly run. Jack Hays will soon be here with his Regt, of Rangers and I have no doubt that Santa Anna will be in a tight place. If I had my revolving pistols I should feel strong hopes of capturing him or killing him. I have written three times to the different officers at Vera Cruz to forward them and two commands have come up since they arrived at Vera Cruz but I have no hope of getting them until Jack Hays comes up. I have allso made repeated applications to go for them but without success. My company however is well drilled in saber exercise and use the rifle very well. My company is reduced by deaths and discharges to seventy men but this is by far the largest number of effective men of any company in the service [of mounted men].

I have written to you several times giving you all particulars of matters and things in general but I doubt very much whether you have received anything from me or not, if not you will learn by the bearer of this everything of interest.

I shall forward allso by A. West who has been discharged for disability the amt. due Wesson for the Rifle which I have not heard of since you wrote to me about them and will forward you a draft for the amt. due you as soon as practicable. I have, however, almost made up my mind to send David home, as he is in bad health and has been for some time past, the result of home sickness in a great measure I have no doubt. He has been but little service to me thus far, and nothing but his honesty and attachment to me would induce me to keep him with me any longer. He desires to have his best wishes sent to you all. I gave him his choice to return home or go on with me. He says that he would like very well to go home but does not wish to leave me for fear something may happen to me.

I have just received a pair of Colts Pistols which he sent to me as a present, there is not an officer who has seen them but what speaks in the highest terms of them and all of the Cavalry officers are determined to get them if possible. Col. Harney says they are the best arm in the world. They are as effective as the common rifle at one hundred yards. Everybody is allso pleased with Wessons Rifle and are anxious to obtain them.

My love and best wishes to Mother and Relatives, Mr. Smith, and all enquiring friends and be assured of my high regards, etc., in haste.

S. H. Walker

P. S. I have been one month under arrest by Col. F. N. Wynkoop the cowardly creature who was the first to retreat since the commencement of the war and that from an insignificant force of the enemy. Gen. Lane has ordered me to duty and given the command of three other companies not withstanding the Cols, protest. I asked for a court of enquiry which Gen. Lane would not grant for want of time.[231]

On that morning of October 5, under General Lane's orders, Walker—with his new revolvers in his saddle holsters—would gallop out of Perote Fortress with his command, in search of Gen. Santa Anna's army. Five days later, he would find it.

CHAPTER 10

The Death of Capt. Samuel H. Walker

Lt. Thomas Claiborne gave this description of Samuel Walker while serving with him:

> His figure was spare, slightly rounded shoulders, his weight 145, hair sandy, beard reddish, eyes blue and penetrating, manner grave, not communicative. I never saw him drink or play cards. He appeared at his best when on horseback he eagerly led his company in search of a fight.[1]

After his death, some of his men commented:

> War was his element, the bivouac his delight, and the battle-field his play-ground, his perfection and inspiration; he could fight and chase the guerillas all day, and dance the highland fling at night; he was a splendid horseman and unsurpassed for firm riding and endurance.[2]

An unknown officer of the Pennsylvania Regiment, possibly the previously mentioned Lieutenant Goff, who said he was an intimate friend of Walker, wrote:

> I wish to give you Captain Walker's character—He was a carpenter, and one of the most unassuming and feeling men that I have ever come across, with the highest notions of right, and not the fire-eater that people suppose at home. He had more feeling for those poor Mexicans than any officer I have seen in the army; and he would not allow one of his men to impose on them with impunity. He said they were ground down by their rulers and it was a pity to oppress them more. He never exercised any of this summary justice on them, that you see in the papers, and the only instance in which he shot any … prisoners was at Sante Fe when he caught a parcel of them who had murdered some Americans who had been left sick on the road, and he shot six of them … General Scott told him he had done perfectly right.[3]

Upon Gen. Joseph Lane's arrival in the late morning at Perote on October 4, he ordered Walker released from arrest and, as previously mentioned, placed him in command of all mounted men in his force: Capt. John Loyall's Georgia Dragoons, a small unit under Captain Besanson of Natchez and another small number under Captain Lewis of Louisiana. But according to Claiborne, they were "raw and unused to guerrilla fighting." In all they numbered 185 men with 57 men from Walker's Company C divided into squadrons as the core.[4] According to Claiborne, Walker was "full of joy" as he prepared to lead his mounted troops into battle.[5] Lane had received word that General Santa Anna was advancing toward Puebla with several

Captain Samuel H. Walker. (Photograph in the public domain)

thousand cavalry and some artillery. Lane was ordered to proceed to Puebla and support Col. Thomas F. Childs's forces there.

A reliable spy brought the information that Santa Anna was at nearby Huamantla with 4,000 cavalry, 100 artillery men, 8 artillery pieces, 20 odd cargoes of ammunition, and 70 infantry. Santa Anna had heard that the American forces would march directly to Puebla and bypass Huamantla. According to the spy, he planned to leave 500 lancers early the next day and leave some infantry to guard the rear of his ammunition and artillery train.

According to Sergeant Myers, Lane's force left Perote on October 5 at 9 a.m. encamping that night at Tafraewalthe (Tepiacualca). On the 6th, it arrived at the hacienda of Veareas and encamped there for the night. On the 7th, under heavy rain, the force proceeded to a hacienda, San Antonio Samaris—about two and half leagues from the town of Nopaluca—and encamped.[6]

Claiborne recalled when the American force left Perote:

> It passed the warm springs west of Mt. Pizzarre called Tepeagualpa, a most desolate place; further on camped at Ojo de Aqua, a fine spring and improved country, and camped on the evening of October 8th at the large hacienda of Tamaris. We had only four miles further to enter Nopaluca and eight miles beyond it, to enter the fortified pass of the Penal; off to the right at the distance of twelve miles, lay the town of Huamantla.[7]

According to one newspaper account, General Lane sent a spy to the town of Huamantla that night, having received information that Santa Anna was there the day before. The next morning the spy returned and reported that the cavalry of the enemy had left town, leaving behind six pieces of artillery. Santa Anna's plan was to attack Lane's force between Perote and Puebla. Lane, with about 3,300 men—including Wynkoop's Pennsylvanians and Walker's combined mounted force—and with seven artillery pieces, left Perote for Puebla via Huamantla, hoping to drive off the Mexican rear guard and attack Santa Anna's main force.[8]

Orders were immediately issued for the cavalry, under Captain Walker; Col. Willis A. Gorman's regiment; Maj. Folliott T. Lally's battalion; Colonel Wynkoop's regiment; Capt. Charles Taylor's battery; and Capt. Samuel P. Heitzelman's battalion, to be in readiness to march for the town, leaving the train (at hacienda of Tamaris) with about eleven hundred men and two pieces of artillery, under the command of Col. John Brough.[9]

After a breakfast of hard crackers and coffee the next morning, Lane placed a guard for their baggage and at 10 a.m. began their preparation to leave for Huamantla with about two thousand men and Captain Walker leading the van.[10]

Walker convinced General Lane that he could attack the reduced troops in the city with his cavalry and keep them under attack until Lane could arrive with his infantry. An impatient Walker, with Claiborne at his side, led their cavalry to just outside Huamantla.

The following was the report in the *Flag of Freedom* newspaper:

> At 11 o'clock the whole moved off in fine style. The cavalry were ordered to keep some distance in advance. We had gone about two miles when Capt. Walker determined to push on at a gallop and surprise the enemy. For five miles the cavalry moved at a very rapid pace until we reached the outskirts of the town, when Capt. Walker gave orders to form fours and close up. He then entered a very narrow lane, both sides of which were lined with thick maguey,[11] so narrow in many places that the sets of fours had to be broken and the column moved by twos. On we went at a trot, until the lane opened into the main street leading to the plaza, when, in column of four, the order was given to draw sabres and charge. Then rose a wild yell, and such a charge! The flashing of the sabres, the thundering of the horses' feet over the paved streets, were enough to strike terror into the hearts of the enemy. Two of their cannon were pointed up the street, another pointed down a cross street, and the fuse was burning in it. The terrified artillerymen moved merely to the sides of the houses, at whom our men made their thrusts and right and left cuts, killing many in this manner.[12]

Santa Anna had left a few guards over the artillery. Many Mexican artillerymen were sabered as the Mounted Riflemen galloped into the plaza.

The eyewitness account continued:

> Our men separated into small parties, pursuing them beyond the town, on the outskirts of which a good many were killed. Capt. Walker went beyond the town for the purpose of overtaking the artillery which had left the place. Capt. Lewis went in another direction for the same purpose. Capt. Besancon was ordered to follow the road to see if the artillery could be overtaken. In the mean time, most of our men having gone in pursuit, Capt. Loyall with a few men, assisted by Adj. Claiborne, secured some fifty or sixty prisoners at their quarters, together with their arms, &c. Lieut. Claiborne then proceeded to secure and bring up the plaza the cannon [three pieces] we had captured. Capt. Walker returned about this … [illegible] … brother of the general's, and a lieutenant; these he delivered to Capt. Walker. Lieut. Claiborne, assisted by Corporal Hescock and private [Sergeant] Myers and one or two others, limbered up the six pounder and brought it to the plaza; leaving it limbered up and the mules standing in it, and returning to get the four pounder [300 yards past the Plaza] the lieutenant was in the act of bringing it up when he was forced to leave it by the appearance of all Santa Anna's cavalry, 2500 strong.

Meanwhile the approaching major American infantry force, about a mile and a half from the city, beheld a large force of Mexican lancers approaching from their left. One of the soldiers recalled:

> They [the lancers] made a most magnificent appearance, dressed as they were in red and green uniforms … Their long and bright lances reflected like a sea of diamonds. The crimson pennons of their lances fluttered gracefully from their staffs, while above the rest was the national flag of Mexico …
>
> The lancers dashed toward the city well ahead of the American infantry.

After Claiborne had prepared the captured cannon for action, Corporal Tilghman of Company C, (Rifles), brought up a small howitzer. Private Dusenbery, of Company C, took a lieutenant of artillery prisoner and turned him over to Surgeon Reynolds. "By this time a good many of our men had returned and were in the plaza in scattered groups, when the lancers charged them suddenly and unexpectedly."

Walker, with 14 of the Riflemen, had been pursuing enemy artillerymen who were escaping with two guns. Riding a cream-colored horse, Walker had already returned to the plaza and was collecting some of his men. He and others had captured and disarmed 70 Mexican infantrymen and locked them in their quarters.

Inside the city, the Riflemen received the lancers who began firing at the first Americans they encountered. Then suddenly there was firing from in and beyond the plaza. Fearing Santa Anna's return with a main force, Claiborne ordered the 10 men with him to mount and prepare for action. A regiment of enemy lancers charged down the narrow street toward the plaza.

Walker's men received them with great bravery, and kept the plaza with the exception of a few with the captain, who retired by a street leading west from the plaza—the enemy close on them at a charge; he turned the next street to his left, while the enemy, seeing the 4-pounder, rushed to take it. It was fortunate for the few men with Captain Walker that they saw this piece, for at the very next corner a still larger force met him; he wheeled and dashed swiftly past the rear of those who had cut him off from the plaza, and again entered it. Here the men dismounted and occupied the convent yard, together with a large house on the corner of the square.

Walker, firing at the enemy with his new Colts, led his 15 Riflemen down the street toward Claiborne who was preparing to make a stand at the plaza. There were now some two dozen mounted men formed in fours. With Walker and Claiborne leading them, they rode away from the plaza, turning left down a narrow side street. They continued uphill on this street, passed the building where the enemy infantry was imprisoned, and turned left again back toward the plaza, possibly hoping to exit the town where they came in and join up with General Lane's forces.

As they turned the corner, they suddenly beheld in the distance an even larger force of lancers blocking their way. Walker ordered "right about wheel" and all made an about face. Walker and Claiborne rushed to the head of galloping Riflemen, and headed back down the narrow street from which they had just come. Claiborne yelled to turn back to the right and surprise the lancers between them and the plaza. Being more occupied with reclaiming artillery, the enemy would not expect an attack.

Walker ordered "Draw sabers" and the Riflemen emerged from the narrow street and turned sharply right back toward the plaza some 300 yards away. They rode full tilt toward the two rear companies of the 1st Regiment of Lancers. Cutting and thrusting they rushed through the startled enemy without losing a single man. They then rushed through the gate by the convent and dismounted, filling the inner courtyard with their horses.

Claiborne found the 6-pounder cannon he had previously brought to the gate in the street by the convent yard. With the help of a corporal (Tilghman), he unlimbered the cannon and prepared to fire the piece. It was apparently already loaded as its fuse seemed to be in place. Seizing an extra round and holding it under his arm, Claiborne was determined to get off at least a second shot at the approaching lancers through which they had just ridden. Walker assisted, using his pistol powder flask to sprinkle powder on the vent of the cannon to ensure its firing.

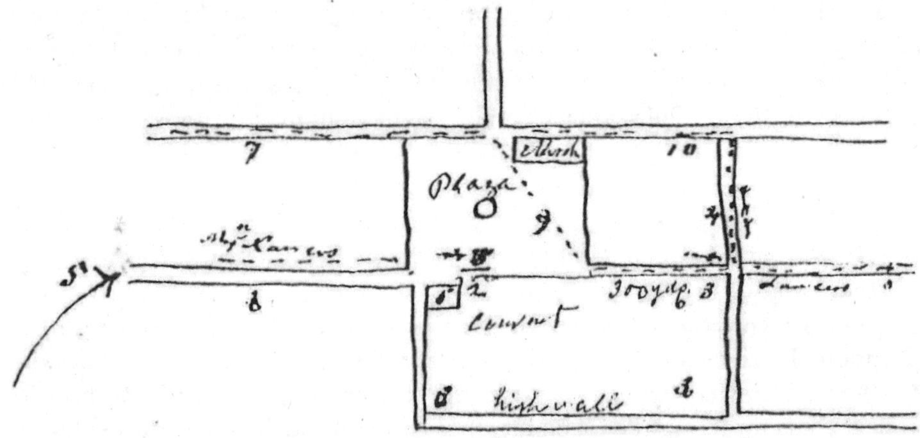

Claiborne's diagram of the situation. No. (1) a church; (2) wide gate; (3) convent and high wall; (4) 70 captured infantry; (5) road leading into the plaza, followed by Walker; (6) lancers forming; (7) road Walker followed out of town after two pieces of artillery, and by which he reentered the plaza; (8) six-pounder in front of the gate to convent; (9) route of Walker when he reentered the plaza, followed by a regiment of lancers; (10) his about wheel from the head of a new regiment, retraced his way, and charged on two rear companies of the 1st regiment, entering the plaza, and seized the gate of the convent yard. At No. 6 he rode over and dispersed the 500 lancers left as rear guard, killing many; at No. 4 he captured and disarmed 70 infantry, piled up the arms on the pavement and locked them in the Quartel. At the points where the artillery was, he sabered many artillery men, while two pieces ran off by No. 7 Street leading to the Penal, these he followed with some 14 men.[13] (Southern Historical Collection, University of North Carolina)

Claiborne waited and watched the lancers advance "with tall shakos and gaudy uniform, their lance points gleaming brightly." Now 60 yards away, the Mexicans saw Claiborne and his artillery piece. The lancer column struggled to part so that the shot would pass down the lane thus opened. Claiborne quickly forced the trail of the cannon to one side so that a ricochet from wall to wall would do more damage. He planned on using the muzzle flash of his dragoon pistol to fire the cannon. His men called out to him to "Fire! Fire!" But his pistol misfired. Calling to one of his men to throw him another pistol, he tried again. The pistol fired but the cannon did not.

Running desperately to escape surely being lanced, Claiborne darted back into the courtyard but was struck in the right thigh by one of the crazed, kicking and biting horses inside the courtyard. He scrambled back on his feet and backed up an outside stairway to an upper room. But the lancers began to withdraw. Lane had arrived with the main force.

Claiborne, looking down from his balcony, saw Walker in the gateway by the convent in the plaza. Suddenly a musket shot struck Walker.

One newspaper reported: "We are assured upon an authority we cannot question that Capt. Walker was struck in the head by one shot, and another in the back, the ball going quite through him. He never spoke, having died gallantly."[14]

Claiborne wrote:

> I now observed Capt. Walker with his left foot planted on the stone sill of the gateway, his hand placed on the side of it, and his head extended and gazing to his right along the high wall, towards the gun before alluded to, which now the enemy were firing at us; so stooping, he was shot from the left, the ball striking him just below the left shoulder, and passing through his body; he fell; a cry of horror went up. "Capt. Walker is killed."[15]

Col. Albert G. Brackett. (contentdm.ad.umbc.edu)

Col. Albert G. Brackett of Lane's Brigade wrote: "Captain Walker wished to preserve the cannon which he had captured, exposed himself. He was struck almost at the same instant by two escopeta balls, one of which passed through his head and the other through his breast. He fell back and died instantly."[16]

Sergeant Myers of Company C wrote:

> About this time Capt. Walker moved out of the gateway for the purpose of giving orders when he was fired upon from the right of the street one ball entering his back coming through his breast—He immediately fell & some of his men ran out & carried him in—His last words were to this effect—Men. Fight to the last, I am dying, do not lose time in attending to me. Go & tell Capt. Lewis not to surrender this place as long as there is a man breathing. He expired in a few minutes.[17]

There are several so-called eyewitness accounts of Walker's death and his alleged last utterances. However, the following from a physician who examined Walker's body leaves little doubt that the wound to his head penetrated his brain and killed him instantly; there would have been no last words.[18]

J. Jacob Oswandel, a private in William F. Smalls's Company C, 1st Pennsylvania Volunteers, who wrote of his wartime experience, was a close friend of Dr. James Reynolds[19] (Oswandel's family physician) who tended to Walker when he was shot. Oswandel wrote:

> Captain Walker was changing his position to a churchyard surrounded by a high stone wall to preserve the two cannon that he had captured, when at the same time a … Mexican from the window or housetop, fired and shot him through the head while another one shot him through the breast … The doctor also states that the ball passed through the right side of his forehead, penetrating to the base of the brain and the escopet ball passed through the lungs.[20]

One account published in a Texas newspaper in 1848, apparently written by an infantryman, gives one more bit of information. In a story entitled "The Correct

Account of the Death of Captain Walker" the soldier recalled that Sam was "shot from the window of a house from which a white flag had been displayed on his [Walker's] entrance into town. One ball entered his head through his eye, another his heart, and a third lodged in his hip."[21] This observer could have very well seen Walker's body and saw three wounds which could have resulted from the four projectiles of one buck and ball round:

> The musket ball passed under his left shoulder blade and the small buckshot round penetrated his right forehead and base of the brain [in a downward path indicating he was shot from above as suggested].[22] The other wound, possibly from buckshot was observed in his hip. If so, Walker was probably killed by one buck and ball round—commonly used by solders of both sides. It had one .69 round lead musket ball which apparently passed through his chest while one of the three .32 buckshot [fixed on top of the musket ball] hit Sam in the head. Another buckshot projectile hit him in the hip.

Reynolds omitted mention of the hip wound, but he would have been more interested in those that he deemed fatal.

Claiborne wrote:

> He fell and a cry arose, "Walker is killed." He was a most popular commander and his death brought a crash of emotions, from the relief of just being saved from sure death to the agony of learning that their commander had just been killed. His body was carried by his men into the convent yard and wrapped in linen.[23]

Another one of Walker's men wrote:

> Capt. Walker was a man universally beloved. No one out of our company could imagine the loss we sustained. He was a father to us in his care, and one of the very best I have met with in my walks through life. Often would he be up two-thirds of the night, when we were on a scout, to see if his men were comfortably quartered, and the horses taken care of, and in the morning, he would be as fresh and vigorous as any of those who had slept undisturbed all the night.[24]

"The same fellow [who Claiborne thought had shot Walker], a few minutes later took a crack at me," Claiborne wrote, "As I stood on the little balcony, the great ounce ball passed the bridge of my nose so very close, it caused sparks to shine."[25] This may indicate that the shooter was also firing from a second story position at roughly the same height as Claiborne on his balcony.

Company C lost one captain, and 18 soldiers killed, wounded, captured or missing in action. With Walker's death, Captain Lewis made a detail of eight men, who went out and brought the 6-pounder and placed it in the gate. "The enemy menaced us [The Mounted Riflemen] a long time, and fired the 4 pounder six or eight times, loaded with grape, one of the discharges shattered the leg of Frederick Raborg, Capt. Walker's interpreter … Capt. Lewis formed the men after Walker fell and by his energy and address assisted materially to suppress disorder."

Walker's slave David was with him in this battle. He was very close to Walker and was beside him and "fanned his fevered brow." When Walker died, David "cried like a child."[26] Soon, David would join Walker in death.

The Austin, Texas *Daily American Star* of November 5, 1847, reported, "Surgeon Lamar[27] who was in the first charge by the side of Walker, was in the plaza when another charge was made, and was saved by the devoted act of Captain Walker's slave David, who caught a lance aimed at him and received it himself. He died in a few minutes. …"[28]

David enjoyed being with Walker on his mounted missions but stayed in the rear when the fighting was ongoing. Walker wrote that summer at Perote, "David has been in bad health for some time and I shall send him home the first opportunity as I fear he will not recover in this climate as it does not agree with him."[29]

Later, when Sam's body was buried for the first time, the coffin had to be remade and David was probably placed in the smaller coffin since both bodies were removed to Perote in November.[30] Walker and David were probably temporarily buried there as Walker's body did not get to Galveston until late December. An unsung hero, David today probably lies in an unmarked grave at Perote while Walker would be interred in four different graves.

Santa Anna's Report of the Battle of Huamantla

Writing to the Minister of War and Marine on October 13, Santa Anna reported that he proposed to attack the American convoy out of Veracruz. He said the enemy camped the night of October 8, between Nopalucan and Guapastla and he planned to attack their rear guard at Pinal when they least expected it. He had begun moving his army for this attack.

> I saw from the watch tower that the enemies train instead of prosecuting its march, was standing towards the place in which I had left all my artillery, camp equipage and stores [Huamantla] … I countermarched with all the celerity I could to meet him. But before I could come up with him, his vanguard had already possessed itself of the place, and its principal buildings and although I attacked him, my columns entering the town itself, yet it was not possible for me to dislodge him from his positions with the dragoons. … In the engagement the enemy lost his commander of cavalry, one officer. … Yet he [the Americans] only succeeded in capturing two pieces of artillery … the four remaining ones were fortunately saved.[31]

Reaction to Walker's Death

Many sought revenge for a cowardly act of shooting the young officer from a house that was flying a white flag. Many simply called his death a murder. His men resolved from that moment on they would take no prisoners, and death to all Mexicans found with firearms in their hands.[32]

One soldier wrote: "General Santa Anna fled to Huamantla, where another battle was fought, and he had to flee again." An unnamed infantry lieutenant wrote to his parents what happened after an officer named Walker was killed in battle:

> General Lane … told us to avenge the death of the gallant Walker, to take all we could lay hands on. And well and fearfully was his mandate obeyed. Grog shops were broken open first, and then, maddened with liquor, every species of outrage was committed. Old women and girls were stripped of their clothing—and many suffered still greater outrages. Men were shot by dozens … their property, churches, stores and dwelling houses ransacked.
>
> Dead horses and men lay about pretty thick, while drunken soldiers, yelling and screeching, were breaking open houses or chasing some poor Mexicans who had abandoned their houses and fled for life. Such a scene I never hope to see again. It gave me a lamentable view of human nature … and made me for the first time ashamed of my country.[33]

One eyewitness recalled that Lane's men exhibited much emotion when they heard of Walker's death and of his company only 12 were uninjured. Colonel Brackett remembered:

> After taking a great many prisoners who had concealed themselves in the houses, we marched to the plaza, where lay a number of dead bodies … All around me was desolation and ruin. Fine houses were, many of them, torn apart … In the arsenal a large amount of ammunition was found, which was by General Lanes's order destroyed. A fine fountain in the plaza was filled with gunpowder which rendered the water unfit for use, and it [the gunpowder] was scattered on the ground to the depth of two to three inches. In this time soldiers were stalking about, smoking cigars which they had taken, unconscious of danger.[34]

His death was mourned throughout the country.

Around this time Lieutenant Claiborne became aware of a slanderous campaign to discredit Captain Walker. Being his friend, he took it upon himself to put the facts as he knew them in a letter to Col. Timothy P. Andrews, Paymaster:

> Vera Cruz, Nov 18th 1847
> To Col T P Andrews
>
> Dear Sir
> Having recd letters from the United States, which state that the conduct of the late Captain Saml H. Walker of Co C, Mtd Riflemen have been falsely represented before the country. I have deemed it due as his second officer no less his friend, to state some facts for the information of his friends. As you are about to visit that part of the country where Captain Walker was born and raised, I address you this letter which you may give to his family.
>
> It was not unknown to Capt W. that letters written from Japlapa had misrepresented what occurred in the skirmish that took place at Santa Fe in May, last. He is said to have hung an Alcalde and summarily shot seventeen prisoner. I was not present myself but I heard him say

repeatedly that it was false, and that he intended to demand a Court of Inquiry, as soon as he joined his regiment.

When the Army under General Scott passed up to Puebla in May, Last, Capt. W. requested to be left at Perote for the purpose of recruiting his horses little expecting to remain there longer than a few weeks. He devoted his energies entirely to his command, drilling daily. In a short time, he was ready to proceed to General headquarters, & although he requested to be ordered forward, he never received orders to that effect. Col. Wynkoop frequently sent him upon scouting expedition, and the conduct of the men became a theme of [illegible]. On the 20th of June, last, he attacked a large Guerilla force at the pass of La Hoya and although he had but forty five men in all he fought & scattered several hundred Guerillas who had assembled to attack Genl Cadwalader. I know that Col Wynkoop was distant a mile & a half from the scene of action with his infantry force and that Capt Walker fought the enemy forty seven minutes. True, Capt Blake of the 2d Drags & the Pa Vols under Col W pursued the enemy, yet the enemy were swept before they came in sight. I make this statement because I understand that holding higher rank than Capt Walker have claimed the honor of the skirmish. A through the Town of Las Vegas the Second Pennsylvania Volunteers (as I learned at the time) at the train passed set fire to many houses which were consumed. Capt W deprecated this reached Jalapa in the strongest terms, & not a single man of his Company assisted in then violation, and yet Captain Walker has the credit of these disgraceful proceedings.

Hearing that Maj Lally's command was seriously annoyed by the Guerillas, Col Wynkoop resolved on or about 23r, last August to take Capt Walker's Company & came two or three hundred Infantry & go to his relief. The command and heard Maj Lally say many were "drunk."

Only one man of Co C was drunk and he recd the usual punishment as for the Infantry I have not to speak of their conduct as I have to do with them. On the 26th Augt Col Wynkoop took command of Capt W's Company. Capt Loyall's Co Georgia Vols, Capt Besancon's La Vols and made a rapid search to the Town Of Coatefree charging for the last three miles at a furious gallop. We found no enemy, not a shot was fired. After passing through the town we returned to the Plaza. Col Wynkoop was just coming out of the Alcalde's store. Meeting me exclaimed that he had caught the Alcalde but he had escaped. He ordered me to search for him, & declared he would hang him as soon as caught. He further ordered me to break into all the houses & search for arms and horses. I proceeded with a detail of men to execute these orders, but I soon found that some persons not connected with the service were pillaging; that some of Capt W's Company had left the ranks for the same purpose. I returned to the Col and reported these facts. Capt Walker reported also the same facts adding that the plunderers alleged thay acted by Col Wynkoop's orders. I was replied to in this way. "Go & report if the will burn" (Lt. Breese of our own Regt heard this order).

At the time Col Wynkoop was sitting in the Alcalde's store his orderly was behind the counter and everything torn down from the shelves. Capt Walker entreated his men to desist at last so violent had the matters gone that Capt W drew his sabre and with the flat of it beat several of his men It was impossible for him to see all that occasion as the men scattered all over the Town. Bering ordered by Col Wynkoop to break open the door of the church in the Plaza and place a sentry in the steeple, I was accompanied by Capt Walker, We had no sooner entered there on looking down by Capt W perceived a man taking something from the wall. He drew his sabre & advancing on him would have killed him, but for the man's haste to escape.

The whole command returned to Jalapa that same evening. Capt Walker was full of anger & declared his determination to charge against Col Wynkoop for what happened. The next day Capt Walker was ordered to command a party which was sent to look for news of a little place one or two miles from Jalapa (the name I forget). Several persons accompanied the expedition to steal & plunder. Among them Smith, the Colonel's interpreter. I saw Walker's determination to restrain all persons from wrong. He searched the church for arms and powder and while doing detected Smith in the act of robbing the Church of a silver cross or a cross having silver upon it. He arrested him & reported him to Col Wynkoop, yet nothing was done by the Col. Capt Walker declared to his men that they had disgraced themselves, held up to them the orders of the Comdg General and assured them that he would bring them before a military commission if they dared to transgress a second time. Walker returned to Perote Castle and on thy 20th day of Sept, last, was ordered to accompany Col W to Jalacingo and Alto Longo, two small villages to the north of Perote. I declined to go mySelf and gave as a reason to Capt Walker that I had heard several say the "towns were to be sacked and the silver mines vented.' Appreciating this I was persuaded by Capt. W to remain in the Castle, I am not a single witness, but I have a hundred times heard Walker speak of it, so will Lt Breese Pa Vols, who was present, and this is true that Col W having arrived at a place some twelve miles more or less from Perote, ordered skirmishers to be thrown out and in this way advanced through a pine woods. He said to the officers that this was the camping ground of the Guerillas. Nothing was discovered and to all appearances nothing had ever been there, as there no signs of Cavalry or fire, nor any water within several miles. Satisfying himself, the Col proceeded to Jolacingo. As at Coatafee. He ordered Capt Walker to charge a distance of 3 miles although it was a mountain road and no enemy inn sight. Capt W proceeded leisurely. The Col repeated his order & started in a gallop. He Arrive a quarter and a half an hour at the Plaza before Walker. Major Besancon came to Capt W. and told he was by order of the Col placed in arrest. Capt W rode up to Col W and told him that he knew he worked to get command of a company but he should not have his to disgrace it so as he had done at Coatofee, He knew the object was to plunder defenseless villages, he had anticipated it and came prepared to prevent a similar disgrace upon the arms of his country, he would not obey his arrest until he returned to the Castle. Col Wynkoop replied that "he [Walker] was a d—d scoundrel." Capt W remarked that he had preferred charges of cowardice aganst him [Col Wynkoop] and everybody believed the truth of him. The discussion was very violent & blows were expected. The parties separated and Walker kept the command of his company. The next day he returned to Castle Perote & gave up the command to me. From that hour he was confined to his quarters in the Castle but until Gen Lane arrived about the 5th of Oct when Walker was placed in command of all the Cavalry with the Genl and Co C ordered to join his command. I will pass over many things and in further vindication of his memory state that at Huamantla he saved the lives of many Mexican soldiers as well as citizens of the place. Sixty prisoners I solemnly believe would never have received quarter had not Capt W exerted his utmost to save them very man fought against as under a black flag having for its device a "Deaths head and bones." These men afterwards escaped. Walker fell shot by an assassin from a house which displayed the White Flag. Let the Army judge who is to blame. Will any one know he was "cold blooded in murder" or "robbed" or committed "Sacrilege." I knew him well and I can truly declare that he was one of the most modest men in the Army & his morals were pure. He was temperate and a most humane man. Many of his men gone home who suffered long at the Castle from sickness. They will bear testimony to his tender kindness. They have also seen him protect Mexican citizens.

His generous & brave man has been attacked and, I learn made this object of the most scurrilous abuse by some newspaper editor. I have deemed it my duty to state the truth in his favor. I will add that there is little doubt I hope but a Court of Inquiry will investigate into all these things & discover who has acted wrong. There are many things to come to light that some will fear to say in public. As I was both the first lieutenant of his Company and his intimate friend, I will be pardoned for intruding myself. His character having been aspersed through malice or envy, it was but a simple act of justice to the dead to give the facts to his friends. Let them hurt whom they may.

Very respectfully
Yr Obt Svt
Thomas Claiborne
1st Lt Co. C, R.M.R.[35]

Colonel Andrews, although wary of Jonathan Thomas Walker's willingness to keep Claiborne's lengthy letter from publication, determined to send it to him with a caution.

Washington, December 15th 1847
J. Thomas Walker, Esq

Dear Sir
I met at Vera Cruz Lieut. Claiborne, the 1st Lieut. of your brother's Company who made to me verbally, the instance of the enclose statement as to the acts and character of his friend & Captain and expressed a wish that I should make them known by knowledge to his friends in the region. I was compelled to decline doing so as I had no official knowledge of his acts he not acted in connection with that part of the Army to which I was attached. But told him if he could commit his statements to writing I would hand them to you. Although we had in the Army & the city many such rumors as Lt Claiborne alludes to, which were to some degree found to be true, I an entirely satisfied for the statements others besides Lt C that the conduct of your gallant Brother was humane as well as laudable I now send you the statement, but some allegations of a strong character are made by Lt. C against officers who outrank him any publication of his letter would have him take to injury under the Articles of War for disrespect to his superiors. At the same time that I do not feel authorized to withhold his statement from you. I would urge that you do not make any publication of it for fear of injury officially a profoundly to your Brother however willing he may be to incur hazzard in defense of his action. I make this suggestion under belief that your Brother's character is not understood to require a defense.

Very respectfully
Your Obt Svt
T. P. Andrews[36]

Myths About Sam's Death

It is amazing how many false reports there were of Walker's demise. One had both of Walker's legs shot off by round shot.[37] Another had a more dramatic tale:

> But the gallant Walker after performing prodigies of valor, and feats of the most daring character, fell in single combat, pierced by the spear of an enraged father, who goaded to actual frenzy, by the death of his son, whose fall beneath the arm of Captain Walker he had just witnessed .... attacking the Captain with almost irresistible violence, plunged his spear into his body.[38]

Fictitious rendering of Walker's death. (Print in the public domain)

This fabrication was even illustrated with a well-known engraving.[39]

Another story circulated that a Mexican guerrilla chief lanced Walker from the back; however, while mortally wounded from the lance and with one leg shot off, Walker killed his attacker with two shots from his new Walker revolver.[40]

One wrote, "He was struck almost at the same time by two balls, one hit him in the forehead and the other pierced his breast; as he fell, he exclaimed, 'Boys, forward, don't flinch a foot, I know I am dying, but don't give way.'"

One story published in the Mexican–American War Veterans periodical, *The Vidette*, states "the brave Captain Samuel Walker was shot through the head from the roof of a building, and was prompt avenged by Sergeant Wilson, of the 4th Indiana volunteers."[41] Whether the sergeant had evidence that he had shot Walker's killer or one of the many who reacted to his death with a rampage and sacking of the city is not known.

David Haines, private, Company F, 6th U.S. Infantry, painted his version of Walker's death. In his unpublished, "Battle of Huamantla. Brilliant Victory and Capture of Mexican Artillery. Santa Anna again beaten, and two of his Aids made Prisoners. Gallant Conduct of our Mounted Riflemen and Dragoons and Death of the Heroic Captain Walker," Haines stated Walker was shot from a house that was flying the white flag, but was outside the walled compound and not only was he shot and killed, but his horse, as well.

An unpublished print by David Haines, an alleged eyewitness of Walker's death. (https://tinyurl.com/yauvnz7t)

The Assassin Story

The New Orleans *Daily Picayune* had an interesting item in its November 6, 1847, edition. It notes that, "The [Mexican] Government has decreed a curiously wrought spear to the man who killed Capt. Walker." This report came in the same edition that reported Walker was killed by an enraged father whose son the captain had killed in battle at Huamantla. Maybe the Mexicans honored someone who claimed he had killed Walker in retaliation of his son's death. The assassin story circulated soon after Sam's death.

Col. Albert G. Brackett, who described Sam's body previous to his burial, wrote in a letter to the Walker family in 1892:

> It is said that Captain Euallio of the Mexican Army knew Walker well, and taking deliberate aim shot him through the body from the effects of which he soon died—For this act he was promoted to the rank of major.[42]

The most interesting story of Sam being shot by an assassin was printed in a Texas newspaper six years after Walker's death. William E. Richards, a member of Walker's Company C, states that in Mexico at the time, the story was circulated that Walker was shot by a Captain Euallio of the Mexican Army who was promoted to major for his claim. A rank, Richards adds, Euallio "still holds in the Mexican army." But Richards states:

> The man who shot him [Walker] was an American by the name of Armitage, who was a deserter from our army, and was a prisoner in Perote Castle, about four weeks prior to the battle of Huamantla.

> This man Armitage took the name of Norryagway, and was made a major in the Mexican Army some two months after the death of Walker—while the undersigned [Richards] was a prisoner in their [the Mexicans] hands. He received his commission at the city of Salamenca, 45 miles from Querretaro, and about the same distance from Guanaxuata. There were present, at the time his promotion was announced in General Orders, three of Walker's men besides myself—Thos. H.
>
> Goslin, John McLean Collins, and Isaac P. Darlington:[43] all of whom can testify that Armitage received his promotion in consequence of his killing Walker.
>
> When your informant takes another trip to Mexico, if he will inquire the facts of General Francisco Parez, he will find that I am correct.[44]

Based on Claiborne's eyewitness account, Walker was shot while standing at the convent gate. It could have been anybody firing a musket using the buck and ball round common for both sides. For one buckshot to hit him in the hip and another in the head, it can be assumed that the shooter was within about 50 yards. They had to get close enough so that the buckshot would not spread out too much to be effective and the musket ball itself would still have some accuracy.

A Personal Epilogue for Sam Walker—His Horse

While he had been purchasing mounts for his men, Walker already had his own mount. On May 13, 1846, citizens of New Orleans presented him with Tornado, a bay gelding 5 years old and about 15 hands high with "great substance and vigor." This was the horse that Walker thought was lost when he rode at a full gallop in the dark of night into an iron picket fence in June 1847.[45]

Apparently, Tornado was rescued. After Walker's death in October 1847, a letter dated December 24, 1847, to Walker's brother Jonathan Thomas states that Tornado was alive and in the United States. Another report a month later indicates Tornado was on a plantation in Mississippi and "is now looking tolerably well but is not in a perfect healthy state." The letter does not indicate whether the horse was ill or injured. He was scheduled to be sent east to Jonathan Walker in the spring. These letters were from Harry T. Hays in New Orleans—brother of Walker's close friend, the commander of the Texas Rangers, Jack Hays. Harry Hays was making sure that Walker's horse would be taken care of.[46]

Walker's Four Graves

The monthly report of Company C of the Mounted Riflemen lists the casualties of that battle as:

> Killed in Action—Samuel H. Walker, Capt.; Joseph E. Merriken, Corp and Almon Tarbox, Pvt. Died of wounds—William B. Glanding, Corp (12 October) and Charles R. Meacham, Pvt. (26 October).[47]

Listed in other sources as Killed in Action is Walker's slave David.

The First Grave

As evening of that fatal day approached, the soldiers assembled in the Huamantla plaza and began placing the dead and wounded in wagons. Walker's body was carried back to the hacienda where the baggage was left. He was placed in a coach belonging to the Catholic priests at Huamantla.[48] At the hacienda the dead were laid out in a row in a room. One soldier said:

> I went in and there lay Walker, with dried blood in streams over his face, and his faithful servant David who was killed with him not far off. The other dead of Company C lay stretched out in their blue jackets, awaiting burial.[49]

There were no coffins with the army, so a large pit was dug for the dead. All except Walker—he was buried alone. A company of Ohio volunteers, under Captain Robinson, fired three volleys of musketry over his grave; Colonel Wynkoop read the funeral service. There Walker would be left "in silent repose" until retrieved later that month.[50]

On October 27, when the army returned to retrieve Sam's body, five men of Company C including Captain Walker and David were buried at hacienda San de Esora.[51] (Brackett called this hacienda San Antonio Tamaris.)

One soldier's drawings (Shannon's sketchbook), now in the University of Texas Special Collection, contain a sketch with ink wash over graphite of the burial place of Captain Walker.[52] There are five graves portrayed along with Captain Walker's grave. Brackett notes that all, save Walker, were buried in a mass grave. Apparently, the artist learned the number from the company that died from the battle (including

Shannon sketchbook drawing of Walker's first grave site. (Southern Historical Collection, University of North Carolina)

David) and painted that number of graves. Yet the background may as well be drawn from an eyewitness's memory.[53]

Oswandel wrote in his diary of the removal of Sam and David's bodies:

> Wednesday, October 27, 1847. This morning we left Napaluco at daylight, and took the back or *ciegro ruta* [blind road, so-called], and marched on until we came to the hacienda *San de Esora*, where we dug up the remains of Capt. Samuel H. Walker, who was killed at the battle of Huamantla, near this spot. He was wrapped up in fine linen and placed in a neat coffin which we brought with us from Puebla, and then placed into a wagon and brought him with us to Vera Cruz, from there to be shipped to Baltimore, Maryland, his native home.
>
> When the officer took the measurement of Capt. Walker's body when first buried, he took it too small and the carpenter made a botch of it; whereupon, Lieut. Wm. Clinton, of Co. H. First Regiment Pennsylvania Volunteers, off with his uniform coat, rolled up his sleeves and went to work and made him, Capt. Walker, a coffin himself. Lieut. Clinton is a carpenter, and I am informed hails from Southwark, Philadelphia, Pa. Lieut. S.D. Breece, of the same company, who is a blacksmith, entered a smithy and made nails for the coffin, and in about a half hour, the whole coffin was completed, and well finished. So much for Philadelphia's mechanics and Pennsylvania's volunteers.[54]

Walker's Second Grave

"The remains of the lamented Captain Walker and his faithful servant David were in the Castle of Perote on the 5th [November 5]—having been brought from Huamantla by order of Col. Wynkoop, and will be forwarded to the United States."[55]

In November, Claiborne was ordered back to Veracruz to bring with him the Walker Colt pistols and ammunition for Company C.[56]

Walker's body arrived in Galveston on December 21.

> [The] funeral was conducted by the Odd Fellows and the Galveston authorities and other participated—large procession received the remains from a steamer and proceeded to the Baptist Church—services performed by Rev. Huckins, address by Capt. Robert Howard—procession took the corpse to the steamer to be taken to Houston, then San Antonio.[57]

Another funeral procession was held in Austin with the body lying in state in the Representative Hall with the governor and representatives of both houses of the legislature in attendance.[58]

The local newspaper reported, "The remains of Capt. Walker are expected to arrive here [New Orleans] tomorrow [early Jan] and committees have been appointed by the Legislature to make suitable arrangements for their reception with appropriate honors."[59]

Walker's Third Grave

[Samuel H. Walker]. E. W. Taylor autograph letter signed to Texas Ranger Francis M. Willingham in Waco Village, Houston, December 29, 1847, reports how the city of Houston paid its respects to the remains of the heroic Texas Ranger Samuel Walker. In part as written:

> We have [Samuel] Walker's Remains here some 10 days since & I assure you the city done the decent up about right, the way they turned out. The body was taken to the Baptist Church where

> an address was delivered by Peter Grey Esq. The body was accompanied by the Odd Fellows, Masons, etc—through the City to the outskirts of the town, on the Austin Road—where all took a last long lingering look of the Box that contain the Brave Chieftain—and it passed on its way to San Antonio, there to be deposited by the side of the ever lamented Gillespie—and their bodies mingle together with the Mother Earth.

The *Free American* wrote on December 21, 1847:

> The remains of the late gallant Capt. Walker have been received in Galveston, whence they are to be conveyed to San Antonio. At the request of the deceased, his remains will be laid by the side of those of his friend Gillespie, who was killed at Monterey. Their countrymen propose to erect a monument over the remains of their young heroes.[60]

The San Antonio funeral for Walker was held on Saturday, January 8, 1848.[61] Miss Angelina Ney, who came to Texas from France in 1846, helped make the wreaths that were placed on the coffin.[62]

Walker was buried on the north side of East Commerce Street that runs within two blocks of the Alamo, next to his fellow Ranger and close friend Ad Gillespie. According to one newspaper account, two rows of large cottonwood trees stood on each side of the street called the Alameda that ran from Spahn's Bakery east to a ditch on Commerce Street. Walker and Ad Gillespie would be buried beneath the shade of these trees with a chain railing around the graves. In 1849, a storm blew down most of the trees and soon no cottonwood trees at all stood there.[63]

He was a loyal member of the Odd Fellows and often mentioned the organization in his letters. In 1850, the Order of the Odd Fellows of San Antonio erected a monument over his grave in San Antonio. According to a newspaper account it was finely polished and looked like marble. The article acknowledged that Ranger Ad Gillespie was buried beside Sam but there was no marker over Gillespie's grave.

Walker's Fourth Grave

According to a San Antonio newspaper, the Odd Fellows and the Masonic Fraternity removed the remains of Captains Walker and Gillespie from their resting places "beneath the cottonwood trees east to the river" to the Odd Fellows Cemetery, in 1856. An oration by Col. J. C. Wilson, one of the other two Mier escapees with Walker, brought focus to the event.[64] He commented on Walker's reputation that he had never heard him curse nor drink even a glass of wine. Yet in battle he was a trusted and fearless leader who "had no sense of fear." "Sweet be their sleep in the land they loved," he concluded.[65]

Monument at the final burial site of Capts. Samuel H. Walker and Robert A. Gillespie. (James Worsham collection)

A Fifth Grave?

Walker almost had a fifth grave in Waco, Texas, in 1995. But circumstances, including a lady serious about preserving both Texas history as well as the dead from the Alamo, prevented this fifth removal.

On January 5, 1995, the *San Antonio Express-News* announced that Sam Walker's body would be removed to the Texas Rangers Hall of Fame and Museum in Waco. The article states "the moving of Walker's remains from the overgrown and neglected cemetery where he has rested since 1856" was authorized by Walker's descendants.

Tom Burks, curator of the Waco Texas Ranger Museum, is quoted in the article as being unaware of the forthcoming move but knew of discussions to rebury Walker next to Capt. Thomas Barron—the first Ranger commander of Fort Fisher in Waco. Clyde Booth, assistant manager of the Sunset Funeral Home, said that the exhumation would begin at 10 a.m. (Saturday, January 7) and not take long. He also said that Ed Mangum, general manager of the Connally Compton Funeral Home in Waco, was contacted on Monday (January 2) about moving the remains, which were to be taken to the funeral home until ceremonies could be arranged for the reburial the following week. The article stated that some were concerned about the secrecy of the move.

The next day, San Antonio Mayor Nelson Wolff requested a delay of the removal of the Ranger's body. Jim Ables, president of the Texas Ranger Association, had appealed to Sam Walker's own request to be buried next to his fellow Ranger Ad Gillespie in San Antonio. He added that five other Rangers were buried in the city and was concerned that perhaps they too would be exhumed after the Walker precedent.

On Friday, January 6, the day before the scheduled exhumation, the plans for the removal of Sam Walker's body were stopped in their tracks by a petite Texas lady with a Texas-sized determination. Just as the Bexar County Courthouse was closing, attorneys for Lee Spencer White were able to get 131st District Judge John D. Gabriel to hear witnesses and to sign a temporary restraining order halting the exhumation scheduled for the next day.

For Lee Spencer White, descendant of Gordon C. Jennings who died at the Alamo, her Texas heritage was serious business. As founder of the Alamo Defenders Descendants, she produced newspaper accounts that some of the remains of the Alamo defenders were reburied between Walker and Gillespie's grave—right where the exhumers were digging.

Leo Bradshaw, a former board member of the Texas Rangers Hall of Fame, is cited for spearheading the effort to get Walker's remains moved to Waco. In addition, Frank N. Graves of San Antonio was active in the project, saying it was a favor to the Walker family.

The evidence presented to the judge to stop the exhumation was two newspaper accounts from the 1906 and 1911 editions of the *San Antonio Express-News*. The 1906 story tells of August Bzensenbach, City Clerk of San Antonio, who stated that as an 8-year-old-boy playing in the Alameda (now East Commerce Street near

St. Joseph's Church), he witnessed the exhumation of the remains—ashes, bones, and fragments of bones of the victims of the siege of the Alamo—and saw them taken to the Odd Fellows Cemetery where Sam Walker and Ad Gillespie were buried in the spring of 1856. These remains were buried midway between the graves of Walker and Gillespie.

Although the exhumation was scheduled for Saturday January 7, a mound of dirt had already been dug by a backhoe on January 4 and was right between the Walker and Gillespie graves.

Apparently, the Walker family was moved by the unfolding events. Through the legally appointed spokesman for the family, John McWilliams, the Walker family announced they wanted Sam Walker to stay where he was. And the city of San Antonio would clean up the grave site.[66] Walker stayed in San Antonio, a town that had meant so much to him as a young Ranger. True to her dedication to preserve her Texas heritage, on December 6, 2003, Lee Spencer White held a rededication of the Capt. Samuel H. Walker grave site to raise money to clean up the area in addition to what the city of San Antonio had done.[67] Walker is at rest in his last and permanent grave.

Battery Samuel H. Walker

At the turn of the 20th century, the United States embarked upon a program of constructing new and improved coastal defense works. Walker was remembered.

Entrance to Battery Samuel H. Walker. (Courtesy of the author)

Battery Samuel H. Walker is a concrete Endicott Period Battery located on Fort Worden, Jefferson County, Washington. It was named in G.O. 194, December 27, 1904, for Capt. Samuel H. Walker, 1st Regiment, U.S. Mounted Riflemen. The battery was begun in June 1903, completed in 1906, and transferred to the Coast Artillery for use May 21, 1907 at a total cost of $12,000.[68] The guns and mounts were removed about 1946 after the close of World War II. Part of the Harbor Defense of Puget Sound, the battery was designed to protect both the Strait of Juan De Fuca and the Admiralty Inlet to Puget Sound.

It was built with two 3-inch rapid fire M1903 guns on M1903 pedestal mounts in a concrete battery, it is a relatively small one with three rooms between the gun mounts. Each gun position has a magazine with a common storeroom between them.

Battery Samuel H. Walker remained armed throughout World War I and World War II, but the guns were declared obsolete on October 18, 1945, and processed for salvage on March 7, 1946.

A World War II Liberty ship was christened with Sam Walker's name. The Liberty ship *Samuel H. Walker* with hull number 1949 was appropriately made in Houston, Texas, under the supervision of the MCA (Marine and Coast Guard Agency). The U.S. Maritime Commission reports that the Houston Shipbuilding Corporation and Todd-Houston Shipbuilding Corporation, Houston Texas from 1941–45 built 208 Liberty ships. The SS *Samuel H. Walker* was chartered or operated by ATS (Army Transportation Service).

Vacated gun position. Coast Defense Study Group. (Photograph in the public domain)

The keel was laid on July 16 and it was launched August 31, 1943. It was delivered September 16, 1943. On duty the *Sam H. Walker* was damaged by a torpedo along the U.S. East Coast on October 22, 1943. The vessel was repaired and continued in service. The ship was scrapped in 1964.

APPENDIX I

Samuel H. Walker Files a Grievance to the American Public

INDIAN AND SEMINOLE WARS

Brief observations on the conduct of the officers, and on the discipline of the army of the United States.

Washington city, July 1, 1840.

As a native American, a lover of my country, and a true friend to the principles of freedom and justice—such as our forefathers so gallantly fought and bled to establish—and one who has been, twelve months a soldier in the United States service, I feel it a duty incumbent upon me, which I cannot longer forbear to fulfill, to give my fellow-citizens a few statements concerning the abuses of power and the tyrannical treatment of soldiers in the United States service, such as is commonly practiced and countenanced from the lowest to the highest grade in command. It is not merely to gratify my own personal feelings, because I have been a sufferer from the tyranny practiced in the army, that I should, after a lapse of more than three years, be stimulated to raise, my feeble voice against the minions of power now in the United States service, but every day's experience teaches me that it is the duty of every true friend to the cause of freedom and justice, to cry aloud and expose every injustice and usurpation of power that may come within his knowledge, especially when there is a probability of such usurpation and injustice, at some future day, affecting the happiness of a large portion of his fellow citizens; and I, think the probability is so great, that I consider it the duty of every freeman and lover of his country to consider seriously on what I shall relate, and then make further inquiry from persons whom they know to be unprejudiced, as I must confess that my feelings have been so deeply wounded by the punishment and injustice inflicted on me, that I do not believe that I can ever forget it; though I should not have attempted any publication of this subject, was it not for the militia system proposed by the Secretary of War and recommended by the president, and particularly the clause in the bill prohibiting the men who may be draughted the privilege of choosing their principal officers, as I shall contend that all republican armies should be conducted on purely republican and democratic principles by giving them the privilege of all the all the officers destined to command them in the field; and, besides this, for all persona in such service to have the right of trial by jury for any violation of the regulations of the army, and not to be thrown on the mercy of officers, who receive their situations from those who are not immediately interested in the welfare of the private soldier.

As the curiosity of every reader to know something about the writer when he raises his voice on matters of importance is natural, I consider it my duty to gratify those who may read this before I proceed further, I am the son of Nathan Walker, who resides ten miles from this city, now in the eighty-third year of his age. He was a short time in. the revolutionary army as a militiaman; he was a house carpenter by trade, though & farmer by occupation for the last twenty years, and always a true friend to the cause of freedom and justice between man and man; and these principles he always endeavored to instill into the minds of his children, which he in a great measure succeeded, so far as relates to the true principles of freedom and fair dealing. My father raised nine children, five sons and four daughters, and being in moderate circumstances, he gave us a common country education, and brought us up to hard work, having taught the eldest son the business of a house carpenter, he in turn has taught the rest, so that we are all mechanics, a distinction which I am proud to acknowledge. I am aware that aristocrats and lovers of power and tyranny will turn their noses up, as the old saying is, to my remarks, but I care not for that, as my wish is to warn the workingmen of the country to watch with unceasing vigilance every movement of those in power, who, instead of being public servants as they should be, would rather make the public their servants.

Having been sent to school very young, I soon learned to read, and nothing so much interested me, as to read of the chivalry and noble deeds of our forefathers in the wars with Great Britain; and being naturally fond of military glory, I determined to try my fortune on the field of battle on the first opportunity that presented itself. Such was my determination, and at the age of nineteen, in May 1836, I came to this city and joined the Washington City Volunteers, raised by Captain B[enjamin] L. Beall.[1] I volunteered from purely patriotic motives. Almost every mail brought intelligence of the massacre of our citizens and soldiers in the Creek nation and in Florida, and I considered it a duty for those who had it in their power to march to the rescue of their fellow-citizens.

Such was my feelings on this occasion; after the company was mustered into the service of the United States, Captain Beall, who had pledged himself to remain with it during the campaign, resigned, having received a captaincy in the 2d regiment of dragoons. E[dward] B[ranch] Robinson being next in command, offered himself as captain and was elected by the company. It may be well here to remark, that this Robinson had formerly been a soldier in the U.S. Army, and was tolerable expert in drilling, but entirely destitute of moral principles and behavior, as the sequel will show.[2] I shall not enter into a detail of every occurrence to show the villainy of Robinson, and the injustice a soldier meets with in the army, but will merely mention a few prominent facts as they occurred. On the 1st June, 1836, (the Marines under Colonel [Archibald] Henderson[3] having left for the Creek nation,) our company took possession of the Marine barracks for the purpose of properly organizing; we had been there but a few nights, when this Robinson attempted to force the door of the quarters where some of the absent soldiers' families were, their cries however alarmed some of his own company who repaired to the spot, and he jumped the wall and escaped. On the next day inquiry was made into the matter, but he found men who stated that he was absent on that night, and thus he escaped punishment at that time.

During the time we were in, the Creek nation I had got completely barefooted, (this was the case with many others,) and having moved to a new encampment, where the earth was covered with briars, the orderly sergeant [George Cochran] did not detail me, on that account, to clear up the encampment, I was sitting down writing on a drumhead; Captain Robinson asked the orderly sergeant why he did not detail me, and when he told him, he swore I should go any how; he said he did not care a d—n if I was barefooted, and ordered me to go forthwith and help to clear off the parade ground, which was covered with briars. I told him if he insisted on it. I would go, and immediately started, telling him I supposed he thought I was writing a letter to obtain my discharge, and assured him that such was not the case, and spoke in a very respectful manner. He immediately called for the guard and ordered them to take me to the guard tent, and preferred the charge of *"insolence and disobedience"* against me. I was called up before Colonel [Archibald] Henderson to answer to this charge. I told him that I had not given Captain Robinson any insolence, neither had I disobeyed him. He asked me if there was any person present. I referred him to the orderly sergeant; he was sent for, and declared that the charge was not correct. The Colonel then said that he did not want to hear any thing more, and told me that I must beg Captain Robinson's pardon, and promise never to do so again. I told him I was not guilty of the charge, and that I would not do as required. A gag [a round piece of wood, or iron bolt, which is forced between the teeth and pushed back, until the mouth is stretched to an enormous size, and fastened with a cord around the back of the head, and generally have the person ironed or tied at the same time, so that it is impossible for them to remove the gag] was now ordered to be got ready to gag me with if I dared to speak in such positive terms. On the next day I was called before Colonel Henderson again; he made a great many threats what he would do with me, and threatened to gag me, and when I told him I thought I ought to have the privilege of speaking in my own defence without being gagged, he told me I had no right to think. I was taken back to the guard tent, and ordered out to wash some dirty filthy clothes that belonged to some poor miserable creatures who had been confined for some time, and kept in double irons except while marching, and their wrists and ankles had become sore from the wearing the irons; their skin was thickly covered with dirt and filth, being compelled to lay in the dirt for weeks, and sometimes months in that hot climate; and it is no uncommon thing to sea them swarming in lice, as it was in some measure the case with these. I had two sentinels placed over me with fixed bayonets and loaded muskets, to force me to wash their miserably dirty, lousy clothes. I washed them, but not for fear of the threatened death provided I did not wash them; but, for the hope of satisfaction at some future day, when I could have a more equal chance than I had there. On the third day after I was confined, I was again marched up before Colonel Henderson, and he still continued to threaten me with severe punishment and again had his gag got ready to fasten in my mouth. A true lover of freedom and justice may, perhaps, judge what my feelings were on this occasion; to be arraigned before a man under a false charge, and that after I had proved it false to the satisfaction of every sensible man present, and yet to be reviled and threatened with the most severe punishments, and even dared to say I was not guilty with a gag ready to stick in my month. The reader may judge what my feelings were on this occasion, I cannot find language to express it, but the injustice of that punishment has cast its sting deeply into my bosom, and I fear it never will be forgot, and I had almost said forgiven.

On the same day, Colonel Henderson ordered me back to the guard tent and told them to keep me till 12 o'clock, and if I did not beg the Captain's pardon, and promise to do so no more, to take and tie me to a tree for the space of two hours, and pin a large label on my back, with the following letters wrote thereon: "For insolence and disobedience to his commanding officer;" after I stood the two hours with my arms hugged around a tree and tied, with the large label on my back, I was released, and procured a fine-tooth comb, and combed out the cattle which had crawled from the heads of my miserable bed-fellows. The reader must recollect that we were all four compelled to stay in a tent only six feet square at bottom, and sloping off to about seven feet high; here we were compelled to lay night and day, without even the privilege of hoisting the sides of our tent to get free circulation of air, and this in a sultry climate in the mouth of July. It may be well to remark that Colonel Henderson is a man whose character stands very fair, and as for his general character I shall not undertake to delineate, but I must say conscientiously, that his course of conduct towards me was any thing but that becoming a gentleman, and were it not for his grey hairs I should seek that satisfaction which the law cannot give under existing circumstances. About the first of August, we left Colonel Henderson's camp, and joined Major [Greenleaf] Dearborn's[4] command, which was close by; this consisted of a detachment of 2d infantry. While we were here we had another occurrence, which plainly shows the rascality that an officer may be guilty of, and yet countenanced and supported in it by his superiors, regardless of justice, or any thing honorable towards the soldiers. One day, while under Major Dearborn's command, Captain Robinson, being officer of the day, went to the village of Tallassee [Alabama], got quite intoxicated, and returned into camp, and commenced a quarrel with one of his men, (who was also under the influence of liquor) and ordered the guard to take him and put him in irons. This order was obeyed; he then went and commenced cursing the prisoner after he was put in irons, and received pretty much such language as he gave. He drew his sword and rushed up and stabbed him in the breast; the prisoner fell down, and was, from appearance, in the agonies of death; the sharp point of the sword had pierced the breast, and created the most excruciating pain, though the wound was not mortal. However there was myself and several others who supposed it was, and we did not think it prudent to let any man that was drunk and quarrelsome have a sword to use in that way; so that myself and several others [probably eight or ten] went to our tents and got our muskets with the intention of disarming the Captain, and placing him under care that no further danger might be apprehended from him, as we did not consider our own lives safe under such circumstances; but, taking the second thought after I entered my tent, I did not load my musket, as I thought he would certainly be punished for such conduct, and I thought it best that it should be done according to the regular routine of business. My companions, however, were loading their muskets, when the orderly sergeant [Cochran] came and ordered them to put their muskets away, telling them that was not a proper way of doing business, and then went and reported it to Major Dearborn. Captain Robinson saw him, and immediately started and hallooed to Major Dearborn, and said his company was ill a state of mutiny, and the orderly sergeant was at the head of it; and the orderly sergeant was immediately confined, and kept in close confinement far something like two months, when in fact there was no contemplation of mutiny no farther than what I have stated, and he was the first to stop that.[5] Major Dearborn ordered his detachment under arms, and kept them in ranks till about 10 o'clock; Colonel [Alexander S.] Brook's[6] regiment was also informed by Major Dearborn and Captain Robinson of the intended mutiny. This regiment was about one hundred and fifty yards from us, the field piece was got ready, and ordered to lay on their arms that night, all from the mere say-so of a drunken man, and without any appearance to justify the belief, as those who loaded their muskets did not bring them out of their tents. This I consider was rather a pitiful movement in these regular officers; to order seven or eight companies under arms to frighten us. However this was reasonable enough, as our company was at least equal to seven companies of regulars, which they in fact acknowledged by ordering out seven or eight companies to contend with us; for the reader must understand that after the sick, lame, and lazy, was deducted from the regulars, they always had a very small effective force. Though it was said here that our company had many of the nuisances of Washington in it, I can assure the reader, without any exaggeration, that our company, with the exception of our captain, who had been a regular soldier, was a company extraordinary genteel, when compared with the regulars. As well as I recollect, the three companies under Major Dearborn one morning while with us only reported eleven men for duty, while we reported daily between fifty and sixty or more from one company; but before I conclude, I shall give the reader my general views of the composition of that portion of the army which has been under my observation. I shall not relate every particular that occurred, as it would occupy too much space for the people to read in the present stale of political excitement; for I can assure the reader that this is not intended for political speculation, although I may speak freely in rotation to the misdeeds and bad management of our public servants before I close my remarks. The next thing I shall speak of is General [Thomas S.] Jesup's[7] conduct towards us. About the last of September, being encamped on the Hatchachubbee swamp about thirty miles from Fort Mitchell, and attached to company G, 4th Regiment of Artillery, under command of Captain John Monroe [Munroe].[8] This company was the first company we had been with that was entitled to the respect which soldiers ought to command; and the first officer that we had been commanded by that was worthy the appellation of a gentleman. A good man's character requires but few words to delineate it; his general characteristic is firmness, decision, and open, unassumed genteel behavior towards every person. This, I would judge, was the reason he had the most genteel company in the service. He was not disposed to countenance every black deed and lie that an officer should be guilty of, as had been done before by them; his prerogative was justice to the soldiers as well as the officer; this insured him the respect of all under his command. While we were at the above-mentioned place, we received orders to repair forthwith to Fort Mitchell to take up the line of march to Florida; and having a longtime previous presented the folio wing list of charges to General Jesup in relation to Captain Robinson's conduct, the following is a copy from the original charges which was presented to General Jesup:

Charges and specification of charges preferred against Capt. E. B. Robinson of the Washington City Volunteers, by Wm. A. T. Maddox, 1st Lieutenant of the same.

CHARGE FIRST.

Unofficerlike and ungentlemanly conduct.

Specification 1st. In this, that the said Capt, E. B. Robinson did, on or about June 19th, while his company remained at Charleston, S. C., at night, in a bawdy house, when in full uniform, draw his sword against a citizen, threatened his life, and probably would have killed him but for the interference of those in company with him.

Spec. 2d. That the said Capt. E. B. Robinson did, on or about the 21st June, resist the civil authority of Charleston, S. C., by ordering his company to take arms against an officer having a civil process to serve against one or more of his men.

Spec. 3d. That on or about 25th June, on the march from Augusta to Columbus, he, the said Capt E. B. Robinson requested Lieut. Maddox to prevail on four or five of his men to desert.

Spec. 4th. That on or about Sunday, 10th July, at Columbus, Georgia, he, the said Capt. E. B. Robinson, being in a state of intoxication, marched and countermarched, drilled and redrilled the company while he was unable to articulate the words of command so as to be understood, and whilst staggering to and fro; repeatedly opened the falls of his pantaloons to give vent to the ordinary functions of nature, within view of many females and a large concourse of spectators, many of whom evinced their displeasure by hisses and groans; and that between Columbus and Fort Mitchell, on the. evening of the same day, he being apparently apprehensive of an attack from the Indians, ordered his men to load their arms, and had the drum and fife beat on march through the woods, at night, until remonstrated with by the orderly sergeant, who pointed out to him the great indiscretion of such conduct, in the vicinity of a savage foe, telling him that such a course of conduct was intended to evade an attack, or inviting one which would prove advantageous to the enemy.

Spec. 5th. That on or about the 6th August, he, the said Capt. E. B. Robinson, did quarrel and fight with a private of the United States Marine Corps in a public store in Tallassee.

CHARGE SECOND.

Repeated drunkenness.

Spec. lst. In this, that the said Capt. E, B Robinson on the march from Augusta to Columbus, Georgia, was constantly in a state of inebriation, would watch the men who purchased liquor and drink from their canteens.

Spec. 2d. That on or about August 6ih, at camp near the village of Tallassee, was highly inebriated, being *officer of the day,* under Major Dearborn, commanding detachment 3d Infantry, and Washington City Volunteers.

Witnesses—Sergeants Hamill and Sheppard, Corporals Irvine and Hart, Privates Kinslow, H. Thomas, W. Morin, G. W. Howard, Wetherill, Faidley, Djunison, W. Thomas, VV. Williams, Walker, and Bignell.

Camp near Stone's 23d August 1833.

And yet he [General Jesup] had not done us the justice to call a court of inquiry; his excuse was that he had not officers enough, and therefore he did not wish to have any of them broke. This was a pitiful excuse, as must be apparent to every one; and we now cams to the conclusion to try more effectual means to get rid of the nuisance of a Captain that was still imposed on us, against all reason and justice, as the charges does not embrace half of his disgraceful conduct. A meeting of the company was called immediately after receiving the foregoing orders, and myself and four others were appointed as a committee to draw up some resolutions to be approved and adopted by the company, and their signatures attached to it, and all of the company signed it, except two or three who had not the hearts of brave men. Our resolution contained in it a positive declaration that we would not march to Florida under Captain Robinson, but was accompanied with a very respectful petition to the Gen., stating our great objections to Captain Robinson, and the impositions, he had practiced on us, and begging him at the same time to relieve us from the disagreeable necessity of being commanded by so odious a character. When we arrived at Fort Mitchell the petition was presented; and, instead of his complying with the request made, he ordered Major [Mann P.] Lomax's[9] command under arms to frighten us into measures of his own; but when he found that his threats were of no avail, and our resolutions unmoved by the display of the regular troops, (which was encamped on our left,) he finally agreed to suspend him from the command. We were now attached to three companies of artillery under command of Major [William L.] McClintock,[10] who I must say proved to be very much of a gentleman, as we remained under his command about three months, and during that time no person had cause to complain of him—a very rare circumstance in the army. We arrived in Tampa Bay on the fifteenth of October, and a few days after General Jesup was so lost to a sense of justice, that he again gave Robinson command of the company. We again refused to come under his orders; when General Jesup now, for the first time, took the trouble to inquire into the affairs of the company to know who was right or wrong.

He then told Captain Robinson that he could resign or stand a court-martial; and not being disposed to have an investigation of his villainous conduct, he resigned, and in a short time afterwards the company elected Charles Irvine in his place, who proved to be a man of a noble disposition, and was much esteemed by his men. After we arrived in Florida, we were kept cutting of wood, to supply the steamboats that were running, for some time. We afterwards helped to rebuild Fort Alabama, which is since called Fort Foster, in honor of Colonel Foster[11] who commanded at the time of its rebuilding. Colonel Foster, I think, is a very meritorious officer, and one amongst the few who reflects honor on the United States army. On the 25th of December, General Jesup sent out orders to Colonel Foster, stating that we should repair to Tampa Bay, and all those who choose to enter the quartermaster's department for public service, as teamsters und artificers, should receive the sum of two dollars per day, and those who remained at the Fort should receive but one dollar per day; so that we all entered the quartermaster's department under the above-mentioned conditions. I do not think that our company would have taken this offer if there had been any chance to have distinguished ourselves in battle; but not being quite so lazy as regulars, our services seemed to be in great demand; so we agreed to take up the offer, as we knew we should have to do a great deal of work any how, and we thought it a wise plan to get paid for it, as we done a good dual that we never got paid for. It will be recollected by the Washingtonians that the company was under the impression that their term of service was only six months, as there were objections by a good many to serve over six months; and Captain Robinson informed them that the President, had agreed to accept their services for that time, and many of them produced their certificates received from magistrates who swore them in, which certified that it was for six months. They contended that they were entitled to their discharge at the end of six months; and besides, it was understood in our enlistment that our service was to be in the Creek nation, Alabama, as it was particularly mentioned; so that it was, in fact, an arbitrary act to compel us to go to Florida after the Creek campaign was ended; however, I had no objections to go myself, neither had I any certificate to certify the period of my enlistment, to be only six months, so I rested quiet on these matters, but it was not the case with the majority; therefore I contend that it was an imposition, both in sending us to Florida, and in keeping us in the service over six months; as I do not believe that one-third of the company would have went if they had known that the original muster roll, that we wore mustered in by, was for twelve months. And it is an indisputable fact, that this was kept a secret until after we left Washington, as the officer who mustered us in never read the head of the muster roll; and yet this was what they, or General Jesup rather, considered sufficient to justify him in keeping us in the service; though I understood that he said that our services was so valuable that he could not do without us. This was certainly saying a good deal for us; in fact the General seemed now to think as much of us as he had before thought little of us; and I must confess that, upon the whole, I like the old General pretty well, though his conduct, in my opinion, was highly censurable in several instances, while I was in the service. In the first place, his neglect or carelessness in relation to the charges against Robinson; in the next place, his management at the Cypress swamp, in sending a messenger to the Indians and inviting them to terms of peace, instead of rushing ahead and forcing them to terms, as he had good reason to suppose that their families were in the vicinity. He had taken between 12 and 1,300 head of cattle, which would have lasted until a fresh supply of provision could have been procured; and it is my opinion that proper exertion at that time would probably have brought the war to a close. But instead of that, four or five days was spent in talking with them, and even paid so much respect to the negroes and Indians, that they thought he was afraid of them; and it is my opinion, that it had a very bad tendency from the time this treaty commenced. I was disgusted with the management of the whole affair; the tobacco was all taken out of the sutler's stores and given to the Indians; and soldiers, who could scarcely live without it in any peace or comfort, were compelled to go without; and also gave them some bread while at the Cypress swamp, and the soldiers were reduced to four ounces per day. They were also allowed free excess to the camp, and allowed to trade with the friendly Indians; they were also allowed ammunition to hunt with, but how much I am not prepared to say. But I suppose, including what was allowed them to hunt with, and the privilege of trading with the friendly Indians for several months, that it is reasonable to suppose that they must have acquired a good supply. But there is a plain fact which no one can deny, that there was a great many thousand rations given out to them, as they were continually drawing of rations from the 18th February until about the 3d of June, when they all cleared themselves, being much better supplied than when they first commenced the war; for all they had to do, was for two or three to come in and report that they had so many people, and they drew their rations accordingly. The officers did not require that they should fetch their people in before they gave them rations, as they should have done; and the probability is, that at the same time the most of their people were a long ways into the interior making of corn for another war. They would carry in their ponies, such mostly as they had no use for, and sell them for enormous prices, from twenty to fifty dollars in specie, trade it out with a sutler for such articles as they wanted and carry it out, and in some instances return at night and steal good horses in place of the ponies they had sold; it was thought to be a wise plan to give them a high price for their ponies and cattle, as that would be some inducement to bring them in; and it seemed to me that the officers in general courted favors of the Indians, instead of exercising that authority and decision which they should have done; but no, every negro and Indian who would condescend to put himself upon an equality with the officers, was taken by the hand and welcomed in the kindest manner; for it may be well to remark that many of them considered themselves far superior to our officers. But our officers seemed disposed to put them on an equality with themselves, by mingling with them and introducing the system of amalgamation. This might possibly be a wise plan, but I do not think it looks very honorable to see our United States officers using such familiarities with a savage foe whom they are sent to fight; the way I found this out, was by seeing the Indian squaws frequently about the officers' quarters, sometimes late of evenings and early of mornings; and sometimes I would see them riding in and fetching a squaw behind them; the negroes, who could mostly talk English, were employed as pimps by the officers to make the engagements on such occasions. Being at work as carpenter, at the same time these movements were going on, we had several very large cots to make, and of most extraordinary width; I asked Mr. Bradley, the boss carpenter, what they were for? And he told me that the officers were all going to take Indian wives; which corroborated the opinion I had formed. Sometime during the month of April, the quartermaster gave orders that we should work the remainder of our time for fifteen cents per day; knowing this to be unlawful and arbitrary in the highest degree, I quit work and persuaded the rest of my companions in arms to do the same; how-, ever there was only one or two others that would follow my example. Lieutenant [James H.] Simpson,[12] who was assistant quartermaster, came in search of us, and ordered myself and another one of our company to be put in stocks; I told [him] I would see my Captain about it firsthand [and] he followed me along, having a file of the guard with him.

I informed Captain [Charles] Irvine [commanding officer, Washington City Volunteers] of the matter, and he told me to go with him and he would attend to it so I went with him to the guard-house, and he again ordered me to be put in stocks. I told him he was a pretty fellow to have men put under guard, and put in stocks for resisting his arbitrary power. He cursed, and told me if I did not hush he would give me a damn good thrashing. I told him if he thought he could do it I was perfectly willing to give him a fair trial for it; but he was not disposed, and ordered the guard to put us in the shocks forthwith. The reader must recollect that they have stocks, wooden horses to ride, shackles, and handcuffs, and almost every invention that the capacity of their genius can invent, for; the punishment of their fellow-men; and in some instances they even go so far as to strip them to the bare back and whip them until the blood streams from them, put a moss collar round their neck, drum them round camp, playing the rogues march after them, and still keep them in the service. This was done to a man by the name of Price, for forging an officer's name to an order for liquor for himself, when at the same time there was such abuses of the use of ardent spirits amongst the officers themselves, that General Jesup had to place restrictions on the sutlers to keep them sober. It may be that this man deserved the punishment; but I ask the question, why keep such men in the army? Is it not a disgrace to hold in the service of our country men who deserve such degrading punishment as this most assuredly was? However, we were put in the stocks, and Lieutenant Simpson was met by Captain Irvine, who asked him what was the cause of so much disturbance with his men? He told Captain Charles Irvine it was none of his business; the Captain called him a damn'd [*sic*] insignificant puppy, and told him he would let him see that it was his business; he then went to Captain [Lorenzo] Thomas,[13] who was principal quartermaster, and asked him what relation his men stood to his department? He replied that they were turned over by general order. Captain Irvine told him it was a general order with his own consent; and he said he supposed it was. Captain Irvine then asked him if it was right that a whole company should be forced to work for the small pittance of fifteen cents per day? He said no, it was not. He then told Captain Thomas he would go and see General Jesup about it. Captain Thomas told him he need not go, that he had just seen General Jesup, and arranged it so that we were to receive a dollar per day.

I do not believe that General Jesup had been consulted about the matter at all, as I am certain the order never originated with him; and therefore there would have been no occasion for Captain Thomas seeing General Jesup about it; my humble opinion is, that it was a scheme to benefit themselves by pocketing the eighty-five cents per day, and returning a false duplicate to Washington; this is my opinion about these gentlemen. I could, if it was necessary, relate a good many small matters in relation to quartermasters and other United States officers, which would go far to show the condition of our army, and the rascality practiced in it.

I resided in Florida near four years, and became tolerably conversant with the affairs of the army; and I must say, with regret, that the present composition of the army is worthless far beyond the conception of our fellow-citizens, whom it is destined to protect, and I can assure them that they never need expect protection from it in its present state. According to my views, I will state the condition of the army. In the first place, the majority of the enlisted men in the service are the worthless dregs of society from almost every European nation; but few, very few indeed, of our own countrymen, except those who are outcasts from society, and brought to degradation from habits of dissipation, will be satisfied to be placed on an equality with those worthless serfs of European nations, who, in many instances, have been from their infancy brought up slaves as it were, and consequently strangers to equality and justice, and consequently they feel no degradation at being cuffed and kicked about by a petty officer, who in a great many instances are fond of abusing their authority. I say that none of our own countrymen, with but few exceptions, unless they be lost to all sense of the principles of freedom and justice, will condescend to undergo such miserable degradation as they have to undergo in the army; the fact is, that no man with purely patriotic feelings can content himself to remain long in the United States army, under the present abuses of power which is daily practiced in it.

In the first place, I am opposed to enlisting men in the service of our country who are outcasts of society, and unworthy of good treatment.

In the next place, I am. opposed to the appointment of officers by any persons except those they are destined to command; as under the present system it is too commonly the case that men receive appointments in the army, without any proof that they have the proper qualifications to fulfill it, more than the recommendation of some influential friend who is anxious to acquire for him distinction and the emoluments of office, without knowing that he is possessed of the qualifications which an officer ought to have. I contend that none but. those in the field are proper judges of the requisite qualifications of a noble officer; and whenever the army shall be established on the principles of merit, instead of favor, we will have a good one, and not until then. I also contend that a man must be a good soldier, or he will not make a good officer to command soldiers; therefore I contend for the principle of raising men from the ranks, according to their merits; and none but those who are daily observers of their conduct and behavior can be proper judges.

I ask how many tyrannical, pitiful, cowardly, disgusting, and contemptible scamps there are who now hold offices of distinction in the United States service, both army and navy? I think that, if every soldier was allowed to answer to this question; you would hear of a good many such fellows, as not a few have come within my own small observation. What I have said, and shall say, I am responsible to any respectable man who may think that I have done him injustice in my remarks; and if my fellow-citizens are not satisfied with my limited expositions of the tyrannies and rascality practiced in the army, in which I have been an eye witness in part,

I will give them a more lengthened detail of the particulars. And I hope, from the bottom of my heart, that the militia system proposed by the Secretary of War and recommended by the President will never be carried into effect, for the probability is that it will prove oppressive in the highest degree, without any advantages whatever; for I do not believe that here would be any occasion for such a scheme as the one proposed, even if our land was invaded, provided there was a proper code of regulations for United States volunteers and regulars. I mean such as would insure to the honest and true-hearted patriot that distinction and justice which he merits, while engaged in the common cause and service of his country; for I believe that the gallant sons of our republic would flock to the standard of freedom and liberty by scores and thousands, if there was any occasion for it, and there was a system of military regulations which would, under all circumstances, insure to him that respect and justice that his conduct might merit. I say, under these circumstances, our gallant sons of America would flock to the standard of liberty and freedom, and there offer their lives as a sacrifice in behalf of the just cause of their country; for where is the true hearted patriot who has read with attention the history of this country, and has learned to appreciate the value of our blood-bought treasures, who would not be ready to sacrifice his life in maintaining the rights of his country, which was established by the price of many lives and much blood. I say that those who have considered well on these things, and would not lend their aid in time of war, when the cause of their country demanded it, are not' true-hearted patriots. I am one of the last who would oppose military discipline when conducted on proper principles, so as to increase the chivalry and military pride of our countrymen, and at the same time create that union and good feeling between the men and their officers, which should always characterize a free and independent nation; but will the scheme proposed by the Secretary have any such tendency? Most assuredly not. It would be attended with wrangling, and quarrelling, and mutiny and create the most bitter feelings imaginable amongst our fellow-men, and might eventually terminate in disgrace to our country. I therefore hope that my fellow-citizens will discountenance the measure proposed by the Secretary of War and recommended by the President, for I view them ridiculous in the highest degree, and well calculated to affect the peace and happiness of our beloved country.

Before I conclude I will, for the information of the public, state that Captain Robinson, whose disgraceful conduct I have spoken of, is now in an important office under our Government; he is employed as traveling mail agent, and I have no hesitation in saying, that I do not believe him any too honest to rob the, mail. My reasons for thinking him dishonest are various. While I was under his command, he often told his men that he did not care a damn how much they stole if they were not caught at it, and would always partake of such plunder when he could get it; and while in Alabama, I knew him to take a jug of liquor from a drunken, Indian, and I was informed made use of some of it, but finding that it was likely to create a disturbance with the friendly Indians that were in the vicinity, he gave it up. Had he been a temperate man, would he have taken it for his own use? He also received fifty dollars from the quartermaster at Augusta or Charleston, I am not certain which, to pay the expenses of the company, as they had no tents; and the fifty dollars was intended to pay for quarters on the road, which was never done, as in many instances, instead of laying in houses, we laid out by the fire under the broad canopy of heaven. I am very certain *that* [emphasis in the original] fifty dollars was never accounted for but in a fraudulent manner, which I think was done in the way of charging it as rations which we never got; for we were at one time compelled to do without any coffee or sugar for something like three or four weeks, and confined to a short allowance of sour flour and fat pork. He argued that we had used it too lavishly, and overdrawn our rations and that it was nothing more than right that we should suffer for it; but I think that if the accounts he kept against the company had been examined, that there would be something found charged to the company's account that they had never received, to account to Government for the fifty-dollars that I have spoken of. There is another circumstance of which I shall speak; a young man by the name of [Joseph C.] Hill [who] belonged to our company, and through the interposition of friends his mother obtained his discharge, and sent fifty dollars to him in a letter directed to Robinson; the letter was franked in the War Department. Robinson received the letter, and presented it to Hill after the seal had been broken, and there was no money in it, though the letter mentioned it. Mr. Hill said he was certain in his own mind that Robinson stole the money. Mr. Hill has since resided in Texas, though I have been informed lately that he was here last summer and made the same declaration, and the reason why he did not enter suit against Robinson, was that he had to return to Texas immediately, and he did not think it worthwhile to undertake it unless he had time to attend to it. In addition to these things, he is certainly the greatest liar in existence; and I do riot believe he ever tells the truth, only when it suits his convenience better than a lie. A pretty fellow this for the U.S. mail guard! I wish it to be understood that l am accountable for what I say.

Fellow-citizens I ask is such a man as this fit to fulfill the offices of our Government? I say God forbid; and I hope the time will soon arrive when all United States officers, both civil and military, from the highest to the lowest, will receive office according to their merit and qualification to fulfill them.

S. H. W.

APPENDIX II

Samuel H. Walker's Texas Ranger Company

Walker would eventually have a total of 97 men in his command for three months from April to July 1846. Six would be killed in action; four captured; one deserted, three dishonorably discharged, and three honorably discharged. Captain Walker resigned from this company on June 30, and Lt. Joseph P. Wells served as commander until the company mustered out on July 16. On the official roster was the following notation:

> Capt. Walker of the Texas Mounted Rangers was called into service during the month of April by Brig. Gen. Z. Taylor, U.S.A. under the authority which the latter received from the Executive of the U.S. in August 1845 to call from the States of Texas, Louisiana, … for … Volunteer troops when he deemed such forced necessary. The Co. thus called in was mustered into service April 21, 1846 under the militia laws then in force. … Capt. Walker was at the same time verbally authorized by General Taylor to increase the strength of his company to any number of [men] within the limits prescribed by law. … The Co. during its enrollment was chiefly used by the commanding general in scouting, conveying intelligence … since the first of May have been kept in the immediate vicinity of the Camp of the Army of Occupation. Compiled and transcribed by James J. Worsham.[1]

Roster, Captain Sam Walker's Texas Mounted Ranger Company April–July, 1846

Name	Date Mustered	Comments
1. Pvt. Barton, John	May 20	Repairing Rifle—Charge $1.00. Absent at muster.
2. Pvt. Beal, Harrison	June 18	
3. Pvt. Beardslee, Louis	June 13	
4. Pvt. Berry, Montgomery	May 20	
5. Pvt. Blair, J. F.	May 16	

6. Pvt. Bowman, Matthew J.	May 20	
7. Pvt. Bowyer, A.	June 25	
8. Pvt. Bradley, John	May 20	Repairing arms—Charge $ .50.
9. Pvt. Brannum, John	June 20	
10. Pvt. Bullard, George	April 21	Deserted in attack on the Enemy's picket guard May 3, 1846. Due U.S. for 1 Colt's Pistol, 1 Carbine, 1 Tube wrench, 1 Bullet mould, 1 cap box. [Henceforth when a Colts pistol and accessories are mention, etc., will be used]
11. Pvt. Cardwell, William	April 21	Due U.S. 1 Colt's pistol, etc. Service commenced May 16
12. Pvt. Clark, James	June 13	
13. Pvt. Coe, John	April 21	Due U.S. for 1 Colt's Pistol, etc. Service commenced May 18. Horse supplied by US [The Army supplied five of Walker's Rangers horses—all such records have a line through this statement perhaps indicating that the Rangers found their own horse but perhaps kept some of the equipment.]
14. Pvt. Comeyngs, John	June 6	
15. Pvt. Crabb, W.A.	May 20	
16. Pvt. Crawford, W. H.	May 20	
17. Pvt. Criswell, J.T.	June 20	
18. Pvt. Dolan, Joseph	June 2	
19. Pvt. Dwyer, Dennis	June 20	
20. Pvt. Eaton, Beal	May 13	
21. Pvt. Frier, E.	May 16	

22. Pvt. Gaines, John	May 12	
23. Pvt. Gicker, C. B.	April 21	Dishonorably discharged May 4, 1846.
24. Pvt. Glass, William S.	May 20	Repairing pistol & wiper—$1.50.
25. Pvt. Goodloe, William	May 9	Absent at muster
26. Pvt. Goodrich, John	May 1	Due U.S. bridles, etc.
27. Pvt. Hamilton, William	May 9	
28. Pvt. Hardy, E.	June 25	
29. Pvt. Harris, E.	April 27	Killed in action, April 28, 1846.
31. 1st Sgt. Hastings, D.M.	May 1	Appointed 1st Sgt., May 16 by Capt. Walker Supplied one horse by US, etc.
31. Pvt. Hastings, H. H.	April 27	Killed in action, April 28, 1846.
32. Pvt. Hatch, D. W.	May 20	Repairing pistol $1.50
33. Pvt. Hickock, George W.	April 16	
24. Pvt. Hodal, Jacob	June 25	
35. Pvt. Holbert, H.	April	Taken prisoner April 28—Exchanged May 11
36. Pvt. Hornsby, C. C.	May 4	Supplied one horse by US, etc.
37. Pvt. Hurd, J. Wesley	April 29	Hon. Discharge May 29.
38. Pvt. Humphries, J. J.	May 12	Due U.S. for 1 Colt's pistol, etc.
39. Pvt. James, Isaac	June 20	
40. Pvt. January, J.B.P.	May 20	Due U.S. for 1 Colt's pistol, etc. Repairing sights of gun $2.00
41. Pvt. Kearney, Charles E.	April 27	Hon. Discharge, May 27 Due US one bridle, bradoon, martingale
42. Pvt. Kinsey, John	April 21	Due U.S. for 1 Colt's pistol, etc.
43. Pvt. Lewis, G.K.	June 13	

44. Pvt. Mabry, Gray	June 20	
42.[2] 2nd Sgt Kinsey, John	April 21	2nd Sgt. Due U.S. for 1 Colt's pistol, etc.
44. Pvt. Mabry, Gray	June 20	
45. Pvt. Mangel, Prosper	May 10	
46. Pvt. McCleester, H. B.	April 16	Taken prisoner April 28. Exchanged May 11, Discharged June 3
47. Pvt. McDonald, D.	April 16	Repairing rifle—$2.00.
48. Pvt. McKay, D.	June 13	
49. McMahon, J.	May 6	
50. Pvt. McWaters, J.A.	May 18	
51. Pvt. Mills, John	May 12	Due U.S. for 1 Colt's pistol, etc.
52. Pvt. Mills, Lawson F.	April 21	Due U. S. for 1 Colt's pistol, etc.
53. Pvt. Mills, Menan	May 20	Exchanged into Washington Rgt La Vol June 7.
54. Pvt. Moore, William E.	April 16	Absent on furlough; reported to be killed
55. Cpl. Neely, James	April 21	Due U.S. for 1 Colt's pistol, etc., Repair arms $1.00.
56. Pvt. Owen, A. G.	April 21	
57. Pvt. Page, Daniel	May 13	
58. 2nd Lt. Page, John	May 4	Due U.S. for 1 Colt's pistol, etc. Appt. 2nd Lt. June 30.
59. Pvt. Paul, P. C.	June 20	
60. Pvt. Peratt, Ary.	June 20	
61. Pvt. Petigree, George W.	June 20	
62. Pvt. Prostoski, Joseph	April 21	Killed in action April 28, Service commenced April 16.
63. Pvt. Quinn, Patrick	June 25	
64. 1st Sgt Radcliffe, Edward S.	April 21	Killed in action Apr. 28.
65. Pvt. Redmond	April 21	Dishonorably discharged May 2.

66. Pvt. Reese, J.	April 21	Taken prisoner April 28—Exchanged May 11—Discharged May 20. Service commenced April 16.
67. Pvt. Reynolds, Hal.	June 11	Sick on furlough.
68. Pvt. Reynolds, R. A.	June 11	
69. Pvt. Richards, William	June 20	
70. Pvt. Roark, Jackson	June 13	
71. Pvt. Robinson, J.	April 21	Killed in action April 28.
72. Pvt. Ryan, M.	June 20	
73. Pvt. Sayres, William B.	May 23	Due US 1 shot pouch, 1 bullet mould, 1 tube wrench Repairing rifle $2.00.
74. Pvt. Scarrett, M.B.	June 1	
75. Pvt. Simons, Morris	April 21	Service commenced April 16 [This could have been Maurice K. Simons, 2nd, 1st Lt. Co. K., 2nd Texas Inf. CSA, Maj. & ACS, Staff, CSA.]
76. Pvt. Simons, Thomas	June 20	
77. Pvt. Snucks, John	April 30	Dishonorably discharged May 2.
78. Pvt. Sovering, Joseph	April 20	Honorable discharge May 25.
79. Pvt. Strade, John	June 5	
80. Pvt. Sutton, J.S.	June 1	
81. Pvt. Taylor, Creed	April 21	Absent purchasing horses Due one bradoon & Martingale. Service commenced April 16.
82. Pvt. Taylor, James	April 21	Due US for one halter and chain Service commenced April 16.
83. Pvt. Taylor, Josiah	May 16	Detached as guide for Capt Gillespie Due U.S. for 1 Colt's pistol.
84. Pvt. Taylor, Pitkin	April 21	Service commenced April 16

85. Pvt. Terry, David	May 13	
86. Pvt. Terry, J.A.	June 9	Due U.S. for 1 Colt's pistol, etc. Repairing guns $2.00.
87. Pvt. Thompson, James	June 23	
88. 1st Lt. Threhan, George W.	April 21	Due U.S. for 2 Colt's pistols, etc. Appt. 1 Lt. June 30—Absent at muster On det. service near Matamoras by order of Gen Taylor. Services commenced April 16.
89. Pvt. Townsend, John	May 15	
90. Pvt. Treadgill, J.	June 13	
91. Cpl. Trimble, Moffett E.	April 21	Due U.S. for 1 Colt's Pistol, etc., one bridle. Service commenced April 16.
92. Pvt. Van Goren, D. F.	April 27	
93. Pvt. Van Reed, L.	April 21	Taken prisoner April 28, Exchanged May 11 Due US one bridle, bridoon, & martingale.
94. Capt. Walker, Samuel H.	April 21	Due U.S. for 1 Colt's pistol, etc.—Resigned June 30.
95. Pvt. Waters, William	April 27	Killed in action April 28.
96. Capt. Wells, Joseph P.	April 21	Vice Walker—Resigned June 30. Due U.S. for 2 Colt's pistols, etc. flask, bridle bit & bridoon. One martingale. Repair of rifle 2.00. Payment due 1st Lt Apr 16—June 30. Supplied horse by US. service commenced April 16. June 1846 on det. service near Matamoras by order of General Taylor.
97. Pvt. White, Charles	May 13	Due U.S. for 1 Colt's pistols, etc.

Supplies and Services for Capt. Sam Walker's Texas Ranger Company, Point Isabel 1846

20 April 1846 Point Isabel, Texas

Signed over to Capt. Walker:

8 Carbines,	Halls
6 screwdrivers & nipple wrenches	
6 wipers	
1 spring vice	
400 musket percussion caps	
32 Pistols	Colts patent
32 screwdrivers	Colts patent
32 Flasks	Colts patent
32 percussion priming boxes	Colts patent
32 Bullet molds	Colts patent
1200 Percussion Caps	Colts patent
6 Rifles …	
6 Screwdrivers	
6 wipers	
1 Ball screw [A "ball screw" is used to remove a ball when the barrel must be cleared without firing.]	
230 Rifle …	
300 Carbine Buck & Ball Cartridges	
300 Carbine B …	
2 Arms Chests	
10 Cartridge Boxes, Carbine	
7 Rifle pouches	
6 Waist Belts, Infantry	
6 … & belt plates, rifle	
7 flasks	
25 musket balls	
7 copper blanks, rifle	

22 April 1846 Point Isabel, Texas

6 axes felling
6 ax handles
6 spades
2 shovels
2 axes pick
6 blankets (saddle)
61 grain sacks

28 April [the following captured by the enemy]

6 axes felling
6 blankets
6 spades
2 shovels
2 axes pick
6 blankets (saddle)
61 grain sacks

28 April To Capt. Walker, Texas Ranger

One hickory shirt & one pair of drawers	2.00
One pair Kinky Jeans pantaloons	3.00

29 April 1846 to SHW at Point Isabel, Texas

6 horses
6 chain halters

[There is an interesting story here as an example of Sam's thoroughness. On July 26, Sam complains that while he was accountable for six horses in this receipt, it should have been five. "The black stallion, you will remember," Sam writes, "I returned without taking any receipt from Capt Montgomery." Sam requested a correct receipt so he could close his accounts with the US Army for his company.]

29 April 1846 to SHW at Point Isabel, Texas

To C. W. Hasting For making sacks	$1.50
10 yards domestic	$1.50

2 May 1846 to SHW at Point Isabel, Texas

12 qt tin cups	ea 3.00
6 frying pans	5.25

6 coffee pots	ea 5.25
1 coffe mill	ea 1.75
2 tin dippers	.50
12 tin plates	3.50
2 water buckets	1.20
2 tin pans	1.25
1 oven	3.50
TOTAL	24.50

5 May 1846 to SHW at Point Isabel, Texas

8 bridles (bit & b.....)
8 martingales
1 [?]

6 May 1846 to SHW at Point Isabel, Texas

20 nose bags
2 camps kettles
3 mess pans

13 May 1846 to SHW at Point Isbal, Texas

6 horse blankets
6 pack saddles complete
6 C ....C ... [?]
6 horse brushes
1 blank book
2 . ...writing paper
½ . ...b. ... [?]

14 May 1846 to SHW at Point Isbal, Texas

6 mules [captured from Mexicans]

23 June–27 June 1846 Forage return for 57 horses and 4 mules for 39 12/32 bushels of corn and 59 2/32 bushels of oats for Capt. SH Walker Texican Rangers—Fort Brown Texas

Undated invoice for Capt S. H. Walker's Company of Texican Rangers

13 nose bags
6 pack saddle blankets
500 grain sacks
6 brushes and curry combs
3 mess pans

30 June 1846

Arms belong to Capt Walker's Company of Texas Rangers repaired by Wm Gammel during the months of May and June 1846 by direction of Major H K Craig, Ordinance Department

1.	McCrea White	Rifle repaired	2.00
2.	James Neely	Rifle repaired	1.00
3.	Daniel McDonald	Rifle repaired	2.00
4.	Joseph Wells	Rifle repaired	2.00
5.	John Mills	Pistols and Rifle repaired	3.75
6.	J. A. Terry	Gun Repaired	2.00
7.	January, J.B.P.	Sight Repaired	1.00
8.	C.A. Glass	Pistols and wipers repaired	1.75
9.	William Tegres	Rifle Repaired	2.00
10.	D.W. Hatch	Pistol Repaired	1.50
11.	Montgomery Berry	Rifle	1.50
12.	John Barton	Rifle Repaired	1.00
13.	James Bradley	Rifle repaired	.50

22 July 1846

Arms turned in by Capt Walker at Matamoras

9 Colts revolving carbines
3 contract brown full stock rifles
6 Halls carbines
9 carbine or rifle cartridge boxes
3″ waist belts
7″ waist plates
4 Colts bullet moulds
3 pistol flasks
3 Percussion primers
3 Colt wrenches and screw drivers
3 rifle wipers
4 copper flasks
5 Rifle pouches

APPENDIX III

Walker Leads a Tribute to Robert Addison Gillespie; his Friend; Fellow Texas Ranger and Brother-in-Arms

Democratic Telegraph and Texas Register (Houston, Tex.), Vol. 11, No. 46, Ed. 1, Monday, November 16, 1846.

Public Meeting

In pursuance of previous notice, a meeting of the citizens of Bexar County was assembled at the courthouse in the city of San Antonio at five o'clock on this the 17th day of October 1846 for the purpose of adopting suitable resolutions expressive of the deep regret felt on the part of the citizens of this counting on hearing the intelligence of the death of Capt. R.A Gillespie late of the Bexar Rangers as well as in testimony of the high respect which the deceased during his lifetime is held by his friends and acquaintances on account of his many admirable qualities exalted virtues.

The meeting was organized by calling Capt. Samuel H. Walker into the chair and appointing as secretary James R Trueheart.

On motion of J A Pascal Esquire seconded by WG Crump Esquire it was resolved that the chair appointed five persons for the purpose of drafting resolutions expressivity of the sense of this meeting and the same to report as soon as practicable.

Whereas the chair appointed J A Pascal, Samuel S Smith, WG Crump Esquire, William S Oury and CF King who after having retired a short time reported the following resolutions which having been read at the clerk's table work on motion of JA Paschal seconded by WG Crump unanimously adopted.

Resolved that this meeting feels the deepest sorrow and regret on learning of the melancholy fate of the late Capt. R.A. Gillespie was recently killed while gallantly charging at the head of the Rangers in an assault upon one of the batteries of the enemy at the battle of Monterey.

Resolved that in the death of Capt. R.A. Gillespie of Texas is also one of the noblest and most gallant sons; society has been deprived of one of its brightest ornaments and his fellow soldiers in arms, of one of their dearest companions and most intrepid and skillful leaders.

Resolved that this meeting sincerely and truly sympathize with the surviving relatives and companions in arms of the deceased as a tribute of respect to his memory the members of this meeting will wear the uniform badger morning, left arm for 30 days.

Resolved that the secretary of this meeting be directed to forward to the nearest relatives of the deceased as early as the day as practical a copy of these proceedings and that the papers throughout the state be requested to be published the same.

Resolved that a committee of eight persons be appointed to draft a biological sketch of the life and services of the late Capt. R.A. Gillespie in defense of the of the country of his adoption and that the same be published in the newspapers of the state.

The chair appointed as said committee Messrs. J A Paschal, Samuel S Smith, W G Crump, William S Oury, CF King, G H Nelson, Thomas Green, John C Hays, V E Howard, and John McMullin.

The chair, on motion of J A Paschal, was added to said committee.

Moved that the thanks of the committee be tendered to the chair.

Moved by WG Crump Esquire that the meeting now be adjourned.
Samuel H Walker chairman
James L Trueheart secretary

APPENDIX IV

Thomas J. Green's Accusation that President Samuel Houston Lied in his Public and Private Letters Concerning the Mier Expedition

To the People of Texas—However unpleasant it may be to appear before you through the columns of a newspaper, it is a matter in which I have at present no choice. The President of your Republic on the one hand, and your countrymen now in chains, and the most odious slavery in Mexico on the other, are the parties at issue. I, more fortunate than they, favoured by an all-wise Providence, and an energy befitting the fearful task, with some few of my comrades, escaped through the walls of Perote some weeks since. A solemn duty I owe myself, my unfortunate fellow- prisoners, and my country, demands of me, with the evidences in my possession, to disabuse the public mind in what has been affirmed on one hand, and unblushingly denied by President Houston and his partisans on the other, to wit: That he wrote, or caused to be written, to Mexico, by Captain Charles Elliott, her Britannic majesty's chargé d'affaires at Galveston, that the Mier prisoners had entered Mexico contrary to law and authority.

Whatever may have been the ostensible pretext of General Houston's communication-and he pretends to ask mercy for his countrymen—yet his high authority that the Mier men had entered Mexico contrary to law and authority furnished the tyrant of that country all the legal pretext he could have desired in slaking his bloodthirsty vengeance upon the citizens of our country. It would, indeed, be an unjust denial of that personal and political acumen which General Houston's friends claim for him, to say that he could not foresee the consequences of that communication. The murder of our twenty-seven countrymen at Tampico, of Colonel Fannin and his brave four hundred, of many of the Santa Fe prisoners, and a thousand other acts of savage cruelty inflicted upon us during this war by Mexico, all too plainly told General Houston that his asking mercy for the Mier men' would not weigh a feather in the balance against Santa Anna's cold-blooded vindictiveness, after he [Houston] had in effect pronounced them brigands and marauders upon Mexico. One year previous to the battle of Mier the bloody tyrant had published a decree that in future the war with Texas should be conducted upon the principles of civilized warfare, and the Mier men, under their articles of capitulation, were guaranteed in a full observance of this decree. It was necessary, then, before he could once more, in the face of these solemn guarantees and the civilized world, dip his hands in the blood of your countrymen, to have some legal pretext for so doing. General Houston furnished him that pretext, and the murder of the brave Cameron, Cocke, Dunham, Ogden, Eastland, Jones, and their comrades in death, is the consequence, and their blood is upon his head.

While myself and companions were incarcerated in the vilest dungeon in Mexico, and had no power of speaking upon this subject, General Houston and his partisans boldly denied the charge, and referred exultingly to the secretary of state's letter, published in June, to the Hon. Ashbel Smith, our minister in London. One word of this letter-wherefore put it off from the battle of Mier in December up to June? All the evils which it sought to remedy was of six months' standing. From the date of our inglorious surrender at Mier on the 26th of December, up to the middle of March, we had been treated with all the consideration which our articles of capitulation guarantied; then comes this "merciful" death warrant of General Houston. Santa Anna forthwith orders General Mexier, Governor of Cohuilla, to shoot the whole of our prisoners in his charge, numbering one hundred and seventy odd. This brave soldier refused positively so to do; and three days after, the order, through the influence of the foreign ministers, was countermanded. Governor Mexier was then ordered to decimate them, which he also refused to do, for which he was broke of his commission, and banished the country; when a murderous wretch was specially charged with the execution of this horrible black bean lottery, and thus fell those brave men, who had so often staked their lives in defence of your liberty. After this most unjust and infamous butchery, which was on the 25th of March, the balance of the Mier men were still in the most imminent peril. On the 25th of April, the brave and lamented Cameron was taken out and shot without any cause being given. Immediately, however, after the first order for shooting our men had gone forth, we lost no time in writing home for evidences of General Houston's falsehood. They were furnished by the bushel. Among these were his ridiculous and bombastic newspaper gasconade, in answer to Santa Anna's letter to General Hamilton—his numerous war proclamations—his bloody war speeches at Galveston and elsewhere—his proclamation of the 16th of September, 1842, calling upon all of the first class of militia of the counties west of the Trinity, and under which proclamation we came out, and in which he authorized the men to call to their lead a man of wisdom, valour, and experience, and "pursue the enemy into Mexico, and chastise him for his insolence and wrongs." Also the law of Texas of January,

1840, authorizing us to elect our commander, and last, though not least, the Constitution of your country, by which foreigners, at least, are taught to believe that President Houston's dictum is not superior to that sacred instrument. These were the evidences which General Thompson so humanely alludes to in his letter of the 10th of June, to his Excellency Mr. Doyle, and which armed him so completely against the machinations of your President and the bloodthirsty vengeance of his friend Santa Anna. "Feeling now that the last blood had flowed which it was in the power of General Houston's vindictiveness to the Mier command to shed, and many of my prison companions looking to me to vindicate them against the foul aspersions of their unjust President, on the 29th of May I wrote to General Thompson to preserve me a copy of the letter which General Houston had caused to be written to Mexico. In doing so, I felt a duty more weighty, and far more sacred, than any obligation to the living. The honest reputation of the dead was the only legacy bequeathed by these murdered heroes to their mourning friends and destitute wives and children: that I shall be in any way instrumental in perpetuating the record that their husbands and fathers did not die robbers, as President Houston pronounced them, will be to me a lasting gratification; while to them, in long years to come, they may look back upon the fact as their proudest recollection, that the traducer of the dead was proved their slanderer and murderer.

Can it be possible that President Houston has a friend so blinded in his party zeal as not to know that Commodore Moore and the whole of his crew would have been shot, had they by any chance of war fallen into the hands of the Mexicans, after President Houston's proclamation of piracy against him? Yet the Mier case is one point, with this difference, that they were already in the hands of the Mexicans, and it suited General Houston's policy to have them killed off more secretly, and under some pretence of mercy.

My letter to General Thompson of the 29th of May, above alluded to, produced the following correspondence between him and the Hon. Mr. Doyle … and from General Thompson to. … By this correspondence it will be seen that I am first referred to the author of the letter for a copy, and in the event of refusal, then General Thompson promises his statement of its contents. Upon my arrival in Galveston, I addressed letter … to Captain Elliott. His answer, … shows his refusal to furnish said letter, which brought forth my reply. I should then have applied to President Houston for the copy in question, but Mr. S. H. Walker, one of my fellow-prisoners lately escaped from Mexico, having applied to General Houston for the same, received General Houston's verbal denial of the existence of such letter. This correspondence will show that Captain Elliott, Mr. Doyle, General Thompson-all, except your President, are too honourable to deny the existence of the letter, and he does it with the same unblushing hardihood which has caused him to deny a thousand things he has uttered. Vice and crime delight in darkness, and General Houston may have supposed that his blunt denial would stop all inquiry upon the subject, but in this he adds moral turpitude to heinous guilt, and therefore deserves the more the execrations of his countrymen. "Fellow-citizens, well may you ponder upon the political condition of your country, and some seek refuge in acknowledging the supremacy of degraded Mexico, some in abolition, some in annexation, when such things are allowed. What a commentary upon our government! If the poorest man were to commit murder upon his neighbour, he would be hanged therefor but President Houston, in the unchecked practice of every political enormity, can do so by the regiment and fleet without punishment. I am, very respectfully, your old friend,

Thomas J. Green
November 10th, 1845.[1]

Galveston, Nov. 6th, 1843.
To his Excellency Charles Elliott,
H. B. M. Chargé d'Affaires for Texas.

Sir,
Feeling a deep interest in the fate of my late fellow-prisoners, and that it is a duty I owe my country that the causes which led to the foul murder of a portion of them, under the order of President Santa Anna, should be known, and believing that their massacre was the result of the correspondence of President Houston with your excellency, which was forwarded by you to Mr. Packenham, I respectfully ask a copy of General Houston's letter to you, and of yours to Mr. Packenham. You will see from the enclosed copy of correspondence between General Thompson and Mr. Doyle, that the contingency upon which I am authorized to make General Thompson's statement public is the failure to procure those letters. I am, very respectfully,

your ob't serv't,
Thomas J. Green[2]

Galveston, Nov. 7th, 1843.

Sir, I have the honour to acknowledge your letter of the 6th instant, and, as a general rule, I must decline to furnish you with copies of any correspondence between other persons and myself. I have the honour to remain, sir, your obedient servant,

Charles Elliott[3]

Galveston, Nov. 7th, 1843.
To his Excellency Charles Elliott,
H. B. M. Chargé d'Affaires for Texas.

Sir, I have the honour to acknowledge your note of yesterday in answer to mine of the 6th instant, and can readily allow, as a "general rule," the propriety of your not furnishing copies of your correspondence; but the correspondence I requested was of such an extraordinary character, I cannot believe it should come under such "general rule." Your excellency, therefore, will allow me most respectfully to state more at length the reasons of that application. Upon the arrival of myself and companions at Tacubaya, near the city of Mexico, about the 15th of March last, we were several times informed by gentlemen who had it direct from General Thompson, the United States minister near that court, that you had, at the request of President Houston, written to H. B. M. minister, Mr. Packenham, to this purport, "that though the Mier prisoners had entered Mexico contrary to law and authority, yet he, Houston, begged mercy for them," &c. The high authority of President Houston, that the Mier prisoners were brigands, endorsed by the still higher authority of her Britannic majesty's chargé d'affaires residing at their homes, gave the President of Mexico all the legal right he desired to shoot them. The whole history of our war shows that he could desire nothing more than such legal pretext to execute upon Texians the bloodiest vengeance. We had been prisoners of war from the 26th of December up to the middle of March, and under our articles of capitulation had been treated as such. Then comes, to say the least of it, your unfortunate letter, which took from us all protection of that capitulation, which legalized our murders, and proved a death warrant to the whole of my brave companions. Most fortunately for them, three days after the bloody order had gone into the hands of a soldier too just and too brave to execute it, the remonstrance of the foreign ministers got it countermanded; but still, their influence could not prevent the execution of your countryman, the brave Cameron, and his seventeen companions. Justice to the memory of these brave spirits and their destitute wives and children calls loudly upon me to place their murder where it rightly belongs. With this view, before leaving Perote, I wrote to the American minister near Mexico to procure me a copy of your letter from Mr. Doyle, H. B. M. minister, who succeeded Mr. Packenham, which correspondence I had the honour of enclosing to your excellency yesterday. It is not my desire to criminate your excellency with a foreknowledge of the consequences of this unfortunate letter; of your humanity I have a more exalted opinion but when your excellency has been made the unwitting instrument of communication by which this melancholy, bloody, hellish tragedy has been perpetrated upon the best men of our country, justice, both to yourself and government, requires that the whole truth should be told, and the blame rest upon the head of him who projected it. Your excellency has been sufficiently unfortunate in being the innocent medium of this fell execution, and its cruel author, the least of all men, deserves screening at your hands by the suppression of the least portion of the truth; and I have yet to learn how such suppression can promote the ends of justice. I must be allowed the opinion, that whatever rule of diplomacy governs your official station, you have no right to hold anything as private to myself or companions which affect our lives or liberty Very respectfully, your excellency's obedient servant

Thomas J. Green.[4]

"To the Public."

Duty to our brave and unfortunate countrymen in the dungeons of Mexico caused me to lay before the public, some months since, the correspondence between the United States and English ministers in that country, relative to the letter which General Houston had written to Mexico, denouncing the Mier prisoners as brigands, and which caused their decimation and subsequent suffering. No honest man, even of the most blinded partisans of President Houston, who read that correspondence, doubted for a moment the statement of the facts therein set forth, though President Houston and his forces in Texas had for months previous to that time denied most solemnly that he had ever written or caused to be written such a letter to Mexico. As soon as he found that I had returned from that country, armed with the proofs of his bloody murder of our countrymen, he, in his speech in the Presbyterian Church at Houston, in November, for the first time admitted the fact, and said "it was not, my friends, Captain Elliott's letter which produced the mischief;" but charges the murder upon General Hunt and the Telegraph, 'for publishing a letter of the former, on the 18th of January previous.

This subterfuge of President Houston in falsely quoting said letter, and so preposterous and unjust a supposition as that the publication of the letter of a private gentleman in a Texas newspaper could be sufficient with the Mexican Government for such a shocking deed, did not satisfy the public mind. On the 12th of December, a few days thereafter, President Houston, in his annual message to Congress, changed his ground of defence, and said "that it was a retaliation on account of those under General Somerville, who robbed Laredo"; thus charging this bloody deed to his particular friends of Washington and Montgomery counties, who returned under Colonel Bennett from that place. This last defence of the

President, more frivolous than the former, shows under what awkward extremes guilt will seek shelter.

Perhaps it would have been unnecessary for me to have said more upon this subject, so well convinced was the public mind of President Houston's criminal and malicious agency in having my comrades shot, and others starved for the want of bread, had not some newspapers in his interest recently insulted public intelligence by speaking of "his kind feelings for those men." This most unblushing and barefaced insult, as well to the memories of those hundred and odd whose deaths he caused, as to the remaining half in chains and slavery, is my excuse, if one were necessary, for again obtruding myself upon the public.

Though our last Congress placed to the credit of our prisoners in Mexico thirty thousand dollars, under the most positive and peremptory injunctions upon President Houston "forthwith" to supply them, not one dollar has been sent them. When the President is asked why he has not sent the money to these men, he adds insult to their misfortunes by saying that they are better off than they would be at their homes.

No man of sane intellect, whatever may be his devotion, personal or political, to President Houston, after reading the annexed correspondence, can for a moment doubt that he was the malicious, vindictive, coldblooded author of the execution.

Very respectfully, your obedient servant,
Thomas J. Green.[5]

Mexico, Dec. 20th, 1843.

Shortly after I heard of the capture of the Texian prisoners at Mier, and having serious apprehensions that their rights as prisoners of war might be violated, I called upon the Hon. Richard Packenham to request that he would, if necessary, add his great and well-deserved influence with the Mexican government to mine, for the protection of those men. He expressed at once a willingness to do so, but said that, from what he had heard, he was afraid they were not strictly entitled to the rights of prisoners of war, because the expedition had not been authorized by the Texian government. I told him that I was very certain he was mistaken. In a subsequent interview with Mr. Packenham on the subject, he told me that he had received a letter from Captain Elliott, H. B. M. chargé d'affaires in Texas, saying that General Houston requested him (Mr. P.) to interpose his good offices in behalf of the Mier prisoners, although they might not, in strictness, be entitled to be regarded as prisoners of war, as the expedition had not been authorized by the Texian government. Shortly after the arrival of Mr. Percy W. Doyle in Mexico, I had a conversation with him on the subject, in which he made the same statement as to the letter of Captain Elliott; and in a subsequent conversation upon the subject, he added, that he thought it probable, in saying that the expedition was not authorized, that President Houston alluded not to the original expedition, but to the continuance of it after the return to Texas of General Somerville. Although I am very sure that in this I cannot be mistaken, yet if I am, it is very easy to prove it by the production of the letter, or a statement of Mr. Packenham.

W. Thompson.[6]

New-Orleans, April 14th, 1844.

Sir, I have had the honour to receive your letter of the 8th of November, in which you inform me that President Houston not only disavows having authorized Captain Elliott to write such a letter to the Hon. Richard Packenham, as it was reported that he had done, but that he also asserts that no communication to that effect had ever been made to me by Mr. Packenham or Mr. Doyle. If President Houston had confined himself to the disavowal of having authorized such a letter to have been written, I do not know that, upon mature reflection, I should have considered it my duty to have made any statement upon the subject; but as the matter now stands, I have no alternative left me. I therefore send you the accompanying statement, with a note from Benjamin E. Green, Esq., and another addressed by me to Mr. Doyle. I trust that nothing farther can be required of me in the matter. You, sir, very well know that my name has been involved in the affair by no officious interference in it, and it has been made public contrary to my advice and wishes. The fact of such a letter having been written came to my knowledge while endeavouring, under the express orders of my government (given in a similar case), to protect those brave and unfortunate men, the prisoners of Mier. It was a matter of such a character that it was impossible I could have been either indifferent or mistaken about it. I have furnished General Houston with a copy of this statement. I have the honour to be, very respectfully, your obedient servant,

Waddy Thompson[7]

Mexico, December 21st, 1843.

General W. Thompson
Dear Sir,—In compliance with your request, I called yesterday upon the Honourable Percy W. Doyle with the statement which is copied above, and which you propose to send to General T. J. Green, upon

the subject of Captain Elliott's letter to Mr. Packenham, relative to the Texians taken prisoners at Mier. Mr. Doyle declined giving me a copy of Captain Elliott's letter, on the ground that it was a private letter, and not addressed to him; and after retiring to another room to compare your statement with that letter, he admitted that the statement was in every respect correct. Very respectfully, your obedient servant,

Ben. E. Green.

The following protest from a committee of our countrymen, prisoners in the Castle of Perote, dated July, 1844, to the British minister near the government of Mexico, has immediate reference to the agency which President Houston had in the decimation of our men:

His Excellency Charles Bankhead:

Sir,—The undersigned, a committee of the prisoners now confined in the Castle of Perote, believing that we are abandoned by our own government, have only the alternative left of appealing to the minister of her Britannic majesty at the court of Mexico to interfere with a view of putting a termination to our suffering and imprisonment. The evidence upon which our opinion is based, that we are surrendered by our government, are, first, the letter to your predecessor by the Executive of Texas, denouncing the Mier Expedition as a lawless band of adventurers, unsanctioned by the authorities of the country whence it came, and therefore unentitled to the consideration and protection which, by civilized usage and of right, belong to prisoners of war. Secondly, his withholding the means appropriated by Congress for our relief, when well apprized of our destitute and unfortunate situation. Thirdly, his entire neglect to make any exertion in our behalf, either by way of mitigating our hard fate or procuring our release. The only anxiety, within the knowledge of the undersigned, evinced by President Houston for the Texian prisoners, is to be found in the letter above referred to, which resulted in the melancholy, tragic scene at the Ranch Salado, where were executed in cold blood seventeen as brave men as ever enlisted in the holy cause and under the sacred banner of liberty. Whether this solicitude was for our weal or wo, the probable tendency of its operation, and its actual lamentable consequences, will show, not only to the satisfaction of those who executed, but those who prompted the horrid act. From this it will appear that this appeal properly emanates from the undersigned, and the sequel will show that it is appropriately addressed to your excellency the British minister.

We believe, sir, that the government of Great Britain is under official obligation to demand our liberation. Under the auspices, and through the avowed agency of the chargé d'affaires of your government to Texas, a treaty for the mutual exchange of prisoners was entered into and solemnly ratified by the contracting parties. Texas had confidence in this treaty from the fact that your government became incidentally a party to it—

The undersigned do not rest their grounds for the interference of your excellency in their behalf upon the foregoing showing alone. They appeal to you, and the whole corps diplomatique, as conservators of international law. Diplomatic agents, clothed with ministerial powers, are called ministers to the different courts to which they are sent, which term, conjoined to their official duties, implies the possession of judicial authority.

If this position be true, you are bound to notice all infractions of the great law of nations, either in a state of peace or in the turmoils of war. It is your prerogative to control and regulate the operations of the latter state when not conducted according to the principles of humanity and the common mild usages of civilized nations.

In the undersigned and their unfortunate comrades you have a case which solicits the controlling influence of foreign ministers. The humane maxims of international law, the acknowledged customs of civilized nations, have all alike been violated and disregarded in our cruel treatment and unjust detention. When taken at Mier, under treaty stipulations guarantying to us safety and consideration, we were marched on foot, through sunshine and through storm, and a portion of the way handcuffed in couples, under the tauntings and lash of merciless Mexican soldiery. In the villages and towns through which we passed, instead of being treated with the kind courtesy usually extended by generous captors to vanquished enemies, we were received amid the hisses and maledictions of the infuriated rabble, with placards staring us in the face, commemorating the defeat of the Texian adventurers and robbers, as they termed us. The bloody tragedies enacted on the road the undersigned refrain from recapitulating; their minds shrink with horror from the recital. Language is inadequate to express the deep agony of the heart in the bare review of such inhuman acts. Such has been our treatment on the way to Mexico, and the same harshness still continues. Only a few days since, one of our men, a Lieutenant Clopton, returned from the hospital in which he had been confined for five or six weeks from the wounds and bruises inflicted upon him by a large bludgeon in the hands of Captain Arroya, commandant of the castle. A few weeks ago, a pale and sickly boy was so severely beaten by the same weapon. in the hands of the same officer, as to be compelled to carry his arm in a sling for some time. In a word, we are miserably fed, badly clothed, and worked like beasts of burden. Our hard fate is rendered yet more intolerable by the fact that neither of the contending parties appear to make any active demonstrations to bring the war to a close, but rather prefer becoming the clients of Great Britain, the United States, and France. The time necessary to render their mediation effective must necessarily be long; and during this state of nominal peace we have suffered, and still continue to suffer, all the hardships of an actual state of warfare.

Very respectfully.
Fenton M. Gibson
Claudius Buster
William S. Fisher
William Ryan
Samuel C. Lyon
Committee.[8]

Upon the release of Thomas J. Greens account of the Mier Expedition and the sufferings of those who had surrendered, Sam Houston, believing he had been wrongfully accused of labeling the prisoners as "banditi," giving Santa Anna justification to murder every tenth unfortunate, retaliated with his own account of the lengths he went to on behalf of them.

Galveston, Texas, Dec. 21, 1845.
Mr. H[amilton] Stuart:[9]

Dear Sir,—Believing that I should be delinquent in duty to others as well as to myself, if I were longer to remain silent, touching the facts connected with the Mier Prisoners, subsequent to their capitulation, I will now express myself. Although I have but seldom read the gratuitous misrepresentations, which have been reiterated upon this subject, I nevertheless, have seen and know sufficient of them to suppose, that many honest readers may be inclined to believe that there was some foundation for the charges made, by those who regard notoriety more than honest fame, I will not now stoop to a vindication of my course, but will state facts. On account of the relations and friends of those noble fellows, who fell by decimation it is proper that their acts should be vindicated, as it was not by their own conduct that they perished, but that of others, on whom punishment might have deservedly fallen. Soon after the General in command had ordered the army back from Guerero, to the San Antonio River, it was reported at Washington, that a portion of the troops had disobeyed the order and elected a leader. Then came in quick succession the news of the surrender at Mier. Our Congress was in session, and adjourned without taking any action upon the case of our men. All persons whom I heard speak of the prisoners seemed to regard their destruction as inevitable, as the fact was known that they had crossed the Rio Grande, to invade Mexico without orders. And although others seemed to despair of their rescue, as a man, and as an Executive, I did not. Instructions were immediately sent through Hon. Anson Jones, Secretary of State, to our Minister at Washington City, as well as our Minister to England and France, directing them to make urgent request of those Governments to interpose their kind offices in behalf of the prisoners, and if possible to obtain their immediate restoration to their friends and their country. The despatch from the Texian Secretary of State was the first intimation which our Minister to England had, of the disaster of Mier. There was surely no "betrayal of the brave sufferers," by this timely application in their behalf, urging such reasons as could be suggested, to cause the immediate action of all the friendly powers, in favor of their safety and release. Not satisfied while it seemed to me that any thing more might be done, I addressed a letter to Captain [Charles] Elliot, H. B. M. Charge d'Affaires, then, at this place, requesting him to address H. B. M. Minister at Mexico in behalf of the prisoners, stating that no matter under what circumstances they might have crossed the Rio Grande, whether with or without orders, the moment that the terms of capitulation proposed by Mexico were accepted by the troops at Mier, that moment they were entitled to all the rights and benefits of prisoners of war, and I hoped, if these reasons were timely presented and urged, that they might all be saved. Previous to the receipt of my letter by Captain Elliot, the newspapers had stated to the world all the facts of the expedition, and that the army of General Somerville had returned, and that those who marched to Mier, had gone "contrary to orders!" Whatever complection some may have tried to give the facts connected with this matter, it is proper to state (notwithstanding what may have been his course, or statements, after wards,) the Hon. Waddy Thompson, the American meteoric diplomatist, stated in a letter to the Hon. Bailey. Peyton of New Orleans, that so soon as he heard of the situation of the Mier prisoners, and of the order for their execution, that he called on the British Minister, Mr. Packenham, who promptly interposed in their behalf, and rendered every aid in his power. This is substantially Mr. Thompson's remark in the letter referred to. Now, it would seem that my letter had not induced Captain Elliot to make such representation to Mr. Packenham as caused the decimation of the prisoners. The cause of their decimation will be stated in the conclusion of my letter. It would seem very ridiculous in an executive who had labored under the most disadvantageous circumstances to obtain the release of the Santa Fe prisoners, to conspire against the lives of gallant men in misfortune, many of whom were sons and kindred of the friends of his early life. The misrepresentations relative to the Mier prisoners do not stop here. When Congress made the appropriation for the relief of the prisoners, by secret act, it has been charged that the Executive had prevented means from being applied to the relief of the prisoners, with a view to aggravate their sufferings. Time will be the best refutation of this calumny. With the return of the members of Congress to Galveston, came the letter of notification, and instructions to the agent Mr. [L. S] Hargous [U.S. Consul at Veracruz], from the Secretary of the Treasury, and was forthwith sent to him at Veracruz. He declined acting in behalf of the prisoners, as the agent of the Government, and assigned, among other reasons, that a General Thomas Jefferson Green, had swindled him out of several hundred dollars, by giving him drafts to the Treasury of Texas, and on his brother in New Orleans, and that on application, he found that Green had no right to draw on the Treasury, and that he had no brother in New Orleans. That kindness he had rendered Green, and his subsequent vain glorious letter, through the New Orleans papers, thanking Mr. Hargous for his kindness, &c., had endangered his life, and caused a prosecution against him, which cost him five thousand dollars before he could extricate himself. Under these circumstances, the Government was compelled to send a special agent. Mr. Porter was sent to Mexico as an agent from this Government, carrying with him $2,500 in specie. Immediately on his arrival from Veracruz, he wrote for $2,000 more, which was placed in the hands of Messrs. Schmidt & Co. at New Orleans, subject to the order of the agent in Mexico. He was recognized and had to escape to Havana, where he had an attack of yellow fever, which nearly cost him his life. None of this action was required by the act of Congress; yet so great was the anxiety of the Government to relieve the wants of the prisoners, that the Executive assumed the responsibility of acting in the case where the law was not sufficient for the emergencies which arose. Were it not that persons who have been friendly to Texas and the prisoners, would be exposed and endangered in their lives, and subjected to the confiscation of their estates, I could present many facts which would convince any man of the difficulties under which the Executive labored. The act of the Congress required that all drafts over one thousand dollars should not be paid by the collector, until thirty days after sight. On the 19th day of October, 1844, one was drawn for $3,740, and information given with the draft, that the money was necessary for the comforts and needs of the prisoners who were suffering of want. On this representation of the collector, I directed him to pay the draft forthwith, and told him that for his indemnity, I would pledge $2,512 for which I had taken a draft on the Custom House for my salary, and the contingent fund of the Executive which was $2,500. This was the course which was pursued by me, and this presents the facts which are imputed to me, as evincing hostility to the sufferers at Mier. It has been sheer falsehood and slander, that ever gave rise to imputations, intended to create a prejudice in the community, while it would exasperate the minds of the Mier prisoners against me; and when they were circulated, they were known to be untrue by their authors. There was but one cause assigned for the decimation of the prisoners by General Santa Anna, and upon which alone he placed his justification before H. B. M. Minister. It was not the attempt made by the prisoners to escape, for that, he said, prisoners had the right to do, but it was the conduct perpetrated by certain followers of the army at Laredo. It had been represented to him, that after the submission of the inhabitants of that place, some persons broke open houses, and robbed the inhabitants and for this reason, he ordered the decimation. It has been solemnly asserted by hundreds of the army, and cannot with truth be denied, that Thomas Jefferson Green was the first man who broke open a house, and incited the men to outrage. Such acts, or saca (as they were termed) are unknown even in Mexico, unless a town or city is taken by storm. The inhabitants of Laredo surrendered at the first summons, and contributed every thing in their power to the comfort and support of the Troops. It should be noted that General Somerville previous to leaving Laredo, ordered the stolen goods to be brought forward and restored to the authorities of the place; (if not all) "a large pile," was handed over. No reflection can be made on the character, of a man who had hung on the skirts of an army, without command, and availed himself of the first opportunity to outrage the rules of civilized nations by warfare on defenseless women and children, acts which were to be visited upon brave men, who subsequently fell martyrs to the dastardly crimes of others. Now, Sir, I assure you, that I have been induced to notice the slanders against me, only because I am aware that many worthy men, for whose feelings, I cherish a regard and for whose opinions, I entertain respect, have laboured under misconceptions of the truth. The facts may go for what they are worth. I did all that was in my power to save and to serve, and nothing to injure the prisoners. I have at all times been satisfied, that my course in relation to the Mier prisoners, has been such as I have pursued in the discharge of other duties, which have devolved upon me. The day will come, when it will be shown, that I obtained the release of the Mier prisoners. Now, it is not proper that it should be made manifest, nor is it necessary. I will not envy any man, who may have it in his power to render more numerous and important services to my country, and to mankind than I have done. I trust that he will not have to exclaim with Lear, "The little dogs and all, Tray, Blanche, and sweet-heart, see, they bark at me."

Sam Houston.[10]

Executive Department,
Washington, October 3, 1842.
To Brigadier General A. Somervell:

Sir—Your official communication from San Felipe, under date of 29th Ultimo, reached me late last night. I seize the first opportunity to communicate my orders.

You will proceed to the most eligible point on the Southwestern frontier of Texas, and concentrate with the force now under your command, all troops who may submit to your orders, and if you can advance with a prospect of success into the enemy's territory, you will do so forthwith. You are at liberty to take one or two pieces of ordnance now at Gonzales. For my own part I have but little confidence in cannon on a march. They will do on a retreat where the forces are nearly equal, but they embarrass the advance of an army. And if pressed hard on a retreat, the great aversion that troops have to leave their artillery may induce delay and embarrass all the movements of the army. Our greatest reliance will be upon light troops, and the celerity of our movements. Hence, the necessity of discipline and subordination. You will therefore receive no troops into service, but such as will be subordinate to your orders and the rules of war.

You will receive no troops into your command but such as will march across the Rio Grande under your orders if required by you so to do [emphasis by the author]. If you cross the Rio Grande you must suffer no surprise, but be always on the alert. Let your arms be inspected night and morning, and your scouts always on the lookout. You will be controlled by the rules of the most civilized war fare, and you will find the advantage of exercising great humanity towards the common people. In battle let the enemy feel the fierceness of just resentment and retribution.

The orders of the government of the 15th ultimo, having been disregarded by those who have gone to Bexar, in never having reported or communicated with the Department of War, the Executive will not recognize their conduct, and you alone will be held responsible to the government and be sustained by its resources. You will report as often as possible your operations.

You may rely upon the gallant Hays and his companions; and I desire that you should obtain his services and cooperation and assure him and all the brave and subordinate men in the field that the troops of the country and the confidence of the Executive point to them as objects of constant solicitude. Insubordination and a disregard of command will bring ruin and disgrace upon our arms.

God speed you!
Sam Houston.

Special order No. 52
Department of War and Marine,
Washington, 13th Octr. 1842.
To Brigr General A. Somervell,

Sir: Should this order meet you on your way to this place, you will reach here as soon as practicable: If at Matagorda, you will proceed without delay to the South Western frontier, and select the most eligible position on the Cibolo or elsewhere, as your judgment may direct, and proceed to the organization and drill of all the troops who may report to you, with a firm resolve to be obedient to orders, and, if required, to cross the Rio Grande None others will be received into the service; nor will supplies of any kind be issued to such, as they would only consume the substance of the frontier inhabitants, without securing to them the corresponding benefit [emphasis by the author]. The greatest care and economy must be observed under any circumstances, or starvation will be the consequence. To insure even probable success, it will be necessary to conduct all your movements with secrecy; for this reason, San Antonio is not deemed a proper place for concentration. If possible, the enemy should be kept in ignorance of our designs; otherwise all our efforts will be counteracted and prove abortive. Too much care cannot be observed to prevent the approach or entrance into your encampment of the native Mexicans of San Antonio. If free ingress and egress is permitted there, your operations, strength, and resources will most certainly reach the enemy. When the force shall have assembled, if their strength and condition will warrant a movement upon the enemy, it is desirable that it should be executed with promptness and efficiency. A plan of the organization for the army will be forwarded to you - Meantime, you will allow only the requisite number of Officers to the men in the field, one soldier who fights well, and does his duty is worth two officers who fight indifferently, and who neither understand, nor will discharge their duty. Officers sometimes embarrass men, who in private stations, would do well, and render efficient service to their country. You will find enclosed an extract from the Law of 18th January 1841 to complete the organization of the militia. If the troops wish to organize under it, they will of course be permitted to do so on application to you, and may elect all their officers, excepting only the commandant of the expedition. You will keep the Department constantly advised of your progress, and success in the execution of your orders.

By order of the President:
M[organ] C. Hamilton,
Acting Sec. War &Marine.

APPENDIX V

Walker's Weapons

His Rifle

Walker never succeeded in arming his company with the Clarke (Wesson) rifles. But on October 5, 1847, Sam wrote his brother Jonathan Thomas that he was sending him the "amount due for Wesson for the Rifle."[1] He also told him that he had not heard anything about the Wesson rifles he had purchased for the two of them. General Lane brought him only the Walker Colt pistols from Sam Colt.[2] But that is the last mention of Walker's rifle in any record yet found. According to Edwin Wesson's Order Book a cast steel barrel rifle was made for Captain Walker, serial number 531. A second one, serial number 532, was made for Walker's brother, Jonathan Thomas. It is thought these rifles were made in 1846.[3]

His Sword

Walker's personal sword appears to have been a Model 1833 Foot Artillery Sword.[4] This old-style artillery sword was probably in storage at Baton Rouge, and issued to Walker. Ironically, the man who wanted the most modern firearm for his men chose a Roman gladius style foot artillery sword. After Walker's death on October 9, 1847, his personal sword was given to one of his friends, Maj. Philip F. Bowman.[5] He was with Walker during their Mier imprisonment. Bowman, a major in the 4th Pennsylvania Regiment, was military commander at Perote where Walker's Mounted Riflemen Company was based. Bowman gave the sword to the museum of the Wyoming Historical Society at Wilkes-Barre, Pennsylvania (which states that it no longer has it). As described in an article written in 1882, "The scabbard is deeply indented, the edge of the blade is hacked and on the inner side of the well-worn belt appears, amidst blood stains, the name written in his own hand, of SAMUEL H. WALKER."[6]

It seems relatively certain, then, that this is the sword that Walker personally used. The name on the scabbard and the well-worn belt indicates heavy personal use by Walker. The notch in the blade also gives further indication that this was Walker's sword. On June 20, 1847, at 3 a.m. at La Hoya Pass in Mexico, Walker and part of his company were ordered to scout for the enemy and encountered them suddenly in the dark. Walker ordered a charge and routed them. Following them down the road—according to his second-in-command—Walker rode at the head of his men, four abreast, with his sword in hand, when they came upon a campfire by the road which blinded them to the road's sudden turn. Walker and his men then rode at full gallop into a fence. He and seven others were unhorsed. Walker reported eight horses—including Tornado—lost in the darkness. According to one source it was this collision with the picket fence that bent and indented the sword scabbard.[7] The sword that was once in the collection of the Wyoming Historical Society had a deep notch and if Walker had it in hand as indicated, this notch is possibly the end result of his mishap.

The Pennsylvania museum has what is believed to be one of Walker's swords but not the sheath. There is evidence that the scabbard was returned to the family. In the family collection of Walker letters is a letter dated March 25, 1915, that tells of a house fire in which all was consumed by fire, inlcuding "Uncle Sam's sword scabbard."[8] No mention of a sword, just the scabbard is recalled, indicating it was of special value.

Some[9] have considered the sword in the Pennsylvania museum as the one presented to Walker on May 22, 1846, by the ladies of New Orleans. However, a newspaper account about this sword indicated it was "a very elegant and serviceable sword, with an appropriate inscription."[10] If the inscription meant an engraving on the blade, then this was not the sword now in Pennsylvania. The sword at Wilkes-Barre has no engraving on the blade whatsoever.[11]

It would seem that Colonel Wynkoop was looking for Walker's sword about two weeks after his death. On October 25, 1847, he wrote Colonel Childs in Puebla, "Will Col Childs[12] ... please to hand the bearer for me the sword belonging to the late Capt. Walker. I have all of his effects with that exception."[13] This, in all likelihood, referred to the engraved presentation sword.[14]

On March 4, 1848—six months after Sam's death—Adj. Gen. Roger Jones wrote Childs about Walker's sword. Childs replied that Colonel Wynkoop was "accountable for the effects of Capt. Walker. I have sent the communication of the Adjutant General to Col Wynkoop."[15]

Walker's Personal Colt Whitney Walker Revolvers

A few days before he was killed in action, Capt. Samuel Walker did indeed receive a pair of the Colt revolvers he helped design. That is fact. What has been uncertain is what happened to them after he was killed.

One tradition has it that 2d Lt. Bedney F. McDonald (3d U.S. Artillery), the son of the former Governor of Georgia Charles J. McDonald,[16] was given a Walker Colt by Walker before he died and McDonald, in turn, sent it back to the maker, Sam Colt himself. There is a letter to Colt from McDonald commenting on this

Walker revolver and Colt accepted it as one of Walker's personal pistols.[17]

It is fact that Bedney McDonald was at the battle of Huamantla where Walker was killed. In Gen. Joseph Lane's official report of the engagement at Huamantla, he wrote: "Lieut. B. P. McDonald, 3d Artillery [Lane's assistant quartermaster], ... was sent with an order into the town previous to my entry, accompanied by Mr. Bradley, of the quartermaster's department. He was surrounded by lancers, but succeeded in escaping."[18]

Bedney F. McDonald. (From a private collection)

When McDonald did join up with Walker's command, there could have been several at Huamantla who would have recognized McDonald. Surgeon J. T. Lamar of Georgia who treated Walker, as well as men in Loyall's Georgia Dragoons who were attached to Walker's battalion probably knew who he was.

One reason McDonald sent the pistol to Colt was their friendship.[19] When McDonald wrote Colt that the two gift revolvers Colt had sent him were destroyed by fire, Colt had sent McDonald another pair of presentation pistols within three weeks. That would certainly imply Colt and McDonald's friendship was in good standing.

Further indications of a Colt–McDonald friendship are indicated by another gift from McDonald to Colt, an English-made "escopeta" carbine that he captured from a Mexican lancer at Huamantla during the battle in which Walker was killed.[20]

McDonald claimed that the presentation pistol he was returning to Colt was in fact one that Colt had sent Sam Walker. McDonald claimed Walker "gave" the pistol to him before he died. This story would have been even more believable had the serial number of the pistol been either 1009 or 1010. Moreover, the instantaneous death of Walker precludes that possibility that Walker passed one of his pistols to him.

When Colt had finally finished his production of Walker Colt revolvers, he had 100 set aside with plain serial numbers without company numbers stamped on them. These were to be presentation pairs. The revolver McDonald sent Colt had such a number.

The saga of the six special presentation pistols that included the one destined for Sam Walker began with a ship's cargo. Sam Colt's brother James wrote the quartermaster at Veracruz that he was sending six pairs of presentation pistols on the *Martha Washington* to be sent to six certain officers he listed in his letter. These officers were Colonel Harney, General Twiggs, General Smith, General Scott, General Worth, and Captain Walker.[21] James also wrote a letter directly to Sam Walker on

July 28, stating he had sent his pair of presentation Walker Colts in this shipment on the steamer *Martha Washington*.[22] The *Martha Washington* left New York on July 20 and arrived at Veracruz in late August.[23]

This shipment of six "small boxes" (as compared to large crates of firearms) was received on August 24 by 1st Lt. Edward G. Elliot[24] of the Quartermaster's Office at Veracruz. His directions were to send them to the officers that James Colt had specified in his letter.[25]

However, the route to Mexico City—where most of these officers were stationed—was so dangerous with guerrilla activity that it had been weeks since an army wagon train had risked travel. But an opportunity to send the pistols to the new owners would soon present itself.

In the early fall of 1847, Gen. Joseph Lane and his brigade were on their way to relieve the besieged American force at Puebla. En route Lane felt it would be prudent to add to his brigade's munition holdings extra ammunition to resupply the army at Puebla. Lane's forces, however, were at National Bridge, 60 miles west of the port of Veracruz where ammunition was stored.

Lieut. McDonald, acting assistant quartermaster of the brigade, was dispatched to Veracruz to secure more ammunition which arrived on the 29th of September. Gen Lane had enough ammunition to have carried him through to the city of Mexico, but wished to supply the garrison at Puebla.[26]

When McDonald signed for the ammunition, he also had to sign for the six boxes of presentation pistols from Colt that arrived at Veracruz one month earlier. Only by McDonald's signing for the presentation pistols could General Lane finally be able to present Sam Walker with his namesake pair from Colt. General Lane brought these pistols with him and personally gave them to Captain Walker when he arrived at Perote.

In a letter to his brother Jonathan, Walker mentioned how delighted he was with them and how effective the new Walker Colts were. But he would have had only an afternoon and evening to try his new pistols, and even possibly his new Wesson rifle. General Lane brought them to Sam sometime after his arrival at Perote at 11 a.m. October 4,[27] but Walker would be leaving in command of all General Lane's mounted men the next day at 9 a.m.[28]

On the morning of October 5, Captain Walker—under General Lane's orders—with his new revolvers in his saddle holsters, would gallop out of Perote Fortress in search of General Santa Anna's army. Five days later, Walker would lead his saddle soldiers in his final battle at the point of General Lane's attack on Santa Anna's army at Huamantla. There, with one of his new Walker revolvers in his hand, he would die in battle.

But did Bedney McDonald retrieve that pistol from Sam and send it to Sam Colt? The problem with this assumption is the second tradition of what happened to Walker's personal revolvers. Walker's family also received not one but a pair of pistols that were also supposedly taken from Sam's body. Colonel Wynkoop had both Walker's personal pistols two weeks after his death. These had to be the pistols the army officially sent to the Walker family. Wynkoop wrote that on October 25, 1847, he had all of Sam Walker's effects (except his sword).[29] That would be 16 days after Sam's death. Sgt. George Myers wrote that William Ashbaugh (possibly a family friend) was seen with Walker's pistols shortly after his death and two weeks later Claiborne took them away from Ashbaugh.[30] Wynkoop stated that he had these pistols for two weeks and two days after Sam's death.

The solution to this conflict perhaps lies in the list of which officers were to receive their presentation Walker Colts. Those specifically listed in Colt's letter to the quartermaster at Veracruz to receive the presentation pistols again were: Harney, Twiggs, Smith, Scott, Worth, and Capt. Samuel Walker.[31] Also, Colt had sent pistols directly to other officers. Three pistol pairs had already been delivered to Col. Jack Hays in June[32] and General Taylor in August.[33] General Twiggs also already had received his presentation Walker Colts sent directly by Colt on June 10.[34]

But General Twiggs was also one of the six officers on Colt's list sent to Veracruz.

Lieutenant McDonald, as General Lane's acting assistant quartermaster who had signed off on the six presentation pistols, was therefore responsible for them. Eventually as Lane's Brigade arrived at Mexico City, McDonald had to learn that General Twiggs already had his presentation pistols and that would mean that the young quartermaster lieutenant had an extra pair of pistols. If this was the case, McDonald had this opportunity to further his relationship with Sam Colt as well as General Lane.

McDonald sent a Walker Colt with the right presentation serial number to Samuel Colt. And it was a splendid opportunity to claim that this was one of the

A perfect example of presentation Walker Colt, serial number 1017. Note the engraved cylinder. (Courtesy of The Metropolitan Museum of Art. Gif of John E. Parsons, 1958 [58.171.]. Photograph by Steve Bluto)

Walker Colt 1009. (Photograph courtesy of the author)

Colt revolvers that Walker actually used and died with in his hand. McDonald had several witnesses that saw him there when Walker was killed. And then to give one to his commanding officer General Lane was a wise move, especially when he might later need favors from the general.[35] In September 1848, he wrote Lane, "Have you written to Colt acknowledging the receipt of the pistol?"[36] Note this is one pistol and not a pair. If McDonald had not given the pistol to Lane, why would he be asking him if he had written Colt?

The serial numbers of a limited number of just over 100 Walker Colts were separate from the production revolvers designated for Companies A, B, C, or D. They were simply a four-digit number beginning with 1000. The Walker Colt revolvers sent to the Walker family were serial numbered 1009 and 1010.

If boxes were in order by serial number and Walker's personal revolvers (1009–10) were the first box to be retrieved when Lane presented them to Walker at Perote, then the box set aside for the next officer on the list would be serial number 1011–12. The sixth box with nobody's name on it would have contained 1019–20. The Walker Colt revolver sent to Sam Colt by McDonald was serial numbered 1020 with the serial number 1019 on the cylinder. That being the case, his claim that it was taken from Walker's hand is false.

In 1849, Lane wrote Colt acknowledging the receipt of "a fine six-shooter [revolver pistol] by the hands of Lt McDonald." He praised this new Colt revolver saying he was very familiar with the Walker Colt six-shot revolver and had seen it tested in

Walker Colt 1010. (Photograph courtesy of the author)

Walker Model serial number 1020; steel and walnut, 5 ½ × 15 inches (13.97 × 38.10 cm), .44 caliber, six shots; the Elizabeth Hart Jarvis Colt Collection, 1905.988; Wadsworth Atheneum and Museum and Art, Hartford, Connecticut. This is the pistol Bedney McDonald claimed he received from the dying Captain Walker. (Photograph by Herb Houtze)

several conflicts. He even stated only Texas Ranger Commander Jack Hays could speak of this weapon with more experience. Lane commented that, "No weapon is equal to it."[37]

According to historian Herbert Houze, who had an opportunity to dissemble the Walker Colt revolver sent to Colt by McDonald, the pistol was virtually pristine and apparently had never been fired.[38] This could imply that this revolver was a presentation pistol never presented to any officer thus shedding further doubt on McDonald's claim that it was taken from Walker at the time of his death.

The Walker family received one pair of Walker Colt revolvers (1009 and 1010).[39] The revolvers stayed in the family for nearly a century. A great-niece of Sam Walker recalled cracking walnuts with Uncle Sam's big pistols.[40] One (1010) disappeared in the 1940s[41] and appeared in a firearms collection in California. Recently the pistols were reunited in the hands of a single collector.

Another Whitney Walker Revolver Belonging to Samuel H. Walker

Sam Walker's namesake, his nephew Samuel Hamilton Walker, was born on June 7, 1844[42]—one day before Texas Ranger Sam Walker was nearly killed by a Comanche lance. This Sam Walker lived near Washington DC. According to family letters,[43] he had two special revolvers; one at least is still in possession of the family. The revolver is a Whitney revolver without a serial number. It would be a logical assumption that Whitney, who made the original Walker Colt, would present revolvers of his own design to Sam Walker's nephew.

Endnotes

Foreword

1. When referring to residents of Texas, there are three categories. The first is "Texicans," those who had resided in Texas before its idependence from Mexico. The second is Texian for residents of Texas between the date of independence and the date of statehood. The third is Texan, which applies to the date of statehood to the present.

Chapter 1: Deep American Roots

1. Kent Walker reported this interesting insight in his posting on September 7, 2011. "9 … The 1st time Charles Walker, Sr., came in contact with Ninian Beall was in 1696 when Charles Walker gives a court deposition saying that he wanted to buy some land from Col. Henry Darnell and Darnell introduced him to a certain Col. Beall to show him the land bounds. They walked the land and Beall pointed out the bounded trees of Darnell's land." http://genforum.genealogy.com/walker/messages/29197.html.
2. "Serving since 1678 when Captain Bealle led his mounted militia to range about the head of the Patuxent River to insure the safety and defense of the neighboring plantations offering 'no violence unless provoked.'" An old settlement account dated February 6, 1700, indicates Colonel Beall was indeed a veteran Mounted Ranger having ranged 141 days in the saddle. C. C. Magruder, Jr., "Colonel Ninian Beall," *Historical Papers of the Society of Colonial Wars in the District of Columbia*, no. 6 (1911): 12, 22. www.archive.org; http://archive.org/stream/colonelninianbea00magr/colonelninianbea00magr_djvu.txt
3. Col. Ninian Beall lived a long and interesting life. He was born in Largo, Fifes Shire, Scotland, in 1625. There he had been an officer in the Scottish–English Army that fought for the Stuarts against Cromwell; he was made a prisoner at the battle of Dunbar, September 3, 1650, and sentenced to five years' servitude in the Barbados, West Indies. Many gentlemen were so sentenced as political prisoners and sent out as industrial servants at that time. He was eventually sent to Maryland, where, after completing his term of servitude, he proved his right to 50 acres of land, and received many hundreds more for bringing out immigrants and settling there. See John Bedell, Stuart Fiedel, Charles Lee Decker, "Bold, Rocky, and Picturesque," *Archeological Identification and Evaluation Study of Rock Creek Park, I,* Prepared for: National Park Service Capital Region, (Washington, DC: National Park Service, 2008), I: 23; Hester Dorsey Richardson, *Side-lights on Maryland History: With Sketches of Early Maryland Families* (Centreville, MD: Tidewater Publishing, 1967), 7; Sally Somervell Mackall, *Early days of Washington* (Washington, DC: Neal and Company, 1891), 48.
4. Martha Sprigg Poole, "Ninian Beall," in *Descendants of John and Priscilla Poole*, compiled and edited by Allen Alger and Alger Clan (Towson, MD: John Poole Association, 2001), http://www.algerclan.org/getperson.php?personID=I36096&tree=alger.
5. The military connection between commanders named Beale and the Walkers continued from the Revolution down to the Seminole War. Sam and his father both served under a captain named Beall. (True, the spelling is slightly different, yet an interesting coincidence.) Sam's father Nathan served as a private in Capt. Thomas Beall's Company of the Upper Battalion of Militia in Prince George's County, Maryland. At the age of 19, Sam was enlisted as a private in the Washington City Volunteers by Capt. Benjamin L. Beall in May 1836.

6. Toping Castle was simply the name of a 48-acre tract of land patented by Isaac Walker in 1754. In no way does it relate to Scotland and in no way does it or should it signify a separate branch of the greater Walker family of Prince George's County. It is important to point out that Toping Castle lies approximately one mile southeast of the land of Charles Walker, Sr., called Bacon Hall, patented in 1709. Charles Walker, Sr., died in 1730 and his will divided Bacon Hall between his eldest son Charles Walker, Jr. (b. 1698), and his youngest son Joseph Walker (b. 1715). DNA evidence shows Isaac Walker's descendants match genetically to those directly descended from brothers Charles Walker Jr., and Joseph Walker of Bacon Hall. http://genforum.genealogy.com/md/princegeorges/messages/1137.html.
7. The following letter from John Hart to King George I provides the details surrounding the fate of the 55 men transported to Maryland:

Maryland, 28th April, 1717.

Sire:

I am honored with the Favour of yours of the 16th of August post, Signifying His Royall Highness, his Pleasure, to return exact Lists of the Rebel Prisoners that have been landed in this Province.

In obedience to His Royall Highness, to whose Commands I shall ever pay a most dutifull Submission, I have inclosed you exact Lists of all the Rebel Prisoners that are come to this Province, Indorsed on the Proclamations I published by the advice of the Councill here which were formed from the Letters I had the honur to receive from the Right

Honourable Mr. Secretary Stanhope on that occasion, And exprest in such a manner as might be consonant to his Majesty's merciful Intentions of sparing the Rebels' lives, and securing their Persons for the space of seven years in the plantations, and also to give due encouragement to the Inhabitants of this Province to Purchase them for servants.

I was comanded by Mr. Secretary Stanhope's Letters (which I answered,) to oblige the Rebel Prisoners to enter into Induentures serve for seven years, and upon their Refusing to Indent, I published the Inclosed Proclamation, which had the effect propos'd, of their being immediately purchased by the Respective Persons whose names are likewise sent to you for your further sattisfaction, that his Majesty's Pleasure has been punctually obey'd.

Some of the Rebel Prisoners have run away from their Service, but on Complaint of their Masters I have given strict orders for the Apprehending of them whereever they shall be found in the Province.

I hope that what I have transacted in relation to the Rebel Prisoners will be considered by you as agreeable to that Duty I owe to his Sacred Majesty's Commands for whose Service I have a most Inviolable Zeal, and shall embrace all occasions to demonstrate it, and that I am with very great respect, Sir,

Your most obedient and most faithfull humble Servant,

Jn. Hart.

Prison List: Court of King's Bench: Crown Side: Baga de Secretis, KB 8 66, 17–102. (1715 Jacobite Rebellion); Embarkation List: Colonial Office Records Book, CO 5 190, 363. (Goodspeed, Liverpool y 14, 1716); Debarkation List: Colonial Office, Maryland, Correspondence, Secretary of State. CO 5/720, # 24 (October 18, 1716), http://immigrantships.net/v2/1700v2/goodspeed17161018.html;

Sold List: Maryland Land Records, Lib. TP 4, 405–7. ("purchased ye Rebells" October 26, 1716), http://freepages.genealogy.rootsweb.ancestry.com/~tornabene.

Isaac's wife Elizabeth Ferguson was born May 3, 1730 in King George's Parish, Prince George's County, Maryland. She was the daughter of Duncan Ferguson and Catherine Clark Cameron (Per church records). Duncan was living in Maryland by 1716 and his daughter Elizabeth was born in Maryland, not Scotland or France. http://genforum.genealogy.com/md/princegeorges/messages/1137.html:

Recorded 29 Mar 1760 I Catharine Farguson do send Greeting. Know ye that I Catherine Ferguson of Prince Georges County in the Province of Maryland for and in consideration of the Love and good will and Natural affection which I have and do bear towards my daughter Elizabeth Walker, have given granted unto the said Elizabeth during her Natural Life the use of my Negro Girl named Eastor with her future Increase and after the decease of my said Daughter Elizabeth I give the said Negro with her future Increase to be equally divided between my said Daughter Elizabeth Walker's children that she now as or hereafter may have by her present Husband Isaac Walker as their Proper goods and chattels absolutely without any manner of Condition. In Witness whereof I have hereunto put my hand and seal this third Day of March 1760. Signed Catherine (her mark) Farguson in the presence of Josa. Beall and Andrew Beall. Frederick County, Maryland Deed Book BB2, 236.

8. Wills and deeds that prove relationships among Elizabeth Walker, Catherine Cameron Ferguson, Isaac Walker, Nathan Walker, John Walker, Ann Skinner Ferguson, and Catherine Lanham:

1769—Catherine Ferguson gives a gift of a slave named Ester to her daughter, Elizabeth Walker, wife of Isaac Walker. Deed requested by Elizabeth Walker in Prince George's County, Maryland. Maryland Deed Book BB2, 236.

1774—Catherine Ferguson gives her granddaughter Ann Skinner Ferguson a one-year-old slave named Jane. (Prince George's County). Catherine Ferguson gives her granddaughter Ann Lanham, wife of William Lanham, a two-year-old slave named Lucy (Prince George's County).

1776—On the census of 1776, Isaac Walker is seen as owning four slaves and two females are 3 and 4 years old.

1779—Catherine Ferguson wills her three granddaughters slaves. Catherine Lovelace receives Esther and it is reiterated that Catherine Lanham receives Lucy and Ann Skinner Ferguson receives Jenny (nickname for Jane listed above). These slaves are in the possession of Isaac Walker according to the will. Will is in Montgomery County, Maryland, but states that Catherine lived in Frederick County, Maryland. Her son, John Ferguson, is named the executor.

1791—Isaac Walker sells several slaves to his son Nathan Walker as well as transferring Toaping Castle. Among the slaves are those originally named in Catherine Ferguson's will as gift to her granddaughters: Esther (Ester), Lucy, and Jane. This would indicate Isaac Walker bought the slaves from Catherine Ferguson's granddaughters at some point (Prince George's County, Maryland.) To conclude, in the 1769 document Catherine Ferguson deeds a slave to daughter, Elizabeth Walker, wife of Isaac Walker. Catherine gives slaves to three granddaughters in deeds and wills. The slaves, Ester, Lucy, and Jane are said to be held by Isaac Walker in the 1779 will. In 1791, Ester, Lucy, and Jane are deeded to Nathan Walker, son of Isaac Walker. All relationships among individuals are stated in the documents verifying that Elizabeth Ferguson is the wife of Isaac Walker and the mother of Nathan Walker. Researched by Sheila Rusher Best.

9. See Mary Lou Williams, *Greenbelt: History of a New Town, 1937–1987* (Norfolk, VA: The Donning Company, 1987), 18–19 for basic information and photos of Toaping Castle and a photo of the

drawing for the original 1757 64-acre plantation. See also James S. C. Wilfong, Jr., "A Grass Roots Research Project," *News Leader* (Laurel, Maryland), September 26; October 3, 1963. Also Wilfong, "Legend on the Local Scene," *News Leader* (Laurel, Maryland), April 13, 1967, and Wilfong, "Paths of Glory," April 20 and 27, 1967, *The Prince Georges Post* (Upper Marlboro, Maryland). These articles tell more about the structure and show photos of the building before it was pulled down in August 1966. Because of Nathan Walker's (Sam's father) Revolutionary War heritage, a College Park chapter of the D. A. R. is named after Toaping Castle.

10. Samuel Hamilton Walker (Sam's namesake—his nephew), "The Walkers of Toaping Castle," 1883, Ironically, this Sam Walker was born on June 7, 1844, the day before Ranger Sam was nearly killed by a Comanche lance at the battle of Walker Creek.
11. Prince George's County, with its county seat of Upper Marlboro was established out of Charles and Calvert Counties in 1695. In February 1754, Isaac Walker I received a large patent of land from the Lord Baron of Baltimore. The estate was known as Tugwelltown ... On August 26, 1771, Elizabeth Walker waived dower, and Isaac, on that date, conveyed to their son, Nathan Walker (1756–1842) (Sam Walker's father), the Toaping Castle estate consisting of 188 acres of land. Also, Nathan Walker owned 10 slaves, their total value being $574, and 317 acres of land worth $794. Of these 317 acres, 169 were in the tract known as "Toaping Castle" and worth $388.70. See the 1828 Tax List, Prince George's County, Maryland, compiled by Prince George's Co. Genealogical Society in 1985. See also, *Directory of Maryland DAR and Ancestors*, published by Maryland State Society, DAR, *ca.* 1966, 727, and Jean A. Sargent, ed., *Stones and Bones; Cemetery Records of Prince George's Co., Maryland* (Bowie, MD: Prince George's Co. Genealogical Society, *ca.* 1984), "When the first thirteen states were formed in 1776, an original state census was taken by Captain Thomas Dent on August 31, 1776, (Bettie S. Carothers, compiler, 1776 Census of Maryland), Isaac was then 55 years old and his wife Elizabeth, 42. They had three sons living with them, ages 18, 18, and 15, and no daughters. When Isaac Walker I died in 1807, he left a modest estate, with his personal inventory having been appraised at $109.49. Elizabeth died between 1800–10. It is assumed that Isaac and Elizabeth made their home with Nathan, their son, until their deaths. They are buried in Walker Cemetery, on the south corner of Capital Beltway and Kenilworth Ave. near Greenbelt, off Walker Drive. Toaping Castle remained in the Walker family until the Federal Government purchased it in 1936. The house deteriorated, was vandalized and fell into such decay, it was eventually demolished. The land was cleared for what is now the Golden Triangle Business Park." http://www.users.qwest.net/~willmurray/Walker/isaac_walker_I.htm. This heritage of this Walker homestead is preserved in the Toaping Castle Chapter, Daughters of the American Revolution (DAR), Hyattsville, Maryland, organized, June 22, 1945.

Chapter 2: The Young Patriot and the Second Seminole War

1. Charles Walker, (son of Isaac and Elizabeth), served in the 7th Maryland Regiment, under Captain Benj. Spykes and Capt. John Gundy. Samuel Isaac Walker enlisted as a private in the 3d Regiment, Maryland Line, May 2, 1777, and served to August 16, 1780.
2. Thomas Beall (*ca.*1742–1818) was commissioned second lieutenant January 2, 1776, Independent Company of Maryland Regulars, Capt. Rezin Beall, commanding, Maryland Archive Volume XVIII, folio 20. Second lieutenant, Capt. John Bracoss's 2d Independent Company of Maryland Regulars, December 10, 1776. First lieutenant, 2d Maryland Infantry; resigned April 17, 1777. First lieutenant, http://gausschildren.org/genwiki/index.php?title=JSB-p307 own company, May 24, 1779, in Upper Battalion of Militia, Prince George's County, Maryland Archive Volume XXI, 414.
3. [Clerk of Council to S. Nichols.] In Council Annapolis, April 29, 1778, Commissions issued to ... Capt, Thomas Beall; First Lieut. Isaac Walker, Journal and Correspondence of the Maryland Council of Safety, January 1–March 20, 1777 (Annapolis, MD), 62. Isaac Walker was first commissioned as an ensign in the 25th Battalion of Militia, Prince George's County, Maryland, September 5, 1775; second lieutenant, Capt. Thomas Richardson's Company, Upper Battalion of Militia, Prince George's

County, to rank from May 2, 1778; and as a first lieutenant in Capt. Thomas Beall's Company, Upper Battalion of Militia, Prince George's County, May 24, 1779. See http://www.users.uswest.net/~willmurray/Walker/isaacwalkeri.htm; http://www.mdarchives.state.md.us/megafile/msa/speccol/sc2900/sc2908/000001/000016/html/index.html; and the application of Milton Thurston Townshend (great-grandson of Nathan Walker) for membership in the Maryland Society of the Sons of the American Revolution, U.S. Sons of the American Revolution Membership Applications, 1889–1970, www.ancestry.com.

4. This Nathan Walker appears to have died in infancy. Nathan and Elizabeth had a son also named Nathan. Sam wrote his father raised nine children, omitting the first Nathan Walker.
5. http://gausschildren.org/genwiki/index.php?title=JSB-p307 Letter, Adelaide Baggerly Chase, January 19, 1932, to Baggerly. Sadie J. Baggarly, The de Baggerley, Baggiley, Baguley, Baggerly, Baggarly family of England and America: England 1066, America 1748: the letters and papers of Miss Sadie J. Baggarly, 1925–1931, comp., Frank Sutherland (Dallas, TX: by the author, 1983). Elizabeth Walker, daughter of Nathan and Nancy Baggerly Walker, married Rezin Beck, her schoolteacher. Rezin Beck was a nephew of John Beck, Elizabeth Walker's deceased first husband. Beck taught school for many years in Good Luck, Maryland.
6. Sam's half-sister from Nathan's first marriage.
7. S. H. Walker, *Brief observations on the conduct of the officers, and on the discipline of the army of the United States* (Washington, DC: by the author, 1840) (hereafter Walker, *Brief observations*). The full text of Walker's pamphlet is reproduced in Appendix I.
8. Ibid.
9. This appellation was bestowed upon an unruly, independent band known as the Alatchaway, by British Indian Agent John Stuart. The term became synonymous with all Florida indigenous people after 1810. John K. Mahon, *History of the Second Seminole War 1835–1842* (Gainesville, FL: University of Florida Press, 1985), 7.
10. Richard W. Scott (*ca.* 1795–1817) entered the U.S. Army as an ensign in the 35th Infantry Regiment, March 31, 1813. Promoted 3d lieutenant, March 3, 1814; 2d lieutenant, October 1, 184; and 1st lieutenant, April 30, 1817. Tortured to death by Seminoles, September 19, 1817. Francis B. Heitman, *Historical Register and Dictionary of the United States Army from its Organization, September 29, 1789, to March 2, 1903* (Washington, DC: Government Printing Office, 1903), I: 869 (hereafter Heitman, *Historical Register*).
11. The Seminole leader Nehemathla Micco ordered Lieutenant Scott to be subjected to the fire torture in every conceivable form before being put to death. During all this time Nehemathla Micco stood by and enjoyed the prisoner's agony. The enormity of this act was too great for pardon, and four months later the day of reckoning came. In April 1818, he and Josiah Francis were both captured and executed. The torture of Lieutenant Scott was the very charge upon which Nehemathla was hanged by order of General Jackson. *American State Papers, Military Affairs* (1832), 1: 700; General Thomas S. Woodward, *Woodward's Reminiscences of the Creek or Muscogee Indians* (Montgomery, AL: Barrett and Wimbish, 1859), 43, 53–54, 97; James Parton, *Life of Andrew Jackson in Three Volumes* (New York: Mason Brothers, 1860), 2: 430–31, 455–58; Augustus C. Buell, *History of Andrew Jackson: Pioneer, Patriot, Soldier, Politician, President* (New York: Charles Schribner's Sons, 1904), 2: 123–25.
12. Duncan Lamont Clinch (1787–1849) was commissioned a first lieutenant, July 1, 1808. Promoted captain, December 31, 1810; lieutenant colonel, August 4, 1813; colonel, April 20, 1819; and brevetted brigadier general for faithful service in one grade for ten years, April 20, 1929. He resigned September 21, 1836. Heitman, *Historical Register*, I: 310.
13. Francis Langhorne Dade (1792–1835) entered the U.S. Army as a third lieutenant, 12th U.S. Infantry Regiment, March 29, 1813. Promoted second lieutenant, January 31, 1814; first lieutenant, September 4, 1816; and captain, February 24, 1818. Brevetted major for ten years faithful service in one grade, February 24, 1828. Heitman, *Historical Register*, I: 350.
14. Militia units that served in Florida during the Second Seminole War were primarily from southern states. In addition to the Washington City Volunteers, the following states provided troops for the Florida

War: Alabama, Florida, Georgia, Louisiana, Missouri, New York, Pennsylvania, South Carolina, and Tennessee. Indian units also served: Col. John Lane's Regiment of Creek Indian Volunteers, Captain Park's Delaware and Shawnee Volunteers, and a battalion of Choctaw. See Militia and Volunteer Units in the Seminole Wars, http://www.floridafrontierguard.com/id18.html.

15. Charles J. Peterson, *The Military Heroes of the War with Mexico* (Philadelphia: J. B. Smith, 1848), 27. Walker was described as "one of Colonel Harney's picked men; for with that daring soldier his boldness and energy rendered him a favorite." Fayette Robinson, "Captain Samuel Walker," *Graham's Magazine* (June 1848): 26, goes into great detail of Harney's use of his picked men from the 2d Dragoons of 1840 in Florida. Sam Walker never served in the dragoons in the Seminole War. He was indeed in Florida in 1840 after his military service and he was living a "dull life" in Iola, Florida, where he had lived with his brother Nathan. Samuel H. Walker to "Dear Brother" [Nathan Walker], February 24, 1840, Samuel H. Walker Papers, Texas State Archives, Austin, Texas (hereafter Samuel H. Walker Papers).
16. Walker, *Brief observations.*
17. Benjamin Lloyd Beall (1797–1863) was a cadet at West Point from 1814–18. His name was dropped from rolls when he absented himself without permission upon the death of his father. Beall was a captain in the Washington City Volunteers, recruiting for the Florida War in 1836. He resigned on June 8, 1836, to become a captain in the 2d U.S. Dragoons. See, "Official List of the changes as casualties which have taken place among the Officers of the Third Brigade of the District of Columbia Militia since June 1831," www.fold3.com. Promoted major, February 16, 1847; lieutenant colonel, March 3, 1855; and colonel May 13, 1861. He would earn a brevet promotion to major for his gallantry and successful service in action, Florida, March 15, 1737, and another to lieutenant colonel, March 16, 1848, for meritorious conduct at the battle of Santa Cruz de Rosales during the Mexican–American War. He retired as colonel, 1st U.S. Cavalry Regiment, February 15, 1862. Heitman, *Historical Register,* I: 202. See also Orlando Wilcox: *Forgotten Valor,* ed., Robert Scott (Manhattan: Kansas State University Press, 1999), 137.
18. Edward Branch Robinson, born Chesterfield Co., Virginia, *ca.* 1803. Printer in Washington, DC, at the time of his enlistment as a private in Company C, 3d U.S. Artillery, by Maj. James H. Hook, October 5, 1826. Served in the detachment of orderlies, Washington, DC, where he undoubtedly gained his expertise in drilling troops, until discharged on surgeon's certificate on October 31, 1827. He was a first lieutenant in Capt. Francis A. Dickins's Company, 2d Regiment, 3d Brigade, District of Columbia Militia, prior to succeeding to the command of Captain Beall's Company on June 1, 1836.
19. On October 7, 1820, Capt. Archibald Henderson was appointed as Lieutenant Colonel, Commandant of the Marine Corps at the age of 37. He served in this position for a little over 38 years—the longest of any officer to hold that position. The years 1820 to 1835 were marked by no very unusual or outstanding activities on the part of the Marine Corps other than its part in the suppression of piracy in the West Indies, and the operations in the early 1830s against the pirates of Quallah Battoo, East Indies. During the 1836–37 war with the Creek and Seminoles in Georgia and Florida in which the Marine Corps took an active part, Colonel Henderson, as Commandant, went into the field with his command, sharing in the dangers and exposures of that campaign. For his services in checking Indian hostilities, he was advanced to the brevet rank of brigadier general. On May 21, 1836, Colonel Henderson sent letters to the commanders of Marine Barracks to prepare their detachments for service and rendezvous at Washington. Office of the Commandant, Historical Section, 1836, May–August to 1837, May–August, Record of the U.S. Marine Corps, Record Group 127, National Archives, Washington, DC.
20. Walker, *Brief Observations.*
21. Ibid.
22. Sam described the gag as "a round piece of wood, or iron bolt, which was forced between the teeth and pushed as far back unto the mouth until the mouth was stretched to tremendous size, and fastened with a cord around the back of the head, and generally have the person ironed or tied at the same time, so it is impossible for them to remove the gag." See Walker, *Brief observations.*
23. Walker, *Brief observations.*

24. Ibid.
25. Letters Received by the Office of the Adjutant General, 1822–1860, National Archives Microfilm Publication M567, www.fold3.com, images 248/291545531-248/291545533.
26. Roger Jones (1789–1852) was appointed second lieutenant, U.S. Marine Corps, January 26, 1809, and promoted to first lieutenant, July 7, 1809. Appointed captain 3d U.S. Artillery, July 12, 1812. Promoted major, February 17, 1827; lieutenant colonel, November 17, 1834; colonel and adjutant general, August 10, 1818–June 1, 1821, and March 7, 1825; brevet brigadier general, June 7, 1832; and brevet major general, May 30, 1848. He died in service, the longest serving adjutant general in the Army's history. Heitman, *Historical Register*, I: 582.
27. Records of the Adjutant General's Office, 1789–1917, Record Group 94, National Archives, Washington, DC.
28. Letters Received by the Office of the Adjutant General, 1822–1860, www.fold3.com, images 248/291545646–248/29154648.
29. Greenleaf Dearborn (1786–1846), entered the U.S. Army as a second lieutenant, 3d Artillery Regiment, March 12, 1812. Promoted first lieutenant, October 1, 1813; captain, September 30, 1819; major, November 27, 1839; and lieutenant colonel, November 26, 1845. He held the rank of lieutenant colonel, 2d Infantry Regiment when he died on September 9, 1846. Heitman, *Historical Register*, I: 363.
30. George Cochran, who enlisted in Washington some time prior to the June 1, 1861, mustering into federal service, is noted, "In confinement at Camp Mitchell, on the August–September 1836 muster roll for Capt. Robinson's Company, Washington City Volunteers. Restored to duty per muster roll for October–November, he deserted from Ft. Brooke, East Florida, on December 12, 1836. District of Columbia Militia, Creek War, 1836–37, Indian Wars, 1817–58, Compiled Military Service Records, Records of the Adjutant General's Office, 1789–1917, Record Group 94, National Archives, Washington, DC (hereafter CSMR, District of Columbia Militia, 1836–1837). He may be the same George Cochran who served as a private in the 3d U.S. Artillery from 1813–18.
31. William Alfred Truman Maddox (1815–89) was commissioned ensign, Washington Volunteer Militia, June 1, 1836, and subsequently promoted to first lieutenant. Upon arriving in Florida, he was taken ill, and was granted leave to recover on November 23, 1836. He returned to Washington and never rejoined his company. Apparently resigning his commission, he was subsequently commissioned second lieutenant of Marines from Maryland to rank from October 14, 1837. Promoted first lieutenant to rank from March 3, 1847, he was brevetted captain to date from January 3, 1847, for meritorious service at the battle of Santa Clara and for suppressing an insurrection at Monterrey during the California campaign of the Mexican–American War. Promoted assistant quartermaster and captain to rank from October 26, 1857, remaining in that capacity until his retirement on January 3, 1880.
32. Thomas Sidney Jesup was appointed second lieutenant May 3, 1808. Promoted, first lieutenant, December 1, 1809; captain, January 20, 1813; major, April 6, 1813; lieutenant colonel, April 30, 1817; brigadier general March 8, 1818; quartermaster, May 8, 1818; and major general quartermaster, 8 May, 1828—a rank he would hold until his death on June 10, 1860. Heitman, *Historical Register*, I: 573.
33. General Jesup's kindness to Robinson went beyond allowing the captain to escape being tried before a military court, allowing him to discretely resign his commission as captain of the Washington Volunteers. He allowed him to continue receiving his pay as a captain "until he heard from the President." E. B. Robinson to "Dear Sir," probably Bvt. Brig. Gen. Roger Jones, Adjutant General of the Army, Washington, January 7, 1837, Letters Received by the Office of the Adjutant General, 1822–1860, www.fold3.com/images 248/291585199–248/291282203. Robinson alleged he, from the start of his company's service against the natives, sought posts of danger, including a "Spy Company of Indians." He further claimed all of his men were malcontents who served in Alabama and Florida with reluctance and assured himself their attitude would "neither honor me or the Country." Denied his glory with the Washington City Volunteers, he submitted a claim that after leaving the Washington City Volunteers, he served as a private in Capt. John Roberts's Company, Colonel Lane's Tennessee Brigade, and took part in several engagements before returning to Washington. There is no record of Robinson having served in Captain Roberts's Company.

34. John Munroe (1796–1861), a Scottish-born graduate of the U.S. Military Academy, fourth in the Class of 1814, was commissioned third lieutenant, 1st U.S. Artillery, March 11, 1814. Promoted second lieutenant, May 1, 1814; first lieutenant, April 20, 1818; captain, March 2, 1825; major, August 18, 1846; and lieutenant colonel, November 11, 1856. Munroe earned the following brevets: major, February 13, 1838, for conspicuous uniformly meritorious and efficiency during the campaigns against the Florida natives; lieutenant colonel, September 23, 1846, for gallant and meritorious conduct for conflicts at Monterrey, Mexico; and colonel, February 23, 1847, for gallant and meritorious conduct at the battle of Buena Vista, Mexico. He died in service, April 28, 1861. Heitman, *Historical Register*, I: 736.
35. Walker, *Brief observations.*
36. Robinson was granted a leave of absence by General Jesup on October 19, 1836, and carried in the company muster roll through December 31, 1836. Robinson, CSMR, District of Columbia Militia, 1836–37.
37. Samuel H. Walker to "Dear Brother," Fort Mitchell, Alabama October 2, 1836, Samuel H. Walker Papers.
38. Charles Irvine was mustered into federal service as a corporal, Washington City Volunteers, on June 1, 1836. Promoted sergeant, December 12, 1836. Commissioned captain, December 31, 1836 to take rank from November 20, 1836. Irwin, CSMR, District of Columbia Militia, 1836–37.
39. Walker, *Brief observations.*
40. Samuel Hamilton Walker to "Dear Brother" [John Thomas Walker], Fort Dade, Florida, March 5, 1837, Samuel H. Walker Papers.
41. Ironically this same general would become one of Sam's supporters when he served in the U.S. Mounted Rifles during the Mexican–American War.
42. Walker, *Brief observations.*
43. S. H. Walker to "Dear Brother" [Jonathan Thomas Walker], Tampa Bay E[ast] F[lorida] headquarters Army of the South, May 10, 1837.
44. Walker, *Brief observations.*
45. G. W. M. (Sgt. George W. Myers, USMR, Co. C), "Battle of Huamantla," *Brooklyn Daily Eagle*, December 3, 1850, 4.
46. This is based on a family tradition passed on by a Walker descendant, Warren Simonds.

Chapter 3: The Florida Civilian Years

1. Sam's brother, Jonathan Thomas Walker, born in 1811, was the eldest son of Nathan and Elizabeth, and the recipient of most of Sam's letters. At the age of 18, Jonathan Thomas moved to Washington City where he worked as a carpenter. In 1833, he married. And with a "little means left [to] his wife by her father" he built his home at 709 6th Street, N.W., in Washington. His carpenter shop was located on 8th and K Streets, N.W. After the Mexican–American War and Sam's death, Jonathan was convinced by Gen. John C. Fremont that he should try his fortune in California. He spent a year trying to develop the first stamping mill in California but lost his means and his wealth in poor investments. He returned in feeble health but opened lumber yards on B, 10th, and 12th Streets, N.W. He, like Sam, was devoted to the Odd Fellowship and was also very active in the Methodist Church. He lived at Toaping Castle until 1866 when he bought "Pleasant Prospect" in Prince George's County where he retired and spent the rest of his days. See Samuel H. Walker (II), *Walkers of Toaping Castle, Md* (Washington, DC: by the author, 1889), 10–13.
2. Walker, *Walkers of Toaping Castle, Md*, 6–7.
3. Nathan Walker to "Dear Brother" [Jonathan Thomas Walker], March 20, 1837, Samuel H. Walker Papers.
4. S. H. Walker to "Dear Brother" [Jonathan Thomas Walker], New Orleans, July 7, 1837, Samuel H. Walker Papers.
5. S. H. Walker to "Dear Brother" [Jonathan Thomas Walker], New Orleans, July 13, 1837, Samuel H. Walker Papers. Sam's brother Charles was one year older than Sam. He was married twice and

lived in Washington, DC. He had one son and eight daughters. See Walker, *Walkers of Toaping Castle, Md*, 7.

6. George Meade, *The Life and Letters of George Gordon Meade: Major-General, United States Army* (New York: Charles Scribner's Sons, 1913) I: 14.
7. Ibid., 75.
8. S. H. Walker to "Dear Brother," February 16, 1837 [1838], Samuel H. Walker Papers.
9. Miss Stone's father was Col. Henry D. Stone, who settled Iola, served with Andrew Jackson, and was later President of the Territorial Council of Florida. He was born about 1767, in Charleston, South Carolina. Colonel Henry Stone died December 24, 1840, and was buried in the Iola Cemetery.
10. S. H. Walker to "My Dear Brother [Charles E. Walker], Iola W Florida July 22, 1838, Samuel H. Walker Papers.
11. Iola was visited by steamers running tri-weekly. Occupations included shingle-makers, sawmills and brickyards. Both Iola and Port St. Joseph on the coast were established in 1835, both were flourishing at the same time, and both dying out at about the same time. Iola is in the northern end of what is presently Gulf County just north of the present City of Wewahitchka. Iola served for three years as the northern terminus of the busy St. Joseph and Iola Railroad. In 1838, a post office was established, and Iola was designated as a voting precinct. The post office was discontinued in 1845, about the same time as the demise of the St. Joseph Railroad, which stopped in Iola. This town was "the home place" of the Stone Family homestead, prominent throughout the history of Jackson, Calhoun and Gulf Counties. Col. Henry D. Stone, who settled Iola, was buried in the Iola Cemetery. http://www.rootsweb.com/~flcalhou/gulf/history/Iola1.htm.
12. Iola was visited by steamers running tri-weekly. Occupations included shingle-makers, sawmills and brickyards. Both Iola and Port St. Joseph on the coast were established in 1835, both were flourishing at the same time, and both dying out at about the same time. Iola is in the northern end of what is presently Gulf County just north of the present City of Wewahitchka. Iola served for three years as the northern terminus of the busy St. Joseph and Iola Railroad. In 1838, a post office was established, and Iola was designated as a voting precinct. The post office was discontinued in 1845, about the same time as the demise of the St. Joseph Railroad, which stopped in Iola. This town was "the home place" of the Stone Family homestead, prominent throughout the history of Jackson, Calhoun and Gulf Counties. Col. Henry D. Stone, who settled Iola, was buried in the Iola Cemetery. http://www.rootsweb.com/~flcalhou/gulf/history/Iola1.htm.
13. Cotton had been shipped down the Apalachicola River on flatboats since 1822; by steamboat after 1828. Apalachicola became the third largest cotton port on the Gulf Coast, ranking after New Orleans and Mobile. Some 15 steamboats on average plied the river to Columbus, Georgia. Cotton would be shipped down river, compressed at some 43 cotton warehouses in town, and taken across the shallow bay by lighter vessels to three-masted sailing ships off West Pass between the St. Vincent and St. George Islands. These vessels would go to New England, England, France, Belgium, or wherever there were cotton mills or lace manufacturing centers. They tended to sail a triangular route among Boston or New York, Apalachicola, and Liverpool or Le Havre. There were even foreign consulates in Apalachicola. Goods were also shipped upriver to towns and plantations.http://www.baynavigator.com/BriefHistory/briefhistory8.cfm
14. The Port of St. Joseph was established in 1836. Florida's first railroad (1839) from Iola to St. Joseph was intended to draw the cotton trade from the Apalachicola River.
15. Dorothy Dodd, "Railroad Projects in Territorial Florida," (Master's thesis, Florida State College for Women, 1929), 17–25.
16. S. H. Walker to "Dear Brother" [Charles E. Walker], Iola, W. Florida, October 21, 1838, Samuel H. Walker Papers.
17. S. H. Walker to "Dear Brother" [Charles E. Walker], Iola, Calhoun Coty, Florida, January 16, 1839, Samuel H. Walker Papers.
18. Samuel H. Walker to "Dear Father & Mother," Iola, April 20, 1839, Samuel H. Walker Papers.

19. James Hudson (Iola's postmaster) to Nathan Walker, Sr., Iola, November 18, 1839, Samuel H. Walker Papers.

> Iola, November 18, 1839
> Mr. Walker
>
> Dear Sir
> The intention of this is to hand you the proceedings of Respect which the friends and acquaintances bore toward your son Mr. Nathan Walker—in life & in death. Hoping that it will be a comfort to you even in death to see the Respect which he merited. …
>
> Very Truly.
> Your Svnt
> James Hudson.

20. Jonathan T. Walker to James Hudson, December 5, 1839, Samuel H. Walker Papers.
21. S. H. Walker to "Dear Brother" [Jonathan Thomas Walker], December 29, 1939, Samuel H. Walker Papers.
22. Manuel Navarro (*ca.* 1816–after 1880) was a Spanish-born friend and brother Odd Fellow who worked and traveled with Sam Walker during his years in Florida. He was last noted in the 1880 federal census living in Key West, Florida.
23. S. H. Walker to "Dear Brother" [Jonathan Thomas Walker], Iola Florida, January 17, 1840, Samuel H. Walker Papers.
24. S. H. Walker to "Dear Brother" [Jonathan Thomas Walker], Charleston, SC, February 24, 1840, Samuel H. Walker Papers.
25. John C. Taylor, a native of Providence, Rhode Island, was a 34-year-old carpenter and Iola business associate of Walker in 1840.
26. Lackland McIntosh Stone and William DeSaix Stone were the late Nathan Walker's brothers-in-law. Lackland M. Stone arrived in St. Joseph from Coosa County, Alabama, in 1840. In addition to the bank established with his brother William, he was also an attorney. http://freepages.genealogy.rootsweb.ancestry.com/~crackerbarrel/3bHenry.html.
27. J. C. Taylor to S H Walker, Iola, March 15th, 1840, Samuel H. Walker Papers.
28. John C. Taylor to S H Walker, Iola, March 17th, 1840, Samuel H. Walker Papers.
29. S. H. Walker to "Dear sister in law" [Ann Stone Walker], Washington City, May 18th 1840, Samuel H. Walker Papers.
30. Ann M. Walker to "Dear Brother" [S. H. Walker], Iola, May 24, 1840, Samuel H. Walker Papers.
31. This is exactly what happened six years later. Walker received a commission in the Mounted Riflemen during the Mexican–American War and was appointed by the president over many other experienced officers. The neglected officers petitioned, complaining Walker and the others appointed to the regiment were political appointees. The original purpose of the forming of the regiment was to protect westward bound settlers from natives. The War with Mexico diverted them to the battlefield instead.

> To the Senators and Representatives of the United States in Congress assembled: Your petitioners, officers of the Regular Army on duty in Texas and Mexico respectfully represent: that having sustained to the utmost of our ability our country's flag in the recent operations upon the Rio Grande and with success which it is believed could not be more complete. We are notwithstanding compelled to feel ourselves at present in the position of men upon whom some stigma rests by which they were disqualified from further advancement in the country's service. This most painful and mortifying conclusion is inevitable when we look at the course pursued toward us in making appointments to the just created Regiment of Mounted Riflemen—to the selections and exclusions which these appointments present. By reference to the list it will be seen not only that not a single officer of the Regular Army who shared in the recent victories has been deemed worthy of promotion into this new regiment but that not an officer of the volunteers

> engaged in the same duty, present at the same battles, and who has been less than three months in the service is rewarded with the rank of Captain. The conclusion seemed irresistible that officers in the army mentioned in official despatches in terms of at least equal honor on the same occupations and who in addition have been many years in this country's service must have received a like reward but from some secret cause which renders them unworthy of confidence.
>
> To be relieved of that position which we feel to be equally unworthy and unjust is the object of this our present petition. As are evidence of confidence and approbation as a token which now and in after years will prove that we have maintained the honor of our glorious flag and shown ourselves worthy to fight beneath it we respectfully entreat that the Congress of the United States will be pleased to pass a resolution authorizing those Regiments of the Regular Army which took part in the defense of Fort Brown; in the victories of Palo Alto and Resaca de las Palinas to bear the names henceforth upon their Regimental Colors
>
> And you petitioners as in duty bound, &c, &c.

The last page of the petition was torn in half omitting the names of the signers and leaving only their regiments: four from the 3d Artillery; two from the 5th Infantry; and one from the 3d Infantry. It is not known whether the petition was ever delivered to Congress, but the nominations and appointments to the Regiment of Mounted Riflemen were unchanged.

32. Since Sam's Washington City unit was recruited locally, this implies that when Sam returned to Florida, he kept in touch with friends and neighbors who were now residing with him in Florida. He mentions several by name in his correspondence.
33. S. H. Walker to "Dear sister in law" [Mrs. Anne M. Walker], Washington City, DC, June 6, 1840, Samuel H. Walker Papers.
34. Ann M. Walker to "Dear Brother" [S. H. Walker], Iola, July 11, 1840, Samuel H. Walker Papers.
35. Ann M. Walker to "Dear Brother" [S. H. Walker], Iola, September 3, 1840, Samuel H. Walker Papers.
36. Sam, who is later to be supported by Democrats in power, ironically is an outspoken supporter of the Whig Party and especially Henry Clay's candidacy for the presidency in the 1840s.
37. S. H. Walker to "Dear Brother" [Jonathan Thomas Walker], Iola, Florida, October 20, 1840.
38. James O. Knauss, "St. Joseph: An Episode of the Economic and Political History of Florida," *Florida Historical Quarterly*: 5: no. 4, Article 4, 12–13, 18.
39. S. H. Walker to "Dear Brother" [Jonathan Thomas Walker], Near Tallahasse Florida, March 7, 1841. Some contemporary accounts of Walker's life report him as a superintendent of a Florida railroad. See J. Frost, *The Mexican War and Its Warriors* (New Haven and Philadelphia: H. Mansfield, 1850), 299. As one can see from this study that was hardly the case, although he seems to have worked as a construction foreman for the Tallahassee Railroad Company. His $60 per month salary indicates he was more than a member of a construction gang.
40. S. H. Walker to "Dear Brother" [Jonathan T. Walker], Tallahassee, Florida, April 20, 1841, Samuel H. Walker Papers.
41. S. H. Walker to "Dear Sister," Leon Coty Fla., May 24, 1841, Samuel H. Walker Papers.
42. S. H. Walker to "Dear Brother" [Jonathan T. Walker], Tallahassee, June 16, 1841, Samuel H. Walker Papers.
43. Zadoc McKnew (1800–72) was a Prince George's County, Maryland, native. His mother was the former Sarah Sally Walker, which may indicate the possibility of a family relationship between him and Samuel H. Walker. McKnew was postmaster in Bladensburg, Maryland, from 1836, and doorkeeper of the House of Representatives in Washington from 1851 to 1855.
44. St. Joseph had a splendid location, harbor, and cooling breezes from the Gulf of Mexico, and attracted traders from all parts of the world. In a short time after its founding it was a thriving city of several thousand inhabitants. The seashore had long wharves extending as far as three-quarters of a mile into the sea; large warehouses; and a shipyard. The *St. Joseph Times* stated up to December 23, 1839, the cotton shipments alone would exceed 50,000 bales the first year the railroad was in operation. In 1839, an important body of Florida's leading men assembled in St. Joseph to write a State Constitution. It

would not be saying too much to state St. Joseph would undoubtedly have been the capital of Florida had it not been destroyed. Along with the great growth of wealth of St. Joseph, there came hand-in-hand wickedness. Finally, on account of its growth in means, St. Joseph received the well-deserved reputation of being the "wickedest city in America." But amidst the laughter of pretty women, the loud shouts from the racetracks, and the clinking of glasses there came a visitor—death. In the summer of 1841, there sailed a ship from some southern point bringing to Old St. Joe, the then dreaded disease of yellow fever. At this time the marshy lagoons and swamps around St. Joseph were filled with lukewarm water which served as breeding places for millions of mosquitoes. And in a short time the disease, which then meant certain death, spread to such an extent that graves could scarcely be dug rapidly enough. Families were broken up, only to be gathered shortly in death. The survivors fled as soon as possible, leaving in truth a deserted village of the once queen city. Old St. Joe never recovered from the terrible scourge. For two or three years the palatial homes, fine public buildings, and full warehouses, awaited their owners never to return. Only a few venturesome fishermen, attracted by the stories of great treasures, dared to come near the city. In 1844, a great hurricane followed by a tidal wave, swept over the deserted homes. For three days and nights the fierce winds as if maddened by their lost prey raged through Old St. Joe. Brick and marble were swept miles inland or carried into the sea by the same receding tidal wave. At the end of the third day the storm abated, but only after there was no more damage it could do to Old St. Joe. Even today, there are no homes within miles of the old town which might have been the capital of Florida. http://members.aol.com/bettymaes/OLDSTJOE.htm.

45. Like the Black Death of medieval Europe, those who remained in the town had to dispose of many of the dead from the "Yellow Death," sometimes in trenches. Others who were well-known had their names preserved at least at the cemetery where they were buried. A roadside historical marker in Florida near this site lists the names of the victims at one cemetery, titled: "BURIAL REGISTER" and "OLD ST. JOSEPH CEMETERY."
46. A mercury compound used as a purgative.
47. Walker's attack was short. The following describes what it was like to have yellow fever. Three to six days after being bitten by an Aedes aegypti mosquito carrying the virus, the disease would have finished incubating, and symptoms would manifest themselves suddenly. They would start with a headache, backache, and fever, followed by nausea and vomiting. The body temperature would return to normal for a few days, but then it would rise again. The skin of the victim would turn yellow from an accumulation of yellow bile pigments in the body. Then the afflicted would start to bleed from the nose and vomit blood. (It was called "black vomit.") The kidneys, liver, and heart would begin to fail, and death would come between the fourth and eighth day after symptoms started. If by some miracle the victim survived (and some did), convalescence would be quick. The jaundice would persist, but the survivor would have a lifetime of immunity to yellow fever. http://www.bansemer.com/florida_lighthouses/st_joseph_bay_lighthouse.htm.
48. S. H. Walker to Zadoc McKnew, New Town, 4 miles from Tallahassee, August 8, 1841, Samuel H. Walker Papers.
49. Knauss "St. Joseph: An Episode of the Economic and Political History of Florida," *Florida Historical Quarterly*, 6, no.1 (July 1927): 14–17.
50. James H. Boss (*ca.* 1817–97), in addition to being a brother Odd Fellow, was a family friend and, like Walker, a carpenter by trade.
51. S. H. Walker to James H Boss, from Leon County near Tallahassee, August 22, 1841, Samuel H. Walker Papers.
52. S. H. Walker to "Dear Sister" [Ann M. Walker], Tallahassee, January 22, 1842, Samuel H. Walker Papers.

Chapter 4: The Long Ordeal, 1842–43

1. http://www.tamu.edu/faculty/ccbn/dewitt/treatyvelasco.
2. Thomas Toby and Brother to D. G. Burnet, New Orleans, July 12, 1836, Executive Department Journals, March–September 1836, 347–49.

3. Gen. Felix Huston to Gen. Sam Houston, *Texas Telegraph and Register*, August 30, 1836.
4. Ibid.
5. See Sam W. Haynes, *Soldiers of Misfortune: The Somervell and Mier Expeditions* (Austin: University of Texas Press, 1990, hereafter Haynes, *Soldiers of Misfortune*), for an interesting political analysis of the events.
6. Samuel C. Reid, Jr., *The Scouting Expeditions of McCulloch's Texas Rangers* (Philadelphia: G. B. Zieber and Co., 1847), 199.
7. Ráfael Vásquez (1804–54), began his career a captain of patriots of the Hacienda de Ciénega de Mata on February 20, 1827. A commander of the Mexican centralist forces, he was appointed brevet brigadier general in 1839. Later, he sought to draw a force of Texans and Mexicans serving with Antonio Canales Rosillo in the breakaway Republic of the Rio Grande, into ambush near Saltillo. In spite of treachery the federalists under Col. Samuel W. Jordan routed the centralist forces, https://tshaonline.org/handbook/online/articles/fva22.
8. According to Joseph Milton Nance, *Attack and Counterattack* (Austin, University Press, 1964), 27, 30. Vasquez's force consisted of "450 cavalry, including volunteers from Béxar, two companies of infantry, 25 artillerymen, and 30 Caddo, commanded by Vincente Córdova"; also reported as "about 700 men—400 regular cavalry; 200 rancheros, partly from the Rio Grande 'but principally of our own Mexican Citizens'; 70 infantrymen; and 30 Caddo Indians." Walker likely cites the latter figure.
9. Edwin Ward Moore (1810–65) entered the United States Navy as a midshipman on January 1, 1825, and was promoted to lieutenant in 1835. In July 1839, he resigned from the Navy to become commander of the Texas Navy.
10. It is not clear which company Walker was serving with during the emergency. He would later claim he had been serving under Hays since he arrived in Texas. Hays did command the Bexar County Rangers from March 10 to September 1, 1842. In his book *Savage Frontier, vol. IV, 1842–1845, Rangers, Riflemen, and Indian Wars in Texas* (Denton, TX: University of North Texas Press, 2010) author Steven L. Moore placed Walker in this company, but without specific documentation, stating, "Reported to have served; extant records unavailable to confirm dates." In this letter to his sister, Walker wrote he had been in Galveston for three weeks prior to March 10, 1842. If Walker did take part in the emergency, it was likely he joined a Galveston company; however, his name does not appear in extant muster rolls for companies organized in that city during that period.
11. S. H. Walker to "Dear Sister," Galveston, Texas, March 10, 1842, Samuel H. Walker Papers.
12. Alexander Somervell (1796–1854), moved to Texas in 1833 and was granted land in Stephen F. Austin's second colony. Somervell engaged in the mercantile business at San Felipe with James F. Perry. In October 1835 Somervell joined the volunteers marching from Gonzales to Bexar and was elected major. He participated in the siege of Bexar. He enrolled in the Texas Army on March 12, 1836, and on April 8 was elected lieutenant colonel of the 1st Regiment of Texas Mounted Rifle Volunteers, succeeding Sidney Sherman. He participated in the battle of San Jacinto and remained in the army until June 7, 1836. He served briefly as secretary of war in David G. Burnet's cabinet. Somervell represented Colorado and Austin counties in the Senate of the First and Second Congresses, October 3, 1836, to May 4, 1838. By the time he was elected brigadier general on November 18, 1839, he was living in Fort Bend County. He was named county clerk in Austin County. In 1842, Houston gave him command of the Somervell Expedition, https://tshaonline.org/handbook/online/articles/fso04.
13. *Austin City Gazette*, March 30, 1842.
14. Houston to Santa Anna, March 12, 1842, *The Writings of Sam Houston, 1813–1863*, vol. 2, Amelia W. Williams and Eugene C. Barker, eds. (Austin: University of Texas Press, 1938), 107.
15. On December 15, 1841, Houston had ordered the Texas Navy to return to Galveston. However, when war with Mexico seemed evident, he changed his mind and ordered Commodore Moore to commence the blockade of Mexico. Jim Dan Hill, *The Texas Navy; In Forgotten Battles and Shirtsleeve Diplomacy* (New York: A. S. Barnes, 1962), 156.
16. Antonio Canales Rosillo (1802–52) commanded Federalist forces in opposition to Santa Anna and raised armed forces from both sides of the Rio Grande to defend the Republic of the Rio Grande. He was defeated at Monterrey by Centralist forces. Canales eventually capitulated to Centralist forces

and forsook his Texan allies, a move for which he received a commission as brigadier general in Santa Anna's army, https://tshaonline.org/handbook/online/articles/fca38.

17. Ewen Cameron (1811?–43) was born in Scotland about 1811. During the Texas Revolution and served two terms in the Texas Army; April 29–October 21, 1836. On October 20, 1836, he reenlisted as a private in Capt. Clark L. Owen's Company A of Joseph H. D. Rogers's 1st Regiment, Permanent Volunteers, serving until the company was mustered out on December 31, 1836. He won renown as a leader of the "cowboys" prominent in frontier defense in South Texas. The *Telegraph and Texas Register* hailed him on September 14, 1842, as "a bold and chivalrous leader" who promised to become "the Bruce of the West," https://tshaonline.org/handbook/online/articles/fca25.
18. James Davis (1790–1859) was an officer during the War of 1812 and fought at the battle of New Orleans, and was elected major general, 2d Division, Alabama Militia, in 1833. Davis was appointed United States consul at Santa Fe in November 1831 and moved to Texas about 1834. He served on Gen. Sam Houston's staff in 1836 and served as adjutant general of the Army of the Republic of Texas from May to July 1842, https://tshaonline.org/handbook/online/articles/fda39.
19. Adrián Woll (1795–1876) served as a distinguished private in the 2d Guard Regiment of Napoleon's Imperial Army in 1813. Promoted to sublieutenant, 4th Battalion, 10th National Regiment, April 14, 1814; and captain, April 17, 1814. Fled to the United States in 1815 and reportedly enlisted in the U.S. Army as a sergeant major, serving on the staff of Gen. Winfield Scott. Deserted in 1816 to become a filibusterer in Mexico. Joined the Mexican Army in 1823 as a lieutenant colonel. In 1846, Woll served as quartermaster of Santa Anna's Army of Operations in Texas. He was among those who supported Archduke Maximilian's brief reign as emperor of Mexico, 1863–65, and served as his field adjutant, http://www.tamu.edu/faculty/ccbn/dewitt/woll.htm.
20. William Alexander Anderson (Bigfoot) Wallace, (1817–99) was descended from Highlanders William Wallace and Robert Bruce. When he learned that a brother and a cousin had been shot down in the Goliad Massacre, he set out for Texas to "take pay out of the Mexicans." A good many years later he told John C. Duval that he believed the account had been squared. Wallace was a magnificent physical specimen. In his prime he stood six feet two inches "in his moccasins," and weighed 240 pounds without surplus fat. He was with the Texans who fought Gen. Adrián Woll's invading Mexican army near San Antonio in 1842, and then volunteered for the Somervell and Mier expeditions and was among those who were surrendered at Mier. Some of his most graphic memories were of his experiences in Perote Prison. As soon as he was released, he joined the Texas Rangers under John Coffee (Jack) Hays and was with the Rangers in the Mexican–American War. In the 1850s Wallace commanded, as captain, a Ranger company of his own, fighting border bandits as well as natives. During the Civil War he helped guard the frontier against the Comanche Indians, https://tshaonline.org/handbook/online/articles/fwa36.
21. John Coffee Hays (1817–83) migrated to Texas 1836 and joined the troops under Thomas J. Rusk to bury the remains of victims of the Goliad Massacre. General Houston advised Hays to join a company of Rangers under Erastus (Deaf) Smith for service from San Antonio to the Rio Grande, under the orders of Col. Henry W. Karnes. In this role Hays took part in an engagement with Mexican cavalry near Laredo, assisted in the capture of Juan Sánchez, and rose to the rank of sergeant. After appointment as deputy surveyor of the Bexar District, Hays combined soldiering and surveying for several years. In the three-way struggle of Anglo colonists, Hispanic settlers, and indigenous people, Hays proved to be an able leader and fearless fighter who gained the respect of the rank and file of the Texas Rangers. From 1840 through 1846 Hays, at first a captain, then a major, and his Ranger companies engaged the Comanche and Mexican troops in small skirmishes and major battles. Important military actions took place at Plum Creek, Cañón de Ugalde, Salado, and Walker's Creek. In these battles Hays and his Rangers were usually outnumbered, and their effective use of revolvers revolutionized warfare against natives. The 1st Regiment of Texas Mounted Rifle Volunteers, commanded by now Colonel Hays, served with the U.S. Army of Gen. Zachary Taylor, and took part in the attack on Monterrey in 1846. The next year Hays formed another regiment that participated in keeping communication and supply lines open between Veracruz and Mexico City for the troops under the command of Gen.

Winfield Scott. In doing so, Hays's Rangers fought Mexican guerrillas near Veracruz and at such places as Teotihuacán and Sequalteplán.

In the years that followed the Mexican–American War, Hays pioneered trails through the Southwest to California and became a prominent citizen of that state. He was elected sheriff of San Francisco County in 1850, appointed United States surveyor general for California in 1853, and became one of the founders of the city of Oakland, https://tshaonline.org/handbook/online/articles/fhabq.

22. Mathew Caldwell (1798–1842) was a signer of the Texas Declaration of Independence. On January 15, 1839, Caldwell was named captain of a company of Rangers to be raised for the defense of Goliad. On March 23, 1839, he became captain of a company in the 1st Regiment of Infantry. Wounded at the Council House Fight in March 1840, he returned to duty and headed a company at the battle of Plum Creek on August 12. As captain of Company D of the scouting force on the Texan Santa Fe expedition in 1841, he was captured with the expedition and imprisoned in Mexico. Upon release he hastened to the relief of San Antonio.
23. Zachariah N. (Wildcat) Morrell (1803–83), traveling Baptist preacher and missionary, church founder, journalist, and historian, moved his family to Texas in April 1836 and settled near the Falls of the Brazos. Indian raids and unsettled political conditions subsequently forced the family to move to Washington-on-the-Brazos, where Morrell helped to form one of the first Baptist churches in Texas in 1837. In the early years of the new Republic of Texas, Morrell fought natives and devoted himself to land speculation, a merchandising business, school teaching, and politics, https://tshaonline.org/handbook/online/articles/fmo53.
24. John William Smith (1792–1845), a Virginian, came to Texas in 1826. Between 1827 and 1836 Smith served as a military storekeeper, developed mercantile interests, and received a sizable Mexican land grant. He also worked as a civil engineer and surveyor. In December 1835, he escaped the occupying Mexican army of Gen. Martín Perfecto de Cos and joined Gen. Edward Burleson and the Texas Army in besieging San Antonio. Smith used his familiarity with the town and his surveying skills to draw the detailed plat that made possible the successful house-to-house attack; he also acted as a guide for one of the assaulting parties. In early 1836, he joined William B. Travis in defense of the Alamo; he was sent by Travis as the final messenger to the Convention of 1836. Subsequently Smith continued as an army scout and participated in the battle of San Jacinto. After Texas independence was gained, he and his family returned to San Antonio, where Smith became an influential citizen and held a number of offices. He was mayor of San Antonio for three one-year terms during the 1830s and 1840s. He was also alderman, Bexar County tax assessor, clerk of the Bexar County Court, clerk of the Board of Land Commissioners of Bexar County, clerk of the Bexar County Probate Court, treasurer of Bexar County, postmaster of San Antonio, Indian commissioner of the Republic of Texas, and senator from 1842 to January 12, 1845. At one time he held as many as 11 different commissions under presidents Sam Houston and Mirabeau B. Lamar, https://tshaonline.org/handbook/online/articles/fsm30.
25. Henry Eustace McCulloch (1816–95) joined the Texas Rangers in the heyday of their role as citizen soldiers against indigenous people and Mexican troops. In the battle of Plum Creek in 1840 against the Comanche, he scouted, fought with distinction, and was wounded. In addition, he served as a lieutenant in Hays's Rangers in their military operations against the Comanche and Mexican nationals. During the Mexican–American War and afterward, he served as a captain of a volunteer company guarding the Indian frontier. In the early 1850s McCulloch served in the state legislature (both houses) from Guadalupe County, and at the end of the decade he accepted an appointment as United States marshal for the Eastern District of Texas. As Texas left the Union, he assumed command of the posts on the northwestern frontier from Camp Colorado to the Red River and used Texas secessionist troops to accept the surrender of federal forces. Given the rank of colonel by the Confederate Congress, McCulloch organized the 1st Regiment, Texas Mounted Riflemen, in 1861. After promotion to brigadier general, McCulloch commanded the Northern Sub-District of Texas from 1863 to the end of the war. He was the brother of Benjamin McCulloch, https://tshaonline.org/handbook/online/articles/fmc35.
26. Z. N. Morrell, *Flowers and Fruits in the Wilderness* (St. Louis: Commercial Printing Company, 1872), 84–90.

27. Andrew Jackson Sowell (1815–83) moved with his family from Tennessee to Missouri, and then to Texas, settling in Gonzales in 1829. During the Texas Revolution he took part in the battles of Gonzales and Concepción, and the Grass Fight. Sowell served in the garrison of the Alamo but shortly before the final battle he and Byrd Lockhart were ordered out to obtain supplies. They were delayed by Gonzales buying cattle and other supplies and did not return to the Alamo before its fall. After Texas gained its independence, Sowell enjoyed a long career with the Texas Rangers. He took part in the Mexican–American War and served in the Confederate Army during the Civil War, https://tshaonline.org/handbook/online/articles/fso12.
28. Vicente Córdova (1798–1842) was among the largest landholders in Nacogdoches in the late Mexican period. He served at various times as alcalde, primary judge, and regidor. For several years, he was captain of a militia company. He supported the Texas Revolution as long as it espoused a return to the Constitution of 1824 but opposed the call for Texas independence. In the fall of 1835, Córdova secretly began to organize local resistance to the Texan revolutionaries. During this period, he kept the Mexican government informed of his attempts to "foster the favorable feelings which the faithful Mexicans here have always entertained" toward Mexico. He assembled a large group of Mexican loyalists and indigenous people on an island in the Angelina River in August 1838 but the Córdova Rebellion, as it was called, was quickly suppressed. Afterward, Córdova, accompanied by a small group of Mexicans, indigenous people, and Black people, attempted to flee to Matamoros, Tamaulipas. The group was discovered encamped near Waterloo (now Austin) and several days later fought a battle with the Colorado volunteers led by Edward Burleson on Mill Creek near the Guadalupe River. Córdova was apparently severely wounded but managed eventually to make his way to Mexico. He returned to Texas with Gen. Adrián Woll and assisted in the occupation of San Antonio in September 1842. He was killed shortly thereafter in the battle of Salado Creek, September 18, 1842, https://tshaonline.org/handbook/online/articles/fco71.
29. A. J. Sowell, *Rangers and Pioneers of Texas* [. . .] (San Antonio: Shepard Bros. & Co., 1884) 213–17.
30. Nicholas Mosby Dawson (1808–42) moved to Texas in 1834 and settled in Fayette County. He enlisted in the revolutionary on January 24, 1836, and within a week was elected to the rank of second lieutenant of Company B, Texas Volunteers. He participated in the battle of San Jacinto. He served as captain of a militia company in 1840 during an Indian campaign in what is now Mitchell County. In August 1837, he was a lieutenant in Company C and in 1842 was captain of a company of volunteers under John H. Moore. When Gen. Adrián Woll invaded Texas in the fall of 1842, Dawson organized a small company of some 15 men and left La Grange on September 16, 1842. Soon his company numbered 53 men, recruited from settlements in Fayette, Gonzales, and DeWitt Counties. While attempting to join Texas forces under Mathew Caldwell on Salado near San Antonio, Dawson and his men were surrounded by a large number of Mexican cavalry on September 18. The following battle, known as the Dawson Massacre, resulted in the death or capture of nearly all the Texans. Dawson was among the casualties. On September 18, 1848, his remains and those of 35 other victims of the battle were buried along with casualties from the Mier Expedition in a vault on Monument Hill near La Grange, Texas, https://tshaonline.org/handbook/online/articles/fda53.
31. John Henry Brown (1820–95) moved to Texas in November 1837 and participated as a private in the battle of Plum Creek in August 1840. By 1841, he had been elected first sergeant of a company of minutemen. He moved to Victoria the same year, but he remained active in frontier warfare. In the spring of 1842, he joined John C. Hays's company following the battle of Salado Creek. He then took part in the Somervell expedition and afterward returned to San Antonio, on January 7, 1843. With the outbreak of the Civil War he became a member of Brig. Gen. Benjamin McCulloch's staff; he advanced from private to major and published the *War Bulletin* from McCulloch's camp in Arkansas. When the general was killed at the battle of Pea Ridge, Arkansas, in 1862, Brown was transferred to the staff of Brig. Gen. Henry E. McCulloch, where he served as assistant adjutant general. But poor health forced him, in 1863, to rejoin his family, then in Austin. During the remainder of the war Brown served with the Texas militia and commanded the Third Frontier District. He participated with Col. John S. Ford in the last engagement of the war, the battle of Palmito Ranch, on May 13, 1865.

32. John Henry Brown, *History of Texas from 1685 to 1892* (St. Louis: L. E. Daniel, 1893), 225–27.
33. Letters from Mexican Imprisonment, http://www.sonsofdewittcolony.org.
34. Jesse Billingsley (1810–80) migrated to Mina, Texas, in 1834. On November 17, 1835, he joined Capt. Robert M. Coleman's company of Mina Volunteers—49 Bastrop County men. Billingsley served until December 17. When this unit mustered into Sam Houston's army at the beginning of the Texas Revolution, it was designated Company B of Col. Edward Burleson's 1st Regiment, and on March 1, 1836, Billingsley was elected its captain. He commanded the company at the battle of San Jacinto, where he received a wound that crippled his left hand for life. The company disbanded at Mina on June 1. Billingsley thereafter served as a private in John C. Hunt's Ranger company, from July 1 through October 1, 1836. He was elected from Bastrop County to the House of Representatives of the First Congress of the Republic of Texas and is said to have "furnished his own grub, slept on his own blanket, and wor[e] a buckskin suit that he took from a Comanche Indian whom he killed in battle." Billingsley was reelected to the House of the Second Congress in 1837. In February 1839, he commanded a company of volunteers under Edward Burleson that pursued and engaged the band of Comanche raiders who had killed the widow of Robert Coleman and their son Albert, and kidnapped their five-year-old son, Thomas. In 1842, Billingsley recruited volunteers to aid in the repulse of the invasion of Adrián Woll, and fought with John C. Hays at the battle of Salado Creek, https://tshaonline.org/handbook/online/articles/fbi10.
35. Walker served from three weeks in Capt. Jesse Billingsley's company during the Woll campaign in September 1842 and was due $15.75. When the men serving in the company were sent certificates for payment dated September 1, 1851, Walker had been dead for almost four years. Jesse Billingsley, Public Documents, R 137 F 280–89.
36. James S. Mayfield (1809–?) served as secretary of state under President Mirabeau B. Lamar and seemingly had no military background. Nevertheless, on September 16, 1842, Mayfield assembled a company of volunteers from La Grange, to follow Capt. Nicholas Dawson in an attempt to repel Gen. Adrián Woll's Mexican army from San Antonio. His group, joined by others under the command of Jesse Billingsley and W. J. Wallace, arrived at the scene of the Dawson massacre on Salado Creek while it was occurring. Mayfield, as the commanding officer, determined that his group was too far outnumbered and remained in the distance until the following day, when he joined the command of Mathew Caldwell. In 1842, Mayfield was a member of the Somervell Expedition but did not join the subsequent Mier Expedition. In 1843, he presented himself as a candidate for major general of the Texas army but removed himself from consideration because, he said, of ill health. It is probable, however, that accusations of cowardice during the Woll invasion leveled by Mathew Caldwell and Edward Burleson had much to do with his decision. Mayfield represented Fayette County at the Convention of 1845 and during the same year challenged Burleson to a duel but did not go through with the engagement, https://tshaonline.org/handbook/online/articles/fma92.
37. Brown, *History of Texas*, 227–28.
38. Morrell, *Flowers and Fruits*, 91–92.
39. *Recollections of Early Texas: The Memoirs of John Holland Jenkins*, John Holmes Jenkins, III, ed. (Austin: University of Texas Press, 1958), 100–1.
40. Edward Burleson (1798–1851) served as a private in the War of 1812 in his father's company, part of Perkin's Regiment, Alabama. He was appointed a captain of militia in Howard County, Missouri, was commissioned colonel in Saline County on June 13, 1821, and was colonel of militia from 1823 to 1830 in Hardeman County, Tennessee. He arrived in Texas on May 1, 1830. On December 7, 1832, he was elected lieutenant colonel of the militia of Austin Municipality. On October 10, 1835, he was elected lieutenant colonel of the infantry in Gen. Stephen F. Austin's army. On November 24, 1835, Burleson became general of the volunteer army and replaced Austin. On November 26, 1835, he fought in the Grass Fight during the siege of Bexar. On December 1, 1835, Burleson was commissioned commander in chief of the volunteer army by the provisional government. By March 10, he had been officially elected colonel of the infantry, 1st Regiment. On April 21, 1836, he commanded the First Regiment, which was placed opposite Mexican breastworks and was the first to charge them. Burleson

accepted the sword and surrender of Gen. Juan N. Almonte at the battle of San Jacinto. From July 12 to December 1836 he was colonel of the frontier Rangers. On June 12, 1837, he became brigadier general of the militia. In 1838, he was colonel of the 1st Regiment of Infantry in the new Regular Army of Texas and on April 4, 1838, defeated Mexican insurrectionists under Vicente Córdova. On January 19, 1839, at President Mirabeau B. Lamar's request, took command of the Frontier Regiment. He defeated the Cherokees under Chief Bowl in July 1839, and again on Christmas Day, 1839, and defeated the Comanches in the battle of Plum Creek. In 1841 he was elected vice president of the republic. In the fall of 1842 Mexican Gen. Adrián Woll invaded Texas. Burleson raised troops for defense but yielded the command to General Somervell who was sent by President Houston. In 1844 Burleson made an unsuccessful bid for the presidency against Anson Jones. During the Mexican–American War, Burleson went to Monterrey, Nuevo León, and was appointed senior aide-de-camp, held the rank of major, and served as a spy during the siege of Monterrey and at Buena Vista. https://tshaonline.org/handbook/online/articles/fbu40.

41. Joseph D. McCutchan, Joseph Milton Nance, eds., *Mier Expedition Diary; A Texan Prisoner's Account* (Austin: University of Texas Press, 1978), 13–14. Joseph D. McCutchan (1823–53) a Tennessean, arrived in Galveston early in January 1841. On October 17, 1842, at the age of 19, he was enrolled as a second lieutenant in Capt. William P. Rutledge's company and went with that company to San Antonio. Upon the organization of the troops in the vicinity of San Antonio on November 7, 1842, into the 1st Regiment of the South Western Army, Capt. Jerome B. Robertson was elected to command the company; however, McCutchan continued to serve as second lieutenant of the company and was mustered into the South Western Army of Operations under the command of Brig. Gen. Alexander Somervell on November 21, 1842. Upon the decision of Somervell to end the campaign and return to Texas, McCutchan withdrew from Robertson's company and enlisted as a private in Capt. William S. Fisher's company on December 11. Too ill to travel when the prisoners left Matamoros for Mexico City on January 14, he regained his health and rejoined his comrades on May 30.

42. William Gordon Cooke (1808–47) was a resident of New Orleans, and on October 13, 1835, he volunteered for the New Orleans Greys. He arrived with the second company at Velasco, Texas, on October 25, 1835, and was elected first lieutenant the next day at Quintana. After arrival at Bexar on November 8, 1835, Cooke was elected captain of his company and raised volunteers to storm the town. Cooke led the party that captured the priest's house on the main plaza, thus forcing the Mexican capitulation, and received the flag of surrender.

Cooke then volunteered for the Matamoros expedition of 1835–36. As captain, he led the reformed San Antonio Greys to Goliad. Shortly after Sam Houston's arrival and impassioned speech there, Cooke offered his services to the Texas Army and was sent with his company to Refugio, where they were joined by Col. James Walker Fannin, Jr., and the Georgia Battalion. Fannin ordered Cooke to San Patricio to reinforce Maj. Robert C. Morris. He later joined Houston's staff as assistant inspector general. Cooke went with Houston to Gonzales and assisted in organizing the troops. At the battle of San Jacinto he served on Houston's staff with the rank of major. Cooke was in charge of the guard on the prisoners when Antonio López de Santa Anna was captured. He prevented the angry Texans from executing Santa Anna so he could be brought before General Houston.

In November 1836, Houston appointed Cooke acting secretary of war, and on January 31, 1837, inspector general—an office he held until July 31, 1837. Cooke then retired from the army because of ill health and opened two drugstores in Houston. Cooke reenlisted in the army around October 1838 and received a commission as quartermaster general of the republic. In March 1840, Mirabeau B. Lamar named him commissioner to sign treaties with the Comanche, and in this role, he took part in the Council House Fight in San Antonio on March 19, 1840.

On August 18, 1840, Cooke was appointed colonel of the 1st Regiment of Infantry. In April 1841 he was appointed senior commissioner on the Texan Santa Fe expedition and was to have been the chief civil authority in Santa Fe. On September 17, 1841, he was deceived by the traitor Capt. William G. Lewis and surrendered the Texans' arms. Cooke and his men were marched to Mexico City and imprisoned in Santiago Prison on December 26, 1841. They were released on June 14, 1842.

Ignoring his pledge not to take arms against Mexico under pain of death, he immediately joined with Gen. Edward Burleson to expel Gen. Adrián Woll from San Antonio. On September 22, 1842, Cooke was wounded in Capt. John C. Hays's charge on the cannon at Arroyo Hondo. On October 25, 1842, Houston appointed him quartermaster general and chief of the subsistence department, in which capacity Cooke helped organize the infamous Snively expedition and the Somervell expedition, of which he was a member until February 1, 1843.

Seeking further revenge, Cooke went to New Orleans to join Commo. Edwin Ward Moore on his expedition to the Yucatan. They sailed on April 15, 1843, in the sloop-of-war *Austin*. Cooke, as a captain, Texas Marine Corps, participated in engagements with the Mexican steamships *Montezuma* and *Guadalupe*, and after the *Independence* joined the Texan fleet, he twice accompanied this ship on raiding expeditions, hoping to capture prisoners to exchange for those held in Mexican prisons. The first expedition resulted in the capture of the Mexican ship *Glide*, and the second brought back news to Moore that Houston had declared him a pirate, charges against which Cooke later defended him. They returned to Galveston on July 14, 1843, and Cooke received an appointment from Gen. Sidney Sherman as adjutant general of the Texas militia.

Cooke was appointed secretary of war by President Anson Jones in December 1844, serving in this office until the spring of 1846. On April 27, 1846, Cooke was appointed the first adjutant general of the state of Texas by Governor James Pinckney Henderson. He served in this office until his death, https://tshaonline.org/handbook/online/articles/fcobv.

43. William S. Fisher, (?–1845) moved to Texas from Virginia in 1834 and settled in Green DeWitt's colony at Gonzales. On March 10, 1836, he joined the Texas Army and on March 26 reinforced Houston's army with the company that he had raised—Company I, 1st Regiment of Texas Volunteers—and participated in the battle of San Jacinto. He remained in the army until June 10, 1836, and served again from June 27 to September 27, 1836. Appointed secretary of war of the Republic of Texas, he served from December 21, 1836, to November 13, 1837. On March 19, 1840, he was in command of two companies of regulars at San Antonio at the time of the Council House Fight. Later in 1840, he was attracted to the Republic of the Rio Grande and led 200 men to join the army of that organization at San Patricio. Returning to Texas after a few months of unsuccessful campaigning, he joined the Somervell expedition in 1842 and was elected captain. With Alexander Somervell's abandonment of the enterprise, Fisher was elected leader of those members of the expedition who continued on into Mexico on the Mier expedition. During the attack on Mier, Fisher was wounded and imprisoned with his men by Mexican Gen. Pedro de Ampudia. Fisher was marched to Perote Prison. He was released in 1843 and returned to Texas. https://tshaonline.org/handbook/online/articles/ffi24.
44. Joseph M. Nance, *Attack and Counterattack: The Texas-Mexican Frontier, 1842* (Austin: University of Texas Press, 1964), 565. Those that departed with Somervell were what remained of the militiamen of Montgomery and Washington Counties, the staff officers, and some of the Houston volunteers.
45. Thomas Jefferson Green (1802–63) was appointed to the United States Military Academy at West Point in 1822 but did not graduate. He organized the Texas Land Company and moved to Texas in 1836 but abandoned the colonization project to serve in the Texas Army. After being commissioned brigadier general, he returned to the United States to raise volunteers, money, and ammunition for the Texas cause. As a member of the Somervell expedition in 1842, he remained on the Rio Grande when Alexander Somervell turned back. Green was second in command on the Mier expedition. He surrendered to Gen. Pedro de Ampudia and was held at Perote Prison. He escaped and returned to Velasco, Texas, where he was elected to represent Brazoria County in the Eighth Congress. He returned to the United States just before the annexation of Texas, and moved to California in 1849. He later became major general of the California militia. https://tshaonline.org/handbook/online/articles/fgr39.
46. Benjamin McCulloch (1811–62), the elder brother of Henry Eustace McCulloch, joined Houston's army on its retreat into East Texas. At the battle of San Jacinto, he commanded one of the famed Twin Sisters and won a battlefield commission as first lieutenant. He soon left the army, and joined the Texas Rangers and, as first lieutenant under John Coffee Hays, won a considerable reputation as an Indian fighter. At the battle of Plum Creek on August 12, 1840, he distinguished himself as a scout and as commander of the right wing of the Texas Army. In February 1842, when the Mexican government

launched a raid against Texas that seized the strategic town of San Antonio, McCulloch rendered invaluable service by scouting enemy positions and taking a prominent role in the fighting that harried Rafael Vásquez's raiders back below the Rio Grande. On September 11, 1842, McCulloch again did valuable scouting service and joined in the pursuit of Adrián Woll's invading troops to the Hondo River, where Hays's Rangers engaged them on September 21. After the repulse of the second Mexican invasion, McCulloch remained with the Ranger company that formed the nucleus of an army with which the Texans planned to invade Mexico. Ben and Henry were part of the Somervell expedition but left it on the Rio Grande before the fight at Mier.

At the outbreak of the Mexican–American War, he raised a command of Texas Rangers that became Company A of Col. Jack Hays's First Regiment, Texas Mounted Volunteers. He was ordered to report to the United States Army on the Rio Grande and was soon named Zachary Taylor's chief of scouts. His work in Mexico earned him the rank of major of United States volunteers. When secession came to Texas, McCulloch was commissioned a colonel and authorized to demand the surrender of all federal posts in the Military District of Texas. On May 11, 1861, Jefferson Davis appointed McCulloch a brigadier general and assigned to the command of Indian Territory. On August 10, 1861, he won an impressive victory over the army of Brig. Gen. Nathaniel Lyon at Wilson's Creek, or Oak Hills, in southwest Missouri. McCulloch commanded the Confederate right wing in the battle of Pea Ridge, or Elkhorn Tavern, on March 7, 1862. At 10:30 a.m., McCulloch rode forward through the thick underbrush to determine the location of the enemy line and was shot and killed by enemy fire, https://tshaonline.org/handbook/online/articles/fmc34.

47. Leaving the expedition were: Lt. Ben McCulloch, Privates Henry McCulloch [Ben's brother], Ephriam W. McLean, Thomas Green, Capt. James H. Gillespie, C. C. Cady, possibly Dr. Edmund J. Felder, and perhaps one more. Joseph Milton Nance, *Dare-Devils All: The Texan Mier Expedition* (Austin; Eakin Press, 1998), 31.
48. An affidavit admitted for payment by William G. Cooke, Secretary of War and Marine, dated December 31, 1845, and filed by Walker for compensation for his time as a prisoner of the Mexicans states he appeared on the muster roll of Cameron's Company at the time of the surrender at Mier. Jack Hays was his attorney. Walker received $25, a mere pittance for his eight months of suffering. Texas State Library and Archives, Auditor's Department, file 2917.
49. *The Perote Prisoners; Being the Diary of James L. Truehart*, Frederick C. Chabot, ed. (San Antonio: The Naylor Co., 1934), 71–72.
50. Gen. Thomas J. Green, *Journal of the Texian Expedition Against Mier* (New York: Harper & Brothers, 1845), Appendix IV, 474–76.
51. Israel Canfield (1808–50) a native of New Jersey, came to Texas before 1840. He served as a deputy sheriff in Refugio County and later as district clerk. He served a 60-day enlistment in the Refugio County Minute Men, and a three-month volunteer in Capt. John M. Smith's Company during the Canales raid of March 1842. He then joined a spy company under Capt. Ewen Cameron and took part in the Somervell Expedition.
52. James M. Day, ed., "Israel Canfield on the Mier Expedition," *Texas Military History*, 3, no. 3 (Fall 1963): 170–71.
53. George Bernard Erath (1813–91) was an Austrian who arrived in Texas in 1833. In 1835, he joined John H. Moore's Ranger company to deal with marauding natives, and on March 1, 1836, he enlisted as a private in Capt. Jesse Billingsley's Company C of Col. Edward Burleson's 1st Regiment, Texan Volunteers, for service in the Texas Revolution. After fighting in the battle of San Jacinto he joined Capt. William H. Hill's Ranger company. By 1841, he had become the captain of the Milam County minute company. In 1842, he participated in the Somervell and Mier expeditions but was on guard duty on the Rio Grande during the battle of Mier and thus escaped capture.

At the outbreak of the Civil War, Erath raised a company for Col. Joseph W. Speight's 15th Texas Infantry Regiment, but was discharged due to ill health and returned to his home at Waco. In 1864, however, Governor Pendleton Murrah appointed him to the command of a regiment in the Second Frontier District with the rank of major. https://tshaonline.org/handbook/online/articles/fer01, *Notes and Fragments of the Mier Expedition*, Houston Wade, comp., (LaGrange, TX: LaGrange Journal, 1936), 102–8.

54. William Oldham (1798–1868) was born in Kentucky in 1798. He volunteered for the Texas Army on October 8, 1835, and was elected a major in the Texian Infantry. He served in Capt. James G. Swisher's company until December 22, 1835, and participated in the siege of Bexar. He also served in the 1st Company of Texas Cavalry from May 29, 1836, to August 2, 1836. On October 17, 1842, he volunteered for the Somervell expedition and was appointed paymaster of the regiment commanded by Col. James Cook. He also participated in the Mier expedition and was taken prisoner on December 25, 1842. When the Texans tried to escape on February 11, 1843, Oldham, along with John Rufus Alexander, was able to make his way back to San Antonio on or about April 5, 1843, https://tshaonline.org/handbook/online/articles/fol16.
55. *Notes and Fragments of the Mier Expedition*, 29.
56. McCutchan, *Mier Expedition Diary: A Texan Prisoner's Account* (Austin: University of Texas Press, 1978), 72.
57. William Preston Stapp, *The Prisoners of Perote Containing a Journal Kept by the Author Who Was Captured by the Mexicans at Mier, December 25, 1842, and Released from Perote, May 16, 1844* (Philadelphia: G. B. Ziebner, 1845, repr. Austin: University of Texas Press, 1977), 53–54. William Preston Stapp (1812–61) a native Kentuckian, moved with this family to Texas in 1830. He participated in an Indian campaign in 1831. From October 3 through November 23, 1835, he served in Capt. John Allen's company of Lavaca Volunteers. On March 1, 1836, he returned to the service as a second lieutenant in Jacob Eberly's company, stationed on Galveston Island. Stapp was discharged on May 29. In the spring of 1842, he enrolled as a private in Capt. Alexander Stevenson's company of Missouri Invincibles for a planned invasion of Mexico, and later that year he joined Capt. Isaac N. Mitchell's company under Alexander Somervell. When Mitchell and 24 of his men left the army in December, Stapp joined the company of Capt. Charles K. Reese. He participated in the Mier expedition and was imprisoned at Perote. He was released on May 16, 1844, at the instigation of his uncle, Gen. Milton Stapp of Madison, Indiana. He remained for a time in Mexico recovering his health, and enjoying his leisure and the pleasures of Mexico City. Before returning to the United States, Stapp paid a farewell visit to his comrades still in prison on July 5 and then, on July 12, 1844, sailed from Veracruz bound for New Orleans.
58. John Crittenden Duval, *The Adventures of Big-Foot Wallace, the Texas Ranger and Hunter* (Macon, GA: The J. W. Burke Co., 1921), 188.
59. Day, "Israel Canfield on the Mier Expedition," 173.
60. Ibid., 174.
61. https://tshaonline.org/handbook/online/articles/fdi19.
62. Day, "Israel Canfield on the Mier Expedition," 175–76.
63. *Notes and Fragments of the Mier Expedition*, 32–33.
64. Ibid., 34–35.
65. Ibid., 35–36.
66. McCutchan, *Mier Expedition Diary*, 58.
67. Day, "Israel Canfield on the Mier Expedition," 176.
68. Joseph Milton Nance, *Dare-Devils All*, 237–38.
69. Samuel W. Jordan, soldier and adventurer, was a captain in the Texas army from 1836 to 1838. In May 1839, he went to East Texas and participated in campaigns against the Cherokee. He resigned from the army on September 2, 1839. The same year, with the rank of colonel, he and Reuben Ross led 180 Texans to join the Mexican Federalists under Antonio Canales in the effort to establish the Republic of the Rio Grande. Jordan won a victory over the Centralists in the battle of Alcantra, 12 miles southwest of Mier, Nuevo León. In June 1840, he joined Canales again, after which Jordan and his volunteers occupied towns along the Rio Grande and moved into the Mexican interior. He later discovered that Mexican leaders had betrayed him and were directing the Texan forces toward the enemy. The volunteers met Centralist forces in Saltillo and scored a victory against overwhelming odds. They returned to Texas afterwards. In December 1840, Jordan was back in Austin, Texas, when his attempt to kill Sam

Houston with an ax was prevented by Adolphus Sterne. In the summer of 1841, Jordan was in New Orleans enlisting men for Mariano Arista's expedition to gain control of Yucatan. When the boat for Yucatan sailed without him and his recruits, Jordan, in a fit of depression, committed suicide by taking an overdose of laudanum on June 22, 1841. http://www.tshaonline.org/handbook/online/articles/fjo73.

70. Wade, *Notes and Fragments of the Mier Expedition*, 40.
71. McCutchan, *Mier Expedition Diary*, 86.
72. Wade, *Notes and Fragments*, 42.
73. John McMullen (1824–?), was born in Baltimore, Maryland, and immigrated to Texas in 1839. He was residing in Galveston in 1842 when he volunteered for the Somervell expedition, perhaps in company with Samuel H. Walker. He is likely the same John McMullen who served as a Texas Ranger under Capt. Jack Hays prior to the Mexican–American War. McMullen is the same John McMullan who served as fourth corporal of Capt. Zaccheus Wilson's company of Col. Joseph L. Bennett's First Regiment, South Western Army. McMullen was one of the command who refused to heed Brig. Gen. Alexander Somervell's order to disband and return to San Antonio, but remained with the rump of the army under Col. William S. Fisher. When Fisher reorganized the army, McMullen became a private in Capt. Ewen Cameron's Company A. He was captured at the battle of Mier and marched to Perote Prison, but according to fellow prisoner Joseph D. McCutchan, McMullen was among "those who have money" and thus was able to board at his own expense in what McCutchan referred to as "a first rate Hotell well furnished and supplied with good eatables." Of McMullen and his fellows outside of the prison, McCutchan wrote, "These fellows live high and do not feel so sharp twitches of a keen cutting and unsatiated appetite." McMullen was released from captivity on September 16, 1844, and sailed from Veracruz on September 22; he arrived 13 days later at New Orleans. On September 28, 1845—the same day as Walker and just prior to the outbreak of the Mexican–American War—McMullen was mustered into federal service as a private in Capt. Robert A. Gillespie's Company I of Col. John C. Hays's First Regiment, Texas Mounted Rifles, in which he served until March 28, 1846. He was elected first lieutenant in Capt. Benjamin McCulloch's Company A of Hays's regiment during the Monterrey campaign and served from June 13 until August 18, 1846. Thereafter he returned to Gillespie's company and served as a private from August 30 to September 29. In 1849, in company with John C. Hays and William Sanders Oury, McMullen left for the gold regions of California. He settled in San Francisco, where he is said to have become wealthy and socially prominent. In 1880, his daughter, Anna, married Jack Hays, the son of his former commander. https://tshaonline.org/handbook/online.
74. James M. Day, ed., *A Narrative of the Capture and Subsequent Sufferings of the Mier Prisoners in Mexico, Captured in the Cause of Texas … by Thomas W. Bell, One of the Captives* (Waco, TX: Texian Press, 1964), 35, hereafter *Bell Narrative*.
75. Canfield Diary March 1, 1843, as quoted in Joseph Milton Nance, *Dare Devils All, The Texas Mier Expedition, 1842–1844*, 273.
76. Day, *Bell Narrative*, 36.
77. Stapp, *Prisoners of Perote*, 89.
78. Fenton M. Gibson enlisted in the Texas Army on December 25, 1835, and was transferred by order of James W. Fannin, Jr., to the Republic of Texas Marine Corps and commissioned captain. He commanded the Marine detachment aboard the Texas war sloop *Invincible* that guarded Santa Anna when he was held prisoner on that ship in June 1836. In November 1836, he was informed that his services were no longer required. Gibson served in Capt. William Ryon's Company during the Somervell Expedition. When Somervell broke up his expedition in December, those who wished to press forward elected William S. Fisher to command them. Gibson was appointed second quartermaster by Fisher. He was among those who escaped during the breakout of February 11, 1843, but was recaptured. He was held in Perote until September 16, 1844.
79. *Notes and Fragments of the Mier Expedition*, 154–58, quoting the *Northern Standard* (Clarkesville, Texas), February 10, 1844.
80. Stapp, *Prisoners of Perote*, 97.
81. *Daily Picayune* (New Orleans), May 24, 1843.
82. Stapp, *Prisoners of Perote*, 76.

83. Ibid., 99.
84. Day, *Bell Narrative*, 41.
85. *Notes and Fragments of the Mier Expedition*, 158, quoting the *Northern Standard* (Clarkesville, Texas), February 10, 1844.
86. McCutchan, *Mier Expedition Diary*, 92.
87. H. Yoakum, *History of Texas from its First Settlement in 1685 to its Annexation to the United States in 1846* (New York: Redfield, 1855) II: 377–78.
88. George Bibb Crittendon (1812–80) was a graduate of the United States Military Academy in 1832. He resigned his commission as a brevet second lieutenant on April 30, 1833. After several years as a lawyer, he moved to Texas in 1842. Returning to the U.S. Army in 1846, he was appointed captain of Mounted Rifles on May 27. He resigned his commission as a lieutenant colonel on June 10, 1861. He served the Confederate States as a colonel, brigadier general and major general until 1865.
89. Walker to Gen. Albert Sidney Johnston. Army Correspondence, May 1843, file 1308–12, Texas State Archives, Austin, TX.
90. Walker to Ann M. Walker, Samuel H. Walker Papers.
91. Letters from Mexican Imprisonment. www.sonsofdewittcolony.org. Barkley made good on his pledge. He was among the group of 15 who escaped with General Thomas Green from Perote Prison on January 27, 1844, by digging through a 6-foot-thick wall.
92. Walker to Jonathan Thomas Walker, Samuel H. Walker Papers.
93. Day, *Bell Narrative*, 46.
94. Ibid., 47–48.
95. Letters from Mexican Imprisonment. www.sonsofdewittcolony.org.
96. Here is the full text of Houston's proclamation from *The Writings of Sam Houston, 1813–1863*, vol. 3, Amelia W. Williams and Eugene C. Barker, eds. (Austin, TX: University of Texas Press, 1938–43), 409–10:

> WHEREAS, an official communication has been received at the Department of State, from Her Britanic Majesty's Chargé d'Affaires near this Government, founded upon a dispatch he had received from Her Majesty's Chargé d'Affaires in Mexico, announcing to this Government the fact that the President of *Mexico* would forthwith order a cessation of hostilities, on his part and the establishment of an armistice between Mexico and Texas and requested that the President of Texas would send similar orders to the different officers, commanding the Texian forces: And WHEREAS, the President of Texas has felt justified from the dispositions evinced by this act of the President of Mexico, and the nature of those dispositions, in adopting the proposed measure, and ordering the cessation of hostilities on the part of Texas.
>
> Therefore, be it known, that I, San Houston, President of the Republic of Texas, and Commander in Chief of the Army and Navy of the same, do hereby declare and proclaim that an ARMISTICE is established between Texas and Mexico, to continue during the pendency of negotiations between the two countries for peace, and until the notice of an intention to resume hostilities (should such an intention hereafter be entertained either party,) shall have been formally announced through H, B. M. Charges d'Affaires at the respective Governments, and the revocation of this proclamation; and all officers, commanding the forces of Texas, or acting by authority of this Government are hereby ordered to observe the same.
>
> In testimony whereof, I have hereunto set my hand and caused the Great Seal of the Republic to be affixed.
>
> Done at Washington the fifteenth day of June, A. D. 1843, and of the Independence of the Republic the eighth.
>
> By the President
> Sam Houston

Anson Jones, Secretary of State. *The Writings of Sam Houston, 1813–1863*, vol. 3, Amelia W. Williams and Eugene C. Barker, eds. (Austin, TX: University of Texas Press, 1938–43), 409–10.

97. John Christopher Columbus Hill (1828–1904) served in the Mier Expedition and was made prisoner upon the surrender of Texas forces. "He displayed such bravery and audacity at the age of 14 in the battle of Mier, Gen. Pedro Ampudia befriended him and sent him with special military escort to President Antonio López de Santa Anna in Mexico." Characterized as "a brave and handsome little fellow" by William Preston Stapp, veteran of the Mier Expedition, and as "a very shrewd and handsome boy" by Waddy Thompson, United States Minister to Mexico, he so endeared himself to generals Santa Anna, Valentín Gómez Farías, and José María Tornel that they persuaded him to remain in Mexico. Although he was in no position to bargain, his agreement was based upon their promise to release his father and brother, Jeffrey, who were also prisoners of war. https://tshaonline.org/handbook.
98. McCutchan, *Mier Expedition Diary*, 18.
99. Houston to Elliot, January 24, 1843, *Writings of Sam Houston*, 3: 299–302.
100. H. Yoakum, Esq., *History of Texas from its First Settlement in 1685 to its Annexation to the United States in 1846* (New York: Redfield, 1855), I: 398.
101. Walker to Houston, October 28, 1843. Thomas J. Green Papers, Southern Historical Collection, University of North Carolina, Chapel Hill.
102. Samuel Houston, *The Writings of Sam Houston*, vol. 3, Amelia W. Williams and Eugene C. Barker, eds., (Austin: University of Texas Press, 1940), 170.
103. Ibid., 177.
104. J. H. Kuykendall, "Sketches of Early Texians," 8. typed ms, University of Texas, Austin.
105. The original document on microfilm in Texas State Archives. It is witnessed by Thomas H. Addicks, Notary Public.

Chapter 5: The Rangers of Texas

1. A very interesting history of the America's earliest Rangers was written by Col. Robert W. Black, *Ranger Dawn: The American Ranger from the Colonial Era to the Mexican War* (Mechanicsburg, PA: Stackpole Books, 2009). Unfortunately, in relation to this study he does not include details of the Maryland Rangers. For information about the Maryland Rangers see William Hand Browne (ed.), *Archives of Maryland: Proceedings and Acts of the General Assembly of Maryland, April 1666–January 1676, II* (Baltimore: Maryland Historical Society, 1884).
2. Black, *Ranger Dawn*, 7. John Smith mentions some small-scale Ranger operation in 1622.
3. See the Introduction of this work.
4. Black, *Ranger Dawn*, 6.
5. William Hand Browne (ed.), *Archives of Maryland* (Baltimore: Maryland State Archives, 1883), 493; Richard L. Morton, *Colonial Virginia* (Chapel Hill: University of North Carolina Press, 1956), I: 306–7; Vernon W. Crane, *The Southern Frontier* (Ann Arbor: University of Michigan Press, 1956), 187–90; William Stephens, *Journal of the Proceedings in Georgia* (Ann Arbor: University Microfilm, Inc., 1966), II: 193.
6. Burt G. Loesher, *History of Rogers Rangers* (San Francisco: By the author, 1946). Loesher's work is a most comprehensive study of Rogers Rangers with a depth of research seldom reached by colonial military historians.
7. Rev. John Entick, *The General History of the Late War* (London: 1763).
8. Loesher, *History of Rogers Rangers*, xiv; Lawrence Henry Gipson, *The British Empire Before the Revolution* (New York: Alfred A. Knopf, Inc., 1949), VII: 154–55. Examples of the difficulty to control early Texas Rangers are given later in this work.
9. http://historyreconsidered.net/VirginiaRangers1754–1763.html.
10. The Ranger originally was not a soldier. In this Quaker-controlled colony, he was a political official appointed in each county by proprietary governors. His duty was to range the county and seize stray animals—especially horses—which were then sold at auction as a source of revenue for the colony.

See W. R. Shepherd, *History of the Proprietary Government of Pennsylvania* (New York: Columbia University Press, 1896), VI: 77n.

11. See Samuel J. Newland, *The Pennsylvania Militia: The Early Years, 1699–1792* (Commonwealth of Pennsylvania, Department of Military and Veterans Affairs, 1997); Gary Zaboly, *American Colonial Ranger: The Northern Colonies, 1724–1763* (Osprey Publishing, 2004).
12. Later, after the Revolutionary War, Rangers were still used to protect Pennsylvanians from Indian attack. The State Legislature seemed to be making up for what the colonial Quaker lawmakers did not do. In 1792, Virginia Ranger Capt. William McMakin complained: "I have great difficulty in raising men … owing to the liberal wages given by the State of Pennsylvania to their Rangers … this difference gives the people great uneasiness, as it has drawn a number of our own best men from the frontier in their service." *Calendar of Virginia State Papers*, V: 490; VI: 246.
13. Brian D. Carroll, "'Savages' in the Service of Empire: Native American Soldiers in Gorham's Rangers, 1744–1762," *The New England Quarterly*, 85, no. 3 (September 2012): 383.
14. Harold L. Peterson, *The Book of the Continental Soldier* (Harrisburg, PA: The Stackpole Co., 1968), 222–23.
15. The majority of the shoulder weapons of the Revolutionary War were smooth-bore muskets, which were relatively fast-loading in the hands of an experienced shooter, but lacked any effective accuracy beyond 50 yards. The British riflemen (with the exception of Major Patrick Ferguson's rifle company) were represented by German *Jaeger* riflemen whose weapon was sighted in for 100 yards. According to contemporary sources, the American rifleman were known to have hit British soldiers in the head easily at 200 yards. For an interesting analysis of these colonial marksmen and their weapon see Harold L. Peterson, "The Kentucky Rifle," *The American Rifleman* (November 1964): 28–32.
16. Bernhard A. Uhlendorf (trans.), *Revolution in America–Confidential Letters and Journals, 1776–84, of the Adjutant General Major Baurmeister of the Hessian Forces* (New Brunswick, New Jersey: Rutgers University Press, 1957), 37. See also Porter R. Sweet, "Rangers Four, Part Two," *Infantry*, 56 (March–April 1966): 12. Sweet points out the effect of the riflemen on the battle of Saratoga in 1777. On the other hand, while the American riflemen were deadly at a distance, in close-in combat they were relatively helpless—especially against a British bayonet attack. The Americans' long, slender rifles were without bayonets and made fragile clubs. American Gen. Anthony Wayne observed this condition in combat and wrote: "the enemy knowing the Defenseless State of our Riflemen rush on—they [the riflemen] fly—mix with or pass Thro' the Other Troops." This observation and other liabilities of the riflemen are cited in Colonel J. W. Wright, "The Rifle in the American Revolution," *The American Historical Review*, 29 (January 1924): 296.
17. Eric I. Manders, "Butler's Rangers, 1777–1784," MUIA plate 196, *Military Collector & Historian*, 13, no. 4 (Winter 1961): 118.
18. Darby Erd, "The Third South Carolina Regiment (Rangers) 1775–1780)," MUIA plate 494, *Military Collector & Historian*, 32, no. 2 (Summer 1980): 73.
19. Alec R. Gilpin, *The War of 1812 in the Old Northwest* (East Lansing, MI: Michigan State University Press, 1958), 34.
20. Captain Larry Ives, "Rangers in Florida, 1818," *Infantry*, 53 (September–October 1963): 37.
21. *American State Papers*, Military Affairs, V: 31. See also, Randy Steffen, *The Horse Soldier: 1776–1943* (Norman: University of Oklahoma Press, 1977), I: 84–87; Otis E. Young, "The United States Mounted Ranger Battalion, 1832–1833," *Mississippi Valley Historical Review*, 41 (December, 1954): 453–70; and Francis Paul Prucha, *The Sword of the Republic: The United States Army on the Frontier, 1783–1846* (Bloomington: Indiana University Press, 1977), 240–45.
22. Many of the Ranger officers transferred to the dragoons, as the mounted Rangers were disbanded in 1833.The 2d Regiment of Dragoons was formed in 1836. See Steffen, I: 110. The first two regiments of the United States Cavalry (after the Legions of the Revolution) were called Dragoons. The next was called the Mounted Rifles. Then, in 1855, the War Department changed the 1st and 2d Dragoons to the 1st and 2d Cavalry; the Mounted Rifles became the 3d Cavalry. Richard Wormser, *The Yellowlegs: The Story of the United States Cavalry* (Garden City, NY: Doubleday & Company, Inc. 1966), ix.

23. Henry Barton, "The United States Cavalry and the Texas Rangers," *Southwestern Historical Quarterly*, 63, no. 4 (April 1960): 497–98.
24. Many medieval Spaniards adopted not only the Moorish horse but also his saddle. Instead of the low cantle, small, pommeled saddle with long stirrups used by the ancient Spanish knights, they chose the short stirrup, high Moorish designed saddle. In those early years before the Spanish reconquest of their land from the Moors in the 15th century, raids on horseback were common and the Spaniards of that age became a breed of horsemen.
25. T. R. Fehrenback, *The Lone Star: A History of Texas and the Texans* (New York: The MacMillan Co., 1968), 22.
26. Ibid., 29.
27. See James Worsham, "The Comanche, the Horse and the Buffalo: A Study in Dependence and Independence," unpublished manuscript, 1991.
28. See Ernest Wallace and E. Adamson Hoebel, *The Comanches: Lords of the South Plains* (Norman: University of Oklahoma Press, 1952).
29. Fehrenback, *The Lone Star*, 31.
30. Eugene C. Barker, *The Life of Stephen F. Austin* (Nashville: The Cokesbury Press, 1925), 102.
31. Ibid., 165–66.
32. Ray Allen Billington, *Westward Expansion* (New York: The Macmillan Company, 1960), 494.
33. Aminta Inelda Perez, "*Tejano Rangers: The Development and Evolution of Ranging Tradition, 1540–1880.*" Abstract, PhD diss., University of Iowa, 2012.
34. Eugene C. Barker, "The Texan Revolutionary Army," *The Southwestern Historical Quarterly*, 9 (April 1906): 232.
35. Rena Maverick Green (ed.), *Samuel Maverick, Texan: 1803–1870; A Collection of Journals and Memoirs* (San Antonio: Privately Printed, 1952), 103.
36. Randy Steffen, "Texas Rangers, 1839," MUIA plate 150, *Military Collector & Historian*, 10. no. 3 (Fall 1958): 79.
37. Webb, *The Texas Rangers: A Century in Frontier Defense*, 79.
38. J. K. Greer, *Col. Jack Hays: Texas Frontier Leader and California Builder* (New York: E. P. Dutton and Co., Inc., 1952), 42.
39. Frederick W. Olmsted, *A Journey Through Texas; Or, a Saddle-Trip on the Southwestern Frontier* (Austin, University of Texas Press, 1978), 300–1.
40. Rupert Norval Richardson, *The Comanche Barrier* (Glendale, CA: Arthur H. Clark Co., 1933), 93.
41. C. W. Webber, *Tales of the Southern Border* (Philadelphia: J. B. Lippincott Company, 1887), 53. Although this work is a novel, Webber describes the Rangers of the Republic from his own experiences as a Ranger with Hays.
42. Ibid., 64.
43. Greer, *Col. Jack Hays*, 22.
44. Ibid.
45. Green, *Samuel Maverick, Texan*, 102.
46. Webb, *The Texas Rangers*, 65.
47. Greer, *Col. Jack Hays*, 31–32.
48. Jack Hays and Flacco became very good friends with a deep mutual respect for each other; they would often go on patrols together. In fact, Flacco was made a Texas Ranger captain with his own company. Some historians have speculated that Hays and Flacco could have been considered the original Lone Ranger and Tonto. Flacco was murdered in 1842 and Hays was deeply saddened. Sam Houston even wrote a moving eulogy on Flacco. See http://www.texasranger.org/history/RangersRepublic.htm.
49. Greer, *Col. Jack Hays*, 35.
50. Webber, *Tales of the Southern Border*, 59.
51. Reid, *The Scouting Expeditions of McCulloch's Texas Rangers*, 69, 71.
52. Ibid., 110; William B. Edwards, "Shootin' Irons," *This Is the West*, ed. Robert West Howard (New York: Rand McNally and Co., 1957), 183.

53. J. Evetts Haley, *Charles Goodnight; Cowman and Plainsman* (Norman: University of Oklahoma Press, 1949), 37.
54. Ibid. Either by a leather thong around their necks or in their pockets, Rangers who armed themselves with the early Colt Paterson revolvers carried loading levers and cappers to facilitate placing fresh percussion caps on their weapons. The Paterson powder and bullet flask was probably carried in the Ranger's "wallet" on his saddle; in a fight the Ranger would only have time to exchange a loaded cylinder for his empty one. The loading tool served to disassemble the weapon and capper was needed in case any caps were lost in the process and had to be replaced.
55. James E. Serven, *Colt Firearms, 1836–1960* (Santa Anna, CA: Serven Books, 1960), 12.
56. Maskell E. Curwin, *Campaign Sketches of the War with Mexico* (New York: George P. Putnam and Co., 1853), 97–98.
57. J. Frank Dobie, *The Mustangs* (Boston: Little, Brown, and Co., 1952), I: 61–62.
58. Lt. Col. George T. Denison, Jr., *Modern Cavalry: Its Organization, Armament, and Employment in War* (London: Thomas Bosworth, Publisher, 1868), 370–72.
59. Haley, *Charles Goodnight*, 38.
60. Catherine W. McDowell, ed., *Now You Hear My Horn: The Journal of James Wilson Nichols 1820–87* (Austin: University of Texas Press, 1968), 80–81.
61. Haley, *Charles Goodnight*, 38–39.
62. McDowell, *Now You Hear My Horn*, 80.
63. J. C. Duval, *Early Times in Texas* (Austin: Steck-Vaughn Co., 1967), 70.
64. Ibid., 71.
65. Ibid., 72.
66. Grace Jackson, *Cynthia Ann Parker* (San, Antonio: The Naylor Co., 1959), 53.
67. Wallace, *The Comanches*, 126.
68. Ibid., 37, 253.
69. Jackson, *Cynthia Ann Parker*, 50.
70. Wallace, *The Comanches*, 156.
71. Ibid., 252.
72. Jackson, *Cynthia Ann Parker*, 47
73. Wallace, *The Comanches*, 257.
74. Greer, *Col. Jack Hays*, 28.
75. Wallace, *The Comanches*, 258.
76. Ralph K. Andrist, *The Long Death: The Last Days of the Plains Indians* (New York: The Macmillan Company, 1964), 21.

Chapter 6: The Battle of Walker Creek, June 8, 1844

1. "The Battle of Walker Creek, June 8, 1844, Tall Tales and Myths Removed, This is the Documented Drama of the Day the Texas Frontier Changed Forever." MS, n.d., Walker Vertical, Texas Ranger Hall of Fame & Museum File.
2. George Catlin, *Letters and Notes on the Manners, Customs, and Conditions of the North American Indians* (New York: Wiley & Putnam, 1842), II: 65–66.
3. Clive Cussler, founder of the National Underwater and Marine Agency, located the hull of *Zavala* (archaeological site 41GV95) beneath a parking lot in the former Bean's Wharf area of Galveston Harbor in 1986.
4. *Journals of the Ninth Congress of the Republic of Texas* (Washington, TX: Miller & Cushing, Public Printers, 1845), Appendix A, 32–33.
5. Robert Addison Gillespie was born June 12, 1815, in Blount County, Tennessee, and migrated to Texas with his extended family. He left his mercantile business from time to time when called upon to deal with marauding Comanche.

Gillespie participated in the 1840 upper Colorado River expedition with John Henry Moore of the Old Three Hundred, during the period when Moore was engaging the Comanche in battle. Gillespie enlisted as a private in Capt. Jack Hays' Company of Texas Rangers in September 1842, serving until January 7, 1843, and participated in the September 17, 1842, battle of Salado Creek. He reenlisted June 1, 1843, in the Hays Spy Company. He remained in Hays' Company until September 28, 1845, when he formed the San Antonio Mounted Rangers, as part of the Hays Battalion of Texas Mounted Rangers, and served as its Captain until March 28, 1846. At the battle of Monterrey during the Mexican–American War, he was the first Ranger to breach the fort at the Independence Hill summit. Later, Gillespie was wounded during the assault on Bishop's Palace of September 22, 1846. He succumbed to his wounds on September 23.

6. *Memoirs of Mary A. Maverick*, Rena Maverick Green, ed. (San Antonio, TX: Alamo Publishing Company, 1921), 81–83.
7. *Northern Star* (Gainesville, Texas), July 24, 1844, copying the Houston *Morning Star* of June 23, 1844.
8. Greer, *Col. Jack Hays*, 96–99.
9. J. M. Morphis, *History of Texas, from its Discovery and Settlement, with a Description of its Principal Cities and Counties, and the Agricultural, Mineral, and Material Resources of the State* (New York: U.S. Publishing Company, 1872), 431.
10. "[…] Tall Tales and Myths Removed […]"
11. Letter Ben McCulloch to T. Greene as appeared in the *Northern Standard* (Gainesville, Texas), July 10, 1844. McColloch was, at that time, a first lieutenant in Hays's Company. Born in Tennessee in 1811, he and his brother Henry decided to move to Texas. On their way, the met up with Davy Crockett and his group. Had McCulloch not come down with the measles, he would have joined the defenders of the Alamo and suffered their fate. Upon reaching Texas after his recovery, he was active with the Texas Rangers and in politics. He was subsequently appointed a major general of Texas Militia. During the War with Mexico, McCulloch was appointed a major of U.S. Volunteers. After the end of the war, he was appointed U.S. Marshall for Eastern Texas, a post he held until the start of the Civil War. He was appointed brigadier general in the Confederate service and was killed in action at the battle of Pea Ridge, March 7, 1862.

Chapter 7: Matamoros to Monterrey: Early Ranger Wartime Service, 1844–46

1. William Ourey was not on the roll with the men who served at the battle of Walker Creek but when he later joined, he probably got many details from the men who were there. See, Edmund L. Dana, "Incidents in the Life of Capt. Samuel H. Walker, Texan Ranger," *Proceedings and Collection of the Wyoming County Historical and Geological Society*, vol. 1 (1882): 49–50.
2. Muster Rolls at State Archives; Texas Rangers Service Records 1830–46, Compiled and indexed by Frances Terry Ingmire, 1982, 154–55. According to the *New York Observer* May 23, 1846, Sam served with the Texas revenue service before commanding his company of Rangers for General Taylor. This is a mistake by the reporter. Walker never served in the Texas revenue service.
3. Ibid.; Quartermaster Records, 1845, San Antonio Ranging Corps, Voucher No. 3, $30, Republic of Texas to Sam H. Walker, October 24, 1845.
4. Homer S. Thrall, *History of Texas* (New York: University Pub. Co., *ca.* 1876), 276, states that Sam was wounded when he helped overpower the guard at Salado during his Mier imprisonment. This is doubtful as Sam does not mention it in his diary or in his application for a pension for his Mier imprisonment.
5. Samuel H. Walker to Ann Stone Walker, August 26, 1845, Samuel H. Walker Papers, Texas State Archives, Austin, Texas.
6. Letters Received by the Office of the Adjutant General, 1822–1860, National Archives Microfilm Publication M567, www.fold3.com, images 292741268–292741270.

7. Message from President James K. Polk, May 22, 1846, *Journal of the Executive Proceedings of the Senate of the United States of America*, vol. 7, 74–75, http;//memory/loc.gov/cgi-bin/ampage. Among those nominated at the same time and later associated with Company C, USMR, were Benjamin S. Roberts, first lieutenant; John G. Walker, first lieutenant; Spear S. Tipton, first lieutenant; Thomas Claiborne, Jr., second lieutenant; and George McLane, second lieutenant.
8. Ibid., J. G. Chalmers to Samuel H. Walker, May 4, 1846.
9. Odie Faulk, *General Tom Green: Fightin' Texan* (Waco, Texian Press, 1963), 31. Unfortunately for Sam, after his three-month service with the Ranger Regiment at Monterrey, he left for Maryland to recruit for his Mounted Rifles in October 1846. On January 1, 1847, Dr. Chalmers was walking home from a New Year's Eve Party with his friend Joshua Holden. They became involved in a quarrel and Holden killed Chalmers with his cane sword. The family of Dr. Chalmers, the former Secretary of Treasury of the Republic of Texas, would now be poverty-stricken with no income. So, on January 31, 1847, Ranger Tom Green married Mary Chalmers and took under his wing her mother and six brothers. Tom and Mary took their responsibility of their large family seriously. In addition to taking care of Mary's family, together they raised five daughters and a son.
10. The Handbook of Texas Online, http://www.tsha.utexas.edu/handbook/online/articles/FF/qbf7.html.
11. Walter Prescott Webb, "The Texas Rangers in the Mexican War," (Master's Thesis, University of Texas, 1920), 2.
12. Ibid., 7.
13. Ibid., 9.
14. *Matamoros Reveille* (Mexico), July 15, 1846. https://lccn.loc.gov/2003241178.
15. This would be Walker's first command as a captain. He would serve in this position for three months. On June 6, Walker was elected lieutenant colonel of Hays's Texas Ranger Regiment. He had also been nominated and confirmed by the United States Senate as a captain and assigned to the United States Regiment of Mounted Rifles. He would not accept this position until October—after he completed his commitment with Hays.
16. Record of events, Walker's Company, Texas Mounted Rangers, April 21 to July 16, 1846.
17. Official Rosters of Capt. Walker's Company of Texas Rangers; Capt. Hays Rangers (February 25–June 26, 1844); and Capt. Cameron's Company, Mier Expedition, Texas State Archives, Austin, TX.
18. A. Russell Buchanan, ed, "George Washington Trahern: Texan Cowboy Soldier from Mier to Buena Vista," *Southwestern Historical Quarterly*, 70 (July 1966): 68–69.
19. Detailed History of Marshall Trimble, http://www.marshalltrimble.com/detailed_history_of_marshall_tri.htm. See also Randy Steffen, *The Horse Soldier, 1776–1943: The United States Cavalryman-His Uniforms, Arms, Accoutrements, and Equipments* (Norman: University of Oklahoma Press, 1977), 84–87.
20. Buchanan, "George Washington Trahern," 77.
21. Walker Papers, Texas State Archives.
22. James K. Holland, "Diary of a Texan Volunteer in the Mexican War," *The Southwestern Historical Quarterly*, vol. 30, no. 1 (July 1926): 13.
23. Walker Papers, Texas State Archives.
24. *Jeffersonian* (New Orleans), May 4, 1846.
25. Ibid., "Letters from the Army" no. 2, July 9, 1846.
26. 1st Lt. Napoleon Jackson Tecumseh Dana, USA, wrote "I have three hickory shirts now. They are first-rate for marching in." Robert H. Ferrell, ed., *Monterrey is Ours: The Mexican War Letters of Lieutenant Dana* (Lexington: University Press of Kentucky, 1990), 112.
27. Invoice, to Behan & Jenkins, Dr. Quartermaster Records, Texas State Archives.
28. According to this newspaper account he was riding a "fine war steed, presented to him by Mr. Harrison." In this same article it is mentioned that this same "fine horse" had been at the camp at Lagoon Iran Pelon to rest and was captured by the Mexicans, *Matamoros Reveille* (Mexico), July 15, 1846. This newspaper is unique. Its publisher Sam Bangs had an interesting history himself. See Lota M. Spell, "Samuel Bangs: The First Printer in Texas," 35, no. 4, *Southwestern Historical Quarterly Online*, http://www.tsha.utexas.edu/publications/journals/shq/online/v035/n4/contrib_DIVL3270.html. Of special

interest are the names on this issue's masthead. It reads *Matamoros Reveille*, Published Wednesdays and Saturdays, (publishers) Samuel Bangs and G. (Gideon) K. Lewis. Lewis was one of Walker's Rangers, mustering in on June 13. He got his information from fellow Rangers who were eyewitnesses. See Official Muster Roll Sam Walker's Company. He would later serve as a Texas Ranger captain himself. Not only that, but Lewis was in Walker's company during the Mier imprisonment. One of Sam's Rangers, George Washington Trahern, knew Lewis from the Mier captivity as "Legs" Lewis for his long strides when marching. See Buchanan, "George Washington Trahern," 64. (See also Official Muster Roll of Cameron's Co.) Ironically, later Lewis and Richard King were co-founders (1853) of the famous King Ranch—the largest in Texas—but Lewis was shot and killed by a jealous husband in 1855. For details see: http://www.tsha.utexas.edu/handbook/online/articles/LL/fle40_print.html.

29. T. B. Thorpe, *Our Army on the Rio Grande*, (Philadelphia: Carey and Hart, 1846), 47–48.
30. Washington, DC, *Vedette*, April 6, 1880, hereafter *Vedette*.
31. *Matamoros Reveille* (Mexico), July 15, 1846.
32. *Jeffersonian* (New Orleans), May 14, 1846.
33. *American Flag* (Matamoros, Mexico), January 20, 1847.
34. Walker Papers. Official Roster of Walker's Company. H. B. McCluster/McCleester, exchanged May 11, discharged June 30. J. Reese was exchanged May 11 and discharged May 30. L. Van Reed was exchanged May 11. H. Holbert was exchanged May 11. The fifth Ranger's name has not been found.
35. *Matamoros Reveille* (Mexico), July 15, 1846.
36. Ibid.
37. The *American Flag* (Matamoros, Mexico), January 20, 1847.
38. *House Executive Document No. 60*, 289; Buchanan, "George Washington Trahern," 71; and Haskel E. Curwin, *Campaign Sketches of the War with Mexico* (New York: George P. Putnam and Co., 1853), 97–98; Justin H. Smith, *War with Mexico* (New York: Macmillan, 1919), II, 423, comments it was common practice for guerrillas to mutilate wounded Americans by dragging the victims with a lasso.
39. Commercial Bulletin of New Orleans, May 11, 1846. According to the Roster of Walker's Company, McCluster survived, but had been captured. He was exchanged May 11 and discharged June 3.
40. *Houston Texas Telegraph*, June 31, 1846.
41. According to the Official Roster of Walker's Company, Lieutenant Trahern was issued two five-shot Colt Peterson revolvers. Neither one was turned in.
42. Buchanan, "George Washington Trahern," 71.
43. *Matamoros Reveille* (Mexico), July 15, 1846.
44. Walker Papers. Of the 32 Colts pistols issued to Sam's men, 20 were never turned in by the men to whom they were issued; 12 were lost in action. The U.S. lost all 32 Colts pistols to Walker's men.
45. Taylor to Adjutant General May 3, 1846. Letters Received by the Office of the Adjutant General, Main Series, 1822–1860, National Archives Microfilm Publication M567, Record Group 94, National Archives, Washington, DC.
46. Walker's official roster bears this out. George H. Bullard deserted in an attack on the enemy's picket guard on May 3. He took with him one Colt pistol and one carbine. C. B. Gicker was dishonorably discharged May 4, and (No first name on roll) Redmond and John Smucks were dishonorably discharged May 2.
47. *Niles National Register*, October 3, 1846.
48. Thorpe, *Our Army on the Rio Grande*, 60–61.
49. *Matamoros Reveille* (Mexico), July 15, 1846.
50. Robert N. Pruyn as told to James E. Edmond, "Campaigning Through Mexico with Old Rough and Ready," *Civil War Times*, vol. 2 (Oct 1963): 11.
51. Major Jacob Brown, at Fort Texas opposite Matamoros, Mexico, to Captain W. W. S. Bliss, Assistant Adjutant General, Point Isabel. Dispatch communicating the start of a Mexican siege and artillery bombardment of Fort Texas. https://www.dmwv.org/mexwar/documents.php.
52. *Matamoros Reveille* (Mexico), July 15, 1846.
53. Frost, *The Mexican War and Its Warriors*, 31.
54. Probably Creed Taylor and Pipkin Taylor.

55. *Matamoros Reveille* (Mexico), July 15, 1846.
56. Robert W. Johansen, *To the Halls of Montezumas: The Mexican War in the American Imagination* (New York: Oxford University Press, 1985). On the other hand, some other officers were jealous. One lieutenant (Lt. Napoleon Jackson Tecumseh) made the following observation: "The man Walker whom the papers make so much ridiculous fiction." Ferrell, *Monterrey is Ours,* 111.
57. Ibid., 135–36.
58. *New York Sun,* December 8, 1846; Joseph Leach, *The Typical Texan; Biography of an American Myth* (Dallas: Southern Methodist University Press, 1952), 46.
59. *Spirit of the Times,* December 19, 1846.
60. Leach, *The Typical Texan,* 90.
61. Johannsen, *To the Halls of Montezumas,* 136, 219, 233.
62. Samuel C. Reid, *The Scouting Expeditions of McCulloch's Texas Rangers or, The Summer and Fall Campaign of the Army of the United States in Mexico, 1846* (Philadelphia: G. G. Evans, 1859).
63. George Lippard, *Legends of Mexico* (Philadelphia: T. B. Peterson, 1847).
64. Emerson Bennett, *Clara Moreland or, Adventures in the far South-West* (Philadelphia: T. B. Petersen, 1853).
65. He was named Tornado because he was purchased on the day of the great tornado in Natchez. Walker Papers, May 15, 1846.
66. *Niles Nation Register,* May 15, May 30, and June 27, 1846; *Newport Mercury* (Rhode Island), May 30, 1846. William S. Henry, *Campaign Sketches of the War with Mexico* (New York: Harper, 1847), 115, 202.
67. *Niles National Register,* copying "Letters from the Corporal at Matamoros, May 25, 1846.
68. *Daily Picayune* (New Orleans), May 16, 1846.
69. *Weekly Reveille* (St. Louis), II, 46. While Walker's family received his pistols at his death, this engraved presentation sword was never found.
70. Ibid., III, 9, 988, Tuesday Morning, September 1, 1846, Missouri Historical Society. Ironically, Sam's legacy would extend to a century later during World War II, a Liberty ship would be named SS *Samuel H. Walker.* She was launched in 1949 and scrapped in 1964.
71. Ulysses S. Grant, *Personal Memoirs of U. S. Grant* (New York: C. L. Webster & Company, 1885), http://www.perseus.tufts.edu/hopper/text?doc=Perseus:text:2001.05.0019.
72. Thorpe, *Our Army on the Rio Grande,* 77.
73. Ibid., I: 93–98.
74. *Niles National Register,* June 13, and July 11, 1846.
75. Grant, *Personal Memoirs.*
76. Thorpe, *Our Army on the Rio Grande,* 125.
77. Grant, *Personal Memoirs.*
78. Ian B. Lyles, *Mixed Blessing: The Role of the Texas Rangers in the Mexican War, 1846–1848* (Cascadia, WA: Normandy Press, 2014), 34.
79. *House Executive Document No. 60,* 288.
80. Ibid., 321.
81. Texas Democrat Austin, May 6, 1846. John Price was a veteran Ranger who received his commission in 1840, the same year Hays became a Ranger captain. See Webb, "The Texas Rangers in the Mexican War," 32, 69.
82. Reid, *The Scouting Expeditions of McCulloch's Texas Rangers,* 41.
83. *Daily Picayune* (New Orleans), August 9, 1846. See Reid, 44. Walker's Company turned in their weapons at Matamoros and Maj. H. K. Craig reported that the Texas were here "armed partly with revolving pistols, Rifles and Carbines issued from our Depots. Many of these have been damaged and ought not to be received again into the Depot."
84. Reid, *The Scouting Expeditions of McCulloch's Texas Rangers,* 33.
85. Greer, *Col. Jack Hays,* 126–27.
86. Zenas Matthews Diary, Sunday June 14, 1846, Walker was elected lieutenant colonel. http://beta.fromthepage.com/display/display_page?ol=d_act_page&page_id=2655.

87. Executive Journal, United States Senate, May 25, 1846, A Century of Lawmaking for a New Nation: U.S. Congressional Documents and Debates 1774–1875, Library of Congress, Washington, DC.
88. Walker to Jones, Adjutant General, June 30, 1846. Record Group 94—Records of the Adjutant General's Office, National Archives, Washington, DC.
89. Walker to Jones, Adjutant General, June 30, 1846; ibid.
90. Ibid.
91. Walker to Dear Brother, July 1, 1846. Walker Papers, Texas State Archives.
92. Jaques to Walker, San Antonio, July 16, 1846. Walker Papers, Texas State Archives.
93. Regimental Order August 27, 1846, Headquarters 1st Regt, Texas Mounted Riflemen, SH Walker, Lieut. Col., Comdg. the Regiment. Texas State Archives, Austin, TX.
94. *Niles National Register*, August 1, 1846. Meanwhile in Washington, in a few weeks, Sam Walker's brother Jonathan Thomas would be caught up in the war enthusiasm and wrote to the Army for a copy of Army Regulations and Tactics. AGO Papers No. 1377, September 16, 1846, The National Archives.
95. *Niles National Register*, August 1, 1846.
96. James K. Greer, ed., *A Texas Ranger and Frontiersman: The Days of Buck Barry in Texas* (Lincoln and London: University of Nebraska Press, 1978), 33–34.
97. Ibid., 34.
98. Ibid.
99. Ibid., 35.
100. *American Flag* (Matamoros, Mexico), October 14, 1846.
101. Ferrell, *Monterrey is Ours*, 131; see also Reid, *Scouting Expeditions with McCulloch's Texas Rangers*, 158, states Walker's horse was severely wounded.
102. Reid, *Scouting Expeditions with McCulloch's Texas Rangers*, 181.
103. Greer, *Col. Jack Hays*, 145.
104. Reid, *Scouting Expeditions with McCulloch's Texas Rangers*, 182.
105. Lyles, *Mixed Blessing*, 46. Years later, when author James K. Greer, was collecting material for his biography of Hays, the subject of Gillespie's wound and his reaction came up. The published version was, "Gillespie—educated, gallant, close friend of Hays—had pretended to be only slightly wounded and had waved his men on into the struggle when several sought to help him." None of those Greer contacted recalled any heroic, stirring last words. He must have said something and Lyles's version is as good as any. Gillespie's body apparently was disinterred once before he was removed to be buried by Sam in San Antonio. See: *Niles National Register*, January 16, 1847. "In your paper of the 4th ult. I saw a biographical sketch of Capt. Gillespie, and on showing it to an acquaintance, he informed me that about four weeks after the battle, he went to the graves of Capt. Gillespie and young [Herman S.] Thomas [one of McCulloch's men—ironically, like Sam, from Maryland], and found that the bodies had been dug up by the Mexicans, and stripped of every vestige of clothing. The bones were reentered and the graves covered over with large flat rocks.—When it is generally known by these groveling wretches, that nothing but the bones of the heroes are left in the grave." Later Gillespie's body would be moved to San Antonio and Sam Walker would be buried beside him—and is today. One Pennsylvania soldier in New Orleans reported that on January 7, 1847, the steamer *Fashion* brought the body of Gillespie to New Orleans for transfer to San Antonio, Texas. J. Jacob Oswandel, *Notes on the Mexican War, 1846–47–48* (Philadelphia: n.p., 1885), 35.
106. Greer, *The Days of Buck Barry*, 37.
107. Walter P. Lane, *The Adventures and Recollections of General Walter P. Lane, a San Jacinto Veteran* (Marshall, TX: Tri-Weekly Herald, 1887), 49.
108. Reid, *Scouting Expeditions with McCulloch's Texas Rangers*, 185–86.
109. Reid, *The Scouting Expeditions of McCulloch's Texas Rangers*, 186.
110. Samuel Chamberlain, *My Confessions: Recollections of a Rogue* (New York: Harper & Brothers, 1956), 67. Chamberlain's *My Confessions* has been described as a "vivid recording of what a soldier would see and feel" as he actually participated in the Mexican–American War. Yet while the young New England cavalry soldier who wrote and gloriously illustrated this recollection (not diary) was in combat, he was

not in all of the fighting he describes. Many have considered his work mostly fantasy but research by Pulitzer Prize winning historian Dr. William H. Goetzmann revealed that much can be documented as factual. In reference to this study Chamberlain actually portrays himself at the battle of Monterrey with Samuel H. Walker. In fact, he was still at San Antonio when the battle took place. Yet as Goetzmann observes, Chamberlain greatly admired the Texas Rangers who fought under Ben McCulloch and Sam Walker. As Goetzmann described it, "He must have discussed it [the battle of Monterrey] with Ranger participants [so] that it burned in his brain" as well as having Reid's *Scouting Expeditions of McCulloch's Texas Rangers*, published in 1847. (Chamberlain's work was written after the Civil War.) William H. Goetzmann, William N. Goetzmann, *The West of the Imagination* (Norman: University of Oklahoma Press, 2009). It is because of his accurate portrayal of many events as well as his respect of the Rangers that we include Goetzmann's edition of Chamberlain's presentation as insight into Sam Walker's participation.

111. Reid, *The Scouting Expeditions of McCulloch's Texas Rangers*, 186.
112. Chamberlain, *My Confessions*, 76–77.
113. Stephen Hardin and Richard Hook, *The Texas Rangers* (Oxford, UK: Osprey Publishing, 1991), 16.
114. Chamberlain, *My Confessions*, 78–81.
115. John C. Duval, *The Adventures of Big-Foot Wallace, The Texas Ranger and Hunter* (Macon, GA: The J. W. Burke Company, 1921), xv.
116. Reid, *The Scouting Expeditions of McCulloch's Texas Rangers*, 200.
117. T. B. Thorpe, *Our Army at Monterey* (Philadelphia: Carey and Hart, 1848), 96–97.
118. John R. Kenly, *Memoirs of a Maryland Volunteer. War with Mexico, in the Years 1846–8* (Philadelphia. J. B. Lippincott & Co., 1873), 144–45.

Chapter 8: The Walker Colt Revolver

1. Charles T. Haven and Frank A. Belden, *History of Colt's Revolver* …, (New York: Bonanza Books, 1978), 18.
2. James E. Servin, *Colt Firearms 1836–1960* (La Habra, CA: Foundation Press Publications, 1972), 9.
3. Ibid.
4. Major B. R. Lewis, "Sam Colt's Repeating Pistol," *The American Rifleman*, 95 (May 1947): 32–33. This is the same General Jessup that Walker met in the Seminole War in Florida. Ironically, although Jessup was very hesitant to help young Private Walker in the Seminole War, for Captain Walker, Texas Ranger, he was able to authorize horses for his Mounted Rifle company.
5. Maj. Gabriel Jones Rains of the 7th Infantry wrote the War Department strongly urging the adoption of the Colt revolvers by the Army. A decade later, Gen. W. S. Harney of the 2d Dragoons, testified that in his 10 years of experience with them, Colt's revolvers had no equal in reliability. He recommended that all members of the cavalry be armed with them. See Haven and Belden, *History of Colt's Revolver*, 33, 301; Servin, *Colt Firearms*, 9, 51.
6. Texas Ranger Ben McCulloch personally wrote President Polk on March 26, 1848, recommending Colt revolvers, and in the letter mentioned that revolvers on the frontier sold for as much as $150 each. Even from a dealer they sold for about $30 each while a single-shot pistol cost only $6.50 and the pepperbox pistols cost $10. So many of the large size Patersons, Model No. 5, ended up in Texas that they were later called the "Texas Arm." See Haven and Belden, *History of Colt's Revolver*, 24; Servin, *Colt Firearms*, 9, 16, 40; William B. Edwards, *The Story of Colt's Revolver* (Harrisburg, PA: The Stackpole Company, 1957), 241.
7. Servin, *Colt Firearms*, 10.
8. Edwards, *The Story of Colt's Revolver*, 95.
9. Edwards, *The Story of Colt's Revolver*, 216.
10. Lewis, "Sam Colt's Repeating Pistol," 33.
11. Haven and Belden, *History of Colt's Revolver*, 273. In Walker's papers was an invoice dated April 28, 1846, for 32 Colt pistols issued by the Army to Walker's Rangers.

12. Colt to Levi D. Slamm, undated, but certainly July 1846. John E. Parsons, comp., *Saml Colt's Own Record of Transactions with Captain Walker and Eli Whitney, Jr. in 1847* (Hartford: Connecticut Historical Society, 1949), 5–7.
13. Ibid., 6–7.
14. *House Executive Document No. 60, Thirtieth Congress, First Session, Serial 520*, 538.
15. Haven and. Belden, *History of Colt's Revolver*, 273; Edwards, *The Story of Colt's Revolver*, 216. Fish was the manufacturer of quality short-barreled rifles but was unable to furnish Walker any in quantity. The original note Walker carried with him in his pocket to New York City is in the Walker Papers.
16. While in New Orleans, Hays and Walker paid a visit to the "Commercial Reading Room" where their names were added to those of other notables who had signed the register of visitors. https://historical.ha.com/itm/militaria/-john-coffee-jack-hays-and-samuel-h-walker-page-from-the-commercial-reading-room-with-texas-rangers-jack-hays-and-samu/a/6104-44037.s?ic4=GalleryView-Thumbnail-071515.
17. *Niles National Register*, November 28, 1846, 208.
18. Lt. Col. George Talcott to Capt. W. A. Thornton, November 18, 1846, Letters to Ord Officers, V, 8, 348–49, Office of the Chief of Ordnance (OCO), Record Group 156, National Archives, Washington, DC, (NARA).
19. James K. Polk, *The Diary of a President, 1845–49* (London: Longmars, Green, 1952), 252.
20. Leach, *The Typical Texan*, 46.
21. Ibid.
22. Walker Papers, Texas State Archives.
23. Edwards, *The Story of Colt's Revolver*, 217.
24. Parsons, comp., *Sam Colt's Own Record*, 7–10.
25. It was once thought that Colt and Walker had met as early as 1839 and designed the Walker Colt Revolver. See W. F. Webb, *The Texas Rangers*, 85–86.
26. Edwards, *The Story of Colt's Revolver*, 216.
27. Ibid., 218.
28. Walker Papers, Texas State Archives.
29. Edwards, *The Story of Colt's Revolver*, 218.
30. Ibid.
31. Leach, *The Typical Texan*, 89–90; Johannsen, *To the Halls of Montezuma*, 135–36.
32. Samuel Walker to Jonathan Walker, May 29, 1843, Walker Papers.
33. Samuel Walker to Young Men's Henry Clay Association, December 29, 1846. Walker Papers.
34. Haven and Belden, *History of Colt's Revolver*, 274. This would be followed by a letter from Brig. Gen. Roger Jones, Adjutant General, to Captain Walker (dated December 19, 1846) ordering him to New York to "superintend the preparation of suitable models for your pistol." He stressed that this New York visit should be brief as "your services will soon be required at the head of your company." Volume 23, 209, Letters Sent, Office of the Adjutant General (AGO), RG 94, NARA.
35. Parsons, *Colt's Own Record*, 12.
36. Ibid., 13.
37. Edwin Wesson to Capt. S. H. Walker, December 16, 1846, Letters Received, 1846, W.D.564, OCO, RG 156, NARA.
38. Wesson was not to supply the pistols barrels either. Slate and Brown machinists were responsible for forging and drilling the barrels and cylinders supplied by Naylor and Co. Parsons, *Colt's Own Record*, 65–66.
39. Ibid., 24–27.
40. Ibid., 29.
41. Ibid., 30.
42. Ibid., 36–37.
43. Ibid., 40–42.
44. Roy G. Jinks, *History of Smith and Wesson* (North Hollywood, CA: Benfeld Publishing, Inc., 1977).
45. Parsons, *Colt's Own Record*, 42–43.
46. Ibid., 44.

47. Ibid., 46–48.
48. Ibid., 48.
49. Ibid., 54.
50. Ibid., 55.
51. Ibid., 58–59.
52. Ibid., 60–61.
53. Ibid., 64–65.
54. Ibid., 71–72.
55. Ibid., 73–74.
56. Ibid., 74–76.
57. Ibid., 21.
58. Karyl Lee Kibler Hall and Carolyn Cooper, *Window on the Works: Industry on the Eli Whitney Site 1798–1979* (New York: Denison Olmsted Arno Press 1972), 28–29.
59. Interestingly, another great symbol of American national progress, the Star-Spangled Banner flag at Fort McHenry, (when Sam Walker was recruited) was made of English wool.
60. G. S. *Cesari*, "*American Arms-making Machine Tool Development*, 1798–1855." (PhD diss., University of Pennsylvania, 1970), 191; Edwards, *The Story of Colt's Revolver*, 230–32.
61. Cooper, *Window on the Works*, 32.
62. Edwin Wesson to Capt. S. H. Walker, December 16, 1846. This was attached to a letter to Secretary of War Marcy on December 22, 1846, requesting him to order the rifles for his company. Letters Received, 564 (W.D.), OCO, RG 156, NARA.
63. Jinks, *History of Smith and Wesson*, 8. Interestingly, Walker would get his Wesson rifle and his Walker Colt revolvers shortly before he was killed.
64. During Sam Walker's time, there were no metallic cartridges, so with different powder charges from their powder flasks, it would be most advantageous to fire the same conical bullet from one's pistol and rifle. In later years, many Rangers carried the larger rifle rounds on their pistol belt as the rifle was the most used weapon of choice. Following the Civil War many Rangers carried the Winchester 73 and the 44–40 revolver: both could use the same cartridge. Bern Keating, *An Illustrated History of the Texas Rangers* (Victoria, Canada: Promontory Press, 1980), 186.
65. As explained later in detail, Wesson was the only rifle maker authorized to make the patented Clarke rifle.
66. *Daily Advertiser* (Newark, New Jersey), January 20, 1847.
67. Walker even tried to get the federal government to pay for his rifles, more pistols and saddles too. On January 15, 1847, Timothy Pillsbury, U.S. Representative from Texas, entered a memorial of Capt. S. H. Walker, of the first regiment of mounted riflemen, praying that provision be made by law for the purchase of one thousand "Clark's rifles," two thousand Colt's revolving pistols, and one thousand saddles and bridles, for the use of the Texan regiment of volunteers. On February 10, consideration of the memorial of S. H. Walker, relative to the arming of a rifle regiment, and was laid upon the table. See Journal of the House of Representatives Second Session 39th Congress, 172, 324. Apparently, the Maryland Legislature rejected the request also.
68. Jinks, *History of Smith and Wesson*, 9.
69. See James Worsham, "The Quest for Interchangeable Parts in American Firearms," unpublished manuscript, 1993.
70. Cesari, "American Arms-Making Machine Tool Development," 187.
71. Ibid., 183.
72. See Dr. Robert B. Gordon, Patrick M. Malone, eds., *The Texture of Industry* [...] (New York: Oxford University Press, 1994) for a detailed evaluation of Whitney's role.
73. Samuel Colt to Jonathan Walker, December 16, 1847, Texas State Archives.
74. Ironically, back in Texas Dr. Chalmers, Walker's potential father-in-law, was killed on January 1, 1847, and fellow Texas Ranger Tom Green would marry Mary Chalmers (a lady Walker had been courting before he left for his home in Maryland). Green and Ms. Chalmers married in late January 1847.

75. One delay in the delivery of the revolvers was due to a copyist's error. On the original memorandum that Colt and Walker drew up on January 4, 1847, the contract called for "one Powder Flask, ... for each pair of pistols." On the contract filed with the Ordnance Department, the statement read, "One powder flask ... for each pistol." The Ordnance Department threatened to delay shipping of the revolvers until Colt complied with their contract and produce 500 more loading implements for the revolvers. See Edwards, *The Story of Colt's Revolver*, 222; Haven and Belden, *History of Colt's Revolver*, 277, 290.
76. The 9-inch barrel—the same as the Ranger's Paterson Colts from the Texas Navy—was probably decided upon because the extra inch over the conventional 8-inch barrel was just that much more aid in accuracy. See Haven and Belden, *History of Colt's Revolver*, 277.
77. Ibid.
78. Walker to Colt, December 1, 1846, Parsons, *Colt's Own Record*, 10–11. See also final contract of January 4, 1847.
79. Reid, *Scouting Expedition*, 111.
80. *Senate Executive Document No. 56, Thirtieth Congress, First Session, Serial 518*, 402.
81. Edwards, *The Story of Colt's Revolver*, 220.
82. Haven and. Belden, *History of Colt's Revolver*, 281.
83. W. E. Rosebush, *Frontier Steel* (Spokane, WA: C. C. Nelson Publishing Company, 1958), 62.
84. Haven and. Belden, *History of Colt's Revolver*, 281.
85. Parsons, *Colt's Own Record*, 25. This was from the original Colt–Walker contract.
86. Parsons, *Colt's Own Record*, 25.
87. Arthur Tobias, Ed. D., *Colt Cylinder Scenes 1847–1851* (Los Angeles: By the Author, 2011), 13.
88. Ibid., 38–40.
89. Ibid.
90. Ibid., 40–44.
91. Edwards, *The Story of Colt's Revolver*, 225; Tobias, *Colt Cylinder Scenes*, 55.
92. Tobias, *Colt Cylinder Scenes*, 45.
93. Ibid., 20.
94. Parsons, *Colt's Own Record*, 57, 78.
95. Ibid., 69.
96. For a photograph of rare Grimsley Dragoon Saddle pommel holsters for the Walker Colt revolvers see R. Stephen Dorsey and Kenneth L. McPheeters, *The American Military Saddle, 1776–1945* (New York: Collectors' Library, 1999), 26.
97. Haven and Belden, *History of Colt's Revolver*, 283.
98. Parsons, *Colt's Own Record*, 46.
99. Cesari, "American Arms-Making Machine Tool Development," 184.
100. Ibid.
101. Rosebush, *Frontier Steel*, 68.
102. John H. Thillmann, "An Early Pair of Colt Walker Saddle Holsters," *Military Collector & Historian*, 65, no. 2 (Summer 2013): 168–82.
103. Ibid., 64.
104. Haven and Belden, *History of Colt's Revolver*, 285.
105. Cesari, "American Arms-Making Machine Tool Development," 185.
106. Parsons, *Colt's Own Record*, 60.
107. Rosebush, *Frontier Steel*, 69.
108. Haven and Belden, *History of Colt's Revolver*, 286.
109. Ibid., 287. According to one historian, "Talcott would set his own policies from day-to-day in an arrogant disrespect for higher authority as well as his subordinates and private arms contractors." See LTC Robert D. Whittington, *The Colt Whitneyville-Walker Pistol* (Dallas, TX: Taylor Publishing Co., 1984), 17. Talcott would eventually be caught and be found guilty in a General Court Martial in 1851 and stripped of rank and position. See General Orders No. 36.
110. Ibid., 288.

111. Whittington, *The Colt Whitneyville-Walker Pistol*, 50–57.
112. Ibid., 66, 72–75.
113. Lane to Colt, Oregon City, August 29, 1848. Samuel Colt Papers, Connecticut Historical Society, Hartford, CT.
114. Parsons, *Colt's Own Record*, 145n60.
115. http://www.colt.com/Company/History.aspx.
116. Walter Prescott Webb, *The Great Frontier* (Boston: Houghton Mifflin Company, 1952), 241–45.
117. Roy Jinks, *History of Smith and Wesson*, 9.
118. *The American Star*, February 4, 1848, quoting an article in the *Hartford Times.*

Chapter 9: Capt. Samuel H. Walker, Regiment of Mounted Riflemen

1. Henry Barton, "The United States Cavalry and the Texas Rangers," 495.
2. *American State Papers, Military Affairs* 7 vols. (Washington, DC: Gales and Seaton, 1838–61), 4: 5–6.
3. Ibid., 279.
4. Francis Paul Prucha, *The Sword of the Republic: The United States Army on the Frontier, 1783–1846* (New York: Macmillan, 1968), 361.
5. Theophilus F. Rodenbough and William L. Haskin, eds., *The Army of the United States: Historical Sketches of the Staff and Line with Portraits of Generals-in-Chief* (New York: Maynard, Merrill, & Co., 1896), 193.
6. "Regiment of Mounted Riflemen, Now the Third United States Calvary," *Army and Navy Journal*, 981, no. 3 and 982 (May 27, 1882); Marcus Cunliffe, *Soldiers & Civilians, The Martial Spirit in America, 1775–1865* (New York: The Free Press, 1973), 307. See also letters by Capt. Thomas W. Gibson of the 3d Indiana Volunteers, all to his wife, Mary, in Charlestown, Indiana, July 1846–May 1847 complaining that President James K. Polk's new officer appointments seem to be political gifts rather than rewards for service. Interestingly one Whig got the appointment, Sam Walker. Many Regular Army officers were also very upset over his appointment over them; they felt he was given the appointment because of his popularity. In fact, in the Walker papers is a copy of a petition by these officers to Congress objecting to political appointees over professionals.
7. Edwin Vose Sumner, born in Boston, Massachusetts, January 30, 1797. He entered the Army in 1819, as a second lieutenant of infantry. Served in the Black Hawk, Mexican–American, and Indian wars. He was the governor of New Mexico, 1851–53. In 1855, he was promoted colonel of 1st Cavalry and made a successful expedition against the Cheyennes. He was as in Kansas during the territorial troubles. In 1862, he commanded the I Corps of the Army of the Potomac. He was relieved at his own request in 1863, and being appointed to the Department of the Missouri, he was on his way there when he died at Syracuse, New York, March 21, 1863. Appleton's *Cyclopedia of American Biography*, 5: 750.
8. Rodenbough and Haskin, eds., *The Army of the United States*, 194.
9. "Regiment of Mounted Riflemen, Now the Third United States Calvary," *Army and Navy Journal*, 981, no. 3 and 982, no. 1 (May 27, 1882).
10. From the Thomas Claiborne Reminiscences, #152, 8 in the Southern Historical Collection, University of North Carolina Library, Chapel Hill, NC. Claiborne was a politically appointed second lieutenant in the regiment.
11. Justin H. Smith, *War with Mexico* (New York: Macmillan, 1919), 207.
12. Personal correspondence between co-author Worsham and Kenneth S. Roberts, July 19, 1989. See also Randy Steffen, *The Horse Soldier 1776–1943.*
13. Probably Halls breech-loading flintlock carbines.
14. This was the standard Ringgold saddle, so criticized by dragoon soldiers. See Steffen, *The Horse Soldier 1776–1943* 1: 154, 156–59, 165.
15. Col. Persifor Smith to Brig. Gen. Roger Jones, October 2, 1846, #S-501, Letters Received, 1846 (Microcopy M567; roll 326, Commence Frame 562), AGO; NARA RG 94.

16. Ibid. The continuing insistence for a hunting knife for his regiment eventually resulted in the manufacture of the first combat knife for issue to American troops. See James S. Hutchins, "The United States Mounted Rifleman's Knife," *Man at Arms: The NRA Journal* (March/April 1991): 10–21.
17. Jones to Walker, Washington December 19, 1847, AGO, RG 94, NARA. Colonel Smith was notified of Walker's orders in a letter from Jones dated the same.
18. Charles Frederick Ruff was born in Philadelphia, and graduated from West Point in 1838. He served with the 2d Dragoons on the frontier. As with Walker, he was an experienced Indian fighter who also left a lieutenant colonel position (the Missouri Volunteers) to accept a captaincy with the Mounted Rifles. See Capt. Charles Morton, *The Third Regiment of Cavalry,* 193, https://history.army.mil/books/R&H/R&H-3CV.htm; Heitman, 1: 850.
19. Ironically, nearly a century later during World War II, one of the 2,751 Liberty ships made to haul cargo was named the *Samuel H. Walker.* It became one of the 13 Liberty ships destined to carry mules. See Bud Shortridge, "Important Cargo 'Mules.'" http://navalmerchantshiparticles.blogspot.com/2010/09/important-cargo-mules.html.
20. Disappointing as it was to fight dismounted for most of the regiment, it saved them from being left behind to escort trains for General Taylor's army and chase guerrillas on the chaparral, and thus see very little action. By fighting on foot, the regiment was able to participate in much combat. In fact, it was on foot that the regiment earned its nickname, "Brave Rifles" when at the battle of Chapultepec, Gen. Winfield Scott was impressed by their bravery in action and called out: "Brave Rifles! Veterans! You have been baptized in fire and blood and come out steel." See Rodenbough and Haskin, *The Army of the United States,* 197 and "Regiment of Mounted Riflemen, now the Third United States Calvary," *Army and Navy Journal,* May 27, 1882, vol. 981, 3 and vol. 982, 1.
21. Capt. S. H. Walker to Col. Roger Stanton, February 11, 1847, Letters Received. 1846–47, Book 4, A9-Y1, entry 1004, AGO, RG 94, NARA.
22. Lacey H. Phillips, Philadelphia, January 14, 1847. Walker Papers.
23. *Washington Weekly Union,* January 23, 1847.
24. Capt. S. H. Walker to Secretary of War William Marcy, February 11, 1847, OQMG, Consolidated Correspondence File: Walker, Samuel H. RG 92, NARA.
25. Capt. S. H. Walker to Col. George Talcott, February 18, 1847, entry 21, W. D. 40, Records of the Office of the Chief of Ordnance (OCO). 1847, RG 156.
26. Ned H. Roberts, *The Muzzle-Loading Cap Lock Rifle* (New York: Bonanza Books, 1952), 66.
27. The gain twist means that the rifling twists less at the breech of the barrel therefore the bullet has less friction, and starts easier and quicker, and holds the bullet in position better than in the uniform twist.
28. Roberts, *The Muzzle-Loading Cap Lock Rifle,* 15, 32.
29. Wayne R. Austerman, "A Lost Heritage: The Personal Arms of Samuel H. Walker," *Man at Arms,* 2, no. 5 (September/October 1980): 27.
30. Walker to Jones, Washington, February 2, 1847. AGO, RG 94.
31. Parsons, *Colt's Own Record,* 44.
32. Tarleton to Walker, New Orleans December 19, 1846. Walker Papers.
33. S. H. Walker to Adjutant General Roger Jones, February 13, 1847, AGO, Consolidated Correspondence File: Walker, Samuel H., RG 94.
34. Walker to R. Jones, Adj. Gen., Washington, January 29, 1847. RG 94.
35. Jones to QM Dept, Washington, 16 February 1847, letter Sent v. 23, 304–5, National Archives Microfilm Publication 565, roll 15, AGO, RG 94.
36. S. H. Walker to Adjutant General Roger Jones, February 13, 1847, AGO, Consolidated Correspondence File: Walker, Samuel H., RG 94.
37. Capt. S. H. Walker to Capt. W. G. Freeman, February 18, 1847, OQMG Consolidated Correspondence File: Walker, Samuel H., RG 92.
38. Capt. S. H. Walker to Col. Henry Stanton, March 6, 1847, entry 1004, Bk 4, Letters Received, OQMG-Clothing & Equipage Branch, RG 92, NARA.
39. Capt. S. H. Walker to Col. Henry Stanton, February 23, 1847, Box 1197 Consolidated Correspondence File: Walker, Samuel H., OQMG, RG 92. See US Patent: 18, 691.

40. *Boston Daily Advertiser*, Boston, MA., February 10, 1847.
41. Mexican War Diary of Sergeant George W. Myers, U.S. Mounted Rifles, Walker's Co. "C," dated from February 26, 1847, through July 5, 1848. Courtesy of the Patrick Stewart, Rees-Jones Collection.
42. Ibid., 1. (Actual page number in the diary.)
43. *Boston Daily Advertiser* Boston, MA., February 27, 1847.
44. Myers Diary, 2.
45. Parsons, *Colt's Own Record*, 48.
46. Ibid., 54.
47. Capt. S. H. Walker to Gen Jones, March 6, 1847, Letters Received by AGO Main Series National Archives Microfilm Publication M567, R 365 RG 364.
48. Myers Diary, 5.
49. Ibid., 6.
50. Jesup to Walker, Head Quarters, Qr Master Genls Dept., New Orleans, January 28, 1847, OQMG, RG 92. NARA. Quartermaster General Thomas Sidney Jesup was the same General Jesup that Walker encountered earlier in Florida.
51. Charles F. Ruff of Missouri, late lieutenant in the U.S. 1st Dragoons.
52. Ruff to Capt. [Robert H. K.] Whitely, Baton Rouge Arsenal, April 3, 1847. OQMG, RG 92, NARA.
53. Capt. S. H. Walker contract with Gilmore and Egbert, March 10, 1847, Register of Contracts, v. 10, 42, 5 OQMG, RG 92, NARA.
54. Myers Diary, 7–8, 10.
55. Capt. S. H. Walker to Col. Roger Stanton, April 2, 1847, Consolidated Correspondence. File: Walker, Samuel H., OQMG, RG 92, NARA.
56. Capt. S. H. Walker to Gen. R. Jones, Adj. Gen., March 11, 1847, Office of the Adjutant General (AGO) 1780s–1917, RG 94 NARA.
57. Walker to Jones, Cumberland, Maryland, March 1, 1847. AGO RG 94.
58. Walker to Jones, Newport, Kentucky, March 6, 1847, Letters Received, 1847, National Archives Microfilm Publication M567, Roll 365, 4–6. AGO, RG 94.
59. Walker to Jones, Newport Barracks, March 11, 1847, National Archives Microfilm Publication M567, Roll 365, 23–26, Letters Received, AGO, RG 94.
60. Jones to Walker, Washington, March 18, 1847, Letters Sent vol. 23, 352, AGO, RG 94.
61. Parsons, *Colt's Own Record*, 55; Myers Diary, 11, 14.
62. Myers Diary, 15.
63. Parsons, *Colt's Own Record*, 58–59.
64. Ibid., 55, 59.
65. Capt. Samuel H. Walker to Gen. R. Jones, Adj. Gen., March 24, 1847, AGO, RG 94. NARA.
66. NNR vol. 72, March 20, 1847, account of the mounted riflemen at Jefferson Barracks.
67. Walker to Jones, Newport Barracks, March 24, 1847. Letters Received, 1847. National Archives Microfilm Publication M567, Roll 365, 183–89, AGO, RG 94.
68. Ibid., March 27, 1847.
69. Myers Diary, 16. Perhaps one reason Myers was made sergeant was that he was quick to act in an emergency. He alone jumped overboard into the Ohio River in early March and rescued a 10-year-old boy from drowning. Myers Diary, 12.
70. Erving to Jones, Newport, Kentucky, April 1, 1847, AGO, RG 94.
71. Parsons, *Colt's Own Record*, 64–65.
72. Ibid.
73. Myers Diary, 20.
74. Oswandel, *Notes of the Mexican War 1846–47–48*, 25. One of these recruits was William P. Wood of Washington. See Hamersly, L.R., "The Regiment of Mounted Riflemen," *The United Service*, (October 1895), 22–23. William P. Wood was the first director of the United States Secret Service.
75. Myers Diary, 21.

76. Ibid., 22.
77. Jones to Walker, Washington, April 5, 1847. Letters Sent, vol 23. National Archives Microfilm Publication M567, Roll 365, 407–8, AGO, RG 94.
78. Ibid., 413.
79. Morton, *Third Regiment of Cavalry*, 193, 196. See also https://friendsofmountmoriahcemetery.org/about/notable-burials/col-charles-frederick-ruff-brevet-brig-general.
80. This was either Ann Margaret Mackall or Mary "Betty" Elizabeth. "Betty" married Maj. William W. S. Bliss in 1849. Major Bliss had served under Taylor in Texas and at the battle of Monterrey. Another more famous sister had died in 1835: The daughter of the future President of the United States, Sarah Knox "Knoxie" Taylor, became the wife of future Confederate President Jefferson Davis.
81. Myers Diary, 25.
82. Ibid., 26.
83. See Dr. Alvin P. Stauffer, "The Quartermaster's Department and the Mexican War," *Quartermaster Review*, May–June 1950, https://www.quartermasterfoundation.org/the-quartermasters-department-and-the-mexican-war.
84. Capt. S. H. Walker to Col. Henry Stanton, April 2, 1847, Consolidated Correspondence File: Walker, Samuel H., QMG, RG 92. NARA.
85. Personal correspondence with Kenneth S. Roberts, July 19, 1989. See also Randy Steffen, *The Horse Soldier 1776–1943: The U.S. Cavalryman: His Uniform, Arms, Accoutrements and Equipment.*
86. General Orders No. 18, June 4, 1846, Headquarters of the Army, AGO, RG 94, NARA.
87. These items were shipped on February 18, 1846. Adj. Gen. Roger Jones to Maj. D. D. Tompkin, February 17, 1847, AGO Letters Sent, v. 23, 304–5, National Archives Microfilm Publication 565, Roll 15, 195, RG 94, NARA.
88. Capt. R. H. K. Whitely, Baton Rouge Arsenal to Col. George Talcott, April 3, 1847, OCO 1847 RG 156 W-197 entry 21.
89. Brig. Gen. R. Jones, Adj. Gen. to Capt. Walker, RMR (under cover to Gen. Brooke, New Orleans, requesting him to forward, April 7, 1847). It is unknown when Walker actually received this communication.
90. Walker to Jonathan Walker, April 18, 1847. Walker Papers.
91. Box 25, OCO, Papers of Capt. Benjamin Huger, Chief of Ordnance, General Scott's Army in Mexico, 1847–48, RG 156, NARA.
92. Ruff's company of Jefferson Barracks' trained recruits was organized at New Orleans on April 1, 1847. See Morton, *Third Regiment of Cavalry*, 194.
93. Capt. C. S. Ruff to Capt. R. H. K. Whitely, Baton Rouge Arsenal, April 3, 1847, Letters Received, V. 17 (1847), OCO RG 156.
94. Entry 21, W-161, 1847, OCO, RG 156.
95. Lt. Col Talcott to Capt. W. A. Thornton at the New York Depot on October 30, 1847, Letters to Ordnance Officers, v. 9, 318–19, OCO, RG 156.
96. This was the .54-caliber Model 1841 single-shot percussion muzzle-loading rifle. It was the last rifle designed to use the traditional round ball. See Randy Steffen, *The Horse Soldier 1776–1943*, 1: 136, and Larry Koller, *The Fireside Book of Guns, A Ridge Press Book* (New York Simon and Shuster, 1959), 65.
97. "Regiment of Mounted Riflemen, now the Third United States Calvary," *Army and Navy Journal*, May 27, 1882, vol. 981, 3 and vol. 982, 1. See also Talcott to Ord. Lt. McNutt, Fort Polk, February 19, 1847, M-84, recd. 22 March 1847, 1847, OCO, RG 156.
98. Myers Diary, 28.
99. This was the U.S. Model 1836 smoothbore .54-caliber flintlock pistol that was issued the Rifles. See Randy Steffen, *The Horse Soldier 1776–1943*, 1: 136.
100. Invoice turned over by Walker for rifles, etc. to Capt. B. Huger at Veracruz, 11 May 1847. Entry 1032, Box 6, Papers of Capt. Benj. Huger, Chief of Ordnance, Gen. Scott's Army in Mexico, OCO, RG 156; Ibid., Entry 1032, Box 25, Cartridges and sabers received by Walker, RG 156.
101. Myers Diary, 30.
102. Ibid., 31.

103. AGO Register Letters Received, May 12, 1847, 336, National Archives Microfilm Publication M-711, Fr 0536–7, RG 94, NARA.
104. Walker to Jonathan Walker, June 6, 1847, Walker Papers.
105. *Mary Kingsland* would have the unfortunate history of its boilers exploding three times. The last disaster occurred near New Orleans on March 1, 1852. See *Lloyd's Steamboat Directory*, 282. See also the *New York Times*, March 4, 1852.
106. Myers Diary, 37.
107. Smith, *War with Mexico*, I: 173.
108. Ibid., 421. During the American Civil War, the Confederacy passed the Partisan Ranger Act which basically had the same goal. Yet the Confederate guerrillas were partisans who fought in uniform and according to the civilized rules of warfare. Most were disbanded as they got out of hand; however, not to the excesses of the Mexican guerrillas. One battalion company by Col. John S. Mosby were most effective and praised by General Lee in his reports. See James J. Worsham and Maj. R. B. Anderson, "Mosby: The Model Partisan, Special Warfare," *The Professional Bulletin of the John F. Kennedy Special Warfare Center*, 2, no. 1 (Winter 1989): 34–38.
109. Myers Diary, 55–56.
110. Ibid., 56.
111. Smith, *War with Mexico*, I: 423.
112. Ibid., 2: 423.
113. James Knox Polk, Milo Milton Quaife, ed., *The Diary of James K. Polk During his Presidency, 1845 to 1849* (Chicago: A. C. McClurg & Co., 1910), July 16, 1847.
114. Robert Marshall Utley, *Lone Star Justice: The First Century of the Texas Rangers* (New York: Oxford University Press, 2002), 84.
115. *Whig and Public Advertiser* (Richmond, Virginia), May 28, 1847.
116. Ibid.
117. Myers Diary, 41.
118. The (Veracruz) *American Eagle*, June 13, 1847.
119. Myers Diary, 41.
120. Ibid., 42.
121. Walker to Col. [Henry] Wilson, Commanding officer at Vera Cruz, May 15, 1847.
122. *The Vidette*, 8, no. 1 (March 1887): 14.
123. The mayor or chief magistrate of a town in a Spanish-speaking area.
124. It is worthwhile noting that Walker and General Scott had met face-to-face and the general knew who he was when he later wrote directly to him concerning problems that Walker felt the general needed to be aware of.
125. Myers Diary, 47.
126. On July 30, 1847, Captain Ruff's company defeated a large superior force at San Juan de los Llanos, killing 40 and wounding 50; winning praise from Smith and Scott, and for Ruff to major, August 1, 1847, "for Gallant and Meritorious Conduct." He went on to fight in the battles of Contreras, Molino del Rey (where he was wounded), Chapultepec, and the assault and capture of the City of Mexico, September 13, 1847. See Morton, *Third Regiment of Cavalry*, 194, 196.
127. Capt. Samuel H. Walker to Jonathan Walker, June 6, 1847. Walker Papers.
128. Myers Diary, 48.
129. Ibid., 48–49.
130. As mentioned earlier in this work, Walker is clean shaven for his photographs but grows a short beard in the field both with the Texas Rangers early in the war and later with the Mounted Riflemen. Walker's portrait was probably taken by Joseph Rinehart, who was listed as a daguerreian in York, PA., *ca.* May, 1847. He advertised that he was a daguerreian from Virginia who included in his display daguerreotypes of Daniel Webster and Captain Walker of the Texas Rangers, images which had been taken on his recent visit to Philadelphia. http://www.daguerreotype.com/r_table.htm#Rinehart,%20 Joseph. Information corrected to November 1997; © 1996, 1997 John S. Craig.

131. Smith, *The War with Mexico*, I: 177.
132. Steffen, *The Horse Soldier 1776–1943*, 1: 161. Claiborne described his first view of the Grimsley saddle that Walker brought with him as "a most wonderful equipment of saddle furniture, high, goose neck pommels, with seat and sides glittering with patent leather, horse hair girth and immense wooden stirrups," Thomas Claiborne Papers, 1845–1935, Collection Number: 00152, Wilson Library, University of North Carolina, Chapel Hill, NC, 24. However, in a letter to his brother Jonathan on June 6, 1847, Walker wrote, "I found out that my saddles would not be sent to me and I had a set of botched saddles made in New Orleans which have hurt a good many of my horses backs. I am in hopes those I had made in Washington will be sent out to Vera Cruz," Walker Papers. See R. Stephen Dorsey and Kenneth L. McPheeters, *The American Military Saddle, 1776–1945* (New York: The Collector's Library, 1999), 19–21, for a discussion of the Grimsley saddle used by the Mounted Rifles.
133. See James Worsham, "Nashville's Col. Thomas Claiborne, Jr.—The Last of the Mexican War Mounted Rifles," unpublished manuscript, 1994.
134. One family name mentioned is "Eschbaugh." Claiborne, "Memories of the Past" *The Vidette*, 7, no. 4 (April 1886): 12. After Walker's death, one of his company wrote Jonathan Walker, Sam's brother, that before he died he gave his pistols to young Ashbaugh of his company. See George C. Myers to Mrs. Jane A. Walker, January 10, 1849; See also John M. L. Collins to Mrs. Jane A. Walker, January 9, 1849. Walker Papers.
135. See George C. Myers to Mrs. Jane A. Walker, January 10, 1849.
136. Benjamin Stone Roberts of Vermont, a graduate of the U.S. Military Academy, would continue to serve with the Mounted Rifles after Walker replaced him as company commanding officer. Roberts would be awarded the rank of brevet major on September 13, 1847, for gallantry in action in the battle of Chapultepec, Mexico. With Walker's death in October 1847, Roberts would again command Company C. He would later serve during the Civil War and would be recognized for his bravery with the rank of brevet major general of the volunteers in March 1865.
137. Company C, RMR, Monthly Report for October 1847, AGO, RG 94.
138. See G. O. #10, 12 March 47.
139. Walker to Jones, New Orleans, May 3, 1847, AGO, RG 94.
140. Company C, RMR, Monthly Report for May 1847, AGO, RG 94. Lieutenant Claiborne with 2 NCOs and 16 privates were detached on May 21 to escort a (wagon) train.
141. Oswandel, *Notes of the Mexican War*, 161.
142. Randy Hackenburg, *Pennsylvania in The War with Mexico: The Volunteer Regiments* (Shippensburg, PA: White Mane Publishing Co., 1992), 45.
143. Ibid. In a June 6, 1847, letter to his brother Jonathan, Walker wrote, "I could if permitted to do so keep the roads open to Vera Cruz with my company." If he said the same thing to General Scott when they met on May 21 at Xalapa, it would appear he got his wish.
144. Utley, *Lone Star, Justice*, 79.
145. Orizaba is the highest mountain in Mexico; and the third highest in North America at 18,490 feet.
146. Capt. Samuel H. Walker to Jonathan Walker, June 6, 1847. Walker Papers.
147. See Edmund Dana, "Incidents in the Life of Capt. Samuel H. Walker, Texas Ranger," 49, for reference to Sam as "Unlucky Walker." Dana served with Walker in Mexico and corresponded with others who served with Walker in the Rangers. See Lee, *Three Years Among the Comanches*, 70, for comment on Sam's being called "Mad Walker." While Nelson Lee's name could not be found on the Ranger muster roll for some of the events he described, Texas historian Walter Prescott Webb wrote the foreword in the book and on page ix writes: "There is little doubt that he served with Ben McCulloch, Jack Hays, and Samuel H. Walker." Whether he was on the official roll or not, he lived at the right place and time to have heard of Walker's reputation from Rangers who served with him.
148. Hackenberg, *Pennsylvania in the War with Mexico*, 42–46.
149. Myers Diary, 81. Myers wrote that most died of dysentery or inflammation of the bowels. So many died daily that as many as eight or ten were buried in the same grave.

150. Mary C. Gillett, *The Army Medical Department, 1818–1865* (CreateSpace Independent Publishing Platform, 2015), 119, 124.
151. Myers Diary, 82.
152. Oswandel, *Notes of the Mexican War*, 176.
153. Myers learned of this story, perhaps from this tour, as he wrote about it in his diary (pages 57–58), retelling the Walker story. Apparently, after learning the truth, he came back to his diary and drew a line through all that he had written about the Walker Perote imprisonment tale.
154. Oswandel, *Notes of the Mexican War*, 176–77.
155. Randy Hackenburg, *Pennsylvania in The War with Mexico*, 45.
156. Oswandel, *Notes of the Mexican War*, 178.
157. Myers Diary, 60, cites the company drilled on horseback with live fire on June 9 to "get the horses used to stand the fire."
158. Company C, RMR Monthly Report for June 1847, AGO, RG 94.
159. Capt. Samuel H. Walker to Jonathan Walker, June 6, 1847. Walker Papers.
160. Oswandel, *Notes of the Mexican War*, 183–84. Later in July, Sgt. Harry Haugh drilled the company with the saber on horse who, according to Sergeant Myers "appears to know his business very well." Myers Diary, 82.
161. Claiborne Reminiscences, 31.
162. Oswandel, *Notes of the Mexican War*, 184, 187.
163. Ibid., 185.
164. Ibid., 186.
165. Myers Diary, 59.
166. Walker to Jonathan T. Walker, June 6, 1847. Walker Papers.
167. Wynkoop to Capt. Scott A.A.A. Genl., June 23, 1847. Wynkoop comments on Walker's "singularly voluminous reports" that were attached to Wynkoop's report to be forwarded to the General in Chief. He also adds that "the Hospital Department at this place has been under admirable control and that from the commencement of the command; no pains have been spared to secure the comfort and convenience of the sick. In this disposition I have been ably seconded by Dr. Reynolds and am convinced the medical direction, Dr. McLaren will continue and improve upon the course."
168. Allan Peskin, ed., *Volunteers: The Mexican War Journals of Private Richard Coulter and Sergeant Thomas Barclay, Company E, Second Pennsylvania Infantry* (Kent, OH: Kent State University Press, 1991), 110. This was recorded in Barclay's journal during Walker's first month at Perote and could be a reflection of newspaper accounts. This same soldier also recorded Walker's being imprisoned at Perote by the Mexicans—a myth that circulated even when Walker was stationed at Perote. (See 113–14.)
169. Ibid., 302–3.
170. *Niles National Register*, vol. 72, June 19, 1847.
171. A career West Point graduate of 1814, Thomas Childs served in the Seminole and Mexican–American War. He was a man of "stout lusty appearance, black eyes, and black mustache and a splendid horseman." Yet he also was "a little too fond of his liquor." He is described as being "recklessly brave." He was later brevetted brigadier general for his defense of Puebla later in 1847. The men had mixed feeling about him as he was considerate of them on the march and gave them frequent rest periods. Yet, as a strict disciplinarian, he enforced corporal punishments in their full measure. See Peskin, *Volunteers*, 97, 119.
172. Smith, *The War with Mexico*, 2: 422. On June 4, McIntosh left Veracruz with 132 wagons, 500 pack mules, 170 dragoons, 100 dismounted dragoons and 450 infantrymen. The wagon horses were weak mustangs, the mules unbroken and vicious, the teamsters Mexicans new to the business. The wagons became too much separated. The dragoons acted imprudently."
173. Myers Diary, 71.
174. Oswandel, *Notes of the Mexican War*, 188.
175. Myers Diary, 67.

176. For some reason Walker chose to use an 1833 artillery sword designed very similar to the Roman short sword. Ironically, the outspoken soldier, who insisted his men have the latest development in firearms, himself used an edged weapon very much like those used by the ancients.
177. In Walker's monthly report he wrote that he gave up the search and recorded Tornado as killed.
178. Oswandel, *Notes of the Mexican War*, 190.
179. *Niles National Register*, vol. 72, August 7, 1847, 359–60. The events described were dated in the newspaper as June 22, 1847.
180. Dana, "Incidents in the Life of Capt. Samuel H. Walker," 47–48.
181. Walker to Jonathan Walker, August 4, 1847. Walker Papers.
182. Sergeant Myers of Walker's company said it was to "our surprise and mortification we were ordered to countermarch for home." Myers Diary, 69.
183. Walker to Jonathan Walker, August 4, 1847. Walker Papers.
184. Claiborne Reminiscences, 27.
185. Walker wrote his brother "our Gallant Col F M Wynkoop I know that he was not under fire during the whole of the affair, yet He assumes to boast of his exploits and make himself a hero out of the affair and criticize my report." Walker to Jonathan Walker, August 4, 1847. Walker Papers.
186. Ibid.
187. Myers Diary, 70.
188. Claiborne Reminiscences, 28.
189. Myers Diary, 71.
190. Ibid., 71–72.
191. Claiborne Reminiscences, 28.
192. Myers Diary, 73, 83. The Mexicans reported a loss of one hundred killed. A number of the dead were from the Perote area, and one lieutenant was brought back to Perote for burial.
193. Claiborne, "Memories of the Past," *The Vidette*, 7, no. 4 (April 1886): 12. Wynkoop in his report said the fighting had been going on for 10 minutes before he arrived to save the day. Hackenberg, *Pennsylvania in the War with Mexico*, 328–29.
194. SHW to Jonathan Walker, August 4, 1847. Walker Papers.
195. Oswandel, *Notes of the Mexican War*, 192.
196. "Troops from Jalapa reach Perote," *Niles National Register*, 72, August 7, 1846, 359–60.
197. Wynkoop to Capt. H. L. Scott, A.A.A. Genl., Head Quarters, Dept. Of Perote, June 23, 1847, AGO, RG 94.
198. Walker to Wynkoop, Perote, June 21, 1847, AGO, RG 94.
199. Oswandel, *Notes of the Mexican War*, 195, 197.
200. George Ballentine, *Autobiography of an English Soldier in the United States Army* (New York, Stringer & Townsend, 1853), 241–42.
201. Ibid.
202. Myers Diary, 81.
203. Ibid., 87.
204. *Albany Patriot* (New York), April 16, 1845–Nov 1847. Microfilm extract from the Washington Correspondent of the (GA) *Columbus Times* nd. This article would imply that Lally concurred with Wynkoop arrest order: "The arrest of Walker (late) Ranger, by the order of Major Lally has created considerable feeling among the good people of Washington-W. being himself a Washingtonian. You will recollect, that Walker had just recaptured the mail, entrusted to the care of Major L., of which the Guerrillas had eased him. This mail is believed to have contained the last, and perhaps the most important budget of dispatches intended for Trist."
205. Oswandel, *Notes of the Mexican War*, 235.
206. Ibid., 258, 316.
207. SHW to Jonathan Walker, August 17, 1847. Walker Papers.
208. http://www.climate.org/topics/climate/mexico-climate-observatory.shtml. Currently the site is being considered as the highest radio telescope site in the world.
209. Myers Diary, 89.

210. SHW to Jonathan Walker, August 17, 1847. Walker Papers.
211. Ibid.
212. Myers Diary, 91–93.
213. SHW to Jonathan Thomas Walker, September 5, 1847. Walker Papers.
214. Ibid.
215. Myers Diary, 108.
216. In late July 1847, Gen. Franklin Pierce (later President) wrote in his diary: "Captain Walker's elegant company of mounted riflemen. Captain Walker is the same who gained (*earned* is the better word, for officers sometimes *gain* what they do not merit) such an enviable reputation on the Rio Grande. His company is in all respects worthy of their efficient, gentlemanly, modest, and daring commander." See Nathaniel Hawthorne, *The Life of Franklin Pierce* (Honolulu HI: University Press of the Pacific, 2002), Chapter 4 "The Mexican War—His Journal of the March from Vera Cruz."
217. Box 9, Letters Received from Officers, L–Z. Mexican War, Army of Occupation, AGO, RG 94.
218. Surg. John Reynolds of the Pennsylvania Volunteers did not sign and later seems to support Wynkoop (Wynkoop to Capt. Scott A.A.A. Genl June 23, 1847) while both Bunting and Reynolds joined the Pennsylvania unit together (Reynolds to Wynkoop April 26, 1847), Bunting seems more outspoken. Surg. John T. Lamar of Augusta, Georgia, first entered service with the Macon Guards. He subsequently received the appointment of surgeon in the Regular Army from President Polk.
219. One of Wynkoop's men once wrote in his diary that on one occasion Wynkoop was in a "glorious state of intoxication"—which meant his men suffered at his decisions. Peskin, *Volunteers*, 315. This combined diary of two friends give insight from two points of view from eyewitnesses in the company that was stationed at Perote while Sam Walker was there. Private Coulter would later become a major general of volunteers in the Civil War; Sergeant Barclay would become a successful banker.
220. Box 9, Letters Received from Officers, L-Z, Mexican War, Army of Occupation, RG 94.
221. On May 14, 1847, the water in the fountains began to flow slowly. Wynkoop ordered the Alcalde of Perote to restore the flow or the artillery in the fort would shell the town. Soon the water began to flow faster. Perhaps the fountains were continually sabotaged by guerrillas. See Oswandel, *Notes of the Mexican War*, 164.
222. Claiborne, "Memories of the Past," *Nashville Union* (Tennessee), April 1886. See Myers Diary.
223. Myers Diary, 58. Sergeant Myers of Walker's Company confirms the taking of these 19 prisoners on June 4.
224. "Capt. Samuel Hamilton Walker's retaliation on Mexican guerrillas," *Niles National Register*, July 3, 1847, 72, 277.
225. Myers Diary, 159. After Walker's death at Huamantla on November 16, Myers was separated from his company (Company C, RMR) and "detailed by Colonel [John Coffee] Hays to act as his Sergeant Major of his Texas Rangers."
226. Haven and Belden, *A History of the Colt Revolver* 292–93.
227. See Robin J. Rapley, *Colt Percussion Accouterments 1834–1873* (Newport Beach, CA: GRAPHIC: Publishers: 1994), 107–15, http://www.icollector.com/Colt-Civilian-Walker-Powder-Flask_i13827732.
228. Ibid.
229. G. W. M., (Sgt. George W. Myers) "Battle of Huamantla," *Brooklyn Daily Eagle*, December 3, 1850.
230. Ibid.
231. SHW to "Dear Brother," October 5, 1847.

Chapter 10: The Death of Capt. Samuel H. Walker

1. *The Vidette*, 7, no. 4 (April 1886): 13.
2. Oswandel, *Notes of the Mexican War*, 354.
3. Undated contemporary newspaper clipping found in the diary of George Myers, one of Walker's men. See http://historical.ha.com/itm/autographs/-samuel-h-walker-mexican-war-diary-of-sergeant-george-w-myers-us-mounted-rifles-walker-s-co-c-dated-from-february/a/6109–34090.s#1101111011540.

4. Claiborne Reminiscences, 35.
5. Claiborne, "Memoirs of the Past," *The Vidette*, no. 4 (April 1886): 7.
6. Brackett, *General Lane's Brigade in Central Mexico*, 78.
7. G. W. M., (Sgt. George W. Myers) "Battle of Huamantla," *Brooklyn Daily Eagle*, December 3, 1850.
8. Claiborne Reminiscences, 35.
9. *Flag of Freedom* (Puebla, Mexico), October 24, 1847.
10. Brackett, *General Lane's Brigade*, 89.
11. A tropical plant that forms a cluster of 20–50 stiff upright leaves edged with prickles.
12. *Flag of Freedom* (Puebla, Mexico), October 24, 1847.
13. Claiborne Reminiscences, 27.
14. *The American Star* from the *Daily Picayune* (New Orleans), January 12, 1848.
15. Claiborne Reminiscences, 35.
16. Brackett, *General Lane's Brigade*, 92.
17. Myers Diary.
18. *Genius of Liberty* (Leesburg, Virginia), November 3, 1847. See also *The American Star*, January 12, 1848.
19. Dr. Reynolds died after the war of diseases contracted in Mexico. *Miners' Journal and Pottsville General Advertiser* (Pottsville, Pennsylvania), August 25, 1860.
20. Oswandel, *Notes of the Mexican War*, 350.
21. *Northern Standard* (Clarkesville, Texas), January 8, 1848. Capt. Loyall. We are indebted to the Editors of the *Muscogee Democrat* of the 13th inst, for an extra containing the following letter from a correspondent at Veracruz.

> Vera Cruz, Friday, 5th Nov, 1847.
>
> Dr. Andrews:
>
> Dear Sir:—I was awakened this morning about 7 o'clock, by a loud rap at my door, and who should be there but Capt. Loyall, looking as well as I ever say him. I hope the report of his death may not reach his family. His friends all believed him dead. He sat down and gave Lieut. McCurdy [McCardy?] and myself a long account of the fight at Huamantla, which may be relied upon. Capt. Walker was in command of only 175 cavalry. They charged the town when the infantry was 5 or 6 miles off, and captured three pieces of artillery. The Mexicans were commanded by Santa Anna. He had near 2500 men. They fled in every direction but were rallied and made fight. Capt. Walker was shot in the breast with a small ball in less than ten feet of Capt. Loyall and did not live more than 15 minutes. He told the command to fight on even if the odds were against them, but that the infantry would soon be there. Capt. Walker was shot from a house which had raised a white flag. Capt. Loyall then took command. Soon the infantry arrived and the Mexicans cut out.

22. Sgt. George W. Myers, who apparently saw Walker's wounds, noted in addition to his chest wound, he apparently struck his forehead on the ground when he fell. G. W. M., (Sgt. George W. Myers) "Battle of Huamantla," *Brooklyn Daily Eagle*, December 3, 1850.
23. Oswandel, *Notes of the Mexican War*, 350.
24. G. W. M., (Sgt. George W. Myers) "Battle of Huamantla," *Brooklyn Daily Eagle*, December 3, 1850.
25. Claiborne, Reminiscences.
26. Oswandel, *Notes of the Mexican War*, 348.
27. The Augusta *Daily Constitutionalist* of 2 December 1847 reported:

> Surgeon J. T. LAMAR of this State was among the Georgians who distinguished themselves at the battles of Hunalo and Huamantla in addition to those already mentioned. The lamented WALKER in his report of the former battle, pays a

merited and well-deserved tribute to the bravery and good conduct of Surgeon LAMAR throughout the engagement. He was also with Capt. WALKER, engaged hand to hand with the Mexicans, when that brave officer was killed, and narrowly escaped with his life. After the death of Capt. WALKER, his faithful servant DAVID saved Mr. LAMAR'S life by receiving in his own breast a lance aimed at the life of the friend who had so gallantly fought by the side of his master. Surgeon LAMAR, is the son of G. W. LAMAR, Esq. Of Augusta, and first entered service-with the Macon Guards, the company made up by the lamented HOLMES, in this city. He subsequently received from President Polk the appointment of Surgeon in the regular army where he has always distinguished himself whenever an opportunity has offered. We notice that some of our contemporaries have fallen into an error in publishing these despatches-giving the name of Surgeon LANEUR-for that of Surgeon LAMAR. In justice to this gallant young Georgian we trust they will correct the error.

28. *Daily American Star*, "The battle of Huamantla," November 5, 1847. (See also *The North American*, same story, November 9, 1847).
29. SHW to Jonathan T. Walker, August 17, 1847. Walker Papers.
30. SHW to Jonathan T. Walker, August 17, 1847. Walker Papers.
31. *Niles National Register*, November 20, 1847.
32. Oswandel, *Notes of the Mexican War*, 350–51.
33. Howard Zinn, "We Take Nothing by Conquest, Thank God," *A Peoples' History of the United States* (New York: The New Press, 1997), chapter 8.
34. Brackett, *General Lane's Brigades in Central Mexico*, 92–93.
35. 1st Lt. Thomas Claiborne to Col. T. P. Andrews November 18, 1847. Walker Papers.
36. T. P. Andrews to J. Thomas Walker, December 15, 1847. Walker Papers.
37. *American Star*, 19 October 1847.
38. *Genius of Liberty* (Leesburg, Virginia), October 25, 1847. It is ironic that such a myth was spread. In fact, Sam Walker was indeed lanced and *almost* killed but by a Comanche warrior in June 1844. Perhaps the story of his being attacked again by a lance-bearing enemy and his Comanche encounter merged into a tempting tale to pass on.
39. James Baille's well-known lithograph by Magee, published in 1847, is entitled "Death of Capt. Walker at Huamantla in Mexico." He is shown on horseback being lanced by a Mexican on foot who is then shot by a fellow Rifleman. It is reproduced in Thomas H. Flaherty, ed., *The War with Mexico*, "Old West Series" (Alexandria, VA: Time-Life Books, 1978), 220. See also another engraving of Sam on foot being shot by a Mexican soldier. Again, an American soldier is on hand to avenge Walker with his rifle stock. Oswandel, *Notes of the Mexican War*, 347.
40. *Macon Weekly Telegraph* (Georgia), November 12, 1847.
41. *The Vidette*, 3, no. 9, (June 15, 1882): 15.
42. Col. A. G. Brackett to S. H. Walker (Sam's namesake nephew), September 4, 1892.
43. The Monthly Report of Company C lists William E. Richards, Thomas Goslin, John McL. Collins, and Isaac P. Darlington as missing in action after the battle of Huamantla.
44. *The Texas Ranger* (Washington, TX.), October 22, 1853. If an American deserter killed Walker, how did he get to Huamantla before Lane's foot soldiers got there?
45. SHW to Jonathan Thomas Walker, August 4, 1847. Walker Papers.
46. Harry T. Hays to Jonathan Walker, December 24, 1847, and January 29, 1948, Walker Papers.
47. Monthly Report, Company C, Mounted Riflemen, RG 94, NARA.
48. Brackett, *General Lane's Brigade in Central Mexico*, 94.
49. Ibid., 96.
50. Ibid.
51. Oswandel, *Notes of the Mexican War*, 376.

52. James Thomas Shannon, *Eyewitness to War: Prints and Daguerreotypes of the Mexican War, 1846–1848* (Washington, DC: Smithsonian Books, 1989), 350. Shannon was with Company A, 1st Regiment, Pennsylvania Volunteers, during service in the Mexican–American War. He participated in the engagements at Cerro Gordo, Perote, and Puebla under the command of Col. Francis M. Wynkoop. This 37-page sketchbook is composed of scenes of Mexico, the Mexican–American War, including the Castle at Perote, burial place of Capt. Samuel H. Walker, view from Xalapa, and the quarters of the U.S. Army after the battle of Cerro Gordo, as drawn by Shannon and others.
53. Oswandel, *Notes of the Mexican War*, 409.
54. Ibid., 376.
55. *Niles National Register*, November 20, 1847.
56. Whittington, *The Colt Whitneyville Pistol*, 84.
57. *Daily Advertiser* (Newark, New Jersey), December 24, 1847.
58. *Northern Standard* (Clarkesville, Texas), January 22, 1848; *Texas Democrat* (Austin), n.d.
59. *Daily American Star*, January 22, 1848, from the *Daily Picayune* (New Orleans), January 10, 1848.
60. *Free American*, December 21, 1847.
61. *San Antonio City Council Minutes*, 1848, 132.
62. Andrew J. Sowell, *Early Settlers and Indian Fighters of Southwest Texas* (Austin, TX: B. C. Jones, 1900), 186–87.
63. *Daily Express* (San Antonio, Texas), May 2, 1918.
64. *Texas State Gazette* (Austin), November 2, 1850.
65. The San Antonio *Daily Herald*, April 26, 1856. See also "Address on the Occasion of the Removing the Remains of Captains Walker and Gillespie on the Twenty-First of April, A. D. 1856," by James C. Wilson.
66. The above newspaper accounts came from the *News-Express* (San Antonio, Texas), January 5–7, 10, and 19, 1995.
67. Personal communication with Lee Spencer White, October 18, 2003.
68. U.S. Army, *Supplement to the Harbor Defense Project, Harbor Defenses of Puget Sound* (CCA-AN-PS), August 12, 1945, CDSG.

Appendix I: Samuel H. Walker Files a Grievance to the American Public

1. Benjamin Lloyd Beall (1797–1863), the son of Revolutionary War and War of 1812 veteran Maj. Lloyd Beall, attended the U.S. Military Academy from 1814–18. He was captain of his company in the Washington City Volunteers until his resignation on June 1, 1836, when he was commissioned captain, 2d U.S. Dragoons, ranking from June 8, 1836. He was brevetted major for gallantry during the Seminole War and lieutenant colonel for meritorious conduct at the battle of Santa Cruz de Rosales during the Mexican–American War. He retired as colonel, 1st U.S. Cavalry Regiment, February 15, 1862. Heitman, *Historical Register*, I: 202.
2. Edward Branch Robinson, born Chesterfield Co., Virginia, *ca.* 1803. Printer in Washington, DC, at time of enlistment in Company C. 3d U.S. Artillery by Maj. James H. Hook, October 5, 1826. Served in the detachment of orderlies, Washington, DC, where he undoubtedly gained his expertise in drilling troops, until discharged on surgeon's certificate, October 31, 1827. He was a first lieutenant in Capt. Francis A. Dickins' Company, 2d Regiment, 3d Brigade, District of Columbia Militia, prior to succeeding to the command of Captain Beall's Company on June 1, 1836. After his resignation as captain of his company *ca.* November 1836, Robinson attached himself to Capt. Joseph Roberts's Company, Colonel (Benjamin Kendrick) Pierce's Regiment Mounted Creek Volunteers and fought in the ill-fated battle of Wahoo Swamp, November 21, 1836. He successfully filed a claim for Seminole War service bounty land and received 80 acres in 1855. Printer in Washington, DC, until his death on October 21, 1880.
3. Archibald Henderson (1783–1859) was commissioned second lieutenant, U.S. Marine Corps, June 4, 1806. Promoted first lieutenant, March 6, 1807; and captain, April 1, 1811. He bypassed the rank of major when he was appointed Lieutenant Colonel, Commandant of the Corps, October 17, 1820,

and Colonel, Commandant, July 1, 1854. He was brevetted brigadier general to rank from January 27, 1837, for meritorious service during the Creek and Second Seminole Wars. He died in office January 6, 1859. Edward W. Callahan ed., *List of Officers of the Navy of the United States and of the Marine Corps from 1775 to 1900*, (New York: L. R. Hamersley & Co., 1901), 679.

4. Greenleaf Dearborn (1786–1846), entered the U.S. Army as a second lieutenant, 3d Artillery Regiment, March 12, 1812. Rising up the grades, he held the rank of lieutenant colonel, 2d Infantry Regiment when he died on September 9, 1846. Heitman, *List of Officers*, I: 363.
5. George Cochran, who enlisted in Washington on June 1, 1861, is noted, "In confinement at Camp Mitchell, on the August–September 1836 muster roll for Capt. Robinson's Company, Washington City Volunteers. Restored to duty per muster roll for October–November, he deserted from Ft. Brooke, East Florida, on December 12, 1836. District of Columbia Militia, Creek War, 1836–37, Indian Wars, 1817–58, Compiled Military Service Records, Record Group 94, Records of the Adjutant General's Office, 1802–1917, National Archives, Washington, DC. He may be the same George Cochran who served as a private in the 3d U.S. Artillery from 1813–18.
6. Alexander Scammell Brooks (1781–1836), entered the service as first lieutenant, 3d U.S. Artillery, May 3, 1808. Promoted captain June 11, 1809, he resigned his commission on May 2, 1810. When the War of 1812 broke out, he returned to the Army as captain and was brevetted major for gallant conduct at the battle of Plattsburg, September 11, 1814. Promoted major of the line, April 26, 1832; and lieutenant colonel, April 6, 1835. Brooks was killed in a steamboat explosion on December 17, 1836. Heitman, *List of Officers*, I: 248.
7. Thomas Sidney Jesup (1788–1860) entered the U.S. Army as a second lieutenant, 7th Infantry Regiment, May 3, 1808. Promoted first lieutenant, December 1, 1809; captain, January 20, 1813; major, April 6, 1813; lieutenant colonel, April 30, 1817; colonel, March 27, 1818; and brigadier general and quartermaster general, May 8, 1818. He was brevetted lieutenant colonel for distinguished and meritorious service at the battle of Chippewa, July 5, 1814; colonel for gallant conduct and distinguished skill for the battle of Niagara, July 25, 1814; and major general for 10 years faithful service in one grade, May 8, 1828. He died in service as Quartermaster General of the Army, a position he held for 42 years, on June 10, 1860.
8. John Munroe (1796–1861), a Scottish-born graduate of the U.S. Military Academy, fourth in the Class of 1814, was commissioned third lieutenant, 1st U.S. Artillery, March 11, 1814. Promoted second lieutenant, May 1, 1814; first lieutenant, April 20, 1818; captain, March 2, 1825, major, August 18, 1846; and lieutenant colonel, November 11, 1856. Munroe earned the following brevets: major, February 13, 1838, for conspicuous uniformly meritorious and efficiency during the campaigns against the Florida indigenous people; lieutenant colonel, September 23, 1846, for gallant and meritorious conduct for conflicts at Monterrey, Mexico; and colonel, February23, 1847, for gallant and meritorious conduct at the battle of Buena Vista, Mexico. He died in service, April 28, 1861. Heitman, *List of Officers*, I: 736.
9. Mann Page Lomax (1787–1842) entered the Army as a second lieutenant, artillery, June 10, 1807. Promoted first lieutenant, June 30, 1811; captain, May 12, 1814; major, July 7, 1838. He died in service March 27, 1842. Heitman, *List of Officers*, I: 639.
10. William L. McClintock (*ca.* 1791–1848) enlisted in the Army as a private and sergeant, 3d U.S. Artillery, July 1, 1812. Commissioned from the ranks as third lieutenant, May 20, 1813. Promoted second lieutenant, June 20, 1813; first lieutenant, September 29, 1817; captain, August 11, 1823; and major, June 27, 1843, Brevetted major for 10 years faithful service in one grade, August 11, 1833. Died in service, October 29, 1848. Heitman, *List of Officers*, I: 657.
11. William Sewell (Stanhope) Foster (1789–1839) entered the Army as a first lieutenant, 11th U.S. Infantry Regiment, March 12, 1812. Promoted captain, March 13, 1813; major, July 7, 1826; and lieutenant colonel, June 8, 1836. Foster earned the following brevets: major, August 15, 1814, for conspicuous gallantry in the defense of Fort Erie, and colonel, December 25, 1837, for distinguished service in Florida, particularly in the battle of Kissimmee. Died in service, November 29, 1838. Heitman, *List of Officers*, I: 432.

12. James Hervey Simpson (1813–83) graduated eighteenth in the U.S. Military Academy Class of 1832. Entered Army service as a brevet second lieutenant, 3d U.S. Artillery Regiment, July 1, 1832, Promoted second lieutenant, November 30, 1833; first lieutenant, April 30, 1837; captain, March 3, 1853; major, August 6, 1861; lieutenant colonel, June 1, 1863; and colonel March 7, 1867. During the Civil War, Simpson served as colonel of the 4th New Jersey Infantry from August 12, 1861, to August 24, 1862. He was brevetted brigadier general for faithful and meritorious service during the war, March 13, 1865. He died in service, March 2, 1883. Heitman, *List of Officers*, I: 888.
13. Lorenzo Thomas (1804–75) entered the U.S. Military Academy on September 1, 1819, and graduated 17th in the Class of 1823 as a second lieutenant. Promoted first lieutenant, March 17, 1829; captain, September 23, 1836; major, January 1, 1848; lieutenant colonel and acting assistant adjutant general, July 15, 1852; colonel and adjutant general, March 7, 1861; and brigadier general and adjutant general, August 3, 1861. He received the following brevets: lieutenant colonel for gallantry and meritorious conduct for conflicts at Monterrey, Mexico, September 23, 1846; brigadier general, May 7, 1861, and major general, March 2, 1875, for faithful and meritorious service during the Civil War. He retired February 22, 1869. Heitman, *List of Officers*, I: 954.

Appendix II: Samuel H. Walker's Texas Ranger Company

1. Walker Papers, Texas State Archives.
2. Erroneous numbering is true to the original.

Appendix IV: Thomas J. Green's Accusation that President Samuel Houston Lied in his Public and Private Letters Concerning the Mier Expedition

1. Gen. Thomas J. Green, *Journal of the Texian Expedition Against Mier; Subsequent Imprisonment of the Author; His Suffering, and Final Escape from the Castle of Perote With Reflections Upon the Present Political and Probable Future Relations of Texas, Mexico, and the United States* (New York; Harper and Brothers, 1845), Appendix No. II, 450–53.
2. Ibid., 456.
3. Ibid.
4. Ibid., 456–57.
5. Ibid., 458–59.
6. Ibid., 459–60.
7. Ibid., 460.
8. Ibid., 460–62.
9. Hamilton Stuart was the sole editor of The *Civilian and Gazette* in Galveston, Texas, from 1838 until 1847, when Samuel Durnett joined him. Stuart was born in Kentucky in 1813, and learned the printing trade in Georgetown, where he published and edited a local newspaper at age 22. The *Civilian and Gazette* was known for its support of Sam Houston until 1861.
10. Houston, Samuel, *The Writings of Sam Houston*, vol. 4, Amelia W. Williams and Eugene C. Barker eds., (Austin: University of Texas Press, 1942) archive.texashistorytrust.org/view/728684636/.

Appendix V: Walker's Weapons

1. Austerman, "A Lost Heritage," 26.
2. SHW to "Dear Brother," dated October 5, 1847. Walker dates this letter at 10 p.m. and says that the next day he would be leaving with General Lane. Lane left on the morning of October 5, so Walker had the wrong date on his letter.

3. Ibid.; James E. Serven, "Samuel Walker: Indian Fighter, Texas Ranger, Mexican War hero—the man who helped make Samuel Colt famous," in *The Gun Digest, 23rd edition, 1969,* J. T. Amber, ed., (*Chicago, IL: Gun Digest* Books, 1968), 135.
4. Austerman, "A Lost Heritage," 26.
5. Marilyn McAdams Sibley, ed., *Samuel H. Walker's Account of the Mier Expedition,* (Austin: The Texas State Historical Association, 1978), 17–19. Bowman recruited and organized the militia artillery unit, the Wyoming (Pennsylvania) Artillerists in 1842 in northeast Pennsylvania. His first lieutenant was Edmund L. Dana who later was to write an article on Sam Walker after Bowman donated the sword to a museum in Wilkes-Barre, Pennsylvania. Wynkoop had been the Governor of Perote but Bowman was the military commander. Hackenberg, *Pennsylvania in The War with Mexico,* 46.
6. Dana, "Incidents in the Life of Capt. Samuel H. Walker," 42.
7. Claiborne, Reminiscences, 27, and Dana, "Incidents in the Life of Capt. Samuel H. Walker," 56.
8. E. W. Lester to Maj. S. H. Walker, March 25, 1915. Walker Papers.
9. Austerman, "A Lost Heritage," 26.
10. *Weekly Reveille* (St. Louis), May 25, 1846, 870.
11. Interestingly, within a year of Samuel Walker's death, his family was contacted by a George Myers on January 10, 1849, stating that he had taken Walker's sword (he said he knew it to be Walker's favorite war sword) from him at his death but was relieved of it two weeks later by Lieutenant Claiborne. John M. L. Collins wrote on the day before, January 9, 1849, that he understood that Myers had taken the sword (lending credence to Myers's story) and thought that Myers still had it. Collins was taken prisoner by the Mexican at the battle of Huamantla, and not returned to Company C until March 5, 1848, in Mexico City after Myers had left Company C. John M. L. Collins to Mrs. Jane A. Walker, January 9, 1849, George C. Myers to Mrs. Jane A. Walker, January 10, 1849, Walker Papers. March 1848, Monthly Report, Company C, Mounted Rifles, RG 94, NARA.
12. Thomas Childs, a West Point graduate, was reaching the height of his career with his defense of Puebla. However, many of the soldiers disliked his severe disciplinary measures. See Peskin, *Volunteers.* Walker did not like him. He wrote: "The Gallant Col Childs who always takes Lions share of the Laurels which the men win who had his forces judiciously up on a high and commanding position about one and a half miles behind the retreating enemy." SHW to Jonathan Walker, August 4, 1847. If Childs did indeed take Walker's sword, it is ironic that Childs would end up suffering where Walker once suffered. He would die six years later (almost six years to the day Walker died on October 9, 1847). Childs died of yellow fever, October 8, 1853, at his headquarters at Fort Brooke, Florida, where Sam himself received such harsh punishment.
13. Mexican War, Army of Occupation, RG 94, NARA.
14. If Childs had Walker's sword (probably his presentation engraved sword), he perhaps kept it. Its location since Walker had it in his own possession is a mystery. Childs was military governor of Puebla. He held this post during the battles for Mexico City. The day before Mexico City surrendered, Childs' garrison at Puebla came under siege. During the following siege of Puebla, Childs repeatedly refused to surrender and was able to successfully repulse the Mexican attacks until a relief force under Gen. Joseph Lane arrived and defeated the besiegers. For his defense of the city, Childs was brevetted brigadier general. It is possible that some officer felt that Childs, the hero, deserved Walker's sword and sent it to him or even that Childs requested it himself. If he did have the sword, he did not keep it long. After the war, he was placed in command of Fort McHenry in Baltimore Harbor (where Walker once recruited men for his RMR company). He was then placed in charge of military operations in Florida. He died in his headquarters at Fort Brooke (Walker's last station of duty in the Seminole War) on October 8, 1853. Childs' family may have the sword or some collector in Florida.
15. Mexican War, Army of Occupation, RG 94, NARA.
16. Macon *Weekly Telegraph* (Georgia), February 1, 1848. "Lieut. Rodney (Bedney) F. McDonald. This gallant young officer arrived here [Macon, Georgia] on Thursday last, from Vera Cruz. Lieut. McDonald, … a native of this town, a son of our late worthy fellow-citizen Ex-Governor McDonald. … After serving out his time in Col. Jackson's Regiment, he received from the President in May last, a commission in

the Third U.S. Artillery, since which time he has been with Gen. Lane, among those who bore the brunt and danger of opening the way, on more than one occasion, between Veracruz and the main body of the Army in the interior. In this service he was much with, and around the gallant Ranger of Texas, and lamented Walker, of whom he speaks with the most devoted affection. He bears upon his body honorable testimony of his gallantry at Vera Cruz. In each of the engagements of Huamantla, Alisco, Tlascala, Matamoras, and Galaxara, he was in the thickest of the fight, and was three times wounded in these skirmishes."

17. See the complete text of the original letter James L. Mitchell, *Colt: The Man, the Arm and the Company* (Harrisburg, PA; Stackpole *Company*, 1959): 99.
18. *Niles National Register*, December 4, 1847, 73, 222–23.
19. Herbert Houze, *Samuel Colt: Arms, Art, and Invention* (New Haven, CT: Yale University Press, 2006), 75–77.
20. Ibid., 76. This carbine, with the documentation that McDonald sent to Colt after taking it from a lancer at Huamantla, is in the Museum of the Connecticut Historical Society (CHS).
21. Edwards, *The Story of Colt's Revolver*, 226, reprinted letter in Connecticut Historical Society.
22. Parsons, *Colt's Own Record*, 97–98.
23. Elliot to Colt, August 23, 1847, CHS.
24. Heitman, *Historical Register*, 401.
25. Edwards, *The Story of Colt's Revolver*, 226, reprinted letter in CHS.
26. *Free American*, February 7, 1848.
27. G. W. M. (George W. Myers), "Battle of Huamantla," *Brooklyn Daily Eagle*, December 3, 1850.
28. Brackett, *General Lane's Brigade*, 76.
29. Mexican War, Army of Occupation, RG 94, NARA.
30. George C. Myers to Mrs. Jane A. Walker, January 10, 1849; Claiborne, Reminiscences, 34.
31. Edwards, *The Story of Colt's Revolver*, 226, Whittington, *The Colt Whitneyville Pistol*, 34.
32. *The Colt Whitneyville-Walker Pistol.*
33. Received August 17, Whittington, *The Colt Whitneyville-Walker Pistol*, 34, 39.
34. Parsons, *Colt's Own Record*, 84.
35. McDonald asked several favors of General Lane. See MacDonald to Lane, Nov 13, 1852: Asking Lane as Governor of Oregon Territory to support a friend of McDonald, a Thomas Selly, who wished to be appointed Surveyor General of California. MacDonald to Lane January 30, 1856: Asking General Lane to support his appointment as a captain in the new regiment authorized by Congress. See Joseph Lane Papers, Mss1146, Oregon Historical Society Research Library, Portland, Oregon.
36. McDonald to Lane, September 4, 1848, Joseph Lane Papers, Mss1146, Oregon Historical Society Research Library.
37. Haven and Belden, *History of Colt's Revolver*, 304.
38. Herbert Houze, *Samuel Colt: Arms, Art, and Invention* (New Haven, CT: Yale University Press, 2006), 75–77.
39. Apparently, the pistols and eventually Sam's sword sheath was all the family received (other than Sam's horse Tornado). According to a letter (no. 830, April 25, 1848) in the AGO files from Gen. R. Jones Adjutant General to the Paymaster of the U.S. Army, Sam had money on him when he was killed. The Army seized the $140.83, according to Regulations, and sent to the U.S. Treasury. See James Worsham, "Walker's Personal Colt Whitney Walker Revolvers," *Military Collector & Historian*, no. 2 (Summer 2015): 67, 118–23.
40. Personal communication with Walker great-niece, Nancy Bouiver.
41. Personal correspondence with Walker's great-nephew Warren O. Simonds, January 22, 1994, indicated further details of the disappearance of this revolver.
42. Samuel Hamilton Walker, *Walkers of Toaping Castle, MD*, 16.
43. Author Worsham has a copy of this letter in his files but as requested by the family, he will not reveal who actually owns the pistol. He does have permission to publish the photographs that he has taken.

Bibliography

Articles

Austerman, Wayne R. "A Lost Heritage: The Personal Arms of Samuel H. Walker." *Man at Arms*, no. 5 (September/October 1980): 2.

Barker, Eugene C. "The Texan Revolutionary Army." *The Southwestern Historical Quarterly*, (April 1906): 9.

Barton, Henry. "The United States Cavalry and the Texas Rangers." *Southwestern Historical Quarterly*, no. 4 (April 1960): 63.

Buchanan, A. Russell ed. "George Washington Trahern: Texan Cowboy Soldier from Mier to Buena Vista." *Southwestern Historical Quarterly*, (July 1966): 70.

Carroll, Brian D. "'Savages' in the Service of Empire: Native American Soldiers in Gorham's Rangers, 1744–1762," *The New England Quarterly*, no. 3 (September 2012): 85.

Dana, Edmund L. "Incidents in the Life of Capt. Samuel H. Walker, Texan Ranger." *Proceedings and Collection of the Wyoming County Historical and Geological Society*, no.1 (1882).

Day, James M., ed. "Israel Canfield on the Mier Expedition." *Texas Military History*, no. 3 (Fall 1963): 3.

Erd, Darby. "The Third South Carolina Regiment (Rangers) 1775–1780." MUIA plate 494, *Military Collector & Historian*, no. 2 (Summer 1980): 32.

Hamersly, L.R. "The Regiment of Mounted Riflemen." *The United Service*, (October 1895).

Hutchins, James S. "The United States Mounted Rifleman's Knife." *Man at Arms: The NRA Journal* (March/April 1991).

Ives, Captain Larry. "Rangers in Florida, 1818." *Infantry*, 53 (September–October 1963).

Knauss, James O. "St. Joseph: An Episode of the Economic and Political History of Florida." *Florida Historical Quarterly*: 5: no. 4, Article 4, 12–13, 18; 6, no. 1 (July 1927).

Lewis, Major B. R. "Sam Colt's Repeating Pistol." *The American Rifleman*, (May 1947): 95.

Magruder, Jr. C. C. "Colonel Ninian Beall." *Historical Papers of the Society of Colonial Wars in the District of Columbia*, no. 6 (1911).

Manders, Eric I. "Butler's Rangers, 1777–1784." MUIA plate 196, *Military Collector & Historian*, no. 4 (Winter 1961): 13.

Peterson, Harold L. "The Kentucky Rifle." *The American Rifleman* (November 1964).

Pruyn, Robert N., as told to James E. Edmond. "Campaigning Through Mexico with Old Rough and Ready." *Civil War Times*, (October 1963): 2.

"Regiment of Mounted Riflemen, Now the Third United States Calvary." *Army and Navy Journal*, 981 and 982 (May 27, 1882).

Robinson, Fayette. "Captain Samuel Walker." *Graham's Magazine* (June 1848).

Spell, Lota M. "Samuel Bangs: The First Printer in Texas." no. 4, *Southwestern Historical Quarterly* (April 1932): 35.

Stauffer, Dr. Alvin P. "The Quartermaster's Department and the Mexican War." *Quartermaster Review*, (May–June 1950).

Steffen, Randy. "Texas Rangers, 1839." MUIA plate 150, *Military Collector & Historian*, no. 3 (Fall 1958): 10.

Thillmann, John H. "An Early Pair of Colt Walker Saddle Holsters." *Military Collector & Historian*, no. 2 (Summer 2013): 65.

Worsham, James J. and Maj. R. B. Anderson. "Mosby: The Model Partisan, Special Warfare." *The Professional Bulletin of the John F. Kennedy Special Warfare Center*, no.1 (Winter 1989): 2.

Worsham, James. "Walker's Personal Colt Whitney Walker Revolvers." *Military Collector & Historian*, no. 2 (Summer 2015): 67.

Young, Otis E. "The United States Mounted Ranger Battalion, 1832–1833." *Mississippi Valley Historical Review* (December, 1954): 41.

Books

1828 Tax List, Prince George's County, Maryland, compiled by Prince George's Co. Genealogical Society in 1985.

Amber, J. T. ed. *The Gun Digest, 23rd edition, 1969. Chicago, IL: Gun Digest* Books, 1968.

Ralph K. Andrist. *The Long Death: The Last Days of the Plains Indians*. New York: The Macmillan Company, 1964.

Appleton's Cyclopedia of American Biography.

Barker, Eugene C. *The Life of Stephen F. Austin.* Nashville: The Cokesbury Press, 1925.

Barton, Henry W. *Texas Volunteers in the Mexican War.* Wichita Falls, TX: Texian Press, 1970.

Billington, Ray Allen. *Westward Expansion.* New York: The Macmillan Company, 1960.

Black, Col. Robert W. *Ranger Dawn: The American Ranger from the Colonial Era to the Mexican War.* Mechanicsburg, PA: Stackpole Books, 2009.

Brown, John Henry. *History of Texas from 1685 to 1892.* St. Louis: L. E. Daniel, 1893.

Browne, William Hand, ed. *Archives of Maryland: Proceedings and Acts of the General Assembly of Maryland, April 1666–January 1676, II.* Baltimore: Maryland Historical Society, 1884.

Browne, William Hand, ed. *Archives of Maryland* (Baltimore: Maryland State Archives, 1883.

Ballentine, George. *Autobiography of an English Soldier in the United States Army.* New York, Stringer & Townsend, 1853.

Bennett, Emerson. *Clara Moreland or, Adventures in the far South-West.* Philadelphia: T. B. Petersen, 1853.

Buell, Augustus C. *History of Andrew Jackson: Pioneer, Patriot, Soldier, Politician, President.* New York: Charles Schribner's Sons, 1904.

Callahan, Edward W., ed. *List of Officers of the Navy of the United States and of the Marine Corps from 1775 to 1900*, New York: L. R. Hamersley & Co., 1901.

Catlin, George. *Letters and Notes on the Manners, Customs, and Conditions of the North American Indians.* New York: Wiley & Putnam, 1842.

Chabot, Frederick C., ed. *The Perote Prisoners; Being the Diary of James L. Truehart.* San Antonio: The Naylor Co., 1934.

Chamberlain, Samuel. *My Confessions: Recollections of a Rogue.* New York: Harper & Brothers, 1956.

Crane, Vernon W. *The Southern Frontier.* Ann Arbor: University of Michigan Press, 1956.

Cunliffe, Marcus. *Soldiers & Civilians, The Martial Spirit in America, 1775–1865.* New York: The Free Press, 1973.

Curwin, Maskell E. *Campaign Sketches of the War with Mexico.* New York: George P. Putnam and Co., 1853.

Day, James M., ed. *A Narrative of the Capture and Subsequent sufferings of the Mier Prisoners in Mexico, Captured in the Cause of Texas … by Thomas W. Bell, One of the Captives.* Waco, TX: Texian Press, 1964.

Denison, Lt. Col. George T. Jr. *Modern Cavalry: Its Organization, Armament, and Employment in War.* London: Thomas Bosworth, 1868.

Directory of Maryland DAR and Ancestors. Maryland State Society, DAR: *ca.* 1966.

Dobie, J. Frank. *The Mustangs.* Boston: Little, Brown, and Co., 1952.

Dorsey, Stephen R. and Kenneth L, McPheeters, *The American Military Saddle, 1776–1945.* New York: Collectors' Library, 1999.

Duval, John Crittenden. *The Adventures of Big-Foot Wallace, the Texas Ranger and Hunter.* Macon, GA: The J. W. Burke Co., 1921.

Edwards, William B. "Shootin' Irons," *This Is the West.* New York: Rand McNally and Co., 1957.

Edwards, William B. *The Story of Colt's Revolver.* Harrisburg, PA: The Stackpole Company, 1957.

Entick, Rev. John. *The General History of the Late War.* London: 1763.

Faulk, Odie. *General Tom Green: Fightin' Texan.* Waco: Texian Press, 1963.

Fehrenback, T. R. *The Lone Star: A History of Texas and the Texans.* New York: The MacMillan Co., 1968.

Ferrell, Robert H., ed. *Monterrey is Ours: The Mexican War Letters of Lieutenant Dana.* Lexington: University Press of Kentucky, 1990.

Frost, J. *The Mexican War and Its Warriors.* New Haven and Philadelphia: H. Mansfield, 1850.

Gillett, Mary C. *The Army Medical Department, 1818–1865.* CreateSpace Independent Publishing Platform, 2015.

Gilpin, Alec R. *The War of 1812 in the Old Northwest.* East Lansing, MI: Michigan State University Press, 1958, 34.

Goetzmann, William N. *The West of the Imagination.* Norman: University of Oklahoma Press, 2009.

Gordon, Dr. Robert B. Patrick M. Malone, eds., *The Texture of Industry* [...]. New York: Oxford University Press, 1994.

Grant, Ulysses S. *Personal Memoirs of U. S. Grant.* New York: C. L. Webster & Company, 1885.

Green, Gen. Thomas J. *Journal of the Texian Expedition Against Mier.* New York: Harper & Brothers, 1845.

Green, Rena Maverick, ed. *Samuel Maverick, Texan: 1803–1870; A Collection of Journals and Memoirs.* San Antonio: Privately Printed, 1952.

Greer, J. K. *Col. Jack Hays; Texas Frontier Leader and California Builder.* New York: E. P. Dutton and Co., Inc., 1952.

Greer, J. K., ed. *A Texas Ranger and Frontiersman: The Days of Buck Barry in Texas.* Lincoln and London: University of Nebraska Press, 1978.

Hackenburg, Randy. *Pennsylvania in The War with Mexico: The Volunteer Regiments.* Shippensburg, PA: White Mane Publishing Co., 1992.

Haley, J. Evetts. *Charles Goodnight; Cowman and Plainsman.* Norman: University of Oklahoma Press, 1949.

Hall, Karyl Lee Kibler and Carolyn Cooper, *Window on the Works: Industry on the Eli Whitney Site 1798–1979.* New York: Denison Olmsted Arno Press, 1972.

Hardin, Stephen and Richard Hook *The Texas Rangers.* Oxford, UK: Osprey Publishing, 1991.

Haven, Charles T. and Frank A. Belden. *History of Colt's Revolver.* New York: Bonanza Books, 1978.

Hawthorne, Nathaniel. *The Life of Franklin Pierce.*Honolulu HI: University Press of the Pacific, 2002.

Haynes, Sam W. *Soldiers of Misfortune: The Somervell and Mier Expeditions.* Austin: University of Texas Press, 1990.

Heitman, Francis B. *Historical Register and Dictionary of the United States Army from its Organization, September 29, 1789, to March 2, 1903.* Washington, DC: Government Printing Office, 1903.

Henry, William S. *Campaign Sketches of the War with Mexico.* New York: Harper, 1847.

Hill, Jim Dan. *The Texas Navy; In Forgotten Battles and Shirtsleeve Diplomacy.* New York: A. S. Barnes, 1962.

Houze, Herbert. *Samuel Colt: Arms, Art, and Invention*. New Haven, CT: Yale University Press, 2006.

Jackson, Grace. *Cynthia Ann Parker*. San, Antonio: The Naylor Co., 1959.

Jenkins, John Holmes III, ed. *Recollections of Early Texas: The Memoirs of John Holland Jenkins*. Austin: University of Texas Press, 1958.

Jinks, Roy G., *History of Smith and Wesson*. North Hollywood, CA: Benfeld Publishing, Inc., 1977.

Johansen, Robert W. *To the Halls of Montezumas: The Mexican War in the American Imagination*. New York: Oxford University Press, 1985.

Journal of Major Robert Rogers. London: 1765.

Kenly, John R. *Memoirs of a Maryland Volunteer. War with Mexico, in the Years 1846–8*. Philadelphia: J. B. Lippincott & Co., 1873.

Koller, Larry. *The Fireside Book of Guns, A Ridge Press Book*. New York: Simon and Shuster, 1959

Lane, Walter P. *The Adventures and Recollections of General Walter P. Lane, a San Jacinto Veteran*. Marshall, TX: Tri-Weekly Herald, 1887.

Leach, Joseph. *The Typical Texan; Biography of an American Myth*. Dallas: Southern Methodist University Press, 1952.

Lee, Nelson. *Three Years Among the Comanches: The Narrative of Nelson Lee, Texas Ranger*. Norman: Oklahoma Press, 1957.

Lippard, George. *Legends of Mexico*. Philadelphia: T. B. Peterson, 1847.

Loesher, Burt G. *History of Rogers Rangers*. San Francisco: By the author, 1946.

Lyles, Ian B. *Mixed Blessing: The Role of the Texas Rangers in the Mexican War, 1846–1848*. Cascadia, WA: Normandy Press, 2014.

Mackall, Sally Somervell. *Early Days of Washington*. Washington, DC: Neal and Company, 1891.

McCutchan, Joseph D., Joseph Milton Nance, eds., *Mier Expedition Diary; A Texan Prisoner's Account*. Austin: University of Texas Press, 1978.

Mahon, John K. *History of the Second Seminole War 1835–1842*. Gainesville, FL: University of Florida Press, 1985.

McDowell, Catherine W., ed. *Now You Hear My Horn: The Journal of James Wilson Nichols 1820–87*. Austin: University of Texas Press, 1968.

Meade, George Gordon. *The Life and Letter of George Gordon Mead*. New York: Charles Scribner's Sons, 1913.

Moore, Steven L. *Savage Frontier, vol. IV, 1842–1845, Rangers, Riflemen, and Indian Wars in Texas*. Denton, TX: University of North Texas Press, 2010.

Morphis, J. M. *History of Texas, from its Discovery and Settlement, with a Description of its Principal Cities and Counties, and the Agricultural, Mineral, and Material Resources of the State*. New York: U.S. Publishing Company, 1872.

Morrell, Z. N. *Flowers and Fruits in the Wilderness*. St. Louis: Commercial Printing Company, 1872.

Morton, Richard L. *Colonial Virginia*. Chapel Hill: University of North Carolina Press, 1956.

Nance, Joseph Milton. *Attack and Counterattack. The Texas-Mexican Frontier, 1842*. Austin: University Press, 1964.

Nance, Joseph Milton. *Dare-Devils All: The Texan Mier Expedition*. Austin: Eakin Press, 1998.

Newland, Samuel J. *The Pennsylvania Militia: The Early Years, 1699–1792*. Commonwealth of Pennsylvania, Department of Military and Veterans Affairs, 1997.

Olmsted, Frederick W. *A Journey Through Texas; Or, a Saddle-Trip on the Southwestern Frontier*. Austin: University of Texas Press, 1978.

Oswandel, J. Jacob. *Notes on the Mexican War, 1846–47–48*. Philadelphia: n.p., 1885.

Parsons, John E. comp. *Saml Colt's Own Record of Transactions with Captain Walker and Eli Whitney, Jr. in 1847*. Hartford: Connecticut Historical Society, 1949.

Parton, James. *Life of Andrew Jackson in Three Volumes*. New York: Mason Brothers, 1860.

Peskin, Allan ed. *Volunteers: The Mexican War Journals of Private Richard Coulter and Sergeant Thomas Barclay, Company E, Second Pennsylvania Infantry*. Kent, OH: Kent State University Press, 1991.

Peterson, Charles J. *The Military Heroes of the War with Mexico*. Philadelphia: J. B. Smith, 1848.

Peterson, Harold L. *The Book of the Continental Soldier*. Harrisburg, PA: The Stackpole Co., 1968.

Phillips, Philip R. and R. L. Wilson. *Paterson Colt Pistol Variations*. Dallas: Jackson Arms, 1979.

Polk, James K. *The Diary of a President, 1845–49*. London: Longmars, Green, 1952.

Poole, Martha Sprigg. "Ninian Beall," in *Descendants of John and Priscilla Poole*, compiled and edited by Allen Alger and Alger Clan. Towson, MD: John Poole Association, 2001.

Prucha, Francis Paul. *The Sword of the Republic: The United States Army on the Frontier, 1783–1846*. Bloomington: Indiana University Press, 1977.

Quaife, Milo Milton ed. *The Diary of James K. Polk During his Presidency, 1845 to 1849*. Chicago: A. C. McClurg & Co., 1910.

Reid, Samuel C. Jr. *The Scouting Expeditions of McCulloch's Texas Rangers*. Philadelphia: G. B. Zieber and Co., 1847.

Richardson, Hester Dorsey. *Side-lights on Maryland History: With Sketches of Early Maryland Families*. Centreville, MD: Tidewater Publishing, 1967.

Richardson, Rupert Norval. *The Comanche Barrier*. Glendale, CA: Arthur H. Clark Co., 1933.

Roberts, Ned H. *The Muzzle-Loading Cap Lock Rifle*. New York: Bonanza Books, 1952.

Rodenbough, Theophilus F. and William L. Haskin, eds. *The Army of the United States: Historical Sketches of the Staff and Line with Portraits of Generals-in-Chief*. New York: Maynard, Merrill, & Co., 1896.

Rosebush, W. E. *Frontier Steel*. Spokane, WA: C. C. Nelson Publishing Company, 1958.

Sargent, Jean A., ed. *Stones and Bones; Cemetery Records of Prince George's Co., Maryland*. Bowie, MD: Prince George's Co. Genealogical Society, *ca.* 1984.

Serven, James E. *Colt Firearms, 1836–1960*. Santa Anna, CA: Serven Books, 1960.

Shannon, James Thomas. *Eyewitness to War: Prints and Daguerreotypes of the Mexican War, 1846–1848*. Washington, DC: Smithsonian Books, 1989.

Shepherd, W.R. *History of the Proprietary Government of Pennsylvania*. New York: Columbia University Press, 1896.

Sibley, Marilyn McAdams ed. *Samuel H. Walker's Account of the Mier Expedition*. Austin: The Texas State Historical Association, 1978.

Smith, Justin H. *War with Mexico*. New York: Macmillan, 1919.

Sowell, A. J. *Rangers and Pioneers of Texas* [...]. San Antonio: Shepard Bros. & Co., 1884.

Stapp, William Preston. *The Prisoners of Perote Containing a Journal Kept by the Author Who Was Captured by the Mexicans at Mier, December 25, 1842, and Released from Perote, May 16, 1844*. Philadelphia: G. B. Ziebner, 1845.

Steffen, Randy. *The Horse Soldier: 1776–1943*. Norman: University of Oklahoma Press, 1977.

Stephens, William. *Journal of the Proceedings in Georgia*. Ann Arbor: University Microfilm, Inc., 1966.

Thrall, Homer S., History of Texas. New York: University Pub. Co., *ca.* 1876.

Tobias, Arthur Ed. D. *Colt Cylinder Scenes 1847–1851*. Los Angeles: By the Author, 2011.

Uhlendorf, Bernhard A. (trans.). *Revolution in America–Confidential Letters and Journals–1776–84–of the Adjutant General Major Baurmeister of the Hessian Forces*. New Brunswick, NJ: Rutgers University Press, 1957.

Utley, Robert Marshall. *Lone Star Justice: The First Century of the Texas Rangers*. New York: Oxford University Press, 2002

Wade, Houston comp. *Notes and Fragments of the Mier Expedition*. LaGrange, TX: LaGrange Journal, 1936.

Walker, Samuel H., (II). *Walkers of Toaping Castle, Md.* Washington, DC: By the author, 1889.

Wallace, Ernest and E. Adamson Hoebel. *The Comanches: Lords of the South Plains*. Norman: University of Oklahoma Press, 1952.

Webb, Walter Prescott. *The Great Frontier*. Boston: Houghton Mifflin Company, 1952.

Webber, C.W. *Tales of the Southern Border*. Philadelphia: J. B. Lippincott Company, 1887.

Whittington, LTC Robert D. *The Colt Whitneyville-Walker Pistol*. Dallas, TX: Taylor Publishing Co., 1984.

Williams, Amelia W. & Eugene C. Barker, eds. *The Writings of Sam Houston, 1813–1863*. Austin: University of Texas Press, 1938.

Williams, Mary Lou. *Greenbelt: History of a New Town, 1937–1987*. Norfolk, VA: The Donning Company, 1987.

Wilson, R. L. *Book of Colt Firearms*. Minneapolis, MN: Blue Book Publications Inc., 2008.

Woodward, Thomas S. *Woodward's Reminiscences of the Creek or Muscogee Indians*. Montgomery, AL: Barrett and Wimbish, 1859.

Wormser, Richard. *The Yellowlegs: The Story of the United States Cavalry*. Garden City, NY: Doubleday & Company, Inc., 1966.

Yoakum, H. *History of Texas from its First Settlement in 1685 to its Annexation to the United States in 1846*. New York: Redfield, 1855.

Zaboly, Gary. *American Colonial Ranger: The Northern Colonies, 1724–1763* (Oxford, UK: Osprey Publishing, 2004).

Zinn, Howard. "We Take Nothing by Conquest, Thank God" *A Peoples' History of the United States*. New York: The New Press, 1997.

Manuscripts

Cesari, G. S. "American Arms-making Machine Tool Development, 1798–1855." PhD diss., University of Pennsylvania, 1970.

Dodd, Dorothy. "Railroad Projects in Territorial Florida." Master's thesis, Florida State College for Women, 1929.

Kuykendall, J. H. "Sketches of Early Texians." 8. Typed manuscript, University of Texas, Austin.

Lyles, Ian B. "Mixed Blessing: The Role of the Texas Rangers in the Mexican War, 1846–1848." Master's thesis, Army Command and General Staff College, Fort Leavenworth, Kansas, 2003.

Perez, Aminta Inelda. "*Tejano Rangers: The Development and Evolution of Ranging Tradition, 1540–1880.*" PhD diss., University of Iowa, 2012.

"The Battle of Walker Creek, June 8, 1844, Tall Tales and Myths Removed, This is the Documented Drama of the Day the Texas Frontier Changed Forever." MS, n.d., Walker Vertical, Texas Ranger Hall of Fame & Museum File.

Webb, Walter Prescott. "The Texas Rangers in the Mexican War." Master's Thesis, University of Texas, 1920.

Worsham, James. "The Quest for Interchangeable Parts in American Firearms." Unpublished manuscript, 1993.

Worsham, James. "Nashville's Col. Thomas Claiborne, Jr.—The Last of the Mexican War Mounted Rifles." Unpublished manuscript, 1994.

Newspapers

Albany Patriot (New York), April 16, 1845–November 1847.

American Flag (Matamoros, Mexico), January 20, 1847.

Austin City Gazette, March 30, 1842.

Boston Daily Advertiser, February 10, 1847.

Brooklyn Daily Eagle, December 3, 1850.
Commercial Bulletin of New Orleans, May 11, 1846.
Daily Advertiser (Newark, New Jersey), January 20, 1847; December 24, 1847.
Daily American Star, (Austin, Texas), November 5, 1847; February 4, 1848.
Daily Express (San Antonio, Texas), May 2, 1918.
Daily Picayune (New Orleans), May 14, 1846; January 10, January 12, 1848.
Flag of Freedom (Puebla, Mexico), October 24, October 27, 1847.
Free American, December 21, 1847; February 7, 1848.
Genius of Liberty (Leesburg, Virginia), November 3, 1847.
Houston Texas Telegraph, June 31, 1846.
Jeffersonian (New Orleans), May 14, 1846.
Macon Weekly Telegraph (Georgia), November 12, 1847; February 1, 1848.
Matamoros Reveille (Mexico), July 15, 1846.
Miners' Journal and Pottsville General Advertiser (Pottsville, Pennsylvania), August 25, 1860.
Nashville Union (Tennessee), April 1886.
Newport Mercury (Rhode Island), May 30, 1846.
News Leader (Laurel, Maryland), September 26; October 3, 1963; and April 13, 20, 1967.
New York Observer, May 23, 1846.
New York Sun, December 8, 1846.
New York Times, March 4, 1852.
News-Express (San Antonio, Texas), January 5–7, 10, and 19, 1995.
Niles National Register, May 15–16, 30; June 13, 27; July 11; August 1; October 3; November 28, 1846; and June 19, July 3, August 7, November 20, 1847.
North American, February 8, 1848
Northern Standard (Clarkesville, Texas), January 22, 1848.
Northern Star (Gainesville, Texas), July 24, 1844; January 8, 1848.
Spirit of the Times (Ironton, Ohio), December 19, 1846.
Texas Democrat (Austin), May 6, 1846.
Texas State Gazette (Austin), November 2, 1850.
Texas Telegraph and Register, August 30, 1836.
The Vidette (Washington, DC), June 1882, April 1886, March 1887.
Washington Weekly Union, January 23, 1847.
Weekly Reveille (St. Louis), May 25, 1846.
Whig and Public Advertiser (Richmond, Virginia), May 28, 1847.

Official Records

American State Papers, Military Affairs, 1832.
Executive Journal, United States Senate, May 25, 1846, *A Century of Lawmaking for a New Nation: U.S. Congressional Documents and Debates 1774–1875*, Library of Congress, Washington, DC.
Journal of the Executive Proceedings of the Senate of the United States of America.
Journals of the Ninth Congress of the Republic of Texas. Washington, TX: Miller & Cushing, Public Printers, 1845.
Letters Received by the Office of the Adjutant General, 1822–1860, National Archives Microfilm Publication M567, Washington, DC.
Militia and Volunteer Units in the Seminole Wars, http://www.floridafrontierguard.com/id18.html.
Record Group 92, Records of the Office of the Quartermaster General, National Archives, Washington, DC.

Record Group 127, Records of the U.S. Marine Corps, National Archives, Washington, DC.
Record Group 156, Records of the Office of the Chief of Ordnance, National Archives, Washington, DC.
San Antonio City Council Minutes, 1848.
Senate Executive Document No. 56, Thirtieth Congress, First Session, Serial 518, 402.
Texas Rangers Service Records 1830–1846, Muster Rolls at Texas State Library and Archives, Austin, TX.
Texas State Library and Archives, Austin, TX. Official Rosters of Capt. Walker's Company of Texas Rangers.
Texas State Library and Archives, Austin, TX. Capt. Hays Rangers (February 25–June 26, 1844).
Texas State Library and Archives, Austin, TX. Capt. Cameron's Company, Mier Expedition.
Upper Battalion of Militia, Prince George's County, Maryland, Maryland Archive Volume XXI, 62; captain of his own company, May 24, 1779, in Upper Battalion of Militia, Prince George's County, Maryland Archive Volume XXI, 414.

Personal Papers/Diaries

Mexican War Diary of Sergeant George W. Myers, U.S. Mounted Rifles, Walker's Co. "C," dated from February 26, 1847, to July 5, 1848.
Samuel Colt Papers, Connecticut Historical Society, Hartford, CT.
Samuel H. Walker Papers, Texas State Archives, Austin, Texas.
Thomas Claiborne Papers, Southern Historical Collection, University of North Carolina Library, Chapel Hill, NC.
Zenas Matthews Diary.

Letters

Letters from Mexican Imprisonment. www.sonsofdewittcolony.org.
Peter Maxwell to Samuel H. Walker, Perote Castle, Mexico, October 11, 1843.
Thomas Claiborne to Col. T. Andrews, Vera Cruz November 18, 1847.
T. P. Andrews to J. Thomas Walker, Washington, December 15, 1847.

Index

Note: References in *italic* refer to figures. References followed by "n" refer to endnotes.